The CAREER ARCHITECT® Development Planner

AN EXPERT SYSTEM OFFERING 95 RESEARCH BASED AND EXPERIENCE TESTED DEVELOPMENT PLANS AND COACHING TIPS

FOR:

LEARNERS,

SUPERVISORS,

MANAGERS,

MENTORS, AND

FEEDBACK GIVERS

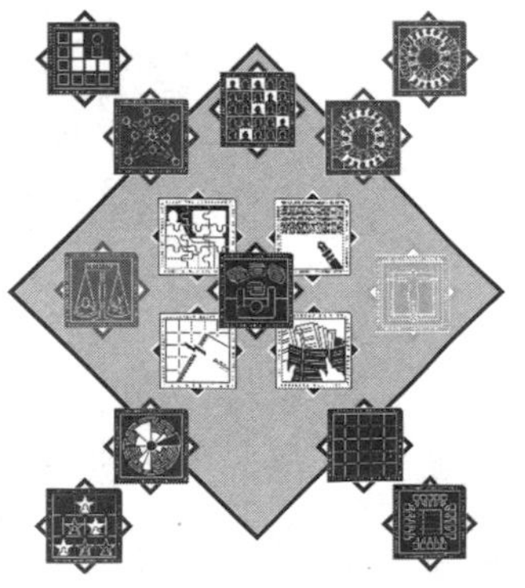

Michael M. Lombardo
Robert W. Eichinger

5320 Cedar Lake Road South
Minneapolis, MN 55416

http://www.lominger.com

ISBN 0-9655712-4-6

TABLE OF CONTENTS

**Note: Italicized words are not alphabetized.*

There are no competencies 68–80. Those numbers are reserved for future additions.

PERFOMANCE MANAGEMENT DIMENSIONS

CAREER STALLERS AND STOPPERS

APPENDIX A

INTRODUCTION

WHO IS THE CAREER ARCHITECT® DEVELOPMENT PLANNER FOR?

- ☐ For individual learners working on their own development
- ☐ For bosses, supervisors and managers working on the development of someone who works with or for them
- ☐ For coaches, mentors and feedback givers helping others work on their development

WHAT IS THE CAREER ARCHITECT® DEVELOPMENT PLANNER ABOUT?

This is a book about building and developing the skills and competencies needed to enhance current job performance and to prepare for future career opportunities. It provides development menus for 67 competencies research indicates are related to career success, 9 universal performance dimensions and 19 menus for stallers and stoppers that can halt otherwise promising careers.

NEW IN THIS EDITION

PERFORMANCE MANAGEMENT ARCHITECT® Chapters

We have added 9 chapters, one for each of the common performance dimensions that we have seen under various names on countless performance evaluation forms.

BOOK RECOMMENDATIONS

In previous editions, we included some book references and were told by users that they would like references for each competency, performance dimension or staller. Accordingly, we have added hundreds of books and audiotapes to help you go beyond the tips we present in these pages. Each of the 95 chapters in the CAREER ARCHITECT® Development Planner has 4 to 15 sources for further reading or listening.

We used these selection criteria:

1. ROI - Is there a significant and immediate payoff for reading this book? Are there suggestions busy people can implement?
2. Organization - Is the book well laid out? Is this easy to find what you are looking for?
3. Ease - Is it well written?
4. Solid - Is the advice more than opinion?
5. Prolific - Are there lots of tips and examples?
6. Available - Can the book (or audio tape) be found without a search?

To insure that the books were solid, we relied heavily on the Library Journal, which reviews and recommends the best business books every year. So the books are substantive and mostly available through your local public library.

Second, we relied on Soundview so many of the books would be conveniently available in eight page summaries. (Soundview Executive Book Summaries, 10 LaCrue Avenue, Concordville PA 19331. 1-800-521-1227. International calls outside the US and Canada 1-610-558-9495, www.summary.com).

Third, we checked major booksellers (Barnes&Noble, B.Dalton, Borders) to see what they stock. In general, they are similar in coverage to Soundview.

Finally, we checked MBA syllabi to see what universities regard as substantive for business people.

The list is also partly eclectic and some sources are "dated" (*The Prince* by Machiavelli is pretty fresh 500 years after publication so we included it). Some come from history, biography and foreign affairs, particularly for competencies like Perspective (46) and Political Savvy (48). There is even a novel or two. Plenty for you to choose from!

WHERE DID THESE 67 SKILLS AND COMPETENCIES, 9 PERFORMANCE DIMENSIONS AND 19 CAREER STALLERS AND STOPPERS (95 NEEDS) COME FROM?

The 67 LEADERSHIP ARCHITECT® competencies come from a content analysis of many sources: the major and continuing studies at the Center for Creative Leadership, long-term studies at AT&T and Sears, studies by Harry and Daniel Levinson, Kotter, Gabarro, Jaques, Kouzes and Posner, Bennis, Tichy and a compendium of empirical studies contained in *The Handbook of Leadership*.

Developing competencies is straightforward – you're not good (unskilled) at *#47 Planning* and would like to get better (skilled) or you overdo (overused skill) *#47 Planning* and need to compensate for that by using other competencies to balance the overuse.

From our experience with performance systems, we developed nine dimensions of performance that apply in most, if not all jobs, from entry to the boardroom. We have numbered them from 81-89, fitting them in-between the 1-67 Core Competencies (with space for more at some future time), and the 101-119 Career Stallers and Stoppers.

Working on performance dimensions is also straightforward - you're not good or average at #81 Quantity of Work and would like to get better (skilled) or you overdo Quantity and need to compensate for this by using other competencies to balance this off.

The 19 career stallers and stoppers come primarily from three sources – the continuing work of the Center for Creative Leadership, the work of Jon

Bentz while he was at Sears and the executive development work and experiences of the authors.

Working on stallers and stoppers is a bit different. If you receive feedback that you are *#112 Insensitive to Others*, this is a serious problem where your goal is to neutralize this potentially career stopping criticism. Working on a staller is not the same as building a competency. A staller is much more serious and likely results from many sources – what you underdo such as *#31 Interpersonal Savvy* and what you overdo such as *#53* Drive for *Results* or *#9 Command Skills*. For this reason, we have written separate development material for the stallers and stoppers that cover tips you won't find if you simply go to *#31 Interpersonal Savvy*, for example.

DO THE 67 SKILLS AND COMPETENCIES REALLY MEASURE SUCCESS?

Research across many companies and industries with **VOICES®**, Lominger's 360° feedback instrument using these 67 competencies and 19 stallers and stoppers indicates they can be measured reliably and most are significantly related to current job performance.

Some are also related to potential for promotion as well.

HOW MANY DIFFERENT KINDS OF NEEDS ARE THERE?

There are five kinds of needs you may be addressing:

1. You are average in something that is critical to your success and it needs to be higher.
2. You are weak or below par in an important area.
3. You are untested (you may be unskilled, but don't really know) in an important area.
4. You overuse a strength that turns into a weakness for you.
5. You have a career staller or stopper that's getting in your way.

HOW DO I KNOW THAT I'M WORKING ON THE RIGHT NEED?

There is a Table of Contents (an index of the 67 Competencies, 9 Performance Dimensions, and 19 Career Stallers and Stoppers). Scan this to see if you can find the need you are interested in working on. Each need has a positive (skilled), a negative (unskilled) definition, and an overused skill definition. When you think you have found your need, go to that page and see if two or more of the things listed in the unskilled definition are true for you and you are not like more than one or two of the things listed in the skilled definition. Sometimes troubles in a skill might show up as overuse instead of as unskilled, since you apply the skill so forcefully that the strength may appear as unskilled as well.

In the case of an untested need (number 3 above), the unskilled statements wouldn't really describe you because you have never had an occasion to try or apply the skills. But if you had the opportunity to apply that skill, some of the unskilled descriptions would likely describe how you would do.

Overall, you can think of the definitions as this is more what I am today or would be if I had to do this (the unskilled or perhaps overused definitions) and this is what I would like to be (the skilled definition). It's a before and after snapshot.

Watch Out For Phantom Needs

Sometimes even excellent feedback can identify the wrong need. Even if everyone agrees that you have problems getting *#53* Drive for *Results*, the question is why? Maybe the real problem is *#11 Composure* or *#57 Standing Alone* or *#18 Delegation*. Perhaps you only have trouble with results when one of these is demanded. So if none or only a few of the remedies for your identified need seem to make sense to you, check all the cross references in **Section 2** (Developmental Remedies) to see if your need is more likely one of those referenced. Then go back to your sources and see if you can discover the true underlying need.

UNDERSTANDING YOUR NEED

The Development Planner offers two unique features to help you or someone else understand the mechanics and reasons for any need.

The Causes:

In our feedback work, we find that many people know their needs before the feedback. What they don't know or understand is why they have the need. This feature lists the most likely causes for each of the 95 needs. We have found that many times knowing the causes provides the breakthrough for people to get energized about working on their needs.

The Map:

Each of the 95 chapters has a map which sets the context of the need. How does it work in the real world? What else is it connected to? What does it look like? Why is it important?

The map should help the learner understand why it's important to have the skills and attitudes reflected in this competency.

HOW MANY NEEDS SHOULD YOU WORK ON AT ONCE?

The typical answer is three, for no particular reason we know of other than that's a nice number and sounds doable! The actual answer is that it depends on four factors:

1. How difficult is the need to develop? How hard it is to get objective feedback on the need? Not all competencies are equal when it comes to development.
2. How similar is it to other needs? You would have a much greater chance of success working on *#31 Interpersonal Savvy*, *#3 Approachability*, and *#7 Caring about Direct Reports* than you would on *#3 Approachability*, *#58 Strategic Agility* and *#47 Planning*. Why? Because the remedies will be similar for the first set and quite dissimilar for the second. Do the common sense test. Read through the remedies for your proposed needs. If you see similar remedies, you can probably work on multiple needs. If you don't, we would advise picking your number one need and going with that for awhile. You can always add more later.
3. Are you (or the person you are working with) a motivated adult? Do you accept your needs and take ownership of them? Yes answers mean more needs can be tackled at once.
4. Do you (or the person you are working with) have access to the developmental resources needed to address multiple needs? In a resource rich and supportive developmental culture, a learner could work on more needs simultaneously.

WHAT DOES THE RESEARCH SAY ABOUT DEVELOPMENT?

The research on development has come down pretty firmly around learning from all types of experience like courses, readings, projects, feedback, assignments or jobs. No one type does the job alone, but in concert they are powerful.

Development generally begins with a realization of current or future need and the motivation to do something about it. This might come from feedback, a mistake, watching other people's reactions, failing at or not being up to a task – in other words, from experience. The odds are that development will be about 70% from on the job experiences, working on tasks and problems; about 20% from feedback or working around good and bad examples of the need, and 10% from courses and reading.

Where the realization of the need comes from is less important than having it, and once you know this, what is critical is to go after the need(s) with all the developmental remedies. Feedback alone won't do it; it only sets the stage. Just doing it won't work – experience by itself is a lousy teacher; it's too involving, too fragmented. People have trouble setting goals and measures to benchmark against or they're simply too busy. Neither courses nor reading will work alone. At best they are knowing what to do better or differently and perhaps practicing in the safe environment of a course. Transfer to the job is difficult.

In short, the developmental remedies work best when orchestrated together. Alone, they are single instruments.

According to the studies we participated in at the Center for Creative Leadership (CCL), development specifically involves:

- ☐ Knowing what the target looks like – what the competency or skill looks like when done well (the after picture).
- ☐ Knowing where you stand against the target (the before picture) – getting feedback.
- ☐ Seeing some consequence or reason to develop – you have to be a motivated person in order to really make progress on a need.
- ☐ Having experiences that test you in that area – not just practice, not just make-work, but stressful experiences where you get better at the area or you fail or don't cope well with the experience. So part of development is a demand pull on you to do something different or you fail or stumble. The task, saying running a task force where the members are experts and you are not, demands that you listen, learn from others, curb any defensiveness you may usually exhibit and so on. Not doing them isn't a reasonable option.
- ☐ Hitting the need with every learning method available – seek out role models, get more feedback, analyze your mistakes, go to a course, whatever it takes to find some new, different and better things to do.
- ☐ Making sense of it all – developing some rules of thumb, guidelines, do's and don't's so the behaviors and attitudes can become part of your repertoire, not things you do once or twice and then forget to do going forward.

HOW IS THE CAREER ARCHITECT® DEVELOPMENT PLANNER ORGANIZED?

The book has 95 chapters, one each for the 67 competencies, 9 performance dimensions, and 19 career stallers and stoppers.

The format in each chapter is organized around the research findings on development.

Each of the 95 development menus in each chapter has six sections:

1. **Scoping out the need –** what does it look like in its skilled version and its unskilled version? The Unskilled (the before picture) definition is used to assess yourself or another person; if most or many of the descriptors fit, it may be a need for you or them. Skilled (the after picture) is to give you a target of what success looks like. The Overuse definition points to the possible negative consequences of using a skill too much or with too much force. If the problem is an overuse, it directs you to other competencies by chapter number which would help balance the overuse.
2. **Ten remedies for development –** Here, we summarize research and our 50 years of experience on your need, boiling it down to ten likely remedies you should consider. Each of the ten remedies or avenues of building the competency have multiple tips and suggestions to follow.

Not all will apply, but some will hit your need squarely. This will be your preferred source when in a hurry. It covers all the developmental remedies needed to write a good plan.

3. **Best feedback sources –** Who is likely to know the most about you and your need? The majority of feedback processes are boss driven, but as you'll see, many other sources are equally or more relevant. Sometimes we don't even list the boss, because research doesn't back up the boss as a good source for feedback.
4. **Best developmental tasks –** As we said, 70% of development tends to be job based. In this section, you'll find up to ten of the best tasks to help you develop.
5. **Best jobs –** We really develop our competencies under moderate to high pressure, not under less stressful conditions. This section details the best jobs to grow your skills.
6. **Other development hints to assure your plan is successful –** Here we cover a variety of learning enhancers to help you make sense of your development: tips on feedback, courses, learning from others, learning from mistakes, and numerous ways to cement learning.

HOW TO THINK ABOUT AND USE EACH SECTION

Section 1 – Skilled, Unskilled and Overuse Definitions

You have little chance of efficient development without a clear target. What are you like? Look to the Unskilled or the Overuse definitions to form a before picture. What do you want to be like? Look to the Skilled definition. Take a few minutes to detail your need. Which unskilled descriptors apply? How and why do they apply? With whom? In what situations?

Look to the causes. Why do you do what you do related to this need? What drives the need?

Look at the map. What does it say that you didn't know or realize before? Does it put the need in a brighter context for you? Does it lead to any aha's! for you?

The more time you invest up front the easier it will be to use the materials in the developmental menus.

Section 2 – Ten Remedies for Development

This section contains ten complete mini-plans. It covers all the developmental remedies from feedback to stretching tasks, as well as cross-references to related competencies. It often includes some readings. This section's guiding principles are brief tips, get a fast start, and see some quick results from your development efforts. In most cases, only some of the ten will apply. Sometimes one of the ten will lead you to another competency. It may be that that is really your need.

Section 3 – Best Feedback Sources

Without continued feedback, even the best plans usually fail, according to research studies. We roll along, think we're getting better, don't realize what impact we may be having on others and pronounce the effort over. Or we think we've improved greatly, go on "autopilot" and six months later we're back to our old behavior. Getting further feedback keeps you growing. This section lists the most accurate sources for your need or needs.

Section 4 – Best Developmental Tasks

Unless you have challenging job tasks where you either perform against the need or fail, not much development will occur. This is the essence of action learning or learning from experience – not practice, not trying things out, but getting better in order to perform. Take the example of listening skills, a common need. Everyone's had a million chances (practices) to listen better but they don't, usually because there are some people or some situations where they don't want to listen and have gotten away with it. To listen better, then, how about if they were in a tough negotiation or running a task force of experts when they're not an expert. Get the idea? It's listen or else you can't do the job. Any plan you write must have "perform this or else" tasks in it to work. Otherwise you'll revert to your old ways.

To use these tasks, shape them to your job and organization. What tasks like these are available?

If you have a significant need (you are really weak or untested in this area), start with the smaller challenges and build up to the tougher ones.

Section 5 – Best Jobs

Lots of people pause at this section. Why have a job in here? I already have a job or I don't want to do this one or it would be risky for me to get in such a job (e.g. a strategic planning job when I'm lousy at strategy).

First, if this is your last job or you have no career ambition to do anything different or at a higher level, skip to section 6. Otherwise read on.

This section is here because:

- ☐ The number one developer of competencies by far is stretching, challenging jobs – not feedback, not courses, not role models, but jobs where you develop and exercise significant and varied competencies. If you really want to grow, these are the best places to do it.
- ☐ If you are ambitious, these are the jobs that matter most for long-term success. In the CCL studies, executives who remained successful had been tested in many of the jobs you'll see in section 5.
- ☐ No one is going to promote you to a significant role unless you prove you can perform these competencies under moderate to high pressure. *#33 Listening* or *#47 Planning* or *#12 Conflict Management* for low stakes is not that impressive to most talent scouts; they want to know

one thing – Can you do it under high pressure? These jobs are as high pressure as it gets.

To use this section:

- ☐ If you have a job which lacks some of the necessary elements for development, see if you can add to the job or enrich it with some of the challenges listed under the relevant full job(s).
- ☐ If you are already in one of the jobs suggested for development, you have a rich opportunity to use it to learn better from experience. What specifically about the job demands that you work on this need? Write down these challenges; focus your development plan on them.
- ☐ Use all other remedies to qualify yourself for one of these jobs. Particularly if you are ambitious, this is the best thing you can do. Use the other remedies to get ready, then show the decision makers you can handle a tough test. This will prove to them that you can handle different kinds of jobs and overcome a competency deficiency.

A final note: in one company, managers were asked to select a job from this list that they'd like to do – because it seemed exciting, because it would take a lot of personal growth, or because they wanted to get noticed. Although none of them was qualified for their "dream" job at that time, 40% qualified themselves for and got this type of job within two years.

Section 6 – Development Plan Enhancers

This section contains up to ten tips on learning better from experience. The tips include learning from other people, learning from mistakes, learning from feedback and course work, and methods of learning to make better sense of your experiences so you can make your new behaviors part of your long-term behavioral repertoire.

Using the six sections together, you can create a research supported and experience tested plan for any of the 95 needs. In addition, The CAREER ARCHITECT® Development Planner contains a General Plan (see page xvii) which gives you the road map to work on any need.

QUICK REFERENCE TO WRITING A GOOD DEVELOPMENT PLAN

1. Try to determine what your real need is. Many times you may have to select a few that together equal your real need. Recall that if you are working on an overused competency that you should select a balancing competency from the list provided with each overused definition.
2. Read the unskilled definition (or overused). Which bullet points describe you the best? Look to the skilled definition. What would you like to be able to do when you're done working on this need? This is your before and after picture.

3. Look to the causes. Why do you do what you do related to this need? What drives the need?
4. Look at the map. What does it say that you didn't know or realize before. Does it put the need in a brighter context for you? Does it lead to any aha's! for you?

Use 2 – 4 to detail your need(s).

5. Look at the General Plan on page xvii which lists ten ways to develop in any area and pick any of those that seem to fit. This universal plan can be used as a basic core for any plan.
6. Look through and select tips and tasks from the five remaining sections. Please seriously consider all sections. Remember that the developmental remedies are much more powerful in concert than by themselves. There is a form in Appendix A designed to capture your plan. You can use this to write plans for single or multiple needs at once.
7. Lay out a plan and a schedule. Your plan should include at least three items you will work on immediately. You should measure the number of times you did this or didn't do that and record these efforts so you can track your improvement. Set a specific timeframe of no more than a month to try these items repeatedly; if your timeframe is longer or indefinite, you'll be less likely to do anything. Start today.

HOW DO YOU KNOW WHEN DEVELOPMENT IS OCCURRING (HAS OCCURRED)?

You or the people you're working with:

1. Refer to the need as "my need;" take ownership of the need.
2. Are a motivated adult on a mission; show some passion about fixing the problem.
3. Demonstrate a broad conceptual understanding of the need being worked on.
4. Converse easily on the topic; views are credible to more experienced people
5. The supervisor's or the coach's role is becoming less directive or coaching, and is switching more to a collegial one in this area.
6. Mistakes, unanticipated problems and consequences of working on the need have been dealt with.
7. Have repeatedly demonstrated the new skill across varied settings.
8. Are working mostly on follow through, checking, tidying up.
9. Are looking actively for other needs to tackle.
10. Are not asking nearly as many questions as before.
11. Exude self-confidence in the area.

BEING A BOSS / MENTOR / COACH

A coach has six possible jobs or tasks to do. These phases of coaching have to be accomplished in linear order to be of any worth.

To help the learner:

1. Understand the need
2. Take personal ownership
3. Find the right plan
4. Get the resources
5. Support the process
6. Celebrate the successes

1. Helping the learner understand each need.

Use the Table of Contents to select the key needs of the person.

Refer to the unskilled definitions of each need to help form a picture of how the person looks now. Scan the overuse definitions to make sure the negative consequences of this competency aren't due to too much use rather than too little. This will be the before picture.

Use the skilled definitions to form how the person should look. That will form the after picture. Note the nature and the size of the gap between them for each need. Add examples you're aware of – the more the better, the more specific the better.

Check the person's five greatest strengths. See if any of them are in overuse. Do those overuses relate to the unskilled needs in any way. Are there any common themes? For example, do they overuse *#53* Drive for *Results* and have a need in *#7 Caring About Direct Reports*?

Check the causes for each need. Are there any causes in common between needs?

Check the map for each need to see if there is any value in looking at the context for the needs. Are there any common themes in the maps? Do the needs all play in one arena?

You can't spend too much time defining the need(s). Much effort is lost if people try to work on a wrong or ill-defined need.

Engage the learner in extensive dialogue and reflection to define the need(s).

2. Helping the learner take ownership of the need.

Only motivated adults with a need make progress building competencies. A boss, coach or mentor needs to help the learner accept need(s). That's where the examples come in. Share personal stories about your own needs from the problems you have had to face. Share stories about people you both know who did or did not take ownership of their needs. Talk about the consequences of being defensive or trying to rationalize away the need(s).

In extreme cases, send the person to talk to someone he/she respects who is several levels higher in the organization. Have this more senior person reinforce the need and why it is critical to rise above it. Also ask the person to observe him/herself in situations where this need plays out and describe to you the consequences of not being skilled in this area. Until the person says, "This need plays out in ways that are unacceptable for me and for my performance," nothing much will happen.

So show some patience. Some people have a hard time acknowledging flaws or admitting that they matter.

COACHING FOR ACCEPTANCE WITH DEFENSIVE PEOPLE

- ☐ Typical reactions to feedback: 33% – deniers, devastated or hostile; defensive and rationalizing; 33% – basically OK – they know they have the need but aren't really motivated to do much and 33% energized by finally figuring out what it was that wasn't working for them and how to fix it.
- ☐ If someone is really a denier, ask why she/he would say this about someone else, ask who on earth has her/his best interests at heart and get a commitment to checking out the need with that person. Recite your view (and that of others) and what people mean by saying it. Ask what the consequences of people believing this are.
- ☐ If someone is really down, say "Only crazy people keep doing things that don't pay off. How has doing that worked for you in the past?" Explain how strengths left ungoverned sometimes tip over to weaknesses. So turn the negative energy into a positive – get the person to see his/her downsides as consequences of strengths.
- ☐ If someone is hostile, let him/her talk; give the person a calm mirror. Then take whatever is said and exaggerate it ("So there's no accuracy to this rating;" "So this is unfair"). Often this will get the person to acknowledge the issue.
- ☐ Go after the toughest issue first unless the person is really hurting. Pick what the person is most likely to remember.
- ☐ There are three basic styles of how people like to understand their needs: bit by bit, surprises, and strengths and weaknesses (thematic). Figure out what your customer is like and provide that choice.
- ☐ Try to sell the person on a balance strategy, and advise not to do less of a strength. It usually doesn't make much sense to say "Hide your intelligence or hide your creativity." Ordinarily, we will fall back on our strengths under pressure anyway. A more productive strategy is to leave strengths alone and develop a counter balance as in a seesaw. An intelligent person might work on her listening skills to be seen as more open; a creative person might work on follow through so he won't run off and leave loose ends and confused people in his wake.

- ☐ When someone is clearly poor at something like team building or strategy, ask what's getting in the way. What does the person not like to do? What's his/her conception of the area? You will generally find the person has a poor understanding and needs a fresh mental map before much progress can be made. For example, poor team builders usually lack not only skill – they lack attitude, may not see the value of teams, don't think like team builders think, and aren't tuned in to reading and learning from other people.
- ☐ Have the person describe tough situations that are stumbling blocks. "Take me inside a meeting where that happened. What did you say? When did you first notice...? What triggers you? What are your hot buttons?" Identify with the person what is getting in the way and what touches his/her hot buttons. Have the person focus on triggers to let him know when he's losing control or she's feeling blocked, and devise simple counters to do as soon as he/she feels that way. For example, "If you get angry when someone attacks you, ask a question, find something in their statement you can agree with, imagine yourself running in slow motion."
- ☐ The essence of acceptance is when the person can vividly describe consequences that are unacceptable to him/her. He or she takes you inside situations, tells you what was done, how that had a bad impact, etc. That's when a person is ready for growth.

3. Helping the learner create a plan.

When you have a motivated adult with a need – a learner – he or she generally wants to launch into fixing the need in a hurry.

Look first at the General Plan on page xvii which lists ten ways to develop in any area and pick any of those that seem to fit for the learner. This universal plan can be used as a basic core for any coaching session.

Then look through and select tips and tasks from the remaining sections for each need. Please seriously consider all sections. Remember that the developmental remedies are much more powerful in concert than by themselves.

Lay out a plan and a schedule with the person. His/her action plan should include at least three items to be worked on immediately and refreshed every time one task gets completed. Agree on measures for the number of times the person did this or didn't do that and a method of recording these efforts so improvement can be tracked. Set a specific timeframe of no more than a month to try these items repeatedly; if the person's timeframe is longer or indefinite, he/she will be less likely to do anything.

The 95 plans are really developmental menus. No one will ever do all of the things listed. In selecting specific steps, consider:

- ☐ The energy of the learner
- ☐ How much time the learner has to spend on development
- ☐ How practical each selected step is in the organization

- ☐ Start small and build up strategies
- ☐ Build in some early successes

4. Help the learner with necessary developmental resources.

Development costs time and money. The learner needs access to tasks, projects and assignments. The need may call for expensive courses or time off work for parallel tasks (such as working on listening by serving on community projects). You can help by running interference in the organization and helping the learner negotiate with the organization and his/her boss. You can also help arrange for the learner to work with others in the organization who could be helpful.

5. Help the learner by supporting the process.

The learner will need continuous feedback, emotional support and reinforcement. When developing any skill, most actually get worse before they get better. It can be a real emotional struggle. In order to work on any need with a big gap, the person has to let go of one trapeze – the past – and grab for the other trapeze – the future – before any progress is possible. In between the two trapezes is nothing but air with no safety net. Many never let go of the first trapeze. You have to help the person realize that forgetting past habits is just as important as learning new ones.

Many times all that's necessary is that you listen and provide a shoulder to rest on, but don't make yourself the sole source of feedback or comfort. Developmental remedies work best in multiples – encourage the learner to get the maximum number of perspectives, not just yours.

People who have made a negative appraisal of the learner's skills will be slow to recognize incremental differences. The person may get demoralized when others don't recognize progress. You may have to chart and mark off progress on the gap ruler to keep up his/her spirit. Use suggestion 10 in the Universal Development Plan – have the learner get feedback from people he/she hasn't been around very much or very long and who haven't formed a negative opinion of the person in this area. Sometimes this can only happen in other work units or off the job.

6. Helping the learner celebrate the successes.

You may be the only person who really knows what the learner has gone through. Find ways for the learner to demonstrate to long term and short term people that he or she is now skilled in the area of the need. Take the measures and milestones the two of you have set up seriously. When one is met or exceeded, celebrate it!

GENERAL TIPS ON COACHING

If You are the Expert Coach for the Person

- ☐ Being an expert is a matter of theme and pattern recognition and applying insights from that recognition. It is not just giving answers. What are you an expert in? What keys do you look at? How can you pass those on?
- ☐ Always explain your thinking. The role of a coach is to teach someone how to think/act in new ways. Giving the person solutions won't help unless she or he knows why and how you came up with them.
- ☐ Before you give advice, ask yourself why this is a strength for you or others you know. What are the first items (keys) you would teach as the keys to help the person form umbrellas for understanding? How did you learn to do this? What were your key experiences? Who helped you? Use these insights and the skilled definition of the competencies to write a list of key behaviors that the person can use as targets.

If You are the Person Being Coached

- ☐ Remember that it is the coach's role to help you grow. Your coach may be an expert in the developmental process and/or an expert in your need area. You will gain most if you focus less on the coach's solutions and more on why and how the coach arrived at the solution. Ask him/her to explain – many people won't do this unless you ask.
- ☐ How does your coach teach? What adjustments does she/he make for you as a learner? Ask for feedback on you as a learner.
- ☐ Set projects for yourself that give you feedback on how well you are gaining expertise in an area. If you are working on listening, set five specific situations in which you attentively listen. Set in advance what would be evidence of effectiveness with your coach.
- ☐ In the case of a boss/mentor as a coach, distance your feelings from the relationship and try to study things that work for this person. Focus on what the person does well.
- ☐ More effective learners reduce insights to rules of thumb. If your coach is an expert, what five things does the coach do that you think you could do? If you have a developmental coach, what have you learned about how to learn and develop that you can use again?

All good coaching requires a good learner – it's always a two-way process!

Before you enter the coaching relationship, read #*108 Defensiveness* and any other chapter that deals with blocks to learning. Until you get in the right frame of mind, your coach can't help you much.

ABOUT THE AUTHORS

Mike Lombardo (left) has over 20 years experience in executive and management research and has conducted over 1,000 individual feedback sessions. Some of the advice in this book results from his research background. During his 15 years at the Center for Creative Leadership, Mike was a co-author of ***The Lessons of Experience****, which detailed which learnings from experience can teach the competencies needed to be successful. He also co-authored the research on executive derailment revealing how personal flaws and overdone strengths caused otherwise effective executives to get into career trouble. After leaving the Center in 1990, Mike has continued his research efforts into issues of learning and competency improvement. During his career Mike has authored over 30 publications dealing with various issues of development. His feedback experience is both as an author – of BENCHMARKS®, VOICES® (which he and Bob Eichinger developed), and LOOKING GLASS® – and as a counselor. Mike has designed and conducted programs in the United States and abroad (which included these data sources), and given feedback both as a part of these programs and in individual sessions.*

Bob Eichinger (right) has been working with managers and executives on personal development for over 30 years. He has been a one-on-one feedback giver from both inside (at PepsiCo and Pillsbury) and from outside organizations using a number of publicly available 360° instruments (like BENCHMARKS®, MSP™, Profiler™ and VOICES®) as well as customized and tailored feedback instruments. He has also served on feedback teams within courses and off-site in various organizations and public courses. He has lectured extensively on the topic of executive and management development and has served on the Board of the Human Resource Planning Society, a professional association of people charged with the responsibility of management and executive development in their organizations. Bob has worked personally with well over 1,000 managers and executives over his career providing developmental suggestions contained in this book.

UNIVERSAL DEVELOPMENT PLAN FOR ANY COMPETENCY

☐ **1. Get specific.** Get more detailed and behavioral feedback on the need. Most of the time, people are weak in some aspect of a competency. It's almost never all interpersonal skills. It's usually something specific – for example, interpersonal skills with upper management under the pressure of tough questions from two of the seven on the management committee on topics you care deeply about. To find out more about what your need is specifically, go to a few people who know and who will tell you if you ask. Accept that you have a need. Don't be defensive or try to rationalize away the need. Say you are concerned about the need and request more detailed information so you can focus on an efficient plan for growth and development. Ask them for specific examples. When? Where? With whom? In what settings? Under what conditions? How many times? Might anyone they know be of help? Get as specific as you can. Listen, don't rebut. Take notes. Thank them for the input.

☐ **2. Creating the plan.** If you have accepted the need as true and you are ready to do something about it, you need three kinds of action plans. You need to know what to stop doing, start doing, and keep doing. Since you have a need in this area (you don't do this well), you need to stop some things you are doing that aren't working. In their place, you need to start doing some things you either don't like doing, haven't ever done, or don't even know about. Even if you are bad at something, there are things you do in this area that you are probably good at. Send a form or E-mail to a number of people who would be willing to help you work on this skill. Tell them you have discovered and taken ownership of this need, want to do something about it, list the specific need you discovered in step one, and ask them for the things you should stop doing, start doing and keep doing.

☐ **3. Learning from others.** Research shows that we learn best from others when we: a) Pick multiple models, each of whom excels at one thing rather than looking for the whole package in one person. Think more broadly than your current job for models; add some off work models. b) Take both the student and the teacher role. As a student, study other people – don't just admire or dislike what they do. One key to learning from others is to reduce what they do or don't do to a set of principles or rules of thumb to integrate into your behavior. As a teacher, it's one of the best ways to learn something as it forces you to think it through, and be concise in your explanation. c) Rely on multiple methods of learning – interview people, observe them without speaking with them, study remote models by reading books or watching films, get someone to tutor you, or use a contrast strategy. Sometimes it's hard to see the effects of your behavior because you are too close to the problem. Pick two people, one who is much better than you are at your need and one who is much worse. Copy what the good model does that leads to good outcomes. Get rid of the behaviors that match what the bad model does.

☐ **4. Read the "bible" on this need.** Every skill or competency has had one or more books written about it. How to negotiate to win. How to get along with bad bosses. How to win friends. How to be more creative. Go to a large business book store and buy at least two books covering your need (our recommendations are included at the end of each competency, performance dimension, or staller chapter). Take one hour and scan each book. Just read the first sentence of every paragraph. Don't read to learn. Just read to see the structure of the book. Pick the one that seems to be right for you and read it thoroughly. That book may reference or lead you to other books or articles on the skill. Use your reading to answer the following questions: What's the research on the skill? What are the 10 how to's all the experts would agree to? How is this skill best learned?

☐ **5. Learn from autobiographies and biographies.** Try to find books by or on two famous people who have the skill you are trying to build. Mother Teresa on compassion. Harry Truman on standing alone. Norman Schwarzkopf on leadership. Helen Keller on persistence. Try to see how they wove the skill you are working on into their fabric of skills. Was there a point in their lives when they weren't good at this skill? What was the turning point?

☐ **6. Learn from a course.** Find the best course you have access to. It might be offered in your organization or more likely it will be a public program. Find one that is taught by the author of a book or a series of articles on this need. Be sure to give it enough time. It usually takes three to five days to learn about any skill or competency. One to two day courses are usually not long enough. Find one where you learn the theory and have a lot of practice with the skill. Find one that video tapes if the skill lends itself to the lens. Take your detailed plan with you and take notes against your need. Don't just take notes following the course outline. For example, if you're attending a listening course and one of your need statements is how to listen when people ramble, take notes against that specific statement; or if your need involves a task or project, write down action steps you can take immediately. Throw yourself into the course. No phone calls. Don't take any work with you. No sightseeing. Just do the course. Be the best student in the course and learn the most. Seldom will a course alone be sufficient to address a need. A course always has to be combined with the other remedies in this General Plan, especially stretching tasks so you can perform against your need under pressure.

☐ **7. Get a partner.** Sometimes it's easier to build a skill if you have someone to work with. If you can find someone working on the same need, you can share learnings and support each other. Take turns teaching each other some to do's – one of the best ways to cement your learning. Share books you've found. Courses you've attended. Models you've observed. You can give each other progress feedback. Or get a learning buddy, someone who will help you grow. Have him/her agree to observe and give you feedback against your learning objectives.

☐ **8. Try some stretching tasks, but start small.** Seventy per cent of skills development happens on the job. As you talk with others while building this skill, get them to brainstorm tasks and activities you can try. Write down five tasks you will commit to doing, tasks like: initiate three conversations, make peace with someone you've had problems with, write a business plan for your unit, negotiate a purchase, make a speech, find something to fix. You can try tasks off the job as well: teach someone to read, be a volunteer, join a study group, take up a new hobby – whatever will help you practice your need in a fairly low risk way. After each task, write down the +'s and –'s of your performance and note things you will try to do better or differently next time.

☐ **9. Track your own progress.** You are going to need some extra motivation to get through this. You need to be able to reward yourself for progress you've made. Others may not notice the subtle changes for awhile. Set progress goals and benchmarks for yourself. If you were working on approachability for instance, have a goal of initiating conversations with five new people a week. Keep a log. Make a chart. Celebrate incremental progress. Noting times you didn't interrupt others or made two strategy suggestions that people grabbed and discussed will reinforce your continued efforts.

☐ **10. Get periodic feedback.** Get a group of people who haven't known you for long. They don't have a history of seeing you not do well in this skill over a long period of time. Get feedback from them a third of the way into your skill building plan. Also, go back to the original group who helped you see and accept this need. Their ratings will lag behind the first group because they know your history in this skill. Use both groups to monitor your progress.

1

ACTION ORIENTED

SECTION 1: YOUR DEVELOPMENT NEED(S)

UNSKILLED

- ☐ Slow to act on an opportunity
- ☐ May be overly methodical, a perfectionist, or risk averse
- ☐ May procrastinate
- ☐ May not set very challenging goals
- ☐ May lack confidence to act
- ☐ May know what to do but hesitates to do it
- ☐ May not be motivated; may be bored with the work or burned out

SKILLED

- ☐ Enjoys working hard
- ☐ Is action oriented and full of energy for the things he/she sees as challenging
- ☐ Not fearful of acting with a minimum of planning
- ☐ Seizes more opportunities than others

OVERUSED SKILL

- ☐ May be a workaholic
- ☐ May push solutions before adequate analysis
- ☐ May be non-strategic
- ☐ May overmanage to get things done too quickly
- ☐ May have personal and family problems due to disinterest and neglect
- ☐ May not attend to important but non-challenging duties and tasks
- ☐ May ignore personal life, burn out

Select one to three of the competencies listed below to work on to compensate for an overuse of this skill.

COMPENSATORS: 11, 27, 33, 39, 41, 43, 47, 50, 51, 52, 60, 66

SOME CAUSES

- ☐ Burned out
- ☐ Hang on to too much
- ☐ Not motivated; bored
- ☐ Not passionate enough about your work
- ☐ Not self confident
- ☐ Perfectionist
- ☐ Procrastinate
- ☐ Slow to grab an opportunity
- ☐ Won't take a risk

THE MAP

One mission-critical competency for today and the future is action orientation. The need for speed and agility in the marketplace means that those individuals and organizations who hesitate will be overtaken by those who don't. Most successful senior managers count action orientation as one of their strengths. The hesitation mainly comes from perfectionism, procrastination or risk avoidance. All cause people to delay taking quick and timely action.

SECTION 2: LEARNING ON YOUR OWN

THESE SELF-DEVELOPMENT REMEDIES WILL HELP YOU BUILD YOUR SKILL(S)

SOME REMEDIES

☐ **1. Procrastinate?** Are you a lifelong procrastinator? Do you perform best in crises and impossible deadlines? Do you wait until the last possible moment? If you do, you will miss some deadlines and performance targets. You may be late taking action. Start earlier. Always do 10% of each task immediately after it is assigned so you can better gauge what it is going to take to finish the rest. Break the task down into smaller pieces. Commit to doing a piece a day. Don't even think of the larger goal. Just do something on it each day. One small step for a procrastinator, one giant step forward to being more action oriented. *More help? – See #16* Timely *Decision Making and #47 Planning.*

☐ **2. Perfectionist?** Need to be 100% sure? Perfectionism is tough to let go of because it's a positive trait for most. Worried about what people will say when you mess up? When every "t" isn't crossed? Recognize your perfectionism for what it might be – collecting information to improve your confidence and avoid criticism, examining opportunities so long you miss them, or waiting for the perfect solution. Try to decrease your need for all of the data and your need to be right all the time slightly every week, until you reach a more reasonable balance between thinking it through and taking action. Also, you may hold on to too much of the work, fail to delegate, and are becoming a bottleneck preventing action around you. One way to overcome this is to begin to believe in others and let them do some of the work for you. *More help? – See #18 Delegation and #19 Developing Direct Reports.*

☐ **3. Analysis paralysis?** Break out of your examine-it-to-death mode and just do it. Sometimes you hold back acting because you don't have all the information. Some like to be close to 100% sure before they act. Anyone with a brain and 100% of the data can make good decisions. The real test is who can act the soonest with a reasonable amount but not all of the data. Some studies suggest successful general managers are about 65% correct. If you learn to make smaller decisions more quickly, you can change course along the way to the correct decision.

☐ **4. Build up your confidence.** Maybe you're slow to act because you don't think you're up to the task. If you boldly act, others will shoot you down and find you out. Take a course or work with a tutor to bolster your confidence in one skill or area at a time. Focus on the strengths you do have; think of ways you can use these strengths when making nerve wracking actions. If you are interpersonally skilled, for example, see yourself smoothly dealing with questions and objections to your actions. The only way you will ever know what you can do is to act and find out.

☐ **5. Don't like risk?** Sometimes taking action involves pushing the envelope, taking chances and trying bold new initiatives. Doing those things leads to more misfires and mistakes. Research says that successful executives have made more mistakes in their career than those who didn't make it. Treat any mistakes or failures as chances to learn. Nothing ventured, nothing gained. Up your risk comfort. Start small so you can recover more quickly. Go for small wins. Don't blast into a major task to prove your boldness. Break it down into smaller tasks. Take the easiest one for you first. Then build up to the tougher ones. Review each one to see what you did well and not well, and set goals so you'll do something differently and better each time. End up accomplishing the big goal and taking the bold action. Challenge yourself. See how creative you can be in taking action a number of different ways. *More help? – See #2* Dealing with *Ambiguity, #14 Creativity, and #28 Innovation Management.*

☐ **6. Lost your passion?** Run out of gas? Heart's not in it anymore? Not 100% committed? Doing the same sort of work a long time and you're bored with it? Seen it all; done the same tasks, made the same decisions, worked with the same people? To make the best of this, make a list of what you like and don't like to do. Concentrate on doing at least a couple of liked activities each day. Work to delegate or task trade the things that are no longer motivating to you. Do your least preferred activities first; focus not on the activity, but your sense of accomplishment. Change your work activity to mirror your interests as much as you can. Volunteer for task forces and projects that would be motivating for you.

☐ **7. Set better priorities.** You may not have the correct set of priorities. Some people take action but on the wrong things. Effective managers typically spend about half their time on two or three key priorities. What should you spend half your time on? Can you name five things that you have to do that are less critical? If you can't, you're not differentiating well. People without priorities see their jobs as 97 things that need to be done right now – that will actually slow you down. Pick a few mission-critical things and get them done. Don't get diverted by trivia. *More help? – See #50 Priority Setting.*

☐ **8. Get organized.** Some don't know the best way to get things done. There is a well established set of best practices for getting work done efficiently and effectively. Formally they are known as Total Quality Management and Process Re-Engineering. If you are not disciplined in how you design work for yourself and others, and are late taking action because of it, buy one book on each of these topics. Go to one workshop on efficient and effective work design. *More help? – See #52 Process Management and #63 TQM/Re-Engineering.*

☐ **9. Afraid to get others involved?** Taking action requires that you get others on board. Work on your influence and selling skills. Lay out the business reason for the action. Think about how you can help everybody win with the action. Get others involved before you have to take action. Involved people are easier to influence. Learn better negotiation skills. Learn to bargain and trade. *More help? – See #31 Interpersonal Savvy, #37 Negotiating, and #39 Organizing.*

☐ **10. Not committed?** Maybe you are giving as much to work as you care to give. Maybe you have made a life/work balance decision that leads you to a fair day's work for a fair day's pay mode of operating. No more. No less. That is an admirable decision. Certainly one you can and should make. Problem is, you may be in a job where that's not enough. Otherwise people would not have given you this rating. You might want to talk to your boss to get transferred to a more comfortable job for you; one that doesn't take as much effort and require as much action initiation on your part. You may even think about moving down to the job level where your balance between quality of life, and effort and hours required of you at work are more balanced.

SECTION 3: LEARNING FROM MORE FEEDBACK

THESE SOURCES WOULD GIVE YOU THE MOST ACCURATE AND DETAILED FEEDBACK ON YOUR SKILL(S)

☐ **Direct Boss**

Your direct boss has important information about you, your performance, and your prospects. The challenge is to get this information. There are formal processes (e.g., performance appraisals). There are day-to-day opportunities. To help, signal your boss that you want and can handle direct and timely feedback. Many bosses have trouble giving feedback, so you will have to work at it over a period of time.

☐ **Direct Reports**

Across a variety of settings, your direct reports probably see you the most. They are the recipients of most of your managerial behaviors. They know your work. They can compare you with former bosses. Since they may hesitate to give you negative feedback, you have to set the atmosphere to make it easier for them. You have to ask.

- ☐ **Natural Mentors**
  Natural mentors have a special relationship with you and are interested in your success and your future. Since they are usually not in your direct chain of command, you can have more open, relaxed, and fruitful discussions about yourself and your career prospects. They can be a very important source for candid or critical feedback others may not give you.
- ☐ **Past Associates/Constituencies**
  When confronted with a present performance problem, some claim, "I wasn't like that before; it must be the current situation." When feedback is available from former associates, about 50% support that claim. In the other half of the cases, the people were like that before and probably didn't know it. It sometimes makes sense to access the past to clearly see the present.
- ☐ **Spouse**
  Spouses can be powerful sources of feedback on such things as interpersonal style, values, balance between work, career, and personal life, etc. Many participants attending development programs share their feedback with their spouses for value-adding confirmation or context and for specific examples.

SECTION 4: LEARNING FROM DEVELOP-IN-PLACE ASSIGNMENTS

THESE PART-TIME DEVELOP-IN-PLACE ASSIGNMENTS WILL HELP YOU BUILD YOUR SKILL(S)

- ☐ Plan for and start up something small (secretarial pool, athletic program, suggestion system, program, etc.).
- ☐ Launch a new product, service, or process.
- ☐ Relaunch an existing product or service that's not doing well.
- ☐ Manage an ad hoc, temporary group of balky and resisting people through an unpopular change or project.
- ☐ Manage an ad hoc, temporary group of people involved in tackling a fix-it or turnaround project.
- ☐ Help shut down a plant, regional office, product line, business, operation, etc.
- ☐ Manage a group through a significant business crisis.
- ☐ Take on a tough and undoable project, one where others who have tried it have failed.
- ☐ Take on a task you dislike or hate to do.
- ☐ Resolve an issue in conflict between two people, units, geographies, functions, etc.

SECTION 5: LEARNING FROM FULL-TIME JOBS

THESE FULL-TIME JOBS OFFER THE OPPORTUNITY TO BUILD YOUR SKILL(S)

- ☐ **Fix-its / Turnarounds**

  The core demands to qualify as a Fix-it or Turnaround assignment are: 1) Cleaning up a mess. 2) Serious people issues/problems like credibility/performance/morale. 3) Tight deadline. 4) Serious business performance failure. 5) Last chance to fix. Four Types of Fix-its/Turnarounds: 1) Fixing a failed business/unit involving taking control, stopping losses, managing damage, planning the turnaround, dealing with people problems, installing new processes and systems, and rebuilding the spirit and performance of the unit. 2) Managing sizable disasters like mishandled labor negotiations and strikes, thefts, history of significant business losses, poor staff, failed leadership, hidden problems, fraud, public relations nightmares, etc. 3) Significant reorganization and restructuring (e.g., stabilizing the business, re-forming the unit, introducing new systems, making people changes, resetting strategy and tactics). 4) Significant system/process breakdown (e.g., MIS, financial coordination processes, audits, standards, etc.) across units requiring working to change something from a distant position, providing advice and counsel, and installing or implementing a major process improvement or system change outside your own unit and/or with customers outside the organization.

- ☐ **Influencing Without Authority**

  The core demands to qualify as an Influence Without Authority are: 1) Significant challenge (e.g, start-up, fix-it, scope and/or scale assignment, strategic planning project, changes in management practices/systems). 2) Insufficient direct authority to make it happen. 3) Tight deadlines. 4) Visible to significant others. 5) Sensitive politics.

- ☐ **Start-ups**

  The core demands to qualify as a start from scratch are: 1) Starting something new for you and/or for the organization. 2) Forging a new team. 3) Creating new systems/facilities/staffs/programs/procedures. 4) Contextual adversity (e.g., uncertainty, government regulation, unions, difficult environment). Seven types of start from scratches: 1) Planning, building, hiring, and managing (e.g., building a new facility, opening up a new location, moving a unit or company). 2) Heading something new (e.g., new product, new service, new line of business, new department/function, major new program). 3) Taking over a group/product/service/program that had existed for less than a year and was off to a fast start. 4) Establishing overseas operations. 5) Making major new designs for existing systems. 6) Moving a successful program from one unit to another. 7) Installing a new organization-wide process as a full-time job (e.g., like Total Quality).

SECTION 6: LEARNING MORE FROM YOUR PLAN

THESE ADDITIONAL REMEDIES WILL HELP MAKE THIS DEVELOPMENT PLAN MORE EFFECTIVE FOR YOU

Learning to Learn Better

☐ **Teach Others Something You Don't Know Well**
Commit to a project like teaching something you don't know much about to force you to learn quickly to accomplish the task; pick something new, different, or unfamiliar.

☐ **Commit to a Tight Timeframe to Accomplish Something**
Set some specific goals and tighter than usual timeframes for yourself and go after them with all you've got. Push yourself to stick to the plan; get more done than usual by adhering to a tight plan.

☐ **Do Something on Gut Feel More Than Analysis**
Act on "gut feel;" go with your hunches instead of careful planning. Take a chance on a solution; take some risks; try a number of things by trial and error and learn to deal with making some mistakes.

Learning from Experience, Feedback and Other People

☐ **Taking the Initiative**
People are reluctant to give others direct criticism. Many bosses lack the managerial courage to give their direct reports complete and timely feedback, and especially corrective feedback. Hence, most people report not getting sufficient feedback. To assure continued progress, people must actively seek and orchestrate their own feedback.

☐ **The More the Better**
The more feedback you receive the better. The more credible the sources the better. The more frequent the better. The sooner the better. The more targeted the better. You will want to use as many sources and methods as you can.

☐ **Getting Feedback from Bosses and Superiors**
Many bosses are reluctant to give negative feedback. They lack the managerial courage to face people directly with criticism. You can help by soliciting feedback and setting the tone. Show them you can handle criticism and that you are willing to work on issues they see as important.

☐ **Getting Feedback from Direct Reports**
Direct reports often fear reprisals for giving negative feedback about bosses, whether in a formal process, like a questionnaire, or informally and face-to-face. Even with a guarantee of confidentiality, some are still hesitant. If you want feedback from direct reports, you have to set a positive tone and never act out of revenge.

☐ **Learning from Limited Staff**
Most managers either inherit or hire staff from time to time who are inexperienced, incompetent, not up to the task, resistant, or dispirited. Any of these may create a hardship for you. The lessons to be learned are how to get things done with limited resources and how to fix the people situation. In the short term, this hardship is best addressed by assessing the combined strengths of the team and deploying the best you have against the problem. Almost everyone can do something well. Also, the team can contribute more than the combined individuals can. How can you empower and motivate the team? If you hired the troublesome staff, why did you err? What can you learn from your hiring mistakes? What wasn't there that you thought was present? What led you astray? How can you prevent that same hiring error in the future? What do you need to do to fix the situation? Quick development? Start over? If you inherited the problem, how can you fix it? Can you implement a program of accelerated development? Do you have to start over and get new people? What did the prior manager do or not do that led to this situation in the first place? What can you learn from that? What will you do differently? How does the staff feel? What can you learn from their frustrations over not being able to do the job? How can you be a positive force under negative circumstances? How can you rally them to perform? What lasting lessons can you learn from someone in distress and trouble? If you're going to try accelerated development, how can you get a quick assessment? How can you give the staff motivating feedback? How can you construct and implement development plans that will work? How can you get people on-line feedback for maximum growth? Do you know when to stop trying and start over? If you're going to turn over some staff, how can you do it both rapidly and with the least damage? How can you deliver the message in a constructive way? What can you learn from having to take negative actions against people? How can you prevent this from happening again?

☐ **Learning from Mistakes**
Since we're human, we all make mistakes. The key is to focus on why you made the mistake. Spend more time locating causes and less worrying about the effects. Check how you react to mistakes. How much time do you spend being angry with yourself? Do you waste time stewing or do you move on? More importantly, do you learn? Ask why you made the mistake. Are you likely to repeat it under similar situations? Was it a lack of skill? Judgment? Style? Not enough data? Reading people? Misreading the challenge? Misreading the politics? Or was it just random? A good strategy that just didn't work? Others that let you down? The key is to avoid two common reactions to your mistakes: 1) avoiding similar situations instead of learning and trying again, and 2) trying to repeat what you did, only more diligently and harder, hoping to break through the problem, making the same

mistake again but with greater impact. Neither trap leaves us with better strategies for the future. Neither is a learning strategy. To learn and do something differently, focus on the patterns in your behavior that get you in trouble and go back to first causes, those that tell you something about your shortcomings. Facing ourselves squarely is always the best way to learn.

SUGGESTED READINGS

Bandrowski, James F. *Corporate Imagination Plus – Five steps to translating innovative strategies into action*. New York: Macmillan, Inc., 1990.

Belasco, James A. and Jerre Stead. *Soaring with the Phoenix – Renewing the vision, reviving the spirit, and re-creating the success of your company*. New York: Warner Books, 1999.

Conger, Jay A., Gretchen M. Spreitzer and Edward E. Lawler III, editors. *The leader's change handbook: an essential guide to setting direction and taking action*. San Francisco, CA: Jossey-Bass, 1999.

Kaplan, Robert S. and David P. Norton. *The Balanced Scorecard: Translating strategy into action*. Boston: Harvard Business School Press, 1996.

Powell, Colin L. with Joseph E. Persico. *My American Journey*. New York: Random House, 1995.

Powell, Colin L. with Joseph E. Persico. *My American Journey [sound recording]*. New York: Random House Audiobooks,1995.

...or...

Roth, David. *Sacred Honor: A biography of Colin Powell*. San Francisco: Harper, 1993.

Roth, David. *Sacred Honor: A biography of Colin Powell* [sound recording]. Grand Rapids, Mich.: Audio Pages, 1993.

2

DEALING WITH AMBIGUITY

SECTION 1: YOUR DEVELOPMENT NEED(S)

UNSKILLED

- ☐ Not comfortable with change or uncertainty
- ☐ May not do well on fuzzy problems with no clear solution or outcome
- ☐ May prefer more data than others, and structure over uncertainty
- ☐ Prefers things tacked down and sure
- ☐ Less efficient and productive under ambiguity
- ☐ Too quick to close
- ☐ May have a strong need to finish everything
- ☐ May like to do things the same way time after time

SKILLED

- ☐ Can effectively cope with change
- ☐ Can shift gears comfortably
- ☐ Can decide and act without having the total picture
- ☐ Isn't upset when things are up in the air
- ☐ Doesn't have to finish things before moving on
- ☐ Can comfortably handle risk and uncertainty

OVERUSED SKILL

- ☐ May move to conclusions without enough data
- ☐ May fill in gaps by adding things that aren't there
- ☐ May frustrate others by not getting specific enough
- ☐ May undervalue orderly problem solving
- ☐ May reject precedent and history
- ☐ May err toward the new and risky at the expense of proven solutions
- ☐ May over-complicate things

Select one to three of the competencies listed below to work on to compensate for an overuse of this skill.

COMPENSATORS: 5, 17, 24, 30, 35, 39, 40, 47, 50, 51, 52, 59, 61, 63

SOME CAUSES

- ☐ Avoid criticism
- ☐ Avoid risk
- ☐ Disorganized
- ☐ Get overwhelmed
- ☐ Like structure and control
- ☐ Perfectionist

THE MAP

According to studies, 90% of the problems of middle managers and above are ambiguous – it's neither clear what the problem is nor what the solution is. The higher you go, the more ambiguous things get. Most people with a brain, given unlimited time and 100% of the information, could make accurate and good decisions. Most people, given access to how this specific problem has been solved hundreds of times before, could repeat the right decision. The real rewards go to those who can comfortably make more good decisions than bad with less than all of the information, in less time, with few or no precedents on how it was solved before.

SECTION 2: LEARNING ON YOUR OWN

THESE SELF-DEVELOPMENT REMEDIES WILL HELP YOU BUILD YOUR SKILL(S)

SOME REMEDIES

☐ **1. Incrementalism.** The essence of dealing comfortably with uncertainty is the tolerance of errors and mistakes, and absorbing the possible heat and criticism that follow. Acting on an ill-defined problem with no precedents to follow means shooting in the dark with as informed a decision as you can make at the time. People who are good at this are incrementalists. They make a series of smaller decisions, get instant feedback, correct the course, get a little more data, move forward a little more, until the bigger problem is under control. They don't try to get it right the first time. Many problem-solving studies show that the second or third try is when we really understand the underlying dynamics of problems. They also know that the more uncertain the situation is, the more likely it is they will make mistakes in the beginning. So you need to work on two practices. Start small so you can recover more quickly. Do little somethings as soon as you can and get used to heat.

☐ **2. Perfectionist?** Need or prefer or want to be 100% sure? Lots might prefer that. Perfectionism is tough to let go of because most people see it as a positive trait for themselves. Recognize your perfectionism for what it might be – collecting more information than others to improve your confidence in making a fault-free decision and thereby avoiding risk and criticism. Try to decrease your need for data and your need to be right all the time slightly every week until you reach a more reasonable balance between thinking it through and taking action. Try making some small decisions on little or no data. Anyone with a brain and 100% of the data can make good decisions. The real test is who can act the soonest with a reasonable amount, but not all, of the data. Some studies suggest successful general managers are about 65% correct. Trust your intuition. Let your brain do the calculations.

☐ **3. Stuck with what you know?** Do you feel best when you know everything that's going on around you and are in control. Most do. Few are motivated by uncertainty and chaos. But many are challenged by it. They enjoy solving problems no one has solved before. They enjoy cutting paths where no one has been before. You need to become more comfortable being a pioneer. Explore new ground. Learn new things. Practice in your life. Go to theme restaurants you know nothing about. Vacation at places without doing a lot of research. Go to ethnic festivals for groups you have little knowledge about.

☐ **4. Disorganized?** Under uncertainty, you have to put the keel in the water yourself. You need to set tight priorities. Focus on the mission-critical few. Don't get diverted by trivia. Get better organized and disciplined. There is a well established set of best practices for getting work done efficiently and effectively. If you are not disciplined in how you design work for yourself and others and are late taking action because of it, buy a book on both Total Quality Management and Process Re-Engineering. Go to one workshop on efficient and effective work design. *More help? – See #50 Priority Setting, #52 Process Management, and #63 Total Quality Management/Re-Engineering.*

☐ **5. Problem definition.** Under uncertainty, it really helps to get as firm a handle as possible on the problem. Figure out what causes it. Keep asking why. See how many causes you can come up with and how many organizing buckets you can put them in. This increases the chance of a better solution because you can see more connections. The evidence from decision-making research makes it clear that thorough problem definition with appropriate questions to answer leads to better decisions. Focusing on solutions or information first often slows things down since we have no conceptual buckets in which to organize our thinking. Learn to ask more questions. In one study of problem solving, 7% of comments were questions and about half were solutions.

☐ **6. Visualize the problem.** Complex processes or problems with a lot of uncertainty are hard to understand. They tend to be a hopeless maze unless they are put in a visual format. One technique is a pictorial chart called a storyboard where a process or vision or strategy is illustrated by its components being depicted as pictures. A variation of this is to do the old pro and con, +'s and -'s of a problem and process, then flow chart those according to what's working and not working. Another is the wishbone diagram used in Total Quality Management. It is a method of breaking down the causes of a problem into categories. Buy a flow charting software program like ABC FlowCharter® 4.0 to help you visualize problems quickly.

☐ **7. Develop a philosophical stance toward failure/criticism.** After all, most innovations fail, most proposals fail, most change efforts fail, anything worth doing takes repeated effort. To increase learning from your mistakes, design feedback loops to be as immediate as possible.

The faster and the more frequent the cycles, the more opportunities to learn – if we do one smaller thing a day for three days instead of one bigger thing in three, we triple our learning opportunities. There will be many mistakes and failures; after all, since you're not sure, it's very likely no one else knows what to do either. They just have a right to comment on your errors. The best tack when confronted with a mistake is to say, "What can we learn from this?" *More help? – See #45 Personal Learning*.

☐ **8. Stress.** Some get stressed with increased ambiguity and uncertainty. We lose our anchor. We are not at our best when we are anxious, frustrated, upset or when we lose our cool. What brings out your emotional response? Write down why you get anxious – when you don't know what to do; don't want to make a mistake; afraid of the unknown consequences; don't have the confidence to act. When you get emotional, drop the problem for awhile. Go do something else. Come back to it when you are under better control. Let your brain work on it while you do something safer. *More help? – See #11 Composure and #107* Lack of *Composure*.

☐ **9. Change is letting go** of one trapeze in the air to catch the next one. For a small amount of time, you have hold of nothing but thin air. The second gets you to a new platform and a new place. If you hang on to the first one, afraid you will fall, you will always return to the same old platform; safe but not new or different. Change is letting go. Stay informed about business/technological change and ask what it means for your work. Visualize a different and better outcome. Talk about it. Invite ideas. Interview those who have successfully pulled off changes. Experiment. The more you do this, the more comfortable you'll feel. To better understand dealing with change, read *The Future of Leadership* by White, Hodgson and Crainer.

☐ **10. Finishing.** Do you prefer to finish what you have started? Do you have a high need to complete tasks? Wrap them up in nice clean packages? Working well with ambiguity and under uncertainty means moving from incomplete task to incomplete task. Some may be abandoned, some may never be finished. They'll probably only ever get 80% done and you'll constantly have to edit your actions and decisions. Change your internal reward process toward feeling good about fixing mistakes and moving things forward incrementally, more than finishing any given project.

SECTION 3: LEARNING FROM MORE FEEDBACK

THESE SOURCES WOULD GIVE YOU THE MOST ACCURATE AND DETAILED FEEDBACK ON YOUR SKILL(S)

- ☐ **Natural Mentors**
  Natural mentors have a special relationship with you and are interested in your success and your future. Since they are usually not in your direct chain of command, you can have more open, relaxed, and fruitful discussions about yourself and your career prospects. They can be a very important source for candid or critical feedback others may not give you.
- ☐ **Past Associates/Constituencies**
  When confronted with a present performance problem, some claim, "I wasn't like that before; it must be the current situation." When feedback is available from former associates, about 50% support that claim. In the other half of the cases, the people were like that before and probably didn't know it. It sometimes makes sense to access the past to clearly see the present.
- ☐ **Peers and Colleagues**
  Peers and colleagues have a special social and working relationship. They attend staff meetings together, share private views, get feedback from the same boss, travel together, and are knowledgeable about each other's work. You perhaps let your guard down more around peers and act more like yourself. They can be a valuable source of feedback.

SECTION 4: LEARNING FROM DEVELOP-IN-PLACE ASSIGNMENTS

THESE PART-TIME DEVELOP-IN-PLACE ASSIGNMENTS WILL HELP YOU BUILD YOUR SKILL(S)

- ☐ Integrate diverse systems, processes, or procedures across decentralized and/or dispersed units.
- ☐ Go on a business trip to a foreign country you've not been to before.
- ☐ Relaunch an existing product or service that's not doing well.
- ☐ Manage an ad hoc, temporary group of balky and resisting people through an unpopular change or project.
- ☐ Manage an ad hoc, temporary group of people where the people in the group are towering experts but the temporary manager is not.
- ☐ Assemble an ad hoc team of diverse people to accomplish a difficult task.
- ☐ Take on a tough and undoable project, one where others who have tried it have failed.
- ☐ Take on a task you dislike or hate to do.

- ☐ Make peace with an enemy or someone you've disappointed with a product or service or someone you've had some trouble with or don't get along well with.
- ☐ Build a multifunctional project team to tackle a common business issue or problem.

SECTION 5: LEARNING FROM FULL-TIME JOBS

THESE FULL-TIME JOBS OFFER THE OPPORTUNITY TO BUILD YOUR SKILL(S)

☐ **Chair of Projects/Task Forces**

The core demands for qualifying as a Project/Task Force assignment are: 1) Full-time assignment. 2) Important and specific goal. 3) Tight deadline. 4) Success or failure will be evident. 5) High-visibility sponsor. 6) Learning something on the fly. 7) Must get others to cooperate. 8) Usually six months or more. Four types of Projects/Task Forces: 1) New ideas, products, services, or systems (e.g., product/service/program research and development, creation/installation/launch of a new system, new programs like Total Quality Management, positive discipline). 2) Formal negotiations and relationships (e.g., acquisitions, divestitures, agreements, joint ventures, licensing arrangements, franchising, dealing with unions, governments, communities, charities, customers, and relocations). 3) Big one-time events (e.g., working on a major presentation for the board, organizing significant meetings or conferences, disaster/damage control teams, reorganizations, mergers, acquisitions, or relocations, working on visions, charters, strategies, other time-urgent issues and problems). 4) Troubleshooting (e.g., problems, disasters, crises, product/service failures, accidents, illegal activities, damage control in public relations goofs, shut downs, downsizings, layoffs, abrupt changes in leadership).

☐ **Fix-its/Turnarounds**

The core demands to qualify as a Fix-it or Turnaround assignment are: 1) Cleaning up a mess. 2) Serious people issues/problems like credibility/performance/morale. 3) Tight deadline. 4) Serious business performance failure. 5) Last chance to fix. Four Types of Fix-its/Turnarounds: 1) Fixing a failed business/unit involving taking control, stopping losses, managing damage, planning the turnaround, dealing with people problems, installing new processes and systems, and rebuilding the spirit and performance of the unit. 2) Managing sizable disasters like mishandled labor negotiations and strikes, thefts, history of significant business losses, poor staff, failed leadership, hidden problems, fraud, public relations nightmares, etc. 3) Significant reorganization and restructuring (e.g., stabilizing the business, re-forming unit, introducing new systems, making people changes, resetting strategy and tactics). 4) Significant system/process breakdown (e.g., MIS, financial coordination processes, audits, standards, etc.) across units requiring working to change something from a distant position, providing advice and counsel, and installing or implementing a major process improvement or system change outside your own unit and/or with customers outside the organization.

☐ **Heavy Strategic Demands**
The core demands necessary to qualify as a Heavy Strategic Content assignment are: 1) Requires significant strategic thinking and planning most couldn't do. 2) Charts new ground strategically. 3) Plan must be presented, challenged, adopted, and implemented. 4) Exposure to significant decision-makers and executives. 1) Strategic planning position. 2) Job involving repositioning of a product, service, or organization.

☐ **Influencing Without Authority**
The core demands to qualify as an Influence Without Authority are: 1) Significant challenge (e.g, start-up, fix-it, scope and/or scale assignment, strategic planning project, changes in management practices/ systems). 2) Insufficient direct authority to make it happen. 3) Tight deadlines. 4) Visible to significant others. 5) Sensitive politics.

SECTION 6: LEARNING MORE FROM YOUR PLAN

THESE ADDITIONAL REMEDIES WILL HELP MAKE THIS DEVELOPMENT PLAN MORE EFFECTIVE FOR YOU

Learning to Learn Better

☐ **Monitoring Yourself More Closely and Getting off Your Autopilot**
Past habits are a mixed blessing, sometimes helping, sometimes not. To avoid putting yourself on "autopilot," think afresh about each situation before acting. Consistently monitor yourself with questions. Is this task different? Ask why you would repeat a past action. Are you avoiding anything, like taking a chance? Is there something new you might try?

☐ **Be Alert to Learnings When Faced With Transitions**
To avoid applying rigid habits, be alert to situations that require a transition to a new set of conditions and reactions; check what's similar and what's different; think out which past lessons and rules apply and which need to be changed. Don't apply old solutions because you have missed subtle differences.

☐ **Teach Others Something You Don't Know Well**
Commit to a project like teaching something you don't know much about to force you to learn quickly to accomplish the task; pick something new, different, or unfamiliar.

☐ **Put Yourself in Situations that Call for Your Weaknesses**
Put yourself in situations where you must overcome or neutralize a weakness to be successful. Find opportunities to develop counter coping skills: if you're shy, attend functions where you don't know many people; if you're too aggressive, work with children, etc.

- ☐ **Break Up Your Work Routine When You're Blocked**
When blocked on a problem, intersperse your work routine with dissimilar tasks, activities, or rest breaks. Turn to another task for awhile. In a sequence of tough work, string dissimilar tasks together so you can vary the types of skills used and the work done.

- ☐ **Examine Why You're Blocked on a Key Issue**
Examine what you are worrying/angry about and list all of your thoughts about it; ask why these feelings are holding you back. Why are the feelings overriding your thinking? How are they getting in the way? Why are they important to you? How can you move beyond them and learn to do something different?

Learning from Experience, Feedback and Other People

- ☐ **Being a Student of Others**
While many of us rely on others for information or advice, we do not really study the behavior of other people. Ask what a person does exceptionally well or poorly. What behaviors are particularly effective and ineffective for them? What works for them and what doesn't? As a student of others, you can deduce the rules of thumb for effective and ineffective behavior and include those in your own library. In comparing yourself with this person, in what areas could you most improve? What could you specifically do to improve in ways comfortable for you?

- ☐ **Learning from Bad Situations**
All of us will find ourselves in bad situations from time to time. Good intentions gone bad. Impossible tasks and goals. Hopeless projects. Even though you probably can't perform well, the key is to at least take away some lessons and insights. How did things get to be this way? What factors led to the impasse? How can you make the best of a bad situation? How can you neutralize the negative elements? How can you get the most out of yourself and your staff under the chilling situation? What can you salvage? How can you use coping strategies to minimize the negatives? How can you avoid these situations going forward? In bad situations: 1) Be resourceful. Get the most you can out of the situation. 2) Try to deduce why things got to be that way. 3) Learn from both the situation you inherited and how you react to it. 4) Integrate what you learn into your future behavior.

Learning from Courses

- ☐ **Strategic Courses**
There are a number of courses designed to stretch minds to prepare for future challenges. They include topics such as Workforce Diversity 2000, globalization, the European Union, competitive competencies and strategies, etc. Quality depends upon the following three factors: 1) The quality of the staff. Are they qualified? Are they respected in

their fields? Are they strategic "gurus"? 2) The quality of the participants. Are they the kind of people you could learn from? 3) The quality of the setting. Is it comfortable and free from distractions? Can you learn there?

☐ **Attitude Toward Learning**
In addition to selecting the right course, a learning attitude is required. Be open. Close down your "like/dislike" switch, your "agree/disagree" blinders, and your "like me/not like me" feelings toward the instructors. Learning requires new lessons, change, and new behaviors and perspectives – all scary stuff for most people. Don't resist. Take in all you can during the course. Ask clarifying questions. Discuss concerns with the other participants. Jot down what you learn as you go. After the course is over, take some reflective time to glean the meat. Make the practical decisions about what you can and cannot use.

SUGGESTED READINGS

Handy, Charles. *The Gods of Management*. London: Oxford University Press, 1995.

Kotter, John P. *Leading Change*. Boston: Harvard Business School Press, 1996.

Macdonald, John. *Calling a Halt to Mindless Change*. New York: AMACOM, 1998.

Olesen, Erik. *12 Steps to Mastering the Winds of Change*. New York: Macmillan, 1993.

O'Toole, James. *Leading Change*. Boston: Harvard Business School Press, 1996.

Price Waterhouse Change Integration Team. *Better Change*. Burr Ridge, IL: Irwin Professional Publishing, 1995.

Stone, Florence M. *The Manager's Balancing Act*. New York: AMACOM, 1997.

White, Randall P., Philip Hodgson and Stuart Crainer. *The future of leadership: Riding the corporate rapids into the 21st century*. Washington, DC: Pitman Publishing, 1996.

3

APPROACHABILITY

SECTION 1: YOUR DEVELOPMENT NEED(S)

UNSKILLED

- ☐ Distant, not easy to be around
- ☐ Not comfortable with first contacts
- ☐ May be shy, cool or a person of few words
- ☐ Doesn't reveal much, hard to know what he/she is really like
- ☐ Doesn't build rapport, may be a "let's get on with it" type
- ☐ May be a poor listener or appear uninterested
- ☐ May not pick up on social cues that others would recognize
- ☐ May be tense
- ☐ Transactions don't go smoothly

SKILLED

- ☐ Is easy to approach and talk to
- ☐ Spends the extra effort to put others at ease
- ☐ Can be warm, pleasant, and gracious
- ☐ Is sensitive to and patient with the interpersonal anxieties of others
- ☐ Builds rapport well
- ☐ Is a good listener
- ☐ Is an early knower, getting informal and incomplete information in time to do something about it

OVERUSED SKILL

- ☐ May waste too much time building rapport in meetings
- ☐ May be misinterpreted as easy-going or easy to influence
- ☐ May have too strong a desire to be liked
- ☐ May avoid necessary negative or unpleasant transactions
- ☐ May try to smooth over real issues and problems

Select one to three of the competencies listed below to work on to compensate for an overuse of this skill.

COMPENSATORS: 1, 5, 9, 12, 13, 16, 17, 20, 30, 34, 35, 37, 43, 50, 53, 57, 65

SOME CAUSES

- ☐ Arrogant
- ☐ Insensitive
- ☐ Judgmental
- ☐ Not interpersonally skilled
- ☐ Not self confident
- ☐ Shy
- ☐ Busy, busy, busy
- ☐ Too intense; can't relax

THE MAP

Being approachable means putting others at ease so that they can be at their best. It means initiating rapport, listening, sharing, understanding and comforting. Approachable people get more information, know things earlier, and can get others to do more things. People just like to have them around.

SECTION 2: LEARNING ON YOUR OWN

THESE SELF-DEVELOPMENT REMEDIES WILL HELP YOU BUILD YOUR SKILL(S)

SOME REMEDIES

- ☐ **1. You start.** Being approachable means you have to initiate the transaction. You have to put out your hand first. Make first eye contact. You have to ask the first question or share the first piece of information. You have to make the first three minutes comfortable for the other person or group so they can accomplish what they came to you to do.
- ☐ **2. Listen.** Approachable people are very good at listening. They listen without interrupting. They ask clarifying questions. They don't instantly judge. They listen to understand. Judgment may come later. They restate what the other person has said to signal understanding. They nod. They may jot down notes. Listeners don't always offer advice or solutions unless it's obvious the person wants to know what they would do. *More help? – See #33 Listening.*
- ☐ **3. Sharing.** Approachable people share more information and get more in return. Confide your thinking on a business issue and invite the response of others. Pass on tidbits of information you think will help people do their jobs better or broaden their perspective. Disclose some things about yourself. It's hard for people to relate to an enigma. Reveal things that people don't need to know to do their jobs, but which will be interesting to them – and help them feel valued. *More help? – See #44 Personal Disclosure.*
- ☐ **4. Personalizing.** Approachable people work to know and remember important things about the people they work around, for, and with. Know three things about everybody – their interests or their children or something you can chat about other than the business agenda. Treat life as a small world. If you ask a few questions, you'll find you have something in common with virtually anyone. Establish things you can talk about with each person you work with that go beyond strictly work transactions. These need not be social, they could be issues of strategy, global events, market shifts. The point is to forge common ground and connections.
- ☐ **5. Watch your non-verbals.** Approachable people appear and sound open and relaxed. They smile. They are calm. They keep eye contact. They nod while the other person is talking. They have an open body posture. They speak in a paced and pleasant tone. Eliminate any disrup-

tive habits such as speaking too rapidly or forcefully, using strongly worded or loaded language, or going into too much detail. Watch out for signaling disinterest with actions like glancing at your watch, fiddling with paper work or giving your impatient, "I'm busy" look.

- ☐ **6. The magic of questions.** Many people don't ask enough curiosity questions when in their work mode. There are too many informational statements, conclusions, suggestions and solutions and not enough "what if," "what are you thinking," "how do you see that." In studies, statements outweighed questions eight to one. Ask more questions than others. Make fewer solution statements early in a discussion. Keep probing until you understand what they are trying to tell you.

- ☐ **7. Selective approachability?** Some people are approachable with some and not with others. Some might be approachable to direct reports and tense around senior management. List the people you can be approachable with and those you can't. What do the people you are comfortable around have in common? Not comfortable with? Is it level? Style? Gender? Race? Background? Of course, the principles of being approachable are the same regardless of the audience. Do what you do with the comfortable group with the uncomfortable groups. The results will be the same.

- ☐ **8. Shy?** Trouble with appearing vulnerable? Afraid of how people will react? Not sure of your social skills? Want to appear – while shaking inside – not shy? Hand first. Consistent eye contact. Ask the first question. For low risk practice, talk to strangers off work. Set a goal of meeting 10 new people at a social gathering; find out what you have in common with them. Initiate contact at your place of worship, at PTA meetings, in the neighborhood, at the supermarket, on the plane and on the bus. See if any of the bad and scary things you think might happen to you if you initiate people contact actually happen. *More help? – See #31 Interpersonal Savvy.*

- ☐ **9. Arrogant?** Arrogant people are seen as distant and impersonal loners who prefer their own ideas to anyone else's. They purposefully, or not, devalue others and their contributions. This usually results in people feeling diminished, rejected and angry. Why? Answers. Solutions. Conclusions. Statements. Dictates. That's the staple of arrogant people. No listening. Instant output. Sharp reactions. Don't want to be that way? Read your audience. Do you know what people look like when they are uncomfortable with you? Do they back up? Stumble over words? Cringe? Stand at the door hoping not to get invited in? You should work doubly hard at observing others. Especially during the first three minutes of an important transaction, work to make the person or group comfortable with you before the real agenda starts. Ask a question unrelated to the topic. Offer them something to drink. Share something personal. *More help? – See #104 Arrogant.*

☐ **10. As you become more approachable,** you will invite more conflict. If someone is angry, let him/her vent without saying anything other than you know he/she is upset. It's hard for most people to continue for very long with no encouragement or resistance. If someone is a chronic complainer, ask him/her to write down problems and solutions and then discuss it. This turns down the volume while hopefully moving him/her off complaining. If someone wants to complain about someone else, ask if he/she has talked to the person. Encourage him/her to do so. If that doesn't work, summarize what he/she has said without agreeing or disagreeing. *More help? – See #12 Conflict Management*. You'll also invite more contact along with the conflict, and you don't want to become the local coffee shop. Manage your time by gently interrupting to summarize or asking people to think about it more, then let's continue. Disclose things that can be said quickly. Defer extended conversations to other times. Approachability doesn't mean you have to give up control of your time.

SECTION 3: LEARNING FROM MORE FEEDBACK

THESE SOURCES WOULD GIVE YOU THE MOST ACCURATE AND DETAILED FEEDBACK ON YOUR SKILL(S)

☐ **Direct Reports**
Across a variety of settings, your direct reports probably see you the most. They are the recipients of most of your managerial behaviors. They know your work. They can compare you with former bosses. Since they may hesitate to give you negative feedback, you have to set the atmosphere to make it easier for them. You have to ask.

☐ **Internal and External Customers**
Customers interact with you as a person and as a supplier or vendor of products and services. You're important to them because you can either help address and solve their problems or stand in their way. As customer service and Total Quality programs gain importance, clients and customers become a more prominent source of feedback.

☐ **Off-Work Friends/Associates**
Those who know you socially "with your guard down" can be a good source of feedback to compare with that of work peers and family members. If you're different at work than you are socially, why? If you're the same, feedback from friends just confirms the feedback. In a way, off-work friends may know the "real you."

☐ **Past Associates/Constituencies**
When confronted with a present performance problem, some claim, "I wasn't like that before; it must be the current situation." When feedback is available from former associates, about 50% support that claim. In the other half of the cases, the people were like that before and probably didn't know it. It sometimes makes sense to access the past to clearly see the present.

- ☐ **Peers and Colleagues**
  Peers and colleagues have a special social and working relationship. They attend staff meetings together, share private views, get feedback from the same boss, travel together, and are knowledgeable about each other's work. You perhaps let your guard down more around peers and act more like yourself. They can be a valuable source of feedback.

SECTION 4: LEARNING FROM DEVELOP-IN-PLACE ASSIGNMENTS

THESE PART-TIME DEVELOP-IN-PLACE ASSIGNMENTS WILL HELP YOU BUILD YOUR SKILL(S)

- ☐ Study humor in business settings; read books on the nature of humor; collect cartoons you could use in presentations; study funny people around you; keep a log of funny jokes and sayings you hear; read famous speeches and study how humor was used; attend comedy clubs; ask a funny person to act as your tutor; practice funny lines and jokes with others.
- ☐ Lobby for your organization on a contested issue in local, regional, state, or federal government.
- ☐ Create employee involvement teams.
- ☐ Train customers in the use of the organization's products or services.
- ☐ Manage an ad hoc, temporary group of "green," inexperienced people as their coach, teacher, orienter, etc.
- ☐ Help shut down a plant, regional office, product line, business, operation, etc.
- ☐ Manage a dissatisfied internal or external customer; troubleshoot a performance or quality problem with a product or service.
- ☐ Manage the outplacement of a group of people.
- ☐ Resolve an issue in conflict between two people, units, geographies, functions, etc.
- ☐ Make peace with an enemy or someone you've disappointed with a product or service or someone you've had some trouble with or don't get along well with.

SECTION 5: LEARNING FROM FULL-TIME JOBS

THESE FULL-TIME JOBS OFFER THE OPPORTUNITY TO BUILD YOUR SKILL(S)

☐ **Influencing Without Authority**
The core demands to qualify as an Influence Without Authority are: 1) Significant challenge (e.g, start-up, fix-it, scope and/or scale assignment, strategic planning project, changes in management practices/ systems). 2) Insufficient direct authority to make it happen. 3) Tight deadlines. 4) Visible to significant others. 5) Sensitive politics.

SECTION 6: LEARNING MORE FROM YOUR PLAN

THESE ADDITIONAL REMEDIES WILL HELP MAKE THIS DEVELOPMENT PLAN MORE EFFECTIVE FOR YOU

Learning to Learn Better

☐ **Study Yourself in Detail**
Study your likes and dislikes because they can drive a lot of your thinking, judging, and acting. Ask which like or dislike has gotten in the way or prevented you from moving to a higher level of learning. Are your likes and dislikes really important to you or have you just gone on "autopilot"? Try to address and understand a blocking dislike and change it.

☐ **Examine Why You Judge People the Way You Do**
List the people you like and those you dislike and try to find out why. What do those you like have in common with each other and with you? What do those you dislike have in common with themselves and how do they differ from you? Are your "people buckets" logical and productive or do they interfere? Could you be more effective without putting people into buckets?

Learning from Experience, Feedback and Other People

☐ **Using Multiple Models**
Who do you know who exemplifies how to do whatever your need is? Who, for example, personifies decisiveness or compassion or strategic agility? Think more broadly than your current job and colleagues. For example, clergy, friends, spouses or community leaders are also good sources for potential models. Select your models not on the basis of overall excellence or likability, but on the basis of the one towering strength (or glaring weakness) you are interested in. Even people who are well thought of usually have only one or two towering strengths (or glaring weaknesses). Ordinarily, you won't learn as much from the whole person as you will from one characteristic.

☐ **Being a Student of Others**
While many of us rely on others for information or advice, we do not really study the behavior of other people. Ask what a person does exceptionally well or poorly. What behaviors are particularly effective

and ineffective for them? What works for them and what doesn't? As a student of others, you can deduce the rules of thumb for effective and ineffective behavior and include those in your own library. In comparing yourself with this person, in what areas could you most improve? What could you specifically do to improve in ways comfortable for you?

☐ **Learning from Observing Others**
Observe others. Find opportunities to observe without interacting with your model. This enables you to objectively study the person, note what he/she is doing or not doing, and compare that with what you would typically do in similar situations. Many times you can learn more by watching than asking. Your model may not be able to explain what he/she does or may be an unwilling teacher.

☐ **Learning from Remote Models**
Many times you can learn from people not directly available to you. You can read a book about them, watch tapes of public figures, read analyses of them, etc. The principles of learning are the same. Ask yourself what they do well or poorly and deduce their rules of thumb.

☐ **Getting Feedback from Direct Reports**
Direct reports often fear reprisals for giving negative feedback about bosses, whether in a formal process, like a questionnaire, or informally and face-to-face. Even with a guarantee of confidentiality, some are still hesitant. If you want feedback from direct reports, you have to set a positive tone and never act out of revenge.

☐ **Getting Feedback from Peers/Colleagues**
Your peers and colleagues may not be candid if they are in competition with you. Some may not be willing to be open with you out of fear of giving you an advantage. Some may give you exaggerated feedback to deliberately cause you undue concern. You have to set the tone and gauge the trust level of the relationship and the quality of the feedback.

☐ **Openness to Feedback**
Nothing discourages feedback more than defensiveness, resistance, irritation, and excuses. People don't like giving feedback anyway, and much less to those who don't listen or are unreceptive. To help the feedback giver, be open, listen, ask for examples and details, take notes, keep a journal, and thank them for their interest.

Learning from Courses

☐ **Insight Events**
These are courses designed around assessing skills and providing feedback to the participants. These events can be a powerful source of self-knowledge and can lead to significant development if done right. When selecting a self-insight course, consider the following: 1) Are the

skills assessed the important ones? 2) Are the assessment techniques and instruments sound? 3) Are those who are providing the feedback trained and professional? 4) Is the feedback provided in a user-friendly and "actionable" format? 5) Does the feedback include development planning? 6) Is the setting comfortable and conducive to reflection and learning? 7) Are the other participants the kinds of people you could learn from? 8) Are you in the right frame of mind to learn from this kind of intense experience? Select events on the basis of positive answers to these eight questions.

SUGGESTED READINGS

Bardwick, Judith M. *In Praise of Good Business – How optimizing risk rewards both your bottom line and your people*. New York: John Wiley & Sons, Inc., 1998.

DuBrin, Andrew J. *Personal Magnetism – Developing the charismatic qualities to influence others*. New York: AMACOM, 1997.

Faust, Gerald W, Richard I. Lyles and Will Phillips. *Responsible Managers Get Results*. New York: AMACOM, 1998.

Maslow, Abraham H. *Maslow on Management*. New York: John Wiley & Sons, Inc., 1998.

BOSS RELATIONSHIPS

SECTION 1: YOUR DEVELOPMENT NEED(S)

UNSKILLED

- ☐ Not comfortable with bosses
- ☐ May be tense in boss's presence
- ☐ May not be open to coaching or direction from bosses
- ☐ Problems dealing comfortably with authority
- ☐ Poor boss relationships get in the way of working productively

SKILLED

- ☐ Responds and relates well to bosses
- ☐ Would work harder for a good boss
- ☐ Is open to learning from bosses who are good coaches and who provide latitude
- ☐ Likes to learn from those who have been there before
- ☐ Easy to challenge and develop
- ☐ Is comfortably coachable

OVERUSED SKILL

- ☐ May be overdependent on bosses and high status figures for advice and counsel
- ☐ May shut out other sources of feedback and learning
- ☐ May pick the wrong boss to model

Select one to three of the competencies listed below to work on to compensate for an overuse of this skill.

COMPENSATORS: 1, 17, 34, 38, 45, 51, 53, 54, 57

SOME CAUSES

- ☐ The boss doesn't think you're as good as you think you are
- ☐ Jealousy about the boss getting a job you think you should have had
- ☐ Large gap in skills leading to one undervaluing/not respecting the other; can be in either direction
- ☐ Mismatches in ethics, values and integrity
- ☐ Mismatches in management practices
- ☐ Mismatches in style, philosophy, pace and motivation

THE MAP

Most people have trouble with about 50% of their bosses, so you have lots of company. Remember, you never stay with one boss that long; either he/she will move on or you will. It may be best to try to wait it out; there will be a reorganization shortly. Try to learn from the experience.

SECTION 2: LEARNING ON YOUR OWN

THESE SELF-DEVELOPMENT REMEDIES WILL HELP YOU BUILD YOUR SKILL(S)

SOME REMEDIES

☐ **1. Drive down the rocky road.** The key is to manage the rocky relationship so it leaves behind the least amount of long-term noise for you and the organization. Focus on the three key problems you need to work on with him or her and do them. Keep your head down. Keep your conversations with the boss directed at these core agenda. If you believe the boss is blocking you, access your network for performance help, think of five ways to accomplish anything and try them all. *More help? – See #43 Perseverance.*

☐ **2. Watch out for loose lips.** Unless the cause is related to breaches of ethics or integrity, don't gossip about it with your coworkers. Your boss has a right to expect your loyalty and support on issues of work and performance. If he/she gives you an assignment you view as unfair, how do you know it wasn't dumped on him/her? Even if it wasn't, this is hardly an unusual happening in organizations. Reset your priorities and get on with it. If you have to carry out an unpopular mission, this will hardly be the last time. Keep your eyes on the goal. While it's fine to discuss difficulties you're having in performing with others, it's not wise to question why you're having to perform it at all. All things you say have a way of coming around again. If there is an integrity issue involved, take it to the proper authorities. Remember that in a study of whistleblowers, 100% of those with grand and general causes failed. People who go in with huge issues like integrity, philosophical differences, or the utter incompetence of a person usually fail to back up their charges. Go in with specifics and specific events. If they form a pattern, let others decide what that pattern is.

☐ **3. Learn to depersonalize and be neutral.** Try to separate the person from the boss role he/she is in; try to objectify the situation. Someone made her/him boss for a reason and you are never going to please everyone. Deal with him/her as your boss more than as a person. While you don't ever have to invite her/him to your home, you do have to deal with this person as a boss. Ask yourself why you dislike your boss so much or don't like to work with him/her? What do people think who have a favorable impression of your boss? Do you share any common interests? Write down everything you've heard him/her say that was favorable. Play to the boss's good points. Whatever you do, don't signal what you think. Put your judgments on hold, nod, ask questions, summarize as you would with anyone else. A fly on the wall should not be able to tell whether you're talking to friend or foe. You can always talk less and ask more questions.

☐ **4. Try to learn from the situation.** Honestly, what part did you play in contributing to the rough relationship? What could you have done differently to make the situation more livable? What will you do next time when you see the first signs of trouble like this? Even if your boss would be condemned by many, you are responsible for your reactions. If you respond with anger and blame, you're not learning to do anything different. In fact, you may end up mirroring your boss!

☐ **5. It could be you, too.** Get some feedback from those you trust about who you are. What are your real strengths and weaknesses? You need to have the clearest possible view of the situation. Get advice about managing and improving on the relationship from a trusted mentor, colleague or someone in the Human Resources function. After all, maybe it's you as well. How are you at interpersonal reads? Do you know what drives your boss? Do you talk detail and he's a big picture person? Do you fight her style which is more action oriented than yours? Do you get in unproductive values debates? Do you use words that set the boss off? *More help? – See #31 Interpersonal Savvy.*

☐ **6. Find your triggers.** Keep a journal on what the boss does to irritate or bother you to make sure that when you get promoted, you won't be guilty of the same behaviors. Once you know what triggers you, learn to manage these tense transactions better. If your boss blows up, for example, listen to the venting, but don't react directly. Remember that it's the person who hits back who usually gets in the most trouble. Listen. Nod. Ask, "What could I do to help?" or "So you think I need to..." Restate his/her position periodically to signal you have understood. Even if the boss attacks, separate the person from the problem. Count to 10, then return to the problem, not you. *More help? – See #11 Composure and #12 Conflict Management.*

☐ **7. Know the boss.** Try to objectively describe the boss in terms of strengths and weaknesses. Even bad people have strengths. In confidence, get someone else to help you. Try to determine why the boss does what he/she does, even though you may not agree with the logic or wouldn't do it that way yourself. How would you act in the same circumstance?

☐ **8. Careers are made or broken in adversity.** Even if your boss is a bad one, research strongly indicates that confronting the situation directly usually fails. The best tactics are to view it as a conflict situation (*More help? – See #12 Conflict Management*), see what you can learn from it and try to develop some common ground. If you can't, show some patience. Precipitous actions will probably reflect negatively on you more than on your boss. The book may have already been written on your boss; make sure it doesn't get written on you as well. For more help read *Coping with Difficult Bosses* by Robert Bramson or *How to Manage Your Boss* by Christopher Hegarty.

- ☐ **9. Facing the boss.** If appropriate or possible, equipped with the insights you have come to in the previous steps, try to have a series of informal relaxed discussions with your boss about what the problem might be, leading with your contributions – we are seldom completely in the right – to the problem first; then give him/her an opportunity to add to the discussion. Some rules to follow. Describe. Say "I" not "you." Focus on how to accomplish work better. (If you think the boss is blocking you, instead of saying this, say, "I need help in getting this done. I've tried the following things, but...").

- ☐ **10. Strike a bargain with yourself.** Dedicate yourself to trying to please the boss in his/her role as boss in all legitimate requests by doing your best and not getting distracted by the noise of the relationship. Ask yourself, "What are the performance imperatives of this job?" Make the best of a bad situation. Your career will continue past this boss.

SECTION 3: LEARNING FROM MORE FEEDBACK

THESE SOURCES WOULD GIVE YOU THE MOST ACCURATE AND DETAILED FEEDBACK ON YOUR SKILL(S)

- ☐ **Boss's Boss(es)**
  From a process standpoint, your boss's boss probably has the most influence and control over your progress. He/she has a broader perspective, has more access to data, and stands at the center of decisions about you. To know what he/she thinks, without having to violate the canons of corporate due process to get that information, would be quite useful.

- ☐ **Development Professionals**
  Sometimes it might be valuable to get some analysis and feedback from a professional trained and certified in the area you're working on: possibly a career counselor, a therapist, clergy, a psychologist, etc.

- ☐ **Direct Boss**
  Your direct boss has important information about you, your performance, and your prospects. The challenge is to get this information. There are formal processes (e.g., performance appraisals). There are day-to-day opportunities. To help, signal your boss that you want and can handle direct and timely feedback. Many bosses have trouble giving feedback, so you will have to work at it over a period of time.

SECTION 4: LEARNING FROM DEVELOP-IN-PLACE ASSIGNMENTS

THESE PART-TIME DEVELOP-IN-PLACE ASSIGNMENTS WILL HELP YOU BUILD YOUR SKILL(S)

- ☐ Manage the renovation of an office, floor, building, meeting room, warehouse, etc.
- ☐ Plan an off-site meeting, conference, convention, trade show, event, etc.
- ☐ Write a proposal for a new policy, process, mission, charter, product, service, or system, and present and sell it to top management.
- ☐ Relaunch an existing product or service that's not doing well.
- ☐ Serve on a junior or shadow board.
- ☐ Manage an ad hoc, temporary group of people involved in tackling a fix-it or turnaround project.
- ☐ Manage the interface between consultants and the organization on a critical assignment.
- ☐ Work on a team that's deciding who to keep and who to let go in a layoff, shutdown, delayering, or divestiture.
- ☐ Write a speech for someone higher up in the organization.
- ☐ Build a multifunctional project team to tackle a common business issue or problem.

SECTION 5: LEARNING FROM FULL-TIME JOBS

THESE FULL-TIME JOBS OFFER THE OPPORTUNITY TO BUILD YOUR SKILL(S)

- ☐ **Chair of Projects/Task Forces**

  The core demands for qualifying as a Project/Task Force assignment are: 1) Full-time assignment. 2) Important and specific goal. 3) Tight deadline. 4) Success or failure will be evident. 5) High-visibility sponsor. 6) Learning something on the fly. 7) Must get others to cooperate. 8) Usually six months or more. Four types of Projects/Task Forces: 1) New ideas, products, services, or systems (e.g., product/service/program research and development, creation/installation/launch of a new system, new programs like Total Quality Management, positive discipline). 2) Formal negotiations and relationships (e.g., acquisitions, divestitures, agreements, joint ventures, licensing arrangements, franchising, dealing with unions, governments, communities, charities, customers, and relocations). 3) Big one-time events (e.g., working on a major presentation for the board, organizing significant meetings or conferences, disaster/damage control teams, reorganizations, mergers, acquisitions, or relocations, working on visions, charters, strategies, other time-urgent issues and problems). 4) Troubleshooting (e.g., problems, disasters, crises, product/service failures, accidents, illegal activities, damage control in public relations goofs, shut downs, downsizings, layoffs, abrupt changes in leadership).

☐ **Fix-its/Turnarounds**
The core demands to qualify as a Fix-it or Turnaround assignment are: 1) Cleaning up a mess. 2) Serious people issues/problems like credibility/performance/morale. 3) Tight deadline. 4) Serious business performance failure. 5) Last chance to fix. Four Types of Fix-its/Turnarounds: 1) Fixing a failed business/unit involving taking control, stopping losses, managing damage, planning the turnaround, dealing with people problems, installing new processes and systems, and rebuilding the spirit and performance of the unit. 2) Managing sizable disasters like mishandled labor negotiations and strikes, thefts, history of significant business losses, poor staff, failed leadership, hidden problems, fraud, public relations nightmares, etc. 3) Significant reorganization and restructuring (e.g., stabilizing the business, reforming unit, introducing new systems, making people changes, resetting strategy and tactics). 4) Significant system/process breakdown (e.g., MIS, financial coordination processes, audits, standards, etc.) across units requiring working to change something from a distant position, providing advice and counsel, and installing or implementing a major process improvement or system change outside your own unit and/or with customers outside the organization.

☐ **Influencing Without Authority**
The core demands to qualify as an Influence Without Authority are: 1) Significant challenge (e.g, start-up, fix-it, scope and/or scale assignment, strategic planning project, changes in management practices/systems). 2) Insufficient direct authority to make it happen. 3) Tight deadlines. 4) Visible to significant others. 5) Sensitive politics.

☐ **Scope Assignments**
The core demands for a Scope (complexity) Assignment are: 1) Significant increase in both internal and external scope or complexity. 2) Significant increase in visibility and/or bottom line responsibility. 3) Unfamiliar area, business, technology, or territory. Examples of Scope Assignments involving shifts: 1) Switching into a new function/technology/business. 2) Moving to new organization. 3) Moving to overseas assignment. 4) Moving to a new location. 5) Adding new products/services. 6) Moving between headquarters/field. 7) Switches in ownership/top management of the unit/organization. Examples of Scope Assignments involving "firsts": 1) First-time manager. 2) First-time managing managers. 3) First-time executive. 4) First-time overseas. 5) First-time headquarters/field. 6) First-time team leader. 7) First-time new technology/business/function. Scope Assignments involving increased complexity: 1) Managing a significant expansion of an existing product or service. 2) Managing adding new products/service into an existing unit. 3) Managing a reorganized and more diverse unit. 4) Managing explosive growth. 5) Adding new technologies.

SECTION 6: LEARNING MORE FROM YOUR PLAN

THESE ADDITIONAL REMEDIES WILL HELP MAKE THIS DEVELOPMENT PLAN MORE EFFECTIVE FOR YOU

Learning from Experience, Feedback and Other People

- ☐ **Using Multiple Models**
  Who do you know who exemplifies how to do whatever your need is? Who, for example, personifies decisiveness or compassion or strategic agility? Think more broadly than your current job and colleagues. For example, clergy, friends, spouses or community leaders are also good sources for potential models. Select your models not on the basis of overall excellence or likability, but on the basis of the one towering strength (or glaring weakness) you are interested in. Even people who are well thought of usually have only one or two towering strengths (or glaring weaknesses). Ordinarily, you won't learn as much from the whole person as you will from one characteristic.

- ☐ **Learning from Bosses**
  Bosses can be an excellent and ready source for learning. All bosses do some things exceptionally well and other things poorly. Distance your feelings from the boss/direct report relationship and study things that work and things that don't work for your boss. What would you have done? What could you use, and what should you avoid?

- ☐ **Learning from Mentors and Tutors**
  Mentors and tutors offer a special case for learning since the relationship is specifically formed for learning. You need to be open and nondefensive. You need to solicit and accept feedback. This is a unique opportunity for you to get low-risk, honest, and direct feedback on what you do well and not so well.

- ☐ **Learning from Interviewing Others**
  Interview others. Ask not only what they do, but how and why they do it. What do they think are the rules of thumb they are following? Where did they learn the behaviors? How do they keep them current? How do they monitor the effect they have on others?

- ☐ **Consolidating What You Learn from People**
  After using any source and/or method of learning from others, write down or mentally note the new rules of thumb and the principles involved. How will you remind yourself of the new behaviors in similar situations? How will you prevent yourself from reacting on "autopilot"? How could you share what you have learned from others?

- ☐ **Getting Feedback from Bosses and Superiors**
  Many bosses are reluctant to give negative feedback. They lack the managerial courage to face people directly with criticism. You can help by soliciting feedback and setting the tone. Show them you can handle criticism and that you are willing to work on issues they see as important.

☐ **Soliciting Feedback**
Almost everyone reports they receive less feedback than they need to achieve their career goals. While others may have some interest in your career, it is primarily up to you to take the initiative in soliciting feedback from multiple sources by any methods available. You're the stakeholder who needs feedback to improve and grow.

☐ **Openness to Feedback**
Nothing discourages feedback more than defensiveness, resistance, irritation, and excuses. People don't like giving feedback anyway, and much less to those who don't listen or are unreceptive. To help the feedback giver, be open, listen, ask for examples and details, take notes, keep a journal, and thank them for their interest.

☐ **Learning from Bad Bosses**
First, what does he/she do so well to make him/her your boss? (Even bad bosses have strengths). Then, ask what makes this boss bad for you. Is it his/her behavior? Attitude? Values? Philosophy? Practices? Style? What is the source of the conflict? Why do you react as you do? Do others react the same? How are you part of the problem? What do you do that triggers your boss? If you wanted to, could you reduce the conflict or make it go away by changing something you do? Is there someone around you who doesn't react like you? How are they different? What can you learn from them? What is your emotional reaction to this boss? Why do you react like that? What can you do to cope with these feelings? Can you avoid reacting out of anger and frustration? Can you find something positive about the situation? Can you use someone else as a buffer? Can you learn from your emotions? What lasting lessons of managing others can you take away from this experience? What won't you do as a manager? What will you do differently? How could you teach these principles you've learned to others by the use of this example?

Learning from Courses

☐ **Insight Events**
These are courses designed around assessing skills and providing feedback to the participants. These events can be a powerful source of self-knowledge and can lead to significant development if done right. When selecting a self-insight course, consider the following: 1) Are the skills assessed the important ones? 2) Are the assessment techniques and instruments sound? 3) Are those who are providing the feedback trained and professional? 4) Is the feedback provided in a user-friendly and "actionable" format? 5) Does the feedback include development planning? 6) Is the setting comfortable and conducive to reflection and learning? 7) Are the other participants the kinds of people you could learn from? 8) Are you in the right frame of mind to learn from this kind of intense experience? Select events on the basis of positive answers to these eight questions.

SUGGESTED READINGS

Bern, Paula. *How to work for a woman boss even if you'd rather not.* New York: Dodd, Mead, 1987.

Bing, Stanley. *Crazy Bosses – Spotting them, serving them, surviving them*. New York: William Morrow and Company, Inc., 1992.

Boccialetti, Gene. *It takes two: managing yourself when working with bosses and authority figures*. San Francisco: Jossey-Bass, 1995.

Bramson, Robert Ph.D. *Coping with Difficult Bosses*. New York: Carol Publishing Group, 1992.

Bramson, Robert Ph.D. *Coping with Difficult Bosses [sound recording]*. New York: Simon & Schuster Audio, 1993.

Carson, Kerry, Ph.D. and Paula Phillips Carson, Ph.D. *Defective Bosses – Working for the Dysfunctional Dozen.* New York: The Haworth Press

DesRoches, Brian Ph.D. *Your Boss Is Not Your Mother – Creating autonomy, respect, and success at work*. New York: William Morrow and Company, 1995.

Eigen, Barry. *How to Think Like a Boss*. New York: Carol Publishing Group, 1990.

Fritz, Roger and Kristie Kennard. *How to Manage Your Boss*. Hawthorne, NJ: Career Press, 1994.

Hornstein, Harvey Ph.D. *Brutal Bosses*. New York: Riverhead Books, 1996.

Hughes, Marylou. *Keeping your job while your bosses are losing theirs*. Binghamton, New York: William Neil Publishing, 1998.

5

BUSINESS ACUMEN

SECTION 1: YOUR DEVELOPMENT NEED(S)

UNSKILLED

- ☐ Doesn't understand the broader world of business
- ☐ May be a very dedicated functional or professional expert
- ☐ Doesn't understand the "business" the organization is in
- ☐ May be narrowly tactical
- ☐ Lacks interest or experience in general business

SKILLED

- ☐ Knows how businesses work
- ☐ Knowledgeable in current and possible future policies, practices, trends, and information affecting his/her business and organization
- ☐ Knows the competition
- ☐ Is aware of how strategies and tactics work in the marketplace

OVERUSED SKILL

- ☐ May overdevelop or depend upon industry and business knowledge and skills at the expense of personal, interpersonal, managerial, and leadership skills

Select one to three of the competencies listed below to work on to compensate for an overuse of this skill.

COMPENSATORS: 14, 24, 30, 32, 45, 46, 54, 57, 58, 61

SOME CAUSES

- ☐ Inexperience; new to the organization
- ☐ Lack of interest in general business
- ☐ Narrow perspective
- ☐ No exposure outside the function
- ☐ Overly dedicated to a profession, not the organization
- ☐ Very tactical and here and now oriented

THE MAP

You gotta know the territory! Nothing beats knowing what's going on. When people get business savvy indicated as one of their needs, it usually comes in two flavors. The first is that you don't seem to know enough about business in general. This means some of the statements and suggestions you make don't pass the business practicality test. It may also mean what you're suggesting is known not to work and you are unaware of that. The second is that you don't know enough about this specific business and industry. That usually means you don't understand the agenda, issues and concerns of the people you serve inside your organization, and you make comments and have suggestions that don't match their priorities. Your contributions are limited because you don't see priorities as they do. You don't think in terms of the bigger picture. Unless you walk a mile in their shoes, they're not going to pay attention to you.

SECTION 2: LEARNING ON YOUR OWN

THESE SELF-DEVELOPMENT REMEDIES WILL HELP YOU BUILD YOUR SKILL(S)

SOME REMEDIES

☐ **1. Read the right periodicals.** There are five publications that probably will teach you most of what you need to know about business in general on a continuous basis. They are the *Wall Street Journal*, *Business Week*, *Fortune*, *Barron's*, and the *Harvard Business Review*. Subscribe and begin to scan those publications regularly. Try to see three items per issue that relate to your business. These will be parallels, trends that affect business now, emerging trends that may have a future impact, and general business savvy about how business works.

☐ **2. Watch the right sources.** There are now three or more business channels on cable that carry business news and information full time. They have interviews with business leaders, reviews of industries by Wall Street experts, as well as general reviews of companies. Begin to watch one or two programs a week until you can zero in on what you specifically need to know.

☐ **3. Join the Conference Board.** They are dedicated to creating and distributing information about business to its members. They have wonderful conferences where many top leaders of business come and share their thoughts about business in general and their business specifically. Attend one of the national Conference Board meetings.

☐ **4. Quick study some business books.** Go to any business book store and pick three books on general business principles, one with a financial slant, one with a marketing slant and one about customer service. When you have scanned those, go back and get three more until you have the business knowledge you need. Attend a nighttime advanced business program or get an MBA at a local college or university. Subscribe to *Soundview Executive Book Summaries* (800-521-1227). They summarize in a few pages all the major business books that are on the best-seller lists.

☐ **5. Figure out the rules of the game.** Reduce your understanding of how business operates to personal rules of thumb or insights. Write them down in your own words. An example would be, "What are the drivers in marketing anything?" One executive had 25 such drivers that he continually edited, scratched through and replaced with more up to date thinking. Use these rules of thumb to analyze a business that you know something about, possibly one of your hobbies or a sport you are enthusiastic about. Pick what you know.

- ☐ **6. Don't know enough about your business?** Talk to the person who knows. Ask for lunch or just a meeting with the person who is in charge of the strategic planning process in your company. Have him/her explain the strategic plan for the organization. Particularly have him or her point out the mission-critical functions and capabilities the organization needs to be leading edge in to win.
- ☐ **7. Try some broader tasks.** Volunteer for task forces that include people outside your area of expertise. Work on some Total Quality Management or Process Re-Engineering projects that cross functional or business unit boundaries to learn more about the business.
- ☐ **8. Get close to customers.** Customer service is the best place to learn about the business. Arrange a meeting with a counterpart in customer service. Have him or her explain the function to you. If you can, listen in to customer service calls or even better handle a couple yourself.
- ☐ **9. Join your national association.** Your industry has a national association. Join it and purchase a number of their publications about business in your specific industry. Attend the national conference.
- ☐ **10. Learn to think as an expert in your business does.** Take problems to inside experts or external consultants and ask them what are the keys they look for; observe what they consider significant and not significant. Chunk up data into categories so you can remember it. Devise five key areas or questions you can consider each time a business issue comes up. Don't waste your time just learning facts; they won't be useful unless you have conceptual buckets to put them in. Then present your thinking to experts or write a strategic business plan for your unit and invite their review. There is no need to restrict your choices to just your organization; any astute business person should have some interesting insights.

SECTION 3: LEARNING FROM MORE FEEDBACK

THESE SOURCES WOULD GIVE YOU THE MOST ACCURATE AND DETAILED FEEDBACK ON YOUR SKILL(S)

- ☐ **Boss's Boss(es)**

  From a process standpoint, your boss's boss probably has the most influence and control over your progress. He/she has a broader perspective, has more access to data, and stands at the center of decisions about you. To know what he/she thinks, without having to violate the canons of corporate due process to get that information, would be quite useful.

- ☐ **Direct Boss**
  Your direct boss has important information about you, your performance, and your prospects. The challenge is to get this information. There are formal processes (e.g., performance appraisals). There are day-to-day opportunities. To help, signal your boss that you want and can handle direct and timely feedback. Many bosses have trouble giving feedback, so you will have to work at it over a period of time.
- ☐ **Past Associates/Constituencies**
  When confronted with a present performance problem, some claim, "I wasn't like that before; it must be the current situation." When feedback is available from former associates, about 50% support that claim. In the other half of the cases, the people were like that before and probably didn't know it. It sometimes makes sense to access the past to clearly see the present.

SECTION 4: LEARNING FROM DEVELOP-IN-PLACE ASSIGNMENTS

THESE PART-TIME DEVELOP-IN-PLACE ASSIGNMENTS WILL HELP YOU BUILD YOUR SKILL(S)

- ☐ Work on a team forming a joint venture or partnership.
- ☐ Do a competitive analysis of your organization's products or services or your position in the marketplace and present it to the people involved.
- ☐ Do a customer-satisfaction survey in person or by phone and present it to the people involved.
- ☐ Do a postmortem on a successful project and present it to the people involved.
- ☐ Help someone outside your unit or the organization solve a business problem.
- ☐ Work short rotations in other units, functions, or geographies you've not been exposed to before.
- ☐ Monitor and follow a new product or service through the entire idea, design, test market, and launch cycle.
- ☐ Study and summarize a new trend, product, service, technique, or process and present and sell it to others.
- ☐ Make speeches/be a spokesperson for the organization on the outside.
- ☐ Manage liquidation/sale of products, equipment, materials, a business, furniture, overstock, etc.

SECTION 5: LEARNING FROM FULL-TIME JOBS

THESE FULL-TIME JOBS OFFER THE OPPORTUNITY TO BUILD YOUR SKILL(S)

- ☐ **Cross-Moves**
  The core demands necessary to qualify as a Cross-Move are: 1) Move to a very different set of challenges. 2) Abrupt jump-shift in tasks/activities. 3) Never been there before. 4) New setting/conditions. Examples of Cross-Moves are: 1) Changing divisions. 2) Changing functions. 3) Field/headquarters shifts. 4) Line/staff switches. 5) Country switches. 6) Working with all new people. 7) Changing lines of business.

- ☐ **Member of Projects/Task Forces**
  The core demands for qualifying as a Project/Task Force assignment are: 1) Full-time assignment. 2) Important and specific goal. 3) Tight deadline. 4) Success or failure will be evident. 5) High-visibility sponsor. 6) Learning something on the fly. 7) Must get others to cooperate. 8) Usually six months or more. Four types of Projects/Task Forces: 1) New ideas, products, services, or systems (e.g., product/service/program research and development, creation/installation/launch of a new system, new programs like Total Quality Management, positive discipline). 2) Formal negotiations and relationships (e.g., acquisitions, divestitures, agreements, joint ventures, licensing arrangements, franchising, dealing with unions, governments, communities, charities, customers, and relocations). 3) Big one-time events (e.g., working on a major presentation for the board, organizing significant meetings or conferences, disaster/damage control teams, reorganizations, mergers, acquisitions, or relocations, working on visions, charters, strategies, other time-urgent issues and problems). 4) Troubleshooting (e.g., problems, disasters, crises, product/service failures, accidents, illegal activities, damage control in public relations goofs, shut downs, downsizings, layoffs, abrupt changes in leadership).

- ☐ **Scale Assignments**
  Core requirements to qualify as a Scale (size) shift assignment are: 1) Sizable jump-shift in the size of the job in areas like: number of people, number of layers in the organization, size of the budget, number of locations, volume of activity, tightness of deadlines. 2) Medium to low complexity; mostly repetitive and routine processes and procedures. 3) Stable staff and business. 4) Stable operations. 5) Often slow, steady growth.

SECTION 6: LEARNING MORE FROM YOUR PLAN

THESE ADDITIONAL REMEDIES WILL HELP MAKE THIS DEVELOPMENT PLAN MORE EFFECTIVE FOR YOU

Learning from Experience, Feedback and Other People

- ☐ **Being a Student of Others**
  While many of us rely on others for information or advice, we do not really study the behavior of other people. Ask what a person does exceptionally well or poorly. What behaviors are particularly effective and ineffective for them? What works for them and what doesn't? As a student of others, you can deduce the rules of thumb for effective and ineffective behavior and include those in your own library. In comparing yourself with this person, in what areas could you most improve? What could you specifically do to improve in ways comfortable for you?

- ☐ **Learning from Mentors and Tutors**
  Mentors and tutors offer a special case for learning since the relationship is specifically formed for learning. You need to be open and nondefensive. You need to solicit and accept feedback. This is a unique opportunity for you to get low-risk, honest, and direct feedback on what you do well and not so well.

- ☐ **Learning from Interviewing Others**
  Interview others. Ask not only what they do, but how and why they do it. What do they think are the rules of thumb they are following? Where did they learn the behaviors? How do they keep them current? How do they monitor the effect they have on others?

- ☐ **Learning from Observing Others**
  Observe others. Find opportunities to observe without interacting with your model. This enables you to objectively study the person, note what he/she is doing or not doing, and compare that with what you would typically do in similar situations. Many times you can learn more by watching than asking. Your model may not be able to explain what he/she does or may be an unwilling teacher.

- ☐ **Learning from a Coach or Tutor**
  Ask a person to coach or tutor you directly. This has the additional benefit of skill building coupled with correcting feedback. Also observe the teacher teaching you. How does he/she teach? How does he/she adjust to you as a learner? After the process, ask for feedback about you as a learner.

- ☐ **Learning from Remote Models**
  Many times you can learn from people not directly available to you. You can read a book about them, watch tapes of public figures, read analyses of them, etc. The principles of learning are the same. Ask yourself what they do well or poorly and deduce their rules of thumb.

- ☐ **Getting Feedback from Bosses and Superiors**
  Many bosses are reluctant to give negative feedback. They lack the managerial courage to face people directly with criticism. You can help by soliciting feedback and setting the tone. Show them you can handle criticism and that you are willing to work on issues they see as important.

Learning from Courses

- ☐ **Orientation Events**
  Most organizations offer a variety of orientation events. They are designed to communicate strategies, charters, missions, goals, and general information and offer an opportunity for people to meet each other. They are short in duration and offer limited opportunities for learning anything beyond general context and background.
- ☐ **Survey Courses**
  These are courses designed to give a general overview of an entire area (such as advertising), product or product line, division's activities, process (getting a product to market, Total Quality Management) or geography (doing business in "X"). These types of courses are good for general background and context.
- ☐ **Strategic Courses**
  There are a number of courses designed to stretch minds to prepare for future challenges. They include topics such as Workforce Diversity 2000, globalization, the European Union, competitive competencies and strategies, etc. Quality depends upon the following three factors: 1) The quality of the staff. Are they qualified? Are they respected in their fields? Are they strategic "gurus"? 2) The quality of the participants. Are they the kind of people you could learn from? 3) The quality of the setting. Is it comfortable and free from distractions? Can you learn there?

SUGGESTED READINGS

Barron's. http://www.barrons.com

Business Week. http://www.businessweek.com

Fortune. http://cgi.pathfinder.com/fortune

Harvard Business Review. Phone: 800-988-0886 (U.S. and Canada). Fax: 617-496-1029. Mail: Harvard Business Review. Subscriber Services, P.O. Box 52623. Boulder, CO 80322-2623 USA. http://www.hbsp.harvard.edu/products/hbr

Soundview Executive Book Summaries. 10 LaCrue Avenue, Concordville, PA 19331. 1-800-521-1227 (US and Canada). 610-558-9495 (outside US and Canada). http://www.summary.com

continued

Wall Street Journal. http://www.wsj.com

Jager, Rama Dev and Rafael Ortiz. *In the Company of Giants*. New York: McGraw-Hill, Inc., 1997.

Kanter, Rosabeth Moss. *On the Frontiers of Management*. Boston: Harvard Business School Press, 1992.

Macdonald, John. *Calling a Halt to Mindless Change*. New York: AMACOM, 1998.

Olesen, Erik. *12 Steps to Mastering the Winds of Change*. New York: Macmillan, 1993.

6

CAREER AMBITION

SECTION 1: YOUR DEVELOPMENT NEED(S)

UNSKILLED

- ☐ Unsure what he/she wants out of a career
- ☐ May be bored or in the wrong career or the wrong organization
- ☐ May not want to make sacrifices to get ahead
- ☐ May not understand how careers really work and how people get ahead
- ☐ A poor marketer of self; doesn't know how to get noticed
- ☐ Hesitant to speak up on career wants and needs
- ☐ Stuck in his/her career comfort zone; won't take a career risk

SKILLED

- ☐ Knows what he/she wants from a career and actively works on it
- ☐ Is career knowledgeable
- ☐ Makes things happen for self
- ☐ Markets self for opportunities
- ☐ Doesn't wait for others to open doors

OVERUSED SKILL

- ☐ May make unwise career choices
- ☐ May only select jobs in the can-do comfort zone
- ☐ May be seen as excessively ambitious
- ☐ May not pay enough attention to the job at hand
- ☐ May not take career advice comfortably
- ☐ May not trust the career decisions others make for him/her

Select one to three of the competencies listed below to work on to compensate for an overuse of this skill.

COMPENSATORS: 16, 17, 30, 32, 33, 42, 46, 48, 50, 51, 53, 55, 58, 63, 66

SOME CAUSES

- ☐ Bored
- ☐ Don't trust organization
- ☐ Don't want to make sacrifices
- ☐ Don't know how to market self
- ☐ Don't like to blow own horn
- ☐ Examine things to death
- ☐ Not career knowledgeable
- ☐ Too deep in your comfort zone
- ☐ Wait for things to happen
- ☐ Will only take a promotion
- ☐ Won't take a chance

THE MAP

Being here on this page means someone or a number of people have told you that you are not ambitious enough. That means they think you have more going for you than you are aware of or want to sacrifice to get. They think you are undermanaging your career. The keys to career management are finding out how successful careers are built, figuring out how far you can and want to go, analyzing what's getting in your way, exposing yourself to new tasks that build your skills, and getting noticed by decision makers.

SECTION 2: LEARNING ON YOUR OWN

THESE SELF-DEVELOPMENT REMEDIES WILL HELP YOU BUILD YOUR SKILL(S)

SOME REMEDIES

☐ **1. How good are you?** How good could you be? Are you underselling yourself? You may be too critical of yourself. Get a good, confidential 360°. Are your ratings lower than those of others? Sit down with an experienced facilitator. The process should be, "How good could I be with this foundation of strengths? What do others think are my strengths that I don't see? What should I work on next to progress?" Build up your confidence. Take a course or work with a tutor to bolster your confidence in an area. Remember you don't have to be good at everything to succeed. *More help? – See #55 Self-Knowledge.*

☐ **2. Get and use a career Board of Directors.** Since you're not – at this time – your best career advisor, seek out one or more people who could be. A mentor. Boss you respect. Friend down the street. Spouse. Parent. Clergy. Consultant. Professional colleague. Periodically, pass your career thoughts, assumptions, concerns and opportunities by them for an objective opinion. Listen to them.

☐ **3. Many people don't know how careers are built.** Most are put off by the popular myth of getting ahead. All of us have seen *How to Succeed in Business Without Really Trying* or something like it. It's easy to get cynical and believe that successful people are political or sell out, suck up, knife people in the back, it's who you know, and so on. The facts are dramatically different from this. Those behaviors get people in trouble eventually. What has staying power is performing and problem solving on the current job, having a few notable strengths, and seeking new tasks you don't know how to do. It's solving every problem with tenacity while looking for what you haven't yet done and getting yourself in a position to do it. Read *The Lessons of Experience* by McCall, Lombardo and Morrison for the careers of men and *Breaking the Glass Ceiling* by Morrison, White and Van Velsor for the careers of women to see how successful careers really happen.

☐ **4. Break out of your career comfort zone.** Maybe you haven't seen enough. Pick some activities you haven't done before but might find exciting. Take a course in a new area. Task trade – switch tasks with a peer. Volunteer for task forces and projects that are multifunctional or multibusiness in nature. Read more broadly. *More help? – See #46 Perspective.*

☐ **5. Don't know what it takes?** Think of five successful people in your organization/field who you know well and ask what drives them? What sorts of jobs have they held? What are their technical skills? Behavioral skills? Use The CAREER ARCHITECT® Portfolio Sort™ Cards to determine what the 10 key skills of each person are; compare this list with your own self assessment and feedback. Ask Human Resources if they have a success profile for some of the jobs you may be interested in. Make a list of what you need to work on next.

☐ **6. Not comfortable marketing yourself?** You don't know how to get promoted. You dislike people who blow their own horns. Here's how to do it. Build a performance track record of variety – start up things, fix things, innovate, make plans, come under budget. This is what will get you promoted. All organizations are looking for broad thinkers to give fresh opportunities to. Start by thinking more broadly.

☐ **7. Getting noticed by top decision makers.** Top managers aren't as interested in glitz as many would have you believe. They're interested in people who take care of problems, spot opportunities, ward off disaster, and have a broad repertoire of skills. They are looking for bold performers. But a better mousetrap alone is not enough. Volunteer for projects that will require interacting/presenting with higher management. Focus on activities that are the core of what your organization does. Find a business opportunity and make a reasoned case for it. Pick a big problem and work maniacally to solve it. You need to be seen and heard – but on substance not fluff.

☐ **8. Not willing to make sacrifices?** Many people turn down career opportunities based upon current life comforts only to regret it later when they have been passed by. Studies indicate that the vast majority of moves successful general managers had to make during their careers were not seen as right for them at the time. They tried to turn them down. We all have the problems. Children in school. A house we like. A parent to take care of. A working spouse. A medical issue to manage. A good neighborhood. Most successful careers require moving around during the years that are the most inconvenient and painful – when we have kids in school, not much extra money, and aging parents to manage. Set your mind to it. You must move to grow.

☐ **9. Waiting for your boss to retire and get the big promotion?** It's hard to understand, but a promotion to your boss's job is about the weakest way to build a successful career. Same issues. Same people.

Same customers. Same products and services. Variety is the key to career building. Take laterals. Bury the ego. Work for the long term. Turn down a straight line promotion and ask for a like level job elsewhere.

☐ **10. Following your passion?** Most of us make a very human error in career management. We pursue what we most like to do. Our parents and counselors told us to find something we like and that makes us happy, get really good at it, join a big company who will take care of us and provide us a nice pension. While that may have been good advice in the past, it doesn't fit today very well. Lifelong employment is dead. Layoffs. Virtual corporations. Chaos. Employability is the new term and concept. You have to be good at a lot of things. You will change organizations several times. You will have to move around to where the opportunities are.

SECTION 3: LEARNING FROM MORE FEEDBACK

THESE SOURCES WOULD GIVE YOU THE MOST ACCURATE AND DETAILED FEEDBACK ON YOUR SKILL(S)

☐ **Natural Mentors**

Natural mentors have a special relationship with you and are interested in your success and your future. Since they are usually not in your direct chain of command, you can have more open, relaxed, and fruitful discussions about yourself and your career prospects. They can be a very important source for candid or critical feedback others may not give you.

☐ **Spouse**

Spouses can be powerful sources of feedback on such things as interpersonal style, values, balance between work, career, and personal life, etc. Many participants attending development programs share their feedback with their spouses for value-adding confirmation or context and for specific examples.

☐ **Yourself**

You are an important source of feedback on yourself. But some caution is appropriate. If you have not received much feedback, you may be less accurate than the other sources. We all have blind spots, defense shields, ideal self-views, and fantasies. Before acting on your own self-views, get outside confirmation from other appropriate sources.

SECTION 4: LEARNING FROM DEVELOP-IN-PLACE ASSIGNMENTS

THESE PART-TIME DEVELOP-IN-PLACE ASSIGNMENTS WILL HELP YOU BUILD YOUR SKILL(S)

- ☐ Do a study of successful executives in your organization and report the findings to top management.
- ☐ Do a study of failed executives in your organization, including interviewing people still with the organization who knew or worked with them, and report the findings to top management.
- ☐ Volunteer to fill an open management job temporarily until it's filled.
- ☐ Manage the outplacement of a group of people.
- ☐ Write a speech for someone higher up in the organization.
- ☐ Launch a new product, service, or process.
- ☐ Seek out and use a seed budget to create and pursue a personal idea, product, or service.
- ☐ Manage an ad hoc, temporary group of people in a rapidly expanding operation.
- ☐ Take on a tough and undoable project, one where others who have tried it have failed.
- ☐ Build a multifunctional project team to tackle a common business issue or problem.

SECTION 5: LEARNING FROM FULL-TIME JOBS

THESE FULL-TIME JOBS OFFER THE OPPORTUNITY TO BUILD YOUR SKILL(S)

- ☐ **Line To Staff Switches**
  The core demands to qualify as a Line to Staff switch are: 1) Intellectually/strategically demanding. 2) Highly visible to others. 3) New area/perspective/method/culture/function. 4) Moving away from a bottom line. 5) Moving from field to headquarters. 6) Exposure to high-level executives. Examples: 1) Business/strategic planning. 2) Heading a staff department. 3) Assistant to/chief of staff to a senior executive. 4) Head of a task force. 5) Human resources role.
- ☐ **Off-Shore Assignments**
  The core demands to qualify as an Off-Shore assignment are: 1) First time working in the country. 2) Significant challenges like new language, hardship location, unique business rules/practices, significant cultural/marketplace differences, different functional task, etc. 3) More than a year assignment. 4) No automatic return deal. 5) Not necessarily a change in job challenge, technical content, or responsibilities.
- ☐ **Staff to Line Shifts**
  Core demands necessary to qualify for a Staff to Line shift are: 1) Moving to a job with an easily determined bottom line or results.

2) Managing bigger scope and/or scale. 3) Requires new skills/ perspectives. 4) Unfamiliar aspects of the assignment.

SECTION 6: LEARNING MORE FROM YOUR PLAN

THESE ADDITIONAL REMEDIES WILL HELP MAKE THIS DEVELOPMENT PLAN MORE EFFECTIVE FOR YOU

Learning to Learn Better

☐ **Envision Yourself Succeeding**
Examine the image of success in detail: what you are doing, what you are feeling, how you are reacting to others, how others are reacting to you, how the parts fit together. Can you then play that out in the real situation and get to the same outcome?

Learning from Experience, Feedback and Other People

☐ **Using Multiple Models**
Who do you know who exemplifies how to do whatever your need is? Who, for example, personifies decisiveness or compassion or strategic agility? Think more broadly than your current job and colleagues. For example, clergy, friends, spouses or community leaders are also good sources for potential models. Select your models not on the basis of overall excellence or likability, but on the basis of the one towering strength (or glaring weakness) you are interested in. Even people who are well thought of usually have only one or two towering strengths (or glaring weaknesses). Ordinarily, you won't learn as much from the whole person as you will from one characteristic.

☐ **Learning from Mentors and Tutors**
Mentors and tutors offer a special case for learning since the relationship is specifically formed for learning. You need to be open and nondefensive. You need to solicit and accept feedback. This is a unique opportunity for you to get low-risk, honest, and direct feedback on what you do well and not so well.

☐ **Learning from Interviewing Others**
Interview others. Ask not only what they do, but how and why they do it. What do they think are the rules of thumb they are following? Where did they learn the behaviors? How do they keep them current? How do they monitor the effect they have on others?

☐ **The Power of Feedback**
People learn and grow best through timely and "actionable" feedback on the skills, knowledge, perspectives, and values required to achieve realistic career goals and job objectives. Armed with accurate feedback and the help of others, people can construct, execute, and monitor focused plans for improvement and growth.

☐ **Using Multiple Sources**
The usefulness of feedback varies with the quality of the source and the content of the information. Some give better feedback than others. Feedback on skills directly tied to success is most useful. Different skills are best observed by different groups like peers, bosses, direct reports, or customers. Timing of feedback can be critical; some times to get feedback are better than others.

☐ **Managing Your Own Future**
You can make a difference in the amount and quality of feedback you receive. The more you understand about feedback and the more initiative you take, the more feedback you will receive. From this, you can construct and execute better, on-target development and career plans.

☐ **Feedback on What?**
Although any feedback is useful, it's best to seek and receive feedback on skills the organization feels are the most important for your present and future success. Not all skills are equal in importance. Some common skills may not have much bearing on success at all. If the organization has an official success profile, that may be the best way to focus your growth efforts.

Learning from Courses

☐ **Orientation Events**
Most organizations offer a variety of orientation events. They are designed to communicate strategies, charters, missions, goals, and general information and offer an opportunity for people to meet each other. They are short in duration and offer limited opportunities for learning anything beyond general context and background.

☐ **Personal Skills Courses**
These are courses designed to teach one skill like negotiating or decision making. They are good for people with a need for that skill and a motivation to learn. The value of such courses depends upon the quality of instructors and the accuracy of the content. Check with others who have attended. Ask if they improved in the particular skill being taught.

SUGGESTED READINGS

Barner, Robert. *Lifeboat strategies: how to keep your career above water during tough times – or any time*. New York: American Management Association, 1994.

Bolles, Richard N. *What color is your parachute? 2000*. Berkeley, CA: Ten Speed Press, 1999.

Bridges, William. *Creating You & Co. – Finding work in the dejobbed workplace*. Reading, MA: Addison-Wesley Longman, 1995.

continued

Brim, Gilbert. *Ambition: How we manage success and failure throughout our lives*. New York: Harper Collins, 1992.

DuBrin, Andrew J. *Your own worst enemy: how to overcome career self-sabotage*. New York: American Management Association, 1992.

Holton, Bill and Cher. *The Manager's Short Course: Thirty-three tactics to upgrade your career*. New York: John Wiley & Sons, 1992.

Hunt, Christopher W. and Scott A. Scanlon. *Navigating your Career*. New York: John Wiley & Sons, 1999.

Johnson, Mike. *Getting a Grip on Tomorrow – Your Guide to Survival and Success in the Changed World of Work*. Newton, MA: Butterworth-Heinemann, 1997.

Kaplan, Robert E. with Wilfred H. Drath and Joan Kofodimos. *Beyond Ambition*. San Francisco: Jossey-Bass Publishers, 1991.

Kelley, Robert E. *How to be a Star at Work*. New York: Times Business, 1998.

Kushel, Gerald and Peter Land. *Reaching the Peak: how to motivate yourself and others to excel*. New York: AMACOM 1994.

Levinson, Harry. *Career Mastery*. San Francisco: Berrett-Koehler Publishers, 1992.

McCall, Morgan W., Michael M. Lombardo and Ann M. Morrison. *The Lessons of Experience*. Lexington, MA: Lexington Books, 1988.

Morrison, Ann M., Randall P. White, Ellen Van Velsor, and the Center for Creative Leadership. *Breaking the glass ceiling: Can women reach the top of America's largest corporations?*. Reading, MA: Addison-Wesley Pub. Co., 1992.

Searing, Jill A. and Anne B. Lovett. *The career prescription: how to stop sabotaging your career and put it on a winning track*. Englewood Cliffs, N.J.: Prentice-Hall, 1995.

Stern, Paul G. and Tom Schactman. *Straight to the top: beyond loyalty, gamesmanship, mentors, and other corporate myths*. New York: Warner Books, 1990.

7

CARING ABOUT DIRECT REPORTS

SECTION 1: YOUR DEVELOPMENT NEED(S)

UNSKILLED

- ☐ May not care much about the personal needs of direct reports
- ☐ May be too busy to know much about direct reports
- ☐ May believe work and personal life should be separate
- ☐ May be more work and task oriented than most
- ☐ May be very tense and impersonal with direct reports
- ☐ May lack the listening skills or interest to know people's hopes and problems

SKILLED

- ☐ Is interested in the work and non-work lives of direct reports
- ☐ Asks about their plans, problems, and desires
- ☐ Knows about their concerns and questions
- ☐ Is available for listening to personal problems
- ☐ Monitors workloads and appreciates extra effort

OVERUSED SKILL

- ☐ May have trouble being firm with direct reports
- ☐ May give them too much room for excuses
- ☐ May not challenge them to perform beyond their comfort zone
- ☐ May get too deep into their lives
- ☐ May not be able to make objective calls on performance and potential
- ☐ May not know when to stop showing care when efforts are rejected

Select one to three of the competencies listed below to work on to compensate for an overuse of this skill.

COMPENSATORS: 9, 12, 13, 17, 18, 20, 23, 27, 34, 35, 56, 57, 64

SOME CAUSES

- ☐ Belief that work and personal life should be kept separate
- ☐ Care more for other things than people
- ☐ Fear being taken advantage of
- ☐ Fear of being placed in counselor role
- ☐ Low priority activity
- ☐ Poor listener
- ☐ Too busy

THE MAP

Caring for others is important on a number of levels. At the most basic is that people who are cared about return that care to others. People who are shown care work more effectively with and for the people who show that care. Cared for people feel better and are more positive to be around and work with than people who are ignored. Caring about others doesn't have to be a soft or counselor activity – it simply means trying to show reasonable concern for direct reports in every way possible to help them perform and grow. People who care don't just smile and act friendly. At the mechanical level, good managers know more about their people than just the work they do. They know a little about their history, a little about their current situation, and a little about their dreams, preferences and wishes. They foster two-way information. They pick up the early warning signs for problems before they become serious, and are quick to help others perform better by removing obstacles. Long term they help by developing their direct reports and giving them critical feedback to help them grow. At the deeper level, good managers show care because they care. Either way, managing the whole person will always be rewarded with better performance and a better feeling for you, the manager.

SECTION 2: LEARNING ON YOUR OWN

THESE SELF-DEVELOPMENT REMEDIES WILL HELP YOU BUILD YOUR SKILL(S)

SOME REMEDIES

☐ **1. Caring is listening.** Many bosses are marginal listeners. They are action oriented and more apt to cut off people mid-sentence than listen. They also are impatient and finish people's sentences for them when they hesitate. All of these impatient behaviors come across to others as a lack of caring. It's being insensitive to the needs and feelings of others. So step one in caring is listening longer. *More help? – See #33 Listening.*

☐ **2. Caring is sharing and disclosing.** Share your thinking on a business issue and invite the advice of direct reports. Pass on tidbits of information you think will help people do their jobs better or broaden their perspective. Reveal things people don't need to know to do their jobs, but which will be interesting to them and help them feel valued. Disclose some things about yourself as well. It's hard for people to relate to a stone. Tell them how you arrive at decisions. Explain your intentions, your reasons, and your thinking when announcing decisions. If you offer solutions first, you invite resistance and feelings of not being cared about – "He/she just dumps things on us."

☐ **3. Caring is knowing.** Know three non-work things about everybody – their interests and hobbies or their children or something you can chat about. Life is a small world. If you ask your people a few personal questions, you'll find you have something in common with virtually anyone. Having something in common will help bond the relationship.

- ☐ **4. Caring is accepting.** Try to listen without judging initially. Turn off your "I agree; I don't agree" filter. You don't have to agree with it; just listen to understand. Assume when people tell you something they are looking for understanding; indicate that by being able to summarize what they said. Don't offer advice or solutions unless it's obvious the person wants to know what you would do. While offering instant solutions is a good thing to do in many circumstances, it's chilling where the goal is to get people to talk to you more freely.
- ☐ **5. Caring is understanding.** Study the people you work with. Without judging them, collect evidence on how they think and what they do. What drives them to do what they do? Try to predict what they will do in given situations. Use this to understand how to relate to them. What are their hot buttons? What would they like for you to care about?
- ☐ **6. Caring is wondering.** Show you care what they think. Many people don't ask enough curiosity questions when they are in their work mode. There are too many probing or informational questions and not enough "what if," "what are you learning," "what would you change" questions. In studies, statements outweighed questions eight to one and few questions invited others to really think things through.
- ☐ **7. Caring is treating people differently.** Caring is not treating people equally, it's treating people equitably. People are different. They have different needs. They respond differently to you. They have different dreams and concerns. Each person is unique and feels best when treated uniquely. *More help? – See #21* Managing *Diversity*.
- ☐ **8. Caring is being concerned without becoming a therapist:**
  - If someone brings you all his/her problems on a regular basis, pick one you think you can help with and ask him/her to seek counseling or employee assistance for the others.
  - If someone is a rambler and repeats things, interrupt but summarize. This signals you heard him/her, but keeps him/her from consuming time.
  - If someone is angry, let him/her vent without saying anything other than you know he/she is upset. It's hard for most people to continue very long with no encouragement or resistance. If he/she keeps on, invite him/her to talk with you outside of work hours.
  - If someone is a chronic complainer, ask him/her to write down problems and solutions, and then discuss it. This turns down the volume while hopefully moving him/her off complaining.
  - If someone wants to complain about someone else, ask if he/she has talked to the person. Encourage him/her to do so. If that

doesn't work, summarize what he/she said without agreeing or disagreeing, which will add still more time to the discussion.

- If someone is demotivated, focus on challenging job tasks and variety in his/her work. Ask what excitement on the job looks like to him/her. *More help? – See #19 Developing Direct Reports and #36 Motivating Others.*

☐ **9. Caring is signaling that you care.** Watch out for unintentionally signaling to people that you don't care. A – "I leave the details to others;" B – "I'm not very organized;" C –"I've always believed in taking action then sorting it out later;" might mean A – "What I do isn't important;" B – "I'm left to pick up the pieces;" and C – "I have to deal with the havoc," to your direct reports. Think about impact on them when you speak.

☐ **10. List your last 10 bosses on a piece of paper.** Put five in the "he/she cared the least about me and other members of the team" category and the other five in the "he/she cared the most about me and other members of the team" category. How did the low care group act? What did they do that showed they didn't care? What didn't they do that showed they didn't care? What did the other group do and not do that showed they cared? Compare your analysis to how you behave as a manager.

SECTION 3: LEARNING FROM MORE FEEDBACK

THESE SOURCES WOULD GIVE YOU THE MOST ACCURATE AND DETAILED FEEDBACK ON YOUR SKILL(S)

☐ **Direct Reports**
Across a variety of settings, your direct reports probably see you the most. They are the recipients of most of your managerial behaviors. They know your work. They can compare you with former bosses. Since they may hesitate to give you negative feedback, you have to set the atmosphere to make it easier for them. You have to ask.

☐ **Human Resource Professionals**
Human Resource professionals have both a formal and informal feedback role. Since they have access to unique and confidential information, they can provide the right context for feedback you've received. Sometimes they may be "directed" to give you feedback. Other times, they may pass on feedback just to be helpful to you.

☐ **Past Associates/Constituencies**
When confronted with a present performance problem, some claim, "I wasn't like that before; it must be the current situation." When feedback is available from former associates, about 50% support that claim. In the other half of the cases, the people were like that before and probably didn't know it. It sometimes makes sense to access the past to clearly see the present.

- ☐ **Peers and Colleagues**
  Peers and colleagues have a special social and working relationship. They attend staff meetings together, share private views, get feedback from the same boss, travel together, and are knowledgeable about each other's work. You perhaps let your guard down more around peers and act more like yourself. They can be a valuable source of feedback.

SECTION 4: LEARNING FROM DEVELOP-IN-PLACE ASSIGNMENTS

THESE PART-TIME DEVELOP-IN-PLACE ASSIGNMENTS WILL HELP YOU BUILD YOUR SKILL(S)

- ☐ Create employee involvement teams.
- ☐ Manage an ad hoc, temporary group of "green," inexperienced people as their coach, teacher, orienter, etc.
- ☐ Manage an ad hoc, temporary group of low-competence people through a task they couldn't do by themselves.
- ☐ Help shut down a plant, regional office, product line, business, operation, etc.
- ☐ Manage a project team of people who are older and more experienced than you.
- ☐ Represent the concerns of a group of nonexempt, clerical, or administrative employees to higher management to seek resolution of a difficult issue.
- ☐ Become someone's assigned mentor, coach, sponsor, champion, or orienter.
- ☐ Manage an ad hoc, temporary group of people where the temporary manager is a towering expert and the people in the group are not.
- ☐ Manage an ad hoc, temporary group of people involved in tackling a fix-it or turnaround project.
- ☐ Assemble an ad hoc team of diverse people to accomplish a difficult task.

SECTION 5: LEARNING FROM FULL-TIME JOBS

THESE FULL-TIME JOBS OFFER THE OPPORTUNITY TO BUILD YOUR SKILL(S)

- ☐ **Fix-its/Turnarounds**
  The core demands to qualify as a Fix-it or Turnaround assignment are: 1) Cleaning up a mess. 2) Serious people issues/problems like credibility/performance/morale. 3) Tight deadline. 4) Serious business performance failure. 5) Last chance to fix. Four Types of Fix-its/Turnarounds: 1) Fixing a failed business/unit involving taking control, stopping losses, managing damage, planning the turnaround, dealing

with people problems, installing new processes and systems, and rebuilding the spirit and performance of the unit. 2) Managing sizable disasters like mishandled labor negotiations and strikes, thefts, history of significant business losses, poor staff, failed leadership, hidden problems, fraud, public relations nightmares, etc. 3) Significant reorganization and restructuring (e.g., stabilizing the business, re-forming unit, introducing new systems, making people changes, resetting strategy and tactics). 4) Significant system/process breakdown (e.g., MIS, financial coordination processes, audits, standards, etc.) across units requiring working to change something from a distant position, providing advice and counsel, and installing or implementing a major process improvement or system change outside your own unit and/or with customers outside the organization.

☐ **Significant People Demands**
Core demands required to qualify as a Significant People Responsibilities assignment are: 1) A sizable increase in either the number of people managed and/or the complexity of the challenges involved 2) Longer-term assignment (two or more years). 3) Quality of people management critical to achieving results. 4) Involves groups not worked with before (e.g., union, new technical areas, nationalities).

SECTION 6: LEARNING MORE FROM YOUR PLAN

THESE ADDITIONAL REMEDIES WILL HELP MAKE THIS DEVELOPMENT PLAN MORE EFFECTIVE FOR YOU

Learning to Learn Better

☐ **Examine Why You Judge People the Way You Do**
List the people you like and those you dislike and try to find out why. What do those you like have in common with each other and with you? What do those you dislike have in common with themselves and how do they differ from you? Are your "people buckets" logical and productive or do they interfere? Could you be more effective without putting people into buckets?

Learning from Experience, Feedback and Other People

☐ **Being a Student of Others**
While many of us rely on others for information or advice, we do not really study the behavior of other people. Ask what a person does exceptionally well or poorly. What behaviors are particularly effective and ineffective for them? What works for them and what doesn't? As a student of others, you can deduce the rules of thumb for effective and ineffective behavior and include those in your own library. In comparing yourself with this person, in what areas could you most improve? What could you specifically do to improve in ways comfortable for you?

- ☐ **Learning from Interviewing Others**
  Interview others. Ask not only what they do, but how and why they do it. What do they think are the rules of thumb they are following? Where did they learn the behaviors? How do they keep them current? How do they monitor the effect they have on others?

- ☐ **Learning from a Coach or Tutor**
  Ask a person to coach or tutor you directly. This has the additional benefit of skill building coupled with correcting feedback. Also observe the teacher teaching you. How does he/she teach? How does he/she adjust to you as a learner? After the process, ask for feedback about you as a learner.

- ☐ **Soliciting Feedback**
  Almost everyone reports they receive less feedback than they need to achieve their career goals. While others may have some interest in your career, it is primarily up to you to take the initiative in soliciting feedback from multiple sources by any methods available. You're the stakeholder who needs feedback to improve and grow.

- ☐ **Giving Feedback to Others**
  Most managers complain they don't get enough useful feedback. Ironically, their direct reports and peers offer the same complaint! Getting serious about feedback for yourself involves giving more feedback to those around you. As you practice giving more feedback to others, you will receive more by the example you set and will become more sensitive and receptive to your own.

- ☐ **Learning from Bad Things that Happen**
  Bad things happen to everyone, sometimes because of what we do and sometimes with no help from us. We all have bad bosses, bad staffs, impossible and hopeless situations, impossible tasks, and unintended consequences. Aside from the trouble these bad things cause for you, the key is how can you learn from each of them.

- ☐ **Learning from Limited Staff**
  Most managers either inherit or hire staff from time to time who are inexperienced, incompetent, not up to the task, resistant, or dispirited. Any of these may create a hardship for you. The lessons to be learned are how to get things done with limited resources and how to fix the people situation. In the short term, this hardship is best addressed by assessing the combined strengths of the team and deploying the best you have against the problem. Almost everyone can do something well. Also, the team can contribute more than the combined individuals can. How can you empower and motivate the team? If you hired the troublesome staff, why did you err? What can you learn from your hiring mistakes? What wasn't there that you thought was present? What led you astray? How can you prevent that same hiring error in the future? What do you need to do to fix the situation? Quick development? Start

over? If you inherited the problem, how can you fix it? Can you implement a program of accelerated development? Do you have to start over and get new people? What did the prior manager do or not do that led to this situation in the first place? What can you learn from that? What will you do differently? How does the staff feel? What can you learn from their frustrations over not being able to do the job? How can you be a positive force under negative circumstances? How can you rally them to perform? What lasting lessons can you learn from someone in distress and trouble? If you're going to try accelerated development, how can you get a quick assessment? How can you give the staff motivating feedback? How can you construct and implement development plans that will work? How can you get people on-line feedback for maximum growth? Do you know when to stop trying and start over? If you're going to turn over some staff, how can you do it both rapidly and with the least damage? How can you deliver the message in a constructive way? What can you learn from having to take negative actions against people? How can you prevent this from happening again?

Learning from Courses

☐ **Supervisory Courses**
Most new supervisors go through an "Introduction to Supervision" type course. They are designed to teach the common practices a first-line supervisor needs to know to be effective. The content of most of those courses is standard. There is general agreement on the principles of effective supervision. There are two common problems: 1) Do the students have a strong motivation to learn? Do they know what they don't know? Is there any pain? Because motivated students with a need for the knowledge learn best, participants should have had some trying experiences and some supervisory pain and hardships before attending. 2) Are the instructors experienced supervisors? Have they practiced what they preach? Can they share powerful anecdotes to make key points? Can they answer questions credibly? If possible, select supervisory courses based on the instructors, since the content seems to be the much same for all such courses. Lastly, does the course offer the opportunity for practicing each skill? Does it contain simulations? Are there case studies you could easily identify with? Are there breakout groups? Is there opportunity for action learning? Search for the most interactive course.

☐ **Sending Others to Courses**
If you are responsible for managing someone else's development and, as part of that, sending them to courses, prepare them beforehand. Don't send them as tourists. Meet with them before and after the course. Tell them why they need this course. Tell them what you expect them to learn. Give them feedback on why you think they need the course. Agree ahead of time how you will measure and monitor learn-

ing after they return. If possible, offer a variety of courses for your employee to choose from. Have them give you a report shortly after they return. If appropriate, have them present what they learned to the rest of your staff. After they return, provide opportunities for using the new skills with safe cover and low risk. Give them practice time before expecting full exercise of the new skills. Be supportive during early unsteadiness. Give continuous feedback on progress.

SUGGESTED READINGS

Autry, James A. *The Art of Caring Leadership*. New York: William Morrow and Company, Inc., 1991.

Daniels, Aubrey C. *Bringing out the Best in People*. New York: McGraw-Hill, Inc., 1994.

Garfield, Charles A. *Second to none: how our smartest companies put people first*. Homewood, IL: Business One Irwin, 1992.

Handy, Charles. *The Hungry Spirit*. New York: Doubleday, 1998.

Keneally, Thomas. *Schindler's List*. New York: Simon & Schuster, 1982.

Keneally, Thomas. *Schindler's List [sound recording]*. New York: Simon & Schuster Audio, 1993.

Maslach, Christina and Michael P. Leiter. *The Truth About Burnout*. San Francisco: Jossey-Bass, Inc., 1997.

Mason, Marilyn Ph.D. *Seven Mountains – The inner climb to commitment and caring*. New York: The Penguin Group, 1997.

Pfeffer, Jeffrey. *The Human Equation.* Boston: Harvard Business School Press, 1998.

8

COMFORT AROUND HIGHER MANAGEMENT

SECTION 1: YOUR DEVELOPMENT NEED(S)

UNSKILLED

- ☐ Lacks self confidence in front of more senior people
- ☐ May appear nervous and tense, not at his/her best
- ☐ May lose composure or get rattled when questioned by executives
- ☐ Doesn't know how to influence or impress more senior managers
- ☐ May not understand what top executives are looking for
- ☐ Says and does things that don't fit the situation

SKILLED

- ☐ Can deal comfortably with more senior managers
- ☐ Can present to more senior managers without undue tension and nervousness
- ☐ Understands how senior managers think and work
- ☐ Can determine the best way to get things done with them by talking their language and responding to their needs
- ☐ Can craft approaches likely to be seen as appropriate and positive

OVERUSED SKILL

- ☐ May manage up too much
- ☐ May be seen as too political and ambitious
- ☐ May spend too much time with more senior managers, parrot their positions, overestimate the meaning and usefulness of the relationships
- ☐ Career may be too dependent on champions
- ☐ May be too free with confidential information

Select one to three of the competencies listed below to work on to compensate for an overuse of this skill.

COMPENSATORS: 5, 9, 12, 17, 22, 24, 29, 30, 45, 51, 53, 57

SOME CAUSES

- ☐ Lack of self confidence in front of more powerful people
- ☐ Fear of making a mistake; slipping up and doing something dumb
- ☐ Perfectionism; the fear of not being perfect in the eyes of senior management
- ☐ Lack of proper preparation due to lack of knowledge or skills or a work style deficit
- ☐ Tendency to become more emotional under pressure and stress

THE MAP

Performing in front of one or a number of higher level managers is usually tough; they are all highly skilled in something to get there; don't have much time; ask tough questions and expect answers; sometimes don't care how they make you feel. Many in your situation don't get through unscathed. Many higher level managers will test you to see what you are made of; some may ask tough questions just to see if you can handle them; some may intentionally want to push you to see what you are made of; they are not always going to be nice to you. It seems the higher up they get the less time they spend thinking about or making any effort to make others feel comfortable around them. They all made their share of mistakes when they were in your position. They learned through tough times. They stumbled once in a while. In fact, the research says successful higher level managers made more mistakes on the way up than the people who didn't get there.

SECTION 2: LEARNING ON YOUR OWN

THESE SELF-DEVELOPMENT REMEDIES WILL HELP YOU BUILD YOUR SKILL(S)

SOME REMEDIES

☐ **1. Keep your cool.** Being nervous, anxious and uncomfortable around one or more higher ups is fairly normal; the key is not allowing that to prevent you from doing your best. Being uncomfortable can sometimes lead to physical reactions like sweating, hesitating or stuttering speech, mispronounced words, flushing of the face, grumbling in the stomach, running out of breath while talking, etc. When that happens, stop a second or two, take a deep breath, compose yourself and continue what you were doing; they all have been there before. Remember, all you can do is the best you can do. You probably know more about this topic than they do. You're well prepared – being anxious can prevent you from demonstrating your expertise. *More help? – See #11 Composure.*

☐ **2. Worst case it.** List all of your worst fears; what bad things do you think might happen; envision yourself in each of those situations; mentally practice how you would recover. Can't think of the right words? Pause, don't fill the void with "uhs." Refer to your notes. Feeling defensive? Ask a question. Running overtime? Go straight to the conclusion. Practice the more realistic recoveries live in front of a mirror or with a colleague playing the audience.

☐ **3. Practice, practice, practice.** Rehearse what you are going to do several times so you can do it as naturally as possible; this gives you time to deal with questions and unexpected reactions more comfortably. Record yourself on video tape. Did you speak no longer than five to 10 minutes per major point? Anything you went into with so much detail that you sounded like an almanac? Did you vary tone and volume or was it monotone? Will they remember your key points 15 minutes after the meeting ends? *More help? – See #49 Presentation Skills.*

☐ **4. Visit the setting.** If it's a presentation to a number of higher ups, visit the setting of the event beforehand to get more comfortable in the actual setting; if you can, practice the event there. When you visit, consider the seating. Will people be able to hear you easily or should you speak up? Any spots where line of sight is restricted? Be sure not to stand there. Will your overheads be easy to read from the back? If not, go to fewer points and larger type.

☐ **5. Be time efficient.** Plan what you need to do and say carefully. Take as little time as necessary. Maybe bring more material than you need and will use. Since no one has ever run out of material, take 60 overheads but show 40 and be prepared to show 30. Summary overheads can help with this. Top managers are very busy; everyone loves someone who takes up less time than is planned or on the agenda. Let them ask for more detail; don't drown them.

☐ **6. Be ready for Q&A.** Many people get in trouble during questions and answers. Don't fake answers; most high level managers will tolerate a "Don't know but I'll get back to you on that." Think of all the questions ahead of time; ask someone else to look at what you are going to say and do, and think of questions they would ask. Rehearse the answers to the questions. Another place people get in trouble when challenged is by retreating to a safe recitation of facts; executives are usually asking for logic and problem analysis, not a repackaging of what you've already said. The worst case of course is when an executive rejects your argument. If this happens, draw the person out to see if you've been misunderstood and clarify. If that's not the case, let the disagreement be as it is. Few executives respect someone who drops an argument as soon as challenged. You should listen carefully, and respond with logic in 30 seconds or less per point. Don't repeat the entire argument; long answers often backfire since people have already heard it and few may agree with the questioner. In haste to be thorough, you may just look defensive.

☐ **7. Find a confidant.** Ask a member of top management you know well and trust for advice on how you could feel better and perform more effectively when you transact with him/her and the rest of the team. Share your anxieties with a trusted colleague and ask for suggestions and observations. Find someone who appears comfortable in the settings you find difficult and ask how to do it.

☐ **8. Consider who bothers you.** If only certain higher ups bother you and others don't, take a piece of paper and list the styles of the two groups/individuals. What are the similarities? Why does one style bother you and the other doesn't? With the groups/individuals that bother you, how could you respond more comfortably and effectively? Perhaps you could use some of the techniques you use with the more comfortable groups. Probably you should prime yourself to take nothing in personal terms and no matter what happens, return to a discussion of the problem. *More help? – See #12 Conflict Management.*

☐ **9. Get to know more top managers.** Try to meet and interact with higher ups in informal settings like receptions, social or athletic events, charity events, off-sites, etc.; you will probably learn that higher ups are just regular people who are older and therefore higher than you in the hierarchy. You may then feel more comfortable with them when back in the work setting.

☐ **10. Find out how top managers think.** Read the biographies of five "great" people; see what is said about them and their view of people like you; read five autobiographies and see what they say about themselves and how they viewed people in your position. Write down five things you can do differently or better.

SECTION 3: LEARNING FROM MORE FEEDBACK

THESE SOURCES WOULD GIVE YOU THE MOST ACCURATE AND DETAILED FEEDBACK ON YOUR SKILL(S)

☐ **Boss's Boss(es)**
From a process standpoint, your boss's boss probably has the most influence and control over your progress. He/she has a broader perspective, has more access to data, and stands at the center of decisions about you. To know what he/she thinks, without having to violate the canons of corporate due process to get that information, would be quite useful.

☐ **Direct Boss**
Your direct boss has important information about you, your performance, and your prospects. The challenge is to get this information. There are formal processes (e.g., performance appraisals). There are day-to-day opportunities. To help, signal your boss that you want and can handle direct and timely feedback. Many bosses have trouble giving feedback, so you will have to work at it over a period of time.

☐ **Natural Mentors**
Natural mentors have a special relationship with you and are interested in your success and your future. Since they are usually not in your direct chain of command, you can have more open, relaxed, and fruitful discussions about yourself and your career prospects. They can be a very important source for candid or critical feedback others may not give you.

SECTION 4: LEARNING FROM DEVELOP-IN-PLACE ASSIGNMENTS

THESE PART-TIME DEVELOP-IN-PLACE ASSIGNMENTS WILL HELP YOU BUILD YOUR SKILL(S)

- ☐ Integrate diverse systems, processes, or procedures across decentralized and/or dispersed units.
- ☐ Plan a new site for a building (plant, field office, headquarters, etc.).
- ☐ Represent the concerns of a group of nonexempt, clerical, or administrative employees to higher management to seek resolution of a difficult issue.
- ☐ Write a proposal for a new policy, process, mission, charter, product, service, or system, and present and sell it to top management.
- ☐ Relaunch an existing product or service that's not doing well.
- ☐ Serve on a junior or shadow board.
- ☐ Manage an ad hoc, temporary group of people involved in tackling a fix-it or turnaround project.
- ☐ Prepare and present a proposal of some consequence to top management.
- ☐ Manage a group through a significant business crisis.
- ☐ Write a speech for someone higher up in the organization.

SECTION 5: LEARNING FROM FULL-TIME JOBS

THESE FULL-TIME JOBS OFFER THE OPPORTUNITY TO BUILD YOUR SKILL(S)

- ☐ **Chair of Projects/Task Forces**
  The core demands for qualifying as a Project/Task Force assignment are: 1) Full-time assignment. 2) Important and specific goal. 3) Tight deadline. 4) Success or failure will be evident. 5) High-visibility sponsor. 6) Learning something on the fly. 7) Must get others to cooperate. 8) Usually six months or more. Four types of Projects/Task Forces: 1) New ideas, products, services, or systems (e.g., product/service/program research and development, creation/installation/launch of a new system, new programs like Total Quality Management, positive discipline). 2) Formal negotiations and relationships (e.g., acquisitions, divestitures, agreements, joint ventures, licensing arrangements, franchising, dealing with unions, governments, communities, charities, customers, and relocations). 3) Big one-time events (e.g., working on a major presentation for the board, organizing significant meetings or conferences, disaster/damage control teams, reorganizations, mergers, acquisitions, or relocations, working on visions, charters, strategies, other time-urgent issues and problems). 4) Troubleshooting (e.g., problems, disasters, crises, product/service failures, accidents, illegal activities, damage control in public relations goofs, shut downs, downsizings, layoffs, abrupt changes in leadership).

☐ **Fix-its/Turnarounds**
The core demands to qualify as a Fix-it or Turnaround assignment are: 1) Cleaning up a mess. 2) Serious people issues/problems like credibility/performance/morale. 3) Tight deadline. 4) Serious business performance failure. 5) Last chance to fix. Four Types of Fix-its/Turnarounds: 1) Fixing a failed business/unit involving taking control, stopping losses, managing damage, planning the turnaround, dealing with people problems, installing new processes and systems, and rebuilding the spirit and performance of the unit. 2) Managing sizable disasters like mishandled labor negotiations and strikes, thefts, history of significant business losses, poor staff, failed leadership, hidden problems, fraud, public relations nightmares, etc. 3) Significant reorganization and restructuring (e.g., stabilizing the business, reforming unit, introducing new systems, making people changes, resetting strategy and tactics). 4) Significant system/process breakdown (e.g., MIS, financial coordination processes, audits, standards, etc.) across units requiring working to change something from a distant position, providing advice and counsel, and installing or implementing a major process improvement or system change outside your own unit and/or with customers outside the organization.

☐ **Heavy Strategic Demands**
The core demands necessary to qualify as a Heavy Strategic Content assignment are: 1) Requires significant strategic thinking and planning most couldn't do. 2) Charts new ground strategically. 3) Plan must be presented, challenged, adopted, and implemented. 4) Exposure to significant decision makers and executives. 1) Strategic planning position. 2) Job involving repositioning of a product, service, or organization.

☐ **Scope Assignments**
The core demands for a Scope (complexity) assignment are: 1) Significant increase in both internal and external scope or complexity. 2) Significant increase in visibility and/or bottom line responsibility. 3) Unfamiliar area, business, technology, or territory. Examples of Scope assignments involving shifts: 1) Switching into a new function/technology/business. 2) Moving to new organization. 3) Moving to overseas assignment. 4) Moving to new location. 5) Adding new products/services. 6) Moving between headquarters/field. 7) Switches in ownership/top management of the unit/organization. Examples of Scope assignments involving "firsts": 1) First-time manager. 2) First-time managing managers. 3) First-time executive. 4) First-time overseas. 5) First-time headquarters/field. 6) First-time team leader. 7) First-time new technology/business/function. Scope assignments involving increased complexity: 1) Managing a significant expansion of an existing product or service. 2) Managing adding new products/service into an existing unit. 3) Managing a reorganized and more diverse unit. 4) Managing explosive growth. 5) Adding new technologies.

☐ **Start-ups**
The core demands to qualify as a start from scratch are: 1) Starting something new for you and/or for the organization. 2) Forging a new team. 3) Creating new systems/facilities/staffs/programs/procedures. 4) Contextual adversity (e.g., uncertainty, government regulation, unions, difficult environment). Seven types of start from scratches: 1) Planning, building, hiring, and managing (e.g., building a new facility, opening up a new location, moving a unit or company). 2) Heading something new (e.g., new product, new service, new line of business, new department/function, major new program). 3) Take over a group/product/service/program that had existed for less than a year and was off to a fast start. 4) Establishing overseas operations. 5) Major new designs for existing systems. 6) Moving a successful program from one unit to another. 7) Installing a new organization-wide process as a full-time job (e.g., like Total Quality).

SECTION 6: LEARNING MORE FROM YOUR PLAN

THESE ADDITIONAL REMEDIES WILL HELP MAKE THIS DEVELOPMENT PLAN MORE EFFECTIVE FOR YOU

Learning from Experience, Feedback and Other People

☐ **Using Multiple Models**
Who do you know who exemplifies how to do whatever your need is? Who, for example, personifies decisiveness or compassion or strategic agility? Think more broadly than your current job and colleagues. For example, clergy, friends, spouses or community leaders are also good sources for potential models. Select your models not on the basis of overall excellence or likability, but on the basis of the one towering strength (or glaring weakness) you are interested in. Even people who are well thought of usually have only one or two towering strengths (or glaring weaknesses). Ordinarily, you won't learn as much from the whole person as you will from one characteristic.

☐ **Being a Student of Others**
While many of us rely on others for information or advice, we do not really study the behavior of other people. Ask what a person does exceptionally well or poorly. What behaviors are particularly effective and ineffective for them? What works for them and what doesn't? As a student of others, you can deduce the rules of thumb for effective and ineffective behavior and include those in your own library. In comparing yourself with this person, in what areas could you most improve? What could you specifically do to improve in ways comfortable for you?

☐ **Learning from Bosses**
Bosses can be an excellent and ready source for learning. All bosses do some things exceptionally well and other things poorly. Distance your

feelings from the boss/direct report relationship and study things that work and things that don't work for your boss. What would you have done? What could you use, and what should you avoid?

- ☐ **Learning from Mentors and Tutors**
  Mentors and tutors offer a special case for learning since the relationship is specifically formed for learning. You need to be open and nondefensive. You need to solicit and accept feedback. This is a unique opportunity for you to get low-risk, honest, and direct feedback on what you do well and not so well.

- ☐ **Learning from Remote Models**
  Many times you can learn from people not directly available to you. You can read a book about them, watch tapes of public figures, read analyses of them, etc. The principles of learning are the same. Ask yourself what they do well or poorly and deduce their rules of thumb.

- ☐ **Consolidating What You Learn from People**
  After using any source and/or method of learning from others, write down or mentally note the new rules of thumb and the principles involved. How will you remind yourself of the new behaviors in similar situations? How will you prevent yourself from reacting on "autopilot"? How could you share what you have learned from others?

- ☐ **Getting Feedback from Bosses and Superiors**
  Many bosses are reluctant to give negative feedback. They lack the managerial courage to face people directly with criticism. You can help by soliciting feedback and setting the tone. Show them you can handle criticism and that you are willing to work on issues they see as important.

- ☐ **Openness to Feedback**
  Nothing discourages feedback more than defensiveness, resistance, irritation, and excuses. People don't like giving feedback anyway, and much less to those who don't listen or are unreceptive. To help the feedback giver, be open, listen, ask for examples and details, take notes, keep a journal, and thank them for their interest.

- ☐ **Learning from Bad Bosses**
  First, what does he/she do so well to make him/her your boss? (Even bad bosses have strengths). Then, ask what makes this boss bad for you. Is it his/her behavior? Attitude? Values? Philosophy? Practices? Style? What is the source of the conflict? Why do you react as you do? Do others react the same? How are you part of the problem? What do you do that triggers your boss? If you wanted to, could you reduce the conflict or make it go away by changing something you do? Is there someone around you who doesn't react like you? How are they different? What can you learn from them? What is your emotional reaction to this boss? Why do you react like that? What can you do to cope with these feelings? Can you avoid reacting out of anger and frustra-

tion? Can you find something positive about the situation? Can you use someone else as a buffer? Can you learn from your emotions? What lasting lessons of managing others can you take away from this experience? What won't you do as a manager? What will you do differently? How could you teach these principles you've learned to others by the use of this example?

Learning from Courses

☐ **Strategic Courses**
There are a number of courses designed to stretch minds to prepare for future challenges. They include topics such as Workforce Diversity 2000, globalization, the European Union, competitive competencies and strategies, etc. Quality depends upon the following three factors: 1) The quality of the staff. Are they qualified? Are they respected in their fields? Are they strategic "gurus"? 2) The quality of the participants. Are they the kind of people you could learn from? 3) The quality of the setting. Is it comfortable and free from distractions? Can you learn there?

SUGGESTED READINGS

Bolton, Robert and Dorothy Grover Bolton. *People Styles at Work – Making bad relationships good and good relationships better.* New York: AMACOM, 1996.

Fritz, Roger and Kristie Kennard. *How to Manage Your Boss.* Hawthorne, NJ: Career Press, 1994.

Hegarty, Christopher with Philip Goldberg. *How to manage your boss.* New York: Rawson, Wade Publishers, 1981, 1980.

Kummerow, Jean M., Nancy J. Barger and Linda K. Kirby. *Work Types.* New York: Warner Books, 1997.

COMMAND SKILLS

SECTION 1: YOUR DEVELOPMENT NEED(S)

UNSKILLED

- ☐ More comfortable following
- ☐ May avoid conflict and crises, be unwilling to take the heat, have problems with taking a tough stand
- ☐ Might be laid back and quiet
- ☐ Too concerned about what others may say or think
- ☐ May worry too much about being liked, correct or above criticism
- ☐ May be conflict shy or lack perseverance
- ☐ May not be cool under pressure
- ☐ May not display a sense of urgency

SKILLED

- ☐ Relishes leading
- ☐ Takes unpopular stands if necessary
- ☐ Encourages direct and tough debate but isn't afraid to end it and move on
- ☐ Is looked to for direction in a crisis
- ☐ Faces adversity head on
- ☐ Energized by tough challenges

OVERUSED SKILL

- ☐ May not be a team player
- ☐ May not be tolerant of other people's ways of doing things
- ☐ May choose to strongly lead when other more team-based tactics would do as well or better
- ☐ May not develop other leaders
- ☐ May become controversial and be rejected by others

Select one to three of the competencies listed below to work on to compensate for an overuse of this skill.

COMPENSATORS: 3, 7, 10, 19, 31, 33, 36, 38, 41, 47, 52, 59, 60

SOME CAUSES

- ☐ Avoid crises
- ☐ Can't set common cause
- ☐ Can't take a tough stand
- ☐ Can't take the heat of leading
- ☐ Fear of criticism/failure
- ☐ Getting others to believe
- ☐ Not cool under pressure
- ☐ Not credible leader
- ☐ Shy

THE MAP

Leading makes you more visible and more open to criticism. The heat is the hottest on the nose cone of the rocket. Leading is exciting and puts you in control. Leading in tough or crisis conditions is all about creating aligned and sustained motion. It involves keeping your eye on the goal, setting common causes, dealing with the inevitable heat, managing your emotions, being a role model, taking tough stands and getting others to believe in where you're headed.

SECTION 2: LEARNING ON YOUR OWN

THESE SELF-DEVELOPMENT REMEDIES WILL HELP YOU BUILD YOUR SKILL(S)

SOME REMEDIES

☐ **1. Leading is riskier than following.** While there are a lot of personal rewards for leading, leading puts you in the limelight. Think about what happens to political leaders and the scrutiny they face. Leaders have to be internally secure. Do you feel good about yourself? They have to please themselves first that they are on the right track. Can you defend to a critical and impartial audience the wisdom of what you're doing? They have to accept lightning bolts from detractors. Can you take the heat? People will always say it should have been done differently. Listen to them, but be skeptical. Even great leaders are wrong sometimes. They accept personal responsibility for errors and move on to lead some more. Don't let criticism prevent you from taking the lead. Build up your heat shield. Conduct a postmortem immediately after finishing milestone efforts. This will indicate to all that you're open to continuous improvement whether the result was stellar or not.

☐ **2. Against the grain tough stands.** Taking a tough stand demands utter confidence in what you're saying along with the humility that you might be wrong – one of life's paradoxes. To prepare to take the lead on a tough issue, work on your stand through mental interrogation until you can clearly state in a few sentences what your stand is and why you hold it. Build the business case. How do others win? People don't line up behind laundry lists or ambiguous objectives. Ask others for advice – scope the problem, consider options, pick one, develop a rationale, then go with it until proven wrong. Then redo the process.

☐ **3. Selling your leadership.** While some people may welcome what you say and want to do, others will go after you or even try to minimize the situation. Some will sabotage. To sell your leadership, keep your eyes on the prize but don't specify how to get there. Present the outcomes, targets and goals without the how to's. Welcome their ideas, good and bad. Any negative response is a positive if you learn from it. Allow them to fill in the blanks, ask questions, and disagree without appearing impatient with them. Allow others to save face;

concede small points, invite criticism of your own. Help them figure out how to win. Keep to the facts and the problem before the group; stay away from personal clashes. *More help? – See #12 Conflict Management.*

☐ **4. Keep your cool.** Manage your emotional reactions. Sometimes your emotional reactions lead others to think you have problems with tough leadership situations. In the situations where this happens, what emotional reactions do you have? Do you show impatience or non-verbals like increasing voice volume or drumming your fingers? Learn to recognize those as soon as they start. Substitute something more neutral. If, when uncomfortable with something you tend to disagree, ask a question instead to buy time. Or, tell the person to tell you more about his/her point of view. *More help? – See #11 Composure and #107* Lack of *Composure.*

☐ **5. Develop a philosophical stance toward failure/criticism.** After all, most innovations fail, most proposals fail, most efforts to lead change fail. Anything worth doing takes repeated effort. Anything could always have been done better. Research says that successful general managers have made more mistakes in their careers than the people they were promoted over. They got promoted because they had the guts to lead, not that they were always right. Other studies suggest really good general managers are right about 65% of the time. Put errors, mistakes and failures on your menu. Everyone has to have some spinach for a balanced diet.

☐ **6. One-on-one combat.** Leading always involves dealing with pure one-on-one confrontation. You want one thing, he/she wants something else. When that happens, keep it to the facts. You won't always win. Stay objective. Listen as long as he/she will talk. Ask a lot of questions. Sometimes he/she will talk him/herself to your point of view if you let him/her talk long enough. Always listen to understand first, not judge. Then restate his/her points until he/she says that's right. Then find something to agree with, however small that may be. Refute his/her points starting with the one you have the most objective information on. Then move down the line. You will always have points left that didn't get resolved. Document those and give a copy to your opponent. The objective is to get the list as small as possible. Then decide whether you are going to pull rank and go ahead. Delay and get more data. Go to a higher source for arbitration. *More help? – See #12 Conflict Management.*

☐ **7. Cutting line.** When all else fails, you may have to pull someone aside and say, "I have listened to all of your objections and have tried to understand them, but the train is moving on. Are you on or off?" Always follow the rules of dealing with conflict: depersonalize; keep it on the problem not the person; try one last time to make your case; note the person's objections but don't concede anything; be clear; now is not the time for negotiation; give the person a day to think it over. Worst case, if the person is a direct report, you may have to ask him/her to leave the unit. *More help? – See #13 Confronting Direct Reports.* If the person is a peer or colleague, inform your boss of the impasse and your intention to proceed without his/her support.

☐ **8. Crisis leadership.** Studies says followers really appreciate sound leadership during a crisis. They want to know there is a firm hand on the tiller. During a crisis, time is the enemy. Collect all the data that exists. Make a list of data that could be gathered in a short time. Get it. With the assembled incomplete data, ask others for suggestions and thoughts. Then decide on an action. Think through all of the worst case consequences and assign a person or a team to prepare for them. Then execute the decision with an instant feedback loop. Make adjustments as you go. And communicate, communicate, communicate.

☐ **9. Haven't found your passion to lead?** Try small things. Try some leadership roles and tasks off work. Volunteer for a leadership role in your place of worship, school, or the neighborhood. Volunteer to head a task force. Start up a credit union. Volunteer for the United Way drive. Start a softball league.

☐ **10. Leadership presence.** Leading takes presence. You have to look and sound like a leader. Voice is strong. Eye contact. Intensity. Confidence. A lot of leadership presence has to do with forceful presentation skills. Giving good presentations is a known technology. There are several books and workshops you can take. Look to workshops that use video taping. Join your local Toastmasters club for some low risk training and practice. Look to small things such as do you look like a leader? What colors do you wear? Do you dress the part? Are your glasses right? Is your office configured right? Do you sound confident? Do you whine and complain or do you solve problems? If I met you for the first time in a group of 10 would I pick you as the leader?

SECTION 3: LEARNING FROM MORE FEEDBACK

THESE SOURCES WOULD GIVE YOU THE MOST ACCURATE AND DETAILED FEEDBACK ON YOUR SKILL(S)

☐ **Direct Reports**

Across a variety of settings, your direct reports probably see you the most. They are the recipients of most of your managerial behaviors. They know your work. They can compare you with former bosses. Since they may hesitate to give you negative feedback, you have to set the atmosphere to make it easier for them. You have to ask.

☐ **Human Resource Professionals**

Human Resource professionals have both a formal and informal feedback role. Since they have access to unique and confidential information, they can provide the right context for feedback you've received. Sometimes they may be "directed" to give you feedback. Other times, they may pass on feedback just to be helpful to you.

☐ **Past Associates/Constituencies**
When confronted with a present performance problem, some claim, "I wasn't like that before; it must be the current situation." When feedback is available from former associates, about 50% support that claim. In the other half of the cases, the people were like that before and probably didn't know it. It sometimes makes sense to access the past to clearly see the present.

SECTION 4: LEARNING FROM DEVELOP-IN-PLACE ASSIGNMENTS

THESE PART-TIME DEVELOP-IN-PLACE ASSIGNMENTS WILL HELP YOU BUILD YOUR SKILL(S)

☐ Relaunch an existing product or service that's not doing well.

☐ Assign a project to a group with a tight deadline.

☐ Manage an ad hoc, temporary group of balky and resisting people through an unpopular change or project.

☐ Manage an ad hoc, temporary group of low-competence people through a task they couldn't do by themselves.

☐ Help shut down a plant, regional office, product line, business, operation, etc.

☐ Prepare and present a proposal of some consequence to top management.

☐ Work on a team that's deciding who to keep and who to let go in a layoff, shutdown, delayering, or divestiture.

☐ Take on a tough and undoable project, one where others who have tried it have failed.

☐ Manage a cost-cutting project.

☐ Resolve an issue in conflict between two people, units, geographies, functions, etc.

SECTION 5: LEARNING FROM FULL-TIME JOBS

THESE FULL-TIME JOBS OFFER THE OPPORTUNITY TO BUILD YOUR SKILL(S)

☐ **Fix-its/Turnarounds**
The core demands to qualify as a Fix-it or Turnaround assignment are: 1) Cleaning up a mess. 2) Serious people issues/problems like credibility/performance/morale. 3) Tight deadline. 4) Serious business performance failure. 5) Last chance to fix. Four Types of Fix-its/Turnarounds: 1) Fixing a failed business/unit involving taking control, stopping losses, managing damage, planning the turnaround, dealing

with people problems, installing new processes and systems, and rebuilding the spirit and performance of the unit. 2) Managing sizable disasters like mishandled labor negotiations and strikes, thefts, history of significant business losses, poor staff, failed leadership, hidden problems, fraud, public relations nightmares, etc. 3) Significant reorganization and restructuring (e.g., stabilizing the business, re-forming unit, introducing new systems, making people changes, resetting strategy and tactics). 4) Significant system/process breakdown (e.g., MIS, financial coordination processes, audits, standards, etc.) across units requiring working to change something from a distant position, providing advice and counsel, and installing or implementing a major process improvement or system change outside your own unit and/or with customers outside the organization.

- ☐ **Significant People Demands**
  Core demands required to qualify as a Significant People Responsibilities assignment are: 1) A sizable increase in either the number of people managed and/or the complexity of the challenges involved 2) Longer-term assignment (two or more years). 3) Quality of people management critical to achieving results. 4) Involves groups not worked with before (e.g., union, new technical areas, nationalities).

- ☐ **Start-ups**
  The core demands to qualify as a start from scratch are: 1) Starting something new for you and/or for the organization. 2) Forging a new team. 3) Creating new systems/facilities/staffs/programs/procedures. 4) Contextual adversity (e.g., uncertainty, government regulation, unions, difficult environment). Seven types of start from scratches: 1) Planning, building, hiring, and managing (e.g., building a new facility, opening up a new location, moving a unit or company). 2) Heading something new (e.g., new product, new service, new line of business, new department/function, major new program). 3) Take over a group/product/service/program that had existed for less than a year and was off to a fast start. 4) Establishing overseas operations. 5) Major new designs for existing systems. 6) Moving a successful program from one unit to another. 7) Installing a new organization-wide process as a full-time job (e.g., like Total Quality).

SECTION 6: LEARNING MORE FROM YOUR PLAN

THESE ADDITIONAL REMEDIES WILL HELP MAKE THIS DEVELOPMENT PLAN MORE EFFECTIVE FOR YOU

Learning to Learn Better

☐ **Sell Something to a Tough Group/Audience**
Think of the person or group who will be the toughest to sell, the most critical, skeptical, or resistant, and sell that person or group first. Take time to understand the opposing viewpoints. Find common ground and leverage points; line up your best data and arguments and go for it.

Learning from Experience, Feedback and Other People

☐ **Learning from Bosses**
Bosses can be an excellent and ready source for learning. All bosses do some things exceptionally well and other things poorly. Distance your feelings from the boss/direct report relationship and study things that work and things that don't work for your boss. What would you have done? What could you use, and what should you avoid?

☐ **Learning from Observing Others**
Observe others. Find opportunities to observe without interacting with your model. This enables you to objectively study the person, note what he/she is doing or not doing, and compare that with what you would typically do in similar situations. Many times you can learn more by watching than asking. Your model may not be able to explain what he/she does or may be an unwilling teacher.

☐ **Learning from a Coach or Tutor**
Ask a person to coach or tutor you directly. This has the additional benefit of skill building coupled with correcting feedback. Also observe the teacher teaching you. How does he/she teach? How does he/she adjust to you as a learner? After the process, ask for feedback about you as a learner.

☐ **Getting Feedback from Bosses and Superiors**
Many bosses are reluctant to give negative feedback. They lack the managerial courage to face people directly with criticism. You can help by soliciting feedback and setting the tone. Show them you can handle criticism and that you are willing to work on issues they see as important.

☐ **Getting Feedback from Direct Reports**
Direct reports often fear reprisals for giving negative feedback about bosses, whether in a formal process, like a questionnaire, or informally and face-to-face. Even with a guarantee of confidentiality, some are still hesitant. If you want feedback from direct reports, you have to set a positive tone and never act out of revenge.

☐ **Learning from Limited Staff**
Most managers either inherit or hire staff from time to time who are inexperienced, incompetent, not up to the task, resistant, or dispirited. Any of these may create a hardship for you. The lessons to be learned are how to get things done with limited resources and how to fix the people situation. In the short term, this hardship is best addressed by assessing the combined strengths of the team and deploying the best you have against the problem. Almost everyone can do something well. Also, the team can contribute more than the combined individuals can. How can you empower and motivate the team? If you hired the troublesome staff, why did you err? What can you learn from your hiring mistakes? What wasn't there that you thought was present? What led you astray? How can you prevent that same hiring error in the future? What do you need to do to fix the situation? Quick development? Start over? If you inherited the problem, how can you fix it? Can you implement a program of accelerated development? Do you have to start over and get new people? What did the prior manager do or not do that led to this situation in the first place? What can you learn from that? What will you do differently? How does the staff feel? What can you learn from their frustrations over not being able to do the job? How can you be a positive force under negative circumstances? How can you rally them to perform? What lasting lessons can you learn from someone in distress and trouble? If you're going to try accelerated development, how can you get a quick assessment? How can you give the staff motivating feedback? How can you construct and implement development plans that will work? How can you get people on-line feedback for maximum growth? Do you know when to stop trying and start over? If you're going to turn over some staff, how can you do it both rapidly and with the least damage? How can you deliver the message in a constructive way? What can you learn from having to take negative actions against people? How can you prevent this from happening again?

Learning from Courses

☐ **Supervisory Courses**
Most new supervisors go through an "Introduction to Supervision" type course. They are designed to teach the common practices a first-line supervisor needs to know to be effective. The content of most of those courses is standard. There is general agreement on the principles of effective supervision. There are two common problems: 1) Do the students have a strong motivation to learn? Do they know what they don't know? Is there any pain? Because motivated students with a need for the knowledge learn best, participants should have had some trying experiences and some supervisory pain and hardships before attending. 2) Are the instructors experienced supervisors? Have they practiced what they preach? Can they share powerful anecdotes to

make key points? Can they answer questions credibly? If possible, select supervisory courses based on the instructors, since the content seems to be the much same for all such courses. Lastly, does the course offer the opportunity for practicing each skill? Does it contain simulations? Are there case studies you could easily identify with? Are there breakout groups? Is there opportunity for action learning? Search for the most interactive course.

SUGGESTED READINGS

Albrecht, Steven. *Crisis management for corporate self-defense: how to protect your organization in a crisis – how to stop a crisis before it starts.* New York: AMACOM, 1996.

Beck, John D.W. and Neil M. Yaeger. *The Leader's Window.* New York: John Wiley & Sons, 1994.

Caponigro, Jeffrey R. *The crisis counselor: the executive's guide to avoiding, managing, and thriving on crises that occur in all businesses.* Southfield, Mich.: Barker Business Books, Inc., 1998.

Green, Peter. *Alexander of Macedon, 356–323 B.C. A historical biography.* Los Angeles: University of California Press, 1991.

Horton, Thomas R. *The CEO Paradox – The privilege and accountability of leadership.* New York: AMACOM, 1992.

Hurst, David K. *Crisis & renewal: meeting the challenge of organizational change.* Boston, Mass.: Harvard Business School Press, 1995.

Kraus, Peter (Ed.). *The Book of Leadership Wisdom.* New York: John Wiley & Sons, Inc., 1998.

Marconi, Joe. *Crisis marketing: when bad things happen to good companies.* Chicago: NTC Business Books, 1997.

Meyers, Gerald C. with John Holusha. *When it hits the fan: Managing the nine crises of business.* Boston: Houghton Mifflin, 1986.

Schwarzkopf, H. Norman with Peter Petre. *It doesn't take a hero: General H. Norman Schwarzkopf, the autobiography.* New York: Bantam Books, 1992.

Schwarzkopf, H. Norman with Peter Petre. *It doesn't take a hero: General H. Norman Schwarzkopf, the autobiography [sound recording].* New York: Bantam Audio, 1992.

10

COMPASSION

SECTION 1: YOUR DEVELOPMENT NEED(S)

UNSKILLED

- ☐ May be less caring or empathic than most
- ☐ Doesn't ask personal questions; doesn't respond much when offered
- ☐ Results are all that matters; everything else gets in the way
- ☐ Believes in separation of personal life and business
- ☐ May find the plight of others an inappropriate topic at work
- ☐ Uncomfortable with people in stress and pain
- ☐ May not know how to show compassion or how to deal with people in trouble
- ☐ May have less sympathy than most for the imperfections and problems of others

SKILLED

- ☐ Genuinely cares about people
- ☐ Is concerned about their work and non-work problems
- ☐ Is available and ready to help
- ☐ Is sympathetic to the plight of others not as fortunate
- ☐ Demonstrates real empathy with the joys and pains of others

OVERUSED SKILL

- ☐ May smooth over conflict in the interest of harmony
- ☐ May not be tough enough in the face of malingerers and may make too many concessions
- ☐ May get so close to people that objectivity is affected and they are able to get away with too much
- ☐ May have trouble with close calls on people

Select one to three of the competencies listed below to work on to compensate for an overuse of this skill.

COMPENSATORS: 12, 13, 16, 18, 20, 34, 35, 37, 50, 53, 57, 59, 62

SOME CAUSES

- ☐ Fear of being consumed by non-work matters
- ☐ Fear of not being able to handle disagreements
- ☐ Hard to see the value at work
- ☐ Have trouble dealing with emotionally or politically charged issues
- ☐ See compassion as a weakness
- ☐ Trouble dealing with people/groups who are different
- ☐ Uncomfortable with feelings

THE MAP

Genuinely cares. Empathizes and sympathizes. Hurts for others. Lends an open ear. Work and personal life flowing together. Sounds alien, painful and out of place to many managers. For most managers, compassion and work don't go together comfortably. Work can be a cold and bleak place. The road of life is bumpy and uneven. There is always rough water. There is probably more opportunity for pain and disappointment than pleasure and fulfillment. People need support and help to make it through. They look to family, religion, social friends and mentors for support but they also expect some compassion from bosses and coworkers. But if you don't show some compassion, you are quite likely to be seen as cold or impersonal. People who don't seem to care eventually run out of people to work with. Even when this isn't the case – you do show compassion – some people get into trouble because they don't handle situations involving compassion well.

SECTION 2: LEARNING ON YOUR OWN

THESE SELF-DEVELOPMENT REMEDIES WILL HELP YOU BUILD YOUR SKILL(S)

SOME REMEDIES

☐ **1. Compassion is understanding.** A primary reason for problems with compassion is that you don't know how to deal with strong feelings and appear distant or uninterested. You're uncomfortable with strong displays of emotion and calls for personal help. Simply imagine how you would feel in this situation and respond with that. Tell him/her how sorry you are this has happened or has to be dealt with. Offer whatever help is reasonable. A day off. A loan. A resource.

☐ **2. Compassion is sometimes just listening.** Sometimes people just need to talk it out. Compassion is quiet listening. Nod and maintain eye contact to indicate listening. When he/she pauses, respond with how he/she must feel, and suggest something you could do to help (e.g. if he/she needs to be gone for awhile, you'll see that his/her work is covered).

☐ **3. Compassion is not always advice.** Don't offer advice unless asked. Indicate support through listening and a helpful gesture. There will be time for advice when the situation isn't so emotionally charged. Many times managers are too quick with advice before they really understand the problem. *More help? – See #7 Caring About Direct Reports.*

☐ **4. Study the three most compassionate people you know** or know of: pick one at work, one off work, and one notable figure (such as Mother Teresa). What do they do that you don't? How do they show compassion? What words do they use; what gestures do they make? Do any of them, such as clergy, have to deal with compassion quickly? What does this person do? Can you translate any of these learnings into compassion for yourself?

- [ ] **5. Compassion is not therapy or counseling.** Another reason people have trouble with compassion is thinking that a counselor role isn't appropriate at work. You can be brief and compassionate by following three rules:

  - Let people say what's on their mind without saying anything other than you know they're upset. Don't judge. Don't advise.
  - Summarize when they start repeating. This signals that you heard them, but keeps them from consuming so much time you begin to feel like a counselor.
  - If someone overdoes it, invite him/her to talk with you outside of work hours or refer him/her to another resource like employee assistance.

  This shows others that you cared, you listened and are willing to help if possible while not putting you in the counselor role that is making you uncomfortable.

- [ ] **6. Compassion isn't judgment or agreement.** Be candid with yourself. Is there a group or groups you don't like or are uncomfortable with? Do you judge individual members of that group without really knowing if your stereotype is true? Most of us do. Do you show compassion for one group's problems but not another's? To deal with this:

  - Put yourself in their case. Why would you act that way? What do you think they're trying to achieve? Assume that however they act is rational to them; it must have paid off or they wouldn't be doing it. Don't use your internal standards.
  - Avoid putting groups in buckets. Many of us bucket groups as friendly or unfriendly; good or bad; like me or not like me. Once we do, we generally don't show as much compassion towards them and may question their motives. Apply the logic above of why people belong to the group in the first place. See if you can predict accurately what the group will say or do across situations to test your understanding of the group. Don't use your agreement program.
  - Listen. Even though this tip may seem obvious, many of us tune out when dealing with difficult or not well understood groups, or reject what they're saying before they say it. Just listen. Mentally summarize their views, and see if you can figure out what they want from what they say and mean. The true test is whether you can clearly figure it out even though you don't think that way.

- [ ] **7. Being sensitive.** You need to know what people's compassion hot buttons are because one mistake can get you labeled as insensitive with some people. The only cure here is to see what turns up the volume for them – either literally or what they're concerned about. Be careful of downplaying or demeaning someone else's cause (like the

Native American community trying to remove Indian nicknames from athletic teams).

- ☐ **8. Follow the rules of good listening** if someone is clearly concerned about a lack of compassion related to something such as ethnic, gender concerns, level or status in the organization:
  - Understanding and listening isn't the same thing as agreement.
  - Don't argue if they're emotional about it. You'll lose no matter what you say. Discuss only that you've heard them, they acknowledge you've heard them, and indicate you want to discuss the problem from a rational point of view – what causes it, what it looks and feels like, and what can be done about it.
- ☐ **9. When the other side of a compassion dispute takes a rigid position, don't reject it.** Ask why – what are the principles behind the position, how do we know it's fair, what's the theory of the case. Play out what would happen if their position was accepted. Ask what they would do if they were in your shoes. Ask lots of questions, but make few statements.
- ☐ **10. If someone attacks you for not being compassionate,** rephrase it as an attack on the problem/issue. In response to unreasonable proposals, attacks, or a non-answer to a question, you can always say nothing but acknowledge that you heard what they said. People will usually respond by saying more, coming off their position a bit, or at least revealing their interests. *More help? – See #12 Conflict Management.*

SECTION 3: LEARNING FROM MORE FEEDBACK

THESE SOURCES WOULD GIVE YOU THE MOST ACCURATE AND DETAILED FEEDBACK ON YOUR SKILL(S)

- ☐ **Development Professionals**
  Sometimes it might be valuable to get some analysis and feedback from a professional trained and certified in the area you're working on: possibly a career counselor, a therapist, clergy, a psychologist, etc.
- ☐ **Direct Reports**
  Across a variety of settings, your direct reports probably see you the most. They are the recipients of most of your managerial behaviors. They know your work. They can compare you with former bosses. Since they may hesitate to give you negative feedback, you have to set the atmosphere to make it easier for them. You have to ask.
- ☐ **Natural Mentors**
  Natural mentors have a special relationship with you and are interested in your success and your future. Since they are usually not in your direct chain of command, you can have more open, relaxed, and fruitful discussions about yourself and your career prospects. They can be a

very important source for candid or critical feedback others may not give you.

- ☐ **Spouse**
  Spouses can be powerful sources of feedback on such things as interpersonal style, values, balance between work, career, and personal life, etc. Many participants attending development programs share their feedback with their spouses for value-adding confirmation or context and for specific examples.

SECTION 4: LEARNING FROM DEVELOP-IN-PLACE ASSIGNMENTS

THESE PART-TIME DEVELOP-IN-PLACE ASSIGNMENTS WILL HELP YOU BUILD YOUR SKILL(S)

- ☐ Join a self-help or support group.
- ☐ Represent the concerns of a group of nonexempt, clerical, or administrative employees to higher management to seek resolution of a difficult issue.
- ☐ Work on a team that's deciding who to keep and who to let go in a layoff, shutdown, delayering, or divestiture.
- ☐ Manage the outplacement of a group of people.
- ☐ Work on an affirmative action plan for the organization and present it to management for approval.
- ☐ Do a study of failed executives in your organization, including interviewing people still with the organization who knew or worked with them, and report the findings to top management.
- ☐ Serve for a year or more with a community agency.
- ☐ Coach a children's sports team.
- ☐ Manage the assigning/allocating of office space in a contested situation.
- ☐ Make peace with an enemy or someone you've disappointed with a product or service or someone you've had some trouble with or don't get along well with.

SECTION 5: LEARNING FROM FULL-TIME JOBS

THESE FULL-TIME JOBS OFFER THE OPPORTUNITY TO BUILD YOUR SKILL(S)

- ☐ **Fix-its/Turnarounds**
  The core demands to qualify as a Fix-it or Turnaround assignment are: 1) Cleaning up a mess. 2) Serious people issues/problems like credibility/performance/morale. 3) Tight deadline. 4) Serious business performance failure. 5) Last chance to fix. Four Types of Fix-its/Turnarounds: 1) Fixing a failed business/unit involving taking control,

stopping losses, managing damage, planning the turnaround, dealing with people problems, installing new processes and systems, and rebuilding the spirit and performance of the unit. 2) Managing sizable disasters like mishandled labor negotiations and strikes, thefts, history of significant business losses, poor staff, failed leadership, hidden problems, fraud, public relations nightmares, etc. 3) Significant reorganization and restructuring (e.g., stabilizing the business, re-forming unit, introducing new systems, making people changes, resetting strategy and tactics). 4) Significant system/process breakdown (e.g., MIS, financial coordination processes, audits, standards, etc.) across units requiring working to change something from a distant position, providing advice and counsel, and installing or implementing a major process improvement or system change outside your own unit and/or with customers outside the organization.

☐ **Influencing Without Authority**
The core demands to qualify as an Influence Without Authority are: 1) Significant challenge (e.g, start-up, fix-it, scope and/or scale assignment, strategic planning project, changes in management practices/ systems). 2) Insufficient direct authority to make it happen. 3) Tight deadlines. 4) Visible to significant others. 5) Sensitive politics.

☐ **Significant People Demands**
Core demands required to qualify as a Significant People Responsibilities assignment are: 1) A sizable increase in either the number of people managed and/or the complexity of the challenges involved 2) Longer-term assignment (two or more years). 3) Quality of people management critical to achieving results. 4) Involves groups not worked with before (e.g., union, new technical areas, nationalities).

SECTION 6: LEARNING MORE FROM YOUR PLAN

THESE ADDITIONAL REMEDIES WILL HELP MAKE THIS DEVELOPMENT PLAN MORE EFFECTIVE FOR YOU

Learning to Learn Better

☐ **Observe Someone Worse Than You for Insights**
Find someone you think is even worse at this area than you. Observe them doing it and try to find out why it doesn't work for them. Interview them for their thoughts and insights; compare and contrast with your own thought and action pattern to check for errors.

Learning from Experience, Feedback and Other People

☐ **Using Multiple Models**
Who do you know who exemplifies how to do whatever your need is? Who, for example, personifies decisiveness or compassion or strategic agility? Think more broadly than your current job and colleagues. For example, clergy, friends, spouses or community leaders are also good

sources for potential models. Select your models not on the basis of overall excellence or likability, but on the basis of the one towering strength (or glaring weakness) you are interested in. Even people who are well thought of usually have only one or two towering strengths (or glaring weaknesses). Ordinarily, you won't learn as much from the whole person as you will from one characteristic.

☐ **Learning from Bosses**
Bosses can be an excellent and ready source for learning. All bosses do some things exceptionally well and other things poorly. Distance your feelings from the boss/direct report relationship and study things that work and things that don't work for your boss. What would you have done? What could you use, and what should you avoid?

☐ **Learning from Observing Others**
Observe others. Find opportunities to observe without interacting with your model. This enables you to objectively study the person, note what he/she is doing or not doing, and compare that with what you would typically do in similar situations. Many times you can learn more by watching than asking. Your model may not be able to explain what he/she does or may be an unwilling teacher.

☐ **Learning from Remote Models**
Many times you can learn from people not directly available to you. You can read a book about them, watch tapes of public figures, read analyses of them, etc. The principles of learning are the same. Ask yourself what they do well or poorly and deduce their rules of thumb.

☐ **Consolidating What You Learn from People**
After using any source and/or method of learning from others, write down or mentally note the new rules of thumb and the principles involved. How will you remind yourself of the new behaviors in similar situations? How will you prevent yourself from reacting on "autopilot"? How could you share what you have learned from others?

☐ **Getting Feedback from Direct Reports**
Direct reports often fear reprisals for giving negative feedback about bosses, whether in a formal process, like a questionnaire, or informally and face-to-face. Even with a guarantee of confidentiality, some are still hesitant. If you want feedback from direct reports, you have to set a positive tone and never act out of revenge.

☐ **Feedback in Unusual Contexts/Situations**
Temporary and extreme conditions and contexts may shade interpretations of your behavior and intentions. Demands of the job may drive you outside your normal mode of operating. Hence, feedback you receive may be inaccurate during those times. However, unusual contexts affect our behavior less than most assume. It's usually a weak excuse.

- [ ] **Openness to Feedback**
  Nothing discourages feedback more than defensiveness, resistance, irritation, and excuses. People don't like giving feedback anyway, and much less to those who don't listen or are unreceptive. To help the feedback giver, be open, listen, ask for examples and details, take notes, keep a journal, and thank them for their interest.

- [ ] **Giving Feedback to Others**
  Most managers complain they don't get enough useful feedback. Ironically, their direct reports and peers offer the same complaint! Getting serious about feedback for yourself involves giving more feedback to those around you. As you practice giving more feedback to others, you will receive more by the example you set and will become more sensitive and receptive to your own.

SUGGESTED READINGS

Autry, James A. *The Art of Caring Leadership.* New York: William Morrow and Company, Inc., 1991.

Brehony, Kathleen A. *Ordinary Grace – An examination of the roots of compassion, altruism, and empat*hy. New York: Riverhead Books, 1999.

Noer, David M. *Healing the Wounds.* San Francisco: Jossey-Bass, Inc., 1993.

Roosevelt, Franklin D., Russell D. Buhite and David W. Levy, Editors. *FDR's Fireside Chats.* Norman, Oklahoma: University of Oklahoma Press, 1992.

Sebba, Anne. *Mother Teresa, 1910–1997, Beyond the Image.* New York: Doubleday, 1997.

Wuthnow, Robert. *Acts of Compassion – Caring for others and helping ourselves.* Princeton, NJ: Princeton University Press, 1991.

11

COMPOSURE

SECTION 1: YOUR DEVELOPMENT NEED(S)

UNSKILLED

- ☐ Gets rattled and loses cool under pressure and stress
- ☐ May blow up, say things he/she shouldn't
- ☐ Gets easily overwhelmed and becomes emotional, defensive or withdrawn
- ☐ May be defensive and sensitive to criticism
- ☐ May be cynical or moody
- ☐ May be knocked off balance by surprises and get easily rattled
- ☐ May contribute to others losing composure or being unsettled
- ☐ May let anger, frustration and anxiety show

SKILLED

- ☐ Is cool under pressure
- ☐ Does not become defensive or irritated when times are tough
- ☐ Is considered mature
- ☐ Can be counted on to hold things together during tough times
- ☐ Can handle stress
- ☐ Is not knocked off balance by the unexpected
- ☐ Doesn't show frustration when resisted or blocked
- ☐ Is a settling influence in a crisis

OVERUSED SKILL

- ☐ May not show appropriate emotion
- ☐ May be seen as cold and uncaring
- ☐ May seem flat in situations where others show feelings
- ☐ May be easily misinterpreted
- ☐ May not be able to relate well to those whose actions and decisions are based more on feelings than on thinking

Select one to three of the competencies listed below to work on to compensate for an overuse of this skill.

COMPENSATORS: 3, 10, 14, 26, 27, 31, 44, 60, 66

SOME CAUSES

- ☐ Defensive
- ☐ Easily overwhelmed; very emotional
- ☐ Lack self confidence
- ☐ Perfectionist
- ☐ Sensitive
- ☐ Too much going on
- ☐ Very control oriented
- ☐ Weak impulse control

THE MAP

First about emotions. Emotions are electricity and chemistry. Emotions are designed to help you cope with emergencies and threats. Emotions trigger predictable body changes. Heart pumps faster and with greater pressure. Blood flows faster. Glucose is released into the bloodstream for increased energy and strength. Eyes dilate to take in more light. Breathing rate increases to get more oxygen. Why is that? To either fight or flee from Saber Toothed Tigers, of course. Emotions are designed to help us with the so-called fight or flight response. It makes the body faster and stronger temporarily. The price? In order to increase energy to the muscles, the emotional response decreases resources for the stomach (that's why we get upset stomachs under stress) and the thinking brain (that's why we say and do dumb things under stress). Even though we might be able to lift a heavy object off a trapped person, we can't think of the right thing to say in a tense meeting. Once the emotional response is triggered, it has to run its course. If no threat follows the initial trigger, it lasts from 45–60 seconds in most people. That's why your grandmother told you to count to 10. Trouble is, people have Saber Toothed Tigers in their heads. In modern times, thoughts can trigger this emotional response. Events which are certainly not physically threatening, like being criticized, can trigger the response. Even worse, today people have added a third "f" to the fight or flight response – freeze. Emotions can shut you down and leave you speechless, neither choosing to fight (argue, respond) or flee (calmly shut down the transaction and exit). You'll have to fight these reactions to learn to be cool under pressure.

SECTION 2: LEARNING ON YOUR OWN

THESE SELF-DEVELOPMENT REMEDIES WILL HELP YOU BUILD YOUR SKILL(S)

SOME REMEDIES

☐ **1. Decreasing triggers.** Write down the last 25 times you lost your composure. Most people who have composure problems have three to five repeating triggers. Criticism. Loss of control. A certain kind of a person. An enemy. Being surprised. Spouse. Children. Money. Authority. Try to group 90% of the events into three to five categories. Once you have the groupings, ask yourself why these are a problem. Is it ego? Losing face? Being caught short? Being found out? Causing you more work? In each grouping, what would be a more mature response? Mentally and physically rehearse a better response. Try to decrease by 10% a month the number of times you lose your composure.

☐ **2. Increasing impulse control.** People say and do inappropriate things when they lose their composure. The problem is that they say or do the first thing that occurs to them. Research shows that generally somewhere between the second and third thing you think of to say or do is the best option. Practice holding back your first response long enough to think of a second. When you can do that, wait long enough to think of a third before you choose. By that time 50% of your composure problems should go away.

☐ **3. Count to 10.** Our thinking and judgment are not at their best during the emotional response. Create and practice delaying tactics. Go get a pencil out of your briefcase. Go get a cup of coffee. Ask a question and listen. Go up to the flip chart and write something. Take notes. See yourself in a setting you find calming. Go to the bathroom. You need about a minute to regain your composure after the emotional response is triggered. Don't do or say anything until the minute has passed.

☐ **4. Delay of gratification.** Are you impatient? Do you get upset when the plane is delayed? The food is late? The car isn't ready? Your spouse is behind schedule? For most of us, life is one big delay. We always seem to be waiting for someone else to do something so we can do our something. People with composure problems often can't accept delay of what they want, and think they deserve and have coming. When what they want is delayed, they get belligerent and demanding. Write down the last 25 delays that set you off. Group them into three to five categories. Create and rehearse a more mature response. Relax. Reward yourself with something enjoyable. Adopt a philosophical stance since there's little or nothing you can do about it. Think great thoughts while you're waiting. *More help? – See #41 Patience.*

☐ **5. Defensive?** A lot of loss of composure starts with an intended or even an unintended criticism. There are a lot of perfect people in this world who cannot deal with a piece of negative information about themselves or about something they have or have not done. The rest of us have flaws that most around us know about and once in awhile tell us about. We even know that once in awhile unjust criticism is sent our way. Dealing constructively with criticism is a learnable skill. *More help? – See #108 Defensiveness.*

☐ **6. Controlling?** Are you somewhat of a perfectionist? Need to have everything just so? Create plans and expect them to be followed? Very jealous of your time? Another source of loss of composure is when things do not go exactly as planned. Put slack in your plans. Expect the unexpected. Lengthen the time line. Plan for delays. List worst case scenarios. Most of the time you will be pleasantly surprised and the rest of the time you won't get so upset.

☐ **7. Blame and vengeance?** Do you feel a need to punish the people and groups that set you off? Do you become hostile, angry, sarcastic or vengeful? While all that may be temporarily satisfying to you, they will all backfire and you will lose in the long term. When someone attacks you, rephrase it as an attack on a problem. Reverse the argument – ask what he/she would do if he/she were in your shoes. When the other side takes a rigid position, don't reject it. Ask why – what are the principles behind the offer, how do we know it's fair, what's the theory of the case. Play out what would happen if their position was accepted. Let the other side vent frustration, blow off steam, but don't react.

- ☐ **8. When you do reply to an attack,** keep it to the facts and their impact on you. It's fine for you to draw conclusions about the impact on yourself ("I felt blindsided."). It's not fine for you to tell others their motives ("You blindsided me" means you did it, probably meant to, and I know the meaning of your behavior). So state the meaning for yourself; ask others what their actions meant.
- ☐ **9. Get anxious and jump to conclusions?** Take quick action? Don't like ambiguity and uncertainty and act to wipe it out? Solutions first, understanding second? Take the time to really define the problem. Let people finish. Try not to interrupt. Don't finish others' sentences. Ask clarifying questions. Restate the problem in your own words to everyone's satisfaction. Ask them what they think. Throw out trial solutions for debate. Then decide.
- ☐ **10. Too much invested at work?** Find a release for your pent-up emotions. Get a physical hobby. Start an exercise routine. Jog. Walk. Chop wood. Sometimes people who have flair tempers hold it in too much, the pressure builds, and the teakettle blows. The body stores energy. It has to go somewhere. Work on releasing your work frustration off work.

SECTION 3: LEARNING FROM MORE FEEDBACK

THESE SOURCES WOULD GIVE YOU THE MOST ACCURATE AND DETAILED FEEDBACK ON YOUR SKILL(S)

- ☐ **Development Professionals**
  Sometimes it might be valuable to get some analysis and feedback from a professional trained and certified in the area you're working on: possibly a career counselor, a therapist, clergy, a psychologist, etc.
- ☐ **Direct Reports**
  Across a variety of settings, your direct reports probably see you the most. They are the recipients of most of your managerial behaviors. They know your work. They can compare you with former bosses. Since they may hesitate to give you negative feedback, you have to set the atmosphere to make it easier for them. You have to ask.
- ☐ **Human Resource Professionals**
  Human Resource professionals have both a formal and informal feedback role. Since they have access to unique and confidential information, they can provide the right context for feedback you've received. Sometimes they may be "directed" to give you feedback. Other times, they may pass on feedback just to be helpful to you.

- ☐ **Peers and Colleagues**
  Peers and colleagues have a special social and working relationship. They attend staff meetings together, share private views, get feedback from the same boss, travel together, and are knowledgeable about each other's work. You perhaps let your guard down more around peers and act more like yourself. They can be a valuable source of feedback.

SECTION 4: LEARNING FROM DEVELOP-IN-PLACE ASSIGNMENTS

THESE PART-TIME DEVELOP-IN-PLACE ASSIGNMENTS WILL HELP YOU BUILD YOUR SKILL(S)

- ☐ Study humor in business settings; read books on the nature of humor; collect cartoons you could use in presentations; study funny people around you; keep a log of funny jokes and sayings you hear; read famous speeches and study how humor was used; attend comedy clubs; ask a funny person to act as your tutor; practice funny lines and jokes with others.
- ☐ Manage an ad hoc, temporary group of balky and resisting people through an unpopular change or project.
- ☐ Manage an ad hoc, temporary group of people where the people in the group are towering experts but the temporary manager is not.
- ☐ Handle a tough negotiation with an internal or external client or customer.
- ☐ Help shut down a plant, regional office, product line, business, operation, etc.
- ☐ Prepare and present a proposal of some consequence to top management.
- ☐ Manage a dissatisfied internal or external customer; troubleshoot a performance or quality problem with a product or service.
- ☐ Manage a cost-cutting project.
- ☐ Take on a task you dislike or hate to do.
- ☐ Make peace with an enemy or someone you've disappointed with a product or service or someone you've had some trouble with or don't get along well with.

SECTION 5: LEARNING FROM FULL-TIME JOBS

THESE FULL-TIME JOBS OFFER THE OPPORTUNITY TO BUILD YOUR SKILL(S)

- ☐ **Influencing Without Authority**
  The core demands to qualify as an Influence Without Authority are: 1) Significant challenge (e.g, start-up, fix-it, scope and/or scale assignment, strategic planning project, changes in management practices/

systems). 2) Insufficient direct authority to make it happen. 3) Tight deadlines. 4) Visible to significant others. 5) Sensitive politics.

☐ **Line To Staff Switches**
The core demands to qualify as a Line to Staff switch are:
1) Intellectually/strategically demanding. 2) Highly visible to others.
3) New area/perspective/method/culture/function. 4) Moving away from a bottom line. 5) Moving from field to headquarters. 6) Exposure to high-level executives. Examples: 1) Business/strategic planning.
2) Heading a staff department. 3) Assistant to/chief of staff to a senior executive. 4) Head of a task force. 5) Human resources role.

☐ **Start-ups**
The core demands to qualify as a start from scratch are: 1) Starting something new for you and/or for the organization. 2) Forging a new team. 3) Creating new systems/facilities/staffs/programs/procedures.
4) Contextual adversity (e.g., uncertainty, government regulation, unions, difficult environment). Seven types of start from scratches:
1) Planning, building, hiring, and managing (e.g., building a new facility, opening up a new location, moving a unit or company). 2) Heading something new (e.g., new product, new service, new line of business, new department/function, major new program). 3) Take over a group/product/service/program that had existed for less than a year and was off to a fast start. 4) Establishing overseas operations. 5) Major new designs for existing systems. 6) Moving a successful program from one unit to another. 7) Installing a new organization-wide process as a full-time job (e.g., like Total Quality).

SECTION 6: LEARNING MORE FROM YOUR PLAN

THESE ADDITIONAL REMEDIES WILL HELP MAKE THIS DEVELOPMENT PLAN MORE EFFECTIVE FOR YOU

Learning to Learn Better

☐ **Rehearse Successful Tactics/Strategies/Actions**
Mentally rehearse how you will act before going into the situation. Try to anticipate how others will react, what they will say, and how you'll respond. Check out the best and worst cases; play out both scenes. Check your feelings in conflict or worst-case situations; rehearse staying under control.

☐ **Put Yourself in Situations that Call for Your Weaknesses**
Put yourself in situations where you must overcome or neutralize a weakness to be successful. Find opportunities to develop counter coping skills: if you're shy, attend functions where you don't know many people; if you're too aggressive, work with children, etc.

☐ **Examine Why You're Blocked on a Key Issue**
Examine what you are worrying/angry about and list all of your thoughts about it; ask why these feelings are holding you back. Why are the feelings overriding your thinking? How are they getting in the way? Why are they important to you? How can you move beyond them and learn to do something different?

☐ **Study Your History of Conflicts for Insights**
List the people and situations which cause you trouble. What are the common themes? Why do those kinds of people and/or those kinds of situations set you off? Do they have to? Was the conflict really important? Did it help or block your learning and getting things done? Try to anticipate those people/situations in the future.

☐ **Learn to Separate Opinions From Facts**
Practice separating opinions, beliefs, feelings, attitudes and values from facts and data. Try to base more of your comments and actions on the data side. If there is a need to air subjective information, announce it as such, and label it for what it is. Don't present opinions with the look and sound of data.

Learning from Experience, Feedback and Other People

☐ **Feedback in Unusual Contexts/Situations**
Temporary and extreme conditions and contexts may shade interpretations of your behavior and intentions. Demands of the job may drive you outside your normal mode of operating. Hence, feedback you receive may be inaccurate during those times. However, unusual contexts affect our behavior less than most assume. It's usually a weak excuse.

☐ **Learning from Bad Bosses**
First, what does he/she do so well to make him/her your boss? (Even bad bosses have strengths). Then, ask what makes this boss bad for you. Is it his/her behavior? Attitude? Values? Philosophy? Practices? Style? What is the source of the conflict? Why do you react as you do? Do others react the same? How are you part of the problem? What do you do that triggers your boss? If you wanted to, could you reduce the conflict or make it go away by changing something you do? Is there someone around you who doesn't react like you? How are they different? What can you learn from them? What is your emotional reaction to this boss? Why do you react like that? What can you do to cope with these feelings? Can you avoid reacting out of anger and frustration? Can you find something positive about the situation? Can you use someone else as a buffer? Can you learn from your emotions? What lasting lessons of managing others can you take away from this experience? What won't you do as a manager? What will you do differently? How could you teach these principles you've learned to others by the use of this example?

☐ **Learning from Bad Situations**
All of us will find ourselves in bad situations from time to time. Good intentions gone bad. Impossible tasks and goals. Hopeless projects. Even though you probably can't perform well, the key is to at least take away some lessons and insights. How did things get to be this way? What factors led to the impasse? How can you make the best of a bad situation? How can you neutralize the negative elements? How can you get the most out of yourself and your staff under the chilling situation? What can you salvage? How can you use coping strategies to minimize the negatives? How can you avoid these situations going forward? In bad situations: 1) Be resourceful. Get the most you can out of the situation. 2) Try to deduce why things got to be that way. 3) Learn from both the situation you inherited and how you react to it. 4) Integrate what you learn into your future behavior.

☐ **Learning from Mistakes**
Since we're human, we all make mistakes. The key is to focus on why you made the mistake. Spend more time locating causes and less worrying about the effects. Check how you react to mistakes. How much time do you spend being angry with yourself? Do you waste time stewing or do you move on? More importantly, do you learn? Ask why you made the mistake. Are you likely to repeat it under similar situations? Was it a lack of skill? Judgment? Style? Not enough data? Reading people? Misreading the challenge? Misreading the politics? Or was it just random? A good strategy that just didn't work? Others that let you down? The key is to avoid two common reactions to your mistakes: 1) avoiding similar situations instead of learning and trying again, and 2) trying to repeat what you did, only more diligently and harder, hoping to break through the problem, making the same mistake again but with greater impact. Neither trap leaves us with better strategies for the future. Neither is a learning strategy. To learn and do something differently, focus on the patterns in your behavior that get you in trouble and go back to first causes, those that tell you something about your shortcomings. Facing ourselves squarely is always the best way to learn.

Learning from Courses

☐ **Insight Events**
These are courses designed around assessing skills and providing feedback to the participants. These events can be a powerful source of self-knowledge and can lead to significant development if done right. When selecting a self-insight course, consider the following: 1) Are the skills assessed the important ones? 2) Are the assessment techniques and instruments sound? 3) Are those who are providing the feedback trained and professional? 4) Is the feedback provided in a user-friendly and "actionable" format? 5) Does the feedback include development planning? 6) Is the setting comfortable and conducive to reflection and

learning? 7) Are the other participants the kinds of people you could learn from? 8) Are you in the right frame of mind to learn from this kind of intense experience? Select events on the basis of positive answers to these eight questions.

SUGGESTED READINGS

DuBrin, Andrew J. *Your Own Worst Enemy.* New York: AMACOM, 1992.

Elliot, Robert S., M.D. *From Stress to Strength.* New York: Doubleday, 1994.

Lee, John H. with Bill Stott. *Facing the fire: experiencing and expressing anger appropriately.* New York: Bantam Books, 1993.

Loehr, James E. *Stress for Success.* New York: Times Business, 1997.

Peck, M. Scott, M.D. *A World Waiting to be Born: Civility Rediscovered.* New York: Bantam Books, 1993.

Peck, M. Scott, M.D. *A World Waiting to be Born: Civility Rediscovered [sound recording].* New York: Bantam Doubleday Dell Audio Pub., 1993.

Potter-Efron, Ronald T. *Working anger: preventing and resolving conflict on the job.* Oakland, CA: New Harbinger Publications, 1998.

Tavris, Carol. *Anger: the misunderstood emotion.* New York: Simon & Schuster, 1989.

12

CONFLICT MANAGEMENT

SECTION 1: YOUR DEVELOPMENT NEED(S)

UNSKILLED

- ☐ Avoids conflict in situations and with people
- ☐ May accommodate, want everyone to get along
- ☐ May get upset as a reaction to conflict, takes it personally
- ☐ Can't operate under conflict long enough to get a good deal
- ☐ Gives in and says yes too soon
- ☐ Gets into conflict by accident; doesn't see it coming
- ☐ Will let things fester rather than dealing with them directly
- ☐ Will try to wait long enough for it to go away
- ☐ May be excessively competitive and have to win every dispute

SKILLED

- ☐ Steps up to conflicts, seeing them as opportunities
- ☐ Reads situations quickly
- ☐ Good at focused listening
- ☐ Can hammer out tough agreements and settle disputes equitably
- ☐ Can find common ground and get cooperation with minimum noise

OVERUSED SKILL

- ☐ May be seen as overly aggressive and assertive
- ☐ May get in the middle of everyone else's problems
- ☐ May drive for a solution before others are ready
- ☐ May have a chilling effect on open debate
- ☐ May spend too much time with obstinate people and unsolvable problems

Select one to three of the competencies listed below to work on to compensate for an overuse of this skill.

COMPENSATORS: 2, 3, 31, 33, 34, 36, 37, 40, 41, 51, 52, 56, 60, 64

SOME CAUSES

- ☐ Avoid conflict
- ☐ Can't negotiate
- ☐ Get too emotional
- ☐ Slow to catch on
- ☐ Take things personally
- ☐ Too sensitive

THE MAP

A 1996 survey found that managers were spending 18% of their time dealing with direct face to face conflict. It has doubled since 1986. Most organizations are decentralized and compartmentalized which sets up natural conflict, group to group. Whenever you form two groups, conflict follows. Gender and race inroads have probably brought with them increased conflict. Competition has heated up, making speed and agility more important but also created more conflict and less relaxed reflection. There is data based conflict – my numbers are better than your numbers. There is opinion conflict – my opinion has greater value than yours. There is power conflict – this is mine. And there is unnecessary conflict due to how people position themselves and protect their turf. Dealing with and resolving all these kinds of conflict is more important and frequent than it used to be.

SECTION 2: LEARNING ON YOUR OWN

THESE SELF-DEVELOPMENT REMEDIES WILL HELP YOU BUILD YOUR SKILL(S)

SOME REMEDIES

☐ **1. Cooperative relations.** The opposite of conflict is cooperation. Developing cooperative relationships involves demonstrating real and perceived equity, the other side feeling understood and respected, and taking a problem oriented point of view. To do this more: increase the realities and perceptions of fairness – don't try to win every battle and take all the spoils; focus on the common ground issues and interests of both sides – find wins on both sides, give in on little points; avoid starting with entrenched positions – show respect for them and their positions; and reduce any remaining conflicts to the smallest size possible.

☐ **2. Causing unnecessary conflict.** Language, words and timing set the tone and can cause unnecessary conflict that has to be managed before you can get anything done. Do you use insensitive language? Do you raise your voice often? Do you use terms and phrases that challenge others? Do you use demeaning terms? Do you use negative humor? Do you offer conclusions, solutions, statements, dictates or answers early in the transaction? Give reasons first, solutions last. When you give solutions first, people often directly challenge the solutions instead of defining the problem. Pick words that are other person neutral. Pick words that don't challenge or sound one-sided. Pick tentative and probabilistic words that give others a chance to maneuver and save face. Pick words that are about the problem and not the person. Avoid direct blaming remarks; describe the problem and its impact.

☐ **3. Practice Aikido,** the ancient art of absorbing the energy of your opponent and using it to manage him/her. Let the other side vent frustration, blow off steam, but don't react. Listen. Nod. Ask clarifying questions. Ask open-ended questions like, "What one change could you make so we could achieve our objectives better?" "What could I do that would help the most?" Restate their position periodically to signal you have understood. But don't react. Keep them talking until they run out of venom. When the other side takes a rigid position, don't reject it. Ask why – what are the principles behind the position, how do we know it's fair, what's the theory of the case. Play out what would happen if their position was accepted. Then explore the concern underlying the answer. Separate the people from the problem. When someone attacks you, rephrase it as an attack on the problem. In response to threats, say you'll only negotiate on merit and fairness. If the other side won't play fair, surface their game – "It looks like you're playing good cop, bad cop. Why don't you settle your differences and tell me one thing?" In response to unreasonable proposals, attacks, or a non-answer to a question, you can always say nothing. People will usually respond by saying more, coming off their position a bit, or at least revealing their true interests. Many times, with unlimited venting and your understanding, the actual conflict shrinks.

☐ **4. Downsizing the conflict.** Almost all conflicts have common points that get lost in the heat of the battle. After a conflict has been presented and understood, start by saying that it might be helpful to see if we agree on anything. Write them on the flip chart. Then write down the areas left open. Focus on common goals, priorities and problems. Keep the open conflicts as small as possible and concrete. The more abstract it gets, "we don't trust your unit," the more unmanageable it gets. To this respond, "Tell me your specific concern – why exactly don't you trust us, can you give me an example?" Usually after calm discussion, they don't trust your unit on this specific issue under these specific conditions. That's easier to deal with. Allow others to save face by conceding small points that are not central to the issue, don't try to hit a home run every time. If you can't agree on a solution, agree on a procedure to move forward. Collect more data. Appeal to a higher power. Get a third party arbitrator. Something. This creates some positive motion and breaks stalemates.

☐ **5. Too emotional?** Sometimes our emotional reactions lead others to think we have problems with conflict. In conflict situations, what emotional reactions do you have such as impatience or non-verbals like flushing or drumming your pen or fingers? Learn to recognize those as soon as they start and substitute something more neutral. Most emotional responses to conflict come from personalizing the issue. Separate people issues from the problem at hand and deal with people issues separately and later if they persist. Always return to facts and the problem before the group; stay away from personal clashes. Attack the problem by looking at common interests and underlying concerns, not people and their positions. Try on their views for size, the emotion as well as the content. Ask yourself if you understand their feelings. Ask what they would do if they were in your shoes. See if you can restate each other's position and advocate it for a minute to get inside each other's place. If you get emotional, pause and collect yourself. You are not your best when you get emotional. Then return to the problem. *More help? – See #11 Composure and #107* Lack of *Composure.*

☐ **6. Bargaining and trading.** Since you can't absolutely win all conflicts unless you keep pulling rank, you have to learn to horsetrade and bargain. What do they need that I have? What could I do for them outside this conflict that could allow them to give up something I need now in return? How can we turn this into a win for both of us? *More help? – See #37 Negotiating.*

☐ **7. Clear problem-focused communication.** Follow the rule of equity: explain your thinking and ask them to explain theirs. Be able to state their position as clearly as they do whether you agree or not; give it legitimacy. Separate facts from opinions and assumptions. Generate a variety of possibilities first rather than stake out positions. Keep your speaking to 30–60 seconds bursts. Try to get them to do the same. Don't give the other side the impression you're lecturing or criticizing them. Explain objectively why you hold a view; make the other side do the same. Asks lots of questions, make fewer statements. To identify interests behind positions, ask why they hold them or why they wouldn't want to do something. Always restate their position to their satisfaction before offering a response. *More help? – See #27 Informing.*

☐ **8. Arbitration.** When there is a true impasse, suggest a third equal-power party to resolve the remaining conflicts. Use a third party to write up each side's interests and keep suggesting solutions until you can agree. Or if time is an issue, pass it on to a higher authority. Present both sides calmly and objectively, and let the chips fall where they may.

☐ **9. Selective conflict.** Do specific people, issues, styles, or groups set you off and make you handle the conflict poorly? Write down the last 20 times when you handled conflict poorly. What's common in the situations? Are there three to five common themes? Are the same people involved? Different people but the same style? Certain kinds of issues? Once you have isolated the cause, mentally rehearse a better way of handling it when it comes up next time.

☐ **10. Larger scale organizational conflict.** Organizations are a complex maze of constituencies, issues and rivalries peopled by strong egos, sensitives, and empire protectors. Political mistakes come in a variety of shapes and sizes. The most common is saying things you shouldn't. Next are actions that are politically out of line and not right for the context. Worst are politically unacceptable moves, initiatives, tactics and strategies. Last are unnecessary conflicts, tensions, misunderstandings and rivalries created because you took after a specific person or group. Work to understand the politics of the organization. Who are the movers and shakers in the organization? Who are the major gatekeepers who control the flow of resources, information and decisions? Who are the guides and the helpers? Get to know them better. Do lunch. Who are the major resisters and stoppers? Try to avoid or go around them or make peace with them. In the special case of dealing with top management, sensitivities are high, egos are big, sensitivity traps are set and tensions can be severe. There is a lot of room for making statements or acting in ways that would be seen as exhibiting your poor political judgment and causing conflict. *More help? – See #38 Organizational Agility, #48 Political Savvy and #119 Political Missteps.*

SECTION 3: LEARNING FROM MORE FEEDBACK

THESE SOURCES WOULD GIVE YOU THE MOST ACCURATE AND DETAILED FEEDBACK ON YOUR SKILL(S)

☐ **Development Professionals**
Sometimes it might be valuable to get some analysis and feedback from a professional trained and certified in the area you're working on: possibly a career counselor, a therapist, clergy, a psychologist, etc.

☐ **Human Resource Professionals**
Human Resource professionals have both a formal and informal feedback role. Since they have access to unique and confidential information, they can provide the right context for feedback you've received. Sometimes they may be "directed" to give you feedback. Other times, they may pass on feedback just to be helpful to you.

☐ **Natural Mentors**
Natural mentors have a special relationship with you and are interested in your success and your future. Since they are usually not in your direct chain of command, you can have more open, relaxed, and fruitful discussions about yourself and your career prospects. They can be a very important source for candid or critical feedback others may not give you.

☐ **Peers and Colleagues**
Peers and colleagues have a special social and working relationship. They attend staff meetings together, share private views, get feedback from the same boss, travel together, and are knowledgeable about each other's work. You perhaps let your guard down more around peers and act more like yourself. They can be a valuable source of feedback.

SECTION 4: LEARNING FROM DEVELOP-IN-PLACE ASSIGNMENTS

THESE PART-TIME DEVELOP-IN-PLACE ASSIGNMENTS WILL HELP YOU BUILD YOUR SKILL(S)

☐ Integrate diverse systems, processes, or procedures across decentralized and/or dispersed units.

☐ Manage the furnishing or refurnishing of new or existing offices.

☐ Relaunch an existing product or service that's not doing well.

☐ Handle a tough negotiation with an internal or external client or customer.

☐ Manage a dissatisfied internal or external customer; troubleshoot a performance or quality problem with a product or service.

☐ Resolve an issue in conflict between two people, units, geographies, functions, etc.

☐ Make peace with an enemy or someone you've disappointed with a product or service or someone you've had some trouble with or don't get along well with.

☐ Do a postmortem on a failed project and present it to the people involved.

☐ Be a member of a union-negotiating or grievance-handling team.

☐ Work on a crisis management team.

SECTION 5: LEARNING FROM FULL-TIME JOBS

THESE FULL-TIME JOBS OFFER THE OPPORTUNITY TO BUILD YOUR SKILL(S)

☐ **Chair of Projects/Task Forces**
The core demands for qualifying as a Project/Task Force assignment are: 1) Full-time assignment. 2) Important and specific goal. 3) Tight deadline. 4) Success or failure will be evident. 5) High-visibility sponsor. 6) Learning something on the fly. 7) Must get others to cooperate. 8) Usually six months or more. Four types of Projects/Task Forces: 1) New ideas, products, services, or systems (e.g., product/service/program research and development, creation/installation/launch of a new system, new programs like Total Quality Management, positive discipline). 2) Formal negotiations and relationships (e.g., acquisitions, divestitures, agreements, joint ventures, licensing arrangements, franchising, dealing with unions, governments, communities, charities, customers, and relocations). 3) Big one-time events (e.g., working on a major presentation for the board, organizing significant meetings or conferences, disaster/damage control teams, reorganizations, mergers, acquisitions, or relocations, working on visions, charters, strategies, other time-urgent issues and problems). 4) Troubleshooting (e.g., problems, disasters, crises, product/service failures, accidents, illegal

activities, damage control in public relations goofs, shut downs, downsizings, layoffs, abrupt changes in leadership).

- ☐ **Fix-its/Turnarounds**
The core demands to qualify as a Fix-it or Turnaround assignment are: 1) Cleaning up a mess. 2) Serious people issues/problems like credibility/performance/morale. 3) Tight deadline. 4) Serious business performance failure. 5) Last chance to fix. Four Types of Fix-its/ Turnarounds: 1) Fixing a failed business/unit involving taking control, stopping losses, managing damage, planning the turnaround, dealing with people problems, installing new processes and systems, and rebuilding the spirit and performance of the unit. 2) Managing sizable disasters like mishandled labor negotiations and strikes, thefts, history of significant business losses, poor staff, failed leadership, hidden problems, fraud, public relations nightmares, etc. 3) Significant reorganization and restructuring (e.g., stabilizing the business, reforming unit, introducing new systems, making people changes, resetting strategy and tactics). 4) Significant system/process breakdown (e.g., MIS, financial coordination processes, audits, standards, etc.) across units requiring working to change something from a distant position, providing advice and counsel, and installing or implementing a major process improvement or system change outside your own unit and/or with customers outside the organization.

- ☐ **Off-Shore Assignments**
The core demands to qualify as an Off-Shore assignment are: 1) First time working in the country. 2) Significant challenges like new language, hardship location, unique business rules/practices, significant cultural/marketplace differences, different functional task, etc. 3) More than a year assignment. 4) No automatic return deal. 5) Not necessarily a change in job challenge, technical content, or responsibilities.

- ☐ **Significant People Demands**
Core demands required to qualify as a Significant People Responsibilities assignment are: 1) A sizable increase in either the number of people managed and/or the complexity of the challenges involved 2) Longer-term assignment (two or more years). 3) Quality of people management critical to achieving results. 4) Involves groups not worked with before (e.g., union, new technical areas, nationalities).

SECTION 6: LEARNING MORE FROM YOUR PLAN

THESE ADDITIONAL REMEDIES WILL HELP MAKE THIS DEVELOPMENT PLAN MORE EFFECTIVE FOR YOU

Learning to Learn Better

- ☐ **Rehearse Successful Tactics/Strategies/Actions**
Mentally rehearse how you will act before going into the situation. Try to anticipate how others will react, what they will say, and how you'll

respond. Check out the best and worst cases; play out both scenes. Check your feelings in conflict or worst-case situations; rehearse staying under control.

- ☐ **Study Your History of Conflicts for Insights**
  List the people and situations which cause you trouble. What are the common themes? Why do those kinds of people and/or those kinds of situations set you off? Do they have to? Was the conflict really important? Did it help or block your learning and getting things done? Try to anticipate those people/situations in the future.

- ☐ **Sell Something to a Tough Group/Audience**
  Think of the person or group who will be the toughest to sell, the most critical, skeptical, or resistant, and sell that person or group first. Take time to understand the opposing viewpoints. Find common ground and leverage points; line up your best data and arguments and go for it.

Learning from Experience, Feedback and Other People

- ☐ **Getting Feedback from Peers/Colleagues**
  Your peers and colleagues may not be candid if they are in competition with you. Some may not be willing to be open with you out of fear of giving you an advantage. Some may give you exaggerated feedback to deliberately cause you undue concern. You have to set the tone and gauge the trust level of the relationship and the quality of the feedback.

- ☐ **Feedback in Unusual Contexts/Situations**
  Temporary and extreme conditions and contexts may shade interpretations of your behavior and intentions. Demands of the job may drive you outside your normal mode of operating. Hence, feedback you receive may be inaccurate during those times. However, unusual contexts affect our behavior less than most assume. It's usually a weak excuse.

- ☐ **Openness to Feedback**
  Nothing discourages feedback more than defensiveness, resistance, irritation, and excuses. People don't like giving feedback anyway, and much less to those who don't listen or are unreceptive. To help the feedback giver, be open, listen, ask for examples and details, take notes, keep a journal, and thank them for their interest.

- ☐ **Giving Feedback to Others**
  Most managers complain they don't get enough useful feedback. Ironically, their direct reports and peers offer the same complaint! Getting serious about feedback for yourself involves giving more feedback to those around you. As you practice giving more feedback to others, you will receive more by the example you set and will become more sensitive and receptive to your own.

☐ **Learning from Bad Bosses**
First, what does he/she do so well to make him/her your boss? (Even bad bosses have strengths). Then, ask what makes this boss bad for you. Is it his/her behavior? Attitude? Values? Philosophy? Practices? Style? What is the source of the conflict? Why do you react as you do? Do others react the same? How are you part of the problem? What do you do that triggers your boss? If you wanted to, could you reduce the conflict or make it go away by changing something you do? Is there someone around you who doesn't react like you? How are they different? What can you learn from them? What is your emotional reaction to this boss? Why do you react like that? What can you do to cope with these feelings? Can you avoid reacting out of anger and frustration? Can you find something positive about the situation? Can you use someone else as a buffer? Can you learn from your emotions? What lasting lessons of managing others can you take away from this experience? What won't you do as a manager? What will you do differently? How could you teach these principles you've learned to others by the use of this example?

☐ **Learning from Limited Staff**
Most managers either inherit or hire staff from time to time who are inexperienced, incompetent, not up to the task, resistant, or dispirited. Any of these may create a hardship for you. The lessons to be learned are how to get things done with limited resources and how to fix the people situation. In the short term, this hardship is best addressed by assessing the combined strengths of the team and deploying the best you have against the problem. Almost everyone can do something well. Also, the team can contribute more than the combined individuals can. How can you empower and motivate the team? If you hired the troublesome staff, why did you err? What can you learn from your hiring mistakes? What wasn't there that you thought was present? What led you astray? How can you prevent that same hiring error in the future? What do you need to do to fix the situation? Quick development? Start over? If you inherited the problem, how can you fix it? Can you implement a program of accelerated development? Do you have to start over and get new people? What did the prior manager do or not do that led to this situation in the first place? What can you learn from that? What will you do differently? How does the staff feel? What can you learn from their frustrations over not being able to do the job? How can you be a positive force under negative circumstances? How can you rally them to perform? What lasting lessons can you learn from someone in distress and trouble? If you're going to try accelerated development, how can you get a quick assessment? How can you give the staff motivating feedback? How can you construct and implement development plans that will work? How can you get people on-line feedback for maximum growth? Do you know when to stop trying and start over? If you're going to turn over some staff, how can you do it

both rapidly and with the least damage? How can you deliver the message in a constructive way? What can you learn from having to take negative actions against people? How can you prevent this from happening again?

Learning from Courses

- ☐ **Insight Events**
These are courses designed around assessing skills and providing feedback to the participants. These events can be a powerful source of self-knowledge and can lead to significant development if done right. When selecting a self-insight course, consider the following: 1) Are the skills assessed the important ones? 2) Are the assessment techniques and instruments sound? 3) Are those who are providing the feedback trained and professional? 4) Is the feedback provided in a user-friendly and "actionable" format? 5) Does the feedback include development planning? 6) Is the setting comfortable and conducive to reflection and learning? 7) Are the other participants the kinds of people you could learn from? 8) Are you in the right frame of mind to learn from this kind of intense experience? Select events on the basis of positive answers to these eight questions.

SUGGESTED READINGS

Crowley, Thomas E. *Settle it out of court: how to resolve business and personal disputes using mediation, arbitration, and negotiation.* New York: John Wiley & Sons, Inc., 1994.

Kheel, Theodore W. *The Keys to Conflict Resolution – Proven methods of resolving disputes voluntarily.* New York: Four Walls Eight Windows, 1999.

Levine, Stewart. *Getting to Resolution.* San Francisco: Berrett-Koehler Publishers, 1998.

Neuhauser, Peg. *Tribal Warfare in Organizations.* New York: Harper & Row, 1988.

Van Slyke, Erik J. *Listening to conflict.* New York: AMACOM, 1999.

CONFRONTING DIRECT REPORTS

SECTION 1: YOUR DEVELOPMENT NEED(S)

UNSKILLED

- ☐ Not comfortable delivering negative messages to direct reports
- ☐ Procrastinates and avoids problems until forced to act
- ☐ May not communicate clear standards or provide much feedback
- ☐ Lets problems fester hoping they will go away
- ☐ May give in too soon to excuses
- ☐ May give people too many chances
- ☐ Can't pull the trigger even when all else has failed
- ☐ Has low standards or plays favorites

SKILLED

- ☐ Deals with problem direct reports firmly and in a timely manner
- ☐ Doesn't allow problems to fester
- ☐ Regularly reviews performance and holds timely discussions
- ☐ Can make negative decisions when all other efforts fail
- ☐ Deals effectively with troublemakers

OVERUSED SKILL

- ☐ May be too quick to act on problem direct reports
- ☐ May not put enough developmental effort toward the problem
- ☐ May expect turnarounds in too short a time
- ☐ May expect miracles

Select one to three of the competencies listed below to work on to compensate for an overuse of this skill.

COMPENSATORS: 3, 7, 12, 19, 20, 21, 23, 31, 33, 36, 41, 56, 60, 64

SOME CAUSES

- ☐ Can't deal with face to face conflict
- ☐ Can't turn around resistant people
- ☐ Don't give enough feedback
- ☐ Don't know how to draw the line
- ☐ Don't want the paper work hassle of acting
- ☐ Don't follow up well
- ☐ Have unrealistic expectations
- ☐ Let problems fester
- ☐ Procrastinate or play favorites
- ☐ Won't make the ultimate call
- ☐ Won't take negative actions

THE MAP

Most organizations are running leaner today. With more rapid change and team-based efforts increasing, problem performers can't be hidden as they often were in the past. Overcoming your reluctance to deal with them is a key to your unit's performance and probably your career as well. Managers who excel at confronting direct reports are timely, consistent, focus on performance gaps, pitch in and help the person succeed, and are sensitive to how the person feels. But if the effort fails, taking timely but compassionate action to separate the person from the organization is the true test of management courage.

SECTION 2: LEARNING ON YOUR OWN

THESE SELF-DEVELOPMENT REMEDIES WILL HELP YOU BUILD YOUR SKILL(S)

SOME REMEDIES

☐ **1. Most problem performers don't know it!** Delivering bad news to people face to face came in number one in a survey of what managers hate to do. Survey after survey says employees do not get the feedback they need to correct performance problems. Women, minorities and older people get the least. Most people who are fired or take an honorary resignation have had satisfactory or high performance appraisals up to the point of leaving. It's tough to be the bearer of bad news. Emotions and defensiveness may flare. The consequences could be severe. You may have to defend your actions inside and outside the organization. Long term, it's cruel and unusual punishment not to deliver fair but direct feedback to someone who is struggling or failing. Otherwise he/she can't work on the problems and plan his/her career. The key to overcoming your reluctance is to focus on fairly applied and communicated standards and on gaps between expected and actual performance. Read *Becoming a Manager* by Linda A. Hill for case studies of managers applying standards to others for the first time. Make sure everyone under you knows what you expect of him/her and where he/she stands.

☐ **2. Creating and communicating standards.** Are your problem performers confused? Do they know what's expected of them? You may not set clear enough performance standards, goals and objectives. You may be a seat of the pants manager, and some people are struggling because they don't know what is expected or it changes. You may be a cryptic communicator. You may be too busy to communicate. You may communicate to some and not to others. You may have given up on some and stopped communicating. Or you may think they would know what to do if they're any good, but that's not really true because you have not properly communicated what you want. The first task is to outline the five to 10 key results areas and what indicators of success would be. Involve your problem direct reports on both ends, the standards and the indicators. Provide them with a fair way to measure their own progress. Employees with goals and standards are usually harder on themselves than you'll ever be. Often they set higher standards than you would. *More help? – See #35 Managing and Measuring Work.*

☐ **3. Realism.** They are not performing up to standard? It's common to see 90 day improve-or-else plans that no one can accomplish. Be more strategic, improve your interpersonal skills, learn about the business, be less arrogant. Ask yourself how long did it take you to become proficient at what you are criticizing this person for? Because managers hesitate delivering negative messages, we get to people late. Sometimes the last five managers this person reported to saw the same difficulty, but none of them confronted the person. Get to people as soon as they do not meet agreed upon standards of performance. Don't wait. Early is the easiest time to do it with the highest return on investment for you, them and the organization. Most people who have reached the problem performer status will take one to two years to turn around under the best of circumstances. It's cruel and unusual punishment to require a fixed time turn around or improvement plan. If your organization demands a 90 day wonder, fight it. Tell them that while a bit of improvement can be seen in that period, substantive change is not like producing a quarterly earnings statement.

☐ **4. Starting the improve or you're gone process.** The first meeting. After you have made the assessment that a direct report just isn't making it, document your observations against the standards and arrange the first tough meeting. Experience directs that these first tough meetings should always to be in the beginning of the week and in the mornings. They should not occur on Fridays or the day before holidays when most managers deliver them. They should not be at a time when the unit is on a bomb run getting ready for a big presentation. Start the meeting by saying "we" have a performance issue to talk about and fix. Be succinct. You have limited attention span in tough feedback situations. Don't waste time with a long preamble, just get to it. The recipient is likely to know the feedback is negative anyway so go ahead and say it first. They won't hear or remember anything positive you have to say anyway. Don't overwhelm the person, even if you have a lot to say. Pick the key areas and stick to them. Keep it to the facts and their impact on you, them and your unit. Talk about specific events and situations. Plan for enough time. This is not a process to rush.

☐ **5. Go in with an improvement plan.** Don't criticize without a solution and a plan. Tell the person what you want – paint a different outcome. Don't expect him/her to guess, and don't spend a lot of time rehashing the past. Suggest steps both of you can take to remedy the problem. Be positive but firm. Be constructive. Be optimistic in the beginning. Help him/her see the negative consequences and the potential timing – you can ask what he/she thinks and you can tell him/her what the consequences are from your side. Change starts with seeing an unacceptable consequence and a way out. Improve or else threats don't work. *More help? – See #19 Developing Direct Reports.*

☐ **6. Managing the pushback.** Keep control of the discussion. Don't do fake listening – the obligatory "Now let's hear your side" if you don't think there is another side. Discussions like this will trigger most people's natural defense routines. Expect that. That's not necessarily a sign of true disagreement or denial; it's just a natural thing to do. Say something like, "I understand you have a different view, but the performance just isn't there in this area. We've got to deal with this." The person may have 10 reasons why your appraisal isn't fair or accurate. Listen. Acknowledge that you understand what he/she has said. If the person persists, say, "Let's talk about your view tomorrow after we've both had a chance to reflect on this discussion." Then, return to your agenda. Say, "I'm going to help you perform in this area." The best tack is to immediately schedule new work, trusting that the person will come through this time. You should discuss this as you would any other work assignment and not bring up the past. She/he has already heard what you said. (With a person who, in your opinion, lacks motivation not skill, raise the stakes. Sometimes a person who performs poorly at a C difficulty task performs well at an A difficulty task in exactly the same area.)

☐ **7. Defense condition four.** Emotions can run high. This may truly be a surprise to the person. Even though this problem has been going on for years, this may be the first time a manager has dealt with it directly. Don't take too seriously what people say in that first meeting. He/she is running on emotion. Mentally rehearse for worst case scenarios. Anticipate what the person might say and have responses prepared so as not to be caught off guard. Work on your stands through mental interrogation until you can clearly state in a few sentences what your stand is and why you hold it. Remain composed and don't use words you'll regret. If he/she is not composed, don't respond. Just let him/her vent or even cry, then return to the problem at hand. Don't forget the pathos of the situation – even if you're totally right, feelings will run high. If you have to knock someone down, you can still empathize with how he/she feels or you can help pick him/her up later when the discussion turns more positive. Allow him/her to save face; concede some small points; don't rush the human process of grieving. *More help? – See #12 Conflict Management.*

☐ **8. The next day.** Go by and see the person the next day; don't have him/her come to your office. Ask him/her how he/she feels. Don't back off your points, just allow him/her to talk. Indicate you will pitch in and help, that you consider it your job to remove obstacles to performance, provide information and support, provide structure and advice on how, but not tell the person how to do it, and be available for trouble shooting. Consciously try to maintain the same or a closer relationship after the event. If the person feels written off, the situation can turn hopeless. Schedule regular checkpoints. Use a ruler you can both relate to. Track progress. If appropriate at some later time, ask the person for feedback on you as a manager. *More help? – See #7 Caring About Direct Reports.*

☐ **9. The two-minute warning.** The last chance for the person who isn't really trying. You may have to pull someone aside after a couple of months and say, "I understand all your issues and have tried to help you, but you aren't doing what we agreed. Are you committed or not?" If you have to do something like the above, follow the rules of dealing with conflict: depersonalize; keep it on the problem, not the person. Try one last time to help. Note the person's concerns or objections or description of what's getting in the way but don't concede anything. Be clear; now is not the time for negotiation. Give the person a day to think it over and come in with a believable performance improvement plan. At this point it's his/her problem. Be prepared to act immediately if the plan is insufficient. Obviously, you will have gotten any necessary clearances in advance and sought the help of Human Resources and Legal.

☐ **10. Saying good-bye.** Just because the person can't do this job doesn't mean he/she is incompetent as a person or that he/she can't do 50 other things better than you can do them. Do nothing to generalize one performance failure to other situations, and point to the person's strengths in any way you can. Suggest what would be a better job match. Indicate what you can do to help; if you're willing to be a reference for certain types of work, say so. Make the meeting short. Go back to see the person later and talk about his/her feelings if he/she is willing. You don't have to respond, just listen. Come up with some sort of parting gesture that indicates to the person that you are not rejecting him or her; it was simply a matter of one job that wasn't a fit. A party, a note, a phone call – whatever you can do that's genuine. Even if he/she rejects you, if you meant it, that's all you can do.

SECTION 3: LEARNING FROM MORE FEEDBACK

THESE SOURCES WOULD GIVE YOU THE MOST ACCURATE AND DETAILED FEEDBACK ON YOUR SKILL(S)

☐ **Direct Boss**

Your direct boss has important information about you, your performance, and your prospects. The challenge is to get this information. There are formal processes (e.g., performance appraisals). There are day-to-day opportunities. To help, signal your boss that you want and can handle direct and timely feedback. Many bosses have trouble giving feedback, so you will have to work at it over a period of time.

☐ **Human Resource Professionals**
Human Resource professionals have both a formal and informal feedback role. Since they have access to unique and confidential information, they can provide the right context for feedback you've received. Sometimes they may be "directed" to give you feedback. Other times, they may pass on feedback just to be helpful to you.

☐ **Past Associates/Constituencies**
When confronted with a present performance problem, some claim, "I wasn't like that before; it must be the current situation." When feedback is available from former associates, about 50% support that claim. In the other half of the cases, the people were like that before and probably didn't know it. It sometimes makes sense to access the past to clearly see the present.

SECTION 4: LEARNING FROM DEVELOP-IN-PLACE ASSIGNMENTS

THESE PART-TIME DEVELOP-IN-PLACE ASSIGNMENTS WILL HELP YOU BUILD YOUR SKILL(S)

☐ Manage an ad hoc, temporary group of balky and resisting people through an unpopular change or project.

☐ Hire and manage a temporary group of people to accomplish a tough or time-tight assignment.

☐ Manage the outplacement of a group of people.

☐ Manage an ad hoc, temporary group of people involved in tackling a fix-it or turnaround project.

☐ Coach a children's sports team.

☐ Become a referee for an athletic league or program.

☐ Manage a project team made up of nationals from a number of countries.

☐ Manage an ad hoc, temporary group of "green," inexperienced people as their coach, teacher, orienter, etc.

☐ Manage an ad hoc, temporary group of low-competence people through a task they couldn't do by themselves.

☐ Help shut down a plant, regional office, product line, business, operation, etc.

SECTION 5: LEARNING FROM FULL-TIME JOBS

THESE FULL-TIME JOBS OFFER THE OPPORTUNITY TO BUILD YOUR SKILL(S)

☐ **Fix-its/Turnarounds**
The core demands to qualify as a Fix-it or Turnaround assignment are: 1) Cleaning up a mess. 2) Serious people issues/problems like credibil-

ity/performance/morale. 3) Tight deadline. 4) Serious business performance failure. 5) Last chance to fix. Four Types of Fix-its/ Turnarounds: 1) Fixing a failed business/unit involving taking control, stopping losses, managing damage, planning the turnaround, dealing with people problems, installing new processes and systems, and rebuilding the spirit and performance of the unit. 2) Managing sizable disasters like mishandled labor negotiations and strikes, thefts, history of significant business losses, poor staff, failed leadership, hidden problems, fraud, public relations nightmares, etc. 3) Significant reorganization and restructuring (e.g., stabilizing the business, reforming unit, introducing new systems, making people changes, resetting strategy and tactics). 4) Significant system/process breakdown (e.g., MIS, financial coordination processes, audits, standards, etc.) across units requiring working to change something from a distant position, providing advice and counsel, and installing or implementing a major process improvement or system change outside your own unit and/or with customers outside the organization.

☐ **Significant People Demands**
Core demands required to qualify as a Significant People Responsibilities assignment are: 1) A sizable increase in either the number of people managed and/or the complexity of the challenges involved 2) Longer-term assignment (two or more years). 3) Quality of people management critical to achieving results. 4) Involves groups not worked with before (e.g., union, new technical areas, nationalities).

SECTION 6: LEARNING MORE FROM YOUR PLAN

THESE ADDITIONAL REMEDIES WILL HELP MAKE THIS DEVELOPMENT PLAN MORE EFFECTIVE FOR YOU

Learning to Learn Better

☐ **Examine Why You're Blocked on a Key Issue**
Examine what you are worrying/angry about and list all of your thoughts about it; ask why these feelings are holding you back. Why are the feelings overriding your thinking? How are they getting in the way? Why are they important to you? How can you move beyond them and learn to do something different?

Learning from Experience, Feedback and Other People

☐ **Learning from Bosses**
Bosses can be an excellent and ready source for learning. All bosses do some things exceptionally well and other things poorly. Distance your feelings from the boss/direct report relationship and study things that work and things that don't work for your boss. What would you have done? What could you use, and what should you avoid?

☐ **Getting Feedback from Bosses and Superiors**
Many bosses are reluctant to give negative feedback. They lack the managerial courage to face people directly with criticism. You can help by soliciting feedback and setting the tone. Show them you can handle criticism and that you are willing to work on issues they see as important.

☐ **Getting Feedback from Direct Reports**
Direct reports often fear reprisals for giving negative feedback about bosses, whether in a formal process, like a questionnaire, or informally and face-to-face. Even with a guarantee of confidentiality, some are still hesitant. If you want feedback from direct reports, you have to set a positive tone and never act out of revenge.

☐ **Feedback in Unusual Contexts/Situations**
Temporary and extreme conditions and contexts may shade interpretations of your behavior and intentions. Demands of the job may drive you outside your normal mode of operating. Hence, feedback you receive may be inaccurate during those times. However, unusual contexts affect our behavior less than most assume. It's usually a weak excuse.

☐ **Giving Feedback to Others**
Most managers complain they don't get enough useful feedback. Ironically, their direct reports and peers offer the same complaint! Getting serious about feedback for yourself involves giving more feedback to those around you. As you practice giving more feedback to others, you will receive more by the example you set and will become more sensitive and receptive to your own.

☐ **Learning from Limited Staff**
Most managers either inherit or hire staff from time to time who are inexperienced, incompetent, not up to the task, resistant, or dispirited. Any of these may create a hardship for you. The lessons to be learned are how to get things done with limited resources and how to fix the people situation. In the short term, this hardship is best addressed by assessing the combined strengths of the team and deploying the best you have against the problem. Almost everyone can do something well. Also, the team can contribute more than the combined individuals can. How can you empower and motivate the team? If you hired the troublesome staff, why did you err? What can you learn from your hiring mistakes? What wasn't there that you thought was present? What led you astray? How can you prevent that same hiring error in the future? What do you need to do to fix the situation? Quick development? Start over? If you inherited the problem, how can you fix it? Can you implement a program of accelerated development? Do you have to start over and get new people? What did the prior manager do or not do that led to this situation in the first place? What can you learn from that? What will you do differently? How does the staff feel? What can

you learn from their frustrations over not being able to do the job? How can you be a positive force under negative circumstances? How can you rally them to perform? What lasting lessons can you learn from someone in distress and trouble? If you're going to try accelerated development, how can you get a quick assessment? How can you give the staff motivating feedback? How can you construct and implement development plans that will work? How can you get people on-line feedback for maximum growth? Do you know when to stop trying and start over? If you're going to turn over some staff, how can you do it both rapidly and with the least damage? How can you deliver the message in a constructive way? What can you learn from having to take negative actions against people? How can you prevent this from happening again?

Learning from Courses

☐ **Supervisory Courses**
Most new supervisors go through an "Introduction to Supervision" type course. They are designed to teach the common practices a first-line supervisor needs to know to be effective. The content of most of those courses is standard. There is general agreement on the principles of effective supervision. There are two common problems: 1) Do the students have a strong motivation to learn? Do they know what they don't know? Is there any pain? Because motivated students with a need for the knowledge learn best, participants should have had some trying experiences and some supervisory pain and hardships before attending. 2) Are the instructors experienced supervisors? Have they practiced what they preach? Can they share powerful anecdotes to make key points? Can they answer questions credibly? If possible, select supervisory courses based on the instructors, since the content seems to be the much same for all such courses. Lastly, does the course offer the opportunity for practicing each skill? Does it contain simulations? Are there case studies you could easily identify with? Are there breakout groups? Is there opportunity for action learning? Search for the most interactive course.

☐ **Sending Others to Courses**
If you are responsible for managing someone else's development and, as part of that, sending them to courses, prepare them beforehand. Don't send them as tourists. Meet with them before and after the course. Tell them why they need this course. Tell them what you expect them to learn. Give them feedback on why you think they need the course. Agree ahead of time how you will measure and monitor learning after they return. If possible, offer a variety of courses for your employee to choose from. Have them give you a report shortly after they return. If appropriate, have them present what they learned to the rest of your staff. After they return, provide opportunities for using the new skills with safe cover and low risk. Give them practice time before

expecting full exercise of the new skills. Be supportive during early unsteadiness. Give continuous feedback on progress.

SUGGESTED READINGS

Baron, S. Anthony. *Violence in the workplace: a prevention and management guide for businesses.* Ventura, CA: Pathfinder Publishing of California, 1993.

Chambers, Harry E. *The Bad Attitude Survival Guide.* Reading, MA: Addison-Wesley Publishing Co. Inc., 1998.

Grote, Dick. *Discipline without Punishment.* New York: AMACOM, 1995.

Jellison, Jerald M. *Overcoming Resistance.* New York: Simon & Schuster, 1993.

Lacey, Walt. *How to discipline employees & correct performance problems [sound recording].* Boulder, CO: CareerTrack Publications, 1994.

Solomon, Muriel. *Working with Difficult People.* Paramus, NJ: Prentice-Hall, 1990.

Stone, Florence M. *Coaching, Counseling and Mentoring.* New York: AMACOM, 1999.

Wylie, Dr. Peter and Dr. Mardy Grothe. *Problem Employees – How to Improve their Performance.* Dover, N.H.: Upstart Publishing Company, Inc., 1991.

14

CREATIVITY

SECTION 1: YOUR DEVELOPMENT NEED(S)

UNSKILLED

- ☐ Narrow, tactical, cautious and conservative
- ☐ May be more comfortable with the past, prefer the tried and true
- ☐ Limited background
- ☐ Avoids risk and doesn't seek to be bold or different
- ☐ Doesn't connect with ideas from outside own area
- ☐ May have no idea how creativity works
- ☐ Uses old solutions for new problems
- ☐ May chill the creative initiatives of others

SKILLED

- ☐ Comes up with a lot of new and unique ideas
- ☐ Easily makes connections among previously unrelated notions
- ☐ Tends to be seen as original and value-added in brainstorming settings

OVERUSED SKILL

- ☐ May get so infatuated with marginally productive ideas that he/she wastes time
- ☐ May get involved in too many things at once
- ☐ May not follow through after the idea
- ☐ May be disorganized or poor at detail
- ☐ May be a loner and not a good team player
- ☐ May not relate well to those less creative

Select one to three of the competencies listed below to work on to compensate for an overuse of this skill.

COMPENSATORS: 1, 5, 16, 17, 24, 28, 30, 38, 39, 45, 46, 47, 48, 50, 51, 52, 53, 58, 59, 61, 64

SOME CAUSES

- ☐ Caught in the past
- ☐ Cautious
- ☐ Don't know what it is
- ☐ Limited ways to think
- ☐ Narrow
- ☐ Practical
- ☐ Reject creativity as fanciful
- ☐ Restrained
- ☐ Too focused
- ☐ Too good of a problem solver

THE MAP

Being creative involves: 1) Immersing yourself in a problem; 2) Looking broadly for connections – in the past, what other organizations do, brainstorming with others; 3) Letting your ideas incubate; 4) The breakthrough which usually occurs when you are distracted or in a relaxed state; 5) Picking one or more to pilot. Most of us are capable of being more creative than we demonstrate. Upbringing, schooling and the narrowness of many jobs can have a chilling effect on creativity. Many of us are or have been taught to be restrained, narrow, focused, hesitant, cautious, conservative, afraid to err, and unwilling to make a fool of ourselves. All of that chills the creativity already inside us. One process is to lift those restraints. The other involves adding creative skills. There are research-based and experience-tested techniques that, if followed, will produce a more creative process from a person or a group. Creativity is a valued skill because most organizations need innovation in their products and services to succeed.

SECTION 2: LEARNING ON YOUR OWN

THESE SELF-DEVELOPMENT REMEDIES WILL HELP YOU BUILD YOUR SKILL(S)

SOME REMEDIES

☐ **1. Remove the restraints.** What's preventing you from being more creative? Perfectionist? Being creative operates at well below having everything right. Cautious and reluctant to speculate? Being creative is the opposite. Worried about what people may think? Afraid you won't be able to defend your idea? By its very nature, being creative means throwing uncertain things up for review and critique. Narrow perspective; most comfortable with your technology and profession? Being creative is looking everywhere. More comfortable with what is very practical? Being creative begins as being impractical. Too busy to reflect and ruminate? Being creative takes time. Get out of your comfort zone. Many busy people rely too much on solutions from their own history. They rely on what has happened to them in the past. They see sameness in problems that isn't there. Beware of – "I have always..."or "Usually, I..." Always pause and look under rocks and ask yourself is this really like the problems you have solved in the past? You don't have to change who you are and what you're comfortable with other than when you need to be more creative. Then think and act differently; try new things; break free of your restraints.

☐ **2. Value added approaches.** To be more personally creative, immerse yourself in the problem. Getting fresh ideas is not a speedboating process; it requires looking deeply.

- Carve out dedicated time – study it deeply, talk with others, look for parallels in other organizations and in remote areas totally outside your field. If your response to this is that you don't have the time, that also usually explains why you're not having any fresh ideas.

- Think out loud. Many people don't know what they know until they talk it out. Find a good sounding board and talk to him/her to increase your understanding of a problem or a technical area. Talk to an expert in an unrelated field. Talk to the most irreverent person you know. Your goal is not to get his/her input, but rather his/her help in figuring out what you know – what your principles and rules of thumb are.
- Practice picking out anomalies – unusual facts that don't quite fit, like sales going down when they should have gone up. What do these odd things imply for strategy? Naturally creative people are much more likely to think in opposite cases when confronted with a problem. Turn the problem upside down: ask what is the least likely thing it could be, what the problem is not, what's missing from the problem, or what the mirror image of the problem is.
- Look for distant parallels. Don't fall into the mental trap of searching only in parallel organizations because "Only they would know." Back up and ask a broader question to aid in the search for solutions. When Motorola wanted to find out how to process orders more quickly they went not to other electronics firms, but to Domino's Pizza and Federal Express. For more ideas, an interesting – and fun – book on the topic is *Take The Road To Creativity and Get Off Your Dead End* by David Campbell.

☐ **3. Unearthing creative ideas.** Creative thought processes do not follow the formal rules of logic, where one uses cause and effect to prove or solve something. Some rules of creative thought are:

- Not using concepts but changing them; imagining this were something else
- Move from one concept or way of looking at things to another, such as from economic to political
- Generate ideas without judging them initially
- Use information to restructure and come up with new patterns
- Jump from one idea to another without justifying the jump
- Look for the least likely and odd
- Looking for parallels far from the problem, such as, how is an organization like a big oak tree?
- Ask what's missing or what's not here
- Fascination with mistakes and failure as learning devices

☐ **4. Apply some standard problem-solving skills.** There are many different ways to think through and solve a problem more creatively.

- Ask more questions. In one study of problem solving, 7% of comments were questions and about half were answers. We jump to solutions based on what has worked in the past.

- Complex problems are hard to visualize. They tend to be either oversimplified or too complex to solve unless they are put in a visual format. Cut it up into its component pieces. Examine the pieces to see if a different order would help, or how you could combine three pieces into one.
- Another technique is a pictorial chart called a storyboard where a problem is illustrated by its components being depicted as pictures.
- A variation of this is to tell stories that illustrate the +'s and -'s of a problem, then flow chart those according to what's working and not working. Another is a fishbone diagram used in Total Quality Management.
- Sometimes going to extremes helps. Adding every condition, every worse case you can think of sometimes will suggest a different solution. Taking the present state of affairs and projecting into the future may indicate how and where the system will break down.
- Sleep on it. Take periodic breaks, whether stuck or not. This allows the brain to continue to work on the issue. Most breakthroughs come when we're "not thinking about it." Put it away; give it to someone else; sleep on it. Once you've come up with every idea you can think of, throw them all out and wait for more to occur to you. Force yourself to forget about the issue. For more techniques, read *The Art of Problem Solving* by Russell Ackoff and *Lateral Thinking or Serious Creativity* by Edward de Bono.

☐ **5. Defining the problem.** Instant and early conclusions, solutions and how we solved it in the past are the enemies of creativity. Studies show that defining the problem and taking action occur almost simultaneously for most people, so the more effort you put on the front end, the easier it is to come up with a breakthrough solution. Stop and first define what the problem is and isn't. Since providing answers and solutions is so easy for everyone, it would be nice if they were offering solutions to the right problem. Figure out what causes it. Keep asking why, see how many causes you can come up with and how many organizing buckets you can put them in. This increases the chance of a more creative solution because you can see more connections. Be a chess master. Chess masters recognize thousands of patterns of chess pieces. Look for patterns in data, don't just collect information. Put it in categories that make sense to you. Ask lots of questions. Allot at least 50% of the time to defining the problem. Once you've defined the problem, studies have shown that on average, the most creative solution is somewhere between the second and third one generated. So if you tend to grab the first one, slow down. Discipline yourself to pause for enough time to define the problem better and always think of three solutions before you pick one.

☐ **6. Increasing group creativity: Selecting a group.** During World War II it was discovered that teams of people with the widest diversity of backgrounds produced the most creative solutions to problems. The teams included people who knew absolutely nothing about the area (i.e., an English major working on a costing problem). When attacking a tough problem which has eluded attempts to solve it, get the broadest group you can. Involve different functions, levels, and disciplines. Pull in customers and colleagues from other organizations. Remember that you're looking for fresh approaches; you're not convening a work task force expected to implement or judge the practicality of the notions. Believe it or not, it doesn't matter if they know anything about the problem or the technology required to deal with it. That's your job.

☐ **7. Increasing group creativity: Define the problem first.** A straightforward technique to enable creativity is brainstorming. Anything goes for an agreed upon time. Throw out ideas, record them all, no evaluation allowed. Many people have had bad experiences with brainstorming. Silly ideas. Nothing practical. A waste of time. This usually happens because the problem gets defined in the same old way. So define the problem well first (see tip 5). Allot hours to this, not two minutes to sketch the problem. Challenge your thinking – are you generalizing from one or two cases? How do you know the causes are really causes? They may simply be related. What is fact and what is assumption?

☐ **8. Increasing group creativity: Facilitating the process.** Here are three methods commonly used:

- Brainstorming. Outline the problem for the group, tell them what you've tried and learned from the tries. Include things that may have happened only once. Invite the group to free form respond, any idea is OK, no criticism allowed. Record all ideas on a flip chart. When the group has exhausted the possibilities, take the most interesting ones and ask the group to first name positive features of the ideas, then negative features, and finally what's interesting about the ideas. Follow this process until you've covered all the ideas that interest you. Then ask the group what else they would select as interesting ideas to do a plus, minus, interesting analysis. This process can usually be done in an hour or two.
- The nominal group. After the problem definition above, have the group write down as many ideas as occur to them. Record them all on a flip chart for free wheeling discussion. People can add, combine or clarify – "What were you thinking when you said...," but no criticism allowed. After this, follow the plus, minus, interesting process above.
- Analogies. Lots of creative solutions come from analogies to nature or other fields. Come up with a list (electrical engineering, cats,

trees, the sea, biology, shipbuilding), any list will do, and insert it after you describe the problem to the group in the first or second option. Many times this will trigger novel ideas that no other process will.

- ☐ **9. Experiment and learn.** Whether the ideas come from you or a brainstorming session, encourage yourself to do quick experiments and trials. Studies show that 80% of innovations occur in the wrong place, are created by the wrong people (dye makers developed detergent, Post-it® Notes was a failed glue experiment, Teflon® was created by mistake) and 30–50% of technical innovations fail in tests within the company. Even among those that make it to the marketplace, 70–90% fail. The bottom line on change is a 95% failure rate, and the most successful innovators try lots of quick inexpensive experiments to increase the chances of success. Watch several episodes of *Inventions*, a show on cable, about how unrelated ideas come together to form creative inventions. You can buy the series.

- ☐ **10. The Bottom Line.** Creativity relies on freedom early, but structure later. Once you come up with your best notion of what to do, subject it to all the logical tests and criticism that any other alternative is treated to. Testing out creative ideas is no different than any other problem-solving/evaluation process. The difference is in how the ideas originate.

SECTION 3: LEARNING FROM MORE FEEDBACK

THESE SOURCES WOULD GIVE YOU THE MOST ACCURATE AND DETAILED FEEDBACK ON YOUR SKILL(S)

- ☐ **Direct Reports**
  Across a variety of settings, your direct reports probably see you the most. They are the recipients of most of your managerial behaviors. They know your work. They can compare you with former bosses. Since they may hesitate to give you negative feedback, you have to set the atmosphere to make it easier for them. You have to ask.

- ☐ **Internal and External Customers**
  Customers interact with you as a person and as a supplier or vendor of products and services. You're important to them because you can either help address and solve their problems or stand in their way. As customer service and Total Quality programs gain importance, clients and customers become a more prominent source of feedback.

- ☐ **Past Associates/Constituencies**
  When confronted with a present performance problem, some claim, "I wasn't like that before; it must be the current situation." When feedback is available from former associates, about 50% support that claim. In the other half of the cases, the people were like that before and probably didn't know it. It sometimes makes sense to access the past to clearly see the present.

☐ **Peers and Colleagues**
Peers and colleagues have a special social and working relationship. They attend staff meetings together, share private views, get feedback from the same boss, travel together, and are knowledgeable about each other's work. You perhaps let your guard down more around peers and act more like yourself. They can be a valuable source of feedback.

SECTION 4: LEARNING FROM DEVELOP-IN-PLACE ASSIGNMENTS

THESE PART-TIME DEVELOP-IN-PLACE ASSIGNMENTS WILL HELP YOU BUILD YOUR SKILL(S)

☐ Help someone outside your unit or the organization solve a business problem.

☐ Launch a new product, service, or process.

☐ Relaunch an existing product or service that's not doing well.

☐ Manage an ad hoc, temporary group of balky and resisting people through an unpopular change or project.

☐ Assemble an ad hoc team of diverse people to accomplish a difficult task.

☐ Prepare and present a proposal of some consequence to top management.

☐ Manage a dissatisfied internal or external customer; troubleshoot a performance or quality problem with a product or service.

☐ Manage a group through a significant business crisis.

☐ Take on a tough and undoable project, one where others who have tried it have failed.

☐ Take on a task you dislike or hate to do.

SECTION 5: LEARNING FROM FULL-TIME JOBS

THESE FULL-TIME JOBS OFFER THE OPPORTUNITY TO BUILD YOUR SKILL(S)

☐ **Heavy Strategic Demands**
The core demands necessary to qualify as a Heavy Strategic Content assignment are: 1) Requires significant strategic thinking and planning most couldn't do. 2) Charts new ground strategically. 3) Plan must be presented, challenged, adopted, and implemented. 4) Exposure to significant decision makers and executives. 1) Strategic planning position. 2) Job involving repositioning of a product, service, or organization.

☐ **Line To Staff Switches**
The core demands to qualify as a Line to Staff switch are:
1) Intellectually/strategically demanding. 2) Highly visible to others.

3) New area/perspective/method/culture/function. 4) Moving away from a bottom line. 5) Moving from field to headquarters. 6) Exposure to high-level executives. Examples: 1) Business/strategic planning. 2) Heading a staff department. 3) Assistant to/chief of staff to a senior executive. 4) Head of a task force. 5) Human resources role.

☐ **Scope Assignments**

The core demands for a Scope (complexity) assignment are: 1) Significant increase in both internal and external scope or complexity. 2) Significant increase in visibility and/or bottom line responsibility. 3) Unfamiliar area, business, technology, or territory. Examples of Scope assignments involving shifts: 1) Switching into a new function/technology/business. 2) Moving to new organization. 3) Moving to overseas assignment. 4) Moving to new location. 5) Adding new products/services. 6) Moving between headquarters/field. 7) Switches in ownership/top management of the unit/organization. Examples of Scope assignments involving "firsts": 1) First-time manager. 2) First-time managing managers. 3) First-time executive. 4) First-time overseas. 5) First-time headquarters/field. 6) First-time team leader. 7) First-time new technology/business/function. Scope assignments involving increased complexity: 1) Managing a significant expansion of an existing product or service. 2) Managing adding new products/service into an existing unit. 3) Managing a reorganized and more diverse unit. 4) Managing explosive growth. 5) Adding new technologies.

☐ **Start-ups**

The core demands to qualify as a start from scratch are: 1) Starting something new for you and/or for the organization. 2) Forging a new team. 3) Creating new systems/facilities/staffs/programs/procedures. 4) Contextual adversity (e.g., uncertainty, government regulation, unions, difficult environment). Seven types of start from scratches: 1) Planning, building, hiring, and managing (e.g., building a new facility, opening up a new location, moving a unit or company). 2) Heading something new (e.g., new product, new service, new line of business, new department/function, major new program). 3) Take over a group/product/service/program that had existed for less than a year and was off to a fast start. 4) Establishing overseas operations. 5) Major new designs for existing systems. 6) Moving a successful program from one unit to another. 7) Installing a new organization-wide process as a full-time job (e.g., like Total Quality).

SECTION 6: LEARNING MORE FROM YOUR PLAN

THESE ADDITIONAL REMEDIES WILL HELP MAKE THIS DEVELOPMENT PLAN MORE EFFECTIVE FOR YOU

Learning to Learn Better

☐ **Monitoring Yourself More Closely and Getting off Your Autopilot**
Past habits are a mixed blessing, sometimes helping, sometimes not. To avoid putting yourself on "autopilot," think afresh about each situation before acting. Consistently monitor yourself with questions. Is this task different? Ask why you would repeat a past action. Are you avoiding anything, like taking a chance? Is there something new you might try?

☐ **Find a Parallel to the Current Problem and Learn From It**
Find a parallel with similar situations, whether in your field or in other areas, past or present, and look for comparison or contrast points to see what else has or hasn't worked. Search especially for the reasons why certain things work and others don't across different situations; find the common and uncommon elements.

☐ **Break Up Your Work Routine When You're Blocked**
When blocked on a problem, intersperse your work routine with dissimilar tasks, activities, or rest breaks. Turn to another task for awhile. In a sequence of tough work, string dissimilar tasks together so you can vary the types of skills used and the work done.

☐ **Try New Things, Take Some Chances, Increase Personal Risk Taking**
Engage in some creative problem-solving activities such as brainstorming, free association, analogies to unrelated areas, nominal group techniques, etc. Let yourself go; let your thinking flow freely. Break down the restrictions on yourself; break through old barriers and blockages; try new ways of thinking.

☐ **Debrief Someone Else After a Successful or Non-Successful Event**
Shortly after someone does something particularly well or badly, debrief them on the process they followed. Ask them about the decisions they made and why; find out what they would have done differently. See if you can glean some insights or rules of thumb from the experiences of others.

☐ **Envision Doing Something Well in a Group**
Take the people you want or need to be involved through a envisioning/creativity exercise to come up with different ideas and solutions.

☐ **Skim Data Repeatedly to Find Insights**
When stumped on a problem, take out the available data and information and read it over and over rapidly. Do not impose any order; do not organize or divide the data into categories when you start. Repeat this until an order and solution jumps out at you and forms into a plan.

Learning from Experience, Feedback, and Other People

- [ ] **Getting Feedback from Direct Reports**
Direct reports often fear reprisals for giving negative feedback about bosses, whether in a formal process, like a questionnaire, or informally and face-to-face. Even with a guarantee of confidentiality, some are still hesitant. If you want feedback from direct reports, you have to set a positive tone and never act out of revenge.

- [ ] **Getting Feedback from Peers/Colleagues**
Your peers and colleagues may not be candid if they are in competition with you. Some may not be willing to be open with you out of fear of giving you an advantage. Some may give you exaggerated feedback to deliberately cause you undue concern. You have to set the tone and gauge the trust level of the relationship and the quality of the feedback.

Learning from Courses

- [ ] **Attitude Toward Learning**
In addition to selecting the right course, a learning attitude is required. Be open. Close down your "like/dislike" switch, your "agree/disagree" blinders, and your "like me/not like me" feelings toward the instructors. Learning requires new lessons, change, and new behaviors and perspectives – all scary stuff for most people. Don't resist. Take in all you can during the course. Ask clarifying questions. Discuss concerns with the other participants. Jot down what you learn as you go. After the course is over, take some reflective time to glean the meat. Make the practical decisions about what you can and cannot use.

SUGGESTED READINGS

Ackoff, Russell Lincoln. *The art of problem solving: Accompanied by Ackoff's fables.* New York: Wiley, 1978.

Birch, Paul and Brian Clegg. *Imagination Engineering – The toolkit for business creativity.* London: Pitman Publishing, 1996.

Butler, Ava S. *Team Think.* New York: McGraw-Hill, Inc., 1996.

De Bono, Edward. *Lateral thinking: creativity step by step.* New York: Harper & Row, 1970, 1973.

De Bono, Edward. *Serious creativity: Using the power of lateral thinking to create new ideas.* New York: HarperBusiness,1992.

Firestine, Roger L., Ph.D. *Leading on the Creative Edge – Gaining competitive advantage through the power of creative problem solving.* Colorado Springs, CO: Piñon Press, 1996.

Miller, William C. *Flash of Brilliance.* Reading, MA: Perseus Books Group, 1999.

Morgan, Gareth. *The Art of Creative Management.* Beverly Hills: Sage Publications, 1993.

Rasberry, Salli and Padi Selwyn. *Living your Life Out Loud – How to unlock your creativity and unleash your joy.* New York: Pocket Books, 1995.

Saint-Exupéry, Antoine de [Translated from the French by Katherine Woods]. *The Little Prince.* New York: Harcourt, Brace,1943.

Saint-Exupéry, Antoine de [Translated from the French by Katherine Woods]. *The Little Prince [sound recording].* Redway, CA: Music for Little People, 1993.

15

CUSTOMER FOCUS

SECTION 1: YOUR DEVELOPMENT NEED(S)

UNSKILLED

- ☐ Doesn't think of the customer first
- ☐ May think he/she already knows what they need
- ☐ May focus on internal operations and get blindsided by customer problems
- ☐ May not make the first move – won't meet and get to know customers
- ☐ Uncomfortable with new people contacts
- ☐ May be unwilling to handle criticisms, complaints, and special requests
- ☐ May not listen well to customers, may be defensive
- ☐ May not make the time for customer contact

SKILLED

- ☐ Is dedicated to meeting the expectations and requirements of internal and external customers
- ☐ Gets first-hand customer information and uses it for improvements in products and services
- ☐ Acts with customers in mind
- ☐ Establishes and maintains effective relationships with customers and gains their trust and respect

OVERUSED SKILL

- ☐ May be overly responsive to customer demands
- ☐ May be too willing to change established processes and timetables to respond to unreasonable customer requests
- ☐ May make too many exceptions and not form consistent policies, practices, and processes for others to learn and follow
- ☐ Sticks so close to current customer needs that breakthroughs are missed

Select one to three of the competencies listed below to work on to compensate for an overuse of this skill.

COMPENSATORS: 5, 9, 12, 34, 35, 38, 50, 51, 52, 53, 57, 58, 59, 63, 65

SOME CAUSES

- ☐ Arrogant; know it all; want to do it yourself
- ☐ Defensive in the face of criticism
- ☐ Loner
- ☐ Poor listening skills
- ☐ Poor time management; too busy
- ☐ Self centered
- ☐ Shy; afraid of transacting with new people; lack self confidence

THE MAP

In a free enterprise system, the customer is king. Those who please the customer best win. The same is true with internal customers. Those who please them the most will win. Winners are always customer-oriented and responsive.

SECTION 2: LEARNING ON YOUR OWN

THESE SELF-DEVELOPMENT REMEDIES WILL HELP YOU BUILD YOUR SKILL(S)

SOME REMEDIES

- ☐ **1. Keep in touch.** Pleasing the reasonable needs of customers is fairly straightforward. First you need to know what they want and expect. The best way to do that is to ask them. Then deliver that in a timely way at a price/value that's justified. Find ways to keep in touch with a broad spectrum of your customers to get a balanced view: face to face, phone surveys, questionnaires, response cards with the products and services you render, etc.
- ☐ **2. Customers complain; it's their job.** Be ready for the good news and the bad news; don't be defensive; just listen and respond to legitimate criticisms and note the rest. Vocal customers will usually complain more than compliment; you need to not get overwhelmed by the negative comments; people who have positive opinions speak up less.
- ☐ **3. Anticipate customer needs.** Get in the habit of meeting with your internal or external customers on a regular basis to set up a dialogue; they need to feel free to contact you about problems and you need to be able to contact them for essential information. Use this understanding to get out in front of your customers; try to anticipate their needs for your products and services before they even know about them; provide your customers with positive surprises; features they weren't expecting; delivery in a shorter time; more than they ordered.
- ☐ **4. Put yourself in your customer's shoes.** If you were a customer of yours, what would you expect; what kind of turnaround time would you tolerate; what price would you be willing to pay for the quality of product or service you provide; what would be the top three things you would complain about? Answer all calls from customers in a timely way; if you promise a response, do it; if the timeframe stretches, inform them immediately; after you have responded, ask them if the problem is fixed.
- ☐ **5. Think customer in.** Always design your work and manage your time from the customer in, not from you out. Your best will always be determined by your customers, not you; try not to design and arrange what you do only from your own view; try to always know and take the viewpoint of your customer first; you will always win following that rule.

☐ **6. Create an environment for experimentation and learning.** One principle of these techniques is to drive for continuous improvement. Never be satisfied. Always drive to improve all work processes so they deliver zero defect goods and services the customers want. Don't be afraid to try and fail. *More help? – See #28 Innovation Management and #63 Total Quality Management/Re-Engineering.*

☐ **7. Look at your own personal work habits.** Are they designed for maximum effectiveness and efficiency for your customer or are they designed for your comfort? Is there room for some continuous improvement? Are you applying the principles you have learned to yourself? Remember, this is one of the major reasons why these efforts fail.

☐ **8. Think of yourself as a dissatisfied customer.** Write down all of the unsatisfactory things that have happened to you as a customer during the past month. Things like delays, orders not right, cost not as promised, phone calls not returned, cold food, bad service, inattentive clerks, out of stock items, etc. Are any of these things happening to your customers? Then do a study of your lost customers. Find out what the three key problems were and see how quickly you can eliminate 50% of the difficulties that caused them to depart. Study your competitor's foul ups and see what you can do to both eliminate those and make your organization more attractive.

☐ **9. Think of yourself as a satisfied customer.** Write down all of the satisfactory things that have happened to you as a customer during the past month. What pleased you the most as a customer? Good value? On-time service? Courtesy? Returned phone calls? Are any of your customers experiencing any of these satisfactory transactions with you and your business? Study your successful customer transactions so they can be institutionalized. Then study what your competitors do well and see what you can also do to improve customer service.

☐ **10. Play detective.** Be a student of the work flows and processes around you at airports, restaurants, hotels, supermarkets, government services, etc. As a customer, how would you design those things differently to make them more effective and efficient? What principles did you follow? Apply those same principles to your own work.

SECTION 3: LEARNING FROM MORE FEEDBACK

THESE SOURCES WOULD GIVE YOU THE MOST ACCURATE AND DETAILED FEEDBACK ON YOUR SKILL(S)

☐ **Direct Boss**

Your direct boss has important information about you, your performance, and your prospects. The challenge is to get this information. There are formal processes (e.g., performance appraisals). There are day-to-day opportunities. To help, signal your boss that you want and can handle direct and timely feedback. Many bosses have trouble giving feedback, so you will have to work at it over a period of time.

- ☐ **Internal and External Customers**
  Customers interact with you as a person and as a supplier or vendor of products and services. You're important to them because you can either help address and solve their problems or stand in their way. As customer service and Total Quality programs gain importance, clients and customers become a more prominent source of feedback.

- ☐ **Past Associates/Constituencies**
  When confronted with a present performance problem, some claim, "I wasn't like that before; it must be the current situation." When feedback is available from former associates, about 50% support that claim. In the other half of the cases, the people were like that before and probably didn't know it. It sometimes makes sense to access the past to clearly see the present.

SECTION 4: LEARNING FROM DEVELOP-IN-PLACE ASSIGNMENTS

THESE PART-TIME DEVELOP-IN-PLACE ASSIGNMENTS WILL HELP YOU BUILD YOUR SKILL(S)

- ☐ Study and establish internal or external customer needs, requirements, specifications, and expectations and present it to the people involved.
- ☐ Do a customer-satisfaction survey in person or by phone and present it to the people involved.
- ☐ Visit Malcolm Baldrige National Quality Award or Deming Prize winners and report back on your findings, showing how they would help your organization.
- ☐ Work a few shifts in the telemarketing or customer service department, handling complaints and inquiries from customers.
- ☐ Represent the organization at a trade show, convention, exposition, etc.
- ☐ Spend time with internal or external customers, write a report on your observations, and present it to the people involved with the customers in the organization.
- ☐ Launch a new product, service, or process.
- ☐ Train customers in the use of the organization's products or services.
- ☐ Manage the interface between consultants and the organization on a critical assignment.
- ☐ Manage a dissatisfied internal or external customer; troubleshoot a performance or quality problem with a product or service.

SECTION 5: LEARNING FROM FULL-TIME JOBS

THESE FULL-TIME JOBS OFFER THE OPPORTUNITY TO BUILD YOUR SKILL(S)

☐ **Chair of Projects/Task Forces**

The core demands for qualifying as a Project/Task Force assignment are: 1) Full-time assignment. 2) Important and specific goal. 3) Tight deadline. 4) Success or failure will be evident. 5) High-visibility sponsor. 6) Learning something on the fly. 7) Must get others to cooperate. 8) Usually six months or more. Four types of Projects/Task Forces: 1) New ideas, products, services, or systems (e.g., product/service/program research and development, creation/installation/launch of a new system, new programs like Total Quality Management, positive discipline). 2) Formal negotiations and relationships (e.g., acquisitions, divestitures, agreements, joint ventures; licensing arrangements, franchising; dealing with unions, governments, communities, charities, customers, and relocations). 3) Big one-time events (e.g., working on a major presentation for the board, organizing significant meetings or conferences, disaster/damage control teams; reorganizations, mergers, acquisitions, or relocations, working on visions, charters, strategies, other time-urgent issues and problems). 4) Troubleshooting (e.g., problems, disasters, crises, product/service failures, accidents, illegal activities, damage control in public relations goofs, shut downs, downsizings, layoffs, abrupt changes in leadership).

☐ **Fix-its/Turnarounds**

The core demands to qualify as a Fix-it or Turnaround assignment are: 1) Cleaning up a mess. 2) Serious people issues/problems like credibility/performance/morale. 3) Tight deadline. 4) Serious business performance failure. 5) Last chance to fix. Four Types of Fix-its/Turnarounds: 1) Fixing a failed business/unit involving taking control, stopping losses, managing damage, planning the turnaround, dealing with people problems, installing new processes and systems, and rebuilding the spirit and performance of the unit. 2) Managing sizable disasters like mishandled labor negotiations and strikes, thefts, history of significant business losses, poor staff, failed leadership, hidden problems, fraud, public relations nightmares, etc. 3) Significant reorganization and restructuring (e.g., stabilizing the business, re-forming unit, introducing new systems, making people changes, resetting strategy and tactics). 4) Significant system/process breakdown (e.g., MIS, financial coordination processes, audits, standards, etc.) across units requiring working to change something from a distant position, providing advice and counsel, and installing or implementing a major process improvement or system change outside your own unit and/or with customers outside the organization.

☐ **Scope Assignments**
The core demands for a Scope (complexity) assignment are: 1) Significant increase in both internal and external scope or complexity. 2) Significant increase in visibility and/or bottom line responsibility. 3) Unfamiliar area, business, technology, or territory. Examples of Scope assignments involving shifts: 1) Switching into a new function/technology/business. 2) Moving to new organization. 3) Moving to overseas assignment. 4) Moving to new location. 5) Adding new products/services. 6) Moving between headquarters/field. 7) Switches in ownership/top management of the unit/organization. Examples of Scope assignments involving "firsts": 1) First-time manager. 2) First-time managing managers. 3) First-time executive. 4) First-time overseas. 5) First-time headquarters/field. 6) First-time team leader. 7) First-time new technology/business/function. Scope assignments involving increased complexity: 1) Managing a significant expansion of an existing product or service. 2) Managing adding new products/service into an existing unit. 3) Managing a reorganized and more diverse unit. 4) Managing explosive growth. 5) Adding new technologies.

☐ **Start-ups**
The core demands to qualify as a start from scratch are: 1) Starting something new for you and/or for the organization. 2) Forging a new team. 3) Creating new systems/facilities/staffs/programs/procedures. 4) Contextual adversity (e.g., uncertainty, government regulation, unions, difficult environment). Seven types of start from scratches: 1) Planning, building, hiring, and managing (e.g., building a new facility, opening up a new location, moving a unit or company). 2) Heading something new (e.g., new product, new service, new line of business, new department/function, major new program). 3) Take over a group/product/service/program that had existed for less than a year and was off to a fast start. 4) Establishing overseas operations. 5) Major new designs for existing systems. 6) Moving a successful program from one unit to another. 7) Installing a new organization-wide process as a full-time job (e.g., like Total Quality).

SECTION 6: LEARNING MORE FROM YOUR PLAN

THESE ADDITIONAL REMEDIES WILL HELP MAKE THIS DEVELOPMENT PLAN MORE EFFECTIVE FOR YOU

Learning to Learn Better

☐ **Monitoring Yourself More Closely and Getting off Your Autopilot**
Past habits are a mixed blessing, sometimes helping, sometimes not. To avoid putting yourself on "autopilot," think afresh about each situation before acting. Consistently monitor yourself with questions. Is this task different? Ask why you would repeat a past action. Are you avoiding anything, like taking a chance? Is there something new you might try?

- ☐ **Pre-sell an Idea to a Key Stakeholder**
Identify the key stakeholders – those who will be the most affected by your actions or the most resistant, or whose support you will most need. Collect the information each will find persuasive; marshal your arguments and try to pre-sell your conclusions, recommendations, and solutions.

- ☐ **Sell Something to a Tough Group/Audience**
Think of the person or group who will be the toughest to sell, the most critical, skeptical, or resistant, and sell that person or group first. Take time to understand the opposing viewpoints. Find common ground and leverage points; line up your best data and arguments and go for it.

Learning from Experience, Feedback and Other People

- ☐ **Using Multiple Models**
Who do you know who exemplifies how to do whatever your need is? Who, for example, personifies decisiveness or compassion or strategic agility? Think more broadly than your current job and colleagues. For example, clergy, friends, spouses or community leaders are also good sources for potential models. Select your models not on the basis of overall excellence or likability, but on the basis of the one towering strength (or glaring weakness) you are interested in. Even people who are well thought of usually have only one or two towering strengths (or glaring weaknesses). Ordinarily, you won't learn as much from the whole person as you will from one characteristic.

- ☐ **Learning from Bosses**
Bosses can be an excellent and ready source for learning. All bosses do some things exceptionally well and other things poorly. Distance your feelings from the boss/direct report relationship and study things that work and things that don't work for your boss. What would you have done? What could you use, and what should you avoid?

- ☐ **Getting Feedback from Bosses and Superiors**
Many bosses are reluctant to give negative feedback. They lack the managerial courage to face people directly with criticism. You can help by soliciting feedback and setting the tone. Show them you can handle criticism and that you are willing to work on issues they see as important.

- ☐ **Openness to Feedback**
Nothing discourages feedback more than defensiveness, resistance, irritation, and excuses. People don't like giving feedback anyway, and much less to those who don't listen or are unreceptive. To help the feedback giver, be open, listen, ask for examples and details, take notes, keep a journal, and thank them for their interest.

Learning from Courses

- ☐ **Job Skills**
  Most organizations and professional associations offer job skills training. The key is to find a course that has the right content and offers the opportunity for practicing the jobs skills. It's helpful if the instructors have actually performed the skills in situations similar to your own. Most organizations offer a variety of orientation events. They are designed to communicate strategies, charters, missions, goals, and general information and offer an opportunity for people to meet each other. They are short in duration and offer limited opportunities for learning anything beyond general context and background.

- ☐ **Courses with Feedback**
  Many courses such as negotiating skills and personal influence offer feedback on the subject matter of the course in addition to the content. They either collect data ahead of time or collect it "live" during the course.

- ☐ **Survey Courses**
  These are courses designed to give a general overview of an entire area (such as advertising), product or product line, division's activities, process (getting a product to market, Total Quality Management) or geography (doing business in "X"). These types of courses are good for general background and context.

SUGGESTED READINGS

Albrecht, Karl. *The Only Thing that Matters.* New York: HarperCollins, 1992.

Albrecht, Karl and Ron Zemke. *Service America!.* Burr Ridge, IL: Irwin Professional Publishing, 1985.

Band, William A. *Creating value for customers: designing and implementing a total corporate strategy.* New York: John Wiley and Sons, 1991.

Cannie, Joan Koob. *Turning Lost Customers into Gold.* New York: AMACOM, 1994.

Carlzon, Jan. *Moments of Truth.* Cambridge, MA: Ballinger Publishing Co., 1987.

Connellan, Thomas K. and Ron Zemke. *Sustaining Knock Your Socks Off Service.* New York: AMACOM, 1993.

The Harvard Business Review. *Command Performance.* Boston: Harvard Business School Press, 1987.

Heskett, James L., W. Earl Sasser, Jr., and Leonard A. Schlesinger. *The service profit chain: how leading companies link profit and growth to loyalty, satisfaction, and value.* New York: Free Press, 1997.

Reichheld, Frederick F. with Thomas Teal. *The Loyalty Effect: The hidden force behind growth, profits and lasting value.* Boston: Harvard Business School Press, 1996.

Schaaf, Dick. *Keeping the Edge.* New York: Dutton, 1995.

Whitely, Richard and Diane Hessan. *Customer-Centered Growth.* Reading, MA: Addison-Wesley Publishing Co. Inc., 1996.

16

TIMELY DECISION MAKING

SECTION 1: YOUR DEVELOPMENT NEED(S)

UNSKILLED

- ☐ Slow to decide or to declare
- ☐ Conservative and cautious
- ☐ May procrastinate, seek more information to build confidence and avoid risk
- ☐ May be a perfectionist, needing to be right, protect strongly against criticism
- ☐ May be disorganized and always scrambling to meet decision deadlines
- ☐ May be slow to make decisions on more complex issues

SKILLED

- ☐ Makes decisions in a timely manner, sometimes with incomplete information and under tight deadlines and pressure
- ☐ Able to make a quick decision

OVERUSED SKILL

- ☐ May jump to conclusions and take action before reasonable consideration of the information
- ☐ May get caught up in deciding for its own sake
- ☐ May have a chilling effect on getting everyone's input before deciding
- ☐ Might be considered impulsive and impatient
- ☐ Might have some trouble and freeze on issues and problems that are close calls
- ☐ May make decisions quickly to avoid debate and personal discomfort

Select one to three of the competencies listed below to work on to compensate for an overuse of this skill.

COMPENSATORS: 3, 11, 17, 33, 39, 41, 46, 47, 51, 52, 58, 59, 63, 65

SOME CAUSES

- ☐ Avoid conflict
- ☐ Avoid risk
- ☐ Disorganized
- ☐ Easily intimidated
- ☐ Need too much information
- ☐ Not focused
- ☐ Perfectionist
- ☐ Procrastinate
- ☐ Slow to make decisions
- ☐ Too busy
- ☐ Trouble meeting deadlines

THE MAP

Slow to act? Miss decision deadlines often? Have to scramble to get done? Still weighing the objections? Don't like to pull the trigger? Unless you're lucky and work in a very stable niche, this behavior will get you left behind. You won't respond quickly enough to change; you won't learn new things; people will be increasingly frustrated as you hold them up. The rewards are to the swift. David Ulrich, a top strategic business consultant says that in the past there was a premium on being right. That is shifting to being first. In the past, organizations brought out no product until it was time; they worked to make sure it was right and it had a market. Now organizations put out products as fast as possible and fix them later after they get customer reaction. You may associate timely decisions with sloppy decisions, but this is not the case. Timely means sooner, as soon as possible or by a time certain date but not sloppy. Timely thoughtful decisions can be of high quality. It's quality incrementalism.

SECTION 2: LEARNING ON YOUR OWN

THESE SELF-DEVELOPMENT REMEDIES WILL HELP YOU BUILD YOUR SKILL(S)

SOME REMEDIES

☐ **1. Perfectionist?** Need or prefer or want to be 100% sure? Want to make sure that all or at least most of your decisions are right? A lot of people prefer that. Perfectionism is tough to let go of because most people see it as a positive trait for them. They pride themselves on never being wrong. Recognize perfectionism for what it might be – collecting more information than others do to improve confidence in making a fault-free decision and thereby avoiding the risk and criticism that would come from making decisions faster. Anyone with a brain, unlimited time and 100% of the data can make good decisions. The real test is who can act the soonest, being right the most, with less than all the data. Some studies suggest even successful general managers are about 65% correct. If you need to be more timely, you need to reduce your own internal need for data and the need to be perfect. Try to decrease your need for data and your need to be right all the time slightly every week until you reach a more reasonable balance between thinking it through and taking action. Try making some small decisions on little or no data. Trust your intuition more. You experience won't let you stray too far. Let your brain do the calculations.

☐ **2. Procrastinator?** Are you a procrastinator? Get caught short on deadlines? Do it all at the last minute? Not only will you not be timely, your decision quality and accuracy will be poor. Procrastinators miss deadlines and performance targets. If you procrastinate, you might not produce consistent decisions. Start earlier. Always do 10% of thinking about the decision immediately after it is assigned so you can better gauge what it is going to take to finish the rest. Divide decisions into thirds or fourths and schedule time to work on them spaced over the delivery period. Remember one of Murphy's Laws. It takes 90% of the time to do 90% of the project, and another 90% of the time to finish the remaining 10%. Always leave more time than you think it's going to take. Set up checkpoints for yourself along the way. Schedule early data collection and analysis. Don't wait until the last moment. Set an internal deadline one week before the real one. *More help? – See #47 Planning.*

☐ **3. Disorganized?** Don't always get to everything on time? Forget deadlines? Lose requests for decisions? Under time pressure and increased uncertainty, you have to put the keel in the water yourself. You can't operate helter skelter and make quality timely decisions. You need to set tighter priorities. Focus more on the mission-critical few decisions. Don't get diverted by trivial work and other decisions. Get better organized and disciplined. Keep a decision log. When a decision opportunity surfaces, immediately log it along with the ideal date it needs to be made. Plan backwards to the work necessary to make the decision on time. If you are not disciplined in how you work and are sometimes late making decisions and taking action because of it, buy a book on both Total Quality Management and Process Re-Engineering. Go to one workshop on efficient and effective work design. *More help? – See #50 Priority Setting, #52 Process Management, #62 Time Management and #63 Total Quality Management/Re-Engineering.*

☐ **4. Too cautious and conservative?** Analysis paralysis? Break out of your examine-it-to-death and always take the safest path mode and just do it. Increasing timeliness will increase errors and mistakes but it also will get more done faster. Develop a more philosophical stance toward failure/criticism. After all, most innovations fail, most proposals fail, most change efforts fail, anything worth doing takes repeated effort. The best tack when confronted with a mistake is to say, "What can we learn from this?" Ask yourself if your need to be cautious matches the requirements for speed and timeliness of your job. *More help? – See #45 Personal Learning.*

☐ **5. Selective timeliness.** It's very common for people to be timely in some areas (budget decisions) and untimely in others (give an employee negative feedback). Sometimes we avoid certain areas. Create two columns. Left side are the areas where you seem to make timely and speedy decisions. What's common about those areas? Right side are the areas where you hold back, hesitate and wait too long to decide. What's common to that list? Money's involved? People? Risk? Higher management's involved? Are you avoiding detail or strategy or a technical area you dislike or know little about? Since you already make timely decisions in at least one area, transfer your decision behaviors and practices to the other areas. You already have the skills. You just need to get over the barriers (most likely attitude barriers) in the more difficult areas. If you lack expertise, access your network. Go to the two wisest people you know on the decision, hire a consultant, convene a one-time problem-solving group. You don't have to be an expert in the area, but you do need to know how to access expertise to make timely decisions.

☐ **6. Selective people.** Sometimes we are timely with some people and not with others. Many times it relates to how they react to you. There are easy to approach people and difficult to deal with people. There are supportive people and punishing people. You may naturally adjust your decision-making style to match the decision customer. Sometimes we avoid hard to deal with people, leaving them to the last minute because we want to be right and not get punished or demeaned. Mentally rehearse for worst case scenarios/hard to deal with people. Anticipate what the person might say and have responses prepared so as not to be caught off guard. Focus on two or three key points in conflict situations and stick to those clearly and politely. Try not to bring up everything you can think of, but instead focus on essence. Try trial balloons with difficult people. Sometime before a decision is due, float up a small trial balloon on a direction you are thinking of. You'll take a little heat and maybe a little punishment, but you'll also get information to create a better decision later. *More help? – See #12 Conflict Management.*

☐ **7. Decision incrementalism.** Think of a big decision as a series of smaller ones. The essence of timely decision making is the tolerance of increased errors and mistakes and absorbing the possible heat and criticism that follow. Acting on an ill-defined problem with no precedents to follow in a hurry means shooting in the dark with as informed a decision as you can make at the time. Incrementalists make a series of smaller decisions, get instant feedback, correct the course, get a little more data, move forward a little more, until the bigger decision gets made. They don't try to get it right the first time. They try their best educated guess now, and then correct as feedback comes in. Many problem-solving studies show that the second or third try is when we really understand the underlying dynamics of problems. So you need to work on two practices. Start smaller so you can recover more quickly. Do something as soon as you can and get used to heat.

☐ **8. Stress and conflict under time pressure.** Some are energized by time pressure. Some are stressed with time pressure. It actually slows us down. We lose our anchor. We are not at our best when we are pushed. We get more anxious, frustrated, upset. What brings out your emotional response? Write down why you get anxious under time pressure. What fears does it surface? Don't want to make a mistake. Afraid of the unknown consequences. Don't have the confidence to decide? When you get stressed, drop the problem for a moment. Go do something else. Come back to it when you are under better control. Let your brain work on it while you do something safer. *More help? – See #11 Composure and #107* Lack of *Composure.*

- ☐ **9. Delayed disclosure.** Another common pattern is for a person to have no problem making timely decisions inside one's head; the problem is holding back announcing the decisions until they become untimely. In this case, there is nothing wrong with your decision-making program; it's usually your courage and confidence programs. How soon did you come to the decision you are now finally making public? Two weeks ago? Why did you hold it back? Afraid of the reaction? Getting yourself emotionally prepared for the heat? Trying to find the safest time to declare? People like this don't usually change their minds once the decision is made; they just change their minds about when to tell people what they have decided. To check this out, write down the decisions you would make right now, then compare them with the decisions you actually make and announce later. Are the decisions more the same than different? If they are more the same, you may have this problem. Since the noise and the heat are the same, the simple solution is to declare as soon as you have made the decision. Better to be done with it. If there is any useful data in the noise and heat, you can adjust your decision sooner.

- ☐ **10. Hesitate in the face of resistance and adverse reaction?** Conflict slows you down? Shakes your confidence in your decision? Do you backpedal? Give in too soon? Try to make everyone happy? Do your homework first. Scope the problem, consider options, pick one, develop a rationale, then go to others. Be prepared to defend your selection; know what they will ask, what they will object to, how this decision will affect them. Listen carefully, invite criticism of your idea and revise accordingly in the face of real data. Otherwise, hold your ground.

SECTION 3: LEARNING FROM MORE FEEDBACK

THESE SOURCES WOULD GIVE YOU THE MOST ACCURATE AND DETAILED FEEDBACK ON YOUR SKILL(S)

- ☐ **Direct Boss**
  Your direct boss has important information about you, your performance, and your prospects. The challenge is to get this information. There are formal processes (e.g., performance appraisals). There are day-to-day opportunities. To help, signal your boss that you want and can handle direct and timely feedback. Many bosses have trouble giving feedback, so you will have to work at it over a period of time.

- ☐ **Direct Reports**
  Across a variety of settings, your direct reports probably see you the most. They are the recipients of most of your managerial behaviors. They know your work. They can compare you with former bosses.

Since they may hesitate to give you negative feedback, you have to set the atmosphere to make it easier for them. You have to ask.

☐ **Past Associates/Constituencies**
When confronted with a present performance problem, some claim, "I wasn't like that before; it must be the current situation." When feedback is available from former associates, about 50% support that claim. In the other half of the cases, the people were like that before and probably didn't know it. It sometimes makes sense to access the past to clearly see the present.

☐ **Peers and Colleagues**
Peers and colleagues have a special social and working relationship. They attend staff meetings together, share private views, get feedback from the same boss, travel together, and are knowledgeable about each other's work. You perhaps let your guard down more around peers and act more like yourself. They can be a valuable source of feedback.

SECTION 4: LEARNING FROM DEVELOP-IN-PLACE ASSIGNMENTS

THESE PART-TIME DEVELOP-IN-PLACE ASSIGNMENTS WILL HELP YOU BUILD YOUR SKILL(S)

☐ Manage the renovation of an office, floor, building, meeting room, warehouse, etc.

☐ Plan a new site for a building (plant, field office, headquarters, etc.).

☐ Become a referee for an athletic league or program.

☐ Plan for and start up something small (secretarial pool, athletic program, suggestion system, program, etc.).

☐ Launch a new product, service, or process.

☐ Relaunch an existing product or service that's not doing well.

☐ Manage an ad hoc, temporary group of people involved in tackling a fix-it or turnaround project.

☐ Help shut down a plant, regional office, product line, business, operation, etc.

☐ Manage liquidation/sale of products, equipment, materials, a business, furniture, overstock, etc.

☐ Work on a crisis management team.

SECTION 5: LEARNING FROM FULL-TIME JOBS

THESE FULL-TIME JOBS OFFER THE OPPORTUNITY TO BUILD YOUR SKILL(S)

☐ **Chair of Projects/Task Forces**

The core demands for qualifying as a Project/Task Force assignment are: 1) Full-time assignment. 2) Important and specific goal. 3) Tight deadline. 4) Success or failure will be evident. 5) High-visibility sponsor. 6) Learning something on the fly. 7) Must get others to cooperate. 8) Usually six months or more. Four types of Projects/Task Forces: 1) New ideas, products, services, or systems (e.g., product/service/program research and development, creation/installation/launch of a new system, new programs like Total Quality Management, positive discipline). 2) Formal negotiations and relationships (e.g., acquisitions, divestitures, agreements, joint ventures; licensing arrangements, franchising; dealing with unions, governments, communities, charities, customers, and relocations). 3) Big one-time events (e.g., working on a major presentation for the board, organizing significant meetings or conferences, disaster/damage control teams; reorganizations, mergers, acquisitions, or relocations, working on visions, charters, strategies, other time-urgent issues and problems). 4) Troubleshooting (e.g., problems, disasters, crises, product/service failures, accidents, illegal activities, damage control in public relations goofs, shut downs, downsizings, layoffs, abrupt changes in leadership).

☐ **Fix-its/Turnarounds**

The core demands to qualify as a Fix-it or Turnaround assignment are: 1) Cleaning up a mess. 2) Serious people issues/problems like credibility/performance/morale. 3) Tight deadline. 4) Serious business performance failure. 5) Last chance to fix. Four Types of Fix-its/Turnarounds: 1) Fixing a failed business/unit involving taking control, stopping losses, managing damage, planning the turnaround, dealing with people problems, installing new processes and systems, and rebuilding the spirit and performance of the unit. 2) Managing sizable disasters like mishandled labor negotiations and strikes, thefts, history of significant business losses, poor staff, failed leadership, hidden problems, fraud, public relations nightmares, etc. 3) Significant reorganization and restructuring (e.g., stabilizing the business, reforming unit, introducing new systems, making people changes, resetting strategy and tactics). 4) Significant system/process breakdown (e.g., MIS, financial coordination processes, audits, standards, etc.) across units requiring working to change something from a distant position, providing advice and counsel, and installing or implementing a major process improvement or system change outside your own unit and/or with customers outside the organization.

- ☐ **Start-ups**
  The core demands to qualify as a start from scratch are: 1) Starting something new for you and/or for the organization. 2) Forging a new team. 3) Creating new systems/facilities/staffs/programs/procedures. 4) Contextual adversity (e.g., uncertainty, government regulation, unions, difficult environment). Seven types of start from scratches: 1) Planning, building, hiring, and managing (e.g., building a new facility, opening up a new location, moving a unit or company). 2) Heading something new (e.g., new product, new service, new line of business, new department/function, major new program). 3) Take over a group/product/service/program that had existed for less than a year and was off to a fast start. 4) Establishing overseas operations. 5) Major new designs for existing systems. 6) Moving a successful program from one unit to another. 7) Installing a new organization-wide process as a full-time job (e.g., like Total Quality).

SECTION 6: LEARNING MORE FROM YOUR PLAN

THESE ADDITIONAL REMEDIES WILL HELP MAKE THIS DEVELOPMENT PLAN MORE EFFECTIVE FOR YOU

Learning to Learn Better

- ☐ **Teach Others Something You Don't Know Well**
  Commit to a project like teaching something you don't know much about to force you to learn quickly to accomplish the task; pick something new, different, or unfamiliar.
- ☐ **Think and Talk More in Probabilities and Less in Absolutes**
  Try to be less "0/1," yes and no; don't be so absolute in everything you do or say. Think and talk in terms of probabilities (I'm about 60% sure my viewpoint is correct). Try to face what's real about your suggestions and ideas rather than wishing or projecting you were always 100% correct. Tell people how sure you are before you make a statement.
- ☐ **Commit to a Tight Timeframe to Accomplish Something**
  Set some specific goals and tighter than usual timeframes for yourself and go after them with all you've got. Push yourself to stick to the plan; get more done than usual by adhering to a tight plan.
- ☐ **Do Something on Gut Feel More Than Analysis**
  Act on "gut feel;" go with your hunches instead of careful planning. Take a chance on a solution; take some risks; try a number of things by trial and error and learn to deal with making some mistakes.

Learning from Experience, Feedback and Other People

- ☐ **Getting Feedback from Bosses and Superiors**
  Many bosses are reluctant to give negative feedback. They lack the managerial courage to face people directly with criticism. You can help by soliciting feedback and setting the tone. Show them you can handle criticism and that you are willing to work on issues they see as important.

- ☐ **Getting Feedback from Direct Reports**
  Direct reports often fear reprisals for giving negative feedback about bosses, whether in a formal process, like a questionnaire, or informally and face-to-face. Even with a guarantee of confidentiality, some are still hesitant. If you want feedback from direct reports, you have to set a positive tone and never act out of revenge.

- ☐ **Getting Feedback from Peers/Colleagues**
  Your peers and colleagues may not be candid if they are in competition with you. Some may not be willing to be open with you out of fear of giving you an advantage. Some may give you exaggerated feedback to deliberately cause you undue concern. You have to set the tone and gauge the trust level of the relationship and the quality of the feedback.

- ☐ **Feedback in Unusual Contexts/Situations**
  Temporary and extreme conditions and contexts may shade interpretations of your behavior and intentions. Demands of the job may drive you outside your normal mode of operating. Hence, feedback you receive may be inaccurate during those times. However, unusual contexts affect our behavior less than most assume. It's usually a weak excuse.

SUGGESTED READINGS

Dawson, Roger. *The Confident Decision Maker.* New York: William Morrow and Company, 1993.

Gartner, Scott Sigmund. *Strategic Assessment in War.* New Haven, CN: Yale University Press, 1999.

Klein, Gary. *Sources of Power: How people make decisions.* Boston: MIT Press, 1999.

Maihafer, Harry J. *Brave decisions: Moral courage from the Revolutionary War to Desert Storm.* London, England; Washington: Brassey's, Inc., 1995.

Muirhead, Brian K. and William L. Simon. *High Velocity Leadership – The Mars Pathfinder Approach to Faster, Better, Cheaper*. New York: HarperBusiness, 1999.

O'Dell, William F. *Effective Business Decision Making.* Lincolnwood, IL: NTC Business Books, 1991.

DECISION QUALITY

SECTION 1: YOUR DEVELOPMENT NEED(S)

UNSKILLED

- ☐ Goes first with quick solutions, conclusions and statements before analysis
- ☐ May rely too much on self – doesn't ask for help
- ☐ Making decisions may trigger emotions and impatience
- ☐ May not use orderly decision methods, models or ways to think
- ☐ May jump to conclusions based on prejudices, historical solutions or narrow perspective
- ☐ Doesn't take the time to define the problem before deciding
- ☐ May have trouble with complexity
- ☐ May wait too long, agonize over every detail to avoid risk or error
- ☐ May go for the big elegant decision when five little ones would be better

SKILLED

- ☐ Makes good decisions (without considering how much time it takes) based upon a mixture of analysis, wisdom, experience, and judgment
- ☐ Most of his/her solutions and suggestions turn out to be correct and accurate when judged over time
- ☐ Sought out by others for advice and solutions

OVERUSED SKILL

- ☐ May see him/herself as overly wise or close to perfect, as someone who can't or doesn't make mistakes
- ☐ May be seen as stubborn and not willing to negotiate or compromise
- ☐ May get frustrated when advice is rejected
- ☐ May not relate well to less data-based people

Select one to three of the competencies listed below to work on to compensate for an overuse of this skill.

COMPENSATORS: 2, 5, 12, 16, 30, 32, 33, 37, 45, 51, 52, 58, 61, 63

SOME CAUSES

- ☐ Arrogant
- ☐ Excessive emotionality; avoiding risk and exposure
- ☐ Faulty thinking
- ☐ Impatient; don't wait for the data
- ☐ Narrow perspective
- ☐ Perfectionist; wait too long for all of the data
- ☐ Prejudiced; preconceived solutions; rigid
- ☐ Want to do it all yourself; won't ask for help

THE MAP

Life and work are just a series of big and small decisions followed by action in line with the decisions. Good decisions are based upon a mixture of data, analysis, intuition, wisdom, experience, and judgment. Making good decisions involves being patient enough to collect the available information, being humble enough to ask for other people's opinions and thoughts and then coldly making the decision. No one is ever right all the time; it's the percent correct over time that matters.

SECTION 2: LEARNING ON YOUR OWN

THESE SELF-DEVELOPMENT REMEDIES WILL HELP YOU BUILD YOUR SKILL(S)

SOME REMEDIES

☐ **1. Know your biases.** Be clear and honest with yourself about your attitudes, beliefs, biases, opinions and prejudices and your favorite solutions. We all have them. The key is not to let them affect your objective and cold decision making. Before making any sizable decision, ask yourself, are any of my biases affecting this decision? Do you play favorites, deciding quickly in one area, but holding off in another? Do you avoid certain topics, people, groups, functional areas because you're not comfortable or don't know? Do you drag out your favorite solutions often? Too often?

☐ **2. Check yourself for these common errors in thinking:** Do you state as facts things that are really opinions or assumptions? Are you sure these assertions are facts? State opinions and assumptions as that and don't present them as facts. Do you attribute cause and effect to relationships when you don't know if one causes the other? If sales are down, and we increase advertising and sales go up, this doesn't prove causality. They are simply related. Say we know that the relationship between sales/advertising is about the same as sales/number of employees. If sales go down, we probably wouldn't hire more people, so make sure one thing causes the other before acting on it. Do you generalize from a single example without knowing if that single example does generalize?

☐ **3. Do you do enough analysis?** Thoroughly define the problem. Figure out what causes it. Keep asking why. See how many causes you can come up with and how many organizing buckets you can put them in. This increases the chance of a better solution because you can see more connections. Look for patterns in data, don't just collect information. Put it in categories that make sense to you. A good rule of thumb is to analyze patterns and causes to come up with alternatives. Many of us just collect data, which numerous studies show increases our confidence but doesn't increase decision accuracy. Think out loud with others; see how they view the problem. Studies show that defining the problem and taking action usually occur simultaneously, so to break out of analysis paralysis, figure out what the problem is first. Then when a good alternative appears you're likely to recognize it immediately.

☐ **4. Do a historical analysis.** Do an objective analysis of decisions you have made in the past and what the percentage correct was. Break the decisions into topics or areas of your life. For most of us, we make better decisions in some areas than others. Maybe your decision-making skills need help in one or two limited areas, like decisions about people, decisions about your career, political decisions, technical, etc.

☐ **5. Holster your gun.** Life is a balance between waiting and doing. Many in management put a premium on doing over waiting. Most could make close to 100% good decisions given all of the data and unlimited time. Life affords us neither the data nor the time. You may need to try to discipline yourself to wait just a little longer than you usually do for more, but not all, the data to come in. Push yourself to always get one more piece of data than you did before until your correct decision percent becomes more acceptable. Instead of just doing it, ask what questions would need to be answered before we'd know which way to go. In one study of problem solving, answers outnumbered questions 8 to 1. We jump to solutions based on what has worked in the past. So collect data to answer these questions, then shoot. *More help? – See #51 Problem Solving.*

☐ **6. If you are hesitant to make a decision, maybe you should be.** Play out the consequences in your head to see how the decision would play in real life. Test out a number of decisions. Some research says that the best decision isn't always the first or even the second solution you think of. The highest quality decisions are somewhere between the second and third decision you come to. You may be hesitating because your little voice in your head is telling you something isn't right.

☐ **7. Sleep on it.** The brain works on things even when you are not thinking about them. Take some time, do something completely different, and get back to the decision later. Let a night's sleep go by and return to it in the morning.

☐ **8. Use others to help.** Delegate the decision. Sometime others above, aside, or below you may be in a better position to make the decision. Create a group or task force, present the decision and all you know about it, and let the group decide. Or set up competing groups or find a buddy group in another function or organization which faces a similar problem or consult history – surely this has happened before. Up your odds through others.

☐ **9. Study decision makers.** Who do you admire? Bill Gates? Winston Churchill? Read the biographies and autobiographies of a few people you respect, and pay attention to how they made decisions in their life and careers. Write down five things they did that you can do. For example, Churchill always slept on important decisions no matter what.

He initially only asked questions and tried to understand the problem and argument as given. He kept his views to himself until later.

☐ **10. Go to a model decision maker.** Find someone around you who makes decisions in a way you think you ought to and ask how he/she does it. Go through several decision processes. Try to figure out with the person what questions he/she asks, and what principles are being followed. See how much he/she relies on advice, consults history for parallels, checks in with various constituencies and how she/he gets familiar with unfamiliar areas.

SECTION 3: LEARNING FROM MORE FEEDBACK

THESE SOURCES WOULD GIVE YOU THE MOST ACCURATE AND DETAILED FEEDBACK ON YOUR SKILL(S)

☐ **Boss's Boss(es)**
From a process standpoint, your boss's boss probably has the most influence and control over your progress. He/she has a broader perspective, has more access to data, and stands at the center of decisions about you. To know what he/she thinks, without having to violate the canons of corporate due process to get that information, would be quite useful.

☐ **Direct Boss**
Your direct boss has important information about you, your performance, and your prospects. The challenge is to get this information. There are formal processes (e.g., performance appraisals). There are day-to-day opportunities. To help, signal your boss that you want and can handle direct and timely feedback. Many bosses have trouble giving feedback, so you will have to work at it over a period of time.

☐ **Past Associates/Constituencies**
When confronted with a present performance problem, some claim, "I wasn't like that before; it must be the current situation." When feedback is available from former associates, about 50% support that claim. In the other half of the cases, the people were like that before and probably didn't know it. It sometimes makes sense to access the past to clearly see the present.

☐ **Peers and Colleagues**
Peers and colleagues have a special social and working relationship. They attend staff meetings together, share private views, get feedback from the same boss, travel together, and are knowledgeable about each other's work. You perhaps let your guard down more around peers and act more like yourself. They can be a valuable source of feedback.

SECTION 4: LEARNING FROM DEVELOP-IN-PLACE ASSIGNMENTS

THESE PART-TIME DEVELOP-IN-PLACE ASSIGNMENTS WILL HELP YOU BUILD YOUR SKILL(S)

- ☐ Plan a new site for a building (plant, field office, headquarters, etc.).
- ☐ Manage the purchase of a major product, equipment, materials, program, or system.
- ☐ Launch a new product, service, or process.
- ☐ Relaunch an existing product or service that's not doing well.
- ☐ Hire/staff a team from outside your unit or organization.
- ☐ Work on a team forming a joint venture or partnership.
- ☐ Manage the interface between consultants and the organization on a critical assignment.
- ☐ Handle a tough negotiation with an internal or external client or customer.
- ☐ Manage a dissatisfied internal or external customer; troubleshoot a performance or quality problem with a product or service.
- ☐ Build a multifunctional project team to tackle a common business issue or problem.

SECTION 5: LEARNING FROM FULL-TIME JOBS

THESE FULL-TIME JOBS OFFER THE OPPORTUNITY TO BUILD YOUR SKILL(S)

- ☐ **Fix-its/Turnarounds**

  The core demands to qualify as a Fix-it or Turnaround assignment are: 1) Cleaning up a mess. 2) Serious people issues/problems like credibility/performance/morale. 3) Tight deadline. 4) Serious business performance failure. 5) Last chance to fix. Four Types of Fix-its/Turnarounds: 1) Fixing a failed business/unit involving taking control, stopping losses, managing damage, planning the turnaround, dealing with people problems, installing new processes and systems, and rebuilding the spirit and performance of the unit. 2) Managing sizable disasters like mishandled labor negotiations and strikes, thefts, history of significant business losses, poor staff, failed leadership, hidden problems, fraud, public relations nightmares, etc. 3) Significant reorganization and restructuring (e.g., stabilizing the business, reforming unit, introducing new systems, making people changes, resetting strategy and tactics). 4) Significant system/process breakdown (e.g., MIS, financial coordination processes, audits, standards, etc.) across units requiring working to change something from a distant position, providing advice and counsel, and installing or implementing a major process improvement or system change outside your own unit and/or with customers outside the organization.

☐ **Member of Projects/Task Forces**
The core demands for qualifying as a Project/Task Force assignment are: 1) Full-time assignment. 2) Important and specific goal. 3) Tight deadline. 4) Success or failure will be evident. 5) High-visibility sponsor. 6) Learning something on the fly. 7) Must get others to cooperate. 8) Usually six months or more. Four types of Projects/Task Forces: 1) New ideas, products, services, or systems (e.g., product/service/program research and development, creation/installation/launch of a new system, new programs like Total Quality Management, positive discipline). 2) Formal negotiations and relationships (e.g., acquisitions, divestitures, agreements, joint ventures; licensing arrangements, franchising; dealing with unions, governments, communities, charities, customers, and relocations). 3) Big one-time events (e.g., working on a major presentation for the board, organizing significant meetings or conferences, disaster/damage control teams; reorganizations, mergers, acquisitions, or relocations, working on visions, charters, strategies, other time-urgent issues and problems). 4) Troubleshooting (e.g., problems, disasters, crises, product/service failures, accidents, illegal activities, damage control in public relations goofs, shut downs, downsizings, layoffs, abrupt changes in leadership).

☐ **Scope Assignments**
The core demands for a Scope (complexity) assignment are: 1) Significant increase in both internal and external scope or complexity. 2) Significant increase in visibility and/or bottom line responsibility. 3) Unfamiliar area, business, technology, or territory. Examples of Scope assignments involving shifts: 1) Switching into a new function/technology/business. 2) Moving to new organization. 3) Moving to overseas assignment. 4) Moving to new location. 5) Adding new products/services. 6) Moving between headquarters/field. 7) Switches in ownership/top management of the unit/organization. Examples of Scope assignments involving "firsts": 1) First-time manager. 2) First-time managing managers. 3) First-time executive. 4) First-time overseas. 5) First-time headquarters/field. 6) First-time team leader. 7) First-time new technology/business/function. Scope assignments involving increased complexity: 1) Managing a significant expansion of an existing product or service. 2) Managing adding new products/service into an existing unit. 3) Managing a reorganized and more diverse unit. 4) Managing explosive growth. 5) Adding new technologies.

☐ **Staff to Line Shifts**
Core demands necessary to qualify for a Staff to Line shift are: 1) Moving to a job with an easily determined bottom line or results. 2) Managing bigger scope and/or scale. 3) Requires new skills/perspectives. 4) Unfamiliar aspects of the assignment.

SECTION 6: LEARNING MORE FROM YOUR PLAN

THESE ADDITIONAL REMEDIES WILL HELP MAKE THIS DEVELOPMENT PLAN MORE EFFECTIVE FOR YOU

Learning to Learn Better

☐ **Monitoring Yourself More Closely and Getting off Your Autopilot**
Past habits are a mixed blessing, sometimes helping, sometimes not. To avoid putting yourself on "autopilot," think afresh about each situation before acting. Consistently monitor yourself with questions. Is this task different? Ask why you would repeat a past action. Are you avoiding anything, like taking a chance? Is there something new you might try?

☐ **Plan Backwards from the Ideal**
Envision what an ideal outcome would look like and plan backwards. What is the series of events that would have to take place to get there? What would people do? What would have to be done? How would people react? How would things play out? Could you plan it forward and get to the same outcome?

☐ **Envision Yourself Succeeding**
Examine the image of success in detail: what you are doing, what you are feeling, how you are reacting to others, how others are reacting to you, how the parts fit together. Can you then play that out in the real situation and get to the same outcome?

☐ **Look Beyond Your First Solution to a Problem**
Don't always take the first action you think of. Look further for a second and third. What's different? Might the second or third be more effective? Research shows that the best solution lies somewhere between the second and third strategies or approaches. Your first solution is often an "autopilot" response and may not be the best.

☐ **Examine How You Think and Solve Problems**
Try to outline how you've attacked or solved something. List the things you considered or rejected. How did your thinking flow? Did you use facts or opinions or both? Does it flow properly? Do a flow diagram of the process you followed. Were there any breakdowns? Could you have done it better?

☐ **Do More Pro and Con Analysis Before Deciding and Acting**
When facing a significant challenge, draw up multiple courses of action and list the pros and cons for each; do an analysis of each to see how it would play out. Pick one to try, and see if your predictions were correct.

☐ **Form An Advisory Group to Help You**
Assemble a one-time ad hoc group of people you respect and ask them for help solving or facing a significant issue. Outline what you know about it and ask the team to lay out a plan. Have them examine your thinking and suggest changes and improvements.

☐ **Sort Through Information Multiple Ways**
Collect the data and arrange it in elements or pieces. Come up with definitions, and arrange the data in various ways: chronologically, from most to least, from biggest to smallest, from cold to hot, what you know most about and least about, from known to unknown, etc., until the meaning becomes obvious.

Learning from Experience, Feedback and Other People

☐ **Feedback on What?**
Although any feedback is useful, it's best to seek and receive feedback on skills the organization feels are the most important for your present and future success. Not all skills are equal in importance. Some common skills may not have much bearing on success at all. If the organization has an official success profile, that may be the best way to focus your growth efforts.

Learning from Courses

☐ **Strategic Courses**
There are a number of courses designed to stretch minds to prepare for future challenges. They include topics such as Workforce Diversity 2000, globalization, the European Union, competitive competencies and strategies, etc. Quality depends upon the following three factors: 1) The quality of the staff. Are they qualified? Are they respected in their fields? Are they strategic "gurus"? 2) The quality of the participants. Are they the kind of people you could learn from? 3) The quality of the setting. Is it comfortable and free from distractions? Can you learn there?

SUGGESTED READINGS

Bernstein, Peter L. *Against the gods: the remarkable story of risk.* New York: John Wiley, 1996.

Churchill, Winston, Sir, edited and with an introduction by David Cannadine. *Blood, toil, tears, and sweat: the speeches of Winston Churchill.* Boston: Houghton Mifflin, 1989.

Dawson, Roger. *The Confident Decision Maker.* New York: William Morrow and Company, 1993.

Driver, Michael J., Philip Hunsaker, Kenneth R. Brousseau. *The Dynamic Decision Maker.* New York: Harper & Row, 1998.

Hale, Guy. *The Leader's Edge – Mastering the five skills of breakthrough thinking.* Burr Ridge, IL: Irwin Professional Publishing, 1996.

Hammond, John S., Ralph L. Keeney, Howard Raiffer. *Smart Choices.* Boston: Harvard University Press, 1999.

Heirs, Ben and Peter Farrell. *The Professional Decision Thinker.* New York: Dodd, Mead & Co. Inc., 1987.

Hodgson, Kent. *A Rock and a Hard Place – How to make ethical business decisions when the choices are tough.* New York: AMACOM, 1992

O'Dell, William F. *Effective Business Decision Making.* Lincolnwood, IL: NTC Business Books, 1991.

Strange, Joe with a chapter on Non-traditional military missions by Anthony C. Zinni. *Capital "W" war: a case for strategic principles of war: (because wars are conflicts of societies, not tactical exercises writ large).* Quantico, Va.: Marine Corps University, 1998.

18

DELEGATION

SECTION 1: YOUR DEVELOPMENT NEED(S)

UNSKILLED

- ☐ Doesn't believe in or trust delegation
- ☐ Lacks trust and respect in the talent of direct reports
- ☐ Does most things by him/herself or hoards, keeps the good stuff for him/herself
- ☐ Doesn't want or know how to empower others
- ☐ May delegate but micromanages and looks over shoulders
- ☐ Might delegate but not pass on the authority
- ☐ May lack a plan of how to work through others
- ☐ May just throw tasks at people; doesn't communicate the bigger picture

SKILLED

- ☐ Clearly and comfortably delegates both routine and important tasks and decisions
- ☐ Broadly shares both responsibility and accountability
- ☐ Tends to trust people to perform
- ☐ Lets direct reports finish their own work

OVERUSED SKILL

- ☐ May overdelegate without providing enough direction or help
- ☐ May have unrealistic expectations for direct reports, or may overstructure tasks and decisions before delegating them to the point of limiting individual initiative
- ☐ May not do enough of the work him/herself

Select one to three of the competencies listed below to work on to compensate for an overuse of this skill.

COMPENSATORS: 7, 19, 20, 21, 23, 33, 35, 36, 57, 60, 63, 64

SOME CAUSES

- ☐ Delegate but don't follow up
- ☐ Delegate by throwing tasks at people
- ☐ Delegate little pieces
- ☐ Don't develop your people
- ☐ Hoard most things to self
- ☐ Not plan work
- ☐ Not trust others
- ☐ Overmanage people
- ☐ Too busy
- ☐ Too controlling

THE MAP

Do you hoard tasks, keeping the good ones to yourself? Do you throw tasks at people without any overall plan or follow-up? Do you micro-manage because you don't trust people will perform? Unless you can do the work of the unit all by yourself, both performance and morale will suffer until you learn to delegate.

SECTION 2: LEARNING ON YOUR OWN

THESE SELF-DEVELOPMENT REMEDIES WILL HELP YOU BUILD YOUR SKILL(S)

SOME REMEDIES

☐ **1. Why delegate?** How busy are you? Can't get everything done you would like to get to? Boss on your butt for more? No time for reflection? No time to get to long range planning and strategy? Longer hours? Saturdays? Work at home? Family wondering if you still live there? Postpone vacations? If this sounds familiar, you join the majority of managers. Time is the most precious commodity. There is never enough. One of the main causes of this is that managers do too much themselves. The major fixes are better personal time management and organization, setting better priorities, designing better work flows and delegation. Delegation frees up time. Delegation motivates. Delegation develops people. Delegation gets more done. Learning to delegate is a major transition skill first line supervisors are supposed to learn when they leave the personal contributor role early in their careers. Read *Becoming a Manager* by Linda A. Hill for how that's supposed to work. We say "supposed to" because there are many high level executives who still have not learned to delegate. They generally get to everything tactical and let everything strategic go until last. They also don't have the time to develop others, leading to their reluctance to delegate because their people aren't good enough! No wonder. You cannot fulfill your potential until you learn to delegate more and better.

☐ **2. How to delegate?** Communicate, set timeframes and goals, and get out of the way. People need to know what it is you expect. What does the outcome look like? When do you need it by? What's the budget? What resources do they get? What decisions can they make? Do you want checkpoints along the way? How will we both know and measure how well the task is done? One of the most common problems with delegation is incomplete or cryptic up front communication leading to frustration, a job not well done the first time, rework, and a reluctance to delegate next time. Poor communicators always have to take more time managing because of rework. *More help? – See #27 Informing and #35 Managing and Measuring Work.*

☐ **3. More what and why, less how.** The best delegators are crystal clear on what and when, and more open on how. People are more motivated when they can determine the how for themselves.

Inexperienced delegators include the hows which turns the people into task automatons instead of empowered and energized staff. Tell them what and when and for how long and let them figure out how on their own. Give them leeway. Encourage them to try things. Besides being more motivating, it's also more developmental for them. Add the larger context. Although it is not necessary to get the task done, people are more motivated when they know where this task fits in the bigger picture. Take three extra minutes and tell them why this task needs to be done, where it fits in the grander scheme and its importance to the goals and objectives of the unit.

- ☐ **4. What to delegate?** Delegate as much as you can along with the authority to do it. Delegate more whole tasks than pieces and parts. People are more motivated by complete tasks. Delegate those things that others can do. Delegate those things that are not things you do well. Delegate tactical; keep strategic. Delegate short term; keep long term. One simple and effective way is to ask your people: "What do I do that you could help me with? What do I do that you could do with a little help from me? What do I do that you could do by yourself? What do you do that I could do faster and more effectively (re-delegation)?" You certainly won't agree to everything, but if you are now a poor delegator, they will help you improve by 50%. Pick one or a few things each time and let go.
- ☐ **5. Who to delegate to?** To those who can do it and those who can almost do it! The most common catch-22 we hear from managers is that they can't delegate because their people are not good enough; they can't do the work. We ask, why is that? They say, because they inherited a weak staff from the previous manager. We say, why don't you get rid of the worst and get better people? They say they can't fire anyone because HR and Legal won't let them. (We ask HR and Legal if that's the case. They generally say no, as long as it's done properly.) Or they say they can't afford to have a position open at this time because there is so much to do. We say, but if they are truly poor performers, what's the difference? You can't and shouldn't delegate to poor performers unless it's for their development and motivation. On the other hand, you'll never get out of your bind until you bite the bullet and start releasing the poorest and replacing them with better. Read Covey's (in *The Seven Habits of Successful People*) point on sharpening your saw. A person comes upon a lumberjack sawing a large tree with a hand saw. He is sweating and breathing hard. It's going very, very slowly. The person asks why it's going so poorly. The lumberjack says because his saw isn't sharp. The person asks why he doesn't stop and sharpen the saw. The lumberjack says because there is no time. If your saws (direct reports) aren't sharp enough, switch to more of a teacher role. What are the first things you would tell them to help think about their work more productively, and to think about tasks as you think about them? Always explain your thinking. The role of a coach/teacher

is to teach someone how to think/act as you do. Giving them solutions will make the person dependent at best. You may have to bubble your thinking to the surface first. To do this, work out loud with them on a task. What do you see as important? How do you know? What mental questions are you asking? What steps are you following? Why is this solution better than others? *More help? – See #13 Confronting Direct Reports and #25 Hiring and Staffing.*

- ☐ **6. Delegate for how long?** Allow more time than it would take you. Another common problem is that managers delegate and set time limits based upon their own capabilities and history. For many things, it is probably true that the manager could do the task faster and better. Remember when you started to learn how to do this task. How long did it take you? How did you feel about someone looking over your shoulder? Always allow more time in the schedule than it would take you to do it. Get the person to whom you are delegating to help you set a realistic time schedule. When you are going to delegate, start earlier in the project than you do now. *More help? – See #47 Planning.*

- ☐ **7. Mixing and matching.** All of your people have differing skills and capacities. Good delegators match the size and complexity of the delegated task with the capacity of each person. Delegation is not an equal, one size fits all, activity. Equal opportunity delegators are not as successful as equitable delegators. Most people prefer stretching tasks to those they could do in their sleep; so it's OK to give each person a task slightly bigger than his/her current capabilities might dictate. Engage each person in the sizing task. Ask them. Most will select wisely. *More help? – See #56 Sizing Up People.*

- ☐ **8. Monitoring delegated tasks.** Do you micromanage? If you're constantly looking over shoulders, you're not delegating. A properly communicated and delegated task doesn't need to be monitored. If you must monitor, set time-definite checkpoints by the calendar; every Monday, by percentage, after each 10% is complete or by outcome, such as when you have the first draft. Be approachable for help, but not intrusive. Intervene only when agreed upon criteria are not being followed, or expectations are not being met. This focuses on the task, not the person. Let people finish their work.

- ☐ **9. Delegation as development.** People grow by being assigned stretching complete tasks that contain elements they have not done before. Seventy per cent of development in successful managers comes from doing stretch tasks and jobs. One bind of the poor delegator – my people aren't good enough – won't be solved until they are good enough. Doing most of the work yourself is a poor long-term development strategy and will never solve the problem.

☐ **10. Why aren't you delegating?** Are you hanging on to too much? Are you a perfectionist, wanting everything to be just so? Do you have unrealistic expectations of others? Someone made you leader because you are probably better at doing what the team does than some or most of the members. Do you feel guilty handing out tough work to do? Do you keep it yourself because you feel bad about giving them too much work? They would have to stay late or work on weekends to get it done. Most people enjoy being busy and on the move. If you think the workload is too much, ask. *More help? – See #36 Motivating Others*. Don't want to take the risk? If they don't perform, it will reflect on you? Poor delegation reflects on you, too. Are you really a personal contributor dressed in supervisor's clothes? Really prefer doing it yourself? People just get in the way? You need to examine whether management is the right career path for you. *More help? – See #6 Career Ambition.*

SECTION 3: LEARNING FROM MORE FEEDBACK

THESE SOURCES WOULD GIVE YOU THE MOST ACCURATE AND DETAILED FEEDBACK ON YOUR SKILL(S)

☐ **Direct Boss**
Your direct boss has important information about you, your performance, and your prospects. The challenge is to get this information. There are formal processes (e.g., performance appraisals). There are day-to-day opportunities. To help, signal your boss that you want and can handle direct and timely feedback. Many bosses have trouble giving feedback, so you will have to work at it over a period of time.

☐ **Direct Reports**
Across a variety of settings, your direct reports probably see you the most. They are the recipients of most of your managerial behaviors. They know your work. They can compare you with former bosses. Since they may hesitate to give you negative feedback, you have to set the atmosphere to make it easier for them. You have to ask.

☐ **Past Associates/Constituencies**
When confronted with a present performance problem, some claim, "I wasn't like that before; it must be the current situation." When feedback is available from former associates, about 50% support that claim. In the other half of the cases, the people were like that before and probably didn't know it. It sometimes makes sense to access the past to clearly see the present.

☐ **Peers and Colleagues**
Peers and colleagues have a special social and working relationship. They attend staff meetings together, share private views, get feedback from the same boss, travel together, and are knowledgeable about each other's work. You perhaps let your guard down more around peers and act more like yourself. They can be a valuable source of feedback.

SECTION 4: LEARNING FROM DEVELOP-IN-PLACE ASSIGNMENTS

THESE PART-TIME DEVELOP-IN-PLACE ASSIGNMENTS WILL HELP YOU BUILD YOUR SKILL(S)

- ☐ Manage something "remote," away from your location.
- ☐ Create employee involvement teams.
- ☐ Assign a project to a group with a tight deadline.
- ☐ Manage an ad hoc, temporary group of "green," inexperienced people as their coach, teacher, orienter, etc.
- ☐ Manage an ad hoc, temporary group of balky and resisting people through an unpopular change or project.
- ☐ Manage an ad hoc, temporary group of low-competence people through a task they couldn't do by themselves.
- ☐ Manage an ad hoc, temporary group including former peers to accomplish a task.
- ☐ Manage an ad hoc, temporary group of people who are older and/or more experienced to accomplish a task.
- ☐ Manage an ad hoc, temporary group of people where the temporary manager is a towering expert and the people in the group are not.
- ☐ Build a multifunctional project team to tackle a common business issue or problem.

SECTION 5: LEARNING FROM FULL-TIME JOBS

THESE FULL-TIME JOBS OFFER THE OPPORTUNITY TO BUILD YOUR SKILL(S)

- ☐ **Fix-its / Turnarounds**

  The core demands to qualify as a Fix-it or Turnaround assignment are: 1) Cleaning up a mess. 2) Serious people issues/problems like credibility/performance/morale. 3) Tight deadline. 4) Serious business performance failure. 5) Last chance to fix. Four Types of Fix-its/ Turnarounds: 1) Fixing a failed business/unit involving taking control, stopping losses, managing damage, planning the turnaround, dealing with people problems, installing new processes and systems, and rebuilding the spirit and performance of the unit. 2) Managing sizable disasters like mishandled labor negotiations and strikes, thefts, history of significant business losses, poor staff, failed leadership, hidden problems, fraud, public relations nightmares, etc. 3) Significant reorganization and restructuring (e.g., stabilizing the business, reforming unit, introducing new systems, making people changes, resetting strategy and tactics). 4) Significant system/process breakdown (e.g., MIS, financial coordination processes, audits, standards, etc.) across units requiring working to change something from a distant position, providing advice and counsel, and installing or implementing a major process improvement or system change outside your own unit and/or with customers outside the organization.

- ☐ **Scale Assignments**
  Core requirements to qualify as a Scale (size) shift assignment are: 1) Sizable jump-shift in the size of the job in areas like: number of people, number of layers in organization, size of budget, number of locations, volume of activity, tightness of deadlines. 2) Medium to low complexity; mostly repetitive and routine processes and procedures. 3) Stable staff and business. 4) Stable operations. 5) Often slow, steady growth.

- ☐ **Significant People Demands**
  Core demands required to qualify as a Significant People Responsibilities assignment are: 1) A sizable increase in either the number of people managed and/or the complexity of the challenges involved 2) Longer-term assignment (two or more years). 3) Quality of people management critical to achieving results. 4) Involves groups not worked with before (e.g., union, new technical areas, nationalities).

- ☐ **Start-ups**
  The core demands to qualify as a start from scratch are: 1) Starting something new for you and/or for the organization. 2) Forging a new team. 3) Creating new systems/facilities/staffs/programs/procedures. 4) Contextual adversity (e.g., uncertainty, government regulation, unions, difficult environment). Seven types of start from scratches: 1) Planning, building, hiring, and managing (e.g., building a new facility, opening up a new location, moving a unit or company). 2) Heading something new (e.g., new product, new service, new line of business, new department/function, major new program). 3) Take over a group/product/service/program that had existed for less than a year and was off to a fast start. 4) Establishing overseas operations. 5) Major new designs for existing systems. 6) Moving a successful program from one unit to another. 7) Installing a new organization-wide process as a full-time job (e.g., like Total Quality).

SECTION 6: LEARNING MORE FROM YOUR PLAN

THESE ADDITIONAL REMEDIES WILL HELP MAKE THIS DEVELOPMENT PLAN MORE EFFECTIVE FOR YOU

Learning to Learn Better

- ☐ **Study Yourself in Detail**
  Study your likes and dislikes because they can drive a lot of your thinking, judging, and acting. Ask which like or dislike has gotten in the way or prevented you from moving to a higher level of learning. Are your likes and dislikes really important to you or have you just gone on "autopilot"? Try to address and understand a blocking dislike and change it.

Learning from Experience, Feedback and Other People

- [ ] **Being a Student of Others**
While many of us rely on others for information or advice, we do not really study the behavior of other people. Ask what a person does exceptionally well or poorly. What behaviors are particularly effective and ineffective for them? What works for them and what doesn't? As a student of others, you can deduce the rules of thumb for effective and ineffective behavior and include those in your own library. In comparing yourself with this person, in what areas could you most improve? What could you specifically do to improve in ways comfortable for you?

- [ ] **Learning from Bosses**
Bosses can be an excellent and ready source for learning. All bosses do some things exceptionally well and other things poorly. Distance your feelings from the boss/direct report relationship and study things that work and things that don't work for your boss. What would you have done? What could you use, and what should you avoid?

- [ ] **Learning from Interviewing Others**
Interview others. Ask not only what they do, but how and why they do it. What do they think are the rules of thumb they are following? Where did they learn the behaviors? How do they keep them current? How do they monitor the effect they have on others?

- [ ] **Learning from Remote Models**
Many times you can learn from people not directly available to you. You can read a book about them, watch tapes of public figures, read analyses of them, etc. The principles of learning are the same. Ask yourself what they do well or poorly and deduce their rules of thumb.

- [ ] **Consolidating What You Learn from People**
After using any source and/or method of learning from others, write down or mentally note the new rules of thumb and the principles involved. How will you remind yourself of the new behaviors in similar situations? How will you prevent yourself from reacting on "autopilot"? How could you share what you have learned from others?

- [ ] **Getting Feedback from Direct Reports**
Direct reports often fear reprisals for giving negative feedback about bosses, whether in a formal process, like a questionnaire, or informally and face-to-face. Even with a guarantee of confidentiality, some are still hesitant. If you want feedback from direct reports, you have to set a positive tone and never act out of revenge.

- [ ] **Openness to Feedback**
Nothing discourages feedback more than defensiveness, resistance, irritation, and excuses. People don't like giving feedback anyway, and much less to those who don't listen or are unreceptive. To help the feedback giver, be open, listen, ask for examples and details, take notes, keep a journal, and thank them for their interest.

☐ **Learning from Limited Staff**
Most managers either inherit or hire staff from time to time who are inexperienced, incompetent, not up to the task, resistant, or dispirited. Any of these may create a hardship for you. The lessons to be learned are how to get things done with limited resources and how to fix the people situation. In the short term, this hardship is best addressed by assessing the combined strengths of the team and deploying the best you have against the problem. Almost everyone can do something well. Also, the team can contribute more than the combined individuals can. How can you empower and motivate the team? If you hired the troublesome staff, why did you err? What can you learn from your hiring mistakes? What wasn't there that you thought was present? What led you astray? How can you prevent that same hiring error in the future? What do you need to do to fix the situation? Quick development? Start over? If you inherited the problem, how can you fix it? Can you implement a program of accelerated development? Do you have to start over and get new people? What did the prior manager do or not do that led to this situation in the first place? What can you learn from that? What will you do differently? How does the staff feel? What can you learn from their frustrations over not being able to do the job? How can you be a positive force under negative circumstances? How can you rally them to perform? What lasting lessons can you learn from someone in distress and trouble? If you're going to try accelerated development, how can you get a quick assessment? How can you give the staff motivating feedback? How can you construct and implement development plans that will work? How can you get people on-line feedback for maximum growth? Do you know when to stop trying and start over? If you're going to turn over some staff, how can you do it both rapidly and with the least damage? How can you deliver the message in a constructive way? What can you learn from having to take negative actions against people? How can you prevent this from happening again?

Learning from Courses

☐ **Supervisory Courses**
Most new supervisors go through an "Introduction to Supervision" type course. They are designed to teach the common practices a first-line supervisor needs to know to be effective. The content of most of those courses is standard. There is general agreement on the principles of effective supervision. There are two common problems: 1) Do the students have a strong motivation to learn? Do they know what they don't know? Is there any pain? Because motivated students with a need for the knowledge learn best, participants should have had some trying experiences and some supervisory pain and hardships before attending. 2) Are the instructors experienced supervisors? Have they practiced what they preach? Can they share powerful anecdotes to

make key points? Can they answer questions credibly? If possible, select supervisory courses based on the instructors, since the content seems to be the much same for all such courses. Lastly, does the course offer the opportunity for practicing each skill? Does it contain simulations? Are there case studies you could easily identify with? Are there breakout groups? Is there opportunity for action learning? Search for the most interactive course.

SUGGESTED READINGS

Covey, Stephen R. *The seven habits of highly effective people.* New York: Simon and Schuster, 1989.

Covey, Stephen R. *The seven habits of highly effective people [sound recording].* Provo, UT: Covey Leadership Center, 1997.

Ginnodo, Bill. *The Power of Empowerment.* Arlington Heights, IL: Pride Publications, Inc., 1997.

Huppe, Frank T. *Successful Delegation: How to grow your people, build your team, free up your time and increase profits and productivity.* Hawthorne, N.J.: Career Press, 1994.

Nelson, Robert B. *Delegation.* Glenview, IL: ScottForesman and Co., 1988.

Nelson, Robert B. *Empowering Employees through Delegation.* Burr Ridge, IL: Irwin Professional Publishing, 1994.

19

DEVELOPING DIRECT REPORTS

SECTION 1: YOUR DEVELOPMENT NEED(S)

UNSKILLED

- ☐ Not a people developer or builder
- ☐ Very results driven and tactical; no time for long-term development
- ☐ Doesn't see long-term development as his/her job
- ☐ Plays it safe – can't bring him/herself to assign really stretching (risky) work
- ☐ Thinks development is going to a course – doesn't know how development really happens
- ☐ May not know the aspirations of direct reports, may not hold career discussions, may not push people to take their development seriously
- ☐ May prefer to select for talent rather than develop it

SKILLED

- ☐ Provides challenging and stretching tasks and assignments
- ☐ Holds frequent development discussions
- ☐ Is aware of each direct report's career goals
- ☐ Constructs compelling development plans and executes them
- ☐ Pushes direct reports to accept developmental moves
- ☐ Will take direct reports who need work
- ☐ Is a people builder

OVERUSED SKILL

- ☐ May concentrate on the development of a few direct reports at the expense of the team
- ☐ May create work inequities as challenging assignments are parceled out
- ☐ May be overly optimistic about how far direct reports can grow

Select one to three of the competencies listed below to work on to compensate for an overuse of this skill.

COMPENSATORS: 7, 12, 18, 20, 21, 23, 25, 35, 36, 47, 54, 56

SOME CAUSES

- ☐ Don't believe people really develop
- ☐ Don't get paid to develop others
- ☐ Don't have the time for it
- ☐ Don't know how to develop people
- ☐ Think it's someone else's responsibility

THE MAP

Most people want to grow and develop. Most people have aspirations to do well and be rewarded with more pay and higher positions. Most people have dreams and goals they want to achieve. Development and preparation for positions with greater responsibility is a three-part harmony. The person needs to be ambitious and willing to do what's required to grow and progress. The organization has to have a process in place to help those who want to grow. Those two are usually true in all organizations. The last part of the harmony is usually the problem: the boss has to be an active player in the three-part harmony or development won't happen. Without the boss's time, interest and effort, people will not grow much. People can't develop themselves without help. People won't grow if they don't want to. People won't grow if the organization shows no interest and offers no support. People won't grow if you don't make it a priority.

SECTION 2: LEARNING ON YOUR OWN

THESE SELF-DEVELOPMENT REMEDIES WILL HELP YOU BUILD YOUR SKILL(S)

SOME REMEDIES

☐ **1. You have to invest some time.** For most managers, time is what they have the least of to give. For the purposes of developing others beyond today's job, you need to allocate about eight hours per year per direct report. If you have a normal span of seven direct reports, that's 7 of 220 working days or 3% of your annual time. Two of the eight hours are for an annual in-depth appraisal of the person in terms of current strengths and weaknesses and of the competencies he/she needs to develop to move on to the next step. Two of the eight hours are for an in-depth career discussion with each person. What does he/she want? What will he/she sacrifice to get there? What is his/her own appraisal of his/her skills? Two of the eight hours are for creating a three to five year development plan and sharing it with the person. The last two hours is to present your findings and recommendations to the organization, usually in a succession planning process, and arranging for developmental events for each person.

☐ **2. Appraisal.** You can't help anyone develop if you can't or aren't willing to fairly and accurately appraise people. Sound appraisal starts with the best picture of current strengths and weaknesses. Then you need to know what competencies are going to be necessary going forward. You can find this out by looking at a success profile for the next possible job or two of the person. If there are no formal success profiles, you can ask the Human Resources group for assistance or ask someone you know and trust currently in that next job what he/she use to be successful. *More help? – See #25 Hiring and Staffing and #56 Sizing Up People.*

☐ **3. Feedback.** People need continuous feedback from you and others to grow. Some tips about feedback:

- Arrange for them to get feedback from multiple people, including yourself, on what matters for success in their future jobs; arrange for your direct reports to get 360° feedback about every two years.
- Give them progressively stretching tasks that are first-time and different for them so that they can give themselves feedback as they go.
- If they have direct reports and peers, another technique to recommend is to ask their associates for comments on what they should stop doing, start doing, and keep doing to be more successful.
- You have to be willing to be straight with your people and give them accurate but balanced feedback. They need to know the negatives as soon as possible. *More help? – See #13 Confronting Direct Reports.*
- Set up a buddy system so people can get continuing feedback.

☐ **4. Development planning.** You need to put together a development plan that, if followed, actually would work. At least 70% of reported skill development comes from having challenging, uncomfortable tasks/assignments. Development means that you do the new skill or fail at something important to you. Tasks that develop anything are those in which not doing it is not a viable option. Another 20% comes from studying and working with others to see useful behavior and get feedback. This can take the form of studying a role model, working with a developmental partner, keeping a written summary of what's working and not working or preferably a formal assessment, like a 360° process. Without this continuous feedback, even the best developmental plans fail. About 10% of development comes from thinking differently or having new ways to think about things. Typically these come from coursework, books or mentors; the lion's share is learning from tough tasks, and the learning from other people that comes from feedback. A good plan would have 70% job and task content; 20% people to study, listen to, and work with; and 10% courses and readings.

☐ **5. Equal Opportunity.** If some of your people have limited or disadvantaged backgrounds, it is unrealistic to expect the same developmental procedures will work for them. According to research conducted by the Center for Creative Leadership (see *The New Leaders* by Ann Morrison), people from diverse backgrounds usually need additional support in the form of mentoring, information on how things work around here, greater access to formal organizational information, a critical mass of support from top management, and accountability/enforcement to make developing diversity a reality rather than a statistic. You may also be able to intern/apprentice those with limited backgrounds to begin to provide appropriate job experiences or provide necessary training. *More help? – See #21* Managing *Diversity.*

- ☐ **6. Delegate for development.** You can use parts of your own job to develop others. Take three tasks that are no longer developmental for you, but would be for others, and delegate them. Trade tasks and assignments between two direct reports; have them do each other's work. Make a list of the 20 tasks that need to be done but no one has gotten around to and assign them to the people who would be challenged by them. Think of varied assignments – more of the same isn't developmental.

- ☐ **7. Remember, meaningful development is not the stress reduction business.** It is not cozy or safe; it comes from varied, stressful, even adverse tasks that require we learn to do something new or different or fail. Real development involves real work the person largely hasn't done before. Real development is rewarding but scary.

- ☐ **8. Help them learn.** Have a learning dialogue with your people. Ask them what they have learned to increase their skills and understanding, making them better managers or professionals. Ask them what they can do now that they couldn't do a year ago. Reinforce this and encourage more of it. Developing is learning in as many ways as possible.

- ☐ **9. Selling development.** Part of developing others is convincing people that tough, new, challenging and different assignments are good for them. In follow up studies of successful executives, more than 90% report that a boss in their past nearly forced them to take a scary job assignment they wanted to turn down. That assignment turned out to be the most developmental for them. The peculiar thing about long-term development is that even ambitious people turn down the very assignments they need to grow. They do not have the perspective to understand that. Your job is to help convince people on the way up to get out of their comfort zone and accept jobs they don't initially see as useful or leading anywhere.

- ☐ **10. Build perspective.** Give the people under you who have the potential for bigger and better things assignments that take them outside your function, unit or business. Help them expand their perspectives. Volunteer them for cross boundary task forces. Have them attend meetings that include people from other areas. Open up the world for them so that they can better judge for themselves what's out there and what part of it they want.

SECTION 3: LEARNING FROM MORE FEEDBACK

THESE SOURCES WOULD GIVE YOU THE MOST ACCURATE AND DETAILED FEEDBACK ON YOUR SKILL(S)

☐ **Direct Boss**
Your direct boss has important information about you, your performance, and your prospects. The challenge is to get this information. There are formal processes (e.g., performance appraisals). There are day-to-day opportunities. To help, signal your boss that you want and can handle direct and timely feedback. Many bosses have trouble giving feedback, so you will have to work at it over a period of time.

☐ **Direct Reports**
Across a variety of settings, your direct reports probably see you the most. They are the recipients of most of your managerial behaviors. They know your work. They can compare you with former bosses. Since they may hesitate to give you negative feedback, you have to set the atmosphere to make it easier for them. You have to ask.

☐ **Human Resource Professionals**
Human Resource professionals have both a formal and informal feedback role. Since they have access to unique and confidential information, they can provide the right context for feedback you've received. Sometimes they may be "directed" to give you feedback. Other times, they may pass on feedback just to be helpful to you.

☐ **Past Associates/Constituencies**
When confronted with a present performance problem, some claim, "I wasn't like that before; it must be the current situation." When feedback is available from former associates, about 50% support that claim. In the other half of the cases, the people were like that before and probably didn't know it. It sometimes makes sense to access the past to clearly see the present.

SECTION 4: LEARNING FROM DEVELOP-IN-PLACE ASSIGNMENTS

THESE PART-TIME DEVELOP-IN-PLACE ASSIGNMENTS WILL HELP YOU BUILD YOUR SKILL(S)

☐ Manage an ad hoc, temporary group of "green," inexperienced people as their coach, teacher, orienter, etc.

☐ Manage an ad hoc, temporary group of low-competence people through a task they couldn't do by themselves.

☐ Manage an ad hoc, temporary group of people where the temporary manager is a towering expert and the people in the group are not.

☐ Assign a project to a group with a tight deadline.

☐ Manage an ad hoc, temporary group of balky and resisting people through an unpopular change or project.

- ☐ Manage an ad hoc, temporary group including former peers to accomplish a task.
- ☐ Manage an ad hoc, temporary group of people who are older and/or more experienced to accomplish a task.
- ☐ Manage an ad hoc, temporary group of people involved in tackling a fix-it or turnaround project.
- ☐ Manage an ad hoc, temporary group of people in a rapidly expanding operation.
- ☐ Assemble an ad hoc team of diverse people to accomplish a difficult task.

SECTION 5: LEARNING FROM FULL-TIME JOBS

THESE FULL-TIME JOBS OFFER THE OPPORTUNITY TO BUILD YOUR SKILL(S)

- ☐ **Scale Assignments**
  Core requirements to qualify as a Scale (size) shift assignment are: 1) Sizable jump-shift in the size of the job in areas like: number of people, number of layers in organization, size of budget, number of locations, volume of activity, tightness of deadlines. 2) Medium to low complexity; mostly repetitive and routine processes and procedures. 3) Stable staff and business. 4) Stable operations. 5) Often slow, steady growth.
- ☐ **Significant People Demands**
  Core demands required to qualify as a Significant People Responsibilities assignment are: 1) A sizable increase in either the number of people managed and/or the complexity of the challenges involved 2) Longer-term assignment (two or more years). 3) Quality of people management critical to achieving results. 4) Involves groups not worked with before (e.g., union, new technical areas, nationalities).
- ☐ **Staff to Line Shifts**
  Core demands necessary to qualify for a Staff to Line shift are: 1) Moving to a job with an easily determined bottom line or results. 2) Managing bigger scope and/or scale. 3) Requires new skills/perspectives. 4) Unfamiliar aspects of the assignment.

SECTION 6: LEARNING MORE FROM YOUR PLAN

THESE ADDITIONAL REMEDIES WILL HELP MAKE THIS DEVELOPMENT PLAN MORE EFFECTIVE FOR YOU

Learning to Learn Better

- ☐ **Teach Others Something You Know Well**
  Teach someone to do something you know how to do to check out your own thinking, knowledge, and rules. Watch in detail how others learn; the process will require breaking down your patterns into teachable steps.

- ☐ **Use Objective Data When Judging Others**
  Practice studying other people more than judging or evaluating them. Get the facts, the data, how they think, why they do things, without classifying them into your internal like/dislike or agree/disagree boxes, categories, or buckets. Try to project or predict how they would act/react in various situations and follow up to see how accurate you are.

- ☐ **Examine Why You Judge People the Way You Do**
  List the people you like and those you dislike and try to find out why. What do those you like have in common with each other and with you? What do those you dislike have in common with themselves and how do they differ from you? Are your "people buckets" logical and productive or do they interfere? Could you be more effective without putting people into buckets?

- ☐ **Become a Student of How People Learn**
  Become a student of learning: read some books and articles on child and adult learning; read about how the brain and mind work; study diverse learners of the past for insights; study the teaching techniques of expert teachers and coaches; attend a course on instructional design. Write and deliver a presentation on your findings.

Learning from Experience, Feedback and Other People

- ☐ **Using Multiple Models**
  Who do you know who exemplifies how to do whatever your need is? Who, for example, personifies decisiveness or compassion or strategic agility? Think more broadly than your current job and colleagues. For example, clergy, friends, spouses or community leaders are also good sources for potential models. Select your models not on the basis of overall excellence or likability, but on the basis of the one towering strength (or glaring weakness) you are interested in. Even people who are well thought of usually have only one or two towering strengths (or glaring weaknesses). Ordinarily, you won't learn as much from the whole person as you will from one characteristic.

☐ **Learning from Observing Others**
Observe others. Find opportunities to observe without interacting with your model. This enables you to objectively study the person, note what he/she is doing or not doing, and compare that with what you would typically do in similar situations. Many times you can learn more by watching than asking. Your model may not be able to explain what he/she does or may be an unwilling teacher.

☐ **Giving Feedback to Others**
Most managers complain they don't get enough useful feedback. Ironically, their direct reports and peers offer the same complaint! Getting serious about feedback for yourself involves giving more feedback to those around you. As you practice giving more feedback to others, you will receive more by the example you set and will become more sensitive and receptive to your own.

☐ **Learning from Limited Staff**
Most managers either inherit or hire staff from time to time who are inexperienced, incompetent, not up to the task, resistant, or dispirited. Any of these may create a hardship for you. The lessons to be learned are how to get things done with limited resources and how to fix the people situation. In the short term, this hardship is best addressed by assessing the combined strengths of the team and deploying the best you have against the problem. Almost everyone can do something well. Also, the team can contribute more than the combined individuals can. How can you empower and motivate the team? If you hired the troublesome staff, why did you err? What can you learn from your hiring mistakes? What wasn't there that you thought was present? What led you astray? How can you prevent that same hiring error in the future? What do you need to do to fix the situation? Quick development? Start over? If you inherited the problem, how can you fix it? Can you implement a program of accelerated development? Do you have to start over and get new people? What did the prior manager do or not do that led to this situation in the first place? What can you learn from that? What will you do differently? How does the staff feel? What can you learn from their frustrations over not being able to do the job? How can you be a positive force under negative circumstances? How can you rally them to perform? What lasting lessons can you learn from someone in distress and trouble? If you're going to try accelerated development, how can you get a quick assessment? How can you give the staff motivating feedback? How can you construct and implement development plans that will work? How can you get people on-line feedback for maximum growth? Do you know when to stop trying and start over? If you're going to turn over some staff, how can you do it both rapidly and with the least damage? How can you deliver the message in a constructive way? What can you learn from having to take negative actions against people? How can you prevent this from happening again?

Learning from Courses

- ☐ **Supervisory Courses**
  Most new supervisors go through an "Introduction to Supervision" type course. They are designed to teach the common practices a first-line supervisor needs to know to be effective. The content of most of those courses is standard. There is general agreement on the principles of effective supervision. There are two common problems: 1) Do the students have a strong motivation to learn? Do they know what they don't know? Is there any pain? Because motivated students with a need for the knowledge learn best, participants should have had some trying experiences and some supervisory pain and hardships before attending. 2) Are the instructors experienced supervisors? Have they practiced what they preach? Can they share powerful anecdotes to make key points? Can they answer questions credibly? If possible, select supervisory courses based on the instructors, since the content seems to be the much same for all such courses. Lastly, does the course offer the opportunity for practicing each skill? Does it contain simulations? Are there case studies you could easily identify with? Are there breakout groups? Is there opportunity for action learning? Search for the most interactive course.

- ☐ **Sending Others to Courses**
  If you are responsible for managing someone else's development and, as part of that, sending them to courses, prepare them beforehand. Don't send them as tourists. Meet with them before and after the course. Tell them why they need this course. Tell them what you expect them to learn. Give them feedback on why you think they need the course. Agree ahead of time how you will measure and monitor learning after they return. If possible, offer a variety of courses for your employee to choose from. Have them give you a report shortly after they return. If appropriate, have them present what they learned to the rest of your staff. After they return, provide opportunities for using the new skills with safe cover and low risk. Give them practice time before expecting full exercise of the new skills. Be supportive during early unsteadiness. Give continuous feedback on progress.

SUGGESTED READINGS

Albright, Mary and Clay Carr. *101 biggest mistakes managers make and how to avoid them.* Paramus, N.J.: Prentice Hall, 1997.

Belker, Loren B. *The first-time manager.* New York: AMACOM, 1997.

Bell, Chip R. *Managers as Mentors – Building Partnerships for Learning.* San Francisco: Berrett-Koehler Publishers, Inc., 1996.

Carr, Clay. *The new manager's survival manual.* New York: John Wiley & Sons, Inc., 1995.

Deal, Terrence E. and William A. Jenkins. *Managing the Hidden Organization.* New York: Warner Books, 1994.

Fuller, George. *The first-time supervisor's survival guide.* Englewood Cliffs, NJ: Prentice Hall, 1995.

Gilley, Jerry W. and Nathaniel W. Boughton. *Stop Managing, Start Coaching.* Burr Ridge, IL: Irwin Professional Publishing, 1996.

Hendricks, William [et al.]. *Coaching, mentoring, and managing.* Franklin Lakes, NJ: Career Press, 1996.

Johnson, Harold E. *Mentoring for exceptional performance.* Glendale, CA: Griffin Pub., 1997.

Matejka, Ken. *Why this horse won't drink.* New York: AMACOM, 1991.

Potts, Tom and Arnold Sykes. *Executive Talent – Develop your best people.* Homewood, IL: Business One Irwin, 1993.

Stone, Florence M. *Coaching, Counseling and Mentoring.* New York: AMACOM, 1999.

DIRECTING OTHERS

SECTION 1: YOUR DEVELOPMENT NEED(S)

UNSKILLED

- ☐ Unclear or cryptic communicator to direct reports
- ☐ Doesn't set goals, targets, mileposts and objectives
- ☐ Not very planful giving out work – just gives out tasks
- ☐ Mostly tells and sells; doesn't listen much
- ☐ Plays favorites and is tough on others
- ☐ May be too impatient to structure work for others
- ☐ Doesn't delegate well
- ☐ Doesn't take the time to manage
- ☐ May lack interest in managing and be more eager to work on own assignments

SKILLED

- ☐ Is good at establishing clear directions
- ☐ Sets stretching objectives
- ☐ Distributes the workload appropriately
- ☐ Lays out work in a well-planned and organized manner
- ☐ Maintains two-way dialogue with others on work and results
- ☐ Brings out the best in people
- ☐ Is a clear communicator

OVERUSED SKILL

- ☐ May be overly controlling
- ☐ May have a chilling effect on others, discouraging input and ideas, intolerant of disagreements
- ☐ May only delegate pieces and not share the larger picture
- ☐ May be overly directive and stifle creativity and initiative

Select one to three of the competencies listed below to work on to compensate for an overuse of this skill.

COMPENSATORS: 3, 7, 14, 18, 19, 21, 23, 28, 31, 33, 35, 36, 60, 64

SOME CAUSES

- ☐ Impatient
- ☐ Inappropriate style or temperament
- ☐ Inexperienced; unskilled in managing
- ☐ Lack of interest in managing
- ☐ Major change in direction and mission
- ☐ New members on the team
- ☐ Time management, too busy to manage

THE MAP

Managing others effectively and efficiently is a known technology. There are a number of research and experience verified techniques and practices that lead to groups performing well under a particular manager. There are also some personal styles and temperaments that work better than others.

SECTION 2: LEARNING ON YOUR OWN

THESE SELF-DEVELOPMENT REMEDIES WILL HELP YOU BUILD YOUR SKILL(S)

SOME REMEDIES

☐ **1. Do an inventory of your personal strengths and weaknesses.** Get some input from others. Ask your people what they appreciate about you as a person and as a manager and what they would prefer you change. What do you do well and what don't you do well personally and as a manager of others? Ask for help from the Human Resources function to get a list of the competencies most often related to managing others well. End up with a list of the good news and the bad news. Devise a development plan for the important things on your bad list. *More help? – See #55 Self-Knowledge.*

☐ **2. Do an inventory** of the common management techniques and practices you do well and those that you do not do so well or often enough. You can get a list of those techniques from any introductory text on management, from a course for first time managers, or from the Human Resource function. Ask your people for input on those you do well and those you need to work on. Create a management practices skill building plan for yourself.

☐ **3. Do a communication check on yourself.** Many times the breakdown in effectively managing others is related to poor, inadequate or inconsistent communication. How well do you inform? Listen? Explain? Get back to people? Give feedback? *More help? – See #27 Informing, #33 Listening, #49 Presentation Skills, and #67 Written Communications.*

☐ **4. Do you delegate enough?** Another common breakdown is in not delegating nor empowering. Do you give the people under you the authority to do their work? Do you over or under manage? Periodically, ask your people to give you a list of the things they think you are doing yourself that they believe they could do a good job on; delegate some of the things on everybody's list. *More help? – See #18 Delegation.*

☐ **5. Does your style chill or turn off others?** Common styles that don't work well with others are impatience, devaluing others, public criticism, playing favorites, prejudice toward a class of people, disorganized, emotional, etc. Are you a poor time manager? Is there enough time left over to spend with your people? Are you any of those things? If yes, try to work on being less of that. *More help? – See #11*

Composure, #21 Managing *Diversity, #23 Fairness to Direct Reports, and #41 Patience.*

- ☐ **6. Are you organized and planful?** Can people follow what you want? Do you lay out work and tasks to be done clearly? Do you set clear goals and objectives that can guide their work? *More help? – See #35 Managing and Measuring Work and #47 Planning.*

- ☐ **7. Do you share the credit?** Do you use "we" more often than "I"? Do you celebrate successes with others? Do people want to work with you again? *More help? – See #36 Motivating Others.*

- ☐ **8. Do you confront problems directly and quickly** or do you let things fester? The rest of the team suffers when a manager doesn't step up to problems quickly. *More help? – See #13 Confronting Direct Reports, #34 Managerial Courage, and #57 Standing Alone.*

- ☐ **9. Rather go it alone?** Are you interested in getting work done through others or would you rather do it all yourself? Maybe management isn't for you. Maybe you would be better off being a senior personal contributor. Maybe you don't really care to relate to people very deeply. *More help? – See #7 Caring About Direct Reports, #10 Compassion, and #23 Fairness to Direct Reports.*

- ☐ **10. Study models.** Seek out one or two people around you who others consider to be good managers. Study them. What do they do that you don't? What do you do that they don't? Or, put your last 10 managers on a piece of paper. Create two lists – the five best and the five worst. What characteristics do the best share? The worst? How does that compare to you?

SECTION 3: LEARNING FROM MORE FEEDBACK

THESE SOURCES WOULD GIVE YOU THE MOST ACCURATE AND DETAILED FEEDBACK ON YOUR SKILL(S)

☐ **Direct Boss**

Your direct boss has important information about you, your performance, and your prospects. The challenge is to get this information. There are formal processes (e.g., performance appraisals). There are day-to-day opportunities. To help, signal your boss that you want and can handle direct and timely feedback. Many bosses have trouble giving feedback, so you will have to work at it over a period of time.

☐ **Direct Reports**

Across a variety of settings, your direct reports probably see you the most. They are the recipients of most of your managerial behaviors. They know your work. They can compare you with former bosses. Since they may hesitate to give you negative feedback, you have to set the atmosphere to make it easier for them. You have to ask.

- ☐ **Human Resource Professionals**
  Human Resource professionals have both a formal and informal feedback role. Since they have access to unique and confidential information, they can provide the right context for feedback you've received. Sometimes they may be "directed" to give you feedback. Other times, they may pass on feedback just to be helpful to you.
- ☐ **Past Associates/Constituencies**
  When confronted with a present performance problem, some claim, "I wasn't like that before; it must be the current situation." When feedback is available from former associates, about 50% support that claim. In the other half of the cases, the people were like that before and probably didn't know it. It sometimes makes sense to access the past to clearly see the present.

SECTION 4: LEARNING FROM DEVELOP-IN-PLACE ASSIGNMENTS

THESE PART-TIME DEVELOP-IN-PLACE ASSIGNMENTS WILL HELP YOU BUILD YOUR SKILL(S)

- ☐ Assign a project to a group with a tight deadline.
- ☐ Manage an ad hoc, temporary group of balky and resisting people through an unpopular change or project.
- ☐ Manage an ad hoc, temporary group of low-competence people through a task they couldn't do by themselves.
- ☐ Manage an ad hoc, temporary group including former peers to accomplish a task.
- ☐ Manage an ad hoc, temporary group of people who are older and/or more experienced to accomplish a task.
- ☐ Manage an ad hoc, temporary group of people where the temporary manager is a towering expert and the people in the group are not.
- ☐ Manage an ad hoc, temporary group of people involved in tackling a fix-it or turnaround project.
- ☐ Manage an ad hoc, temporary group of people in a rapidly expanding operation.
- ☐ Assemble an ad hoc team of diverse people to accomplish a difficult task.
- ☐ Build a multifunctional project team to tackle a common business issue or problem.

SECTION 5: LEARNING FROM FULL-TIME JOBS

THESE FULL-TIME JOBS OFFER THE OPPORTUNITY TO BUILD YOUR SKILL(S)

☐ **Scale Assignments**
Core requirements to qualify as a Scale (size) shift assignment are: 1) Sizable jump-shift in the size of the job in areas like: number of people, number of layers in organization, size of budget, number of locations, volume of activity, tightness of deadlines. 2) Medium to low complexity; mostly repetitive and routine processes and procedures. 3) Stable staff and business. 4) Stable operations. 5) Often slow, steady growth.

☐ **Significant People Demands**
Core demands required to qualify as a Significant People Responsibilities assignment are: 1) A sizable increase in either the number of people managed and/or the complexity of the challenges involved 2) Longer-term assignment (two or more years). 3) Quality of people management critical to achieving results. 4) Involves groups not worked with before (e.g., union, new technical areas, nationalities).

☐ **Staff to Line Shifts**
Core demands necessary to qualify for a Staff to Line shift are: 1) Moving to a job with an easily determined bottom line or results. 2) Managing bigger scope and/or scale. 3) Requires new skills/perspectives. 4) Unfamiliar aspects of the assignment.

SECTION 6: LEARNING MORE FROM YOUR PLAN

THESE ADDITIONAL REMEDIES WILL HELP MAKE THIS DEVELOPMENT PLAN MORE EFFECTIVE FOR YOU

Learning to Learn Better

☐ **Examine Why You Judge People the Way You Do**
List the people you like and those you dislike and try to find out why. What do those you like have in common with each other and with you? What do those you dislike have in common with themselves and how do they differ from you? Are your "people buckets" logical and productive or do they interfere? Could you be more effective without putting people into buckets?

Learning from Experience, Feedback and Other People

☐ **Learning from Bosses**
Bosses can be an excellent and ready source for learning. All bosses do some things exceptionally well and other things poorly. Distance your feelings from the boss/direct report relationship and study things that work and things that don't work for your boss. What would you have done? What could you use, and what should you avoid?

- ☐ **Learning from Interviewing Others**
Interview others. Ask not only what they do, but how and why they do it. What do they think are the rules of thumb they are following? Where did they learn the behaviors? How do they keep them current? How do they monitor the effect they have on others?

- ☐ **Learning from Observing Others**
Observe others. Find opportunities to observe without interacting with your model. This enables you to objectively study the person, note what he/she is doing or not doing, and compare that with what you would typically do in similar situations. Many times you can learn more by watching than asking. Your model may not be able to explain what he/she does or may be an unwilling teacher.

- ☐ **Getting Feedback from Direct Reports**
Direct reports often fear reprisals for giving negative feedback about bosses, whether in a formal process, like a questionnaire, or informally and face-to-face. Even with a guarantee of confidentiality, some are still hesitant. If you want feedback from direct reports, you have to set a positive tone and never act out of revenge.

- ☐ **Learning from Limited Staff**
Most managers either inherit or hire staff from time to time who are inexperienced, incompetent, not up to the task, resistant, or dispirited. Any of these may create a hardship for you. The lessons to be learned are how to get things done with limited resources and how to fix the people situation. In the short term, this hardship is best addressed by assessing the combined strengths of the team and deploying the best you have against the problem. Almost everyone can do something well. Also, the team can contribute more than the combined individuals can. How can you empower and motivate the team? If you hired the troublesome staff, why did you err? What can you learn from your hiring mistakes? What wasn't there that you thought was present? What led you astray? How can you prevent that same hiring error in the future? What do you need to do to fix the situation? Quick development? Start over? If you inherited the problem, how can you fix it? Can you implement a program of accelerated development? Do you have to start over and get new people? What did the prior manager do or not do that led to this situation in the first place? What can you learn from that? What will you do differently? How does the staff feel? What can you learn from their frustrations over not being able to do the job? How can you be a positive force under negative circumstances? How can you rally them to perform? What lasting lessons can you learn from someone in distress and trouble? If you're going to try accelerated development, how can you get a quick assessment? How can you give the staff motivating feedback? How can you construct and implement development plans that will work? How can you get people on-line feedback for maximum growth? Do you know when to stop trying and

start over? If you're going to turn over some staff, how can you do it both rapidly and with the least damage? How can you deliver the message in a constructive way? What can you learn from having to take negative actions against people? How can you prevent this from happening again?

Learning from Courses

☐ **Supervisory Courses**
Most new supervisors go through an "Introduction to Supervision" type course. They are designed to teach the common practices a first-line supervisor needs to know to be effective. The content of most of those courses is standard. There is general agreement on the principles of effective supervision. There are two common problems: 1) Do the students have a strong motivation to learn? Do they know what they don't know? Is there any pain? Because motivated students with a need for the knowledge learn best, participants should have had some trying experiences and some supervisory pain and hardships before attending. 2) Are the instructors experienced supervisors? Have they practiced what they preach? Can they share powerful anecdotes to make key points? Can they answer questions credibly? If possible, select supervisory courses based on the instructors, since the content seems to be the much same for all such courses. Lastly, does the course offer the opportunity for practicing each skill? Does it contain simulations? Are there case studies you could easily identify with? Are there breakout groups? Is there opportunity for action learning? Search for the most interactive course.

☐ **Courses with Feedback**
Many courses such as negotiating skills and personal influence offer feedback on the subject matter of the course in addition to the content. They either collect data ahead of time or collect it "live" during the course.

SUGGESTED READINGS

Team Management Briefings (monthly publication). P.O. Box 25755, Alexandria, VA 22313 1-800-722-9221 http://www.briefings.com/tm

Ginnodo, Bill. *The Power of Empowerment.* Arlington Heights, IL: Pride Publications, Inc., 1997.

Huppe, Frank F. *Successful Delegation: How to grow your people, build your team, free up your time and increase profits and productivity.* Hawthorne, N.J.: Career Press, 1994.

Koch, Richard and Ian Godden. *Managing without management: a post-management manifesto for business simplicity.* London; Sonoma, CA: Nicholas Brealey Pub., 1996.

Maurer, Rick. *Caught in the Middle.* Cambridge, MA: Productivity Press, 1992.

Miller, James B. *The Corporate Coach.* New York: St. Martin's Press, 1993.

Parker, Glenn M. *Cross-functional Teams.* San Francisco: Jossey-Bass, Inc., 1994.

Sproull, Lee and Sara Kiesler. *Connections: new ways of working in the networked organization.* Cambridge, MA: MIT Press, 1991.

21

MANAGING DIVERSITY

SECTION 1: YOUR DEVELOPMENT NEED(S)

UNSKILLED

- ☐ Not effective with groups much different from him/her
- ☐ May be uncomfortable with those not like him/her
- ☐ May act inappropriately with those different from him/her
- ☐ Defends turf from outsiders
- ☐ Avoids conflict and the noise of differing views and agendas
- ☐ Doesn't see the business value of diversity
- ☐ Treats everybody the same without regard to their differences
- ☐ Very narrow and ethnocentric; believes his/her group to be superior
- ☐ May carry around negative and demeaning stereotypes he/she has trouble getting rid of

SKILLED

- ☐ Manages all kinds and classes of people equitably
- ☐ Deals effectively with all races, nationalities, cultures, disabilities, ages and both sexes
- ☐ Hires variety and diversity without regard to class
- ☐ Supports equal and fair treatment and opportunity for all

OVERUSED SKILL

- ☐ May make too many allowances for members of a particular class
- ☐ May not apply equal standards and criteria to all classes
- ☐ May show an inappropriate preference for a single class of people
- ☐ May compromise standards to achieve diversity

Select one to three of the competencies listed below to work on to compensate for an overuse of this skill.

COMPENSATORS: 9, 12, 13, 18, 19, 20, 25, 34, 35, 36, 37, 56, 57, 60, 64

SOME CAUSES

- ☐ Are uncomfortable with different groups
- ☐ Believe in diversity, but don't know what to do
- ☐ Can't make the business case for diversity
- ☐ Don't see how diversity helps
- ☐ Narrow and rigid
- ☐ Think diversity means double standards
- ☐ Uncomfortable with the new and different

THE MAP

In the new global world and economy, large, meaning world wide, diversity is king. Markets are now more diverse. The labor pool is more diverse. And almost every global company's greatest opportunities are in cultures different and more diverse than its home country's. Those organizations that best manage large diversity will be the winners. Managing large diversity starts with managing small – home country – diversity. Managing diversity is basically deciding which differences make a difference and enrich, and which differences don't. Once you have figured that out, managing is managing. However, until you see the benefits of large and small diversity, little change is likely. To do this, you'll need to learn to understand without judging other groups, see people more as individuals and less as a member of a group, understand your own subtle stereotyping (if any), make the business case for diversity, make a personal case for diversity by seeing it work, and treat some people a bit differently due to their lack of opportunity in the past.

SECTION 2: LEARNING ON YOUR OWN

THESE SELF-DEVELOPMENT REMEDIES WILL HELP YOU BUILD YOUR SKILL(S)

SOME REMEDIES

☐ **1. Making the business case.** Nothing much will happen until you have the business case in mind for increased diversity in the organization. Are your markets and customers more diverse than your employees? Where are your major new opportunities for volume and share? Are they in your home market? People just like you? Most likely not. Do you know a lot about the people and cultures inside and outside your home country who are going to buy your products and make you successful? As the population becomes more diverse, same culture sales and marketing people have had more success selling (Hispanics to Hispanics, for example). Innovation through diversity. Studies show that heterogeneous or diverse groups are more innovative than homogeneous groups. They view opportunities from different perspectives. The majority of the U.S. labor market will shortly be former minorities. Females and minorities collectively will be in the majority. Companies known in the marketplace for managing diversity well will get their pick of the best and the brightest. A broader talent pool means more to choose from; more effective managers tend to have a more diverse array of people around them. The rest will get the leftovers. Are you known for managing diversity well? Want increased motivation and productivity? There is a positive relationship between perceived equity/feeling valued and the performance of organizations. The business case boils down to more perspectives, more chances to learn, more ways to appeal to different market segments, and a more productive workforce where all employees think merit is what counts in our organization. Read *Making Differences Matter: A New Paradigm for Managing Diversity* by Thomas and Ely in the *Harvard Business Review*, September–October 1996. Also read *Diversity Making the Business Case* by Michael L. Wheeler in *Business Week*, Dec. 9, 1996.

☐ **2. Equal opportunity.** If you don't buy this, you can't learn to be better at managing diversity. Equal opportunity means differential treatment. Equal opportunity does not mean equal treatment. In golf, do you object to handicaps? That's a system designed to even the playing field for golfers with different levels of expertise and experience. Do you object to veterans preference? That's a system of giving veterans a ten point advantage on civil service tests to make up for the lost time and break in their business skill development while they were serving their four years in the military. What about handicap preferences? Do you mind that they have special bathroom stalls to adjust to their handicaps? Close in parking? Ramps to get to work? Special buses? That's all unequal treatment to level the playing field. The same is true then for disadvantaged backgrounds. Never had a father role model at home. Never traveled out of town. Never was a student leader. Couldn't afford to belong to Scouts. Never went to camp. Never studied in Europe for a semester. Never knew anyone in the immediate family who had a regular job that lasted 20 years. Denied other opportunities due to what group they belonged to. But otherwise bright, ambitious and willing to learn. What adjustments would you have to or would you be willing to make to level the playing field? More orientation? More training? A little more patience? More understanding? Special exposures? Forming groups of like people to share common problems? The key is that all of this disadvantage was not the fault of the person sitting before you. He or she now wants to break free of that and have an equitable chance to learn and perform. You can provide the opportunity if you understand unequal treatment is necessary to reach equal opportunity. Read *The New Leaders* by Ann Morrison.

☐ **3. Double standards?** This is tough. Are there double standards at entry? Probably. Due to whatever disadvantage (cultural, economic, physical, language) is at work, there is at entry probably a deficit in the past demonstration of needed skills and background. Are there double standards for treatment? Definitely yes. Should there be double standards long term? Definitely not. Once a person has been given preferential treatment – language training or problem-solving skills enhancement – to balance a disadvantage, the playing field should be equal and the same standards should apply to everyone. The whole point of this is the belief that when given equal opportunity, equal performance will be the result. If performance is not up to standard after some time, then the person will have to live with the consequences the same as anyone else in the same situation.

☐ **4. Differences.** What differences make a difference? Does gender make a difference in performance? Research says no. Some studies actually point to higher ratings for women, probably due to the pioneer effect. Also, research says that gender diverse teams are more creative and innovative. Age? Generally not. Some skills stay strong, others (memory) slowly decrease for some. Race? Not much research yet. Given equal opportunities, looks like not. Handicapped? Some studies show greater performance probably due to special motivation. Culture? Too many variables. Not much research. Certainly cultural background influences how you think about things but all cultures seem to have a sufficient work ethic and ambition to perform against reasonable standards. Some surveys on Asians in the U.S. says they outperform others in grades and academic and scientific achievement, again maybe because of the pioneer effect.

☐ **5. Stereotypes?** You have to understand your own subtle stereotyping. Helen Astin's research showed that both men and women rated women managers at the extremes (very high or very low) while they rate men on a normal curve. Do you think redheads have tempers? Blondes have more fun? Overweight people are lazy? Women are more emotional at work? Men can't show emotion? Find out your own pattern. Attend a course which delves into perception of others. Most stereotyping is false. Even if there are surface differences, they don't make a difference in performance.

☐ **6. Dealing with people equitably.** Try to see people more as individuals than members of a group. Avoid putting people in grouped buckets. Many of us bucket people as can or can't do this. We have good buckets and bad buckets. Buckets I like/am comfortable with and buckets that bother me. Once we bucket, we generally don't relate as well to the off bucket people. Much of the time bucketing is based on like me – the good bucket; not like me – the bad bucket. Across time, the can do/like me bucket gets the majority of your attention, more feedback, stretching tasks, develops the most and performs the best, unfortunately proving your stereotyping again and again. To break this cycle, understand without judging. Be candid with yourself. Is there a group or groups you don't like or are uncomfortable with? Do you judge individual members of that group without really knowing if your stereotype is true? Most of us do. Try to see people as people.

☐ **7. Balancing people processes.** Women and people of color are less likely to get developmental feedback. Senior women haven't had the tough job assignments men have had on the way up. Women and minorities get less informal information. Sometimes women and minorities do not participate equally in off work but organization related socializing – where important business information is exchanged and decisions made in an informal and relaxed environment. Examine each of your people processes. Are there unintentional inequities? Drive special programming to make them more equal. Equal access to information, challenging jobs, relating, skill building and networking is equal opportunity.

☐ **8. The catch-22.** If a group is inequitably treated, it will coalesce into a subgroup and fight back. It's natural. Misery loves company. People who are not in power tend to group together. They form special forums to discuss problems. They may eat together, socialize together and stand as a group united behind a position or a demand. All of this tends to irritate others (who steadfastly claim they have never discriminated against anyone), who may decide this just proves their negative assessments of the group in general. They then put the whole group and all its individual members back in the bad bucket. You have to relax. This is a human process. It happens all over the world at all levels when an identifiable group enters someone else's sandbox, like the Irish in the 1850's coming to New York. Help them form groups and attend and learn and listen. Address their legitimate demands and complaints. Help them out. Teach them to make the business or organizational case first, and to be more tentative and conditional than they actually are so others have room to get comfortable and negotiate and bargain. Figure out what they want and see if you can help them get it. *More help? – See #64 Understanding Others.*

☐ **9. Diversity that matters.** Diversity of viewpoint, background, education, culture, experience, beliefs and attitudes matter, and all help produce a superior product in a diverse and global marketplace. Put diversity to the test yourself; attack problems with diverse task forces, pull in the widest array of thinking you can and see if you get broader, more inventive results. Assemble the most diverse team you can who have the skills to do the job but otherwise are different. Consciously spend more of your time with people around you who are different. Solicit the points of view of each person. How do those background differences lead to viewing problems differently?

☐ **10. The diversity experience.** Not much diversity in your background but want to improve?

- Stage one: talk to people in your organization, neighborhood or place of worship who are different in some way than you. Do lunch. Go to a ballgame. Exchange views. House a foreign student from a country your organization is thinking about entering. Do volunteer work with a group not like you.
- Stage two: visit all ethnic festivals in your geography. Sample the foods. See the costumes and the crafts. Study their history. Talk to them.
- Stage three: vacation in Miami and spend time in the Cuban area. San Diego and San Antonio for Spanish. San Francisco and New York for Chinatown. Toronto for a number of ethnic areas within the city limits.

- Stage four: travel and stay for one week anywhere in the world where you are in the minority and most others do not speak your language. Get away from the tourist areas. See how that feels.

SECTION 3: LEARNING FROM MORE FEEDBACK

THESE SOURCES WOULD GIVE YOU THE MOST ACCURATE AND DETAILED FEEDBACK ON YOUR SKILL(S)

☐ **Direct Reports**
Across a variety of settings, your direct reports probably see you the most. They are the recipients of most of your managerial behaviors. They know your work. They can compare you with former bosses. Since they may hesitate to give you negative feedback, you have to set the atmosphere to make it easier for them. You have to ask.

☐ **Human Resource Professionals**
Human Resource professionals have both a formal and informal feedback role. Since they have access to unique and confidential information, they can provide the right context for feedback you've received. Sometimes they may be "directed" to give you feedback. Other times, they may pass on feedback just to be helpful to you.

☐ **Natural Mentors**
Natural mentors have a special relationship with you and are interested in your success and your future. Since they are usually not in your direct chain of command, you can have more open, relaxed, and fruitful discussions about yourself and your career prospects. They can be a very important source for candid or critical feedback others may not give you.

☐ **Past Associates/Constituencies**
When confronted with a present performance problem, some claim, "I wasn't like that before; it must be the current situation." When feedback is available from former associates, about 50% support that claim. In the other half of the cases, the people were like that before and probably didn't know it. It sometimes makes sense to access the past to clearly see the present.

SECTION 4: LEARNING FROM DEVELOP-IN-PLACE ASSIGNMENTS

THESE PART-TIME DEVELOP-IN-PLACE ASSIGNMENTS WILL HELP YOU BUILD YOUR SKILL(S)

☐ Serve for a year or more with a community agency.

☐ Represent the concerns of a group of nonexempt, clerical, or administrative employees to higher management to seek resolution of a difficult issue.

☐ Work on an affirmative action plan for the organization and present it to management for approval.

- ☐ Manage a project team made up of nationals from a number of countries.
- ☐ Act as a loaned executive to a charity, government, agency, etc.
- ☐ Train and work as an assessor in an assessment center.
- ☐ Become someone's assigned mentor, coach, sponsor, champion, or orienter.
- ☐ Manage an ad hoc, temporary group of balky and resisting people through an unpopular change or project.
- ☐ Manage an ad hoc, temporary group of people where the people in the group are towering experts but the temporary manager is not.
- ☐ Manage a project team of people who are older and more experienced than you.

SECTION 5: LEARNING FROM FULL-TIME JOBS

THESE FULL-TIME JOBS OFFER THE OPPORTUNITY TO BUILD YOUR SKILL(S)

☐ **Off-Shore Assignments**

The core demands to qualify as an Off-Shore assignment are: 1) First time working in the country. 2) Significant challenges like new language, hardship location, unique business rules/practices, significant cultural/marketplace differences, different functional task, etc. 3) More than a year assignment. 4) No automatic return deal. 5) Not necessarily a change in job challenge, technical content, or responsibilities.

☐ **Scope Assignments**

The core demands for a Scope (complexity) assignment are: 1) Significant increase in both internal and external scope or complexity. 2) Significant increase in visibility and/or bottom line responsibility. 3) Unfamiliar area, business, technology, or territory. Examples of Scope assignments involving shifts: 1) Switching into a new function/technology/business. 2) Moving to new organization. 3) Moving to overseas assignment. 4) Moving to new location. 5) Adding new products/services. 6) Moving between headquarters/field. 7) Switches in ownership/top management of the unit/organization. Examples of Scope assignments involving "firsts": 1) First-time manager. 2) First-time managing managers. 3) First-time executive. 4) First-time overseas. 5) First-time headquarters/field. 6) First-time team leader. 7) First-time new technology/business/function. Scope assignments involving increased complexity: 1) Managing a significant expansion of an existing product or service. 2) Managing adding new products/service into an existing unit. 3) Managing a reorganized and more diverse unit. 4) Managing explosive growth. 5) Adding new technologies.

☐ **Significant People Demands**

Core demands required to qualify as a Significant People Responsibilities assignment are: 1) A sizable increase in either the number of people managed and/or the complexity of the challenges involved 2) Longer-term assignment (two or more years). 3) Quality of people management critical to achieving results. 4) Involves groups not worked with before (e.g., union, new technical areas, nationalities).

SECTION 6: LEARNING MORE FROM YOUR PLAN

THESE ADDITIONAL REMEDIES WILL HELP MAKE THIS DEVELOPMENT PLAN MORE EFFECTIVE FOR YOU

Learning to Learn Better

- ☐ **Study Yourself in Detail**
  Study your likes and dislikes because they can drive a lot of your thinking, judging, and acting. Ask which like or dislike has gotten in the way or prevented you from moving to a higher level of learning. Are your likes and dislikes really important to you or have you just gone on "autopilot"? Try to address and understand a blocking dislike and change it.

- ☐ **Examine Why You Judge People the Way You Do**
  List the people you like and those you dislike and try to find out why. What do those you like have in common with each other and with you? What do those you dislike have in common with themselves and how do they differ from you? Are your "people buckets" logical and productive or do they interfere? Could you be more effective without putting people into buckets?

Learning from Experience, Feedback and Other People

- ☐ **Using Multiple Models**
  Who do you know who exemplifies how to do whatever your need is? Who, for example, personifies decisiveness or compassion or strategic agility? Think more broadly than your current job and colleagues. For example, clergy, friends, spouses or community leaders are also good sources for potential models. Select your models not on the basis of overall excellence or likability, but on the basis of the one towering strength (or glaring weakness) you are interested in. Even people who are well thought of usually have only one or two towering strengths (or glaring weaknesses). Ordinarily, you won't learn as much from the whole person as you will from one characteristic.

- ☐ **Getting Feedback from Direct Reports**
  Direct reports often fear reprisals for giving negative feedback about bosses, whether in a formal process, like a questionnaire, or informally and face-to-face. Even with a guarantee of confidentiality, some are still hesitant. If you want feedback from direct reports, you have to set a positive tone and never act out of revenge.

- [ ] **Learning from Limited Staff**
Most managers either inherit or hire staff from time to time who are inexperienced, incompetent, not up to the task, resistant, or dispirited. Any of these may create a hardship for you. The lessons to be learned are how to get things done with limited resources and how to fix the people situation. In the short term, this hardship is best addressed by assessing the combined strengths of the team and deploying the best you have against the problem. Almost everyone can do something well. Also, the team can contribute more than the combined individuals can. How can you empower and motivate the team? If you hired the troublesome staff, why did you err? What can you learn from your hiring mistakes? What wasn't there that you thought was present? What led you astray? How can you prevent that same hiring error in the future? What do you need to do to fix the situation? Quick development? Start over? If you inherited the problem, how can you fix it? Can you implement a program of accelerated development? Do you have to start over and get new people? What did the prior manager do or not do that led to this situation in the first place? What can you learn from that? What will you do differently? How does the staff feel? What can you learn from their frustrations over not being able to do the job? How can you be a positive force under negative circumstances? How can you rally them to perform? What lasting lessons can you learn from someone in distress and trouble? If you're going to try accelerated development, how can you get a quick assessment? How can you give the staff motivating feedback? How can you construct and implement development plans that will work? How can you get people on-line feedback for maximum growth? Do you know when to stop trying and start over? If you're going to turn over some staff, how can you do it both rapidly and with the least damage? How can you deliver the message in a constructive way? What can you learn from having to take negative actions against people? How can you prevent this from happening again?

Learning from Courses

- [ ] **Supervisory Courses**
Most new supervisors go through an "Introduction to Supervision" type course. They are designed to teach the common practices a first-line supervisor needs to know to be effective. The content of most of those courses is standard. There is general agreement on the principles of effective supervision. There are two common problems: 1) Do the students have a strong motivation to learn? Do they know what they don't know? Is there any pain? Because motivated students with a need for the knowledge learn best, participants should have had some trying experiences and some supervisory pain and hardships before attending. 2) Are the instructors experienced supervisors? Have they practiced what they preach? Can they share powerful anecdotes to

make key points? Can they answer questions credibly? If possible, select supervisory courses based on the instructors, since the content seems to be the much same for all such courses. Lastly, does the course offer the opportunity for practicing each skill? Does it contain simulations? Are there case studies you could easily identify with? Are there breakout groups? Is there opportunity for action learning? Search for the most interactive course.

- ☐ **Insight Events**
  These are courses designed around assessing skills and providing feedback to the participants. These events can be a powerful source of self-knowledge and can lead to significant development if done right. When selecting a self-insight course, consider the following: 1) Are the skills assessed the important ones? 2) Are the assessment techniques and instruments sound? 3) Are those who are providing the feedback trained and professional? 4) Is the feedback provided in a user-friendly and "actionable" format? 5) Does the feedback include development planning? 6) Is the setting comfortable and conducive to reflection and learning? 7) Are the other participants the kinds of people you could learn from? 8) Are you in the right frame of mind to learn from this kind of intense experience? Select events on the basis of positive answers to these eight questions.

- ☐ **Strategic Courses**
  There are a number of courses designed to stretch minds to prepare for future challenges. They include topics such as Workforce Diversity 2000, globalization, the European Union, competitive competencies and strategies, etc. Quality depends upon the following three factors: 1) The quality of the staff. Are they qualified? Are they respected in their fields? Are they strategic "gurus"? 2) The quality of the participants. Are they the kind of people you could learn from? 3) The quality of the setting. Is it comfortable and free from distractions? Can you learn there?

- ☐ **Attitude Toward Learning**
  In addition to selecting the right course, a learning attitude is required. Be open. Close down your "like/dislike" switch, your "agree/disagree" blinders, and your "like me/not like me" feelings toward the instructors. Learning requires new lessons, change, and new behaviors and perspectives – all scary stuff for most people. Don't resist. Take in all you can during the course. Ask clarifying questions. Discuss concerns with the other participants. Jot down what you learn as you go. After the course is over, take some reflective time to glean the meat. Make the practical decisions about what you can and cannot use.

- ☐ **Sending Others to Courses**
  If you are responsible for managing someone else's development and, as part of that, sending them to courses, prepare them beforehand. Don't send them as tourists. Meet with them before and after the

course. Tell them why they need this course. Tell them what you expect them to learn. Give them feedback on why you think they need the course. Agree ahead of time how you will measure and monitor learning after they return. If possible, offer a variety of courses for your employee to choose from. Have them give you a report shortly after they return. If appropriate, have them present what they learned to the rest of your staff. After they return, provide opportunities for using the new skills with safe cover and low risk. Give them practice time before expecting full exercise of the new skills. Be supportive during early unsteadiness. Give continuous feedback on progress.

SUGGESTED READINGS

Harvard Business Review. Phone: 800-988-0886 (U.S. and Canada). Fax: 617-496-1029. Mail: Harvard Business Review. Subscriber Services, P.O. Box 52623. Boulder, CO 80322-2623 USA. http://www.hbsp.harvard.edu/products/hbr

Blank, Renee and Sandra Slipp. *Voices of Diversity – Real people talk about problems and solutions in a workplace where everyone is not alike.* New York: AMACOM, 1994.

Griggs, Lewis Brown and Lente-Louise Cor Editors. *Valuing Diversity – New tools for a new reality.* New York: McGraw Hill, 1995.

Leach, Joy with Bette George, Tina Jackson and Arleen Labella. *A Practical Guide to Working with Diversity – The Process The Tools The Resources.* New York: AMACOM, 1995.

Jamieson, David and Julie O'Mara. *Managing Workforce 2000.* San Francisco: Jossey-Bass, Inc., 1991.

Morrison, Ann M. *The New Leaders – Guidelines on Leadership Diversity in America.* San Francisco: Jossey-Bass, Inc., 1992.

Sonnenschein, William. *The Practical Executive and Workforce Diversity.* New York: NTC Business Books, 1997.

ETHICS AND VALUES

SECTION 1: YOUR DEVELOPMENT NEED(S)

UNSKILLED

- ☐ Values may be out of sync with those of the organization
- ☐ Strong individualist with low concern for values of others; may set his/her own rules; make others uncomfortable
- ☐ May play too close or over the edge for the organization
- ☐ May not think about own values much and have no idea how he/she comes across
- ☐ Behavior may vary too much across situations
- ☐ Values may be seen as too self serving
- ☐ He/she doesn't walk the talk; says one thing, does another

SKILLED

- ☐ Adheres to an appropriate (for the setting) and effective set of core values and beliefs during both good and bad times
- ☐ Acts in line with those values
- ☐ Rewards the right values and disapproves of others
- ☐ Practices what he/she preaches

OVERUSED SKILL

- ☐ May go to battle based on beliefs and values when not appropriate
- ☐ May be overly sensitive to situations he/she sees as litmus tests of principles, values, and beliefs
- ☐ May be seen as stubborn and insensitive to the need for change and compromise
- ☐ May be overly critical of those who do not hold the same values
- ☐ May use ethics statements to close off discussion

Select one to three of the competencies listed below to work on to compensate for an overuse of this skill.

COMPENSATORS: 10, 11, 12, 17, 21, 32, 33, 37, 41, 45, 46, 48, 55, 56, 58, 64, 65

SOME CAUSES

- ☐ Inconsistent values/ethical stances
- ☐ Marginal values and ethics; operate close to the edge
- ☐ Old values/ethical stances
- ☐ Overly independent; set own rules
- ☐ Situational ethics
- ☐ Vague about values/ethics

THE MAP

Values and ethics are shorthand statements of the core or underlying principles that guide what you say and do. Do unto others as you would have them do unto you. Although short and sometimes simple – Quality is Job One (Ford), Our customers are always right (Nordstrom), Our employees are our most important asset – values and ethics provide guidance on how we act and how we make choices. We are an equal opportunity employer – simple enough – covers behavior in hiring, firing, promotion, training, development, placement, and employee assistance programming. We all have a set of values and ethics but many times we haven't thought out our values/ethical stances well; we are on autopilot from childhood and our accumulated experience. All organizations have a set of reasonably consistent values and ethics they prefer to operate under. Organizations require reasonable conformity with those collective standards. People who are models of ethics and values have thought their values through, are clear about them, can deal with close calls by applying them, understand other value stances, speak up on these matters, and are reasonably consistent and in tune with those around them.

SECTION 2: LEARNING ON YOUR OWN

THESE SELF-DEVELOPMENT REMEDIES WILL HELP YOU BUILD YOUR SKILL(S)

SOME REMEDIES

☐ **1. Brain, mouth and hand coordination.** Most of the evaluation of your ethics and values comes from people watching what you do. If they have not had the opportunity to see you in action, they will evaluate what you say. If they have both, they will take what you do over what you say. People are bothered by inconsistencies between what you say and what you do. If you tend to say one thing but do another, people will see that as inconsistent and will say of you that you don't walk your talk. Above all, align your actions and your mouth. Inconsistencies come in three kinds, outlined below in points two, three and four.

☐ **2. Don't walk your good talk?** The usual case is that there is a sizable gap between what you say about your ethics and values and what the ethics and values of others should be, and what you actually do in those same situations. We have worked with many who get themselves in trouble by making values and ethics speeches, high toned, inspiring, lofty, passionate, charismatic, gives you goose bumps until you watch that person do the opposite or something quite different in practice. Examine all the things you tend to say in speeches or in meetings or casual conversations that are values and ethics statements about you or what you think others should do. Write them down the left side of a legal pad. For each one, see if you can write three to five examples of when you acted exactly in line with that value or ethic.

Can you write down any that are not exactly like that? If you can, it's the gap that's the problem. Either stop making values and ethics statements you can't or won't model or bring your stated values into alignment with your own actions.

- ☐ **3. Don't walk your bad talk?** Another, though more rare, possibility is that there is a sizable gap between what you say and the language you use, and what you actually think and do. We have worked with many who get themselves in trouble by using language and words that imply marginal values and ethics that make others uncomfortable that are not real. Do you shoot for effect? Fire them all. Do you exaggerate? There are no good vendors. Do you push your statements to the extreme to make a point? Do you overstate negative views? Do you trash talk to fit in? Do you use demeaning words? All consultants are just mercenaries. What if I have never seen you in action? What would I think your values were if I listened to you talk and didn't know what you actually do? Examine the words and the language you tend to use in speeches or in meetings or casual conversations that are values and ethics based. Write them down the left side of a legal pad. For each one, see if you can write three to five examples of when you acted exactly in line with those words. Do you really act like that? Do you really think that way? If you don't, it's the gap that's the problem. Stop using words and language that are not in line with your real thoughts, values and actions.

- ☐ **4. Situational?** Not everyone has a keel in the values water. You might just be inconsistent in your statements and actions across situations. You change your mind based on mood or who you talked with last or what your last experience was. You may express a pro people value in one instance (people you manage) and an anti people value in another (people from another unit). You may rigidly adhere to a high moral code in one transaction (with customers) and play it close to the acceptable margin in another – with vendors. You may match your values with your audience when managing up and not when you're managing down. People are more comfortable with consistency and predictability. Do you do one thing with people you like and quite another with people you don't? Look for the three to five areas where you think these inconsistencies play out. Write down what you did with various people so you can compare. Did you do different things in parallel situations? Do you hold others to a different standard? Do you have so many values positions that they have to clash eventually? Try to balance your behavior so that you are more consistent across situations.

- ☐ **5. Mismatch?** At the least, a low rating for ethics and values means the values and ethics you are operating under are not in line with the commonly held values and ethics of those around you. That's a common problem. You join an organization thinking it has the values you believe in and after you are there for awhile, you find out they are something different. Or the organization makes a big shift in direction, gets acquired, or merges and changes its ethics and values overnight, out of your comfort zone. To some extent, that's life. It's hard to find a perfect match. If the gap is serious, leave. If the gap is just uncomfortable, try to affect it in any way you can by influencing the organization. Try not to challenge others with your discomfort. Maybe you're too independent? You set your own rules, smash through obstacles, see yourself as tough, action and results oriented. You get it done. The problem is you don't often worry about whether others think as you do. You operate from your inside out. What's important to you is what you think and what you judge to be right and just. In a sense, admirable. In a sense, not smart. You live in an organization that has both formal and informal commonly held standards, beliefs, ethics and values. You can't survive long without knowing what they are and bending yours to fit. Try to be a supporter of what you can and just be silent about the rest.

☐ **6. Double standards?** Another common problem is one set of standards for you and a different set of standards for others. Or one set for you and the people you like and another for everyone else. Do you do what you expect others to do? Don't ask anyone to do what you wouldn't do. A common problem with higher level managers is telling the people below them to make tough people calls and fire those who don't meet standards. Then they give everyone reporting to them an above average rating and a bonus even though everyone knows one or two of these people are not up to standard. Do you do anything like this? Do you make close calls in favor of those you like or play favorites?

☐ **7. Clarifying your values.** You may not think much in terms of ethics and values, and your statements may not clearly represent your true values. Since you are having trouble in this area, it might be a good exercise to try to capture your value system on paper so you know what it is and are able to deliver a clear statement of it to others. Think about your past actions. How do you treat people? Think of the last 25 treatment events or opportunities. What did you do? Was it consistent? If it was, what values and ethics would you have shown to others? 25 honesty and straightforwardness opportunities. 25 opportunities to disclose. 25 opportunities to help others. 25 decisions about allocating resources. 25 spending opportunities. 25 hiring and 25 firing or layoff decisions. 25 delegation decisions, and so on. What are the values that underlie your actions? Are they the ones you want to be known for? Are they like the commonly held ethics and values of the organization you are in?

☐ **8. Old values?** This is a tough one. Times change. Do values change? Some think not. That might be your stance. What about humor? Could you tell some ribald jokes ten years ago that would get you in trouble today? Have dating practices and ages changed? Using the example of sexual harassment, what is it to you? What's the difference between poor taste, kidding, flirting and sexual harassment? Has the definition changed over your working career? Do you think your old values are better than today's? When did you form your current values? Over 20 years ago? Maybe it's time to examine your personal commandments in light of the new today to see whether you need to make any midcourse corrections. Others may view your stances as simplistic or rigid. List five common areas where values clash for you at work – quality/cost tradeoffs, work with someone or fire, treat different people differently or all the same. Can you describe how you deal with these situations? What are your tie-breakers? What wins out? Why? If you find yourself coming down on the same side in the same way almost every time, you need an update. Talk to people who would go the other way and begin to see more complexity in the issue. Turn off your judgment programming – listen to understand.

☐ **9. The worst case.** On the more negative side, it could mean you have unacceptable values and ethics, that is, most would reject them. You may operate too close or over the edge for most people to feel comfortable with you. You hedge, sabotage others, play for advantage, set up others and make others look bad. You may be devious and scheming and overly political. You tell yourself it's OK because you're getting results. You really believe the end justifies the means. You tell people what they want to hear and then go off and do something else. If any of this is true, this criticism should be a repeat for you. This is not something that develops overnight. You need to find out if your career with this organization is salvageable. The best way to do this is to admit that you know your ethics and values are not the same as the people you work with and ask a boss or a mentor whether it's fixable. If they say yes, contact everyone you think you've alienated and see how they respond. Tell them the things you're going to do differently. Ask them if the situation can be repaired. Longer term, you need to seek some professional counsel on your values and ethics or find a place that has the same set as you do.

☐ **10. Changing your values and ethics.** Remember behavior is 10 times more important than words. What values do you want? What do you want your ethics to be? Write them down the left hand side of the page. I want to be known as a fair manager. Then down the right side, what would someone with that value do and not do? Wouldn't play favorites. Would offer everyone opportunities to grow and develop. Would listen to everyone's ideas. Would call for everyone's input in a staff meeting. Would apportion my time so everyone gets a piece of it. Hold everyone to the same standards. Have someone you trust check it over to see if you are on the right track. Then start to consistently do the things you have written on the right hand side.

SECTION 3: LEARNING FROM MORE FEEDBACK

THESE SOURCES WOULD GIVE YOU THE MOST ACCURATE AND DETAILED FEEDBACK ON YOUR SKILL(S)

☐ **Direct Reports**
Across a variety of settings, your direct reports probably see you the most. They are the recipients of most of your managerial behaviors. They know your work. They can compare you with former bosses. Since they may hesitate to give you negative feedback, you have to set the atmosphere to make it easier for them. You have to ask.

☐ **Natural Mentors**
Natural mentors have a special relationship with you and are interested in your success and your future. Since they are usually not in your direct chain of command, you can have more open, relaxed, and fruitful discussions about yourself and your career prospects. They can be a very important source for candid or critical feedback others may not give you.

☐ **Past Associates/Constituencies**
When confronted with a present performance problem, some claim, "I wasn't like that before; it must be the current situation." When feedback is available from former associates, about 50% support that claim. In the other half of the cases, the people were like that before and probably didn't know it. It sometimes makes sense to access the past to clearly see the present.

☐ **Peers and Colleagues**
Peers and colleagues have a special social and working relationship. They attend staff meetings together, share private views, get feedback from the same boss, travel together, and are knowledgeable about each other's work. You perhaps let your guard down more around peers and act more like yourself. They can be a valuable source of feedback.

SECTION 4: LEARNING FROM DEVELOP-IN-PLACE ASSIGNMENTS

THESE PART-TIME DEVELOP-IN-PLACE ASSIGNMENTS WILL HELP YOU BUILD YOUR SKILL(S)

☐ Handle a tough negotiation with an internal or external client or customer.

☐ Help shut down a plant, regional office, product line, business, operation, etc.

☐ Manage a dissatisfied internal or external customer; troubleshoot a performance or quality problem with a product or service.

☐ Manage the assigning/allocating of office space in a contested situation.

- ☐ Manage a group through a significant business crisis.
- ☐ Take on a tough and undoable project, one where others who have tried it have failed.
- ☐ Manage the outplacement of a group of people.
- ☐ Resolve an issue in conflict between two people, units, geographies, functions, etc.
- ☐ Make peace with an enemy or someone you've disappointed with a product or service or someone you've had some trouble with or don't get along well with.
- ☐ Be a member of a union-negotiating or grievance-handling team.

SECTION 5: LEARNING FROM FULL-TIME JOBS

THESE FULL-TIME JOBS OFFER THE OPPORTUNITY TO BUILD YOUR SKILL(S)

☐ **Fix-its/Turnarounds**

The core demands to qualify as a Fix-it or Turnaround assignment are: 1) Cleaning up a mess. 2) Serious people issues/problems like credibility/performance/morale. 3) Tight deadline. 4) Serious business performance failure. 5) Last chance to fix. Four Types of Fix-its/ Turnarounds: 1) Fixing a failed business/unit involving taking control, stopping losses, managing damage, planning the turnaround, dealing with people problems, installing new processes and systems, and rebuilding the spirit and performance of the unit. 2) Managing sizable disasters like mishandled labor negotiations and strikes, thefts, history of significant business losses, poor staff, failed leadership, hidden problems, fraud, public relations nightmares, etc. 3) Significant reorganization and restructuring (e.g., stabilizing the business, re-forming unit, introducing new systems, making people changes, resetting strategy and tactics). 4) Significant system/process breakdown (e.g., MIS, financial coordination processes, audits, standards, etc.) across units requiring working to change something from a distant position, providing advice and counsel, and installing or implementing a major process improvement or system change outside your own unit and/or with customers outside the organization.

☐ **Scope Assignments**

The core demands for a Scope (complexity) assignment are: 1) Significant increase in both internal and external scope or complexity. 2) Significant increase in visibility and/or bottom line responsibility. 3) Unfamiliar area, business, technology, or territory. Examples of Scope assignments involving shifts: 1) Switching into a new function/technology/business. 2) Moving to new organization. 3) Moving to overseas assignment. 4) Moving to new location. 5) Adding new products/ services. 6) Moving between headquarters/field. 7) Switches in ownership/top management of the unit/organization. Examples of Scope

assignments involving "firsts": 1) First-time manager. 2) First-time managing managers. 3) First-time executive. 4) First-time overseas. 5) First-time headquarters/field. 6) First-time team leader. 7) First-time new technology/business/function. Scope assignments involving increased complexity: 1) Managing a significant expansion of an existing product or service. 2) Managing adding new products/service into an existing unit. 3) Managing a reorganized and more diverse unit. 4) Managing explosive growth. 5) Adding new technologies.

☐ **Start-ups**
The core demands to qualify as a start from scratch are: 1) Starting something new for you and/or for the organization. 2) Forging a new team. 3) Creating new systems/facilities/staffs/programs/procedures. 4) Contextual adversity (e.g., uncertainty, government regulation, unions, difficult environment). Seven types of start from scratches: 1) Planning, building, hiring, and managing (e.g., building a new facility, opening up a new location, moving a unit or company). 2) Heading something new (e.g., new product, new service, new line of business, new department/function, major new program). 3) Take over a group/product/service/program that had existed for less than a year and was off to a fast start. 4) Establishing overseas operations. 5) Major new designs for existing systems. 6) Moving a successful program from one unit to another. 7) Installing a new organization-wide process as a full-time job (e.g., like Total Quality).

SECTION 6: LEARNING MORE FROM YOUR PLAN

THESE ADDITIONAL REMEDIES WILL HELP MAKE THIS DEVELOPMENT PLAN MORE EFFECTIVE FOR YOU

Learning to Learn Better

☐ **Study Yourself in Detail**
Study your likes and dislikes because they can drive a lot of your thinking, judging, and acting. Ask which like or dislike has gotten in the way or prevented you from moving to a higher level of learning. Are your likes and dislikes really important to you or have you just gone on "autopilot"? Try to address and understand a blocking dislike and change it.

Learning from Experience, Feedback and Other People

☐ **Using Multiple Models**
Who do you know who exemplifies how to do whatever your need is? Who, for example, personifies decisiveness or compassion or strategic agility? Think more broadly than your current job and colleagues. For example, clergy, friends, spouses or community leaders are also good sources for potential models. Select your models not on the basis of overall excellence or likability, but on the basis of the one towering

strength (or glaring weakness) you are interested in. Even people who are well thought of usually have only one or two towering strengths (or glaring weaknesses). Ordinarily, you won't learn as much from the whole person as you will from one characteristic.

☐ **Learning from Bosses**
Bosses can be an excellent and ready source for learning. All bosses do some things exceptionally well and other things poorly. Distance your feelings from the boss/direct report relationship and study things that work and things that don't work for your boss. What would you have done? What could you use, and what should you avoid?

☐ **Learning from Ineffective Behavior**
Seeing things done poorly can be a very potent source of learning for you, especially if the behavior or action affects others negatively. Many times the thing done poorly causes emotional reactions or pain in you and others. Distance yourself from the feelings and explore why the actions didn't work.

☐ **Getting Feedback from Direct Reports**
Direct reports often fear reprisals for giving negative feedback about bosses, whether in a formal process, like a questionnaire, or informally and face-to-face. Even with a guarantee of confidentiality, some are still hesitant. If you want feedback from direct reports, you have to set a positive tone and never act out of revenge.

☐ **Getting Feedback from Peers/Colleagues**
Your peers and colleagues may not be candid if they are in competition with you. Some may not be willing to be open with you out of fear of giving you an advantage. Some may give you exaggerated feedback to deliberately cause you undue concern. You have to set the tone and gauge the trust level of the relationship and the quality of the feedback.

☐ **Feedback in Unusual Contexts/Situations**
Temporary and extreme conditions and contexts may shade interpretations of your behavior and intentions. Demands of the job may drive you outside your normal mode of operating. Hence, feedback you receive may be inaccurate during those times. However, unusual contexts affect our behavior less than most assume. It's usually a weak excuse.

☐ **Learning from Bad Situations**
All of us will find ourselves in bad situations from time to time. Good intentions gone bad. Impossible tasks and goals. Hopeless projects. Even though you probably can't perform well, the key is to at least take away some lessons and insights. How did things get to be this way? What factors led to the impasse? How can you make the best of a bad situation? How can you neutralize the negative elements? How can you get the most out of yourself and your staff under the chilling situation?

What can you salvage? How can you use coping strategies to minimize the negatives? How can you avoid these situations going forward? In bad situations: 1) Be resourceful. Get the most you can out of the situation. 2) Try to deduce why things got to be that way. 3) Learn from both the situation you inherited and how you react to it. 4) Integrate what you learn into your future behavior.

Learning from Courses

☐ **Insight Events**

These are courses designed around assessing skills and providing feedback to the participants. These events can be a powerful source of self-knowledge and can lead to significant development if done right. When selecting a self-insight course, consider the following: 1) Are the skills assessed the important ones? 2) Are the assessment techniques and instruments sound? 3) Are those who are providing the feedback trained and professional? 4) Is the feedback provided in a user-friendly and "actionable" format? 5) Does the feedback include development planning? 6) Is the setting comfortable and conducive to reflection and learning? 7) Are the other participants the kinds of people you could learn from? 8) Are you in the right frame of mind to learn from this kind of intense experience? Select events on the basis of positive answers to these eight questions.

☐ **Attitude Toward Learning**

In addition to selecting the right course, a learning attitude is required. Be open. Close down your "like/dislike" switch, your "agree/disagree" blinders, and your "like me/not like me" feelings toward the instructors. Learning requires new lessons, change, and new behaviors and perspectives – all scary stuff for most people. Don't resist. Take in all you can during the course. Ask clarifying questions. Discuss concerns with the other participants. Jot down what you learn as you go. After the course is over, take some reflective time to glean the meat. Make the practical decisions about what you can and cannot use.

SUGGESTED READINGS

Aguilar, Francis J. *Managing Corporate Ethics – Learning from America's ethical companies how to supercharge business performance.* New York: Oxford University Press, 1994.

Badaracco, Joseph L. Jr. *Defining Moments – When managers must choose between right and right.* Boston: Harvard Business School Press, 1997.

Clark, Ralph W. and Alice Darnell Lattal. *Workplace Ethics – Winning the integrity revolution.* Lanham, MD: Rowman and Littlefield Publishers, Inc., 1993.

Dosick, Rabbi Wayne. *The Business Bible – Ten new commandments for creating an ethical workplace.* New York: William Morrow and Company, Inc., 1993.

Edwards, Owen. *Upward Nobility: How to succeed in business without losing your soul.* New York: Crown Publishers, Inc., 1991.

Sonnenberg, Frank K. *Managing with a Conscience – How to improve performance through integrity, trust and commitment.* New York: McGraw-Hill, Inc., 1994.

23

FAIRNESS TO DIRECT REPORTS

SECTION 1: YOUR DEVELOPMENT NEED(S)

UNSKILLED

- ☐ Is not equitable toward direct reports
- ☐ Doesn't listen to direct reports' concerns and needs
- ☐ May not read people's needs well and not be able to tell how they are responding to his/her treatment
- ☐ Hides or keeps things from his/her people they have a right to know
- ☐ May be inconsistent and play favorites
- ☐ May not think about it or be too busy to pay attention to equity
- ☐ May bucket people into good and bad buckets and treat them accordingly

SKILLED

- ☐ Treats direct reports equitably
- ☐ Acts fairly
- ☐ Has candid discussions
- ☐ Doesn't have hidden agenda
- ☐ Doesn't give preferential treatment

OVERUSED SKILL

- ☐ May spend too much time pleasing everyone
- ☐ May worry about distributing the work evenly and not using, challenging, or developing the best
- ☐ His/her need to be fair may mask real problems and differences

Select one to three of the competencies listed below to work on to compensate for an overuse of this skill.

COMPENSATORS: 9, 12, 13, 18, 19, 20, 21, 25, 34, 35, 36, 37, 51, 52, 56, 57, 64

SOME CAUSES

- ☐ Believe strongly in a meritocracy; rewards to the winners
- ☐ Don't read people well
- ☐ Don't really care about people
- ☐ Inconsistent behavior toward others
- ☐ Play favorites
- ☐ Too busy to treat all equitably

THE MAP

Fairness seems simple; treat all people the same. Lack of fairness plays out in many ways: Do you treat high performers differently than everyone else? Do you have favorite and less favorite groups? Do you develop some but not others? Do your ethics seem variable to direct reports? Does your candor vary? It's usually best to think of fairness as equity toward others and not signaling to others what your assessment is of them in your day to day behavior. A subtler way to think of fairness is to treat each person equitably, that is according to his or her needs. The treatment would actually differ somewhat from person to person but the outcome or effect would be the same; each person would feel fairly treated. A large part of each person's motivation will be determined by his/her feelings about fair treatment. Unfair treatment causes all kinds of noise in the relationship between a boss and a direct report and causes noise in the group. Unfair treatment leads to less productivity, less efficiency and wasted time seeking justice.

SECTION 2: LEARNING ON YOUR OWN

THESE SELF-DEVELOPMENT REMEDIES WILL HELP YOU BUILD YOUR SKILL(S)

SOME REMEDIES

☐ **1. Equity with information.** Follow the rule of equity of information with everyone: explain your thinking and ask them to explain theirs. When discussing issues, give reasons first, solutions last. When you give solutions first, people often don't listen to your reasons. Some people get overly directive with some of their reports, and they in turn feel that you're not interested in what they think. Invite their thinking and their reasons before settling on solutions. Don't provide information selectively. Don't use information as a reward or a relationship builder with one or just a few and not others.

☐ **2. Equity with groups.** Monitor yourself carefully to see if you treat different groups or people differently. Common patterns are to treat low performers, people with less status and people from outside your unit with less respect. Be candid with yourself. Is there a group or individuals you don't like or are uncomfortable with? Have you put them in your not very respected bucket? Many of us do. To break out of this, ask yourself why they behave the way they do and how you would like to be treated if you were in their position. Turn off your judgment program.

☐ **3. Equity with standards.** Check to make sure you are not excusing a behavior in a high performer that you wouldn't tolerate in someone else. Does everyone have the same rules and get held to the same standard?

☐ **4. Equity with demographics.** Check to make sure you are not applying different standards based upon gender, age, nationality, ethnic origin, religion, etc. Do you treat groups more familiar and comfortable to you or like you differently than others? Does one group come in for more praise or criticism than the others? The best way to find out is to ask one or more from each group you work with for feedback. *More help? – See #21* Managing *Diversity.*

☐ **5. In meetings, make sure you include everyone** and don't direct substantially more remarks toward one person or subgroup to the exclusion of others. Make sure you signal nothing negative to others; a neutral observer should not be able to tell from your demeanor who you like and don't like. Help the quiet, shy and reserved have their say. Quiet the loud, assertive and passionate. Give everyone a fair chance to be heard.

☐ **6. Keep fairness conflicts small and concrete.** The more abstract it gets, the more unmanageable it becomes. Separate the people from the problem. Attack fairness problems by looking at the nature of the problem, not the particular positions people take. Try on their views of "what would have been fair" for size, the emotion as well as the content. Don't guess at their motives and intentions. Avoid direct blaming remarks; describe the problem and its impact. If you can't agree on a solution, agree on procedure; or agree on a few things, and agree that there are issues remaining. This creates some motion and breaks fairness stalemates.

☐ **7. Fairness standards.** Install objective standards to determine the fairness of a treatment (pay, office choice, day off) – criteria, statistical models, professional standards, market value, cost models. Set standards anyone could independently measure and come up with the same conclusion.

☐ **8. If you lose your composure with certain people,** but not others, a good practice to follow is when your emotions rise to a challenge of your fairness, count to five in your head, then respond with a clarifying question. This serves the triple purpose of giving the person a second chance, allows you to compose yourself, and may prevent you from jumping to an incorrect conclusion and taking precipitous action.

☐ **9. Fairness norms.** There are as many interpretations of what's fair as there are people in your world. Try to get the whole group involved in questions of fairness. Get everyone's opinion about how fair a particular program or treatment is. Let them tell you what's fair before you make that judgment for them without input. Everyone will feel better treated when they have had a hand in determining the rules.

☐ **10. If a fairness issue hits a core value of yours,** pause to:

- Edit your actions before you act. Before you speak or act in problem situations, ask yourself if you would do the same thing in a parallel situation. Is your value really what should be operating here?

- Pick your battles. Make sure you only pull rank and impose your values on others in really mission-critical situations.

SECTION 3: LEARNING FROM MORE FEEDBACK

THESE SOURCES WOULD GIVE YOU THE MOST ACCURATE AND DETAILED FEEDBACK ON YOUR SKILL(S)

☐ **Direct Reports**
Across a variety of settings, your direct reports probably see you the most. They are the recipients of most of your managerial behaviors. They know your work. They can compare you with former bosses. Since they may hesitate to give you negative feedback, you have to set the atmosphere to make it easier for them. You have to ask.

☐ **Human Resource Professionals**
Human Resource professionals have both a formal and informal feedback role. Since they have access to unique and confidential information, they can provide the right context for feedback you've received. Sometimes they may be "directed" to give you feedback. Other times, they may pass on feedback just to be helpful to you.

☐ **Past Associates/Constituencies**
When confronted with a present performance problem, some claim, "I wasn't like that before; it must be the current situation." When feedback is available from former associates, about 50% support that claim. In the other half of the cases, the people were like that before and probably didn't know it. It sometimes makes sense to access the past to clearly see the present.

SECTION 4: LEARNING FROM DEVELOP-IN-PLACE ASSIGNMENTS

THESE PART-TIME DEVELOP-IN-PLACE ASSIGNMENTS WILL HELP YOU BUILD YOUR SKILL(S)

☐ Represent the concerns of a group of nonexempt, clerical, or administrative employees to higher management to seek resolution of a difficult issue.

☐ Manage an ad hoc, temporary group of "green," inexperienced people as their coach, teacher, orienter, etc.

☐ Manage an ad hoc, temporary group of balky and resisting people through an unpopular change or project.

☐ Manage an ad hoc, temporary group of low-competence people through a task they couldn't do by themselves.

☐ Manage an ad hoc, temporary group including former peers to accomplish a task.

☐ Manage an ad hoc, temporary group of people who are older and/or more experienced to accomplish a task.

- ☐ Manage an ad hoc, temporary group of people where the temporary manager is a towering expert and the people in the group are not.
- ☐ Manage an ad hoc, temporary group of people involved in tackling a fix-it or turnaround project.
- ☐ Help shut down a plant, regional office, product line, business, operation, etc.
- ☐ Manage a project team of people who are older and more experienced than you.

SECTION 5: LEARNING FROM FULL-TIME JOBS

THESE FULL-TIME JOBS OFFER THE OPPORTUNITY TO BUILD YOUR SKILL(S)

☐ **Fix-its/Turnarounds**
The core demands to qualify as a Fix-it or Turnaround assignment are: 1) Cleaning up a mess. 2) Serious people issues/problems like credibility/performance/morale. 3) Tight deadline. 4) Serious business performance failure. 5) Last chance to fix. Four Types of Fix-its/Turnarounds: 1) Fixing a failed business/unit involving taking control, stopping losses, managing damage, planning the turnaround, dealing with people problems, installing new processes and systems, and rebuilding the spirit and performance of the unit. 2) Managing sizable disasters like mishandled labor negotiations and strikes, thefts, history of significant business losses, poor staff, failed leadership, hidden problems, fraud, public relations nightmares, etc. 3) Significant reorganization and restructuring (e.g., stabilizing the business, reforming unit, introducing new systems, making people changes, resetting strategy and tactics). 4) Significant system/process breakdown (e.g., MIS, financial coordination processes, audits, standards, etc.) across units requiring working to change something from a distant position, providing advice and counsel, and installing or implementing a major process improvement or system change outside your own unit and/or with customers outside the organization.

☐ **Scale Assignments**
Core requirements to qualify as a Scale (size) shift assignment are: 1) Sizable jump-shift in the size of the job in areas like: number of people, number of layers in organization, size of budget, number of locations, volume of activity, tightness of deadlines. 2) Medium to low complexity; mostly repetitive and routine processes and procedures. 3) Stable staff and business. 4) Stable operations. 5) Often slow, steady growth.

☐ **Significant People Demands**
Core demands required to qualify as a Significant People Responsibilities assignment are: 1) A sizable increase in either the number of people managed and/or the complexity of the challenges involved 2) Longer-term assignment (two or more years). 3) Quality of

people management critical to achieving results. 4) Involves groups not worked with before (e.g., union, new technical areas, nationalities).

SECTION 6: LEARNING MORE FROM YOUR PLAN

THESE ADDITIONAL REMEDIES WILL HELP MAKE THIS DEVELOPMENT PLAN MORE EFFECTIVE FOR YOU

Learning to Learn Better

☐ **Examine Why You Judge People the Way You Do**
List the people you like and those you dislike and try to find out why. What do those you like have in common with each other and with you? What do those you dislike have in common with themselves and how do they differ from you? Are your "people buckets" logical and productive or do they interfere? Could you be more effective without putting people into buckets?

Learning from Experience, Feedback and Other People

☐ **Using Multiple Models**
Who do you know who exemplifies how to do whatever your need is? Who, for example, personifies decisiveness or compassion or strategic agility? Think more broadly than your current job and colleagues. For example, clergy, friends, spouses or community leaders are also good sources for potential models. Select your models not on the basis of overall excellence or likability, but on the basis of the one towering strength (or glaring weakness) you are interested in. Even people who are well thought of usually have only one or two towering strengths (or glaring weaknesses). Ordinarily, you won't learn as much from the whole person as you will from one characteristic.

☐ **Learning from Interviewing Others**
Interview others. Ask not only what they do, but how and why they do it. What do they think are the rules of thumb they are following? Where did they learn the behaviors? How do they keep them current? How do they monitor the effect they have on others?

☐ **Learning from Observing Others**
Observe others. Find opportunities to observe without interacting with your model. This enables you to objectively study the person, note what he/she is doing or not doing, and compare that with what you would typically do in similar situations. Many times you can learn more by watching than asking. Your model may not be able to explain what he/she does or may be an unwilling teacher.

☐ **Learning from a Coach or Tutor**
Ask a person to coach or tutor you directly. This has the additional benefit of skill building coupled with correcting feedback. Also observe the teacher teaching you. How does he/she teach? How does he/she

adjust to you as a learner? After the process, ask for feedback about you as a learner.

- ☐ **Consolidating What You Learn from People**
After using any source and/or method of learning from others, write down or mentally note the new rules of thumb and the principles involved. How will you remind yourself of the new behaviors in similar situations? How will you prevent yourself from reacting on "autopilot"? How could you share what you have learned from others?

- ☐ **Getting Feedback from Direct Reports**
Direct reports often fear reprisals for giving negative feedback about bosses, whether in a formal process, like a questionnaire, or informally and face-to-face. Even with a guarantee of confidentiality, some are still hesitant. If you want feedback from direct reports, you have to set a positive tone and never act out of revenge.

- ☐ **Learning from Limited Staff**
Most managers either inherit or hire staff from time to time who are inexperienced, incompetent, not up to the task, resistant, or dispirited. Any of these may create a hardship for you. The lessons to be learned are how to get things done with limited resources and how to fix the people situation. In the short term, this hardship is best addressed by assessing the combined strengths of the team and deploying the best you have against the problem. Almost everyone can do something well. Also, the team can contribute more than the combined individuals can. How can you empower and motivate the team? If you hired the troublesome staff, why did you err? What can you learn from your hiring mistakes? What wasn't there that you thought was present? What led you astray? How can you prevent that same hiring error in the future? What do you need to do to fix the situation? Quick development? Start over? If you inherited the problem, how can you fix it? Can you implement a program of accelerated development? Do you have to start over and get new people? What did the prior manager do or not do that led to this situation in the first place? What can you learn from that? What will you do differently? How does the staff feel? What can you learn from their frustrations over not being able to do the job? How can you be a positive force under negative circumstances? How can you rally them to perform? What lasting lessons can you learn from someone in distress and trouble? If you're going to try accelerated development, how can you get a quick assessment? How can you give the staff motivating feedback? How can you construct and implement development plans that will work? How can you get people on-line feedback for maximum growth? Do you know when to stop trying and start over? If you're going to turn over some staff, how can you do it both rapidly and with the least damage? How can you deliver the message in a constructive way? What can you learn from having to take negative actions against people? How can you prevent this from happening again?

Learning from Courses

- ☐ **Supervisory Courses**
  Most new supervisors go through an "Introduction to Supervision" type course. They are designed to teach the common practices a first-line supervisor needs to know to be effective. The content of most of those courses is standard. There is general agreement on the principles of effective supervision. There are two common problems: 1) Do the students have a strong motivation to learn? Do they know what they don't know? Is there any pain? Because motivated students with a need for the knowledge learn best, participants should have had some trying experiences and some supervisory pain and hardships before attending. 2) Are the instructors experienced supervisors? Have they practiced what they preach? Can they share powerful anecdotes to make key points? Can they answer questions credibly? If possible, select supervisory courses based on the instructors, since the content seems to be the much same for all such courses. Lastly, does the course offer the opportunity for practicing each skill? Does it contain simulations? Are there case studies you could easily identify with? Are there breakout groups? Is there opportunity for action learning? Search for the most interactive course.

- ☐ **Sending Others to Courses**
  If you are responsible for managing someone else's development and, as part of that, sending them to courses, prepare them beforehand. Don't send them as tourists. Meet with them before and after the course. Tell them why they need this course. Tell them what you expect them to learn. Give them feedback on why you think they need the course. Agree ahead of time how you will measure and monitor learning after they return. If possible, offer a variety of courses for your employee to choose from. Have them give you a report shortly after they return. If appropriate, have them present what they learned to the rest of your staff. After they return, provide opportunities for using the new skills with safe cover and low risk. Give them practice time before expecting full exercise of the new skills. Be supportive during early unsteadiness. Give continuous feedback on progress.

SUGGESTED READINGS

Bardwick, Judith M. *In Praise of Good Business – How optimizing risk rewards both your bottom line and your people.* New York: John Wiley & Sons, Inc., 1998.

Faust, Gerald W, Richard I Lyles and Will Phillips. *Responsible Managers Get Results.* New York: AMACOM, 1998.

Jellison, Jerald M. *Overcoming Resistance.* New York: Simon & Schuster, 1993.

Maslow, Abraham H. *Maslow on Management.* New York: John Wiley & Sons, Inc., 1998.

24

FUNCTIONAL / TECHNICAL SKILLS

SECTION 1: YOUR DEVELOPMENT NEED(S)

UNSKILLED

- ☐ Not up to functional or technical proficiency
- ☐ Makes technical/functional errors
- ☐ Judgment and decision making marginal because of lack of knowledge
- ☐ May be stuck in past skills and technologies
- ☐ May be inexperienced, new to the area, or lack interest in it
- ☐ Lack of detail orientation to go deep
- ☐ May not make the time to learn

SKILLED

- ☐ Has the functional and technical knowledge and skills to do the job at a high level of accomplishment

OVERUSED SKILL

- ☐ May be seen as too narrow
- ☐ May overdevelop or depend upon technical and functional knowledge and skills at the expense of personal, interpersonal and managerial skills
- ☐ May use deep technical knowledge and skills to avoid ambiguity and risk

Select one to three of the competencies listed below to work on to compensate for an overuse of this skill.

COMPENSATORS: 14, 28, 30, 32, 45, 46, 51, 57, 58

SOME CAUSES

- ☐ Inexperienced; new to the area
- ☐ Lack of detail orientation
- ☐ Lack of interest in the function
- ☐ Time management; haven't gotten around to it
- ☐ Stuck in a past technology

THE MAP

All areas of work have a single or sometimes a few sets of technologies behind doing them well. Doing the work of the function takes a higher level of technical/functional knowledge than managing it. In most functions or technical areas, there are a number of strong pros who know the technology in great depth. They are the experts. Most others have sufficient knowledge to do their jobs. Some have marginal skills and knowledge in the area and hurt the rest of the group.

SECTION 2: LEARNING ON YOUR OWN

THESE SELF-DEVELOPMENT REMEDIES WILL HELP YOU BUILD YOUR SKILL(S)

SOME REMEDIES

☐ **1. Locate a pro.** Find the seasoned master professional in the technology or function and ask whether he/she would mind showing you the ropes and tutoring you. Most don't mind having a few "apprentices" around. Help him or her teach you. Ask, "How do you know what's important? What do you look at first? Second? What are the five keys you always look at or for? What do you read? Who do you go to for advice?"

☐ **2. Sign up.** Almost all functions have national and sometimes regional professional associations made up of hundreds of people who do well what you need to learn every day. Sign up as a member. Buy some of the introductory literature. Go to some of their workshops. Go to the annual conference.

☐ **3. Find the bible on your function/technology.** Almost every function and technology has a book people might call the "bible" in the area. It is the standard reference everyone looks to for knowledge. There is probably a journal in your technology or function. Subscribe for a year or more. See if they have back issues available.

☐ **4. Meet the notables.** Identify some national leaders in your function/technology and buy their books, read their articles, and attend their lectures and workshops.

☐ **5. Learn from those around you.** Ask others in your function/technology which skills and what knowledge is mission-critical and ask them how they learned it. Follow the same or a similar path.

☐ **6. Take a course.** Your local college or university might have some nighttime or weekend courses you could take in your technology. Your organization may have training classes in your technology.

☐ **7. Consult your past.** You might have been good in some previous function or technology. If this isn't the case, consider anything you know well such as a hobby. How did you learn it? *More help? – See #32 Learning on the Fly.*

☐ **8. Find a guru.** Find a consultant in your technology/function and hire him/her to provide a private tutorial to accelerate your learning.

☐ **9. Learn to think as an expert in the technology does.** Take problems to him/her and ask what are the keys he/she looks for; observe what he/she considers significant and not significant. Chunk up data into categories so you can remember it. Devise five key areas or questions you can consider each time a technical issue comes up. Don't waste your time learning facts; they won't be useful unless you have conceptual buckets to put them in.

☐ **10. Teach others.** Form a study group and take turns presenting on new, different or unknown aspects of the technology. Having to teach it will force you to conceptualize and understand it more deeply.

SECTION 3: LEARNING FROM MORE FEEDBACK

THESE SOURCES WOULD GIVE YOU THE MOST ACCURATE AND DETAILED FEEDBACK ON YOUR SKILL(S)

☐ **Direct Boss**
Your direct boss has important information about you, your performance, and your prospects. The challenge is to get this information. There are formal processes (e.g., performance appraisals). There are day-to-day opportunities. To help, signal your boss that you want and can handle direct and timely feedback. Many bosses have trouble giving feedback, so you will have to work at it over a period of time.

☐ **Direct Reports**
Across a variety of settings, your direct reports probably see you the most. They are the recipients of most of your managerial behaviors. They know your work. They can compare you with former bosses. Since they may hesitate to give you negative feedback, you have to set the atmosphere to make it easier for them. You have to ask.

☐ **Past Associates/Constituencies**
When confronted with a present performance problem, some claim, "I wasn't like that before; it must be the current situation." When feedback is available from former associates, about 50% support that claim. In the other half of the cases, the people were like that before and probably didn't know it. It sometimes makes sense to access the past to clearly see the present.

☐ **Peers and Colleagues**
Peers and colleagues have a special social and working relationship. They attend staff meetings together, share private views, get feedback from the same boss, travel together, and are knowledgeable about each other's work. You perhaps let your guard down more around peers and act more like yourself. They can be a valuable source of feedback.

SECTION 4: LEARNING FROM DEVELOP-IN-PLACE ASSIGNMENTS

THESE PART-TIME DEVELOP-IN-PLACE ASSIGNMENTS WILL HELP YOU BUILD YOUR SKILL(S)

☐ Manage the purchase of a major product, equipment, materials, program, or system.

☐ Audit cost overruns to assess the problem and present your findings to the person or people involved.

- ☐ Study some aspect of your job or a new technical area you haven't studied before that you need to be more effective.
- ☐ Do a problem-prevention analysis on a product or service and present it to the people involved.
- ☐ Do a competitive analysis of your organization's products or services or your position in the marketplace and present it to the people involved.
- ☐ Monitor and follow a new product or service through the entire idea, design, test market, and launch cycle.
- ☐ Represent the organization at a trade show, convention, exposition, etc.
- ☐ Seek out and use a seed budget to create and pursue a personal idea, product, or service.
- ☐ Teach a course, seminar, or workshop on something you don't know well.
- ☐ Train customers in the use of the organization's products or services.

SECTION 5: LEARNING FROM FULL-TIME JOBS

THESE FULL-TIME JOBS OFFER THE OPPORTUNITY TO BUILD YOUR SKILL(S)

☐ **Fix-its / Turnarounds**

The core demands to qualify as a Fix-it or Turnaround assignment are: 1) Cleaning up a mess. 2) Serious people issues/problems like credibility/performance/morale. 3) Tight deadline. 4) Serious business performance failure. 5) Last chance to fix. Four Types of Fix-its/ Turnarounds: 1) Fixing a failed business/unit involving taking control, stopping losses, managing damage, planning the turnaround, dealing with people problems, installing new processes and systems, and rebuilding the spirit and performance of the unit. 2) Managing sizable disasters like mishandled labor negotiations and strikes, thefts, history of significant business losses, poor staff, failed leadership, hidden problems, fraud, public relations nightmares, etc. 3) Significant reorganization and restructuring (e.g., stabilizing the business, re-forming unit, introducing new systems, making people changes, resetting strategy and tactics). 4) Significant system/process breakdown (e.g., MIS, financial coordination processes, audits, standards, etc.) across units requiring working to change something from a distant position, providing advice and counsel, and installing or implementing a major process improvement or system change outside your own unit and/or with customers outside the organization.

☐ **Line To Staff Switches**

The core demands to qualify as a Line to Staff switch are: 1) Intellectually/strategically demanding. 2) Highly visible to others. 3) New area/perspective/method/culture/function. 4) Moving away from a bottom line. 5) Moving from field to headquarters. 6) Exposure to high-level executives. Examples: 1) Business/strategic planning.

2) Heading a staff department. 3) Assistant to/chief of staff to a senior executive. 4) Head of a task force. 5) Human resources role.

- ☐ **Member of Projects/Task Forces**
  The core demands for qualifying as a Project/Task Force assignment are: 1) Full-time assignment. 2) Important and specific goal. 3) Tight deadline. 4) Success or failure will be evident. 5) High-visibility sponsor. 6) Learning something on the fly. 7) Must get others to cooperate. 8) Usually six months or more. Four types of Projects/Task Forces: 1) New ideas, products, services, or systems (e.g., product/service/program research and development, creation/installation/launch of a new system, new programs like Total Quality Management, positive discipline). 2) Formal negotiations and relationships (e.g., acquisitions, divestitures, agreements, joint ventures; licensing arrangements, franchising; dealing with unions, governments, communities, charities, customers, and relocations). 3) Big one-time events (e.g., working on a major presentation for the board, organizing significant meetings or conferences, disaster/damage control teams; reorganizations, mergers, acquisitions, or relocations, working on visions, charters, strategies, other time-urgent issues and problems). 4) Troubleshooting (e.g., problems, disasters, crises, product/service failures, accidents, illegal activities, damage control in public relations goofs, shut downs, downsizings, layoffs, abrupt changes in leadership).

- ☐ **Start-ups**
  The core demands to qualify as a start from scratch are: 1) Starting something new for you and/or for the organization. 2) Forging a new team. 3) Creating new systems/facilities/staffs/programs/procedures. 4) Contextual adversity (e.g., uncertainty, government regulation, unions, difficult environment). Seven types of start from scratches: 1) Planning, building, hiring, and managing (e.g., building a new facility, opening up a new location, moving a unit or company). 2) Heading something new (e.g., new product, new service, new line of business, new department/function, major new program). 3) Take over a group/product/service/program that had existed for less than a year and was off to a fast start. 4) Establishing overseas operations. 5) Major new designs for existing systems. 6) Moving a successful program from one unit to another. 7) Installing a new organization-wide process as a full-time job (e.g., like Total Quality).

SECTION 6: LEARNING MORE FROM YOUR PLAN

THESE ADDITIONAL REMEDIES WILL HELP MAKE THIS DEVELOPMENT PLAN MORE EFFECTIVE FOR YOU

Learning from Experience, Feedback and Other People

☐ **Learning from Mentors and Tutors**
Mentors and tutors offer a special case for learning since the relationship is specifically formed for learning. You need to be open and nondefensive. You need to solicit and accept feedback. This is a unique opportunity for you to get low-risk, honest, and direct feedback on what you do well and not so well.

☐ **Learning from Interviewing Others**
Interview others. Ask not only what they do, but how and why they do it. What do they think are the rules of thumb they are following? Where did they learn the behaviors? How do they keep them current? How do they monitor the effect they have on others?

☐ **Getting Feedback from Bosses and Superiors**
Many bosses are reluctant to give negative feedback. They lack the managerial courage to face people directly with criticism. You can help by soliciting feedback and setting the tone. Show them you can handle criticism and that you are willing to work on issues they see as important.

☐ **Getting Feedback from Direct Reports**
Direct reports often fear reprisals for giving negative feedback about bosses, whether in a formal process, like a questionnaire, or informally and face-to-face. Even with a guarantee of confidentiality, some are still hesitant. If you want feedback from direct reports, you have to set a positive tone and never act out of revenge.

☐ **Getting Feedback from Peers/Colleagues**
Your peers and colleagues may not be candid if they are in competition with you. Some may not be willing to be open with you out of fear of giving you an advantage. Some may give you exaggerated feedback to deliberately cause you undue concern. You have to set the tone and gauge the trust level of the relationship and the quality of the feedback.

☐ **Openness to Feedback**
Nothing discourages feedback more than defensiveness, resistance, irritation, and excuses. People don't like giving feedback anyway, and much less to those who don't listen or are unreceptive. To help the feedback giver, be open, listen, ask for examples and details, take notes, keep a journal, and thank them for their interest.

Learning from Courses

- ☐ **Job Skills**
  Most organizations and professional associations offer job skills training. The key is to find a course that has the right content and offers the opportunity for practicing the jobs skills. It's helpful if the instructors have actually performed the skills in situations similar to your own. Most organizations offer a variety of orientation events. They are designed to communicate strategies, charters, missions, goals, and general information and offer an opportunity for people to meet each other. They are short in duration and offer limited opportunities for learning anything beyond general context and background.
- ☐ **Survey Courses**
  These are courses designed to give a general overview of an entire area (such as advertising), product or product line, division's activities, process (getting a product to market, Total Quality Management) or geography (doing business in "X"). These types of courses are good for general background and context.
- ☐ **Strategic Courses**
  There are a number of courses designed to stretch minds to prepare for future challenges. They include topics such as Workforce Diversity 2000, globalization, the European Union, competitive competencies and strategies, etc. Quality depends upon the following three factors: 1) The quality of the staff. Are they qualified? Are they respected in their fields? Are they strategic "gurus"? 2) The quality of the participants. Are they the kind of people you could learn from? 3) The quality of the setting. Is it comfortable and free from distractions? Can you learn there?

SUGGESTED READINGS

There are no suggested readings for this competency as there are thousands of technical/functional skills.

25

HIRING AND STAFFING

SECTION 1: YOUR DEVELOPMENT NEED(S)

UNSKILLED

- ☐ Doesn't have a good track record in hiring and/or staffing
- ☐ May clone him/herself or focus on one or two preferred characteristics
- ☐ May look narrowly for people who are similar to him/her
- ☐ May play it safe with selections
- ☐ Doesn't select much diversity
- ☐ May not know what competence looks like, lack criteria, or assume he/she just knows
- ☐ May lack the patience to wait for a better candidate

SKILLED

- ☐ Has a nose for talent
- ☐ Hires the best people available from inside or outside
- ☐ Is not afraid of selecting strong people
- ☐ Assembles talented staffs

OVERUSED SKILL

- ☐ May overlook slow starters
- ☐ May select on surface characteristics
- ☐ May assemble a team of individual performers who aren't good team players
- ☐ May prefer currently talented people who aren't broad enough for further growth
- ☐ May be too quick to replace rather than work with a person

Select one to three of the competencies listed below to work on to compensate for an overuse of this skill.

COMPENSATORS: 21, 30, 33, 41, 52, 56, 60, 64

SOME CAUSES

- ☐ Fear of being shown up by a better person
- ☐ Inexperience with hiring people
- ☐ Lack of courage to do something different
- ☐ Lack of personal self confidence
- ☐ Narrow perspective on what talent looks like
- ☐ Too impatient to wait for a better candidate

THE MAP

The world runs on talent. The more talent you have personally and the more talented your team is the better. Talented people make big things happen. Working with and around talent is motivating and energizing. Talented people are competitive, most of the time friendly; sometimes not. Managing talented people is sometimes a challenge, albeit maybe a pleasant one. Lots of good things happen when there is talent around.

SECTION 2: LEARNING ON YOUR OWN

THESE SELF-DEVELOPMENT REMEDIES WILL HELP YOU BUILD YOUR SKILL(S)

SOME REMEDIES

☐ **1. Can you tell who is talented and who isn't?** Look around your environment and see who others think the very talented people are and who are not very talented. Do the talented have any common characteristics? Watch out for traps – it is rarely intelligence or pure personality that spells the difference in talent. Most people are smart enough and many personality characteristics don't matter that much for performance. Ask the second question. Look below surface descriptions of smart, approachable, technically skilled.

☐ **2. Can you interview for talent?** There are commonly agreed upon methods to find talent in an interview. See The RECRUITING ARCHITECT® or ask someone in the recruiting and staffing area in your organization for guidance on how to conduct a good interview.

☐ **3. Think back over your career.** Make two lists – one of the most talented people you have worked with and the other of those who were so-so; although they made have had reasonable talents, they didn't really deliver. Do the people on each list have common characteristics? Why did you say one was talented and the other less so? What's the major difference between the two lists?

☐ **4. List all of the bosses you have had.** Divide them into the 33% most talented and the 33% least talented. Do the bosses on the most talented list have common characteristics. Why did you say one list was talented and the other not? What's the major difference between the two lists of bosses? Which list would you like to work for again?

☐ **5. Ask your Human Resource person to share with you** the success profile of successful and talented people in your organization.

☐ **6. When you make a hiring decision** or are deciding who to work with on a problem or project, do you think you have a tendency to clone yourself too much? Do you have a preference for people who think and act as you do? What characteristics do you value too much? What downsides do you ignore or excuse away? This is a common human tendency. The key is to seek balance, variety and diversity. People good at this competency can comfortably surround themselves with people not like them.

- ☐ **7. Are your standards too high or too low?** Do you hire the first close candidate that comes along or do you wait for the perfect candidate and leave the position open too long? Either tendency will probably get you and the organization in trouble. Always try to wait long enough to have choices but not long enough to lose a very good candidate while you wait for the perfect one to come along. Learn how to set reasonable standards with The RECRUITING ARCHITECT® and The COMPETENCY ARCHITECT™.
- ☐ **8. Do you have a long-term view of the talent** it's going to take to produce both current and long-term results? Do you have a replacement plan for yourself? Do you use a success profile with the competencies you know you are going to need? Have you hired someone who now has or will have in a short period of time, the ability to take your job? Have you selected someone you would sponsor for promotion to another job at your level, possibly passing you up in time? The best managers surround themselves with talent and eventually some of the talent turns out to be better than the person who hired and trained them. That's a good thing and reason for a celebration.
- ☐ **9. Read two or three books on personality** or on how people differ from one another (such as *Gifts Differing* by Isabel Myers) or go to a class about how people differ. Check your people assessments with others you trust to give you their real opinion.
- ☐ **10. Some people feel insecure around talented people** and are rightly afraid of being shown up. That's true. You will be, because no one has all possible strengths. Chances are everyone in your unit is better at something than you are. The key is to take this natural fear and use it as a positive – hire people for different talents, study how they think, watch how they go about exercising their strengths and use this knowledge to improve yourself.

SECTION 3: LEARNING FROM MORE FEEDBACK

THESE SOURCES WOULD GIVE YOU THE MOST ACCURATE AND DETAILED FEEDBACK ON YOUR SKILL(S)

☐ **Direct Boss**

Your direct boss has important information about you, your performance, and your prospects. The challenge is to get this information. There are formal processes (e.g., performance appraisals). There are day-to-day opportunities. To help, signal your boss that you want and can handle direct and timely feedback. Many bosses have trouble giving feedback, so you will have to work at it over a period of time.

☐ **Human Resource Professionals**

Human Resource professionals have both a formal and informal feedback role. Since they have access to unique and confidential information, they can provide the right context for feedback you've received. Sometimes they may be "directed" to give you feedback. Other times, they may pass on feedback just to be helpful to you.

- ☐ **Past Associates/Constituencies**
  When confronted with a present performance problem, some claim, "I wasn't like that before; it must be the current situation." When feedback is available from former associates, about 50% support that claim. In the other half of the cases, the people were like that before and probably didn't know it. It sometimes makes sense to access the past to clearly see the present.

SECTION 4: LEARNING FROM DEVELOP-IN-PLACE ASSIGNMENTS

THESE PART-TIME DEVELOP-IN-PLACE ASSIGNMENTS WILL HELP YOU BUILD YOUR SKILL(S)

- ☐ Go to a campus as a recruiter.
- ☐ Train and work as an assessor in an assessment center.
- ☐ Work on a team that's deciding who to keep and who to let go in a layoff, shutdown, delayering, or divestiture.
- ☐ Work on a team looking at a reorganization plan where there will be more people than positions.
- ☐ Build a multifunctional project team to tackle a common business issue or problem.
- ☐ Construct a success and derailment profile for a unit or the entire organization and present it to decision makers for adoption.
- ☐ Do a study of successful executives in your organization and report the findings to top management.
- ☐ Run (chair) a task force on a pressing problem.
- ☐ Serve on the board or operating committee of a credit union.
- ☐ Assemble an ad hoc team of diverse people to accomplish a difficult task.

SECTION 5: LEARNING FROM FULL-TIME JOBS

THESE FULL-TIME JOBS OFFER THE OPPORTUNITY TO BUILD YOUR SKILL(S)

- ☐ **Fix-its/Turnarounds**
  The core demands to qualify as a Fix-it or Turnaround assignment are: 1) Cleaning up a mess. 2) Serious people issues/problems like credibility/performance/morale. 3) Tight deadline. 4) Serious business performance failure. 5) Last chance to fix. Four Types of Fix-its/Turnarounds: 1) Fixing a failed business/unit involving taking control, stopping losses, managing damage, planning the turnaround, dealing

with people problems, installing new processes and systems, and rebuilding the spirit and performance of the unit. 2) Managing sizable disasters like mishandled labor negotiations and strikes, thefts, history of significant business losses, poor staff, failed leadership, hidden problems, fraud, public relations nightmares, etc. 3) Significant reorganization and restructuring (e.g., stabilizing the business, reforming unit, introducing new systems, making people changes, resetting strategy and tactics). 4) Significant system/process breakdown (e.g., MIS, financial coordination processes, audits, standards, etc.) across units requiring working to change something from a distant position, providing advice and counsel, and installing or implementing a major process improvement or system change outside your own unit and/or with customers outside the organization.

☐ **Significant People Demands**
Core demands required to qualify as a Significant People Responsibilities assignment are: 1) A sizable increase in either the number of people managed and/or the complexity of the challenges involved 2) Longer-term assignment (two or more years). 3) Quality of people management critical to achieving results. 4) Involves groups not worked with before (e.g., union, new technical areas, nationalities).

☐ **Start-ups**
The core demands to qualify as a start from scratch are: 1) Starting something new for you and/or for the organization. 2) Forging a new team. 3) Creating new systems/facilities/staffs/programs/procedures. 4) Contextual adversity (e.g., uncertainty, government regulation, unions, difficult environment). Seven types of start from scratches: 1) Planning, building, hiring, and managing (e.g., building a new facility, opening up a new location, moving a unit or company). 2) Heading something new (e.g., new product, new service, new line of business, new department/function, major new program). 3) Take over a group/product/service/program that had existed for less than a year and was off to a fast start. 4) Establishing overseas operations. 5) Major new designs for existing systems. 6) Moving a successful program from one unit to another. 7) Installing a new organization-wide process as a full-time job (e.g., like Total Quality).

SECTION 6: LEARNING MORE FROM YOUR PLAN

THESE ADDITIONAL REMEDIES WILL HELP MAKE THIS DEVELOPMENT PLAN MORE EFFECTIVE FOR YOU

Learning to Learn Better

☐ **Use Objective Data When Judging Others**
Practice studying other people more than judging or evaluating them. Get the facts, the data, how they think, why they do things, without classifying them into your internal like/dislike or agree/disagree boxes,

categories, or buckets. Try to project or predict how they would act/react in various situations and follow up to see how accurate you are.

- ☐ **Examine Why You Judge People the Way You Do**
List the people you like and those you dislike and try to find out why. What do those you like have in common with each other and with you? What do those you dislike have in common with themselves and how do they differ from you? Are your "people buckets" logical and productive or do they interfere? Could you be more effective without putting people into buckets?

Learning from Experience, Feedback and Other People

- ☐ **Learning from Bosses**
Bosses can be an excellent and ready source for learning. All bosses do some things exceptionally well and other things poorly. Distance your feelings from the boss/direct report relationship and study things that work and things that don't work for your boss. What would you have done? What could you use, and what should you avoid?

- ☐ **Learning from Mentors and Tutors**
Mentors and tutors offer a special case for learning since the relationship is specifically formed for learning. You need to be open and nondefensive. You need to solicit and accept feedback. This is a unique opportunity for you to get low-risk, honest, and direct feedback on what you do well and not so well.

- ☐ **Learning from Interviewing Others**
Interview others. Ask not only what they do, but how and why they do it. What do they think are the rules of thumb they are following? Where did they learn the behaviors? How do they keep them current? How do they monitor the effect they have on others?

- ☐ **Consolidating What You Learn from People**
After using any source and/or method of learning from others, write down or mentally note the new rules of thumb and the principles involved. How will you remind yourself of the new behaviors in similar situations? How will you prevent yourself from reacting on "autopilot"? How could you share what you have learned from others?

- ☐ **Getting Feedback from Bosses and Superiors**
Many bosses are reluctant to give negative feedback. They lack the managerial courage to face people directly with criticism. You can help by soliciting feedback and setting the tone. Show them you can handle criticism and that you are willing to work on issues they see as important.

- ☐ **Learning from Limited Staff**
Most managers either inherit or hire staff from time to time who are inexperienced, incompetent, not up to the task, resistant, or dispirited. Any of these may create a hardship for you. The lessons to be learned

are how to get things done with limited resources and how to fix the people situation. In the short term, this hardship is best addressed by assessing the combined strengths of the team and deploying the best you have against the problem. Almost everyone can do something well. Also, the team can contribute more than the combined individuals can. How can you empower and motivate the team? If you hired the troublesome staff, why did you err? What can you learn from your hiring mistakes? What wasn't there that you thought was present? What led you astray? How can you prevent that same hiring error in the future? What do you need to do to fix the situation? Quick development? Start over? If you inherited the problem, how can you fix it? Can you implement a program of accelerated development? Do you have to start over and get new people? What did the prior manager do or not do that led to this situation in the first place? What can you learn from that? What will you do differently? How does the staff feel? What can you learn from their frustrations over not being able to do the job? How can you be a positive force under negative circumstances? How can you rally them to perform? What lasting lessons can you learn from someone in distress and trouble? If you're going to try accelerated development, how can you get a quick assessment? How can you give the staff motivating feedback? How can you construct and implement development plans that will work? How can you get people on-line feedback for maximum growth? Do you know when to stop trying and start over? If you're going to turn over some staff, how can you do it both rapidly and with the least damage? How can you deliver the message in a constructive way? What can you learn from having to take negative actions against people? How can you prevent this from happening again?

Learning from Courses

☐ **Supervisory Courses**

Most new supervisors go through an "Introduction to Supervision" type course. They are designed to teach the common practices a first-line supervisor needs to know to be effective. The content of most of those courses is standard. There is general agreement on the principles of effective supervision. There are two common problems: 1) Do the students have a strong motivation to learn? Do they know what they don't know? Is there any pain? Because motivated students with a need for the knowledge learn best, participants should have had some trying experiences and some supervisory pain and hardships before attending. 2) Are the instructors experienced supervisors? Have they practiced what they preach? Can they share powerful anecdotes to make key points? Can they answer questions credibly? If possible, select supervisory courses based on the instructors, since the content seems to be the much same for all such courses. Lastly, does the course offer the opportunity for practicing each skill? Does it contain simulations? Are there case studies you could easily identify with? Are there breakout groups? Is there opportunity for action learning? Search for the most interactive course.

SUGGESTED READINGS

Bell, Arthur H. *Extraviewing – Innovative ways to hire the best.* Homewood, IL: Business One Irwin, 1992.

Canning, Miles B. *Ready, Aim, Hire!.* OakBrook, IL: PerSysCo. Publishing, Inc., 1992.

Connolly, Kathleen Groll and Paul M. Connolly. *Competing for Employees.* Lexington, MA: Lexington Books, 1991.

Half, Robert. *Finding, Hiring and Keeping the Best Employees.* New York: John Wiley & Sons, Inc., 1993.

Miller, Kathleen D. *Retraining the American Workforce.* Reading, MA: Addison-Wesley Publishing Co. Inc., 1989.

Smart, Bradford D. Pd.D. *Topgrading – How Leading Companies Win Hiring, Coaching and Keeping the Best People.* New York: Prentice-Hall, Inc., 1999.

Yate, Martin. *Hiring the Best.* Holbrook, MA: Adams Media Corp, 1994.

Yate, Martin. *Keeping the Best.* Holbrook, MA: Adams Media Corp, 1991.

26

HUMOR

SECTION 1: YOUR DEVELOPMENT NEED(S)

UNSKILLED

- ☐ Appears humorless
- ☐ Doesn't know how or doesn't want to use humor in the workplace
- ☐ May have problems telling a joke
- ☐ May chill humor in others
- ☐ Thinks humor is out of place in the workplace
- ☐ May be too serious and want to avoid looking or sounding silly
- ☐ May lack a light touch
- ☐ May use sarcastic or politically offensive humor
- ☐ May use humor in the wrong time or wrong place or in the wrong way

SKILLED

- ☐ Has a positive and constructive sense of humor
- ☐ Can laugh at him/herself and with others
- ☐ Is appropriately funny and can use humor to ease tension

OVERUSED SKILL

- ☐ May disrupt group process with untimely or inappropriate humor
- ☐ May use humor to deflect real issues and problems
- ☐ May use humor to criticize others and veil an attack
- ☐ May use humor to deliver sarcasm or cynicism
- ☐ May be perceived as immature or lacking in appropriate seriousness
- ☐ His/her humor may be misinterpreted

Select one to three of the competencies listed below to work on to compensate for an overuse of this skill.

COMPENSATORS: 7, 10, 11, 22, 31, 33, 41, 43, 48, 52, 55

SOME CAUSES

- ☐ Can't tell a joke
- ☐ Don't think you're funny
- ☐ Think humor is out of place in business
- ☐ Avoid looking/sounding silly
- ☐ Too serious
- ☐ Avoid risk

…E MAP

There's good humor and negative humor. There's constructive humor and destructive humor. There are humorous people. There are humorous stories that are funny regardless of who tells them. There are humorous situations that are funny regardless of who brings them to our attention. There are pictures and cartoons that are funny regardless of who shows them. Humor is an essential element to life and work. Properly used and delivered, it can be a constructive influence on those around you. It can increase a feeling of well being and belonging, it can take the bite out of tension, and it can balance a negative situation for someone or the whole team.

SECTION 2: LEARNING ON YOUR OWN

THESE SELF-DEVELOPMENT REMEDIES WILL HELP YOU BUILD YOUR SKILL(S)

SOME REMEDIES

☐ **1. Where to find humor.** There are topics that can be near universally humorous. There are universal traits. Misers, bad drivers, absent-minded people, anything that is understood worldwide as the human condition. There are things that are funny about your life. Have funny kids, pets, hobbies? What's a ridiculous situation you've been caught in lately? There are funny things in the workplace. The jargon of it, memos, ironic rules. Stories from the picnic or the off-site. There is providing relief from our problems. The weather, taxes, any of life's little indignities and embarrassments. And there is always the news. Most programs have at least one humorous tale, and sometimes the news is funny enough as it is. There are cartoons that most find humorous in the work setting (*The Farside* and *Dilbert* currently). There are funny jokes that most find funny. Humor that unites people rather than puts down people or groups is always safe. Begin to look for and remember the humor around you. Begin to pass on your observation to a few safe people to test your humor judgment.

☐ **2. Where not to find humor.** Today, we live in a very politically sensitive world. Many people are turned off by political, sexist or ethnic humor. Humor that's out is anything ribald, sexist, religious or ethnic. Most gender and race humor is unacceptable. Humor that makes fun of entire groups (women) or cultures (Polish jokes) doesn't play well. Any humor about a handicap is out. Basically any humor that makes fun of others, makes others feel bad or diminished, or is at the expense of others is out.

☐ **3. Self humor.** Self humor is usually safe, seen as positive by others, and most of the time leads to increased respect. Funny and embarrassing things that happened to you (when the airlines lost your luggage and you had to wash your underwear in an airport restroom and dry it under the hand dryer). Your flaws and foibles (when you were so stressed over your taxes that you locked the keys in your car with the motor running). Mistakes you've made. Blunders you've committed. Besides adding humor to the situation, it humanizes you and endears people to you. Anything can of course be overdone, so balance it with seriousness.

☐ **4. Negative humor.** Some people use humor to deliver negative messages. They are sarcastic and barbed in their humor. In a tense confrontation with an employee, to say, "I hope your résumé is up to date," instead of saying, "Your performance is not what I expected. It has to improve or I will have to reconsider your continued employment," is not acceptable. There is a very simple rule. Do not use humor to deliver a critical point to a person or a group. Negative humor hurts more than direct statements and is basically chicken on your part. Say directly what you mean.

☐ **5. Avoidance humor.** Some make light of things that make them uncomfortable. It's a very human defense technique. There is a difference between using unrelated humor for tension relief, which can be a good practice, and using direct humor to make light of the person or the issue. Better to say, "I'm uncomfortable with that" than to say through humor that it's less important than you're making it. This can also be seen as a subject change, in effect deflecting the topic.

☐ **6. Timing.** There is a time for everything and sometimes humor is not appropriate. Since you are reading this because you or others don't think you are good at using humor, the best technique is to follow the lead of others. Be second or third to be humorous in a setting until you find your funny legs. *More help? – See #48 Political Savvy.*

☐ **7. Studying humor.** Read *How to Be Funny* by Steve Allen and *Laughing Matters* by Joel Goodman. Saratoga Springs, N.Y.: The HUMOR Project at Sagamore Institute, 1982) Go to three comedy performances at a local comedy club to study how the professionals do it. Study funny people in your organization. What do they do that you don't? Buy all the *Dilbert* and *Far Side* books. Cut out ten from each that really are funny to you. Use them in your presentations and hang them in your office and see how others react.

☐ **8. Being funnier.** There are some basic humor tactics. Use exaggeration, like when Bill Cosby exited the doctor's office in his new trifocals and began an odyssey through a mile-long elevator and across a newly terrifying street. Use reversal, where you turn the situation into its opposite – the paranoid who thinks the world's out to do her good; or the speaker who turned eight ways to help people succeed in their careers into eight ways to ruin the careers of your enemies. Physical or pratfall humor works such as when your hand hits the microphone and lets out a loud boom and you say, "Sorry, Mike." Be brief. Cut out unnecessary words. Humor condenses the essential elements of a situation, just as good writing does. If the time of day or the color of the sky or city it happened in is not relevant, leave it out. Include touches, however, to set a mood. If heat is essential to the humor, let the listener see sweat pouring off people, flowers wilting, whatever it takes to set the stage. Be on the lookout for the ridiculous around you. Jot down funny things that happen around you so you can remember them.

☐ **9. Humbling exercises.** Play silly games (draw a picture with your eyes shut, play any of a number of board games devoted to laughter such as Pictionary®). Play with small children and let them take the lead. Be willing to make a fool of yourself at off-sites, picnics and parties. Volunteer to dress in the clown costume and have employees throw water balloons at you. Learn and demonstrate the Macarena at the company picnic!

☐ **10. Letting others be humorous.** Sometimes people who aren't very humorous (or are very serious) chill and suppress humor in others. Even if you're not going to work on being more humorous or funny, at least let others be. That will actually help you be seen as at least more tolerant of humor than you were in the past. Eventually, you may even be tempted to join in.

SECTION 3: LEARNING FROM MORE FEEDBACK

THESE SOURCES WOULD GIVE YOU THE MOST ACCURATE AND DETAILED FEEDBACK ON YOUR SKILL(S)

☐ **Family Members**
On some issues, like interpersonal style or compassion, it might be helpful to ask various and multiple family members for feedback to add confirmation or context to feedback you've received in the workplace.

☐ **Off-Work Friends/Associates**
Those who know you socially "with your guard down" can be a good source of feedback to compare with that of work peers and family members. If you're different at work than you are socially, why? If you're the same, feedback from friends just confirms the feedback. In a way, off-work friends may know the "real you."

☐ **Past Associates/Constituencies**
When confronted with a present performance problem, some claim, "I wasn't like that before; it must be the current situation." When feedback is available from former associates, about 50% support that claim. In the other half of the cases, the people were like that before and probably didn't know it. It sometimes makes sense to access the past to clearly see the present.

☐ **Peers and Colleagues**
Peers and colleagues have a special social and working relationship. They attend staff meetings together, share private views, get feedback

from the same boss, travel together, and are knowledgeable about each other's work. You perhaps let your guard down more around peers and act more like yourself. They can be a valuable source of feedback.

- ☐ **Spouse**
  Spouses can be powerful sources of feedback on such things as interpersonal style, values, balance between work, career, and personal life, etc. Many participants attending development programs share their feedback with their spouses for value-adding confirmation or context and for specific examples.

SECTION 4: LEARNING FROM DEVELOP-IN-PLACE ASSIGNMENTS

THESE PART-TIME DEVELOP-IN-PLACE ASSIGNMENTS WILL HELP YOU BUILD YOUR SKILL(S)

- ☐ Study humor in business settings; read books on the nature of humor; collect cartoons you could use in presentations; study funny people around you; keep a log of funny jokes and sayings you hear; read famous speeches and study how humor was used; attend comedy clubs; ask a funny person to act as your tutor; practice funny lines and jokes with others.
- ☐ Try to learn something frivolous and fun to see how good you can get (e.g., juggling, square dancing, magic).
- ☐ Plan an off-site meeting, conference, convention, trade show, event, etc.

SECTION 5: LEARNING FROM FULL-TIME JOBS

Humor is generally not learned from any specific kind of job.

SECTION 6: LEARNING MORE FROM YOUR PLAN

THESE ADDITIONAL REMEDIES WILL HELP MAKE THIS DEVELOPMENT PLAN MORE EFFECTIVE FOR YOU

Learning to Learn Better

- ☐ **Learn New and Frivolous Skills to Study How You Learn**
  Practice learning frivolous and fun skills (like juggling, square dancing, skeet shooting, video games, etc.) to see yourself under different and less personal or stressful learning conditions. Ask yourself why that was easy while developing new personal/managerial skills is so hard. Try something harder with the same tactics.

Learning from Experience, Feedback and Other People

- [ ] **Using Multiple Models**
Who do you know who exemplifies how to do whatever your need is? Who, for example, personifies decisiveness or compassion or strategic agility? Think more broadly than your current job and colleagues. For example, clergy, friends, spouses or community leaders are also good sources for potential models. Select your models not on the basis of overall excellence or likability, but on the basis of the one towering strength (or glaring weakness) you are interested in. Even people who are well thought of usually have only one or two towering strengths (or glaring weaknesses). Ordinarily, you won't learn as much from the whole person as you will from one characteristic.

- [ ] **Getting Feedback from Peers/Colleagues**
Your peers and colleagues may not be candid if they are in competition with you. Some may not be willing to be open with you out of fear of giving you an advantage. Some may give you exaggerated feedback to deliberately cause you undue concern. You have to set the tone and gauge the trust level of the relationship and the quality of the feedback.

- [ ] **Learning from Bad Things that Happen**
Bad things happen to everyone, sometimes because of what we do and sometimes with no help from us. We all have bad bosses, bad staffs, impossible and hopeless situations, impossible tasks, and unintended consequences. Aside from the trouble these bad things cause for you, the key is how can you learn from each of them.

- [ ] **Learning from Bad Situations**
All of us will find ourselves in bad situations from time to time. Good intentions gone bad. Impossible tasks and goals. Hopeless projects. Even though you probably can't perform well, the key is to at least take away some lessons and insights. How did things get to be this way? What factors led to the impasse? How can you make the best of a bad situation? How can you neutralize the negative elements? How can you get the most out of yourself and your staff under the chilling situation? What can you salvage? How can you use coping strategies to minimize the negatives? How can you avoid these situations going forward? In bad situations: 1) Be resourceful. Get the most you can out of the situation. 2) Try to deduce why things got to be that way. 3) Learn from both the situation you inherited and how you react to it. 4) Integrate what you learn into your future behavior.

SUGGESTED READINGS

Adams, Scott. *The Joy of Work – Dilbert's guide to finding happiness at the expense of your co-workers.* New York: HarperBusiness, 1998.

Adams, Scott. *The joy of work [sound recording]: [Dilbert's guide to finding happiness at the expense of your co-workers].* New York: HarperCollins, 1998.

Allen, Steve with Jane Wollman. *How to be funny: Discovering the comic you.* New York: McGraw-Hill, 1987.

Antion, Tom. *Wake 'em up: how to use humor and other professional techniques to create alarmingly good business presentations.* Landover Hills, Md.: Anchor Pub.; Minneapolis, MN.: Creative Training Techniques Press, 1997.

Barry, Dave. *Claw your way to the top [sound recording].* Beverly Hills, CA: Dove Audio, 1993.

Barsoux, Jean-Louis. *Funny Business – Humor, Management and Business Culture.* London; New York: Cassell, 1993.

Fahlman, Clyde. *Laughing Nine to Five – The quest for humor in the workplace.* Portland, OR: Steelhead Press, 1997.

Hemsath, Dave and Leslie Yerkes. *301 ways to have fun at work.* San Francisco: Berrett-Koehler Publishers, Inc., 1997

27

INFORMING

SECTION 1: YOUR DEVELOPMENT NEED(S)

UNSKILLED

- ☐ Not a consistent communicator
- ☐ Tells too little or too much
- ☐ Tells too late; timing is off
- ☐ May be unclear, may inform some better than others
- ☐ May not think through who needs to know by when
- ☐ Doesn't seek or listen to the data needs of others
- ☐ May inform but lack follow-through
- ☐ May either hoard information or not see informing as important
- ☐ May only have one mode – written or oral or E-mail

SKILLED

- ☐ Provides the information people need to know to do their jobs and to feel good about being a member of the team, unit, and/or the organization
- ☐ Provides individuals information so that they can make accurate decisions
- ☐ Is timely with information

OVERUSED SKILL

- ☐ May provide too much information
- ☐ May upset people by giving them information they can't handle or preliminary information that turns out not to be true

Select one to three of the competencies listed below to work on to compensate for an overuse of this skill.

COMPENSATORS: 2, 8, 11, 12, 22, 29, 33, 38, 41, 47, 48, 50, 52, 64

SOME CAUSES

- ☐ Don't think it's needed
- ☐ Inform some better than others
- ☐ Little informing
- ☐ Sporadic informing
- ☐ Too busy
- ☐ Too late in informing
- ☐ Unclear informing
- ☐ Use the wrong informing method

THE MAP

Although it seems a simple skill, *Informing* ranks 52nd out of 67 (low) competencies in terms of skill proficiency in our research on The CAREER ARCHITECT®. Informing also has a very high return on investment. Things go better. People are more motivated. Are you too busy? A minimal communicator? Only inform to meet your needs? You don't package information or think through who needs to know what by when? This can lead to some bad consequences for others and you. Maybe that's why they rate *Informing* as 21st of 67 (high) in importance! It's a simple and important skill that many do not do well or enough of.

SECTION 2: LEARNING ON YOUR OWN

THESE SELF-DEVELOPMENT REMEDIES WILL HELP YOU BUILD YOUR SKILL(S)

SOME REMEDIES

☐ **1. Don't inform much if at all.** Do you think a word to the wise is sufficient? Do you think if they were any good they would figure it out themselves? You didn't need much information when you were in their jobs? Information leads to more efficient and effective use of resources. It leads to better decisions. It leads to less rework. It leads to greater motivation. It leads to less of your time monitoring. People need a basic flow of information to do their jobs better. Best thing to do if it's not natural to you is to just ask them what they need to know and provide it.

☐ **2. Don't inform enough.** Are you a minimalist? Do you tell people only what they need to know to do their little piece of the puzzle? People are motivated by being aware of the bigger picture. They want to know what to do to do their jobs and more. How does what they are doing fit into the larger picture? What are the other people working on and why? Many people think that's unnecessary information and that it would take too much time to do. They're wrong. The sense of doing something worthwhile is the number two motivator at work! It results in a high return on motivation and productivity. (Try to increase the amount of more-than-your-job information you share.) Focus on the impact on others by figuring out who information affects. Put five minutes on your meeting agenda. Ask people what they want to know and assuming it's not confidential information, tell them.

☐ **3. A loner.** Do you keep to yourself? Work alone or try to? Do you hold back information? Do you parcel out information on your schedule? Do you share information to get an advantage or to win favor? Do people around you know what you're doing and why? Are you aware of things others would benefit from but you don't take the time to communicate? In most organizations, these things and things like it will get you in trouble. Organizations function on the flow of information.

Being on your own and preferring peace and privacy are OK as long as you communicate things to bosses, peers and teammates that they need to know and would feel better if they knew. Don't be the source of surprises.

☐ **4. Cryptic informer.** Some people just aren't good at informing. Their communication styles are not effective. The most effective communicators, according to behavioral research studies: speak often, but briefly (15–30 seconds); ask more questions than others; make fewer solution statements early in a discussion; headline their points in a sentence or two; summarize frequently, and make more frequent "here's where we are" statements; invite everyone to share their views; typically interject their views after others have had a chance to speak, unless they are passing on decisions. Compare these practices to yours. Work on those that are not up to standard.

☐ **5. Inconsistent informing.** Have an information checklist detailing what information should go to whom; pass on summaries or copies of important communications. Determine the information checklist by: keeping tabs on unpleasant surprises people report to you; ask direct reports what they'd like to know to do their jobs better; and check with boss, peers and customers to see if you pass along too little, enough, or too much of the right kinds of information. It's important to know what to pass, to whom to pass, and when to pass, to become an effective informer.

☐ **6. Poor informing.** Eliminate disruptive habits such as using the same words too often, hesitating, having frequent filler words like "you know" and "uh," speaking too rapidly or forcefully, using strongly judgmental words, or going into too much detail that leaves listeners bored or wondering what the point is. Are you a complexifier? Simplify and emphasize. Vary the volume and length of time spoken to emphasize key points and maintain the interest of others. Outline complex arguments/processes on paper or overheads or charts to make them easy to follow. Use visual aids. Use common action words, simple examples or visual catch phrases to cement information transfer. *More help? – See #49 Presentation Skills and #67 Written Communications.*

☐ **7. Selective informing.** The most common selective pattern is informing up and out but not down or sideways. When these people get their 360° feedback reports, there is a discrepancy among groups on informing. Some groups rate it high and others lower. That means there is not a skills block. You can inform. There is an attitude filter. I will inform some but not others. Why? What do you gain with one group that you lose with another? Is it personal? Are you gaining by sharing? At the expense of others? Why are you avoiding one group? Do you fear debate?

☐ **8. Whistleblowing.** A tough call. Do you know something others should but when they find out, there will be noise and trouble? Saying what needs to be said to the right person in a timely way takes courage. Everybody sees things, observes things, knows things or learns about things that others should know. Many times it's not positive information. Something is about to go wrong. Something is being covered up. Someone is holding back an important piece of information. Someone or something is going off in the wrong direction. It's good news and bad news. If you inform, the organization may gain. But a person or some people may lose. Generally, your best bet is to find the right person and inform. *More help? – See #34 Managerial Courage.*

☐ **9. Dealing with the heat of informing.** Informing is not always benign and friendly. It many times generates heat. Defensiveness. Blame. Attacks. Threats. Many times they want to shoot the messenger. Separate the passion from the message. Avoid direct blaming remarks. Deal with people issues directly but separately and maybe off line. If attacked for delivering bad news, you can always say nothing or ask a clarifying question. People will usually respond by saying more, coming off their position a bit, or at least revealing their interests. *More help? – See #12 Conflict Management.*

☐ **10. Audience sensitivity.** Unfortunately, one method or style of informing does not play equally well across audiences. Many times you will have to adjust the tone, pace, style and even the message and how you couch it for different audiences. If you are delivering the same message to multiple people or audiences, always ask yourself how are they different? Some differences among people or audiences include level of sophistication, friendly vs. unfriendly, time sensitivity, whether they prefer it in writing or not and whether a logical or emotional argument will play better. Write or tell? Writing is usually best for the extremes – complex descriptions complete with background and five or six progressive arguments, or on the other side, straightforward, unambiguous things people need to know. You should generally tell when it requires discussion or you are alerting them to a problem. Make a read on each person and each audience and adjust accordingly. *More help? – See #15 Customer Focus and #45 Personal Learning.*

SECTION 3: LEARNING FROM MORE FEEDBACK

THESE SOURCES WOULD GIVE YOU THE MOST ACCURATE AND DETAILED FEEDBACK ON YOUR SKILL(S)

- ☐ **Direct Reports**
  Across a variety of settings, your direct reports probably see you the most. They are the recipients of most of your managerial behaviors. They know your work. They can compare you with former bosses. Since they may hesitate to give you negative feedback, you have to set the atmosphere to make it easier for them. You have to ask.
- ☐ **Internal and External Customers**
  Customers interact with you as a person and as a supplier or vendor of products and services. You're important to them because you can either help address and solve their problems or stand in their way. As customer service and Total Quality programs gain importance, clients and customers become a more prominent source of feedback.
- ☐ **Peers and Colleagues**
  Peers and colleagues have a special social and working relationship. They attend staff meetings together, share private views, get feedback from the same boss, travel together, and are knowledgeable about each other's work. You perhaps let your guard down more around peers and act more like yourself. They can be a valuable source of feedback.

SECTION 4: LEARNING FROM DEVELOP-IN-PLACE ASSIGNMENTS

THESE PART-TIME DEVELOP-IN-PLACE ASSIGNMENTS WILL HELP YOU BUILD YOUR SKILL(S)

- ☐ Integrate diverse systems, processes, or procedures across decentralized and/or dispersed units.
- ☐ Establish security procedures for a building or floor.
- ☐ Manage something "remote," away from your location.
- ☐ Lobby for your organization on a contested issue in local, regional, state, or federal government.
- ☐ Represent the organization at a trade show, convention, exposition, etc.
- ☐ Be a change agent; create a symbol for change; lead the rallying cry; champion a significant change and implementation.
- ☐ Create employee involvement teams.
- ☐ Teach a course, seminar, or workshop on something you know a lot about.
- ☐ Become someone's assigned mentor, coach, sponsor, champion, or orienter.
- ☐ Take over for someone on vacation or a long trip.

SECTION 5: LEARNING FROM FULL-TIME JOBS

THESE FULL-TIME JOBS OFFER THE OPPORTUNITY TO BUILD YOUR SKILL(S)

☐ **Influencing Without Authority**
The core demands to qualify as an Influence Without Authority are: 1) Significant challenge (e.g, start-up, fix-it, scope and/or scale assignment, strategic planning project, changes in management practices/ systems). 2) Insufficient direct authority to make it happen. 3) Tight deadlines. 4) Visible to significant others. 5) Sensitive politics.

☐ **Scope Assignments**
The core demands for a Scope (complexity) assignment are: 1) Significant increase in both internal and external scope or complexity. 2) Significant increase in visibility and/or bottom line responsibility. 3) Unfamiliar area, business, technology, or territory. Examples of Scope assignments involving shifts: 1) Switching into a new function/technology/business. 2) Moving to new organization. 3) Moving to overseas assignment. 4) Moving to new location. 5) Adding new products/ services. 6) Moving between headquarters/field. 7) Switches in ownership/top management of the unit/organization. Examples of Scope assignments involving "firsts": 1) First-time manager. 2) First-time managing managers. 3) First-time executive. 4) First-time overseas. 5) First-time headquarters/field. 6) First-time team leader. 7) First-time new technology/business/function. Scope assignments involving increased complexity: 1) Managing a significant expansion of an existing product or service. 2) Managing adding new products/service into an existing unit. 3) Managing a reorganized and more diverse unit. 4) Managing explosive growth. 5) Adding new technologies.

☐ **Significant People Demands**
Core demands required to qualify as a Significant People Responsibilities assignment are: 1) A sizable increase in either the number of people managed and/or the complexity of the challenges involved 2) Longer-term assignment (two or more years). 3) Quality of people management critical to achieving results. 4) Involves groups not worked with before (e.g., union, new technical areas, nationalities).

SECTION 6: LEARNING MORE FROM YOUR PLAN

THESE ADDITIONAL REMEDIES WILL HELP MAKE THIS DEVELOPMENT PLAN MORE EFFECTIVE FOR YOU

Learning to Learn Better

☐ **Consult With Expert in the Area of Concern for You**
Consult with an outside expert in the area you're dealing with, someone especially skilled and known; describe your situation the best you can and openly and receptively listen to the advice and counsel the expert provides. Try the advice before you reject it.

- ☐ **Form a Learning Network With Others Working on the Same Problem**
  Look for people in similar situations, and create a process for sharing and learning together. Look for a variety of people inside and outside your organization. Give feedback to each other; try new and different things together; share successes and failures, lessons and learning.
- ☐ **Study People Who Have Successfully Done What You Need to Do**
  Interview people who have already done what you're planning to do and check your plan against what they did. Try to summarize their key tactics, strategies, and insights; adjust your plan accordingly.
- ☐ **Pre-sell an Idea to a Key Stakeholder**
  Identify the key stakeholders – those who will be the most affected by your actions or the most resistant, or whose support you will most need. Collect the information each will find persuasive; marshal your arguments and try to pre-sell your conclusions, recommendations, and solutions.
- ☐ **Work With a Development Partner**
  Find a person you trust to be both candid and constructive and team up with him/her. Construct effective strategies together. Give each other feedback; role-play tactics with each other.
- ☐ **Preview a Plan With a Test Audience**
  Before committing to a plan, find someone agreeable to a wide-ranging discussion about the issue or problem you face. Explore all sides and options; go with the flow; let what you need to do emerge from the process; develop a plan as you go.

Learning from Experience, Feedback and Other People

- ☐ **Being a Teacher of Others**
  Teaching others a skill you possess is a powerful way to learn from your students and about yourself. Decide what skill you have that you could teach direct reports, a child, or a friend. In what areas could you be a mentor or tutor? Ask yourself why this is a strength for you. What are the first items you would teach as the keys to help others form umbrellas for understanding? Get feedback from others on why this is a strength for you and what you do behaviorally that makes it so. When teaching and coaching, watch the students carefully for their reactions. What works and doesn't work for you as a coach? Write down your rules of thumb on what works for you that helps others. Get feedback from your students on what you do well and not so well as a teacher/coach.
- ☐ **Giving Feedback to Others**
  Most managers complain they don't get enough useful feedback. Ironically, their direct reports and peers offer the same complaint! Getting serious about feedback for yourself involves giving more feed-

back to those around you. As you practice giving more feedback to others, you will receive more by the example you set and will become more sensitive and receptive to your own.

Learning from Courses

☐ **Supervisory Courses**
Most new supervisors go through an "Introduction to Supervision" type course. They are designed to teach the common practices a first-line supervisor needs to know to be effective. The content of most of those courses is standard. There is general agreement on the principles of effective supervision. There are two common problems: 1) Do the students have a strong motivation to learn? Do they know what they don't know? Is there any pain? Because motivated students with a need for the knowledge learn best, participants should have had some trying experiences and some supervisory pain and hardships before attending. 2) Are the instructors experienced supervisors? Have they practiced what they preach? Can they share powerful anecdotes to make key points? Can they answer questions credibly? If possible, select supervisory courses based on the instructors, since the content seems to be the much same for all such courses. Lastly, does the course offer the opportunity for practicing each skill? Does it contain simulations? Are there case studies you could easily identify with? Are there breakout groups? Is there opportunity for action learning? Search for the most interactive course.

☐ **Sending Others to Courses**
If you are responsible for managing someone else's development and, as part of that, sending them to courses, prepare them beforehand. Don't send them as tourists. Meet with them before and after the course. Tell them why they need this course. Tell them what you expect them to learn. Give them feedback on why you think they need the course. Agree ahead of time how you will measure and monitor learning after they return. If possible, offer a variety of courses for your employee to choose from. Have them give you a report shortly after they return. If appropriate, have them present what they learned to the rest of your staff. After they return, provide opportunities for using the new skills with safe cover and low risk. Give them practice time before expecting full exercise of the new skills. Be supportive during early unsteadiness. Give continuous feedback on progress.

SUGGESTED READINGS

Dilenschneider, Robert L. A Briefing for Leaders: *Communication as the ultimate exercise of power.* New York: HarperBusiness, 1992.

Elgin, Suzette Haden. *BusinessSpeak: using the gentle art of verbal persuasion to get what you want at work.* New York: McGraw-Hill, 1995.

Kaplan, Burton. *Strategic Communication – The art of making your ideas their ideas.* New York: HarperBusiness, 1991.

Linver, Sandy. *The Leader's Edge – How to use communication to grow your business and yourself.* New York: Simon & Schuster, 1994.

McCallister, Dr. Linda. *Say What You Mean, Get What You Want.* New York: John Wiley & Sons, Inc., 1992.

McCormack, Mark H. *On Communicating.* Los Angeles: Dove Books, 1998.

INNOVATION MANAGEMENT

SECTION 1: YOUR DEVELOPMENT NEED(S)

UNSKILLED

- ☐ Not a good judge of what's creative
- ☐ Doesn't understand the marketplace for innovation
- ☐ Can't select from among creative ideas which one would work the best
- ☐ Doesn't innovate
- ☐ May not be open to the creative suggestions of others
- ☐ May be stuck in his/her comfort zone of tasks and methods of doing them
- ☐ May not understand creativity or the process of innovation
- ☐ May close too soon with solutions and conclusions
- ☐ May be a perfectionist avoiding risk and fearing failures and mistakes
- ☐ May not use experiments to learn and improve, and may block the innovations of others

SKILLED

- ☐ Is good at bringing the creative ideas of others to market
- ☐ Has good judgment about which creative ideas and suggestions will work
- ☐ Has a sense about managing the creative process of others
- ☐ Can facilitate effective brainstorming
- ☐ Can project how potential ideas may play out in the marketplace

OVERUSED SKILL

- ☐ May err toward the new and reject the old
- ☐ May prefer creative people and undervalue those less creative
- ☐ May get too far out in front of others in thinking and planning

Select one to three of the competencies listed below to work on to compensate for an overuse of this skill.

COMPENSATORS: 16, 17, 24, 27, 33, 47, 50, 52, 53, 59, 61, 64

SOME CAUSES

- ☐ Don't understand the market
- ☐ Don't understand creativity
- ☐ Fear mistakes
- ☐ Get it right the first time
- ☐ Perfectionist
- ☐ Too comfortable

THE MAP

Innovation involves three skills. The first is a total understanding of the marketplace for your products and services. That's knowing what sells and why. What more do your customers want? What features would be most attractive to them? And what do your non-customers want that they don't find in your products? The second is being able to select from among many possible creative ideas for new products and services, those which would have the highest likelihood of success in the marketplace. The third skill is taking the raw idea and managing its transition into a successful product in the marketplace.

SECTION 2: LEARNING ON YOUR OWN

THESE SELF-DEVELOPMENT REMEDIES WILL HELP YOU BUILD YOUR SKILL(S)

SOME REMEDIES

☐ **1. The first step to managing innovation** is to understand your markets, historically, today and most importantly tomorrow. What have your customers done in the past? Which new products succeeded and which failed? What do they buy today? Among your current customers, what more do they want and are willing to pay for? For those who did not buy your product or service, what was missing? What do your competitors have that you don't? What are the known future trends that will affect you? Aging of the population? Eating out? Electric cars? Green movement? What are some of the wilder possibilities? Fusion? Free long distance telephoning over the Internet? Space travel? Subscribe to the *Futurist Magazine* put out by the World Future Society. Talk to the strategic planners in your organization for their long-term forecasts. Talk to your key customers. What do they think their needs will be? *More help? – See #15 Customer Focus and #46 Perspective.*

☐ **2. Managing the creative process.** You need raw creative ideas to be able to manage innovation. While you may not and don't need to be the source for the creative ideas, you need to understand the process. Creative thought processes do not follow the formal rules of logic where one uses cause and effect to prove or solve something. The rules of creative thought lie not in using existing concepts but in changing them – moving from one concept or way of looking at things to another. It involves challenging the status quo and generating ideas without judging them initially. Jumping from one idea to another without justifying the jump. Looking for the least likely and the odd. The creative process requires freedom and openness and a non-judgmental environment. The creative process can't be timed. Setting a goal and a time schedule to be creative will most likely chill creativity. *More help? – See #14 Creativity.*

☐ **3. Managing creative people.** Creative people have special gifts but special problems come along with the gifts. Many times you have to buffer and protect creative people from the normal processes and procedures of the organization. Creative people need rumination time undisturbed by the process expectations of others. They need to carve out some portion of their time to study problems deeply, talk with others, look for parallels in other organizations and in remote areas totally outside the field. Naturally creative people are much more likely to think in opposite cases when confronted with a problem. They turn problems upside down. They think differently. They ask what is the least likely thing it could be, what the problem is not, what's missing from the problem, or what the mirror image of the problem is. Creative people can be playful. Playfulness is highly related to coming up with new ideas. Anything goes. Most creative people are not detail oriented, get their expense reports in late and ignore deadlines they consider trivial compared with what they are doing. If you manage creative people, you have to give them room.

☐ **4. Getting creativity out of a group.** Many times the creative idea comes from a group, not single individuals. When working on a new idea for a product or service, have them come up with as many questions about it as you can. Often we think too quickly of solutions. In studies of problem-solving sessions, solutions outweigh questions eight to one. Asking more questions helps people rethink the problem and come to more and different solutions. Have the group take a current product you are dissatisfied with and represent it visually – a flow chart or a series of pictures. Cut it up into its component pieces and shuffle them. Examine the pieces to see if a different order would help, or how you could combine three pieces into one. Try many experiments or trials to find something that will work. Have the group think beyond current boundaries. What are some of the most sacred rules or practices in your organization? Unit? Think about smashing them – what would your unit be doing if you broke the rules? Talk to the most irreverent person you know about this. Buffer the group. It's difficult to work on something new if they are besieged with all the distractions you have to deal with, particularly if people are looking over your shoulder asking why isn't anything happening.

☐ **5. The special case of line extensions.** Very few innovations are pure breakthroughs. They are variations on a theme, borrowed ideas from other fields, or putting old ideas together in new ways. Knowledge and free flow of ideas increase the chance of novel connection, as when a Pizza Hut manager solved a time-to-bake problem by considering how to transfer heat using a child's Erector set as heat transfer probes. Many innovation are mistakes. Post-it® Notes was a glue experiment that failed. Creative ideas may be closer at hand than you think. Before you try for the grand idea, extend everything you now do 24 inches to see what you get.

- ☐ **6. Selecting the idea.** Creativity relies on freedom early, but structure later. Once the unit comes up with its best notion of what to do, subject it to all the logical tests and criticism any other alternative is treated to. Testing out creative ideas is no different than any other problem-solving/evaluation process. The difference is in how the ideas originate.

- ☐ **7. Develop a philosophical stance toward failure/criticism.** After all, most innovations fail, most new products fail, most change efforts fail, anything worth doing takes repeated effort, anything could always have been done better. To increase learning, build in immediate feedback loops. Look for something that is common to each failure and that is never present when there is a success. There will be many mistakes and failures in innovation; after all, no one knows what to do. The best tack is to say what can we learn from this? What caused it? What do we need to do differently? Don't expect to get it right the first time. This leads to safe, less than innovative solutions. Many problem-solving studies show that the second or third try is when we come up with the best solution.

- ☐ **8. Moving an idea through the organization.** Once an idea has been selected, you need to manage it through to the marketplace. Designing processes to get the job done most efficiently and effectively is a known science. Look to the principles of Total Quality Management and Process Re-Engineering. *More help? – See #63 Total Quality Management/Re-Engineering*. Read a book on each. Go to a workshop. Ask for help from the Organizational Effectiveness group in your organization or hire a consultant. Have the team work with you to design the best way to proceed. Teams work better when they have a say in how things will be done.

- ☐ **9. Dealing with the politics.** Sometimes creative ideas are orphans until everyone is convinced they are going to work. Early in the process of turning the ideas into products, resources may be tight. You will also have to deal with many units outside your team to get it done. Organizations can be complex mazes with many turns, dead ends, quick routes and choices. In most organizations, the best path to get somewhere is almost never a straight line. There is a formal organization – the one on the organization chart – where the path may look straight and then there is the informal organization where all paths are zigzagged. Since organizations are staffed with people, they become all that more complex. There are gatekeepers, expediters, stoppers, resisters, guides, good Samaritans and influencers. All of these types live in the organizational maze. The key to being successful in maneuvering an innovation through complex organizations is to find your way through the maze in the least amount of time while making the least noise. *More help? – See #38 Organizational Agility.*

☐ **10. Become a student of innovation outside your field.** Look for and study new products you buy and use. Find out the process that was used to create it. Watch *Inventions* on the Discovery Channel. Read *The Soul of a New Machine* by Tracy Kidder to see how innovation happens from the inside. Write down five things from your research that you can model in your own behavior.

SECTION 3: LEARNING FROM MORE FEEDBACK

THESE SOURCES WOULD GIVE YOU THE MOST ACCURATE AND DETAILED FEEDBACK ON YOUR SKILL(S)

☐ **Boss's Boss(es)**
From a process standpoint, your boss's boss probably has the most influence and control over your progress. He/she has a broader perspective, has more access to data, and stands at the center of decisions about you. To know what he/she thinks, without having to violate the canons of corporate due process to get that information, would be quite useful.

☐ **Direct Boss**
Your direct boss has important information about you, your performance, and your prospects. The challenge is to get this information. There are formal processes (e.g., performance appraisals). There are day-to-day opportunities. To help, signal your boss that you want and can handle direct and timely feedback. Many bosses have trouble giving feedback, so you will have to work at it over a period of time.

☐ **Internal and External Customers**
Customers interact with you as a person and as a supplier or vendor of products and services. You're important to them because you can either help address and solve their problems or stand in their way. As customer service and Total Quality programs gain importance, clients and customers become a more prominent source of feedback.

☐ **Past Associates/Constituencies**
When confronted with a present performance problem, some claim, "I wasn't like that before; it must be the current situation." When feedback is available from former associates, about 50% support that claim. In the other half of the cases, the people were like that before and probably didn't know it. It sometimes makes sense to access the past to clearly see the present.

☐ **Peers and Colleagues**
Peers and colleagues have a special social and working relationship. They attend staff meetings together, share private views, get feedback from the same boss, travel together, and are knowledgeable about each other's work. You perhaps let your guard down more around peers and act more like yourself. They can be a valuable source of feedback.

SECTION 4: LEARNING FROM DEVELOP-IN-PLACE ASSIGNMENTS

THESE PART-TIME DEVELOP-IN-PLACE ASSIGNMENTS WILL HELP YOU BUILD YOUR SKILL(S)

- ☐ Monitor and follow a new product or service through the entire idea, design, test market, and launch cycle.
- ☐ Launch a new product, service, or process.
- ☐ Relaunch an existing product or service that's not doing well.
- ☐ Seek out and use a seed budget to create and pursue a personal idea, product, or service.
- ☐ Do a study of lost customers, including interviewing a sample, and report the findings to the people involved.
- ☐ Plan for and start up something small (secretarial pool, athletic program, suggestion system, program, etc.).
- ☐ Plan a new site for a building (plant, field office, headquarters, etc.).
- ☐ Manage an ad hoc, temporary group of balky and resisting people through an unpopular change or project.
- ☐ Assemble an ad hoc team of diverse people to accomplish a difficult task.
- ☐ Manage the interface between consultants and the organization on a critical assignment.

SECTION 5: LEARNING FROM FULL-TIME JOBS

THESE FULL-TIME JOBS OFFER THE OPPORTUNITY TO BUILD YOUR SKILL(S)

☐ **Heavy Strategic Demands**

The core demands necessary to qualify as a Heavy Strategic Content assignment are: 1) Requires significant strategic thinking and planning most couldn't do. 2) Charts new ground strategically. 3) Plan must be presented, challenged, adopted, and implemented. 4) Exposure to significant decision makers and executives. 1) Strategic planning position. 2) Job involving repositioning of a product, service, or organization.

☐ **Scope Assignments**

The core demands for a Scope (complexity) assignment are: 1) Significant increase in both internal and external scope or complexity. 2) Significant increase in visibility and/or bottom line responsibility. 3) Unfamiliar area, business, technology, or territory. Examples of Scope assignments involving shifts: 1) Switching into a new function/technology/business. 2) Moving to new organization. 3) Moving to overseas assignment. 4) Moving to new location. 5) Adding new products/services. 6) Moving between headquarters/field. 7) Switches in ownership/top management of the unit/organization. Examples of Scope

assignments involving "firsts": 1) First-time manager. 2) First-time managing managers. 3) First-time executive. 4) First-time overseas. 5) First-time headquarters/field. 6) First-time team leader. 7) First-time new technology/business/function. Scope assignments involving increased complexity: 1) Managing a significant expansion of an existing product or service. 2) Managing adding new products/service into an existing unit. 3) Managing a reorganized and more diverse unit. 4) Managing explosive growth. 5) Adding new technologies.

☐ **Start-ups**
The core demands to qualify as a start from scratch are: 1) Starting something new for you and/or for the organization. 2) Forging a new team. 3) Creating new systems/facilities/staffs/programs/procedures. 4) Contextual adversity (e.g., uncertainty, government regulation, unions, difficult environment). Seven types of start from scratches: 1) Planning, building, hiring, and managing (e.g., building a new facility, opening up a new location, moving a unit or company). 2) Heading something new (e.g., new product, new service, new line of business, new department/function, major new program). 3) Take over a group/product/service/program that had existed for less than a year and was off to a fast start. 4) Establishing overseas operations. 5) Major new designs for existing systems. 6) Moving a successful program from one unit to another. 7) Installing a new organization-wide process as a full-time job (e.g., like Total Quality).

SECTION 6: LEARNING MORE FROM YOUR PLAN

THESE ADDITIONAL REMEDIES WILL HELP MAKE THIS DEVELOPMENT PLAN MORE EFFECTIVE FOR YOU

Learning from Experience, Feedback and Other People

☐ **Being a Student of Others**
While many of us rely on others for information or advice, we do not really study the behavior of other people. Ask what a person does exceptionally well or poorly. What behaviors are particularly effective and ineffective for them? What works for them and what doesn't? As a student of others, you can deduce the rules of thumb for effective and ineffective behavior and include those in your own library. In comparing yourself with this person, in what areas could you most improve? What could you specifically do to improve in ways comfortable for you?

☐ **Learning from Bosses**
Bosses can be an excellent and ready source for learning. All bosses do some things exceptionally well and other things poorly. Distance your feelings from the boss/direct report relationship and study things that work and things that don't work for your boss. What would you have done? What could you use, and what should you avoid?

- ☐ **Learning from Observing Others**
  Observe others. Find opportunities to observe without interacting with your model. This enables you to objectively study the person, note what he/she is doing or not doing, and compare that with what you would typically do in similar situations. Many times you can learn more by watching than asking. Your model may not be able to explain what he/she does or may be an unwilling teacher.

- ☐ **Learning from Remote Models**
  Many times you can learn from people not directly available to you. You can read a book about them, watch tapes of public figures, read analyses of them, etc. The principles of learning are the same. Ask yourself what they do well or poorly and deduce their rules of thumb.

- ☐ **Getting Feedback from Bosses and Superiors**
  Many bosses are reluctant to give negative feedback. They lack the managerial courage to face people directly with criticism. You can help by soliciting feedback and setting the tone. Show them you can handle criticism and that you are willing to work on issues they see as important.

Learning from Courses

- ☐ **Survey Courses**
  These are courses designed to give a general overview of an entire area (such as advertising), product or product line, division's activities, process (getting a product to market, Total Quality Management) or geography (doing business in "X"). These types of courses are good for general background and context.

- ☐ **Strategic Courses**
  There are a number of courses designed to stretch minds to prepare for future challenges. They include topics such as Workforce Diversity 2000, globalization, the European Union, competitive competencies and strategies, etc. Quality depends upon the following three factors: 1) The quality of the staff. Are they qualified? Are they respected in their fields? Are they strategic "gurus"? 2) The quality of the participants. Are they the kind of people you could learn from? 3) The quality of the setting. Is it comfortable and free from distractions? Can you learn there?

SUGGESTED READINGS

Futurist Magazine. http://www.wfs.org

Drucker, Peter F. *Innovation and Entrepreneurship.* New York: Harper & Row, 1985.

Drucker, Peter F. *Innovation and Entrepreneurship [sound recording]: practice and principles.* New York: AMACOM; Albuquerque, NM: distributed by Newman, 1985.

Hamel, Gary and C.K. Prahalad. *Competing for the Future.* Boston: Harvard Business School Press, 1994.

Kanter, Rosabeth Moss, John Kao, and Fred Wiersema, Editors. *Innovation: Breakthrough Thinking at 3M, DuPont, GE, Pfizer and Rubbermaid.* New York: Harper Business, 1997.

Kidder, Tracy. *The soul of a new machine.* Boston: Little, Brown, 1981.

Peters, Tom. *The Circle of Innovation – You Can't Shrink Your Way to Greatness.* New York: Alfred A. Knopf, Inc., 1997.

Peters, Tom. *The Circle of Innovation – You Can't Shrink Your Way to Greatness [sound recording].* New York: Random House Audio Pub., 1997.

Peters, Tom. *Liberation Management.* New York: Knopf, 1992.

Peters, Tom. *Liberation Management [sound recording].* New York: Random House Audio, 1992.

Robert, Michel. *Product Innovation Strategy.* New York: McGraw-Hill, Inc., 1995.

Stalk, George Jr. and Thomas M. Hout. *Competing Against Time.* New York: Macmillan, Inc., 1990.

29

INTEGRITY AND TRUST

SECTION 1: YOUR DEVELOPMENT NEED(S)

UNSKILLED

- ☐ Is not widely trusted
- ☐ May hedge or not take a stand
- ☐ May treat others differently or indifferently at times
- ☐ May not walk his/her talk and be seen as inconsistent
- ☐ May have trouble keeping confidences and talks out of school
- ☐ Makes promises he/she doesn't or can't keep
- ☐ May lack follow-through and causes problems for others
- ☐ Blames others for own mistakes
- ☐ Seen as just out for him/herself

SKILLED

- ☐ Is widely trusted
- ☐ Is seen as a direct, truthful individual
- ☐ Can present the unvarnished truth in an appropriate and helpful manner
- ☐ Keeps confidences
- ☐ Admits mistakes
- ☐ Doesn't misrepresent him/herself for personal gain

OVERUSED SKILL

- ☐ May be too direct at times, which may catch people off guard and make them uncomfortable
- ☐ May push openness and honesty to the point of being disruptive
- ☐ May be so "only the facts" driven as to omit drawing reasonable conclusions, rendering opinions, or fixing blame, even when it's reasonable

Select one to three of the competencies listed below to work on to compensate for an overuse of this skill.

COMPENSATORS: 2, 5, 14, 22, 26, 31, 33, 38, 40, 42, 46, 48, 52, 54, 56, 64

SOME CAUSES

- ☐ Avoid conflict
- ☐ Don't "walk your talk"
- ☐ Hedging; holding back
- ☐ Overly ambitious
- ☐ Problems with keeping confidences
- ☐ Spread too thin; can't say no
- ☐ Too anxious to make the sale
- ☐ Treat others differentially
- ☐ Won't take a stand

THE MAP

Integrity and trust are on almost every success profile we see. It is a basic threshold requirement to be a part of the team. Without it, almost nothing else matters. To think that people question our integrity or don't totally trust us is very difficult to accept. The more common causes are personal disorganization, inconsistencies and habits that get us into trouble. Many of us simply haven't thought through the impact of our actions and have little idea how we come across. It can also be a lack of integrity in the bigger sense; people just don't buy what you say.

SECTION 2: LEARNING ON YOUR OWN

THESE SELF-DEVELOPMENT REMEDIES WILL HELP YOU BUILD YOUR SKILL(S)

SOME REMEDIES

☐ **1. Are you a hedger?** Do you hold back and qualify everything? Don't speak up when you should? Do you not know how to say what needs to be said so you go bland and qualify everything to death? Do you hesitate or slow down when you are sharing something that is difficult for you? Even though it's not your intention, do people think you are not disclosing what you really know? Practice coming up with two or three clear statements you are prepared to defend. Test them with people you trust. Keep them on the facts and on the problems. Be specific and don't blame. Don't qualify or make your statements conditional. Just say it. *More help? – See #34 Managerial Courage.*

☐ **2. Overselling?** Trying too hard to make the sale? Does your enthusiasm to make the sale or get your point across cause you to commit to too many things in the heat of the transaction? Do you stretch the truth? Do you embellish? The customer you get by unrealistic commitments is the customer you will lose forever when he/she finds out you can't deliver. Can't say no to customers? Do you want to help so much that you put yourself in impossible situations? Afraid that people will think you're not helpful? Being helpful is not helpful when you don't deliver. If you goof on the time required, go back and tell him/her the problem; either renegotiate or ask what else you should move down his/her list of requests. Don't promise something unless you can deliver. If you don't know for sure, say, "I'll let you know when I do." Either promise or don't – don't say "I'll try." If you don't know, just say so and follow up when you do know. Try to reduce your sales pitches to the actual merits of the case.

☐ **3. Loose lips?** Some people get into trust issues because they share information others intended to be kept confidential. Be clear on what keeping a confidence means. Some rules are:

- Keep personal information confidential.
- Don't agree too quickly to keep performance/ethical/legal matters confidential. Warn others up front, "Before you tell me, I can't promise confidentiality on matters that affect unit performance, ethics or legal matters."
- Ask up front, "Is this to be kept confidential?"
- If someone is complaining about a coworker's ethics, tell him/her you can do nothing since you know nothing directly. Have him/her confront the person or produce evidence before continuing the discussion.
- There is usually no guarantee of confidentiality on matters affecting performance, legal and ethical jeopardy.
- There is usually no guarantee of confidentiality on matters affecting personal safety. Even doctors and psychiatrists pass on warnings of harm to authorities even though they obtained the information in confidence.
- It doesn't take many slip-ups in an organization before people say you can't be trusted with confidential information.

☐ **4. Buying favor?** Do people think you disclose information and use your friendships for personal advantage? Being seen as taking advantage of friendships or using information for personal advantage is hard to deal with. There is a fine line between this and the normal way things get done in organizations: friends tell each other things, deals get struck, people access their networks, and sharing information is part of the process. Some rules of thumb so as to not cross the line are:

- Make sure it is a business request for information, not a personal one.
- Make sure it improves performance or efficiency or adds value; any benefit to you is then a by-product.
- Make sure you would tell this or ask this of someone you didn't know well in your organization.

☐ **5. Taking responsibility.** Trouble admitting mistakes? Look for others to blame? Do people get blindsided because you don't warn them? People who excel at dealing with their own mistakes usually do the following:

- Admit the mistake early and inform everyone affected what could occur because of it.
- Publicly acknowledge the mistake if necessary; take personal responsibility.

- Demonstrate what they have learned so the mistake does not happen again.
- Move on; don't dwell on it.

☐ **6. Trying to avoid conflict?** Do you say what you need to say to get through the meeting or transaction? Do you say things just to go along and not cause trouble? Do you say what you need to say to avoid disagreement or an argument? All these behaviors will eventually backfire when people find out you said something different in another setting or to another person or they notice that you didn't actually follow through and do what you said. *More help? – See #12 Conflict Management.*

☐ **7. A loner.** Do you keep to yourself? Work alone or try to? Do you hold back information? Do you parcel out information on your schedule? Do you keep everything to yourself? Do people around you know what you're doing and why? Even though it may not be your intention, could people think you are holding things back? Do they think you are aware of things others would benefit from but you don't take the time or make the effort to communicate? In most organizations, these things and things like it will get you in trouble. Organizations function on the flow of information. Being on your own and preferring peace and privacy are OK as long as you communicate things to bosses, peers and teammates that they need to know and would feel better if they knew. Make the effort to find out from each group you interact with what it is that they want and need to know and try to comply. *More help? – See #27 Informing.*

☐ **8. Whistleblowing.** A tough call. Do you hesitate blowing the whistle? Do you know something others should but when they find out, there will be noise and trouble? Saying what needs to be said to the right person in a timely way takes courage, being direct and straightforward. Everybody sees things, observes things, knows things or learns about things that others should know. Many times it's not positive information. Something is about to go wrong. Something is being covered up. Someone is holding back an important piece of information. Someone or something is going off in the wrong direction. It's good news and bad news. If you inform, the organization may gain. But a person or some people may lose. Generally, your best bet is to find the right person and inform. *More help? – See #34 Managerial Courage.*

☐ **9. Disorganized.** Do you follow up on simple commitments? Do you return phones calls in a timely manner? Do you forward material that you promised? Do you pass on information you promised to get? Do you carry through on tasks you promised someone you would take care of? Failing to do things like this damages relationships. If you don't follow through well, focus on the receiver. What does this person need to know to implement this change? If you tend to forget, write things down. If you are going to miss a deadline, let people know and give them a second date you will be sure to make. Always out of time? Do you intend to get to things but never have the time? Do you always estimate shorter times to get things done that then take longer? If you run out of time, set up a specific time each day to follow through on commitments. There is a well established science and a set of best practices in time management. There are a number of books you can buy in any business book store, and there are a number of good courses you can attend. Delegating also helps use your time more effectively. *More help? – See #62 Time Management.*

☐ **10. Perhaps you really aren't very trustworthy.** You hedge, sabotage others, play for advantage, set up others, don't intend to follow up. You justify it by saying that things are tough, that you're just doing your job, getting results. After all, the end justifies the means. You use others to get your agenda accomplished. First, you need to examine whether this view of the world is really right and if that is the way you really want to be. Second, you need to find out if your career with this organization is salvageable. Have you burned too many bridges? The best way to do this is to admit you have regularly betrayed trusts and not followed through on your commitments. Talk with your boss or mentor to see if you can redeem yourself. If yes, meet with everyone you think you've alienated and see how they respond. Tell them what you're going to do differently. Ask them what you should stop doing. Ask them if the situation can be repaired. *More help? – See #105 Betrayal of Trust.*

SECTION 3: LEARNING FROM MORE FEEDBACK

THESE SOURCES WOULD GIVE YOU THE MOST ACCURATE AND DETAILED FEEDBACK ON YOUR SKILL(S)

☐ **Direct Boss**

Your direct boss has important information about you, your performance, and your prospects. The challenge is to get this information. There are formal processes (e.g., performance appraisals). There are day-to-day opportunities. To help, signal your boss that you want and can handle direct and timely feedback. Many bosses have trouble giving feedback, so you will have to work at it over a period of time.

☐ **Direct Reports**

Across a variety of settings, your direct reports probably see you the most. They are the recipients of most of your managerial behaviors. They know your work. They can compare you with former bosses. Since they may hesitate to give you negative feedback, you have to set the atmosphere to make it easier for them. You have to ask.

- [ ] **Human Resource Professionals**
Human Resource professionals have both a formal and informal feedback role. Since they have access to unique and confidential information, they can provide the right context for feedback you've received. Sometimes they may be "directed" to give you feedback. Other times, they may pass on feedback just to be helpful to you.

- [ ] **Natural Mentors**
Natural mentors have a special relationship with you and are interested in your success and your future. Since they are usually not in your direct chain of command, you can have more open, relaxed, and fruitful discussions about yourself and your career prospects. They can be a very important source for candid or critical feedback others may not give you.

SECTION 4: LEARNING FROM DEVELOP-IN-PLACE ASSIGNMENTS

THESE PART-TIME DEVELOP-IN-PLACE ASSIGNMENTS WILL HELP YOU BUILD YOUR SKILL(S)

- [ ] Handle a tough negotiation with an internal or external client or customer.
- [ ] Help shut down a plant, regional office, product line, business, operation, etc.
- [ ] Manage a dissatisfied internal or external customer; troubleshoot a performance or quality problem with a product or service.
- [ ] Manage the assigning/allocating of office space in a contested situation.
- [ ] Manage a group through a significant business crisis.
- [ ] Take on a tough and undoable project, one where others who have tried it have failed.
- [ ] Manage the outplacement of a group of people.
- [ ] Resolve an issue in conflict between two people, units, geographies, functions, etc.
- [ ] Make peace with an enemy or someone you've disappointed with a product or service or someone you've had some trouble with or don't get along well with.
- [ ] Be a member of a union-negotiating or grievance-handling team.

SECTION 5: LEARNING FROM FULL-TIME JOBS

THESE FULL-TIME JOBS OFFER THE OPPORTUNITY TO BUILD YOUR SKILL(S)

☐ **Chair of Projects/Task Forces**

The core demands for qualifying as a Project/Task Force assignment are: 1) Full-time assignment. 2) Important and specific goal. 3) Tight deadline. 4) Success or failure will be evident. 5) High-visibility sponsor. 6) Learning something on the fly. 7) Must get others to cooperate. 8) Usually six months or more. Four types of Projects/Task Forces: 1) New ideas, products, services, or systems (e.g., product/service/program research and development, creation/installation/launch of a new system, new programs like Total Quality Management, positive discipline). 2) Formal negotiations and relationships (e.g., acquisitions, divestitures, agreements, joint ventures; licensing arrangements, franchising; dealing with unions, governments, communities, charities, customers, and relocations). 3) Big one-time events (e.g., working on a major presentation for the board, organizing significant meetings or conferences, disaster/damage control teams; reorganizations, mergers, acquisitions, or relocations, working on visions, charters, strategies, other time-urgent issues and problems). 4) Troubleshooting (e.g., problems, disasters, crises, product/service failures, accidents, illegal activities, damage control in public relations goofs, shut downs, downsizings, layoffs, abrupt changes in leadership).

☐ **Fix-its/Turnarounds**

The core demands to qualify as a Fix-it or Turnaround assignment are: 1) Cleaning up a mess. 2) Serious people issues/problems like credibility/performance/morale. 3) Tight deadline. 4) Serious business performance failure. 5) Last chance to fix. Four Types of Fix-its/Turnarounds: 1) Fixing a failed business/unit involving taking control, stopping losses, managing damage, planning the turnaround, dealing with people problems, installing new processes and systems, and rebuilding the spirit and performance of the unit. 2) Managing sizable disasters like mishandled labor negotiations and strikes, thefts, history of significant business losses, poor staff, failed leadership, hidden problems, fraud, public relations nightmares, etc. 3) Significant reorganization and restructuring (e.g., stabilizing the business, reforming unit, introducing new systems, making people changes, resetting strategy and tactics). 4) Significant system/process breakdown (e.g., MIS, financial coordination processes, audits, standards, etc.) across units requiring working to change something from a distant position, providing advice and counsel, and installing or implementing a major process improvement or system change outside your own unit and/or with customers outside the organization.

☐ **Influencing Without Authority**

The core demands to qualify as an Influence Without Authority are: 1) Significant challenge (e.g, start-up, fix-it, scope and/or scale assign-

ment, strategic planning project, changes in management practices/systems). 2) Insufficient direct authority to make it happen. 3) Tight deadlines. 4) Visible to significant others. 5) Sensitive politics.

☐ **Scope Assignments**
The core demands for a Scope (complexity) assignment are:
1) Significant increase in both internal and external scope or complexity. 2) Significant increase in visibility and/or bottom line responsibility. 3) Unfamiliar area, business, technology, or territory. Examples of Scope assignments involving shifts: 1) Switching into a new function/technology/business. 2) Moving to new organization. 3) Moving to overseas assignment. 4) Moving to new location. 5) Adding new products/services. 6) Moving between headquarters/field. 7) Switches in ownership/top management of the unit/organization. Examples of Scope assignments involving "firsts": 1) First-time manager. 2) First-time managing managers. 3) First-time executive. 4) First-time overseas. 5) First-time headquarters/field. 6) First-time team leader. 7) First-time new technology/business/function. Scope assignments involving increased complexity: 1) Managing a significant expansion of an existing product or service. 2) Managing adding new products/service into an existing unit. 3) Managing a reorganized and more diverse unit. 4) Managing explosive growth. 5) Adding new technologies.

SECTION 6: LEARNING MORE FROM YOUR PLAN

THESE ADDITIONAL REMEDIES WILL HELP MAKE THIS DEVELOPMENT PLAN MORE EFFECTIVE FOR YOU

Learning from Experience, Feedback and Other People

☐ **Using Multiple Models**
Who do you know who exemplifies how to do whatever your need is? Who, for example, personifies decisiveness or compassion or strategic agility? Think more broadly than your current job and colleagues. For example, clergy, friends, spouses or community leaders are also good sources for potential models. Select your models not on the basis of overall excellence or likability, but on the basis of the one towering strength (or glaring weakness) you are interested in. Even people who are well thought of usually have only one or two towering strengths (or glaring weaknesses). Ordinarily, you won't learn as much from the whole person as you will from one characteristic.

☐ **Learning from Bosses**
Bosses can be an excellent and ready source for learning. All bosses do some things exceptionally well and other things poorly. Distance your feelings from the boss/direct report relationship and study things that work and things that don't work for your boss. What would you have done? What could you use, and what should you avoid?

☐ **Learning from Mentors and Tutors**
Mentors and tutors offer a special case for learning since the relationship is specifically formed for learning. You need to be open and nondefensive. You need to solicit and accept feedback. This is a unique opportunity for you to get low-risk, honest, and direct feedback on what you do well and not so well.

☐ **Learning from Ineffective Behavior**
Seeing things done poorly can be a very potent source of learning for you, especially if the behavior or action affects others negatively. Many times the thing done poorly causes emotional reactions or pain in you and others. Distance yourself from the feelings and explore why the actions didn't work.

☐ **Learning from Interviewing Others**
Interview others. Ask not only what they do, but how and why they do it. What do they think are the rules of thumb they are following? Where did they learn the behaviors? How do they keep them current? How do they monitor the effect they have on others?

☐ **Learning from Observing Others**
Observe others. Find opportunities to observe without interacting with your model. This enables you to objectively study the person, note what he/she is doing or not doing, and compare that with what you would typically do in similar situations. Many times you can learn more by watching than asking. Your model may not be able to explain what he/she does or may be an unwilling teacher.

☐ **Feedback in Unusual Contexts/Situations**
Temporary and extreme conditions and contexts may shade interpretations of your behavior and intentions. Demands of the job may drive you outside your normal mode of operating. Hence, feedback you receive may be inaccurate during those times. However, unusual contexts affect our behavior less than most assume. It's usually a weak excuse.

☐ **Openness to Feedback**
Nothing discourages feedback more than defensiveness, resistance, irritation, and excuses. People don't like giving feedback anyway, and much less to those who don't listen or are unreceptive. To help the feedback giver, be open, listen, ask for examples and details, take notes, keep a journal, and thank them for their interest.

☐ **Learning from Mistakes**
Since we're human, we all make mistakes. The key is to focus on why you made the mistake. Spend more time locating causes and less worrying about the effects. Check how you react to mistakes. How much time do you spend being angry with yourself? Do you waste time stewing or do you move on? More importantly, do you learn? Ask why you made the mistake. Are you likely to repeat it under similar situa-

tions? Was it a lack of skill? Judgment? Style? Not enough data? Reading people? Misreading the challenge? Misreading the politics? Or was it just random? A good strategy that just didn't work? Others that let you down? The key is to avoid two common reactions to your mistakes: 1) avoiding similar situations instead of learning and trying again, and 2) trying to repeat what you did, only more diligently and harder, hoping to break through the problem, making the same mistake again but with greater impact. Neither trap leaves us with better strategies for the future. Neither is a learning strategy. To learn and do something differently, focus on the patterns in your behavior that get you in trouble and go back to first causes, those that tell you something about your shortcomings. Facing ourselves squarely is always the best way to learn.

Learning from Courses

☐ **Insight Events**

These are courses designed around assessing skills and providing feedback to the participants. These events can be a powerful source of self-knowledge and can lead to significant development if done right. When selecting a self-insight course, consider the following: 1) Are the skills assessed the important ones? 2) Are the assessment techniques and instruments sound? 3) Are those who are providing the feedback trained and professional? 4) Is the feedback provided in a user-friendly and "actionable" format? 5) Does the feedback include development planning? 6) Is the setting comfortable and conducive to reflection and learning? 7) Are the other participants the kinds of people you could learn from? 8) Are you in the right frame of mind to learn from this kind of intense experience? Select events on the basis of positive answers to these eight questions.

SUGGESTED READINGS

Chambers, Harry E. *No fear management: rebuilding trust, performance, and commitment in the new American workplace.* Boca Raton, FL: St. Lucie Press, 1998.

Dorland, Gil and John Dorland. *Duty, Honor, Company – West Point Fundamentals for Business Success.* New York: Henry Holt & Company, 1992.

Dosick, Rabbi Wayne. *The Business Bible – Ten new commandments for creating an ethical workplace.* New York: William Morrow and Company, Inc., 1993.

O'Toole, James. *Leading Change.* Boston: Harvard Business School Press, 1996.

Shaw, Robert Bruce. *Trust in the Balance – Building successful organizations on results, integrity and concern.* San Francisco: Jossey-Bass, Inc., 1997.

Sonnenberg, Frank K. *Managing with a Conscience – How to improve performance through integrity, trust and commitment.* New York: McGraw-Hill, Inc., 1994.

Zand, Dale E. *The Leadership Triad – Knowledge, Trust and Power.* New York: Oxford University Press, 1997.

30

INTELLECTUAL HORSEPOWER

SECTION 1: YOUR DEVELOPMENT NEED(S)

UNSKILLED

- ☐ May be intellectually lazy or disorganized
- ☐ May not think things through carefully
- ☐ Always wants everything to be simple
- ☐ Emotions may get in the way of careful consideration
- ☐ Impatience may get in the way of careful consideration
- ☐ May be mentally inflexible or stale – believing that his/her way is the best and virtually only way to do things or solve problems
- ☐ May get frustrated when others are talking conceptually
- ☐ May be slow to catch on to things

SKILLED

- ☐ Is bright and intelligent
- ☐ Deals with concepts and complexity comfortably
- ☐ Described as intellectually sharp, capable, and agile

OVERUSED SKILL

- ☐ May use intelligence to dominate and intimidate others
- ☐ May not be able to relate to those less intelligent
- ☐ May only accept own solutions
- ☐ May be impatient with due process

Select one to three of the competencies listed below to work on to compensate for an overuse of this skill.

COMPENSATORS: 3, 4, 7, 10, 15, 18, 19, 26, 31, 33, 36, 41, 42, 44

SOME CAUSES

- ☐ Disorganized
- ☐ Excessive emotionality
- ☐ Lack of patience, perseverance or self confidence
- ☐ Lack of cognitive skills
- ☐ Lazy
- ☐ Rigid belief systems

THE MAP

Much of success in life and work is based upon acquiring knowledge and skills and putting them to use solving life's problems and challenges. Although your level of basic intelligence is in a sense set at birth – you have as much as you are ever going to have – popular science writers commonly claim we use only 10% of the brain's capacity. Even though that number probably can't be specifically verified, it's safe to say we all have extra capacity we could put to use. Studies show that intelligence is a use it or lose it competence; those who stay mentally sharp show continuing though slight increases in intelligence throughout their lifetimes.

SECTION 2: LEARNING ON YOUR OWN

THESE SELF-DEVELOPMENT REMEDIES WILL HELP YOU BUILD YOUR SKILL(S)

SOME REMEDIES

- ☐ **1. Cool down.** Excessive emotionality decreases the effective use of brain power. The emotional system hijacks the brain until the threat is removed. The brain works best under cool conditions. If you tend to get emotional about things, wait a minute or two to regain your composure and then try to solve the problem. Decision making under heat is unlikely to be correct over time. *More help? – See #11 Composure.*

- ☐ **2. Take time to think.** Many of us are very action oriented. It's the famous fire-ready-aim. Many mistakes we make would not have happened if we had taken the time to think things through. Try to add one minute to your thinking time. Go through a mental checklist to see if you have thought about all of the ramifications of the problem or challenge. Other research has shown that the first thing or solution you think of is seldom the best choice. Usually somewhere between the second and third choice turns out to be the most effective. If you are an action junkie and jump at the first option, you will be wrong much of the time. *More help? – See #41 Patience and #43 Perseverance.*

- ☐ **3. Rigid or narrow beliefs decrease the use of your brain power.** Much research from anthropology has shown that our brains are trapped inside our belief framework. The Hopi Indians in the Southwest have one word for snow whereas the Inuits of Alaska have 24 different words for 24 different kinds of snow conditions. A Hopi could not survive in Alaska with just one snow concept. Our experience unknowingly creates boundaries for our thinking. Try to think outside your belief boundaries. You don't have to give them up; just turn them off when you are thinking about a problem or challenge.

- ☐ **4. Jump start your mind.** There are all kinds of mental exercises to increase the use of whatever intellectual horsepower you have. You can create checklists so you don't forget anything. You can run scenarios. You can ask what's missing. You can do pro's and con's. You can visualize. You can diagram a problem. You can practice seeing how many patterns you can see in something or how many ways you can mentally organize it. These and many other practices will be in any text on problem solving. *More help? – See #51 Problem Solving and #52 Process Management.*

☐ **5. Learn to separate your opinions from facts you know.** Help others do the same. Read Edward de Bono's *Six Thinking Hats* to learn more about this technique. Opinionated people are seldom clear thinkers and good problem solvers.

☐ **6. Turn off your answer program.** We all have a need to provide answers as soon as possible to questions and problems. We all have preconceived notions, favorite solutions, and prejudices that prevent our intellectual skills from dealing with the real facts of the problem. For one half of the time you have to deal with an issue or a problem, shut off your solution machine and just take in the facts.

☐ **7. Think systems.** Subscribe to *The Systems Thinker*™, Pegasus Communications, Inc., Cambridge, MA, 617-576-1231) This is a group dedicated to finding out how things work and why they work that way. They have a monthly publication as well as workshops, seminars and other materials available to help you see the world as a series of recurring systems or archetypes. They analyze everyday events and processes and try to see why they work the way they do. They take complex problems and try to show how almost all problems are some form of seven classic models.

☐ **8. Exercise your brain.** Buy some beginning crossword puzzle books to do in your spare time. Buy other kinds of mental puzzle materials and practice on them. Get a book on "mind mapping" or better yet, attend a workshop. Mind mapping is a technique that teaches you how to organize concepts.

☐ **9. Visualize.** Try to picture problems and challenges in the form of pictures or flows. Buy a flow charting software program like ABC FlowCharter® 4.0 that does PERT and GANT charts. Become an expert in its use. Use the output of the software to communicate the elements of a problem to others. Use the flow charts in your presentations to explain the problems you've solved.

☐ **10. Access great minds.** Study a few great thinkers and philosophers like John Stuart Mill who outlined the basic logic of problem solving. Read their biographies or autobiographies for clues into how they used their intellectual skills.

SECTION 3: LEARNING FROM MORE FEEDBACK

THESE SOURCES WOULD GIVE YOU THE MOST ACCURATE AND DETAILED FEEDBACK ON YOUR SKILL(S)

- ☐ **Boss's Boss(es)**
  From a process standpoint, your boss's boss probably has the most influence and control over your progress. He/she has a broader perspective, has more access to data, and stands at the center of decisions about you. To know what he/she thinks, without having to violate the canons of corporate due process to get that information, would be quite useful.
- ☐ **Development Professionals**
  Sometimes it might be valuable to get some analysis and feedback from a professional trained and certified in the area you're working on: possibly a career counselor, a therapist, clergy, a psychologist, etc.
- ☐ **Human Resource Professionals**
  Human Resource professionals have both a formal and informal feedback role. Since they have access to unique and confidential information, they can provide the right context for feedback you've received. Sometimes they may be "directed" to give you feedback. Other times, they may pass on feedback just to be helpful to you.
- ☐ **Natural Mentors**
  Natural mentors have a special relationship with you and are interested in your success and your future. Since they are usually not in your direct chain of command, you can have more open, relaxed, and fruitful discussions about yourself and your career prospects. They can be a very important source for candid or critical feedback others may not give you.

SECTION 4: LEARNING FROM DEVELOP-IN-PLACE ASSIGNMENTS

THESE PART-TIME DEVELOP-IN-PLACE ASSIGNMENTS WILL HELP YOU BUILD YOUR SKILL(S)

- ☐ Do a competitive analysis of your organization's products or services or your position in the marketplace and present it to the people involved.
- ☐ Train and work as an assessor in an assessment center.
- ☐ Relaunch an existing product or service that's not doing well.
- ☐ Teach a course, seminar, or workshop on something you don't know well.
- ☐ Teach/coach someone how to do something you are not an expert in.
- ☐ Manage an ad hoc, temporary group of people where the people in the group are towering experts but the temporary manager is not.
- ☐ Assemble an ad hoc team of diverse people to accomplish a difficult task.

- ☐ Manage a group through a significant business crisis.
- ☐ Do a postmortem on a failed project and present it to the people involved.
- ☐ Audit cost overruns to assess the problem and present your findings to the person or people involved.

SECTION 5: LEARNING FROM FULL-TIME JOBS

THESE FULL-TIME JOBS OFFER THE OPPORTUNITY TO BUILD YOUR SKILL(S)

☐ **Fix-its / Turnarounds**

The core demands to qualify as a Fix-it or Turnaround assignment are: 1) Cleaning up a mess. 2) Serious people issues/problems like credibility/performance/morale. 3) Tight deadline. 4) Serious business performance failure. 5) Last chance to fix. Four Types of Fix-its/ Turnarounds: 1) Fixing a failed business/unit involving taking control, stopping losses, managing damage, planning the turnaround, dealing with people problems, installing new processes and systems, and rebuilding the spirit and performance of the unit. 2) Managing sizable disasters like mishandled labor negotiations and strikes, thefts, history of significant business losses, poor staff, failed leadership, hidden problems, fraud, public relations nightmares, etc. 3) Significant reorganization and restructuring (e.g., stabilizing the business, reforming unit, introducing new systems, making people changes, resetting strategy and tactics). 4) Significant system/process breakdown (e.g., MIS, financial coordination processes, audits, standards, etc.) across units requiring working to change something from a distant position, providing advice and counsel, and installing or implementing a major process improvement or system change outside your own unit and/or with customers outside the organization.

☐ **Heavy Strategic Demands**

The core demands necessary to qualify as a Heavy Strategic Content assignment are: 1) Requires significant strategic thinking and planning most couldn't do. 2) Charts new ground strategically. 3) Plan must be presented, challenged, adopted, and implemented. 4) Exposure to significant decision makers and executives. 1) Strategic planning position. 2) Job involving repositioning of a product, service, or organization.

☐ **Scope Assignments**

The core demands for a Scope (complexity) assignment are: 1) Significant increase in both internal and external scope or complexity. 2) Significant increase in visibility and/or bottom line responsibility. 3) Unfamiliar area, business, technology, or territory. Examples of Scope assignments involving shifts: 1) Switching into a new function/technology/business. 2) Moving to new organization. 3) Moving to overseas assignment. 4) Moving to new location. 5) Adding new products/

services. 6) Moving between headquarters/field. 7) Switches in ownership/top management of the unit/organization. Examples of Scope assignments involving "firsts": 1) First-time manager. 2) First-time managing managers. 3) First-time executive. 4) First-time overseas. 5) First-time headquarters/field. 6) First-time team leader. 7) First-time new technology/business/function. Scope assignments involving increased complexity: 1) Managing a significant expansion of an existing product or service. 2) Managing adding new products/service into an existing unit. 3) Managing a reorganized and more diverse unit. 4) Managing explosive growth. 5) Adding new technologies.

SECTION 6: LEARNING MORE FROM YOUR PLAN

THESE ADDITIONAL REMEDIES WILL HELP MAKE THIS DEVELOPMENT PLAN MORE EFFECTIVE FOR YOU

Learning to Learn Better

☐ **Keep a Learning Journal**
Keep a learning log or diary about the issues and opportunities you've faced and how you've acted. Focus on how you've used your strengths and weaknesses. Deduce your effective and successful rules of thumb – what worked and what didn't, and how you would have done it differently.

☐ **Skim Data Repeatedly to Find Insights**
When stumped on a problem, take out the available data and information and read it over and over rapidly. Do not impose any order; do not organize or divide the data into categories when you start. Repeat this until an order and solution jumps out at you and forms into a plan.

Learning from Experience, Feedback and Other People

☐ **Getting Feedback from Bosses and Superiors**
Many bosses are reluctant to give negative feedback. They lack the managerial courage to face people directly with criticism. You can help by soliciting feedback and setting the tone. Show them you can handle criticism and that you are willing to work on issues they see as important.

Learning from Experience, Feedback and Other People

☐ **Insight Events**
These are courses designed around assessing skills and providing feedback to the participants. These events can be a powerful source of self-knowledge and can lead to significant development if done right. When selecting a self-insight course, consider the following: 1) Are the skills assessed the important ones? 2) Are the assessment techniques and instruments sound? 3) Are those who are providing the feedback trained and professional? 4) Is the feedback provided in a user-friendly

and "actionable" format? 5) Does the feedback include development planning? 6) Is the setting comfortable and conducive to reflection and learning? 7) Are the other participants the kinds of people you could learn from? 8) Are you in the right frame of mind to learn from this kind of intense experience? Select events on the basis of positive answers to these eight questions.

SUGGESTED READINGS

The Systems Thinker™. Pegasus Communications, Inc., Waltham, MA. 781-398-9700

Epstein, Seymour, Ph.D. with Archie Brodsky. *You're Smarter Than You Think – How to develop your practical intelligence for success in living.* New York: Simon and Schuster, 1993.

Glassman, Peter J. *J.S. Mill: the evolution of a genius.* Gainesville: University of Florida Press, 1985.

Hale, Guy. *The Leader's Edge – Mastering the five skills of breakthrough thinking.* Burr Ridge, IL: Irwin Professional Publishing, 1996.

Markova, Dawna Ph.D. *Open Mind – Exploring the 6 patterns of natural intelligence.* Berkeley, CA: Conari Press, 1996.

Miller, Marlane. *BrainStyles: change your life without changing who you are.* New York: Simon & Schuster, 1997.

Miller, Paul C. with Tom Gorman. *Big League Business Thinking.* New York: Prentice-Hall, 1994.

Nadler, Gerald Ph.D. and Shozo Hibino, Ph.D., with John Farrell. *Creative Solution Finding: The Triumph of Breakthrough Thinking over Conventional Problem Solving.* Rocklin, CA: Prima Publishing, 1995

Sternberg, Robert J. *Thinking Styles.* Boston: Cambridge University Press, 1997.

Stewart, Thomas A. *Intellectual Capital – The new wealth of organizations.* New York: Doubleday, 1997.

31

INTERPERSONAL SAVVY

SECTION 1: YOUR DEVELOPMENT NEED(S)

UNSKILLED

- ☐ Doesn't relate smoothly to a variety of people
- ☐ May not build relationships easily – may lack approachability or good listening skills
- ☐ Doesn't take the time to build rapport
- ☐ May be too raw and direct at times
- ☐ May be excessively work oriented or intense
- ☐ May be impatient to get on with the agenda; judgmental or arrogant toward others
- ☐ May not read others well
- ☐ May freeze or panic in the face of conflict, attack or criticism
- ☐ May be shy or lack confidence around others

SKILLED

- ☐ Relates well to all kinds of people, up, down, and sideways, inside and outside the organization
- ☐ Builds appropriate rapport
- ☐ Builds constructive and effective relationships
- ☐ Uses diplomacy and tact
- ☐ Can diffuse even high-tension situations comfortably

OVERUSED SKILL

- ☐ May be able to get by with smooth interpersonal skills
- ☐ May spend too much time building networks and glad-handing
- ☐ May not be taken as substantive by some
- ☐ May not be a credible take-charge leader when that's necessary
- ☐ May have some trouble and freeze when facing serious conflict

Select one to three of the competencies listed below to work on to compensate for an overuse of this skill.

COMPENSATORS: 1, 5, 9, 12, 13, 20, 24, 34, 36, 50, 51, 52, 57, 62, 65

SOME CAUSES

- ☐ Arrogant, impatient, insensitive
- ☐ Can't handle disagreement and attacks
- ☐ Defensive in the face of criticism
- ☐ Don't know what to do in various interpersonal situations
- ☐ Judgmental, rigid
- ☐ Narrow
- ☐ Not self confident
- ☐ Poor listening skills

- ☐ Poor time management; too busy
- ☐ Shy; afraid of transacting with new people; lack of self confidence
- ☐ Too intense; can't relax

THE MAP

The key to getting along with all kinds of people is to hold back or neutralize your personal reactions and focus on others first. Being savvy is working from the outside in. Then, interpersonal savvy becomes having a range of interpersonal skills and approaches and knowing when to use what with whom. The outcome is ease of transaction where you get what you need without damaging other parties unnecessarily and leave them wanting to work with you again.

SECTION 2: LEARNING ON YOUR OWN

THESE SELF-DEVELOPMENT REMEDIES WILL HELP YOU BUILD YOUR SKILL(S)

SOME REMEDIES

☐ **1. Why flexible interpersonal skills?** Except from a moral viewpoint (everyone is equal in the eyes of their creator), all people are different. There is a rich variety and diversity of people. Physical is easy to see. Height. Weight. Speed. Some personal characteristics are easy as well. Smart; not so smart. Articulate; not so articulate. Warm; cold. Composed; emotional. Good presenter; poor presenter. Other human characteristics are a little harder to read. Motivated; not so motivated. Good values; not so good values. Integrity? Decisive? Fair? To understand the differences, look to the obvious first. What do they do first? What do they emphasize in their speech? People focus on different things – taking action, details, concepts, feelings, other people. What's their interaction style? People come in different styles – pushy, tough, soft, matter of fact and so on. To figure these out, listen for the values behind their words and note what they have passion and emotion around. One key to getting anything of value done in the work world is the ability to see differences in people and to manage against and use those differences for everyone's benefit. Interpersonal savvy is meeting each person where he/she is to get done what you need to get done. Basically, people respond favorably to ease of transaction. If you make it easy by accepting their normal mode of doing things, not fighting their style, and neither defending your own nor letting style get in the way of performance, things will generally run smoothly. *More help? – See #56 Sizing Up People.*

☐ **2. Does your style chill the transaction?** Arrogant? Insensitive? Distant? Too busy to pay attention? Too quick to get into the agenda? Do you devalue others and dismiss their contributions, resulting in people feeling diminished, rejected and angry? Do you offer: answers, solutions, conclusions, statements, or dictates early in the transaction? That's the staple of people with a non-savvy style. No listening. Instant output. Sharp reactions. Don't want to be that way? Read your audience. Do you know what people look like when they are uncomfortable with you? Do they back up? Stumble over words? Cringe? Stand at the door hoping not to get invited in? You should work doubly hard at observing others. Always select your interpersonal approach from the other person in, not from you out. Your best choice of approach will always be determined by the other person or group, not you. Think about each transaction as if the other person were a customer you wanted. How would you craft an approach? *More help? – See #45 Personal Learning and #112 Insensitive to Others.*

☐ **3. The first three minutes.** Managing the first three minutes is essential. The tone is set. First impressions are formed. Work on being open and approachable, and take in information during the beginning of a transaction. This means putting others at ease so that they feel OK about disclosing. It means initiating rapport, listening, sharing, understanding and comforting. Approachable people get more information, know things earlier, and can get others to do more things. The more you can get them to initiate and say early in the transaction, the more you'll know about where they are coming from, and the better you can tailor your approach. *More help? – See #3 Approachability.*

☐ **4. Listening.** Interpersonally skilled people are very good at listening. They listen to understand and take in information to select their response. They listen without interrupting. They ask clarifying questions. They don't instantly judge. Judgment might come later. They restate what the other person has said to signal understanding. They nod. They might jot down notes. Listeners get more data. *More help? – See #33 Listening.*

☐ **5. Sharing.** Interpersonally skilled people share more information and get more in return. Confide your thinking on a business issue and invite the response of others. Pass on tidbits of information you think will help people do their jobs better or broaden their perspective. Disclose more things about yourself. Reveal things people don't need to know to do their jobs, but which will be interesting to them, and help them feel valued. *More help?– See #44 Personal Disclosure*. Personalize. Work to know and remember important things about the people you work around, for, and with. Know three things about everybody – their interests or their children or something you can chat about other than the business agenda. Establish things you can talk about with each person you work with that go beyond strictly work transactions. These need not be social; they could also be issues of strategy, global events, market shifts. The point is to establish common ground and connections.

☐ **6. Manage your non-verbals.** Interpersonally savvy people understand the critical role of non-verbal communications, of appearing and sounding open and relaxed, smiling and calm. They keep consistent eye contact. They nod while the other person is talking. They speak in a paced and pleasant tone. Work to eliminate any disruptive habits such as speaking too rapidly or forcefully, using strongly worded or loaded language, or going into too much detail. Watch out for signaling disinterest with actions like glancing at your watch, fiddling with paper work or giving your impatient I'm busy look.

☐ **7. Selective interpersonal skills?** Some people are interpersonally comfortable and effective with some and not others. Some might be interpersonally smooth with direct reports and tense around senior management. What do the people you are comfortable around have in common? What about those you're not comfortable with? Is it level? Style? Gender? Race? Background? The principles of interpersonal savvy are the same regardless of the audience. Do what you do with the comfortable group with the uncomfortable groups. The results will generally be the same.

☐ **8. Shy?** Lack self confidence? Generally hold back and let others take the lead? Feelings of being too vulnerable? Afraid of how people will react? Not sure of your social skills? Want to appear – while shaking inside – not shy? Hand first. Consistent eye contact. Ask the first question. For low risk practice, talk to strangers off work. Set a goal of meeting new people at every social gathering; find out what you have in common with them. Initiate contact at your place of worship, at PTA meetings, in the neighborhood, at the supermarket, on the plane and on the bus. See if any of the bad and scary things you think might happen to you if you initiate people contact actually happen. The only way people will know you are shy and nervous is if you tell them through your actions. Watch what non-shy people do that you don't do. Practice those behaviors.

☐ **9. Being savvy with people you don't like.** What do people see in them who do like them or can at least get along with them? What are their strengths? Do you have any common interests with them? Whatever you do, don't signal to them what you think. Put your judgments on hold, nod, ask questions, summarize as you would with anyone else. A fly on the wall should not be able to tell whether you're talking to friend or foe. You can always talk less and ask more questions; and neither apologize nor criticize. Even if they're contentious, you can respond neutrally by restating the problem you're working on.

☐ **10. Tense transactions.** What if you're attacked? What if venom is flowing? What if someone doesn't like you very much? What if everyone is angry and upset? Practice interpersonal Aikido, the ancient art of absorbing the energy of your opponent and using it to manage him/her. Let the other side vent frustration, blow off steam, but don't react directly. Remember that it's the person who hits back who usually gets in the most trouble. Listen. Nod. Ask clarifying questions. Ask open-ended questions like, "Why is this particularly bothersome to you?", "What could I do to help?", "So you think I need to..." Restate his/her position periodically to signal you have understood. But don't react. Don't judge. Keep him/her talking until he/she runs out of venom. When the other side takes a rigid position, don't reject it. Ask why – what's behind the position, what's the theory of the case, what brought this about? Separate the people from the problem. When someone attacks you, rephrase it as an attack on a problem. Keep your cool even though he/she may have lost his/her cool. In response to unreasonable proposals, attacks, or a non-answer to a question, you can always say nothing. People will usually respond by saying more, coming off their position a bit, or at least revealing their true interests. Many times, with unlimited venting and your understanding, the actual conflict shrinks. *More help? – See #12 Conflict Management.*

SECTION 3: LEARNING FROM MORE FEEDBACK

THESE SOURCES WOULD GIVE YOU THE MOST ACCURATE AND DETAILED FEEDBACK ON YOUR SKILL(S)

☐ **Human Resource Professionals**
Human Resource professionals have both a formal and informal feedback role. Since they have access to unique and confidential information, they can provide the right context for feedback you've received. Sometimes they may be "directed" to give you feedback. Other times, they may pass on feedback just to be helpful to you.

☐ **Off-Work Friends/Associates**
Those who know you socially "with your guard down" can be a good source of feedback to compare with that of work peers and family members. If you're different at work than you are socially, why? If you're the same, feedback from friends just confirms the feedback. In a way, off-work friends may know the "real you."

☐ **Past Associates/Constituencies**
When confronted with a present performance problem, some claim, "I wasn't like that before; it must be the current situation." When feedback is available from former associates, about 50% support that claim. In the other half of the cases, the people were like that before and probably didn't know it. It sometimes makes sense to access the past to clearly see the present.

☐ **Peers and Colleagues**
Peers and colleagues have a special social and working relationship. They attend staff meetings together, share private views, get feedback from the same boss, travel together, and are knowledgeable about each other's work. You perhaps let your guard down more around peers and act more like yourself. They can be a valuable source of feedback.

- ☐ **Spouse**
  Spouses can be powerful sources of feedback on such things as interpersonal style, values, balance between work, career, and personal life, etc. Many participants attending development programs share their feedback with their spouses for value-adding confirmation or context and for specific examples.

SECTION 4: LEARNING FROM DEVELOP-IN-PLACE ASSIGNMENTS

THESE PART-TIME DEVELOP-IN-PLACE ASSIGNMENTS WILL HELP YOU BUILD YOUR SKILL(S)

- ☐ Integrate diverse systems, processes, or procedures across decentralized and/or dispersed units.
- ☐ Study humor in business settings; read books on the nature of humor; collect cartoons you could use in presentations; study funny people around you; keep a log of funny jokes and sayings you hear; read famous speeches and study how humor was used; attend comedy clubs; ask a funny person to act as your tutor; practice funny lines and jokes with others.
- ☐ Be a change agent; create a symbol for change; lead the rallying cry; champion a significant change and implementation.
- ☐ Manage an ad hoc, temporary group of people where the temporary manager is a towering expert and the people in the group are not.
- ☐ Manage an ad hoc, temporary group of people where the people in the group are towering experts but the temporary manager is not.
- ☐ Help shut down a plant, regional office, product line, business, operation, etc.
- ☐ Manage a dissatisfied internal or external customer; troubleshoot a performance or quality problem with a product or service.
- ☐ Manage the assigning/allocating of office space in a contested situation.
- ☐ Resolve an issue in conflict between two people, units, geographies, functions, etc.
- ☐ Make peace with an enemy or someone you've disappointed with a product or service or someone you've had some trouble with or don't get along well with.

SECTION 5: LEARNING FROM FULL-TIME JOBS

THESE FULL-TIME JOBS OFFER THE OPPORTUNITY TO BUILD YOUR SKILL(S)

☐ **Cross-Moves**

The core demands necessary to qualify as a Cross-Move are: 1) Move to a very different set of challenges. 2) Abrupt jump-shift in tasks/activities. 3) Never been there before. 4) New setting/conditions. Examples of Cross-Moves are: 1) Changing divisions. 2) Changing functions. 3) Field/headquarters shifts. 4) Line/staff switches. 5) Country switches. 6) Working with all new people. 7) Changing lines of business.

☐ **Influencing Without Authority**

The core demands to qualify as an Influence Without Authority are: 1) Significant challenge (e.g, start-up, fix-it, scope and/or scale assignment, strategic planning project, changes in management practices/ systems). 2) Insufficient direct authority to make it happen. 3) Tight deadlines. 4) Visible to significant others. 5) Sensitive politics.

☐ **Member of Projects/Task Forces**

The core demands for qualifying as a Project/Task Force assignment are: 1) Full-time assignment. 2) Important and specific goal. 3) Tight deadline. 4) Success or failure will be evident. 5) High-visibility sponsor. 6) Learning something on the fly. 7) Must get others to cooperate. 8) Usually six months or more. Four types of Projects/Task Forces: 1) New ideas, products, services, or systems (e.g., product/service/ program research and development, creation/installation/launch of a new system, new programs like Total Quality Management, positive discipline). 2) Formal negotiations and relationships (e.g., acquisitions, divestitures, agreements, joint ventures; licensing arrangements, franchising; dealing with unions, governments, communities, charities, customers, and relocations). 3) Big one-time events (e.g., working on a major presentation for the board, organizing significant meetings or conferences, disaster/damage control teams; reorganizations, mergers, acquisitions, or relocations, working on visions, charters, strategies, other time-urgent issues and problems). 4) Troubleshooting (e.g., problems, disasters, crises, product/service failures, accidents, illegal activities, damage control in public relations goofs, shut downs, downsizings, layoffs, abrupt changes in leadership).

SECTION 6: LEARNING MORE FROM YOUR PLAN

THESE ADDITIONAL REMEDIES WILL HELP MAKE THIS DEVELOPMENT PLAN MORE EFFECTIVE FOR YOU

Learning to Learn Better

☐ **Look Beyond Your First Solution to a Problem**

Don't always take the first action you think of. Look further for a second and third. What's different? Might the second or third be more effective? Research shows that the best solution lies somewhere between the second and third strategies or approaches. Your first solution is often an "autopilot" response and may not be the best.

- ☐ **Use Objective Data When Judging Others**
Practice studying other people more than judging or evaluating them. Get the facts, the data, how they think, why they do things, without classifying them into your internal like/dislike or agree/disagree boxes, categories, or buckets. Try to project or predict how they would act/react in various situations and follow up to see how accurate you are.

- ☐ **Examine Why You Judge People the Way You Do**
List the people you like and those you dislike and try to find out why. What do those you like have in common with each other and with you? What do those you dislike have in common with themselves and how do they differ from you? Are your "people buckets" logical and productive or do they interfere? Could you be more effective without putting people into buckets?

- ☐ **Analyze How You Perform Under Several Roles**
Do an analysis of yourself as a contributor, boss, manager, professional, parent, spouse, and/or friend. Create a list of criteria for each role and evaluate yourself against it. Pick a few things to work on for each role to improve.

Learning from Experience, Feedback and Other People

- ☐ **Using Multiple Models**
Who do you know who exemplifies how to do whatever your need is? Who, for example, personifies decisiveness or compassion or strategic agility? Think more broadly than your current job and colleagues. For example, clergy, friends, spouses or community leaders are also good sources for potential models. Select your models not on the basis of overall excellence or likability, but on the basis of the one towering strength (or glaring weakness) you are interested in. Even people who are well thought of usually have only one or two towering strengths (or glaring weaknesses). Ordinarily, you won't learn as much from the whole person as you will from one characteristic.

- ☐ **Learning from Mentors and Tutors**
Mentors and tutors offer a special case for learning since the relationship is specifically formed for learning. You need to be open and nondefensive. You need to solicit and accept feedback. This is a unique opportunity for you to get low-risk, honest, and direct feedback on what you do well and not so well.

- ☐ **Learning from Ineffective Behavior**
Seeing things done poorly can be a very potent source of learning for you, especially if the behavior or action affects others negatively. Many times the thing done poorly causes emotional reactions or pain in you and others. Distance yourself from the feelings and explore why the actions didn't work.

☐ **Learning from Observing Others**
Observe others. Find opportunities to observe without interacting with your model. This enables you to objectively study the person, note what he/she is doing or not doing, and compare that with what you would typically do in similar situations. Many times you can learn more by watching than asking. Your model may not be able to explain what he/she does or may be an unwilling teacher.

☐ **Learning from Bad Bosses**
First, what does he/she do so well to make him/her your boss? (Even bad bosses have strengths). Then, ask what makes this boss bad for you. Is it his/her behavior? Attitude? Values? Philosophy? Practices? Style? What is the source of the conflict? Why do you react as you do? Do others react the same? How are you part of the problem? What do you do that triggers your boss? If you wanted to, could you reduce the conflict or make it go away by changing something you do? Is there someone around you who doesn't react like you? How are they different? What can you learn from them? What is your emotional reaction to this boss? Why do you react like that? What can you do to cope with these feelings? Can you avoid reacting out of anger and frustration? Can you find something positive about the situation? Can you use someone else as a buffer? Can you learn from your emotions? What lasting lessons of managing others can you take away from this experience? What won't you do as a manager? What will you do differently? How could you teach these principles you've learned to others by the use of this example?

Learning from Courses

☐ **Insight Events**
These are courses designed around assessing skills and providing feedback to the participants. These events can be a powerful source of self-knowledge and can lead to significant development if done right. When selecting a self-insight course, consider the following: 1) Are the skills assessed the important ones? 2) Are the assessment techniques and instruments sound? 3) Are those who are providing the feedback trained and professional? 4) Is the feedback provided in a user-friendly and "actionable" format? 5) Does the feedback include development planning? 6) Is the setting comfortable and conducive to reflection and learning? 7) Are the other participants the kinds of people you could learn from? 8) Are you in the right frame of mind to learn from this kind of intense experience? Select events on the basis of positive answers to these eight questions.

SUGGESTED READINGS

Baker, Wayne E. *Networking Smart.* New York: McGraw-Hill, Inc., 1994.

Bolton, Robert. *People skills: How to assert yourself, listen to others, and resolve conflicts.* New York: Simon & Schuster, 1986.

Foster, D. Glenn and Mary Marshall. *How can I get through to you?: breakthrough communication beyond gender, beyond therapy, beyond deception.* New York: Hyperion, 1994.

Foster, D. Glenn and Mary Marshall. *How can I get through to you?: breakthrough communication beyond gender, beyond therapy, beyond deception [sound recording].* New York: Harper Audio, 1994.

Giovagnoli, Melissa. *Make Your Connections Count.* Chicago: Dearborn Financial Publishing, Inc., 1994.

Hargrove, Robert. *Mastering the Art of Creative Collaboration.* New York: McGraw-Hill, Inc., 1999.

McCallister, Linda Ph.D. *I wish I'd said that!.* New York: John Wiley & Sons, 1992.

Robinson, Margot.. *Egos & eggshells: managing for success in today's workplace.* Greensboro, NC: Stanton & Harper Books, 1993.

Stanley, Thomas J. *Networking with the Affluent.* Homewood, IL: Business One Irwin, 1993.

32

LEARNING ON THE FLY

SECTION 1: YOUR DEVELOPMENT NEED(S)

UNSKILLED

- ☐ Not agile or versatile in learning to deal with first time or unusual problems
- ☐ May not analyze problems carefully or search for multiple clues and parallels
- ☐ May be afraid to take a chance on the unknown
- ☐ Learns new things slowly
- ☐ May be stuck in historical, tried and true methods, uncomfortable with ambiguity and quick to jump to a solution
- ☐ Doesn't look under rocks, just sticks to the obvious
- ☐ Looks for the simplest explanation too soon
- ☐ Gives up too soon and accepts a marginal solution
- ☐ Functions on the surface, doesn't go deep

SKILLED

- ☐ Learns quickly when facing new problems
- ☐ A relentless and versatile learner
- ☐ Open to change
- ☐ Analyzes both successes and failures for clues to improvement
- ☐ Experiments and will try anything to find solutions
- ☐ Enjoys the challenge of unfamiliar tasks
- ☐ Quickly grasps the essence and the underlying structure of anything

OVERUSED SKILL

- ☐ May leave others behind
- ☐ May frustrate others with his/her need for change
- ☐ May tend to change things too often
- ☐ People may interpret openness as indecisiveness or being wishy-washy
- ☐ May seek out change for change's sake regardless of the situation
- ☐ May not be good at routine administration or unchallenging tasks or jobs

Select one to three of the competencies listed below to work on to compensate for an overuse of this skill.

COMPENSATORS: 27, 33, 39, 41, 43, 47, 52, 59

SOME CAUSES

- ☐ Don't analyze successes and failures for clues
- ☐ Historical problem solver
- ☐ Not a risk taker
- ☐ Not self confident

- ☐ Perfectionist
- ☐ Stuck in the past
- ☐ Too narrow in search for parallels

THE MAP

Most of us are good at applying what we have seen and done in the past. Most of us can apply solutions that have worked for us before. We are all pretty good at solving problems we've seen before. A rarer skill is doing things for the first time. Solving problems we've never seen before. Trying solutions we have never tried before. Analyzing problems in new contexts and in new ways. With the increasing pace of change, being quick to learn and apply first time solutions is becoming a crucial skill. It involves taking risks, being less than perfect, discarding the past, going against the grain, and cutting new paths.

SECTION 2: LEARNING ON YOUR OWN

THESE SELF-DEVELOPMENT REMEDIES WILL HELP YOU BUILD YOUR SKILL(S)

SOME REMEDIES

☐ **1. When faced with a new issue,** challenge or problem, figure out what causes it. Keep asking why, see how many causes you can come up with, and how many organizing buckets you can put them in. This increases the chance of a better solution because you can see more connections. Chess masters recognize thousands of possible patterns of chess pieces. Look for patterns in data; don't just collect information. Put it in categories that make sense to you. To better understand new and difficult learning, read *The Future of Leadership* by White, Hodgson and Crainer.

☐ **2. Locate the essence of the problem.** What are the key factors or elements in this problem? Experts usually solve problems by figuring out what the deep underlying principles are and working forward from there; the less adept focus on desired outcomes/solutions and either work backward or concentrate on the surface facts. What are the deep principles of what you're working on? Once you've done this, search the past for parallels – your past, the business past, the historical past. One common mistake here is to search in parallel organizations because "only they would know." Backing up and asking a broader question will aid in the search for solutions. When Motorola wanted to find out how to process orders more quickly, they went not to other electronics firms, but to Domino's Pizza and Federal Express.

☐ **3. Patterns.** Look for patterns in personal, organization, or the world, in general successes and failures. What was common to each success or what was present in each failure but never present in a success? Focus on the successes; failures are easier to analyze but don't in themselves tell you what would work. Comparing successes, while less exciting, yields more information about underlying principles. The bottom line is to reduce your insights to principles or rules of thumb you think might be repeatable. When faced with the next new problem those general underlying principles will apply again.

☐ **4. Don't expect to get it right the first time.** This leads to safe and stale solutions. Many studies show that the second or third try is when we really understand the underlying dynamics of problems. To increase learning, shorten your act and get feedback loops aiming to make them as immediate as possible. The more frequent the cycles, the more opportunities to learn; if we do something in each of three days instead of one thing every three days, we triple our learning opportunities and increase our chances of finding the right answer. Be more willing to experiment.

☐ **5. Use experts.** Find an expert or experts in your functional/technical/business area and go find out how they think and solve new problems. Ask them what are the critical principles/drivers/things they look for. Have them tell you how they thought through a new problem in this area; the major skills they look for in sizing up people's proficiency in this area; key questions they ask about a problem; how they would suggest you go about learning quickly in this area.

☐ **6. People who think in opposite cases** when confronted with a problem tend to do better. Turn the problem upside down. Ask what is the least likely thing it could be, what the problem is not, what's missing from the problem, or what the mirror image of the problem is.

☐ **7. Use others.** Teams of people with the widest diversity of backgrounds produce the most innovative solutions to problems. Get others with different backgrounds to analyze and make sense with you. When working together, come up with as many questions about it as you can. Set up a competition with another group or individual, asking them to work on exactly what you are working on. Set a certain timeframe and have a postmortem to try to deduce some of the practices and procedures that work best. Find a team or individual that faces problems quite similar to what you face and set up dialogues on a number of specific topics.

☐ **8. Use oddball tactics.** What is a direct analogy between something you are working on and a natural occurrence? Ask what in nature parallels your problem. When the terrible surfs and motion of the tide threatened to defeat their massive dam project, the Delta Works, the Dutch used the violence of the North Sea to drive in the pilings, ending the danger of the south of the Netherlands flooding. Practice picking out anomalies – unusual facts that don't quite fit, like sales going down when they should have gone up. What do these odd things imply for strategy?

☐ **9. Encourage yourself to do quick experiments and trials.** Studies show that 80% of innovations occur in the wrong place, are created by the wrong people – dye makers developed detergent; Post-it® Notes was an error in a glue formula – and 30–50% of technical innovations fail in tests within the company. Even among those that make it to the marketplace, 70–90% fail. The bottom line on change is a 95% failure rate, and the most successful innovators try lots of quick, inexpensive experiments to increase the chances of success.

☐ **10. Too often we think first and only of solutions.** In studies of problem-solving sessions, solutions outweigh questions eight to one. Most meetings on a problem start with people offering solutions. Early solutions are not likely to be the best. Set aside 50% of the time for questions and problem definition, and the last 50% for solutions. Asking more questions early helps you rethink the problem and come to more and different solutions.

SECTION 3: LEARNING FROM MORE FEEDBACK

THESE SOURCES WOULD GIVE YOU THE MOST ACCURATE AND DETAILED FEEDBACK ON YOUR SKILL(S)

☐ **Direct Boss**
Your direct boss has important information about you, your performance, and your prospects. The challenge is to get this information. There are formal processes (e.g., performance appraisals). There are day-to-day opportunities. To help, signal your boss that you want and can handle direct and timely feedback. Many bosses have trouble giving feedback, so you will have to work at it over a period of time.

☐ **Human Resource Professionals**
Human Resource professionals have both a formal and informal feedback role. Since they have access to unique and confidential information, they can provide the right context for feedback you've received. Sometimes they may be "directed" to give you feedback. Other times, they may pass on feedback just to be helpful to you.

☐ **Internal and External Customers**
Customers interact with you as a person and as a supplier or vendor of products and services. You're important to them because you can either help address and solve their problems or stand in their way. As customer service and Total Quality programs gain importance, clients and customers become a more prominent source of feedback.

☐ **Natural Mentors**
Natural mentors have a special relationship with you and are interested in your success and your future. Since they are usually not in your direct chain of command, you can have more open, relaxed, and fruitful discussions about yourself and your career prospects. They can be a very important source for candid or critical feedback others may not give you.

- ☐ **Past Associates/Constituencies**
  When confronted with a present performance problem, some claim, "I wasn't like that before; it must be the current situation." When feedback is available from former associates, about 50% support that claim. In the other half of the cases, the people were like that before and probably didn't know it. It sometimes makes sense to access the past to clearly see the present.

SECTION 4: LEARNING FROM DEVELOP-IN-PLACE ASSIGNMENTS

THESE PART-TIME DEVELOP-IN-PLACE ASSIGNMENTS WILL HELP YOU BUILD YOUR SKILL(S)

- ☐ Work short rotations in other units, functions, or geographies you've not been exposed to before.
- ☐ Study and summarize a new trend, product, service, technique, or process and present and sell it to others.
- ☐ Benchmark innovative practices, processes, products, or services of competitors, vendors, suppliers, or customers and present a report to others to create recommendations for change.
- ☐ Work on a project that involves travel and study of an issue, acquisition, or joint venture off-shore or overseas, with a report back to management.
- ☐ Relaunch an existing product or service that's not doing well.
- ☐ Teach a course, seminar, or workshop on something you don't know well.
- ☐ Manage an ad hoc, temporary group of "green," inexperienced people as their coach, teacher, orienter, etc.
- ☐ Volunteer to fill an open management job temporarily until it's filled.
- ☐ Help shut down a plant, regional office, product line, business, operation, etc.
- ☐ Take on a tough and undoable project, one where others who have tried it have failed.

SECTION 5: LEARNING FROM FULL-TIME JOBS

THESE FULL-TIME JOBS OFFER THE OPPORTUNITY TO BUILD YOUR SKILL(S)

- ☐ **Cross-Moves**
  The core demands necessary to qualify as a Cross-Move are: 1) Move to a very different set of challenges. 2) Abrupt jump-shift in tasks/activities. 3) Never been there before. 4) New setting/conditions. Examples of Cross-Moves are: 1) Changing divisions. 2) Changing functions. 3) Field/headquarters shifts. 4) Line/staff switches. 5) Country switches. 6) Working with all new people. 7) Changing lines of business.

☐ **Heavy Strategic Demands**
The core demands necessary to qualify as a Heavy Strategic Content assignment are: 1) Requires significant strategic thinking and planning most couldn't do. 2) Charts new ground strategically. 3) Plan must be presented, challenged, adopted, and implemented. 4) Exposure to significant decision makers and executives. 1) Strategic planning position. 2) Job involving repositioning of a product, service, or organization.

☐ **Member of Projects/Task Forces**
The core demands for qualifying as a Project/Task Force assignment are: 1) Full-time assignment. 2) Important and specific goal. 3) Tight deadline. 4) Success or failure will be evident. 5) High-visibility sponsor. 6) Learning something on the fly. 7) Must get others to cooperate. 8) Usually six months or more. Four types of Projects/Task Forces: 1) New ideas, products, services, or systems (e.g., product/service/program research and development, creation/installation/launch of a new system, new programs like Total Quality Management, positive discipline). 2) Formal negotiations and relationships (e.g., acquisitions, divestitures, agreements, joint ventures; licensing arrangements, franchising; dealing with unions, governments, communities, charities, customers, and relocations). 3) Big one-time events (e.g., working on a major presentation for the board, organizing significant meetings or conferences, disaster/damage control teams; reorganizations, mergers, acquisitions, or relocations, working on visions, charters, strategies, other time-urgent issues and problems). 4) Troubleshooting (e.g., problems, disasters, crises, product/service failures, accidents, illegal activities, damage control in public relations goofs, shut downs, downsizings, layoffs, abrupt changes in leadership).

☐ **Off-Shore Assignments**
The core demands to qualify as an Off-Shore assignment are: 1) First time working in the country. 2) Significant challenges like new language, hardship location, unique business rules/practices, significant cultural/marketplace differences, different functional task, etc. 3) More than a year assignment. 4) No automatic return deal. 5) Not necessarily a change in job challenge, technical content, or responsibilities.

SECTION 6: LEARNING MORE FROM YOUR PLAN

THESE ADDITIONAL REMEDIES WILL HELP MAKE THIS DEVELOPMENT PLAN MORE EFFECTIVE FOR YOU

Learning to Learn Better

☐ **Keep a Learning Journal**
Keep a learning log or diary about the issues and opportunities you've faced and how you've acted. Focus on how you've used your strengths and weaknesses. Deduce your effective and successful rules of

thumb – what worked and what didn't, and how you would have done it differently.

☐ **Learn New and Frivolous Skills to Study How You Learn**
Practice learning frivolous and fun skills (like juggling, square dancing, skeet shooting, video games, etc.) to see yourself under different and less personal or stressful learning conditions. Ask yourself why that was easy while developing new personal/managerial skills is so hard. Try something harder with the same tactics.

☐ **Try Some New Things Out of Your Normal Comfort Zone**
Periodically, practice going against your grain (what's normal for you) and getting out of your comfort zone. Try something different and opposite to your nature; take a learning risk. Explore: if you're a thinker, act; if you're an action person, think. Test the unfamiliar; try the new; go beyond your self-determined limits and boundaries.

☐ **Throw Yourself With More Vigor Than Usual Into Something New**
Throw yourself into a new area, something you've not done before so you will have to learn quickly, such as a new technical area, a new management practice, or a self-development project. Pick something that is out of your skill and strength set.

☐ **Preview a Plan With a Test Audience**
Before committing to a plan, find someone agreeable to a wide-ranging discussion about the issue or problem you face. Explore all sides and options; go with the flow; let what you need to do emerge from the process; develop a plan as you go.

Learning from Experience, Feedback and Other People

☐ **Learning from Bosses**
Bosses can be an excellent and ready source for learning. All bosses do some things exceptionally well and other things poorly. Distance your feelings from the boss/direct report relationship and study things that work and things that don't work for your boss. What would you have done? What could you use, and what should you avoid?

☐ **Getting Feedback from Bosses and Superiors**
Many bosses are reluctant to give negative feedback. They lack the managerial courage to face people directly with criticism. You can help by soliciting feedback and setting the tone. Show them you can handle criticism and that you are willing to work on issues they see as important.

☐ **Openness to Feedback**
Nothing discourages feedback more than defensiveness, resistance, irritation, and excuses. People don't like giving feedback anyway, and much less to those who don't listen or are unreceptive. To help the feedback giver, be open, listen, ask for examples and details, take notes, keep a journal, and thank them for their interest.

☐ **Learning from Mistakes**

Since we're human, we all make mistakes. The key is to focus on why you made the mistake. Spend more time locating causes and less worrying about the effects. Check how you react to mistakes. How much time do you spend being angry with yourself? Do you waste time stewing or do you move on? More importantly, do you learn? Ask why you made the mistake. Are you likely to repeat it under similar situations? Was it a lack of skill? Judgment? Style? Not enough data? Reading people? Misreading the challenge? Misreading the politics? Or was it just random? A good strategy that just didn't work? Others that let you down? The key is to avoid two common reactions to your mistakes: 1) avoiding similar situations instead of learning and trying again, and 2) trying to repeat what you did, only more diligently and harder, hoping to break through the problem, making the same mistake again but with greater impact. Neither trap leaves us with better strategies for the future. Neither is a learning strategy. To learn and do something differently, focus on the patterns in your behavior that get you in trouble and go back to first causes, those that tell you something about your shortcomings. Facing ourselves squarely is always the best way to learn.

Learning from Courses

☐ **Insight Events**

These are courses designed around assessing skills and providing feedback to the participants. These events can be a powerful source of self-knowledge and can lead to significant development if done right. When selecting a self-insight course, consider the following: 1) Are the skills assessed the important ones? 2) Are the assessment techniques and instruments sound? 3) Are those who are providing the feedback trained and professional? 4) Is the feedback provided in a user-friendly and "actionable" format? 5) Does the feedback include development planning? 6) Is the setting comfortable and conducive to reflection and learning? 7) Are the other participants the kinds of people you could learn from? 8) Are you in the right frame of mind to learn from this kind of intense experience? Select events on the basis of positive answers to these eight questions.

SUGGESTED READINGS

Barner, Robert W. *Crossing the Minefield – Tactics for Overcoming Today's Toughest Management Challenges.* New York: AMACOM, 1994.

Fradette, Michael and Steve Michaud. *The Power of Corporate Kinetics.* New York: Simon & Schuster, 1998.

McCall, Morgan W., Michael M. Lombardo and Ann M. Morrison. *The Lessons of Experience.* Lexington, MA: Lexington Books, 1988.

Stone, Florence M. and Randi T. Sachs. *The High-Value Manager – Developing the core competencies your organization needs.* New York: AMACOM, 1995.

White, Randall P., Philip Hodgson, and Stuart Crainer. *The future of leadership: Riding the corporate rapids into the 21st century.* Washington, DC: Pitman Publishing, 1996.

Wick, Calhoun W. and Lu Stanton León. *The learning edge: How smart managers and smart companies stay ahead.* New York: McGraw-Hill, 1993.

33

LISTENING

SECTION 1: YOUR DEVELOPMENT NEED(S)

UNSKILLED

- ☐ Doesn't listen well
- ☐ Cuts people off and finishes their sentences if they hesitate
- ☐ Interrupts to make a pronouncement or render a solution or decision
- ☐ Doesn't learn much from interactions with others
- ☐ Appears not to listen or be too busy constructing his/her own response
- ☐ Many times misses the point others are trying to make
- ☐ May appear arrogant, impatient or uninterested
- ☐ May listen to some groups/people and not to others
- ☐ Inaccurate in restating the case of others

SKILLED

- ☐ Practices attentive and active listening
- ☐ Has the patience to hear people out
- ☐ Can accurately restate the opinions of others even when he/she disagrees

OVERUSED SKILL

- ☐ May spend too much time listening
- ☐ May avoid necessary action
- ☐ Others may confuse listening with agreement

Select one to three of the competencies listed below to work on to compensate for an overuse of this skill.

COMPENSATORS: 1, 9, 12, 13, 16, 17, 27, 34, 37, 38, 50, 57

SOME CAUSES

- ☐ Arrogant
- ☐ Defensive
- ☐ Don't care
- ☐ Don't value others
- ☐ Impatient
- ☐ Insensitive
- ☐ Selective listening
- ☐ Too busy

THE MAP

Listening means knowing what others have said and meant to say and leaving people comfortable that they have had their say. Most people know the techniques of good listening: don't interrupt, be able to paraphrase, listen for underlying meaning, be accepting of other views.

The problem is we all listen well only when we want to or have to. What most need to learn is how to listen when you don't want to. Remember, listening doesn't mean you accept what they have said or even that you have accepted them. It just means listening.

SECTION 2: LEARNING ON YOUR OWN

THESE SELF-DEVELOPMENT REMEDIES WILL HELP YOU BUILD YOUR SKILL(S)

SOME REMEDIES

- ☐ **1. There are three kinds of listening problems:**
  - The first is you don't know how to listen. That's the least likely problem.
  - The second is that you know how to listen but you just don't do it with anyone. That's a little more likely.
  - The third is that you listen intently to some, neutrally to others and not at all to yet others. That's the most likely problem. To test this out, do you listen to anyone? Boss? Chairperson? Mother? Children? Priest/minister/rabbi/clergy? Police officer? Best friend? Mentor? Spouse? Professional colleague outside of work? Has anyone ever complimented you or thanked you for listening? If the answer to any of those questions is yes, you have a selective listening problem. You know how to listen, you just turn it off and on.

- ☐ **2. How do people know you are listening?** First, remember the basics. You have your mouth closed. When your mouth is open, your ears automatically close. You have eye contact. You take notes. You don't frown or fidget. How do people know you've understood? You paraphrase what they have said to their satisfaction. How do people know if you have accepted or rejected what you have understood they have said? You tell them. Hopefully in a tactful way if you reject what they have had to say. Give your reasons.
- ☐ **3. Listening chillers?** Don't interrupt before they have finished. Don't suggest words when they hesitate or pause. Don't finish their sentences for them. Don't wave off any further input by saying, "Yes I know that," "Yes, I know where you're going," "Yes, I have heard that before." If time is really important, you can say, "Let me see if I know where this is going..." or "I wonder if we could summarize to save both of us some time?" Finally, early in a transaction answers, solutions, conclusions, statements, and dictates shut many people down. You've told them your mind's already made up. Listen first, solve second.
- ☐ **4. Questions.** Good listeners ask lots of questions to get to a good understanding. Probing questions. Clarifying questions. Confirming – is this what you are saying – questions. Ask one more question than you do now and add to that until people signal you that they think you are truly listening.

☐ **5. Selective listening.** Who do you listen to? Who don't you listen to? What factors account for the difference? Level? Age? Skills? Smarts? Like you/not like you? Gender? Direction (listen up but not down)? Setting? Situation? Your needs? Time available? Race? People I need/don't need? People who have something to offer/those who don't? Challenge yourself to practice listening to those you don't usually listen to. Listen for content. Separate the content from the person. Try to ferret out some value from everyone.

☐ **6. Listening to those who waste a lot of time.** With those you don't have time to listen to, switch to being a teacher. Try to help them craft their communications to you in a more acceptable way. Interrupt to summarize. Tell them to be shorter next time. Come with more/less data. Structure the conversation by helping them come up with categories and structures to stop their rambling. Good listeners don't signal to the "bad" people that they are not listening or are not interested. Don't signal to anyone what bucket they're in. Put your mind in neutral, nod, ask questions, be helpful.

☐ **7. Listening under duress.** What if you're being criticized or attacked personally? What if people are wrong in what they are saying? The rules remain the same. You need to work on keeping yourself in a calm state when getting negative feedback. You need to shift your thinking. When getting the feedback, your only task is to accurately understand what the person is trying to tell you. It is not, at that point, to accept or refute. That comes later. Practice verbal Aikido, the ancient art of absorbing the energy of your opponent, and using it to manage him/her. Let the other side vent but don't react directly. Listen. Nod. Ask clarifying questions. But don't hit back. Don't judge. Keep him/her talking until he/she runs out of venom. Separate the person from the feedback. *More help? – See Tip #4 in #108 Defensiveness* for help on responding to negative attacks that aren't true. *More help? – See #12 Conflict Management.*

☐ **8. Work on your listening non-verbals.** Most people who are not in fact listening, have one or more non-verbals that signal that to others. It could be the washboard brow, blank stare, body agitation, finger or pencil drumming, interrupting, your impatient, I'm busy look. Most around you know your signs. Do you? Ask someone you trust what it is you do when they think you are not listening. Work on eliminating those chilling non-verbals.

☐ **9. Listening to people you don't like.** What do people see in them who do like them or can at least get along with them? What are their strengths? Do you have any common interests? Talk less and ask more questions to give them a second chance. Don't judge their motives and intentions – do that later.

☐ **10. Listening to people you like but...**

- They are disorganized. Interrupt to summarize and keep the discussion focused. While interrupting is generally not a good tactic, it's necessary here.
- They just want to chat. Ask questions to focus them; don't respond to chatty remarks.
- They want to unload a problem. Assume when people tell you something they are looking for understanding; indicate that by being able to summarize what they said. Don't offer any advice.
- They are chronic complainers. Ask them to write down problems and solutions and then let's discuss it. This turns down the volume while hopefully moving them off complaining.
- They like to complain about others. Ask if they've talked to the person. Encourage them to do so. If that doesn't work, summarize what they have said without agreeing or disagreeing.

SECTION 3: LEARNING FROM MORE FEEDBACK

THESE SOURCES WOULD GIVE YOU THE MOST ACCURATE AND DETAILED FEEDBACK ON YOUR SKILL(S)

☐ **Development Professionals**
Sometimes it might be valuable to get some analysis and feedback from a professional trained and certified in the area you're working on: possibly a career counselor, a therapist, clergy, a psychologist, etc.

☐ **Direct Reports**
Across a variety of settings, your direct reports probably see you the most. They are the recipients of most of your managerial behaviors. They know your work. They can compare you with former bosses. Since they may hesitate to give you negative feedback, you have to set the atmosphere to make it easier for them. You have to ask.

☐ **Human Resource Professionals**
Human Resource professionals have both a formal and informal feedback role. Since they have access to unique and confidential information, they can provide the right context for feedback you've received. Sometimes they may be "directed" to give you feedback. Other times, they may pass on feedback just to be helpful to you.

☐ **Peers and Colleagues**
Peers and colleagues have a special social and working relationship. They attend staff meetings together, share private views, get feedback from the same boss, travel together, and are knowledgeable about each other's work. You perhaps let your guard down more around peers and act more like yourself. They can be a valuable source of feedback.

SECTION 4: LEARNING FROM DEVELOP-IN-PLACE ASSIGNMENTS

THESE PART-TIME DEVELOP-IN-PLACE ASSIGNMENTS WILL HELP YOU BUILD YOUR SKILL(S)

- ☐ Attend a self-awareness/assessment course that includes feedback.
- ☐ Find and spend time with an expert to learn something new to you.
- ☐ Go to a campus as a recruiter.
- ☐ Study and establish internal or external customer needs, requirements, specifications, and expectations and present it to the people involved.
- ☐ Go on a business trip to a foreign country you've not been to before.
- ☐ Interview outsiders on their view of your organization and present your findings to management.
- ☐ Represent the concerns of a group of nonexempt, clerical, or administrative employees to higher management to seek resolution of a difficult issue.
- ☐ Become someone's assigned mentor, coach, sponsor, champion, or orienter.
- ☐ Manage an ad hoc, temporary group of people where the people in the group are towering experts but the temporary manager is not.
- ☐ Make peace with an enemy or someone you've disappointed with a product or service or someone you've had some trouble with or don't get along well with.

SECTION 5: LEARNING FROM FULL-TIME JOBS

THESE FULL-TIME JOBS OFFER THE OPPORTUNITY TO BUILD YOUR SKILL(S)

- ☐ **Fix-its/Turnarounds**

  The core demands to qualify as a Fix-it or Turnaround assignment are: 1) Cleaning up a mess. 2) Serious people issues/problems like credibility/performance/morale. 3) Tight deadline. 4) Serious business performance failure. 5) Last chance to fix. Four Types of Fix-its/Turnarounds: 1) Fixing a failed business/unit involving taking control, stopping losses, managing damage, planning the turnaround, dealing with people problems, installing new processes and systems, and rebuilding the spirit and performance of the unit. 2) Managing sizable disasters like mishandled labor negotiations and strikes, thefts, history of significant business losses, poor staff, failed leadership, hidden problems, fraud, public relations nightmares, etc. 3) Significant reorganization and restructuring (e.g., stabilizing the business, reforming unit, introducing new systems, making people changes, resetting strategy and tactics). 4) Significant system/process breakdown (e.g., MIS, financial coordination processes, audits, standards, etc.) across units requiring working to change something from a distant position, providing advice and counsel, and installing or implementing a major process improvement or system change outside your own unit and/or with customers outside the organization.

- ☐ **Influencing Without Authority**
The core demands to qualify as an Influence Without Authority are: 1) Significant challenge (e.g, start-up, fix-it, scope and/or scale assignment, strategic planning project, changes in management practices/ systems). 2) Insufficient direct authority to make it happen. 3) Tight deadlines. 4) Visible to significant others. 5) Sensitive politics.

- ☐ **Significant People Demands**
Core demands required to qualify as a Significant People Responsibilities assignment are: 1) A sizable increase in either the number of people managed and/or the complexity of the challenges involved 2) Longer-term assignment (two or more years). 3) Quality of people management critical to achieving results. 4) Involves groups not worked with before (e.g., union, new technical areas, nationalities).

SECTION 6: LEARNING MORE FROM YOUR PLAN

THESE ADDITIONAL REMEDIES WILL HELP MAKE THIS DEVELOPMENT PLAN MORE EFFECTIVE FOR YOU

Learning to Learn Better

- ☐ **Consult With Expert in the Area of Concern for You**
Consult with an outside expert in the area you're dealing with, someone especially skilled and known; describe your situation the best you can and openly and receptively listen to the advice and counsel the expert provides. Try the advice before you reject it.

- ☐ **Interview a Model of What You Need to Learn**
Find someone you consider a model in the area you're trying to work on and observe them performing successfully. Interview them for keys, rules of thumb, and insights. Ask how they became good at it. Test their thinking: how do they assess situations to determine when and how to use the skills in this area?

- ☐ **Form a Learning Network With Others Working on the Same Problem**
Look for people in similar situations, and create a process for sharing and learning together. Look for a variety of people inside and outside your organization. Give feedback to each other; try new and different things together; share successes and failures, lessons and learning.

- ☐ **Debrief Someone Else After a Successful or Non-Successful Event**
Shortly after someone does something particularly well or badly, debrief them on the process they followed. Ask them about the decisions they made and why; find out what they would have done differently. See if you can glean some insights or rules of thumb from the experiences of others.

Learning from Experience, Feedback and Other People

- ☐ **Being a Student of Others**
  While many of us rely on others for information or advice, we do not really study the behavior of other people. Ask what a person does exceptionally well or poorly. What behaviors are particularly effective and ineffective for them? What works for them and what doesn't? As a student of others, you can deduce the rules of thumb for effective and ineffective behavior and include those in your own library. In comparing yourself with this person, in what areas could you most improve? What could you specifically do to improve in ways comfortable for you?

- ☐ **Learning from Ineffective Behavior**
  Seeing things done poorly can be a very potent source of learning for you, especially if the behavior or action affects others negatively. Many times the thing done poorly causes emotional reactions or pain in you and others. Distance yourself from the feelings and explore why the actions didn't work.

- ☐ **Learning from Remote Models**
  Many times you can learn from people not directly available to you. You can read a book about them, watch tapes of public figures, read analyses of them, etc. The principles of learning are the same. Ask yourself what they do well or poorly and deduce their rules of thumb.

- ☐ **Getting Feedback from Direct Reports**
  Direct reports often fear reprisals for giving negative feedback about bosses, whether in a formal process, like a questionnaire, or informally and face-to-face. Even with a guarantee of confidentiality, some are still hesitant. If you want feedback from direct reports, you have to set a positive tone and never act out of revenge.

- ☐ **Learning from Limited Staff**
  Most managers either inherit or hire staff from time to time who are inexperienced, incompetent, not up to the task, resistant, or dispirited. Any of these may create a hardship for you. The lessons to be learned are how to get things done with limited resources and how to fix the people situation. In the short term, this hardship is best addressed by assessing the combined strengths of the team and deploying the best you have against the problem. Almost everyone can do something well. Also, the team can contribute more than the combined individuals can. How can you empower and motivate the team? If you hired the troublesome staff, why did you err? What can you learn from your hiring mistakes? What wasn't there that you thought was present? What led you astray? How can you prevent that same hiring error in the future? What do you need to do to fix the situation? Quick development? Start over? If you inherited the problem, how can you fix it? Can you implement a program of accelerated development? Do you have to start over and get new people? What did the prior manager do or not do

that led to this situation in the first place? What can you learn from that? What will you do differently? How does the staff feel? What can you learn from their frustrations over not being able to do the job? How can you be a positive force under negative circumstances? How can you rally them to perform? What lasting lessons can you learn from someone in distress and trouble? If you're going to try accelerated development, how can you get a quick assessment? How can you give the staff motivating feedback? How can you construct and implement development plans that will work? How can you get people on-line feedback for maximum growth? Do you know when to stop trying and start over? If you're going to turn over some staff, how can you do it both rapidly and with the least damage? How can you deliver the message in a constructive way? What can you learn from having to take negative actions against people? How can you prevent this from happening again?

Learning from Courses

- [ ] **Insight Events**

These are courses designed around assessing skills and providing feedback to the participants. These events can be a powerful source of self-knowledge and can lead to significant development if done right. When selecting a self-insight course, consider the following: 1) Are the skills assessed the important ones? 2) Are the assessment techniques and instruments sound? 3) Are those who are providing the feedback trained and professional? 4) Is the feedback provided in a user-friendly and "actionable" format? 5) Does the feedback include development planning? 6) Is the setting comfortable and conducive to reflection and learning? 7) Are the other participants the kinds of people you could learn from? 8) Are you in the right frame of mind to learn from this kind of intense experience? Select events on the basis of positive answers to these eight questions.

SUGGESTED READINGS

Bechler, Curt Ph.D. and Richard L. Weaver II, Ph.D. *Listen to Win – A manager's guide to effective listening.* New York: MasterMedia Limited, 1994.

Burley-Allen, Madelyn. *Listening: The forgotten skill.* New York: John Wiley and Sons, 1995.

Nichols, Michael P. *The Lost Art of Listening.* New York: The Guilford Press, 1995.

Robertson, Arthur. *Language of Effective Listening.* Carmel, IN: ScottForesman Professional Books, 1991.

34

MANAGERIAL COURAGE

SECTION 1: YOUR DEVELOPMENT NEED(S)

UNSKILLED

- ☐ Doesn't take tough stands with others
- ☐ Holds back in tough feedback situations
- ☐ Doesn't know how to present a tough position
- ☐ Knows but doesn't disclose
- ☐ Doesn't step up to issues
- ☐ Intimidated by others in power
- ☐ Hangs back and lets others take the lead
- ☐ Is a conflict avoider unwilling to take the heat of controversy
- ☐ Afraid to be wrong, get in a win/lose situation, or make a tough personnel call

SKILLED

- ☐ Doesn't hold back anything that needs to be said
- ☐ Provides current, direct, complete, and "actionable" positive and corrective feedback to others
- ☐ Lets people know where they stand
- ☐ Faces up to people problems on any person or situation (not including direct reports) quickly and directly
- ☐ Is not afraid to take negative action when necessary

OVERUSED SKILL

- ☐ May be overly critical
- ☐ May be too direct and heavy-handed when providing feedback or addressing issues
- ☐ May provide too much negative and too little positive feedback
- ☐ May put too much emphasis on the dark side
- ☐ May fight too many battles

Select one to three of the competencies listed below to work on to compensate for an overuse of this skill.

COMPENSATORS: 3, 7, 10, 11, 12, 19, 23, 26, 31, 33, 36, 41, 56, 60, 64

SOME CAUSES

- ☐ Avoid conflict
- ☐ Can't take the heat
- ☐ Fear of being wrong
- ☐ Fear of losing
- ☐ Get emotional
- ☐ Like to keep nose in own business

THE MAP

Saying what needs to be said at the right time, to the right person, in the right manner, is managerial courage. Everybody sees things, observes things, knows things or learns things that others need to hear. Many times it's not positive. Something went wrong. Something is being covered up or over. Something is not being done right. Someone isn't performing well. Someone is holding something back. Someone is going off on the wrong track. Some people speak up and maybe take some heat. They have managerial courage. Some people keep it to themselves. They do not.

SECTION 2: LEARNING ON YOUR OWN

THESE SELF-DEVELOPMENT REMEDIES WILL HELP YOU BUILD YOUR SKILL(S)

SOME REMEDIES

☐ **1. Check it out.** It's best to be right when presenting negative information about someone else or someone else's unit or process or mistake. Be careful with hearsay and gossip. Better that you've had direct contact with the data. If it doesn't put anyone else in jeopardy, check it out with other sources. Think of all the things it could be other than your interpretation. Check out those possibilities. Work on your message through mental interrogation until you can clearly state in a few sentences what your stand is and why you hold it. When you end up feeling or better yet knowing you're right, go with it.

☐ **2. Delivering the information.** The basic rule is to deliver it to the person who can do the most with it. Limit your passing of the information to one or as few people as possible. Consider telling the actual person involved and give him/her the opportunity to fix it without any further exposure to risk. If that's not possible, move up the chain of command. Don't pass indirect messages via messengers.

☐ **3. The message.** Be succinct. You have limited attention span in tough feedback situations. Don't waste time with a long preamble, particularly if the feedback is negative. If your feedback is negative and the recipient is likely to know it, go ahead and say it directly. They won't hear anything positive you have to say anyway. Don't overwhelm the person/group, even if you have a lot to say. Go from specific to general points. Keep it to the facts. Don't embellish to make your point. No passion or inflammatory language. Don't do it to harm or out of vengeance. Don't do it in anger. If feelings are involved for you, wait until you can describe them, not show them. Managerial courage comes in search of a better outcome, not destroying others. Stay calm and cool. If others are not composed, don't respond. Just return to the message. *More help? – See #31 Interpersonal Savvy.*

☐ **4. Bring a solution if you can.** Nobody likes a critic. Everybody appreciates a problem solver. Give people ways to improve; don't just dump and leave. Tell others what you think would be better – paint a different outcome. Help others see the consequences – you can ask them what they think and you can tell them what the consequences are from your side if you are personally involved ("I'd be reluctant to work with you on X again.").

☐ **5. Tough concern.** Don't forget the pathos of the situation – even if you're totally right, feelings may run high. If you have to knock someone down, you can still empathize with how he/she feels or you can help pick him/her up later when the discussion turns more positive. Mentally rehearse for worst case scenarios. Anticipate what the person might say and have responses prepared so as not to be caught off guard. *More help? – See #12 Conflict Management.*

☐ **6. Timing.** Organizations are a complex maze of constituencies, issues and rivalries peopled by strong egos, sensitives and empire protectors. Worse yet, they are populated by people – which complicates organizations even further. Political savvy involves delivering negative messages in the maze, with the minimum of noise with the maximum effect. Tread boldly but carefully. Deliver messages in private. Cue the person what you are coming to talk about. "I have a concern over the way X is being treated and I would like to talk to you about it." Consider but don't be deterred by political considerations. Pick the right timing. A relaxed setting. With time to spare, don't try to fit it in the elevator. If possible let the person pick the timing and the setting. *More help? – See #38 Organizational Agility and #48 Political Savvy.*

☐ **7. Laid back?** None of your business? Tend to shy away from managerial courage situations? Why? What's getting in your way? Are you prone to give up in tough situations, fear exposing yourself, don't like conflict, what? Ask yourself – what's the downside of delivering a message you think is right and will eventually help the organization but may cause someone short-term pain. What if it turns out you were wrong? Treat any misinterpretations as chances to learn. What if you were the target person or group? Even though it might hurt, would you appreciate it if someone brought the data to your attention in time for you to fix it with minimal damage? What would you think of a person you later found out knew about it and didn't come forward, and you had to spend inordinate amounts of time and political currency to fix it? Follow your convictions. Follow due process. Step up to the plate and be responsible, win or lose. People will think better of you in the long term. *More help? – See #12 Conflict Management and #57 Standing Alone.*

☐ **8. Is it personal?** If you are personally involved and you are delivering a message to someone who didn't meet your expectations, stick to the facts and the consequences for you. Separate the event from the person. It's OK to be upset with the behavior, less so with the person, unless it's a repetitive transgression. Most of the time he/she won't accept it the first time you deliver the message. "I'm not happy with the way you presented my position in the staff meeting." Many people are defensive. Don't go for the close in every delivery situation. Just deliver the message enough so you are sure he/she understood it. Give him/her time to absorb it. Don't seek instant acceptance. Don't seek a kiss of your ring. Just deliver the message clearly and firmly. Don't threaten. *More help? – See #11 Composure.*

☐ **9. If you must.** Sometimes the seriousness of the situation calls for more drastic action. Keeping in mind you are doing this for the collective benefit of the organization and that personal gain or vengeance is not at stake, be prepared to go all the way, even if it pits you against a colleague or even a boss. If your initial message is rejected, covered, denied, hidden or glossed over and you are still convinced of its accuracy, go up the chain until it's dealt with or someone in power two levels or more above the event or person asks you to stop. If you have a mentor, seek his or her counsel along the way. A caution: in a study of whistleblowers, 100% of the failures spoke in general terms, tying their message to lofty values such as integrity. All the successes dealt with the specific issue as it was – problem and consequences. They didn't generalize at all.

☐ **10. Put balance in your messages.** Don't get the reputation of being the executioner or the official organization critic. Try to deliver as much positive information as negative over time. Keep track of the losers – if you have to work with these people again, do something later to show goodwill. Compliment them on a success, share something, help them achieve something. You have to balance the scales. Pick your battles. If you get the reputation of a Cassandra or a Don Quixote, anything you say will be discounted and you'll meet increasing resistance, even when you're clearly right.

SECTION 3: LEARNING FROM MORE FEEDBACK

THESE SOURCES WOULD GIVE YOU THE MOST ACCURATE AND DETAILED FEEDBACK ON YOUR SKILL(S)

☐ **Development Professionals**
Sometimes it might be valuable to get some analysis and feedback from a professional trained and certified in the area you're working on: possibly a career counselor, a therapist, clergy, a psychologist, etc.

☐ **Direct Reports**
Across a variety of settings, your direct reports probably see you the most. They are the recipients of most of your managerial behaviors. They know your work. They can compare you with former bosses. Since they may hesitate to give you negative feedback, you have to set the atmosphere to make it easier for them. You have to ask.

- ☐ **Past Associates/Constituencies**
  When confronted with a present performance problem, some claim, "I wasn't like that before; it must be the current situation." When feedback is available from former associates, about 50% support that claim. In the other half of the cases, the people were like that before and probably didn't know it. It sometimes makes sense to access the past to clearly see the present.

SECTION 4: LEARNING FROM DEVELOP-IN-PLACE ASSIGNMENTS

THESE PART-TIME DEVELOP-IN-PLACE ASSIGNMENTS WILL HELP YOU BUILD YOUR SKILL(S)

- ☐ Manage an ad hoc, temporary group of balky and resisting people through an unpopular change or project.
- ☐ Manage an ad hoc, temporary group of people involved in tackling a fix-it or turnaround project.
- ☐ Work on a team looking at a reorganization plan where there will be more people than positions.
- ☐ Do a problem-prevention analysis on a product or service and present it to the people involved.
- ☐ Coach a children's sports team.
- ☐ Relaunch an existing product or service that's not doing well.
- ☐ Serve on a product/service/project review committee.
- ☐ Manage a dissatisfied internal or external customer; troubleshoot a performance or quality problem with a product or service.
- ☐ Manage the assigning/allocating of office space in a contested situation.
- ☐ Audit cost overruns to assess the problem and present your findings to the person or people involved.

SECTION 5: LEARNING FROM FULL-TIME JOBS

THESE FULL-TIME JOBS OFFER THE OPPORTUNITY TO BUILD YOUR SKILL(S)

- ☐ **Fix-its/Turnarounds**
  The core demands to qualify as a Fix-it or Turnaround assignment are: 1) Cleaning up a mess. 2) Serious people issues/problems like credibility/performance/morale. 3) Tight deadline. 4) Serious business performance failure. 5) Last chance to fix. Four Types of Fix-its/Turnarounds: 1) Fixing a failed business/unit involving taking control, stopping losses, managing damage, planning the turnaround, dealing with people problems, installing new processes and systems, and rebuilding the spirit and performance of the unit. 2) Managing sizable disasters like mishandled labor negotiations and strikes, thefts, history

of significant business losses, poor staff, failed leadership, hidden problems, fraud, public relations nightmares, etc. 3) Significant reorganization and restructuring (e.g., stabilizing the business, reforming unit, introducing new systems, making people changes, resetting strategy and tactics). 4) Significant system/process breakdown (e.g., MIS, financial coordination processes, audits, standards, etc.) across units requiring working to change something from a distant position, providing advice and counsel, and installing or implementing a major process improvement or system change outside your own unit and/or with customers outside the organization.

☐ **Significant People Demands**
Core demands required to qualify as a Significant People Responsibilities assignment are: 1) A sizable increase in either the number of people managed and/or the complexity of the challenges involved 2) Longer-term assignment (two or more years). 3) Quality of people management critical to achieving results. 4) Involves groups not worked with before (e.g., union, new technical areas, nationalities).

SECTION 6: LEARNING MORE FROM YOUR PLAN

THESE ADDITIONAL REMEDIES WILL HELP MAKE THIS DEVELOPMENT PLAN MORE EFFECTIVE FOR YOU

Learning from Experience, Feedback and Other People

☐ **Learning from Bosses**
Bosses can be an excellent and ready source for learning. All bosses do some things exceptionally well and other things poorly. Distance your feelings from the boss/direct report relationship and study things that work and things that don't work for your boss. What would you have done? What could you use, and what should you avoid?

☐ **Getting Feedback from Bosses and Superiors**
Many bosses are reluctant to give negative feedback. They lack the managerial courage to face people directly with criticism. You can help by soliciting feedback and setting the tone. Show them you can handle criticism and that you are willing to work on issues they see as important.

☐ **Getting Feedback from Direct Reports**
Direct reports often fear reprisals for giving negative feedback about bosses, whether in a formal process, like a questionnaire, or informally and face-to-face. Even with a guarantee of confidentiality, some are still hesitant. If you want feedback from direct reports, you have to set a positive tone and never act out of revenge.

☐ **Feedback in Unusual Contexts/Situations**
Temporary and extreme conditions and contexts may shade interpretations of your behavior and intentions. Demands of the job may drive

you outside your normal mode of operating. Hence, feedback you receive may be inaccurate during those times. However, unusual contexts affect our behavior less than most assume. It's usually a weak excuse.

☐ **Giving Feedback to Others**
Most managers complain they don't get enough useful feedback. Ironically, their direct reports and peers offer the same complaint! Getting serious about feedback for yourself involves giving more feedback to those around you. As you practice giving more feedback to others, you will receive more by the example you set and will become more sensitive and receptive to your own.

☐ **Learning from Limited Staff**
Most managers either inherit or hire staff from time to time who are inexperienced, incompetent, not up to the task, resistant, or dispirited. Any of these may create a hardship for you. The lessons to be learned are how to get things done with limited resources and how to fix the people situation. In the short term, this hardship is best addressed by assessing the combined strengths of the team and deploying the best you have against the problem. Almost everyone can do something well. Also, the team can contribute more than the combined individuals can. How can you empower and motivate the team? If you hired the troublesome staff, why did you err? What can you learn from your hiring mistakes? What wasn't there that you thought was present? What led you astray? How can you prevent that same hiring error in the future? What do you need to do to fix the situation? Quick development? Start over? If you inherited the problem, how can you fix it? Can you implement a program of accelerated development? Do you have to start over and get new people? What did the prior manager do or not do that led to this situation in the first place? What can you learn from that? What will you do differently? How does the staff feel? What can you learn from their frustrations over not being able to do the job? How can you be a positive force under negative circumstances? How can you rally them to perform? What lasting lessons can you learn from someone in distress and trouble? If you're going to try accelerated development, how can you get a quick assessment? How can you give the staff motivating feedback? How can you construct and implement development plans that will work? How can you get people on-line feedback for maximum growth? Do you know when to stop trying and start over? If you're going to turn over some staff, how can you do it both rapidly and with the least damage? How can you deliver the message in a constructive way? What can you learn from having to take negative actions against people? How can you prevent this from happening again?

Learning from Courses

- [ ] **Supervisory Courses**
Most new supervisors go through an "Introduction to Supervision" type course. They are designed to teach the common practices a first-line supervisor needs to know to be effective. The content of most of those courses is standard. There is general agreement on the principles of effective supervision. There are two common problems: 1) Do the students have a strong motivation to learn? Do they know what they don't know? Is there any pain? Because motivated students with a need for the knowledge learn best, participants should have had some trying experiences and some supervisory pain and hardships before attending. 2) Are the instructors experienced supervisors? Have they practiced what they preach? Can they share powerful anecdotes to make key points? Can they answer questions credibly? If possible, select supervisory courses based on the instructors, since the content seems to be the much same for all such courses. Lastly, does the course offer the opportunity for practicing each skill? Does it contain simulations? Are there case studies you could easily identify with? Are there breakout groups? Is there opportunity for action learning? Search for the most interactive course.

- [ ] **Insight Events**
These are courses designed around assessing skills and providing feedback to the participants. These events can be a powerful source of self-knowledge and can lead to significant development if done right. When selecting a self-insight course, consider the following: 1) Are the skills assessed the important ones? 2) Are the assessment techniques and instruments sound? 3) Are those who are providing the feedback trained and professional? 4) Is the feedback provided in a user-friendly and "actionable" format? 5) Does the feedback include development planning? 6) Is the setting comfortable and conducive to reflection and learning? 7) Are the other participants the kinds of people you could learn from? 8) Are you in the right frame of mind to learn from this kind of intense experience? Select events on the basis of positive answers to these eight questions.

- [ ] **Sending Others to Courses**
If you are responsible for managing someone else's development and, as part of that, sending them to courses, prepare them beforehand. Don't send them as tourists. Meet with them before and after the course. Tell them why they need this course. Tell them what you expect them to learn. Give them feedback on why you think they need the course. Agree ahead of time how you will measure and monitor learning after they return. If possible, offer a variety of courses for your employee to choose from. Have them give you a report shortly after they return. If appropriate, have them present what they learned to the rest of your staff. After they return, provide opportunities for using the

new skills with safe cover and low risk. Give them practice time before expecting full exercise of the new skills. Be supportive during early unsteadiness. Give continuous feedback on progress.

SUGGESTED READINGS

Barner, Robert W. *Crossing the Minefield – Tactics for Overcoming Today's Toughest Management Challenges.* New York: AMACOM, 1994.

Bennis, Warren. *Why Leaders Can't Lead.* San Francisco: Jossey-Bass, Inc., 1989.

Calvert, Gene. *Highwire Management.* San Francisco: Jossey-Bass, Inc., 1993.

Silva, Michael and Terry McGann. *Overdrive.* New York: John Wiley & Sons, Inc., 1995.

Webber, Ross Arkell. *Becoming a Courageous Manager.* Englewood Cliffs, Prentice Hall, 1991.

35

MANAGING AND MEASURING WORK

SECTION 1: YOUR DEVELOPMENT NEED(S)

UNSKILLED

- ☐ Doesn't use goals and objectives to manage self or others
- ☐ Not orderly in assigning and measuring work
- ☐ Isn't clear about who is responsible for what
- ☐ May be disorganized, just throw tasks at people, or lack goals or priorities
- ☐ May manage time poorly and not get around to managing in an orderly way
- ☐ Doesn't provide work in progress feedback
- ☐ Doesn't set up benchmarks and ways for people to measure themselves

SKILLED

- ☐ Clearly assigns responsibility for tasks and decisions
- ☐ Sets clear objectives and measures
- ☐ Monitors process, progress, and results
- ☐ Designs feedback loops into work

OVERUSED SKILL

- ☐ May be overcontrolling
- ☐ May look over people's shoulders
- ☐ May prescribe too much and not empower people

Select one to three of the competencies listed below to work on to compensate for an overuse of this skill.

COMPENSATORS: 3, 14, 18, 19, 26, 33, 36, 44, 57, 60, 63, 64, 65

SOME CAUSES

- ☐ Avoid the conflict that goes with setting tough goals
- ☐ Disorganized; not orderly thinking about work and tasks
- ☐ Inexperienced
- ☐ Not personally goal oriented; don't use goals
- ☐ Poor time management; don't get around to it

THE MAP

Most people like to have goals. They like to measure themselves against a standard. They like to see who can run the fastest, score the most, jump the highest, and work the best. They like to be measured by people they respect and who make a difference to them in life and at work. They like goals to be realistic but stretching, goals that you don't know ahead of time you can really reach. Goals can make things fairer, an equitable way to measure one person against the other.

People like it even better when they participate in a fair goal setting process; it's even more motivating to them to have a hand in setting their own stretch goals.

SECTION 2: LEARNING ON YOUR OWN

THESE SELF-DEVELOPMENT REMEDIES WILL HELP YOU BUILD YOUR SKILL(S)

SOME REMEDIES

- ☐ **1. Set goals.** You should set goals before assigning projects, work and tasks. Goals help focus people's time and efforts. It allows people to perform more effectively and efficiently. Most people don't want to waste time. Most people want to perform well. Learn about MBO – managing by objectives. Read a book about it. While you may not be interested in a full-blown application, all of the principles of setting goals will be in the book. Go to a course on goal setting.
- ☐ **2. Focus on measures.** How would you tell if the goal was accomplished? If the things I asked others to do were done right, what outcomes could we all agree on as measures of success? Most groups can easily come up with success measures that are different from, and more important to them, than formal measures. Ask them to do so.
- ☐ **3. Engage your people in the goal setting effort.** People are more motivated when they have a say in how goals are set and measured. Most won't sandbag the effort by lobbying for low goals. They are just as likely to set the goals higher than you might.
- ☐ **4. People are different.** You need to match the goals to each of the people you manage. They each respond differently to goals. Some like stretch goals; some perform better when they are assured of reaching the goal ahead of time. How do you like your goals? Did you ever work with someone who reacted to goals quite differently than you did? What was the difference? Try to relate the goals to everyone's hot button. Don't treat people alike when it comes to what goals you set and how you set them. If you let each person participate in the process, some of the matching will have already taken place.
- ☐ **5. Clarity.** You need to be clear about goals, how they are going to be measured, and what the rewards and consequences will be for those who exceed, just make, or miss their goals. Communicate both verbally and in writing if you can.
- ☐ **6. Visualize.** Set up a process to monitor progress against the goals. People like running measures. They like to gauge their pace. It's like the United Way Thermometer in the lobby.
- ☐ **7. Feedback.** Give as much in process feedback as you have time for. Most people are motivated by process feedback against agreed upon goals for three reasons.

- First, it helps them adjust what they are doing along the way in time to achieve the goal; they can make midcourse corrections.
- Second, it shows them what they are doing is important and that you're eager to help.
- Third, it's not the "gotcha" game of negative and critical feedback after the fact.

☐ **8. Be flexible.** Things change all the time. Be ready to change goals midstream when faced with contrary information. Anticipate what could go wrong. *More help? – See #47 Planning.*

☐ **9. Follow through with positive and negative rewards** and consequences. Celebrate the exceeders, compliment the just made its, and sit down and discuss what happened with the missers. Actually deliver the reward or consequence you communicated. If you don't do what you said you were going to do, no one will pay attention to the next goal and consequence you set.

☐ **10. Set goals for yourself in your job and your career.** Get used to measuring yourself. Ask your boss's help in setting goals and providing you continuous feedback. That way, you'll know better what effect goals have on others.

SECTION 3: LEARNING FROM MORE FEEDBACK

THESE SOURCES WOULD GIVE YOU THE MOST ACCURATE AND DETAILED FEEDBACK ON YOUR SKILL(S)

☐ **Direct Boss**
Your direct boss has important information about you, your performance, and your prospects. The challenge is to get this information. There are formal processes (e.g., performance appraisals). There are day-to-day opportunities. To help, signal your boss that you want and can handle direct and timely feedback. Many bosses have trouble giving feedback, so you will have to work at it over a period of time.

☐ **Direct Reports**
Across a variety of settings, your direct reports probably see you the most. They are the recipients of most of your managerial behaviors. They know your work. They can compare you with former bosses. Since they may hesitate to give you negative feedback, you have to set the atmosphere to make it easier for them. You have to ask.

☐ **Past Associates/Constituencies**
When confronted with a present performance problem, some claim, "I wasn't like that before; it must be the current situation." When feedback is available from former associates, about 50% support that claim. In the other half of the cases, the people were like that before and probably didn't know it. It sometimes makes sense to access the past to clearly see the present.

- ☐ **Peers and Colleagues**
  Peers and colleagues have a special social and working relationship. They attend staff meetings together, share private views, get feedback from the same boss, travel together, and are knowledgeable about each other's work. You perhaps let your guard down more around peers and act more like yourself. They can be a valuable source of feedback.

SECTION 4: LEARNING FROM DEVELOP-IN-PLACE ASSIGNMENTS

THESE PART-TIME DEVELOP-IN-PLACE ASSIGNMENTS WILL HELP YOU BUILD YOUR SKILL(S)

- ☐ Manage an ad hoc, temporary group of balky and resisting people through an unpopular change or project.
- ☐ Manage an ad hoc, temporary group of low-competence people through a task they couldn't do by themselves.
- ☐ Manage an ad hoc, temporary group of people involved in tackling a fix-it or turnaround project.
- ☐ Manage an ad hoc, temporary group of people in a stable and static operation.
- ☐ Manage an ad hoc, temporary group of people in a rapidly expanding operation.
- ☐ Assemble an ad hoc team of diverse people to accomplish a difficult task.
- ☐ Manage a cost-cutting project.
- ☐ Build a multifunctional project team to tackle a common business issue or problem.
- ☐ Audit cost overruns to assess the problem and present your findings to the person or people involved.
- ☐ Work on a team looking at a reorganization plan where there will be more people than positions.

SECTION 5: LEARNING FROM FULL-TIME JOBS

THESE FULL-TIME JOBS OFFER THE OPPORTUNITY TO BUILD YOUR SKILL(S)

- ☐ **Scale Assignments**
  Core requirements to qualify as a Scale (size) shift assignment are: 1) Sizable jump-shift in the size of the job in areas like: number of people, number of layers in organization, size of budget, number of locations, volume of activity, tightness of deadlines. 2) Medium to low complexity; mostly repetitive and routine processes and procedures. 3) Stable staff and business. 4) Stable operations. 5) Often slow, steady growth.

- ☐ **Staff to Line Shifts**
  Core demands necessary to qualify for a Staff to Line shift are: 1) Moving to a job with an easily determined bottom line or results. 2) Managing bigger scope and/or scale. 3) Requires new skills/perspectives. 4) Unfamiliar aspects of the assignment.

- ☐ **Start-ups**
  The core demands to qualify as a start from scratch are: 1) Starting something new for you and/or for the organization. 2) Forging a new team. 3) Creating new systems/facilities/staffs/programs/procedures. 4) Contextual adversity (e.g., uncertainty, government regulation, unions, difficult environment). Seven types of start from scratches: 1) Planning, building, hiring, and managing (e.g., building a new facility, opening up a new location, moving a unit or company). 2) Heading something new (e.g., new product, new service, new line of business, new department/function, major new program). 3) Take over a group/product/service/program that had existed for less than a year and was off to a fast start. 4) Establishing overseas operations. 5) Major new designs for existing systems. 6) Moving a successful program from one unit to another. 7) Installing a new organization-wide process as a full-time job (e.g., like Total Quality).

SECTION 6: LEARNING MORE FROM YOUR PLAN

THESE ADDITIONAL REMEDIES WILL HELP MAKE THIS DEVELOPMENT PLAN MORE EFFECTIVE FOR YOU

Learning to Learn Better

- ☐ **Study People Who Have Successfully Done What You Need to Do**
  Interview people who have already done what you're planning to do and check your plan against what they did. Try to summarize their key tactics, strategies, and insights; adjust your plan accordingly.

Learning from Experience, Feedback and Other People

- ☐ **Learning from Interviewing Others**
  Interview others. Ask not only what they do, but how and why they do it. What do they think are the rules of thumb they are following? Where did they learn the behaviors? How do they keep them current? How do they monitor the effect they have on others?

- ☐ **Learning from Observing Others**
  Observe others. Find opportunities to observe without interacting with your model. This enables you to objectively study the person, note what he/she is doing or not doing, and compare that with what you would typically do in similar situations. Many times you can learn more by watching than asking. Your model may not be able to explain what he/she does or may be an unwilling teacher.

☐ **Getting Feedback from Direct Reports**
Direct reports often fear reprisals for giving negative feedback about bosses, whether in a formal process, like a questionnaire, or informally and face-to-face. Even with a guarantee of confidentiality, some are still hesitant. If you want feedback from direct reports, you have to set a positive tone and never act out of revenge.

☐ **Learning from Limited Staff**
Most managers either inherit or hire staff from time to time who are inexperienced, incompetent, not up to the task, resistant, or dispirited. Any of these may create a hardship for you. The lessons to be learned are how to get things done with limited resources and how to fix the people situation. In the short term, this hardship is best addressed by assessing the combined strengths of the team and deploying the best you have against the problem. Almost everyone can do something well. Also, the team can contribute more than the combined individuals can. How can you empower and motivate the team? If you hired the troublesome staff, why did you err? What can you learn from your hiring mistakes? What wasn't there that you thought was present? What led you astray? How can you prevent that same hiring error in the future? What do you need to do to fix the situation? Quick development? Start over? If you inherited the problem, how can you fix it? Can you implement a program of accelerated development? Do you have to start over and get new people? What did the prior manager do or not do that led to this situation in the first place? What can you learn from that? What will you do differently? How does the staff feel? What can you learn from their frustrations over not being able to do the job? How can you be a positive force under negative circumstances? How can you rally them to perform? What lasting lessons can you learn from someone in distress and trouble? If you're going to try accelerated development, how can you get a quick assessment? How can you give the staff motivating feedback? How can you construct and implement development plans that will work? How can you get people on-line feedback for maximum growth? Do you know when to stop trying and start over? If you're going to turn over some staff, how can you do it both rapidly and with the least damage? How can you deliver the message in a constructive way? What can you learn from having to take negative actions against people? How can you prevent this from happening again?

Learning from Courses

☐ **Supervisory Courses**
Most new supervisors go through an "Introduction to Supervision" type course. They are designed to teach the common practices a first-line supervisor needs to know to be effective. The content of most of those courses is standard. There is general agreement on the principles of effective supervision. There are two common problems: 1) Do the

students have a strong motivation to learn? Do they know what they don't know? Is there any pain? Because motivated students with a need for the knowledge learn best, participants should have had some trying experiences and some supervisory pain and hardships before attending. 2) Are the instructors experienced supervisors? Have they practiced what they preach? Can they share powerful anecdotes to make key points? Can they answer questions credibly? If possible, select supervisory courses based on the instructors, since the content seems to be the much same for all such courses. Lastly, does the course offer the opportunity for practicing each skill? Does it contain simulations? Are there case studies you could easily identify with? Are there breakout groups? Is there opportunity for action learning? Search for the most interactive course.

☐ **Courses with Feedback**
Many courses such as negotiating skills and personal influence offer feedback on the subject matter of the course in addition to the content. They either collect data ahead of time or collect it "live" during the course.

☐ **Sending Others to Courses**
If you are responsible for managing someone else's development and, as part of that, sending them to courses, prepare them beforehand. Don't send them as tourists. Meet with them before and after the course. Tell them why they need this course. Tell them what you expect them to learn. Give them feedback on why you think they need the course. Agree ahead of time how you will measure and monitor learning after they return. If possible, offer a variety of courses for your employee to choose from. Have them give you a report shortly after they return. If appropriate, have them present what they learned to the rest of your staff. After they return, provide opportunities for using the new skills with safe cover and low risk. Give them practice time before expecting full exercise of the new skills. Be supportive during early unsteadiness. Give continuous feedback on progress.

SUGGESTED READINGS

Blohowiak, Donald W. *How's all the work going to get done?*. Franklin Lakes, NJ: Career Press, 1995.

Cooper, Robert K., Ph.D. *The Performance Edge: New strategies to maximize your work effectiveness and competitive advantage.* Boston: Houghton Mifflin Co., 1991.

Dess, Gregory G. and Joseph C. Picken. *Beyond Productivity: How leading companies achieve superior performance by leveraging their human capital.* New York: AMACOM, 1999.

Ghoshal, Sumantra and Christopher A. Bartlett. *The Individualized Corporation.* New York: HarperBusiness, 1997.

Hronec, Steven M. and Arthur Anderson and Company. *Vital Signs – Using quality, time and cost performance measurements to chart your company's future.* AMACOM: 1993.

Keen, Peter G. W. *The Process Edge – Creating value where it counts.* Boston: Harvard Business School Press, 1998.

Lester, Richard K. *The Productive Edge: How U.S. Industries are pointing the way to a new era of economic growth.* New York: W.W. Norton, 1998.

Lynch, Richard L. and Kevin F. Cross. *Measure Up! Yardsticks for continuous improvement.* Cambridge, MA: Basil Blackwell, 1991.

Maurer, Rick. *Caught in the Middle*. Cambridge, MA: Productivity Press, 1992.

Risher, Howard and Charles Fay, Editors. *The Performance Imperative: Strategies for enhancing workforce effectiveness.* San Francisco: Jossey-Bass, 1995.

Sibson, Robert. *Maximizing Employee Productivity.* New York: AMACOM, 1994.

36

MOTIVATING OTHERS

SECTION 1: YOUR DEVELOPMENT NEED(S)

UNSKILLED

- ☐ Doesn't know what motivates others or how to do it
- ☐ People under him/her don't do their best
- ☐ Not empowering and not a person many people want to work for, around or with
- ☐ May be a one style fits all person, have simplistic models of motivation, or may not care as much as most others do; may be a driver just interested in getting the work out
- ☐ May have trouble with people not like him/her
- ☐ May be a poor reader of others, may not pick up on their needs and cues
- ☐ May be judgmental and put people in stereotypic categories
- ☐ Intentionally or unintentionally demotivates others

SKILLED

- ☐ Creates a climate in which people want to do their best
- ☐ Can motivate many kinds of direct reports and team or project members
- ☐ Can assess each person's hot button and use it to get the best out of him/her
- ☐ Pushes tasks and decisions down
- ☐ Empowers others
- ☐ Invites input from each person and shares ownership and visibility
- ☐ Makes each individual feel his/her work is important
- ☐ Is someone people like working for and with

OVERUSED SKILL

- ☐ May not be good at building team spirit because of an emphasis on individuals
- ☐ May be seen as providing inequitable treatment by treating each person individually
- ☐ May not take tough stands when the situation calls for it
- ☐ May take too long getting input
- ☐ May be reluctant to assign work with tough deadlines

Select one to three of the competencies listed below to work on to compensate for an overuse of this skill.

COMPENSATORS: 9, 12, 13, 18, 19, 20, 34, 35, 37, 50, 52, 56, 57, 60

SOME CAUSES

- ☐ A one style fits all
- ☐ Believe everyone should be naturally motivated
- ☐ Don't believe motivation is necessary or important
- ☐ Have trouble talking with people not like you
- ☐ Judgmental about others
- ☐ Prefer to treat everyone the same
- ☐ Too simple views of motivation

THE MAP

Greater things can happen when people are motivated. Think of three accomplishments you're proud of, then ask yourself how motivated you were to accomplish them. Similarly, if you can figure out what motivates others, their accomplishments and yours will be greater. Some managers believe others should be automatically motivated, thinking motivation comes standard with the person. Some managers believe everyone should be as motivated as they are about the job and the organization. That's seldom the case. Fact is, people are different. Each person is different in the way he/she becomes and sustains being motivated. Being good in this area includes believing it's a manager's job to motivate – that all people are different, and that motivating each of them takes a little bit different approach.

SECTION 2: LEARNING ON YOUR OWN

THESE SELF-DEVELOPMENT REMEDIES WILL HELP YOU BUILD YOUR SKILL(S)

SOME REMEDIES

☐ **1. Follow the basic rules of inspiring others** as outlined in classic books like *People Skills* by Robert Bolton or *Thriving on Chaos* by Tom Peters. Communicate to people that what they do is important. Say thanks. Offer help and ask for it. Provide autonomy in how people do their work. Provide a variety of tasks. "Surprise" people with enriching, challenging assignments. Show an interest in their careers. Adopt a learning attitude toward mistakes. Celebrate successes, have visible accepted measures of achievement and so on.

☐ **2. Know and play the motivation odds.** According to research by Rewick and Lawler, the top motivators at work are: 1) Job challenge, 2) Accomplishing something worthwhile, 3) Learning new things, 4) Personal development, 5) Autonomy. Pay (12th), Friendliness (14th), Praise (15th) or Chance of Promotion (17th) are not insignificant but are superficial compared with the more powerful motivators. Provide challenges, paint pictures of why this is worthwhile, create a common mindset, set up chances to learn and grow, and provide autonomy and you'll hit the vast majority of people's hot buttons.

☐ **3. Use goals to motivate.** Most people are turned on by reasonable goals. They like to measure themselves against a standard. They like to see who can run the fastest, score the most, and work the best. They like goals to be realistic but stretching. People try hardest when they have somewhere between ½ and a ⅔ chance of success and some control over how they go about it. People are even more motivated when they participate in setting the goals. Set just out of reach challenges and tasks that will be first time for people – their first negotiation, their first solo presentation, etc. *More help? – See #35 Managing and Measuring Work*.

☐ **4. To better figure out what drives people,** look to: What do they do first? What do they emphasize in their speech? What do they display emotion around? What values play out for them?

- First things. Does this person go to others first, hole up and study, complain, discuss feelings, or take action? These are the basic orientations of people that reveal what's important to them. Use these to motivate.
- Speech content. People might focus on details, concepts, feelings, or other people in their speech. This can tell you again how to appeal to them by mirroring their speech emphasis. Although most of us naturally adjust – we talk details with detail oriented people – chances are good that in problem relationships you're not finding the common ground. She talks detail and you talk people, for example.
- Emotion. You need to know what people's hot buttons are because one mistake can get you labeled as insensitive with some people. The only cure here is to see what turns up the volume for them – either literally or what they're concerned about.
- Values. Apply the same thinking to the values of others. Do they talk about money, recognition, integrity, efficiency in their normal work conversation?

Figuring out what their drivers are tells you another easy way to appeal to anyone. Once you have this basic understanding, you need to follow the basic rules of motivating others covered in this section.

☐ **5. Turn off your judgment program.** In trying to reach someone, work on without judging him/her. You don't have to agree, you just have to understand in order to motivate. The fact that you wouldn't be motivated that way isn't relevant.

☐ **6. Be able to speak their language at their level.** It shows respect for their way of thinking. Speaking their language makes it easier for them to talk with you and give you the information you need to motivate.

- ☐ **7. Bring him/her into your world.** Tell him/her your conceptual categories. To deal with you he/she needs to know how you think and why. Tell him/her your perspective – the questions you ask, the factors you're interested in. If you can't explain your thinking, he/she won't know how to deal with you effectively. It's easier to follow someone and something you understand.
- ☐ **8. Motivating is personal.** Know three non-work things about everybody – their interests and hobbies or their children or something you can chat about. Life is a small world. If you ask people a few personal questions, you'll find you have something in common with virtually anyone. Having something in common will help bond the relationship and allow you to individualize how you motivate.
- ☐ **9. Turn a negative into a motivator.** If a person is touchy about something, he/she will respond to targeted help. If the person responds by being clannish, he/she may need your support to get more in the mainstream. If he/she is demotivated, look for both personal and work causes. This person may respond to job challenge. If the person is naive, help him/her see how things work.
- ☐ **10. The easiest way to motivate someone** is to get him/her involved deeply in the work he/she is doing. Delegate and empower as much as you can. Get him/her involved in setting goals and determining the work process to get there. Ask his/her opinion about decisions that have to be made. Have him/her help appraise the work of the unit. Share the successes. Debrief the failures together. Use his/her full tool set.

SECTION 3: LEARNING FROM MORE FEEDBACK

THESE SOURCES WOULD GIVE YOU THE MOST ACCURATE AND DETAILED FEEDBACK ON YOUR SKILL(S)

☐ **Direct Reports**

Across a variety of settings, your direct reports probably see you the most. They are the recipients of most of your managerial behaviors. They know your work. They can compare you with former bosses. Since they may hesitate to give you negative feedback, you have to set the atmosphere to make it easier for them. You have to ask.

☐ **Human Resource Professionals**

Human Resource professionals have both a formal and informal feedback role. Since they have access to unique and confidential information, they can provide the right context for feedback you've received. Sometimes they may be "directed" to give you feedback. Other times, they may pass on feedback just to be helpful to you.

☐ **Past Associates/Constituencies**
When confronted with a present performance problem, some claim, "I wasn't like that before; it must be the current situation." When feedback is available from former associates, about 50% support that claim. In the other half of the cases, the people were like that before and probably didn't know it. It sometimes makes sense to access the past to clearly see the present.

SECTION 4: LEARNING FROM DEVELOP-IN-PLACE ASSIGNMENTS

THESE PART-TIME DEVELOP-IN-PLACE ASSIGNMENTS WILL HELP YOU BUILD YOUR SKILL(S)

☐ Integrate diverse systems, processes, or procedures across decentralized and/or dispersed units.

☐ Be a change agent; create a symbol for change; lead the rallying cry; champion a significant change and implementation.

☐ Relaunch an existing product or service that's not doing well.

☐ Create employee involvement teams.

☐ Assign a project to a group with a tight deadline.

☐ Manage an ad hoc, temporary group of "green," inexperienced people as their coach, teacher, orienter, etc.

☐ Manage an ad hoc, temporary group of balky and resisting people through an unpopular change or project.

☐ Handle a tough negotiation with an internal or external client or customer.

☐ Prepare and present a proposal of some consequence to top management.

☐ Resolve an issue in conflict between two people, units, geographies, functions, etc.

SECTION 5: LEARNING FROM FULL-TIME JOBS

THESE FULL-TIME JOBS OFFER THE OPPORTUNITY TO BUILD YOUR SKILL(S)

☐ **Fix-its/Turnarounds**
The core demands to qualify as a Fix-it or Turnaround assignment are: 1) Cleaning up a mess. 2) Serious people issues/problems like credibility/performance/morale. 3) Tight deadline. 4) Serious business performance failure. 5) Last chance to fix. Four Types of Fix-its/Turnarounds: 1) Fixing a failed business/unit involving taking control, stopping losses, managing damage, planning the turnaround, dealing with people problems, installing new processes and systems, and rebuilding the spirit and performance of the unit. 2) Managing sizable disasters like mishandled labor negotiations and strikes, thefts, history

of significant business losses, poor staff, failed leadership, hidden problems, fraud, public relations nightmares, etc. 3) Significant reorganization and restructuring (e.g., stabilizing the business, reforming unit, introducing new systems, making people changes, resetting strategy and tactics). 4) Significant system/process breakdown (e.g., MIS, financial coordination processes, audits, standards, etc.) across units requiring working to change something from a distant position, providing advice and counsel, and installing or implementing a major process improvement or system change outside your own unit and/or with customers outside the organization.

- ☐ **Influencing Without Authority**
  The core demands to qualify as an Influence Without Authority are: 1) Significant challenge (e.g, start-up, fix-it, scope and/or scale assignment, strategic planning project, changes in management practices/ systems). 2) Insufficient direct authority to make it happen. 3) Tight deadlines. 4) Visible to significant others. 5) Sensitive politics.

- ☐ **Significant People Demands**
  Core demands required to qualify as a Significant People Responsibilities assignment are: 1) A sizable increase in either the number of people managed and/or the complexity of the challenges involved 2) Longer-term assignment (two or more years). 3) Quality of people management critical to achieving results. 4) Involves groups not worked with before (e.g., union, new technical areas, nationalities).

- ☐ **Start-ups**
  The core demands to qualify as a start from scratch are: 1) Starting something new for you and/or for the organization. 2) Forging a new team. 3) Creating new systems/facilities/staffs/programs/procedures. 4) Contextual adversity (e.g., uncertainty, government regulation, unions, difficult environment). Seven types of start from scratches: 1) Planning, building, hiring, and managing (e.g., building a new facility, opening up a new location, moving a unit or company). 2) Heading something new (e.g., new product, new service, new line of business, new department/function, major new program). 3) Take over a group/ product/service/program that had existed for less than a year and was off to a fast start. 4) Establishing overseas operations. 5) Major new designs for existing systems. 6) Moving a successful program from one unit to another. 7) Installing a new organization-wide process as a full-time job (e.g., like Total Quality).

SECTION 6: LEARNING MORE FROM YOUR PLAN

THESE ADDITIONAL REMEDIES WILL HELP MAKE THIS DEVELOPMENT PLAN MORE EFFECTIVE FOR YOU

Learning to Learn Better

- ☐ **Use Objective Data When Judging Others**
  Practice studying other people more than judging or evaluating them. Get the facts, the data, how they think, why they do things, without classifying them into your internal like/dislike or agree/disagree boxes, categories, or buckets. Try to project or predict how they would act/react in various situations and follow up to see how accurate you are.

- ☐ **Examine Why You Judge People the Way You Do**
  List the people you like and those you dislike and try to find out why. What do those you like have in common with each other and with you? What do those you dislike have in common with themselves and how do they differ from you? Are your "people buckets" logical and productive or do they interfere? Could you be more effective without putting people into buckets?

- ☐ **Pre-sell an Idea to a Key Stakeholder**
  Identify the key stakeholders – those who will be the most affected by your actions or the most resistant, or whose support you will most need. Collect the information each will find persuasive; marshal your arguments and try to pre-sell your conclusions, recommendations, and solutions.

Learning from Experience, Feedback and Other People

- ☐ **Using Multiple Models**
  Who do you know who exemplifies how to do whatever your need is? Who, for example, personifies decisiveness or compassion or strategic agility? Think more broadly than your current job and colleagues. For example, clergy, friends, spouses or community leaders are also good sources for potential models. Select your models not on the basis of overall excellence or likability, but on the basis of the one towering strength (or glaring weakness) you are interested in. Even people who are well thought of usually have only one or two towering strengths (or glaring weaknesses). Ordinarily, you won't learn as much from the whole person as you will from one characteristic.

- ☐ **Learning from Bosses**
  Bosses can be an excellent and ready source for learning. All bosses do some things exceptionally well and other things poorly. Distance your feelings from the boss/direct report relationship and study things that work and things that don't work for your boss. What would you have done? What could you use, and what should you avoid?

- ☐ **Learning from Ineffective Behavior**
Seeing things done poorly can be a very potent source of learning for you, especially if the behavior or action affects others negatively. Many times the thing done poorly causes emotional reactions or pain in you and others. Distance yourself from the feelings and explore why the actions didn't work.

- ☐ **Learning from Interviewing Others**
Interview others. Ask not only what they do, but how and why they do it. What do they think are the rules of thumb they are following? Where did they learn the behaviors? How do they keep them current? How do they monitor the effect they have on others?

- ☐ **Getting Feedback from Direct Reports**
Direct reports often fear reprisals for giving negative feedback about bosses, whether in a formal process, like a questionnaire, or informally and face-to-face. Even with a guarantee of confidentiality, some are still hesitant. If you want feedback from direct reports, you have to set a positive tone and never act out of revenge.

- ☐ **Learning from Limited Staff**
Most managers either inherit or hire staff from time to time who are inexperienced, incompetent, not up to the task, resistant, or dispirited. Any of these may create a hardship for you. The lessons to be learned are how to get things done with limited resources and how to fix the people situation. In the short term, this hardship is best addressed by assessing the combined strengths of the team and deploying the best you have against the problem. Almost everyone can do something well. Also, the team can contribute more than the combined individuals can. How can you empower and motivate the team? If you hired the troublesome staff, why did you err? What can you learn from your hiring mistakes? What wasn't there that you thought was present? What led you astray? How can you prevent that same hiring error in the future? What do you need to do to fix the situation? Quick development? Start over? If you inherited the problem, how can you fix it? Can you implement a program of accelerated development? Do you have to start over and get new people? What did the prior manager do or not do that led to this situation in the first place? What can you learn from that? What will you do differently? How does the staff feel? What can you learn from their frustrations over not being able to do the job? How can you be a positive force under negative circumstances? How can you rally them to perform? What lasting lessons can you learn from someone in distress and trouble? If you're going to try accelerated development, how can you get a quick assessment? How can you give the staff motivating feedback? How can you construct and implement development plans that will work? How can you get people on-line feedback for maximum growth? Do you know when to stop trying and start over? If you're going to turn over some staff, how can you do it

both rapidly and with the least damage? How can you deliver the message in a constructive way? What can you learn from having to take negative actions against people? How can you prevent this from happening again?

Learning from Courses

☐ **Supervisory Courses**
Most new supervisors go through an "Introduction to Supervision" type course. They are designed to teach the common practices a first-line supervisor needs to know to be effective. The content of most of those courses is standard. There is general agreement on the principles of effective supervision. There are two common problems: 1) Do the students have a strong motivation to learn? Do they know what they don't know? Is there any pain? Because motivated students with a need for the knowledge learn best, participants should have had some trying experiences and some supervisory pain and hardships before attending. 2) Are the instructors experienced supervisors? Have they practiced what they preach? Can they share powerful anecdotes to make key points? Can they answer questions credibly? If possible, select supervisory courses based on the instructors, since the content seems to be the much same for all such courses. Lastly, does the course offer the opportunity for practicing each skill? Does it contain simulations? Are there case studies you could easily identify with? Are there breakout groups? Is there opportunity for action learning? Search for the most interactive course.

SUGGESTED READINGS

Bardwick, Judith M. *Danger in the Comfort Zone.* New York: AMACOM, 1991.

Bolton, Robert. *People skills: How to assert yourself, listen to others, and resolve conflicts.* New York: Simon & Schuster, 1986.

Bradford, Lawrence and Claire Raines. *Twenty Something.* New York: MasterMedia Ltd., 1992.

Daniels, Aubrey C. *Bringing out the Best in People.* New York: McGraw-Hill, Inc., 1994.

Deal, Terrence E. and William A. Jenkins. *Managing the Hidden Organization.* New York: Warner Books, 1994.

Lawler, Edward E. *Motivation in work organizations.* San Francisco: Jossey-Bass, Inc., 1994.

Matejka, Ken. *Why this horse won't drink.* New York: AMACOM, 1991.

continued

Maurer, Rick. *Caught in the Middle.* Cambridge, MA: Productivity Press, 1992.

Mullen, James X. *The simple art of greatness: building, managing and motivating a kick-ass workforce.* New York: Viking, 1995.

Spitzer, Dean R. *Supermotivation.* New York: AMACOM, 1995.

Stack, Jack. *The Great Game of Business.* New York: Doubleday, 1992.

NEGOTIATING

SECTION 1: YOUR DEVELOPMENT NEED(S)

UNSKILLED

- ☐ Not a good deal maker; doesn't come away with much
- ☐ May use ineffective tactics – too hard or too soft, may have to win every battle or gives away too much to get the agreement
- ☐ Poor conflict manager, trouble dealing with attack, contention or non-negotiable points
- ☐ May hold back and be afraid to take tough stands
- ☐ Poor listener
- ☐ May not seek or know how to find common ground
- ☐ May be too noisy and do too much damage to relationships
- ☐ May not know how to be diplomatic, direct and polite

SKILLED

- ☐ Can negotiate skillfully in tough situations with both internal and external groups
- ☐ Can settle differences with minimum noise
- ☐ Can win concessions without damaging relationships
- ☐ Can be both direct and forceful as well as diplomatic
- ☐ Gains trust quickly of other parties to the negotiations
- ☐ Has a good sense of timing

OVERUSED SKILL

- ☐ May leave people-damage in his/her wake
- ☐ May walk over people's feelings
- ☐ May always need to win
- ☐ May hang on to a position too long
- ☐ May become overly accommodating and be reluctant to walk away
- ☐ May need to smooth over everything
- ☐ May take too long to get things decided

Select one to three of the competencies listed below to work on to compensate for an overuse of this skill.

COMPENSATORS: 2, 12, 16, 17, 30, 38, 41, 48, 50, 51, 52, 53, 56, 57, 63

SOME CAUSES

- ☐ Can't take the heat
- ☐ Come on too hard/too soft
- ☐ Give in too much; too early
- ☐ Have to win every battle
- ☐ Have trouble reaching equitable agreements
- ☐ Have trouble when the other side is contentious

- ☐ Nervous about negotiating
- ☐ Not a good trader or bargainer
- ☐ Poor interpersonal skills
- ☐ Too serious and intense

THE MAP

Negotiation is getting all you can at the least cost possible while leaving the other side intact and reasonably positive so that they will negotiate with you again. The best case is win-win where both sides go away with exactly what they wanted. A rare happening. More likely is that both sides got enough to feel good about the process. It is something-something. There are win-lose negotiations where one side wins a lot of concessions and the other side leaves with nothing or very little. That's usually only good for one-time events or buying cars. Losers are not happy people. Good win-win negotiators focus on the target, the issues and the underlying interests of both sides. They generally use commonly accepted ethical principles and fairness. They deal with personal issues separately if at all, deflect personal assaults, and stay away from early rigid positions.

SECTION 2: LEARNING ON YOUR OWN

THESE SELF-DEVELOPMENT REMEDIES WILL HELP YOU BUILD YOUR SKILL(S)

SOME REMEDIES

☐ **1. Set rapport and boundaries.** Start slow until you know where the other party is coming from. Pay attention to positioning. You and your team on one side and them on the other sets up a contest. Try to mix team members together on both sides. If you're the host, start with small talk unrelated to the subject of the negotiation. Give everyone time to settle in and get comfortable. When it's time, ask whether it would be useful for each side to lay out its goals, starting positions and any boundaries – such as, we aren't here to negotiate costs at this time. Volunteer to go first. Give reasons first, positions last. When you offer goals and positions, people often don't listen to your reasons. *More help? – See #3 Approachability and #31 Interpersonal Savvy.*

☐ **2. Avoid early rigid positions.** It's just physics. Action gets equal reaction. Strong statements. Strongly worded positions. Casting blame. Absolutes. Lines in the sand. Unnecessary passion. All of these will be responded to in kind, will waste time, cause ill will and possibly prevent a win-win or a something-something. It only has a place in one-time, either/or negotiations and even there it isn't recommended.

☐ **3. Downsize the negotiation.** Make the negotiations as small as possible. Even far apart initial positions will have something in common. Announce that you would first like to see if there are any points on which the two sides could tentatively agree. List those on a board or flip chart. Then ask if there are any tentative trades that could be made. I can give you this, if you could give me that. Document the possible trades, pending other things of course. Then list the seemingly far aparts, the deal stoppers each side has. Take each deal stopper one at a time and have the owner get as specific as possible as to the concessions they are asking for so time isn't wasted on assumed far aparts. See if you can move any of them off the far apart list. Have some things you can give away. Hold out some attractive concessions and giveaways. Release them as you need them during the negotiation process. (Better if you know ahead of time what they would be pleased with.) To bring them out, state them in a proposition, "If I would give in on this point, could I have X in return?" Do this to generate a wider variety of possibilities.

☐ **4. Questions.** In win-win and something-something negotiations, the more information about the other side you have, the more you will have to work with. Ask more questions, make fewer statements. Ask clarifying questions – "What did you mean by that?" Probes – "Why do you say that?" Motives – "What led you to that position?" Explain objectively why you hold a view; make the other side do the same. When the other side takes a rigid position, don't reject it. Ask why – what are the principles behind the offer, how will we know it's fair, what's the theory of the case. Play out what would happen if their position was accepted. Get everything out that you can. Don't negotiate assumptions, negotiate facts.

☐ **5. Dealing with the heat.** Negotiations are not always benign and friendly. Many times they generate heat. Passion. Defensiveness. Blame. Attacks. Innuendoes. Threats. Separate the people from the heat they deliver and the people from the roles they play in the negotiations. Deal with people issues directly but separately and maybe off line during a break. Try to deal candidly with the toughest critic first. Avoid direct blaming remarks; describe the impasse and possible solutions. In response to unreasonable proposals, attacks, or a non-answer to a question, you can always say nothing. People will usually respond by saying more, coming off their position a bit, or at least revealing their interests. If the other side won't play fair, surface their game – "It looks like you're playing good cop, bad cop. Why don't you settle your differences and tell me one thing?" In response to threats, say you'll only negotiate on merit and fairness. Suggest objective standards or throw out ideas of what would be fair parameters for discussion. If someone makes a ridiculous offer, take it seriously. Ask him/her to explain it, then watch him/her squirm. When he/she engages in brinksmanship of the X dollars or nothing variety, treat the statement as a goal or wish or simply go on talking as if he/she hadn't said it. If someone yells at you, lower your voice or move closer to him/her. *More help? – See #12 Conflict Management.* Also read *Getting to Yes* by Fisher and Ury.

☐ **6. Keeping your cool.** Sometimes our emotional reactions lead others to think we are weak and have problems with tough situations. How do you show emotions? In negotiations, what emotional reactions do you have such as impatience, interrupting, denials or non-verbals like fidgeting or drumming your fingers? Learn to recognize those as soon as they start and ask a question instead to bide time, or tell the person to tell you more about his/her point of view. Let the other side vent frustration, blow off steam, but don't react. Return to facts, and the problem before the group, staying away from personal clashes. *More help? – See #11 Composure.*

☐ **7. Small wins.** Figure out ways to keep the other side intact. When they have to report back to their boss, what can they say they got? Allow others to save face; concede small points; don't try to hit a home run every time.

☐ **8. Impasses.** If you can't agree on everything, document the things both were able to agree upon, and delineate all the remaining issues. See if you can least agree on process – design and agree upon definite time, certain follow-up steps. This creates some motion and breaks dead in the water stalemates. *More help? – See #52 Process Management.*

☐ **9. Arbitration.** When there is a true impasse, suggest a third equal power and acceptable to both parties person, to help resolve the remaining conflicts. Use a third party to write up each side's interests and keep suggesting compromises until you can agree. Continue to move closer until each side can improve it no more. Or if time is an issue, pass it up to a higher authority. Present both sides calmly and objectively, and let the chips fall where they may.

☐ **10. Cut line.** The most confident and focused negotiators are those who are comfortable walking away if necessary. Think it through ahead of time. Could you afford to walk away temporarily or permanently? How could you recoup? Do you have the time? Could you get what you need some other way? It's a real confidence builder to know you can say no. Be prepared to cut line and leave the negotiation. *More help? – See #57 Standing Alone.*

SECTION 3: LEARNING FROM MORE FEEDBACK

THESE SOURCES WOULD GIVE YOU THE MOST ACCURATE AND DETAILED FEEDBACK ON YOUR SKILL(S)

☐ **Internal and External Customers**

Customers interact with you as a person and as a supplier or vendor of products and services. You're important to them because you can either help address and solve their problems or stand in their way. As customer service and Total Quality programs gain importance, clients and customers become a more prominent source of feedback.

- ☐ **Past Associates/Constituencies**
  When confronted with a present performance problem, some claim, "I wasn't like that before; it must be the current situation." When feedback is available from former associates, about 50% support that claim. In the other half of the cases, the people were like that before and probably didn't know it. It sometimes makes sense to access the past to clearly see the present.

- ☐ **Peers and Colleagues**
  Peers and colleagues have a special social and working relationship. They attend staff meetings together, share private views, get feedback from the same boss, travel together, and are knowledgeable about each other's work. You perhaps let your guard down more around peers and act more like yourself. They can be a valuable source of feedback.

SECTION 4: LEARNING FROM DEVELOP-IN-PLACE ASSIGNMENTS

THESE PART-TIME DEVELOP-IN-PLACE ASSIGNMENTS WILL HELP YOU BUILD YOUR SKILL(S)

- ☐ Integrate diverse systems, processes, or procedures across decentralized and/or dispersed units.
- ☐ Manage the renovation of an office, floor, building, meeting room, warehouse, etc.
- ☐ Plan a new site for a building (plant, field office, headquarters, etc.).
- ☐ Plan an off-site meeting, conference, convention, trade show, event, etc.
- ☐ Manage the purchase of a major product, equipment, materials, program, or system.
- ☐ Get involved with the negotiation of a contract or agreement with international consequences.
- ☐ Manage an ad hoc, temporary group of balky and resisting people through an unpopular change or project.
- ☐ Handle a tough negotiation with an internal or external client or customer.
- ☐ Manage liquidation/sale of products, equipment, materials, a business, furniture, overstock, etc.
- ☐ Manage a dissatisfied internal or external customer; troubleshoot a performance or quality problem with a product or service.

SECTION 5: LEARNING FROM FULL-TIME JOBS

THESE FULL-TIME JOBS OFFER THE OPPORTUNITY TO BUILD YOUR SKILL(S)

☐ **Influencing Without Authority**

The core demands to qualify as an Influence Without Authority are: 1) Significant challenge (e.g, start-up, fix-it, scope and/or scale assignment, strategic planning project, changes in management practices/ systems). 2) Insufficient direct authority to make it happen. 3) Tight deadlines. 4) Visible to significant others. 5) Sensitive politics.

☐ **Scope Assignments**

The core demands for a Scope (complexity) assignment are: 1) Significant increase in both internal and external scope or complexity. 2) Significant increase in visibility and/or bottom line responsibility. 3) Unfamiliar area, business, technology, or territory. Examples of Scope assignments involving shifts: 1) Switching into a new function/technology/business. 2) Moving to new organization. 3) Moving to overseas assignment. 4) Moving to new location. 5) Adding new products/ services. 6) Moving between headquarters/field. 7) Switches in ownership/top management of the unit/organization. Examples of Scope assignments involving "firsts": 1) First-time manager. 2) First-time managing managers. 3) First-time executive. 4) First-time overseas. 5) First-time headquarters/field. 6) First-time team leader. 7) First-time new technology/business/function. Scope assignments involving increased complexity: 1) Managing a significant expansion of an existing product or service. 2) Managing adding new products/service into an existing unit. 3) Managing a reorganized and more diverse unit. 4) Managing explosive growth. 5) Adding new technologies.

☐ **Start-ups**

The core demands to qualify as a start from scratch are: 1) Starting something new for you and/or for the organization. 2) Forging a new team. 3) Creating new systems/facilities/staffs/programs/procedures. 4) Contextual adversity (e.g., uncertainty, government regulation, unions, difficult environment). Seven types of start from scratches: 1) Planning, building, hiring, and managing (e.g., building a new facility, opening up a new location, moving a unit or company). 2) Heading something new (e.g., new product, new service, new line of business, new department/function, major new program). 3) Take over a group/product/service/program that had existed for less than a year and was off to a fast start. 4) Establishing overseas operations. 5) Major new designs for existing systems. 6) Moving a successful program from one unit to another. 7) Installing a new organization-wide process as a full-time job (e.g., like Total Quality).

SECTION 6: LEARNING MORE FROM YOUR PLAN

THESE ADDITIONAL REMEDIES WILL HELP MAKE THIS DEVELOPMENT PLAN MORE EFFECTIVE FOR YOU

Learning to Learn Better

- ☐ **Envision Yourself Succeeding**
  Examine the image of success in detail: what you are doing, what you are feeling, how you are reacting to others, how others are reacting to you, how the parts fit together. Can you then play that out in the real situation and get to the same outcome?

- ☐ **Rehearse Successful Tactics/Strategies/Actions**
  Mentally rehearse how you will act before going into the situation. Try to anticipate how others will react, what they will say, and how you'll respond. Check out the best and worst cases; play out both scenes. Check your feelings in conflict or worst-case situations; rehearse staying under control.

- ☐ **Look Beyond Your First Solution to a Problem**
  Don't always take the first action you think of. Look further for a second and third. What's different? Might the second or third be more effective? Research shows that the best solution lies somewhere between the second and third strategies or approaches. Your first solution is often an "autopilot" response and may not be the best.

- ☐ **Use Objective Data When Judging Others**
  Practice studying other people more than judging or evaluating them. Get the facts, the data, how they think, why they do things, without classifying them into your internal like/dislike or agree/disagree boxes, categories, or buckets. Try to project or predict how they would act/react in various situations and follow up to see how accurate you are.

- ☐ **Examine Why You Judge People the Way You Do**
  List the people you like and those you dislike and try to find out why. What do those you like have in common with each other and with you? What do those you dislike have in common with themselves and how do they differ from you? Are your "people buckets" logical and productive or do they interfere? Could you be more effective without putting people into buckets?

- ☐ **Learn to Separate Opinions From Facts**
  Practice separating opinions, beliefs, feelings, attitudes and values from facts and data. Try to base more of your comments and actions on the data side. If there is a need to air subjective information, announce it as such, and label it for what it is. Don't present opinions with the look and sound of data.

- ☐ **Think and Talk More in Probabilities and Less in Absolutes**
  Try to be less "0/1," yes and no; don't be so absolute in everything you do or say. Think and talk in terms of probabilities (I'm about 60% sure

my viewpoint is correct). Try to face what's real about your suggestions and ideas rather than wishing or projecting you were always 100% correct. Tell people how sure you are before you make a statement.

- ☐ **Sell Something to a Tough Group/Audience**
  Think of the person or group who will be the toughest to sell, the most critical, skeptical, or resistant, and sell that person or group first. Take time to understand the opposing viewpoints. Find common ground and leverage points; line up your best data and arguments and go for it.

Learning from Experience, Feedback and Other People

- ☐ **Using Multiple Models**
  Who do you know who exemplifies how to do whatever your need is? Who, for example, personifies decisiveness or compassion or strategic agility? Think more broadly than your current job and colleagues. For example, clergy, friends, spouses or community leaders are also good sources for potential models. Select your models not on the basis of overall excellence or likability, but on the basis of the one towering strength (or glaring weakness) you are interested in. Even people who are well thought of usually have only one or two towering strengths (or glaring weaknesses). Ordinarily, you won't learn as much from the whole person as you will from one characteristic.

- ☐ **Learning from Observing Others**
  Observe others. Find opportunities to observe without interacting with your model. This enables you to objectively study the person, note what he/she is doing or not doing, and compare that with what you would typically do in similar situations. Many times you can learn more by watching than asking. Your model may not be able to explain what he/she does or may be an unwilling teacher.

SUGGESTED READINGS

Bazerman, Max H. and Margaret A. Neale. *Negotiating Rationally.* New York: MacMillan Inc., 1992.

Dawson, Roger. *Secrets of Power Negotiating.* Franklin Lakes, NJ: Career Press, 1995.

Dawson, Roger. *Secrets of Power Negotiating [sound recording].* Chicago, IL: Nightingale-Conant Corporation, 1987.

Fisher, Roger and William Ury, with Bruce Patton, editor. *Getting to yes: negotiating agreement without giving in.* New York: Penguin Books, 1991.

Gottlieb, Marvin and William J. Heath. *Making Deals.* New York: Simon & Schuster, 1990.

Skopec, Eric William and Laree S. Keily. *Everything's Negotiable – When You Know How to Play the Game.* New York: AMACOM, 1994.

38

ORGANIZATIONAL AGILITY

SECTION 1: YOUR DEVELOPMENT NEED(S)

UNSKILLED

- ☐ Doesn't get things done in organizations beyond his/her area
- ☐ May lack the interpersonal skills to get things done across boundaries
- ☐ May not negotiate well within organizations
- ☐ May be too timid and laid back to maneuver through organizations
- ☐ May reject the complexity of organizations
- ☐ May lack the experience or simply not know who and where to go
- ☐ May be too impatient to learn
- ☐ May neither know nor care to know the origins of how things work around the organization

SKILLED

- ☐ Knowledgeable about how organizations work
- ☐ Knows how to get things done both through formal channels and the informal network
- ☐ Understands the origin and reasoning behind key policies, practices, and procedures
- ☐ Understands the cultures of organizations

OVERUSED SKILL

- ☐ May spend too much time maneuvering for advantage
- ☐ May spend too much time and energy working on issues that lack substance
- ☐ May be seen as too political

Select one to three of the competencies listed below to work on to compensate for an overuse of this skill.

COMPENSATORS: 4, 5, 8, 12, 17, 22, 27, 29, 51, 52, 53, 57, 63

SOME CAUSES

- ☐ Don't see things in systems
- ☐ Impatient
- ☐ Inexperienced
- ☐ Poor interpersonal skills
- ☐ Resist the reality of complexity
- ☐ Weak negotiator

THE MAP

Organizations can be complex mazes with many turns, dead ends, quick routes and choices. In most organizations, the best path to get somewhere is almost never a straight line. There is a formal organization – the one on the organization chart – where the path may look straight and then there is the informal organization where all paths are zigzagged. Since organizations are staffed with people, they become all the more complex. There are gatekeepers, expediters, stoppers, resisters, guides, good Samaritans and influencers. All of these types live in the organizational maze. The key to being successful in maneuvering through complex organizations is to find your way through the maze to your goal in the least amount of time while making the least noise. The best way to do that is to accept the complexity of organizations rather than fighting it and learn to be a maze-bright person.

SECTION 2: LEARNING ON YOUR OWN

THESE SELF-DEVELOPMENT REMEDIES WILL HELP YOU BUILD YOUR SKILL(S)

SOME REMEDIES

☐ **1. Get an assessment.** Try to do the most honest self-assessment you can on why you aren't skilled at getting things done smoothly and effectively in the organization. Ask at least one person from each group you work with for feedback. *More help? – See #55 Self-Knowledge.*

☐ **2. Shake things up.** What you are doing now apparently isn't working. Do something different. Try things you generally don't do. Look to what others do who are more effective than you. Keep a log on what worked and what didn't.

☐ **3. Personal style can get in the way.** People differ in the impression they leave. Those who leave positive impressions get more things done through the organization than those who leave a negative impression. Positive impressions include listening. *More help? – See #3 Approachability, #31 Interpersonally Savvy, #33 Listening, #37 Negotiating, #39 Organizing and #42 Peer Relationships.*

☐ **4. Think equity.** Relationships that work are built on equity and considering the impact on others. Don't just ask for things; find some common ground where you can provide help, not just ask for it. What does the unit you're contacting need in the way of problem solving or information? Do you really know how they see the issue? Is it even important to them? How does what you're working on affect them? If it affects them negatively and they are balky, can you trade something, appeal to the common good, figure out some way to minimize the work or other impact (volunteering staff help, for example)? *More help? – See #42 Peer Relationships.*

☐ **5. Sometimes the problem is in assessing people.** Who really wants to help? Who is going to get in the way? What do they really want? What price will they ask for helping? *More help? – See #56 Sizing Up People and #64 Understanding Others.*

☐ **6. Sometimes the problem is underestimating the complexity** of organizations. Some people always want to think things are simpler than they are. While it's possible some organizations are simple, most are not. *More help? – See #48 Political Savvy and #59* Managing Through *Systems.*

☐ **7. Sometimes disorganization does you in.** Understanding how organizations function takes some discipline. You have to look beyond what you see to what's really in the background. *More help? – See #47 Planning.*

☐ **8. Lost in the maze?** Some people know the steps necessary to get things done but are too impatient to follow the process. Maneuvering through the maze includes stopping once in awhile to let things run their course. It may mean waiting until a major gatekeeper has the time to pay attention to your needs. *More help? – See #41 Patience.* One additional problem might be in diagnosing the paths, turns, dead ends and zags. *More help? – See #32 Learning on the Fly, #48 Political Savvy and #51 Problem Solving.*

☐ **9. Get rattled when what you try doesn't work or gets rejected?** If you tend to lose your cool and get frustrated, practice responses before the fact. What's the worst that could happen and what will you do? You can pause, count to 10, or ask why it can't be done. You can take in information and develop counter moves. So don't react, learn. *More help? – See #11 Composure.*

☐ **10. Who are the movers and shakers in the organization?** How do they get things done? Who do they rely on for expediting things through the maze? How do you compare to them? Who are the major gatekeepers who control the flow of resources, information and decisions? Who are the guides and the helpers? Get to know them better. Who are the major resisters and stoppers? Try to avoid or go around them.

SECTION 3: LEARNING FROM MORE FEEDBACK

THESE SOURCES WOULD GIVE YOU THE MOST ACCURATE AND DETAILED FEEDBACK ON YOUR SKILL(S)

☐ **Boss's Boss(es)**

From a process standpoint, your boss's boss probably has the most influence and control over your progress. He/she has a broader perspective, has more access to data, and stands at the center of decisions about you. To know what he/she thinks, without having to violate the canons of corporate due process to get that information, would be quite useful.

☐ **Natural Mentors**

Natural mentors have a special relationship with you and are interested in your success and your future. Since they are usually not in your direct chain of command, you can have more open, relaxed, and fruitful discussions about yourself and your career prospects. They can be a very important source for candid or critical feedback others may not give you.

☐ **Past Associates/Constituencies**
When confronted with a present performance problem, some claim, "I wasn't like that before; it must be the current situation." When feedback is available from former associates, about 50% support that claim. In the other half of the cases, the people were like that before and probably didn't know it. It sometimes makes sense to access the past to clearly see the present.

SECTION 4: LEARNING FROM DEVELOP-IN-PLACE ASSIGNMENTS

THESE PART-TIME DEVELOP-IN-PLACE ASSIGNMENTS WILL HELP YOU BUILD YOUR SKILL(S)

☐ Integrate diverse systems, processes, or procedures across decentralized and/or dispersed units.

☐ Manage the renovation of an office, floor, building, meeting room, warehouse, etc.

☐ Plan a new site for a building (plant, field office, headquarters, etc.).

☐ Plan for and start up something small (secretarial pool, athletic program, suggestion system, program, etc.).

☐ Launch a new product, service, or process.

☐ Be a change agent; create a symbol for change; lead the rallying cry; champion a significant change and implementation.

☐ Relaunch an existing product or service that's not doing well.

☐ Help shut down a plant, regional office, product line, business, operation, etc.

☐ Manage the assigning/allocating of office space in a contested situation.

☐ Work on a team looking at a reorganization plan where there will be more people than positions.

SECTION 5: LEARNING FROM FULL-TIME JOBS

THESE FULL-TIME JOBS OFFER THE OPPORTUNITY TO BUILD YOUR SKILL(S)

☐ **Chair of Projects/Task Forces**

The core demands for qualifying as a Project/Task Force assignment are: 1) Full-time assignment. 2) Important and specific goal. 3) Tight deadline. 4) Success or failure will be evident. 5) High-visibility sponsor. 6) Learning something on the fly. 7) Must get others to cooperate. 8) Usually six months or more. Four types of Projects/Task Forces: 1) New ideas, products, services, or systems (e.g., product/service/program research and development, creation/installation/launch of a new system, new programs like Total Quality Management, positive discipline). 2) Formal negotiations and relationships (e.g., acquisitions, divestitures, agreements, joint ventures; licensing arrangements, franchising; dealing with unions, governments, communities, charities, customers, and relocations). 3) Big one-time events (e.g., working on a major presentation for the board, organizing significant meetings or conferences, disaster/damage control teams; reorganizations, mergers, acquisitions, or relocations, working on visions, charters, strategies, other time-urgent issues and problems). 4) Troubleshooting (e.g., problems, disasters, crises, product/service failures, accidents, illegal activities, damage control in public relations goofs, shut downs, downsizings, layoffs, abrupt changes in leadership).

☐ **Fix-its/Turnarounds**

The core demands to qualify as a Fix-it or Turnaround assignment are: 1) Cleaning up a mess. 2) Serious people issues/problems like credibility/performance/morale. 3) Tight deadline. 4) Serious business performance failure. 5) Last chance to fix. Four Types of Fix-its/Turnarounds: 1) Fixing a failed business/unit involving taking control, stopping losses, managing damage, planning the turnaround, dealing with people problems, installing new processes and systems, and rebuilding the spirit and performance of the unit. 2) Managing sizable disasters like mishandled labor negotiations and strikes, thefts, history of significant business losses, poor staff, failed leadership, hidden problems, fraud, public relations nightmares, etc. 3) Significant reorganization and restructuring (e.g., stabilizing the business, reforming unit, introducing new systems, making people changes, resetting strategy and tactics). 4) Significant system/process breakdown (e.g., MIS, financial coordination processes, audits, standards, etc.) across units requiring working to change something from a distant position, providing advice and counsel, and installing or implementing a major process improvement or system change outside your own unit and/or with customers outside the organization.

☐ **Influencing Without Authority**

The core demands to qualify as an Influence Without Authority are: 1) Significant challenge (e.g, start-up, fix-it, scope and/or scale assign-

ment, strategic planning project, changes in management practices/systems). 2) Insufficient direct authority to make it happen. 3) Tight deadlines. 4) Visible to significant others. 5) Sensitive politics.

☐ **Scope Assignments**
The core demands for a Scope (complexity) assignment are: 1) Significant increase in both internal and external scope or complexity. 2) Significant increase in visibility and/or bottom line responsibility. 3) Unfamiliar area, business, technology, or territory. Examples of Scope assignments involving shifts: 1) Switching into a new function/technology/business. 2) Moving to new organization. 3) Moving to overseas assignment. 4) Moving to new location. 5) Adding new products/services. 6) Moving between headquarters/field. 7) Switches in ownership/top management of the unit/organization. Examples of Scope assignments involving "firsts": 1) First-time manager. 2) First-time managing managers. 3) First-time executive. 4) First-time overseas. 5) First-time headquarters/field. 6) First-time team leader. 7) First-time new technology/business/function. Scope assignments involving increased complexity: 1) Managing a significant expansion of an existing product or service. 2) Managing adding new products/service into an existing unit. 3) Managing a reorganized and more diverse unit. 4) Managing explosive growth. 5) Adding new technologies.

☐ **Start-ups**
The core demands to qualify as a start from scratch are: 1) Starting something new for you and/or for the organization. 2) Forging a new team. 3) Creating new systems/facilities/staffs/programs/procedures. 4) Contextual adversity (e.g., uncertainty, government regulation, unions, difficult environment). Seven types of start from scratches: 1) Planning, building, hiring, and managing (e.g., building a new facility, opening up a new location, moving a unit or company). 2) Heading something new (e.g., new product, new service, new line of business, new department/function, major new program). 3) Take over a group/product/service/program that had existed for less than a year and was off to a fast start. 4) Establishing overseas operations. 5) Major new designs for existing systems. 6) Moving a successful program from one unit to another. 7) Installing a new organization-wide process as a full-time job (e.g., like Total Quality).

SECTION 6: LEARNING MORE FROM YOUR PLAN

THESE ADDITIONAL REMEDIES WILL HELP MAKE THIS DEVELOPMENT PLAN MORE EFFECTIVE FOR YOU

Learning to Learn Better

☐ **Monitoring Yourself More Closely and Getting off Your Autopilot**
Past habits are a mixed blessing, sometimes helping, sometimes not. To avoid putting yourself on "autopilot," think afresh about each situation

before acting. Consistently monitor yourself with questions. Is this task different? Ask why you would repeat a past action. Are you avoiding anything, like taking a chance? Is there something new you might try?

- ☐ **Be Alert to Learnings When Faced With Transitions**
To avoid applying rigid habits, be alert to situations that require a transition to a new set of conditions and reactions; check what's similar and what's different; think out which past lessons and rules apply and which need to be changed. Don't apply old solutions because you have missed subtle differences.

- ☐ **Pre-sell an Idea to a Key Stakeholder**
Identify the key stakeholders – those who will be the most affected by your actions or the most resistant, or whose support you will most need. Collect the information each will find persuasive; marshal your arguments and try to pre-sell your conclusions, recommendations, and solutions.

- ☐ **Sell Something to a Tough Group/Audience**
Think of the person or group who will be the toughest to sell, the most critical, skeptical, or resistant, and sell that person or group first. Take time to understand the opposing viewpoints. Find common ground and leverage points; line up your best data and arguments and go for it.

Learning from Experience, Feedback and Other People

- ☐ **Learning from Bosses**
Bosses can be an excellent and ready source for learning. All bosses do some things exceptionally well and other things poorly. Distance your feelings from the boss/direct report relationship and study things that work and things that don't work for your boss. What would you have done? What could you use, and what should you avoid?

- ☐ **Learning from Interviewing Others**
Interview others. Ask not only what they do, but how and why they do it. What do they think are the rules of thumb they are following? Where did they learn the behaviors? How do they keep them current? How do they monitor the effect they have on others?

- ☐ **Learning from Observing Others**
Observe others. Find opportunities to observe without interacting with your model. This enables you to objectively study the person, note what he/she is doing or not doing, and compare that with what you would typically do in similar situations. Many times you can learn more by watching than asking. Your model may not be able to explain what he/she does or may be an unwilling teacher.

- ☐ **Getting Feedback from Peers/Colleagues**
Your peers and colleagues may not be candid if they are in competition with you. Some may not be willing to be open with you out of fear of giving you an advantage. Some may give you exaggerated feedback

to deliberately cause you undue concern. You have to set the tone and gauge the trust level of the relationship and the quality of the feedback.

☐ **Feedback in Unusual Contexts/Situations**
Temporary and extreme conditions and contexts may shade interpretations of your behavior and intentions. Demands of the job may drive you outside your normal mode of operating. Hence, feedback you receive may be inaccurate during those times. However, unusual contexts affect our behavior less than most assume. It's usually a weak excuse.

Learning from Courses

☐ **Orientation Events**
Most organizations offer a variety of orientation events. They are designed to communicate strategies, charters, missions, goals, and general information and offer an opportunity for people to meet each other. They are short in duration and offer limited opportunities for learning anything beyond general context and background.

SUGGESTED READINGS

Annison, Michael H. *Managing the Whirlwind.* Englewood, CO: Medical Group Management Association, 1993.

Ashkenas, Ron, Dave Ulrich, Todd Jick and Steve Kerr. *The Boundaryless Organization.* San Francisco: Jossey-Bass, Inc., 1995.

Belasco, James. *Teaching the Elephant to Dance – empowering change in your organization.* New York: Crown Publishers, 1990.

Belasco, James. *Teaching the Elephant to Dance – empowering change in your organization [sound recording].* Studio City, CA: Dove Books on Tape, 1990.

Drucker, Peter F. *Managing the Non-Profit Organization.* New York: HarperCollins, 1990.

Handy, Charles. *The Age of Unreason.* Boston: Harvard Business School Press, 1989.

Treacy, Michael and Fred Wiersema. *Discipline of Market Leaders.* Reading, MA: Addison-Wesley Publishing Co., 1995.

39

ORGANIZING

SECTION 1: YOUR DEVELOPMENT NEED(S)

UNSKILLED

- ☐ Doesn't pull resources together effectively
- ☐ May not know how to find and arrange people, materials, budget, etc.
- ☐ May be a poor delegator and planner and not very motivating to work with
- ☐ Performance decreases as the number of simultaneous activities increase
- ☐ May rely too much on self
- ☐ May scramble at the last minute and have to work long hours to finish
- ☐ May not anticipate or be able to see how multiple activities come together

SKILLED

- ☐ Can marshal resources (people, funding, material, support) to get things done
- ☐ Can orchestrate multiple activities at once to accomplish a goal
- ☐ Uses resources effectively and efficiently
- ☐ Arranges information and files in a useful manner

OVERUSED SKILL

- ☐ May not be tolerant of normal chaos
- ☐ May too often want to do things his/her own way
- ☐ May not be open to suggestions and input
- ☐ May lose his/her effectiveness when things don't go as planned

Select one to three of the competencies listed below to work on to compensate for an overuse of this skill.

COMPENSATORS: 2, 11, 12, 26, 32, 33, 36, 40, 46, 52, 60

SOME CAUSES

- ☐ Don't delegate
- ☐ Inexperienced
- ☐ Not motivating to work with
- ☐ Not resourceful
- ☐ Poor negotiator
- ☐ Poor planner
- ☐ Too self centered

THE MAP

It is easier to get things done when everybody is pulling in the same direction. It is easier to perform when you have all the tools and resources you need. It is easier to get things done when everyone you need in your corner is supportive and pulling for you. It's fun to be able to work through others even when you don't have direct authority over them. Unless you prefer things to be hard and not much fun, organizing is an essential skill to have.

SECTION 2: LEARNING ON YOUR OWN

THESE SELF-DEVELOPMENT REMEDIES WILL HELP YOU BUILD YOUR SKILL(S)

SOME REMEDIES

☐ **1. Set goals and measures.** Nothing keeps projects on time and on budget like a goal and a measure. Set goals for the whole project and the sub tasks. Set measures so you and others can track progress against the goals. *More help? – See #35 Managing and Measuring Work.*

☐ **2. Laying out the work.** Most resourcefulness starts out with a plan. What do I need to accomplish? What's the timeline? What resources will I need? Who controls the resources – people, funding, tools, materials, support – I need? What's my currency? How can I pay for or repay the resources I need? Who wins if I win? Who might lose? Lay out the work from A to Z. Many people are seen as disorganized because they don't write the sequence or parts of the work and leave something out. Ask others to comment on ordering and what's missing.

☐ **3. Bargaining for resources.** What do I have to trade? What can I buy? What can I borrow? What do I need to trade for? What do I need that I can't pay or trade for?

☐ **4. Rallying support.** Share your mission and goals with the people you need to support you. Try to get their input. People who are asked tend to cooperate more than people who are not asked. Figure out how the people who support your effort can win along with you.

☐ **5. Delegating.** Getting long, complex or multi-tracked projects done involves accomplishing a series of tasks that lead up to the whole. One clear finding in the research is that empowered people work longer and harder. People like to have control over their work, determine how they are going to do it, and have the authority to make decisions. Give away as much as possible along with the authority that goes with it. Another clear finding is to pay attention to the weakest links – usually groups or elements you have the least interface with or control over – perhaps someone in a remote location, a consultant or supplier. Stay doubly in touch with the potential weak links.

☐ **6. Managing multiple tracks.** Many attempts to get complex things done involve managing parallel tracks or multiple tasks at the same time. It helps if you have a master plan. It helps if you delegate some of the work. *More help? – See #47 Planning.*

☐ **7. Manage efficiently.** Watch the budget. Plan spending carefully. Have a reserve if the unanticipated comes up. Set up a funding timeline so you can track ongoing expenditures.

☐ **8. Manage coolly.** Some get flustered when a lot of things are up in the air at the same time. A plan helps. Delegation helps. Goals and measures help. Getting frustrated seldom helps. *More help? – See #11 Composure.*

☐ **9. Celebrating.** Get in the habit of sharing the successes and spreading the wealth. It will make it easier for you to go back to the well the next time you need resources.

☐ **10. Find someone in your environment** who is good at organizing people and things. Watch what he/she does. How does that compare to what you typically do?

SECTION 3: LEARNING FROM MORE FEEDBACK

THESE SOURCES WOULD GIVE YOU THE MOST ACCURATE AND DETAILED FEEDBACK ON YOUR SKILL(S)

☐ **Direct Boss**

Your direct boss has important information about you, your performance, and your prospects. The challenge is to get this information. There are formal processes (e.g., performance appraisals). There are day-to-day opportunities. To help, signal your boss that you want and can handle direct and timely feedback. Many bosses have trouble giving feedback, so you will have to work at it over a period of time.

☐ **Direct Reports**

Across a variety of settings, your direct reports probably see you the most. They are the recipients of most of your managerial behaviors. They know your work. They can compare you with former bosses. Since they may hesitate to give you negative feedback, you have to set the atmosphere to make it easier for them. You have to ask.

☐ **Internal and External Customers**

Customers interact with you as a person and as a supplier or vendor of products and services. You're important to them because you can either help address and solve their problems or stand in their way. As customer service and Total Quality programs gain importance, clients and customers become a more prominent source of feedback.

SECTION 4: LEARNING FROM DEVELOP-IN-PLACE ASSIGNMENTS

THESE PART-TIME DEVELOP-IN-PLACE ASSIGNMENTS WILL HELP YOU BUILD YOUR SKILL(S)

- ☐ Integrate diverse systems, processes, or procedures across decentralized and/or dispersed units.
- ☐ Manage the renovation of an office, floor, building, meeting room, warehouse, etc.
- ☐ Plan a new site for a building (plant, field office, headquarters, etc.).
- ☐ Plan an off-site meeting, conference, convention, trade show, event, etc.
- ☐ Manage the visit of a VIP (member of top management, government official, outside customer, foreign visitor, etc.).
- ☐ Manage an ad hoc, temporary group of "green," inexperienced people as their coach, teacher, orienter, etc.
- ☐ Manage an ad hoc, temporary group of low-competence people through a task they couldn't do by themselves.
- ☐ Help shut down a plant, regional office, product line, business, operation, etc.
- ☐ Manage liquidation/sale of products, equipment, materials, a business, furniture, overstock, etc.
- ☐ Work on a team that's deciding who to keep and who to let go in a layoff, shutdown, delayering, or divestiture.

SECTION 5: LEARNING FROM FULL-TIME JOBS

THESE FULL-TIME JOBS OFFER THE OPPORTUNITY TO BUILD YOUR SKILL(S)

- ☐ **Scale Assignments**
  Core requirements to qualify as a Scale (size) shift assignment are: 1) Sizable jump-shift in the size of the job in areas like: number of people, number of layers in organization, size of budget, number of locations, volume of activity, tightness of deadlines. 2) Medium to low complexity; mostly repetitive and routine processes and procedures. 3) Stable staff and business. 4) Stable operations. 5) Often slow, steady growth.
- ☐ **Scope Assignments**
  The core demands for a Scope (complexity) assignment are: 1) Significant increase in both internal and external scope or complexity. 2) Significant increase in visibility and/or bottom line responsibility. 3) Unfamiliar area, business, technology, or territory. Examples of Scope assignments involving shifts: 1) Switching into a new function/technology/business. 2) Moving to new organization. 3) Moving to overseas assignment. 4) Moving to new location. 5) Adding new products/services. 6) Moving between headquarters/field. 7) Switches in owner-

ship/top management of the unit/organization. Examples of Scope assignments involving "firsts": 1) First-time manager. 2) First-time managing managers. 3) First-time executive. 4) First-time overseas. 5) First-time headquarters/field. 6) First-time team leader. 7) First-time new technology/business/function. Scope assignments involving increased complexity: 1) Managing a significant expansion of an existing product or service. 2) Managing adding new products/service into an existing unit. 3) Managing a reorganized and more diverse unit. 4) Managing explosive growth. 5) Adding new technologies.

☐ **Start-ups**
The core demands to qualify as a start from scratch are: 1) Starting something new for you and/or for the organization. 2) Forging a new team. 3) Creating new systems/facilities/staffs/programs/procedures. 4) Contextual adversity (e.g., uncertainty, government regulation, unions, difficult environment). Seven types of start from scratches: 1) Planning, building, hiring, and managing (e.g., building a new facility, opening up a new location, moving a unit or company). 2) Heading something new (e.g., new product, new service, new line of business, new department/function, major new program). 3) Take over a group/product/service/program that had existed for less than a year and was off to a fast start. 4) Establishing overseas operations. 5) Major new designs for existing systems. 6) Moving a successful program from one unit to another. 7) Installing a new organization-wide process as a full-time job (e.g., like Total Quality).

SECTION 6: LEARNING MORE FROM YOUR PLAN

THESE ADDITIONAL REMEDIES WILL HELP MAKE THIS DEVELOPMENT PLAN MORE EFFECTIVE FOR YOU

Learning to Learn Better

☐ **Study People Who Have Successfully Done What You Need to Do**
Interview people who have already done what you're planning to do and check your plan against what they did. Try to summarize their key tactics, strategies, and insights; adjust your plan accordingly.

Learning from Experience, Feedback and Other People

☐ **Learning from Bosses**
Bosses can be an excellent and ready source for learning. All bosses do some things exceptionally well and other things poorly. Distance your feelings from the boss/direct report relationship and study things that work and things that don't work for your boss. What would you have done? What could you use, and what should you avoid?

☐ **Learning from Observing Others**
Observe others. Find opportunities to observe without interacting with your model. This enables you to objectively study the person, note

what he/she is doing or not doing, and compare that with what you would typically do in similar situations. Many times you can learn more by watching than asking. Your model may not be able to explain what he/she does or may be an unwilling teacher.

- [ ] **Getting Feedback from Bosses and Superiors**
Many bosses are reluctant to give negative feedback. They lack the managerial courage to face people directly with criticism. You can help by soliciting feedback and setting the tone. Show them you can handle criticism and that you are willing to work on issues they see as important.

- [ ] **Getting Feedback from Direct Reports**
Direct reports often fear reprisals for giving negative feedback about bosses, whether in a formal process, like a questionnaire, or informally and face-to-face. Even with a guarantee of confidentiality, some are still hesitant. If you want feedback from direct reports, you have to set a positive tone and never act out of revenge.

- [ ] **Getting Feedback from Peers/Colleagues**
Your peers and colleagues may not be candid if they are in competition with you. Some may not be willing to be open with you out of fear of giving you an advantage. Some may give you exaggerated feedback to deliberately cause you undue concern. You have to set the tone and gauge the trust level of the relationship and the quality of the feedback.

Learning from Courses

- [ ] **Supervisory Courses**
Most new supervisors go through an "Introduction to Supervision" type course. They are designed to teach the common practices a first-line supervisor needs to know to be effective. The content of most of those courses is standard. There is general agreement on the principles of effective supervision. There are two common problems: 1) Do the students have a strong motivation to learn? Do they know what they don't know? Is there any pain? Because motivated students with a need for the knowledge learn best, participants should have had some trying experiences and some supervisory pain and hardships before attending. 2) Are the instructors experienced supervisors? Have they practiced what they preach? Can they share powerful anecdotes to make key points? Can they answer questions credibly? If possible, select supervisory courses based on the instructors, since the content seems to be the much same for all such courses. Lastly, does the course offer the opportunity for practicing each skill? Does it contain simulations? Are there case studies you could easily identify with? Are there breakout groups? Is there opportunity for action learning? Search for the most interactive course.

SUGGESTED READINGS

Henry, Lauchland A. *The Professional's Guide to Working Smarter.* Tenafly, NJ: Burrill-Ellsworth Associates, 1993.

Koch, Richard. *The 80/20 principle: the secret of achieving more with less.* New York: Currency/Doubleday, 1998.

Moskowitz, Robert. *How to organize your work and your life.* New York: Doubleday, 1993.

Pagonis, Lt. Gen. William G. with Jeffrey L. Cruikshank. *Moving Mountains.* Boston: Harvard Business School Press, 1992.

Winston, Stephanie. *The Organized Executive.* New York: Warner Books, 1985.

Winston, Stephanie. *The Organized Executive [sound recording].* New York: Simon & Schuster Sound Ideas, 1987.

40

DEALING WITH PARADOX

SECTION 1: YOUR DEVELOPMENT NEED(S)

UNSKILLED

- ☐ Not very flexible
- ☐ Can't shift gears readily
- ☐ One-trick pony (although may be very good at that one trick)
- ☐ Believes strongly in personal consistency and following a few principles
- ☐ Tries to get everything done one way
- ☐ Doesn't take a balanced approach
- ☐ May be seen as rigidly following and overdoing his/her one best way
- ☐ May rely too much on personal strengths
- ☐ Has trouble shifting modes of behavior in the same meeting or situation

SKILLED

- ☐ Can act in ways that seem contradictory
- ☐ Is very flexible and adaptable when facing tough calls
- ☐ Can combine seeming opposites like being compassionately tough, stand up for self without trampling others, set strong but flexible standards
- ☐ Can act differently depending upon the situation
- ☐ Is seen as balanced despite the conflicting demands of the situation

OVERUSED SKILL

- ☐ May be seen as two-faced or wishy-washy
- ☐ May change too easily from one style or mode to another
- ☐ May misread what skills are called for
- ☐ May confuse people who observe him/her across different settings
- ☐ May be misinterpreted

Select one to three of the competencies listed below to work on to compensate for an overuse of this skill.

COMPENSATORS: 5, 9, 12, 17, 29, 30, 34, 37, 38, 47, 50, 51, 52, 53, 58

SOME CAUSES

- ☐ Abdicate or freeze when situations change quickly
- ☐ Don't read people
- ☐ Don't read situations
- ☐ Not very flexible
- ☐ One "me" fits all
- ☐ Rigid about values and beliefs
- ☐ Run over others
- ☐ Too much of a good thing

THE MAP

Dealing with paradox involves attitudinal and behavioral flexibility – going from a planning discussion to customer complaints to administrative snafus and shifting gears accordingly. People who excel at this are versatile in situations and with others – they can lead and let others lead, know how to apply "tough love," or remain adaptable in the face of crises. They are able to think and act in seemingly contrary ways at the same time or when moving from one task to another. They are flexible and meet the needs of the moment. This requires having some flexibility in approach, tone and style, and then matching those to the demands of the situation.

SECTION 2: LEARNING ON YOUR OWN

THESE SELF-DEVELOPMENT REMEDIES WILL HELP YOU BUILD YOUR SKILL(S)

SOME REMEDIES

☐ **1. Gear shifting and making transitions.** As the song says, "I want to be me." Not many of us have that luxury. Each situation we deal with is a little bit, somewhat, or a lot different. In order to be truly effective across situations and people, we are called upon to act differently. In control at 9, following at 10, quiet at 11 and dominating at noon. It's all in a day's work. Respectful with the boss, critiquing with peers, caring for directs, and responding to customers. No trickery. No blowing with the wind. No Machiavellianism. Just adjusting flexibly to the demands of each situation. Work on first reading the situation and the people. Monitor your gear shifting behavior for a week at work and at home. What switches give you the most trouble? The least? Why? Off work, practice gear shifting transitions. Go from a civic meeting to a water fight with your kids, for example. On the way between activities, if only for a few seconds, think about the transition you're making and the frame of mind needed to make it work well.

☐ **2. Contradictory behaviors.** Tough love is the best example. Deliver a tough message on layoffs but do it in a compassionate way. Dig into the details while trying to establish three basic conceptual drivers in the data. Take strong stands but listen and leave room for others to maneuver. Have a strong personal belief about an issue but loyally implement an organization plan which opposes your view. Being playful but firm. Being loose with parts of the budget but unyielding in others. Many situations in today's complex world call for mixed responses and behaviors. Doing two opposing things at once isn't comfortable for everyone. Many pride themselves on being just one person, believing and following one set of beliefs. Acting paradoxically doesn't really violate that. It just means within your normal range of behaviors and style, you use two of your extremes – as quiet as you can be in the first half of the meeting and as loud as you ever are in the last half – at once.

☐ **3. Overused skills.** A lot of us overdo some of our strengths. We push for results too hard. We analyze data too long. We try to be too nice. For those overdone behaviors, it's difficult for us to do the opposite. Find out what you overdo by getting feedback, either a 360° feedback instrument or by polling your closest associates. Find out how adaptable people think you are under pressure and how well you handle the fragmentation of a typical day. Try to balance your behavior against whatever you overdo. Don't replace what you do – add to it:

- If you get brusque under pressure, take three deep breaths and consciously slow down or use some humor.
- If you get frustrated easily, learn some pause strategies such as visualizing yourself in a more calming setting, asking a question, or asking yourself, "How should I act this instant?"
- If you're too tough, ask yourself how you'd like to be treated in this situation. Stop and ask how the other person is doing or responding.
- If you overmanage, work on setting standards, outcomes and delegating; let your team set the process.
- If you freeze under too much fragmentation, pause, walk around the building and ask yourself how you'd like to behave right now and what is most important. Then come back and start doing the task a piece at a time.
- If you get rigid, set a goal of understanding other people's views well enough that you can present them back to them without inaccuracy.
- If you habitually go into an action frenzy or grind to a halt, ask yourself what would be more effective right now.
- If you run over others, tell them what you're thinking about doing and ask them what they think should be done.

☐ **4. Walking someone else's talk.** A common paradox is having to support someone else's program or idea when you don't really think that way or agree with it. You have to be a member of the loyal opposition. Most of the time, you may be delivering someone else's view of the future. Top management and a consultant created the mission, vision and strategy off somewhere in the woods. You may or may not have been asked for any input. You may even have some doubts about it yourself. Do not offer conditional statements to your audience. Don't let it be known to others that you are not fully on board. Your role is to manage this vision and mission, not your personal one. *More help? – See #22 Ethics and Values.* If you have strong contrary views, be sure to demand a voice next time around.

- [ ] **5. Transitions.** Which transitions are the toughest for you? Write down the five toughest for you. What do you have a hard time switching to and from? Use this knowledge to assist you in making a list of discontinuities (tough transitions) you face such as:

  - Confronting people vs. Being approachable and accepting
  - Leading vs. Following
  - Going from firing someone to a business as usual staff meeting.

  Write down how each of these discontinuities makes you feel and what you may do that gets you in trouble. For example, you may not shift gears well after a confrontation or you may have trouble taking charge again after passively sitting in a meeting all day. Create a plan to attack each of the tough transitions.

- [ ] **6. Go for more variety at work.** Take a risk, then play it safe. Set tasks for yourself that force you to shift gears such as being a spokesperson for your organization when tough questions are expected, making peace with an enemy or managing people who are novices at a task. If you already have these tasks as part of your job, use them to observe yourself and try new behaviors.

- [ ] **7. Models.** Interview people who are good at shifting gears, such as fix-it managers (tear down and build back up), shutdown managers (fire people yet support them and help them find other employment; motivating those who stay), or excellent parents. Talk to an actor or actress to see how he/she can play opposing roles back to back. Talk to people who have recently joined your organization from places quite different than yours. Talk to a therapist who hears a different problem or trauma every hour. See if you can figure out some rules for making comfortable transitions.

- [ ] **8. Be a novice.** Volunteer to teach others something you don't know well the next time a new procedure, policy or technology appears. This will force you to shift from experienced expert to novice.

- [ ] **9. Control your instant responses to shifts.** Many of us respond to the fragmentation and discontinuities of work as if they were threats instead of the way life is. Sometimes our emotions and fears are triggered by switching from active to passive or soft to tough. This initial anxious response lasts 45–60 seconds and we need to buy some time before we say or do something inappropriate. Research shows that generally somewhere between the second and third thing you think to say or do is the best option. Practice holding back your first response long enough to think of a second and a third. Manage your shifts, don't be a prisoner of them. *More help? – See #11 Composure.*

- [ ] **10. Use mental rehearsal** to think about different ways you could carry out a transaction. Try to see yourself acting in opposing ways to get the same thing done – when to be tough, when to let them decide, when to deflect the issue because it's not ready to decide. What cues would you look for to select an approach that matches? Practice trying to get the same thing done with two different groups with two different approaches. Did they both work?

SECTION 3: LEARNING FROM MORE FEEDBACK

THESE SOURCES WOULD GIVE YOU THE MOST ACCURATE AND DETAILED FEEDBACK ON YOUR SKILL(S)

- ☐ **Development Professionals**
  Sometimes it might be valuable to get some analysis and feedback from a professional trained and certified in the area you're working on: possibly a career counselor, a therapist, clergy, a psychologist, etc.
- ☐ **Direct Reports**
  Across a variety of settings, your direct reports probably see you the most. They are the recipients of most of your managerial behaviors. They know your work. They can compare you with former bosses. Since they may hesitate to give you negative feedback, you have to set the atmosphere to make it easier for them. You have to ask.
- ☐ **Natural Mentors**
  Natural mentors have a special relationship with you and are interested in your success and your future. Since they are usually not in your direct chain of command, you can have more open, relaxed, and fruitful discussions about yourself and your career prospects. They can be a very important source for candid or critical feedback others may not give you.
- ☐ **Past Associates/Constituencies**
  When confronted with a present performance problem, some claim, "I wasn't like that before; it must be the current situation." When feedback is available from former associates, about 50% support that claim. In the other half of the cases, the people were like that before and probably didn't know it. It sometimes makes sense to access the past to clearly see the present.

SECTION 4: LEARNING FROM DEVELOP-IN-PLACE ASSIGNMENTS

THESE PART-TIME DEVELOP-IN-PLACE ASSIGNMENTS WILL HELP YOU BUILD YOUR SKILL(S)

- ☐ Make speeches/be a spokesperson for the organization on the outside.
- ☐ Manage an ad hoc, temporary group of balky and resisting people through an unpopular change or project.
- ☐ Manage an ad hoc, temporary group of people where the people in the group are towering experts but the temporary manager is not.
- ☐ Manage an ad hoc, temporary group of people in a rapidly expanding operation.

- ☐ Assemble an ad hoc team of diverse people to accomplish a difficult task.
- ☐ Take on a task you dislike or hate to do.
- ☐ Make peace with an enemy or someone you've disappointed with a product or service or someone you've had some trouble with or don't get along well with.
- ☐ Build a multifunctional project team to tackle a common business issue or problem.
- ☐ Audit cost overruns to assess the problem and present your findings to the person or people involved.
- ☐ Work on a team looking at a reorganization plan where there will be more people than positions.

SECTION 5: LEARNING FROM FULL-TIME JOBS

THESE FULL-TIME JOBS OFFER THE OPPORTUNITY TO BUILD YOUR SKILL(S)

☐ **Fix-its/Turnarounds**

The core demands to qualify as a Fix-it or Turnaround assignment are: 1) Cleaning up a mess. 2) Serious people issues/problems like credibility/performance/morale. 3) Tight deadline. 4) Serious business performance failure. 5) Last chance to fix. Four Types of Fix-its/ Turnarounds: 1) Fixing a failed business/unit involving taking control, stopping losses, managing damage, planning the turnaround, dealing with people problems, installing new processes and systems, and rebuilding the spirit and performance of the unit. 2) Managing sizable disasters like mishandled labor negotiations and strikes, thefts, history of significant business losses, poor staff, failed leadership, hidden problems, fraud, public relations nightmares, etc. 3) Significant reorganization and restructuring (e.g., stabilizing the business, reforming unit, introducing new systems, making people changes, resetting strategy and tactics). 4) Significant system/process breakdown (e.g., MIS, financial coordination processes, audits, standards, etc.) across units requiring working to change something from a distant position, providing advice and counsel, and installing or implementing a major process improvement or system change outside your own unit and/or with customers outside the organization.

☐ **Influencing Without Authority**

The core demands to qualify as an Influence Without Authority are: 1) Significant challenge (e.g, start-up, fix-it, scope and/or scale assignment, strategic planning project, changes in management practices/ systems). 2) Insufficient direct authority to make it happen. 3) Tight deadlines. 4) Visible to significant others. 5) Sensitive politics.

- ☐ **Line To Staff Switches**
  The core demands to qualify as a Line to Staff switch are: 1) Intellectually/strategically demanding. 2) Highly visible to others. 3) New area/perspective/method/culture/function. 4) Moving away from a bottom line. 5) Moving from field to headquarters. 6) Exposure to high-level executives. Examples: 1) Business/strategic planning. 2) Heading a staff department. 3) Assistant to/chief of staff to a senior executive. 4) Head of a task force. 5) Human resources role.

- ☐ **Off-Shore Assignments**
  The core demands to qualify as an Off-Shore assignment are: 1) First time working in the country. 2) Significant challenges like new language, hardship location, unique business rules/practices, significant cultural/marketplace differences, different functional task, etc. 3) More than a year assignment. 4) No automatic return deal. 5) Not necessarily a change in job challenge, technical content, or responsibilities.

SECTION 6: LEARNING MORE FROM YOUR PLAN

THESE ADDITIONAL REMEDIES WILL HELP MAKE THIS DEVELOPMENT PLAN MORE EFFECTIVE FOR YOU

Learning to Learn Better

- ☐ **Teach Others Something You Don't Know Well**
  Commit to a project like teaching something you don't know much about to force you to learn quickly to accomplish the task; pick something new, different, or unfamiliar.

- ☐ **Try Some New Things Out of Your Normal Comfort Zone**
  Periodically, practice going against your grain (what's normal for you) and getting out of your comfort zone. Try something different and opposite to your nature; take a learning risk. Explore: if you're a thinker, act; if you're an action person, think. Test the unfamiliar; try the new; go beyond your self-determined limits and boundaries.

- ☐ **Analyze How You Perform Under Several Roles**
  Do an analysis of yourself as a contributor, boss, manager, professional, parent, spouse, and/or friend. Create a list of criteria for each role and evaluate yourself against it. Pick a few things to work on for each role to improve.

- ☐ **Study Something Unusual or Unexpected**
  Consider the odd and unusual facts or opinions that don't seem to fit in anywhere. If these anomalies comprised the majority opinion, where would that lead? What beliefs or facts would you have to have to state those unusual opinions?

Learning from Experience, Feedback and Other People

☐ **Learning from Mentors and Tutors**
Mentors and tutors offer a special case for learning since the relationship is specifically formed for learning. You need to be open and nondefensive. You need to solicit and accept feedback. This is a unique opportunity for you to get low-risk, honest, and direct feedback on what you do well and not so well.

☐ **Learning from Limited Staff**
Most managers either inherit or hire staff from time to time who are inexperienced, incompetent, not up to the task, resistant, or dispirited. Any of these may create a hardship for you. The lessons to be learned are how to get things done with limited resources and how to fix the people situation. In the short term, this hardship is best addressed by assessing the combined strengths of the team and deploying the best you have against the problem. Almost everyone can do something well. Also, the team can contribute more than the combined individuals can. How can you empower and motivate the team? If you hired the troublesome staff, why did you err? What can you learn from your hiring mistakes? What wasn't there that you thought was present? What led you astray? How can you prevent that same hiring error in the future? What do you need to do to fix the situation? Quick development? Start over? If you inherited the problem, how can you fix it? Can you implement a program of accelerated development? Do you have to start over and get new people? What did the prior manager do or not do that led to this situation in the first place? What can you learn from that? What will you do differently? How does the staff feel? What can you learn from their frustrations over not being able to do the job? How can you be a positive force under negative circumstances? How can you rally them to perform? What lasting lessons can you learn from someone in distress and trouble? If you're going to try accelerated development, how can you get a quick assessment? How can you give the staff motivating feedback? How can you construct and implement development plans that will work? How can you get people on-line feedback for maximum growth? Do you know when to stop trying and start over? If you're going to turn over some staff, how can you do it both rapidly and with the least damage? How can you deliver the message in a constructive way? What can you learn from having to take negative actions against people? How can you prevent this from happening again?

☐ **Learning from Bad Situations**
All of us will find ourselves in bad situations from time to time. Good intentions gone bad. Impossible tasks and goals. Hopeless projects. Even though you probably can't perform well, the key is to at least take away some lessons and insights. How did things get to be this way? What factors led to the impasse? How can you make the best of a bad

situation? How can you neutralize the negative elements? How can you get the most out of yourself and your staff under the chilling situation? What can you salvage? How can you use coping strategies to minimize the negatives? How can you avoid these situations going forward? In bad situations: 1) Be resourceful. Get the most you can out of the situation. 2) Try to deduce why things got to be that way. 3) Learn from both the situation you inherited and how you react to it. 4) Integrate what you learn into your future behavior.

Learning from Courses

☐ **Strategic Courses**
There are a number of courses designed to stretch minds to prepare for future challenges. They include topics such as Workforce Diversity 2000, globalization, the European Union, competitive competencies and strategies, etc. Quality depends upon the following three factors: 1) The quality of the staff. Are they qualified? Are they respected in their fields? Are they strategic "gurus"? 2) The quality of the participants. Are they the kind of people you could learn from? 3) The quality of the setting. Is it comfortable and free from distractions? Can you learn there?

☐ **Attitude Toward Learning**
In addition to selecting the right course, a learning attitude is required. Be open. Close down your "like/dislike" switch, your "agree/disagree" blinders, and your "like me/not like me" feelings toward the instructors. Learning requires new lessons, change, and new behaviors and perspectives – all scary stuff for most people. Don't resist. Take in all you can during the course. Ask clarifying questions. Discuss concerns with the other participants. Jot down what you learn as you go. After the course is over, take some reflective time to glean the meat. Make the practical decisions about what you can and cannot use.

SUGGESTED READINGS

Handy, Charles. *The Age of Paradox.* Boston: Harvard Business School Press, 1994.

Horton, Thomas R. *The CEO Paradox – The privilege and accountability of leadership.* New York: AMACOM, 1992.

Peters, Tom. *Liberation Management.* New York: Knopf, 1992.

Peters, Tom. *Liberation Management [sound recording].* New York, NY: Random House Audio, 1992.

Sebba, Anne. *Mother Teresa, 1910–1997, Beyond the Image.* New York: Doubleday, 1997.

Smith, Kenwyn K. and David N. Berg. *Paradoxes of Group Life.* San Francisco: Jossey-Bass, Inc., 1987.

PATIENCE

SECTION 1: YOUR DEVELOPMENT NEED(S)

UNSKILLED

- ☐ Acts before it's time to act
- ☐ Intolerant of the slow pace and cumbersome processes of others
- ☐ May be seen as a self-centered do it my way and at my speed type
- ☐ Doesn't take the time to listen or understand
- ☐ Thinks almost everything needs to be faster and shorter
- ☐ Disrupts those facilitating meetings with his/her need to finish sooner
- ☐ Frequently interrupts and finishes other people's sentences
- ☐ Makes his/her own process rules; doesn't wait for others
- ☐ May appear to others as arrogant, uninterested or a know it all
- ☐ May be action oriented and resist process and problem complexity
- ☐ May just jump to conclusions rather than thinking things through

SKILLED

- ☐ Is tolerant with people and processes
- ☐ Listens and checks before acting
- ☐ Tries to understand the people and the data before making judgments and acting
- ☐ Waits for others to catch up before acting
- ☐ Sensitive to due process and proper pacing
- ☐ Follows established process

OVERUSED SKILL

- ☐ May wait too long to act
- ☐ May try to please everyone
- ☐ Others may confuse attentive listening with acceptance of their position
- ☐ May waste time when faced with issues too close to a 50-50 proposition
- ☐ May let things fester without acting

Select one to three of the competencies listed below to work on to compensate for an overuse of this skill.

COMPENSATORS: 1, 2, 9, 12, 13, 16, 34, 40, 53, 57

SOME CAUSES

- ☐ Unrealistic standards
- ☐ Don't understand others well
- ☐ Action junkie
- ☐ Very intelligent
- ☐ Lack of composure
- ☐ Poor listener

- ☐ Poor tactical manager/disorganized
- ☐ Arrogant

THE MAP

Many people pride themselves on impatience, thinking of it as high standards and a results orientation. This would be true sometimes, especially when the results just aren't there or standards are slack. In many situations though, impatience is a cover for other problems and has serious long-term consequences. It leads to overmanaging, not developing others, stacking the unit with your solutions, monitoring too much, and people shying away from you because you lack tolerance.

SECTION 2: LEARNING ON YOUR OWN

THESE SELF-DEVELOPMENT REMEDIES WILL HELP YOU BUILD YOUR SKILL(S)

SOME REMEDIES

☐ **1. The simple courtesies.** Impatient people interrupt, finish other people's sentences when they hesitate, ask people to hurry, ask people to skip the next few transparencies and get to the last slide, urge people to finish and get to the point. All these behaviors of the impatient person intimidate, irritate, demotivate and frustrate others and lead to incomplete communications, damaged relationships, a feeling of injustice and leave others demeaned in the process. All for the sake of gaining a few minutes of your valuable time. Add five seconds a month to your average response/interrupt tolerance time until you stop doing these things most of the time. Learn to pause to give people a second chance. People often stumble on words with impatient people, hurrying to get through before their first or next interruption.

☐ **2. Non-verbals.** Impatient people signal their impatience through speech and actions, of course, but they also signal non-verbally. The washboard brow, body shifting, finger and pencil drumming, and glares. What do you do? Ask others you trust for your five most frequent impatience signals. Work to eliminate them.

☐ **3. Delay of gratification.** Impatient people want it now. They are not good waiters. Sometimes impatience flowers into loss of composure. When things don't go as fast as they want, it triggers an emotional response. *More help? – See #11 Composure and #107* Lack of *Composure.*

☐ **4. Impatience triggers.** Some people probably bring out your impatience more than others. Who are they? What is it about them that makes you more impatient? Pace? Language? Thought process? Accent? These people may include people you don't like, who ramble, who whine and complain, or who are repetitive advocates for things you have already rejected. Mentally rehearse some calming tactics before meeting with people who trigger your impatience. Work on understanding their positions without judging them – you can always judge later. In all cases, focus them on the issues or problems to be discussed, return them to the point, interrupt to summarize and state your position. Try to gently train them to be more efficient with you next time without damaging them in the process.

☐ **5. Arrogance is a major blockage to patience.** People who have a towering strength or lots of success get less feedback and keep rolling along and over others until their careers get in trouble. If you are arrogant – you devalue the contributions of others – you should work doubly hard at reading and listening to others. You don't have to accept everything, just listen to understand before you react. You need to submerge your "what I want/think" demeanor and keep asking yourself, "What are they saying; how are they reacting?"

☐ **6. Work on your openness and approachability.** Impatient people don't get as much information as patient listeners do. They are more often surprised by events when others knew they were coming. People are hesitant to talk to impatient people. It's too painful. People don't pass on hunches, unbaked thoughts, maybes, and possibles to impatient people. You will be out of the information loop and miss important information you need to know to be effective. Suspend judgment on informal communications. Just take it in. Acknowledge that you understand. Ask a question or two. Follow up later.

☐ **7. Rein in your horse.** Impatient people provide answers, conclusions, and solutions too early in the process. Others haven't even understood the problem yet. Providing solutions too quickly will make your people dependent and irritated. If you don't teach them how you think and how you can come up with solutions so fast, they will never learn. Take the time to really define the problem – not impatiently throw out a solution. Brainstorm what questions need to be answered in order to resolve it. Give your people the task to think about for a day and come back with some solutions. Be a teacher instead of a dictator of solutions.

☐ **8. Task impatience.** Impatient people check in a lot. How's it coming. Is it done yet? When will it be finished? Let me see what you've done so far. That is disruptive to due process and wastes time. When you give out a task or assign a project, establish agreed upon time checkpoints. You can also assign percentage checkpoints. Check in with me when you are about 25% finished so we can make midcourse corrections and 75% so we can make final corrections. Let them figure out how to do the task. Hold back from checking in at other than the agreed upon times and percentages. *More help? – See #18 Delegation.*

☐ **9. Too dependent upon yourself.** Look at others' solutions more. Invite discussion and disagreement, welcome bad news, ask that people come up with the second and third solution. A useful trick is to assign issues and questions before you have given them any thought. Two weeks before you are due to decide, ask your people to examine that issue and report to you two days before you have to deal with it. That way, you really don't have any solutions yet. This really motivates people and makes you look less impatient.

☐ **10. Read #*19 Developing Direct Reports*** to find out how people actually develop. Your impatience makes it less likely you will develop any deep skills in others since development doesn't operate on brief timeframes and close monitoring. As you'll see, challenging tasks, feedback along the way, and encouraging learning are the keys. Impatient people seldom develop others.

SECTION 3: LEARNING FROM MORE FEEDBACK

THESE SOURCES WOULD GIVE YOU THE MOST ACCURATE AND DETAILED FEEDBACK ON YOUR SKILL(S)

☐ **Development Professionals**
Sometimes it might be valuable to get some analysis and feedback from a professional trained and certified in the area you're working on: possibly a career counselor, a therapist, clergy, a psychologist, etc.

☐ **Direct Reports**
Across a variety of settings, your direct reports probably see you the most. They are the recipients of most of your managerial behaviors. They know your work. They can compare you with former bosses. Since they may hesitate to give you negative feedback, you have to set the atmosphere to make it easier for them. You have to ask.

☐ **Family Members**
On some issues, like interpersonal style or compassion, it might be helpful to ask various and multiple family members for feedback to add confirmation or context to feedback you've received in the workplace.

SECTION 4: LEARNING FROM DEVELOP-IN-PLACE ASSIGNMENTS

THESE PART-TIME DEVELOP-IN-PLACE ASSIGNMENTS WILL HELP YOU BUILD YOUR SKILL(S)

☐ Integrate diverse systems, processes, or procedures across decentralized and/or dispersed units.

☐ Teach a child a new skill (e.g., reading, running a computer, a sport).

☐ Create employee involvement teams.

☐ Manage an ad hoc, temporary group of "green," inexperienced people as their coach, teacher, orienter, etc.

☐ Manage an ad hoc, temporary group of balky and resisting people through an unpopular change or project.

- ☐ Manage a dissatisfied internal or external customer; troubleshoot a performance or quality problem with a product or service.
- ☐ Take on a task you dislike or hate to do.
- ☐ Resolve an issue in conflict between two people, units, geographies, functions, etc.
- ☐ Make peace with an enemy or someone you've disappointed with a product or service or someone you've had some trouble with or don't get along well with.
- ☐ Be a member of a union-negotiating or grievance-handling team.

SECTION 5: LEARNING FROM FULL-TIME JOBS

THESE FULL-TIME JOBS OFFER THE OPPORTUNITY TO BUILD YOUR SKILL(S)

☐ **Influencing Without Authority**
The core demands to qualify as an Influence Without Authority are: 1) Significant challenge (e.g, start-up, fix-it, scope and/or scale assignment, strategic planning project, changes in management practices/ systems). 2) Insufficient direct authority to make it happen. 3) Tight deadlines. 4) Visible to significant others. 5) Sensitive politics.

☐ **Off-Shore Assignments**
The core demands to qualify as an Off-Shore assignment are: 1) First time working in the country. 2) Significant challenges like new language, hardship location, unique business rules/practices, significant cultural/marketplace differences, different functional task, etc. 3) More than a year assignment. 4) No automatic return deal. 5) Not necessarily a change in job challenge, technical content, or responsibilities.

SECTION 6: LEARNING MORE FROM YOUR PLAN

THESE ADDITIONAL REMEDIES WILL HELP MAKE THIS DEVELOPMENT PLAN MORE EFFECTIVE FOR YOU

Learning to Learn Better

☐ **Rehearse Successful Tactics/Strategies/Actions**
Mentally rehearse how you will act before going into the situation. Try to anticipate how others will react, what they will say, and how you'll respond. Check out the best and worst cases; play out both scenes. Check your feelings in conflict or worst-case situations; rehearse staying under control.

☐ **Look Beyond Your First Solution to a Problem**
Don't always take the first action you think of. Look further for a second and third. What's different? Might the second or third be more effective? Research shows that the best solution lies somewhere between the second and third strategies or approaches. Your first solution is often an "autopilot" response and may not be the best.

Learning from Experience, Feedback and Other People

☐ **Learning from Ineffective Behavior**
Seeing things done poorly can be a very potent source of learning for you, especially if the behavior or action affects others negatively. Many times the thing done poorly causes emotional reactions or pain in you and others. Distance yourself from the feelings and explore why the actions didn't work.

☐ **Getting Feedback from Direct Reports**
Direct reports often fear reprisals for giving negative feedback about bosses, whether in a formal process, like a questionnaire, or informally and face-to-face. Even with a guarantee of confidentiality, some are still hesitant. If you want feedback from direct reports, you have to set a positive tone and never act out of revenge.

☐ **Feedback in Unusual Contexts/Situations**
Temporary and extreme conditions and contexts may shade interpretations of your behavior and intentions. Demands of the job may drive you outside your normal mode of operating. Hence, feedback you receive may be inaccurate during those times. However, unusual contexts affect our behavior less than most assume. It's usually a weak excuse.

☐ **Learning from Bad Bosses**
First, what does he/she do so well to make him/her your boss? (Even bad bosses have strengths). Then, ask what makes this boss bad for you. Is it his/her behavior? Attitude? Values? Philosophy? Practices? Style? What is the source of the conflict? Why do you react as you do? Do others react the same? How are you part of the problem? What do you do that triggers your boss? If you wanted to, could you reduce the conflict or make it go away by changing something you do? Is there someone around you who doesn't react like you? How are they different? What can you learn from them? What is your emotional reaction to this boss? Why do you react like that? What can you do to cope with these feelings? Can you avoid reacting out of anger and frustration? Can you find something positive about the situation? Can you use someone else as a buffer? Can you learn from your emotions? What lasting lessons of managing others can you take away from this experience? What won't you do as a manager? What will you do differently? How could you teach these principles you've learned to others by the use of this example?

☐ **Learning from Limited Staff**
Most managers either inherit or hire staff from time to time who are inexperienced, incompetent, not up to the task, resistant, or dispirited. Any of these may create a hardship for you. The lessons to be learned are how to get things done with limited resources and how to fix the people situation. In the short term, this hardship is best addressed by assessing the combined strengths of the team and deploying the best

you have against the problem. Almost everyone can do something well. Also, the team can contribute more than the combined individuals can. How can you empower and motivate the team? If you hired the troublesome staff, why did you err? What can you learn from your hiring mistakes? What wasn't there that you thought was present? What led you astray? How can you prevent that same hiring error in the future? What do you need to do to fix the situation? Quick development? Start over? If you inherited the problem, how can you fix it? Can you implement a program of accelerated development? Do you have to start over and get new people? What did the prior manager do or not do that led to this situation in the first place? What can you learn from that? What will you do differently? How does the staff feel? What can you learn from their frustrations over not being able to do the job? How can you be a positive force under negative circumstances? How can you rally them to perform? What lasting lessons can you learn from someone in distress and trouble? If you're going to try accelerated development, how can you get a quick assessment? How can you give the staff motivating feedback? How can you construct and implement development plans that will work? How can you get people on-line feedback for maximum growth? Do you know when to stop trying and start over? If you're going to turn over some staff, how can you do it both rapidly and with the least damage? How can you deliver the message in a constructive way? What can you learn from having to take negative actions against people? How can you prevent this from happening again?

☐ **Learning from Mistakes**

Since we're human, we all make mistakes. The key is to focus on why you made the mistake. Spend more time locating causes and less worrying about the effects. Check how you react to mistakes. How much time do you spend being angry with yourself? Do you waste time stewing or do you move on? More importantly, do you learn? Ask why you made the mistake. Are you likely to repeat it under similar situations? Was it a lack of skill? Judgment? Style? Not enough data? Reading people? Misreading the challenge? Misreading the politics? Or was it just random? A good strategy that just didn't work? Others that let you down? The key is to avoid two common reactions to your mistakes: 1) avoiding similar situations instead of learning and trying again, and 2) trying to repeat what you did, only more diligently and harder, hoping to break through the problem, making the same mistake again but with greater impact. Neither trap leaves us with better strategies for the future. Neither is a learning strategy. To learn and do something differently, focus on the patterns in your behavior that get you in trouble and go back to first causes, those that tell you something about your shortcomings. Facing ourselves squarely is always the best way to learn.

Learning from Courses

- ☐ **Insight Events**
  These are courses designed around assessing skills and providing feedback to the participants. These events can be a powerful source of self-knowledge and can lead to significant development if done right. When selecting a self-insight course, consider the following: 1) Are the skills assessed the important ones? 2) Are the assessment techniques and instruments sound? 3) Are those who are providing the feedback trained and professional? 4) Is the feedback provided in a user-friendly and "actionable" format? 5) Does the feedback include development planning? 6) Is the setting comfortable and conducive to reflection and learning? 7) Are the other participants the kinds of people you could learn from? 8) Are you in the right frame of mind to learn from this kind of intense experience? Select events on the basis of positive answers to these eight questions.

- ☐ **Attitude Toward Learning**
  In addition to selecting the right course, a learning attitude is required. Be open. Close down your "like/dislike" switch, your "agree/disagree" blinders, and your "like me/not like me" feelings toward the instructors. Learning requires new lessons, change, and new behaviors and perspectives – all scary stuff for most people. Don't resist. Take in all you can during the course. Ask clarifying questions. Discuss concerns with the other participants. Jot down what you learn as you go. After the course is over, take some reflective time to glean the meat. Make the practical decisions about what you can and cannot use.

SUGGESTED READINGS

Parekh, Bhikhu. *Gandhi's Political Philosophy*. Notre Dame, IN: University of Notre Dame Press, 1989.

Peters, Tom. *Thriving on Chaos.* New York: Knopf, Inc., 1987.

Peters, Thomas J. *Thriving on Chaos [sound recording]: handbook for a management revolution.* New York: Random House, 1987.

Plato. *The last days of Socrates*; translated by Hugh Tredennick and Harold Tarrant. London, England; New York: Penguin Books, 1993.

Sebba, Anne. *Mother Teresa, 1910–1997, Beyond the Image.* New York: Doubleday, 1997.

PEER RELATIONSHIPS

SECTION 1: YOUR DEVELOPMENT NEED(S)

UNSKILLED

- ☐ Not good at lateral cross boundary relations
- ☐ Doesn't strike fair bargains or understand what peers expect or need
- ☐ Not open to negotiation
- ☐ A loner, not seen as a team player, doesn't have the greater good in mind
- ☐ May withhold resources from the other team members
- ☐ May not respect their functions or disciplines and somehow communicates that
- ☐ May be very competitive, play and maneuver for advantage and withhold information
- ☐ May have a chilling effect on the entire unit because he/she won't play
- ☐ May deal with lateral conflict noisily or uncooperatively

SKILLED

- ☐ Can quickly find common ground and solve problems for the good of all
- ☐ Can represent his/her own interests and yet be fair to other groups
- ☐ Can solve problems with peers with a minimum of noise
- ☐ Is seen as a team player and is cooperative
- ☐ Easily gains trust and support of peers
- ☐ Encourages collaboration
- ☐ Can be candid with peers

OVERUSED SKILL

- ☐ May touch base with too many peers and be overly concerned with making everyone happy
- ☐ May be too accommodating
- ☐ May invest too much in peer relationships at the expense of others
- ☐ May be uncomfortable with relationships where everyone's not equal
- ☐ May share sensitive information inappropriately just to solidify a relationship
- ☐ May get in trouble by being too candid with peers

Select one to three of the competencies listed below to work on to compensate for an overuse of this skill.

COMPENSATORS: 4, 8, 9, 12, 16, 23, 29, 34, 37, 43, 50, 53, 57

SOME CAUSES

- ☐ Bad experiences with peers in the past
- ☐ Competitive with peers
- ☐ Don't respect other groups
- ☐ Impersonal style
- ☐ Not a team player
- ☐ Not forthcoming with information
- ☐ Poor collegial skills
- ☐ Poor communication skills
- ☐ Poor time management
- ☐ Possessive

THE MAP

Effective lateral or cross boundary (peer) relationships are among the toughest to build in organizations. There is a strong "not invented here" mentality at work between units, businesses, functions, and geographies. There is natural competition between groups. Pay and reward systems many times pit one group against the other. If one group gets more, the other has to get less. One team likes to beat the other. Lots of messy political problems originate as turf disputes. Many people get their lowest scores on 360° feedback from peers because they are uncooperative. Quite often these problems are a result of not finding common ground with peers, failure to understand what they want and need, and failure to understand the nature of the relationship. There is high return on investment for the organization if lateral relationships are working. It leads to more efficient use of time and resources and the easy exchange of ideas and talent. There are wasted resources and suboptimization when they are not.

SECTION 2: LEARNING ON YOUR OWN

THESE SELF-DEVELOPMENT REMEDIES WILL HELP YOU BUILD YOUR SKILL(S)

SOME REMEDIES

☐ **1. Influencing.** Peers generally do not have power over each other. That means that influence skills, understanding, and trading is the currency to use. Don't just ask for things; find some common ground where you can provide help. What do the peers you're contacting need? Do you really know how they see the issue? Is it even important to them? How does what you're working on affect them? If it affects them negatively can you trade something, appeal to the common good, figure out some way to minimize the work (volunteering staff help, for example)? Go into peer relationships with a trading mentality.

☐ **2. Many times, negative personal styles get in the way** of effective peer relationships. People differ in the impression they leave. Those who leave positive impressions get more things done with peers than those who leave cold, insensitive or impersonal negative impressions.

More help? – See #3 Approachability, #31 Interpersonal Savvy, and #33 Listening.

- ☐ **3. Sometimes the problem is in assessing peers.** Do you really understand the peers you need to deal with? Which ones really want to help? Who is going to get in the way? What did they really want? What price will they ask for helping? *More help? – See #56 Sizing Up People and #64 Understanding Others.*

- ☐ **4. Sometimes the problem is maneuvering** through the complex maze called the organization. How do you get things done sideways? Who are the movers and shakers in the organization? How do they get things done? Who do they rely on for expediting things through the maze? Who are the major gatekeepers who control the flow of resources, information and decisions? Who are the guides and the helpers? Get to know them better. Who are the major resisters and stoppers? Try to avoid or go around them. *More help? – See #38 Organizational Agility and #39 Organizing.*

- ☐ **5. If peers see you as excessively competitive,** they will cut you out of the loop and may sabotage your cross border attempts. To be seen as more cooperative, always explain your thinking and invite them to explain theirs. Generate a variety of possibilities first rather than stake out positions. Be tentative, allowing them room to customize the situation. Focus on common goals, priorities and problems. Invite criticism of your ideas.

- ☐ **6. If peers think you lack respect for them** or what they do, try to keep conflicts as small and concrete as possible. Separate the people from the problem. Don't get personal. Don't give peers the impression you're trying to dominate or push something on them. Without agreeing or disagreeing, try on their views for size. Can you understand their viewpoint? When peers blow off steam, don't react; return to facts and the problem, staying away from personal clashes. Allow others to save face; concede small points; don't try to hit a home run every time. When a peer takes a rigid position, don't reject it. Ask why – what are the principles behind the position, how do we know it's fair, what's the theory of the case, play out what would happen if his/her position was accepted.

- ☐ **7. Separate working smoothly with peers** from personal relationships, contests, competing for incentives, one-upsmanship, not invented here, pride and ego. Working well with peers over the long term helps everyone, makes sense for the organization and builds a capacity for the organization to do greater things. Usually the least used resource in an organization is lateral exchanges of information and resources.

☐ **8. If a peer doesn't play fair,** avoid telling others all about it. This often boomerangs. What goes around comes around. Confront the peer directly, politely and privately. Describe the unfair situation; explain the impact on you. Don't blame. Give the peer the chance to explain, ask questions, let him/her save some face and see if you can resolve the matter. Even if you don't totally accept what is said, it's better to solve the problem than win the argument.

☐ **9. Monitor yourself in tough situations** to get a sense of how you are coming across. What's the first thing you attend to? How often do you take a stand vs. make an accommodating gesture? What proportion of your comments deals with relationships vs. the issue to be addressed? Mentally rehearse for worst case scenarios/hard to deal with people. Anticipate what the person might say and have responses prepared so as not to be caught off guard. *More help? – See #12 Conflict Management.*

☐ **10. Make sure the winning and losing is balanced.** Watch out for winning concessions too often. If you win too much, how do the losers fare? Do you want them diminished or would you like them to work willingly with you again? The best tack is to balance the wins and losses. Make sure you are known in the organization as someone who is always ready to help and cooperate, and the favor will be returned.

SECTION 3: LEARNING FROM MORE FEEDBACK

THESE SOURCES WOULD GIVE YOU THE MOST ACCURATE AND DETAILED FEEDBACK ON YOUR SKILL(S)

☐ **Human Resource Professionals**
Human Resource professionals have both a formal and informal feedback role. Since they have access to unique and confidential information, they can provide the right context for feedback you've received. Sometimes they may be "directed" to give you feedback. Other times, they may pass on feedback just to be helpful to you.

☐ **Off-Work Friends/Associates**
Those who know you socially "with your guard down" can be a good source of feedback to compare with that of work peers and family members. If you're different at work than you are socially, why? If you're the same, feedback from friends just confirms the feedback. In a way, off-work friends may know the "real you."

☐ **Past Associates/Constituencies**
When confronted with a present performance problem, some claim, "I wasn't like that before; it must be the current situation." When feedback is available from former associates, about 50% support that claim. In the other half of the cases, the people were like that before and probably didn't know it. It sometimes makes sense to access the past to clearly see the present.

- ☐ **Peers and Colleagues**
  Peers and colleagues have a special social and working relationship. They attend staff meetings together, share private views, get feedback from the same boss, travel together, and are knowledgeable about each other's work. You perhaps let your guard down more around peers and act more like yourself. They can be a valuable source of feedback.

SECTION 4: LEARNING FROM DEVELOP-IN-PLACE ASSIGNMENTS

THESE PART-TIME DEVELOP-IN-PLACE ASSIGNMENTS WILL HELP YOU BUILD YOUR SKILL(S)

- ☐ Join a community board.
- ☐ Manage the assigning/allocating of office space in a contested situation.
- ☐ Resolve an issue in conflict between two people, units, geographies, functions, etc.
- ☐ Work on a team looking at a reorganization plan where there will be more people than positions.
- ☐ Install a new process or system (computer system, new policies, new process, new procedures, etc.).
- ☐ Manage the furnishing or refurnishing of new or existing offices.
- ☐ Study and establish internal or external customer needs, requirements, specifications, and expectations and present it to the people involved.
- ☐ Draft a mission statement, policy proposal, charter, or goal statement and get feedback from others.
- ☐ Serve on a junior or shadow board.
- ☐ Volunteer to fill an open management job temporarily until it's filled.

SECTION 5: LEARNING FROM FULL-TIME JOBS

THESE FULL-TIME JOBS OFFER THE OPPORTUNITY TO BUILD YOUR SKILL(S)

- ☐ **Chair of Projects/Task Forces**
  The core demands for qualifying as a Project/Task Force assignment are: 1) Full-time assignment. 2) Important and specific goal. 3) Tight deadline. 4) Success or failure will be evident. 5) High-visibility sponsor. 6) Learning something on the fly. 7) Must get others to cooperate. 8) Usually six months or more. Four types of Projects/Task Forces: 1) New ideas, products, services, or systems (e.g., product/service/program research and development, creation/installation/launch of a new system, new programs like Total Quality Management, positive discipline). 2) Formal negotiations and relationships (e.g., acquisitions, divestitures, agreements, joint ventures; licensing arrangements, fran-

chising; dealing with unions, governments, communities, charities, customers, and relocations). 3) Big one-time events (e.g., working on a major presentation for the board, organizing significant meetings or conferences, disaster/damage control teams; reorganizations, mergers, acquisitions, or relocations, working on visions, charters, strategies, other time-urgent issues and problems). 4) Troubleshooting (e.g., problems, disasters, crises, product/service failures, accidents, illegal activities, damage control in public relations goofs, shut downs, downsizings, layoffs, abrupt changes in leadership).

☐ **Fix-its / Turnarounds**
The core demands to qualify as a Fix-it or Turnaround assignment are: 1) Cleaning up a mess. 2) Serious people issues/problems like credibility/performance/morale. 3) Tight deadline. 4) Serious business performance failure. 5) Last chance to fix. Four Types of Fix-its/ Turnarounds: 1) Fixing a failed business/unit involving taking control, stopping losses, managing damage, planning the turnaround, dealing with people problems, installing new processes and systems, and rebuilding the spirit and performance of the unit. 2) Managing sizable disasters like mishandled labor negotiations and strikes, thefts, history of significant business losses, poor staff, failed leadership, hidden problems, fraud, public relations nightmares, etc. 3) Significant reorganization and restructuring (e.g., stabilizing the business, reforming unit, introducing new systems, making people changes, resetting strategy and tactics). 4) Significant system/process breakdown (e.g., MIS, financial coordination processes, audits, standards, etc.) across units requiring working to change something from a distant position, providing advice and counsel, and installing or implementing a major process improvement or system change outside your own unit and/or with customers outside the organization.

☐ **Influencing Without Authority**
The core demands to qualify as an Influence Without Authority are: 1) Significant challenge (e.g, start-up, fix-it, scope and/or scale assignment, strategic planning project, changes in management practices/ systems). 2) Insufficient direct authority to make it happen. 3) Tight deadlines. 4) Visible to significant others. 5) Sensitive politics.

SECTION 6: LEARNING MORE FROM YOUR PLAN

THESE ADDITIONAL REMEDIES WILL HELP MAKE THIS DEVELOPMENT PLAN MORE EFFECTIVE FOR YOU

Learning to Learn Better

☐ **Form a Learning Network With Others Working on the Same Problem**
Look for people in similar situations, and create a process for sharing and learning together. Look for a variety of people inside and outside

your organization. Give feedback to each other; try new and different things together; share successes and failures, lessons and learning.

- ☐ **Think and Talk More in Probabilities and Less in Absolutes**
Try to be less "0/1," yes and no; don't be so absolute in everything you do or say. Think and talk in terms of probabilities (I'm about 60% sure my viewpoint is correct). Try to face what's real about your suggestions and ideas rather than wishing or projecting you were always 100% correct. Tell people how sure you are before you make a statement.

- ☐ **Work With a Development Partner**
Find a person you trust to be both candid and constructive and team up with him/her. Construct effective strategies together. Give each other feedback; role-play tactics with each other.

- ☐ **Preview a Plan With a Test Audience**
Before committing to a plan, find someone agreeable to a wide-ranging discussion about the issue or problem you face. Explore all sides and options; go with the flow; let what you need to do emerge from the process; develop a plan as you go.

Learning from Experience, Feedback and Other People

- ☐ **Using Multiple Models**
Who do you know who exemplifies how to do whatever your need is? Who, for example, personifies decisiveness or compassion or strategic agility? Think more broadly than your current job and colleagues. For example, clergy, friends, spouses or community leaders are also good sources for potential models. Select your models not on the basis of overall excellence or likability, but on the basis of the one towering strength (or glaring weakness) you are interested in. Even people who are well thought of usually have only one or two towering strengths (or glaring weaknesses). Ordinarily, you won't learn as much from the whole person as you will from one characteristic.

- ☐ **Getting Feedback from Bosses and Superiors**
Many bosses are reluctant to give negative feedback. They lack the managerial courage to face people directly with criticism. You can help by soliciting feedback and setting the tone. Show them you can handle criticism and that you are willing to work on issues they see as important.

- ☐ **Getting Feedback from Peers/Colleagues**
Your peers and colleagues may not be candid if they are in competition with you. Some may not be willing to be open with you out of fear of giving you an advantage. Some may give you exaggerated feedback to deliberately cause you undue concern. You have to set the tone and gauge the trust level of the relationship and the quality of the feedback.

☐ **Soliciting Feedback**
Almost everyone reports they receive less feedback than they need to achieve their career goals. While others may have some interest in your career, it is primarily up to you to take the initiative in soliciting feedback from multiple sources by any methods available. You're the stakeholder who needs feedback to improve and grow.

Learning from Courses

☐ **Insight Events**
These are courses designed around assessing skills and providing feedback to the participants. These events can be a powerful source of self-knowledge and can lead to significant development if done right. When selecting a self-insight course, consider the following: 1) Are the skills assessed the important ones? 2) Are the assessment techniques and instruments sound? 3) Are those who are providing the feedback trained and professional? 4) Is the feedback provided in a user-friendly and "actionable" format? 5) Does the feedback include development planning? 6) Is the setting comfortable and conducive to reflection and learning? 7) Are the other participants the kinds of people you could learn from? 8) Are you in the right frame of mind to learn from this kind of intense experience? Select events on the basis of positive answers to these eight questions.

SUGGESTED READINGS

Adams, Scott. *The Joy of Work – Dilbert's guide to finding happiness at the expense of your co-workers.* New York: HarperBusiness, 1998.

Adams, Scott. *The joy of work [sound recording]: Dilbert's guide to finding happiness at the expense of your co-workers.* New York: HarperCollins, 1998.

Alessandra, Tony and Michael J. O'Connor with Janice Van Dyke. *People Smarts – Bending the golden rule to give others what they want.* San Diego: Pfeiffer & Company, 1994.

Baber, Anne and Lynne Waymon. *Great connections: small talk and networking for businesspeople*. Woodbridge, VA: Impact Publications, 1991.

Baker, Wayne E. *Networking Smart.* New York: McGraw-Hill, Inc., 1994.

Bolton, Robert and Dorothy Grover Bolton. *People Styles at Work – Making bad relationships good and good relationships better.* New York: AMACOM, 1996.

Brinkman, Rick, Ph.D. and Dr. Rick Kirschner. *Dealing with People You Can't Stand.* New York: McGraw-Hill, Inc., 1994.

DesRoches, Brian Ph.D. *Your Boss Is Not Your Mother – Creating autonomy, respect, and success at work.* New York: William Morrow and Company, 1995.

Dowse, Eileen. *The Naked Manager – How to build open relationships at work.* Greensboro, North Carolina: Oakhill Press, 1998.

Simmons, Annette. *Territorial games: understanding and ending turf wars at work.* New York: American Management Association, 1998.

43

PERSEVERANCE

SECTION 1: YOUR DEVELOPMENT NEED(S)

UNSKILLED

- ☐ Gives up too soon or moves on to something that's going better
- ☐ Doesn't push hard enough to get things done
- ☐ Doesn't go back with different strategies for the third and fourth try
- ☐ May take rejection too personally
- ☐ May hesitate to push when met with conflict, disagreement or attacks
- ☐ May agree too early just to get it over with
- ☐ May compromise for less than the original goal or objective
- ☐ May simply not want to take charge and be out front

SKILLED

- ☐ Pursues everything with energy, drive, and a need to finish
- ☐ Seldom gives up before finishing, especially in the face of resistance or setbacks

OVERUSED SKILL

- ☐ May stick to efforts beyond reason, in the face of overwhelming odds and evidence to the contrary
- ☐ May be seen as stubborn and unyielding
- ☐ May not set appropriate priorities
- ☐ May find it difficult to change course
- ☐ May confuse personal have-to-do's with what most needs to be done

Select one to three of the competencies listed below to work on to compensate for an overuse of this skill.

COMPENSATORS: 2, 14, 26, 33, 41, 45, 46, 50, 51, 54, 60

SOME CAUSES

- ☐ Don't push hard enough
- ☐ Give up too soon
- ☐ Impatient
- ☐ Lost the passion
- ☐ Short span of attention
- ☐ Take things personally
- ☐ Uncomfortable with rejection
- ☐ Wilt in the face of resistance
- ☐ Won't take charge

THE MAP

The need for perseverance comes about because you weren't effective the first time, the thing you are trying to get done is being resisted, or your customers and the audience aren't ready to do what you need; it's not on their agenda. Sticking to the course, especially in the face of pushback, is what perseverance is all about. Going back a second and third time or however many tries are needed. Perseverance is also about using a variety of ways to get things done. Persevering people try it different ways when the first way isn't effective. Why don't people persevere? You may fear the rejection; the persevering don't take it personally even when people try to make it so. You may have trouble taking a stand; the persevering do it as a matter of course to accomplish something worthwhile. You may not be convinced of the worth of what you're doing. You may not be doing it the right way. All in all, persevering people get the job done.

SECTION 2: LEARNING ON YOUR OWN

THESE SELF-DEVELOPMENT REMEDIES WILL HELP YOU BUILD YOUR SKILL(S)

SOME REMEDIES

☐ **1. Give up after one or two tries?** If you have trouble going back the second or third time to get something done, then switch approaches. Sometimes people get stuck in a repeating groove that's not working. Do something different next time. If you visited the office of someone you have difficulties with, invite him/her to your office next time. Think about multiple ways to get the same outcome. For example, to push a decision through, you could meet with stakeholders first, go to a single key stakeholder, study and present the problem to a group, call a problem-solving session, or call in an outside expert. Be prepared to do them all when obstacles arise.

☐ **2. Meeting resistance.** Don't persevere because you prefer to avoid conflict? Hesitate in the face of resistance and adverse reaction? Conflict slows you down? Shakes your confidence in your decision? Do you backpedal? Give in too soon? Try to make everyone happy? When your initiative hits resistance, keep it on the problem and the objectives. Depersonalize. If attacked, return to what you're trying to accomplish and invite people's criticisms and ideas. Listen. Correct if justified. Stick to your point. Push ahead again. Resistance is natural. Some of the time it's legitimate; most of the time it's just human nature. People push back until they understand. They are just protecting territory. *More help? – See #12 Conflict Management.*

☐ **3. Procrastinate?** You don't go back a second time until forced to by deadlines? Less motivated when your first attempt falls flat or meets resistance? Don't get back to people when you said you would? You might not produce results consistently. Some of your work will be marginal because you only had time for one or two attempts before the project was due. Start earlier. Reduce the time between attempts. Always start 10% of each attempt immediately after it is apparent it will be needed so you can better gauge what it is going to take to finish it. Always assume it will take more time than you think it's going to take. *More help? – See #47 Planning.*

☐ **4. Take resistance personally?** If you tend to take rejection or inattention or non-responsiveness personally, focus on why this isn't personal. Develop a philosophical stance toward rejection and failure. After all, most innovations fail, most proposals fail, the majority of efforts to change people fail and most attempts to change organizations fail. Anything really worth doing takes repeated effort, and everything could always be done better. Remember resistance is normal, not abnormal. Even resistance that looks and sounds personal may not be. Keep reminding yourself what you are there to do. Keep making the business case. How can everyone win? Don't get dragged down by personal concerns. Keep it objective. Listen. Absorb the heat. Look for quality feedback and respond appropriately. Always return to the facts and your agenda. The closer you get to success, the more the heat of the naysayers may increase. Work even harder, listen, answer all questions and objections – focus on the work, not yourself. Don't expect everyone to cheer your successes. Some will be jealous. *More help? – See #12 Conflict Management.*

☐ **5. Trouble taking tough stands?** You may have to go back because you didn't make a strong enough case the first time. Do your homework. Be prepared. Don't make it sound like a trial balloon. Use more definite, direct language. Don't be vague or tentative. Don't throw things out without the aircover of the business case and the safety net of how everybody can gain. Prepare by rehearsing for tough questions, attacks, and countering views. Plan as if you're only going to have one shot. Match your style, tone, pace and volume with the feeling that you are right and that this thing must get done. Lead with strength.

☐ **6. Fight the right battles.** Maybe you're pushing on everything and getting tired and frustrated about your low batting average. Some persevere too much. Some persevere on the wrong things. Are you sure this is critical? What's mission-critical versus nice to get done versus not really in the mainstream? Be sure your priorities are right. *More help? – See #50 Priority Setting.*

☐ **7. Disorganized?** Don't always get to everything on time? Forget deadlines? Lose requests for decisions? Forget to follow up on a request for more information? Lose interest in anything not right in front of you? Move from task to task until you find one that's working? Short attention span? You can't operate helter skelter and persevere. Perseverance takes focus and continuity of effort. Get better organized and disciplined. Keep a task progress log. Keep a top ten things I have to do list. Stick with tasks longer than you now do.

☐ **8. Working against the maze.** Organizations can be complex mazes with many turns and dead ends. Even worse, organizations are staffed with people which makes it more complex. Egos. Gatekeepers. Resisters. The best path to get something done may not be direct. The formal organization works only some of the time. Most of the time, the informal organization runs the show. To persevere efficiently, you have to know how to work the maze. You have to be patient with process. Things sometimes take time. People need to be ready to move. Maybe the best way to approach someone is through someone else. Maybe you have to work on your timing. When is the best time to approach someone for a decision or an action? Learn the informal organization. Identify the key players, especially the gatekeepers and the traffic controllers. Ask others the best way to get things done in this organization. Watch others. What path do they follow? *More help? – See #52 Process Management and #38 Organizational Agility.*

☐ **9. Finishing.** While it's true that sometimes you get 80% of what you are pushing for with the first 20% of the effort, it unfortunately then takes another 80% of the time to finish the last 20%. It's not over until the gravity-challenged lady sings. In a fast paced world, it's sometimes tough to pull the cart all the way to the finish line when the race is over. Not all tasks have to be completely finished. For some, 80% would be acceptable. For those who need all the i's dotted and the t's crossed, it will take perseverance. The devil is in the details. When you get caught in this situation, create a checklist with the 20% that remains to be done. Plan to do a little on it each day. Cross things off and celebrate each time you get to take something off the list. Remember, it's going to challenge your motivation and attention. Try to delegate finishing to someone who would see the 20% as a fresh challenge. Get a consultant to finish it. Task trade with someone else's 20% so you both would have something fresh to do.

☐ **10. Burned out.** Lost your passion? Run out of gas? Heart's not in it anymore? Not 100% committed? Maybe you don't persevere because deep down you don't care anymore – you're sick of doing this job or working for this organization or pushing against a particular person or group. Ask what is it that you want. Find your passion again. Prepare yourself for another job. To make the best of your current job, make a list of what you like and don't like to do. Concentrate on doing more liked activities each day. Work to delegate or task trade the things that are no longer motivating to you. Do your least preferred activities first to get them out of the way; focus not on the activity, but on your sense of accomplishment. Change your work activity to mirror your interests as much as you can. Volunteer for task forces and projects that would be motivating for you. *More help? – See #6 Career Ambition.*

SECTION 3: LEARNING FROM MORE FEEDBACK

THESE SOURCES WOULD GIVE YOU THE MOST ACCURATE AND DETAILED FEEDBACK ON YOUR SKILL(S)

- ☐ **Direct Reports**
  Across a variety of settings, your direct reports probably see you the most. They are the recipients of most of your managerial behaviors. They know your work. They can compare you with former bosses. Since they may hesitate to give you negative feedback, you have to set the atmosphere to make it easier for them. You have to ask.

- ☐ **Human Resource Professionals**
  Human Resource professionals have both a formal and informal feedback role. Since they have access to unique and confidential information, they can provide the right context for feedback you've received. Sometimes they may be "directed" to give you feedback. Other times, they may pass on feedback just to be helpful to you.

- ☐ **Spouse**
  Spouses can be powerful sources of feedback on such things as interpersonal style, values, balance between work, career, and personal life, etc. Many participants attending development programs share their feedback with their spouses for value-adding confirmation or context and for specific examples.

SECTION 4: LEARNING FROM DEVELOP-IN-PLACE ASSIGNMENTS

THESE PART-TIME DEVELOP-IN-PLACE ASSIGNMENTS WILL HELP YOU BUILD YOUR SKILL(S)

- ☐ Plan a new site for a building (plant, field office, headquarters, etc.).
- ☐ Be a change agent; create a symbol for change; lead the rallying cry; champion a significant change and implementation.
- ☐ Manage an ad hoc, temporary group of "green," inexperienced people as their coach, teacher, orienter, etc.
- ☐ Manage an ad hoc, temporary group of people involved in tackling a fix-it or turnaround project.
- ☐ Handle a tough negotiation with an internal or external client or customer.
- ☐ Take on a tough and undoable project, one where others who have tried it have failed.
- ☐ Manage the outplacement of a group of people.
- ☐ Take on a task you dislike or hate to do.
- ☐ Resolve an issue in conflict between two people, units, geographies, functions, etc.
- ☐ Work on a crisis management team.

SECTION 5: LEARNING FROM FULL-TIME JOBS

THESE FULL-TIME JOBS OFFER THE OPPORTUNITY TO BUILD YOUR SKILL(S)

☐ **Fix-its/Turnarounds**

The core demands to qualify as a Fix-it or Turnaround assignment are: 1) Cleaning up a mess. 2) Serious people issues/problems like credibility/performance/morale. 3) Tight deadline. 4) Serious business performance failure. 5) Last chance to fix. Four Types of Fix-its/ Turnarounds: 1) Fixing a failed business/unit involving taking control, stopping losses, managing damage, planning the turnaround, dealing with people problems, installing new processes and systems, and rebuilding the spirit and performance of the unit. 2) Managing sizable disasters like mishandled labor negotiations and strikes, thefts, history of significant business losses, poor staff, failed leadership, hidden problems, fraud, public relations nightmares, etc. 3) Significant reorganization and restructuring (e.g., stabilizing the business, reforming unit, introducing new systems, making people changes, resetting strategy and tactics). 4) Significant system/process breakdown (e.g., MIS, financial coordination processes, audits, standards, etc.) across units requiring working to change something from a distant position, providing advice and counsel, and installing or implementing a major process improvement or system change outside your own unit and/or with customers outside the organization.

☐ **Influencing Without Authority**

The core demands to qualify as an Influence Without Authority are: 1) Significant challenge (e.g, start-up, fix-it, scope and/or scale assignment, strategic planning project, changes in management practices/ systems). 2) Insufficient direct authority to make it happen. 3) Tight deadlines. 4) Visible to significant others. 5) Sensitive politics.

☐ **Off-Shore Assignments**

The core demands to qualify as an Off-Shore assignment are: 1) First time working in the country. 2) Significant challenges like new language, hardship location, unique business rules/practices, significant cultural/marketplace differences, different functional task, etc. 3) More than a year assignment. 4) No automatic return deal. 5) Not necessarily a change in job challenge, technical content, or responsibilities.

☐ **Start-ups**

The core demands to qualify as a start from scratch are: 1) Starting something new for you and/or for the organization. 2) Forging a new team. 3) Creating new systems/facilities/staffs/programs/procedures. 4) Contextual adversity (e.g., uncertainty, government regulation, unions, difficult environment). Seven types of start from scratches: 1) Planning, building, hiring, and managing (e.g., building a new facility, opening up a new location, moving a unit or company). 2) Heading something new (e.g., new product, new service, new line of business, new department/function, major new program). 3) Take over a group/product/service/program that had existed for less than a year and was off to a fast start. 4) Establishing overseas operations. 5) Major new designs for existing systems. 6) Moving a successful program from one unit to another. 7) Installing a new organization-wide process as a full-time job (e.g., like Total Quality).

SECTION 6: LEARNING MORE FROM YOUR PLAN

THESE ADDITIONAL REMEDIES WILL HELP MAKE THIS DEVELOPMENT PLAN MORE EFFECTIVE FOR YOU

Learning to Learn Better

☐ **Analyze Mistakes Immediately and Learn from Them**
Avoid mistakes, yes, but don't pass up the opportunity to learn from them. It's important to examine closely the reasons for the negative outcome. Do you need a small adjustment or a major change next time? Were there extenuating circumstances? How much an influence was the context, how much was you?

Learning from Experience, Feedback and Other People

☐ **Getting Feedback from Direct Reports**
Direct reports often fear reprisals for giving negative feedback about bosses, whether in a formal process, like a questionnaire, or informally and face-to-face. Even with a guarantee of confidentiality, some are still hesitant. If you want feedback from direct reports, you have to set a positive tone and never act out of revenge.

☐ **Learning from Bad Things that Happen**
Bad things happen to everyone, sometimes because of what we do and sometimes with no help from us. We all have bad bosses, bad staffs, impossible and hopeless situations, impossible tasks, and unintended consequences. Aside from the trouble these bad things cause for you, the key is how can you learn from each of them.

☐ **Learning from Bad Bosses**
First, what does he/she do so well to make him/her your boss? (Even bad bosses have strengths). Then, ask what makes this boss bad for you. Is it his/her behavior? Attitude? Values? Philosophy? Practices? Style? What is the source of the conflict? Why do you react as you do? Do others react the same? How are you part of the problem? What do you do that triggers your boss? If you wanted to, could you reduce the conflict or make it go away by changing something you do? Is there someone around you who doesn't react like you? How are they different? What can you learn from them? What is your emotional reaction to this boss? Why do you react like that? What can you do to cope with these feelings? Can you avoid reacting out of anger and frustration? Can you find something positive about the situation? Can you use someone else as a buffer? Can you learn from your emotions?

What lasting lessons of managing others can you take away from this experience? What won't you do as a manager? What will you do differently? How could you teach these principles you've learned to others by the use of this example?

☐ **Learning from Bad Situations**
All of us will find ourselves in bad situations from time to time. Good intentions gone bad. Impossible tasks and goals. Hopeless projects. Even though you probably can't perform well, the key is to at least take away some lessons and insights. How did things get to be this way? What factors led to the impasse? How can you make the best of a bad situation? How can you neutralize the negative elements? How can you get the most out of yourself and your staff under the chilling situation? What can you salvage? How can you use coping strategies to minimize the negatives? How can you avoid these situations going forward? In bad situations: 1) Be resourceful. Get the most you can out of the situation. 2) Try to deduce why things got to be that way. 3) Learn from both the situation you inherited and how you react to it. 4) Integrate what you learn into your future behavior.

☐ **Learning from Mistakes**
Since we're human, we all make mistakes. The key is to focus on why you made the mistake. Spend more time locating causes and less worrying about the effects. Check how you react to mistakes. How much time do you spend being angry with yourself? Do you waste time stewing or do you move on? More importantly, do you learn? Ask why you made the mistake. Are you likely to repeat it under similar situations? Was it a lack of skill? Judgment? Style? Not enough data? Reading people? Misreading the challenge? Misreading the politics? Or was it just random? A good strategy that just didn't work? Others that let you down? The key is to avoid two common reactions to your mistakes: 1) avoiding similar situations instead of learning and trying again, and 2) trying to repeat what you did, only more diligently and harder, hoping to break through the problem, making the same mistake again but with greater impact. Neither trap leaves us with better strategies for the future. Neither is a learning strategy. To learn and do something differently, focus on the patterns in your behavior that get you in trouble and go back to first causes, those that tell you something about your shortcomings. Facing ourselves squarely is always the best way to learn.

SUGGESTED READINGS

DuBrin, Andrew J. *Your Own Worst Enemy.* New York: AMACOM, 1992.

Dumas, Alexandre. *Count of Monte Cristo.* New York: Bantam Books, 1981.

Dumas, Alexandre. *Count of Monte Cristo [sound recording].* Salt Lake City, Utah: Audio Books on Cassette, 1988.

Keller, Helen. *The story of my life.* New York: Bantam Books, 1990.

Keller, Helen. *The story of my life [sound recording].* Newport Beach, CA: Books on Tape, 1994.

Olesen, Erik. *12 Steps to Mastering the Winds of Change.* New York: Macmillan, 1993.

Sapadin, Linda with Jack Maguire. *It's about time!: the six styles of procrastination and how to overcome them.* New York: Viking, 1996.

Shackleton, Ernest Henry, Sir. *Shackleton, his Antarctic writings / selected and introduced by Christopher Ralling.* London: British Broadcasting Corp., 1983....or...

Shackleton, Ernest Henry, Sir. *South: the story of Shackleton's last expedition.* Oxford, England; Santa Barbara, CA: 1990.

Troyat, Henri. *Peter the Great.* New York: Dutton, 1987.

PERSONAL DISCLOSURE

SECTION 1: YOUR DEVELOPMENT NEED(S)

UNSKILLED

- ☐ A private person who does not discuss personal information
- ☐ A closed book to most; hard to tell where he/she is coming from
- ☐ May not believe in sharing personal views and foibles
- ☐ Works to keep personal and business separate
- ☐ May fear what will happen if he/she discloses
- ☐ May be shy
- ☐ Doesn't ask others for personal information
- ☐ Doesn't know what is helpful to share or why people find it valuable
- ☐ May believe he/she has something to hide
- ☐ May be defensive and unwilling to share much

SKILLED

- ☐ Shares his/her thoughts about personal strengths, weaknesses, and limitations
- ☐ Admits mistakes and shortcomings
- ☐ Is open about personal beliefs and feelings
- ☐ Is easy to get to know to those who interact with him/her regularly

OVERUSED SKILL

- ☐ May turn off some people by excessive directness
- ☐ May leave him/herself open for criticism because of his/her honesty
- ☐ Openness and directness may actually lead to a lack of trust
- ☐ Open style may lack credibility with some

Select one to three of the competencies listed below to work on to compensate for an overuse of this skill.

COMPENSATORS: 15, 22, 27, 29, 45, 48, 55, 56, 64

SOME CAUSES

- ☐ Believe work and personal should not be mixed
- ☐ Don't have a good sense about what to disclose
- ☐ Don't see the point of disclosing
- ☐ Lack of self confidence; others will find out the real me
- ☐ Perfectionist; don't want to show any weaknesses
- ☐ Seen it done very poorly by others
- ☐ Shy and uncomfortable being personal

THE MAP

Personal relationships are give and take. Warmth is usually responded to with warmth, openness with openness, and coolness with coolness. You get what you give. Personal disclosure is one aspect of any job (like managing others; working on a team) that involves prolonged relationships. Many managers believe that keeping a proper distance from direct reports is the right practice. Their measure of proper is usually too distant and far. A balanced business plus personal relationship works best. People can't relate well to a cold role across time. Disclosing gives people a sense of where you're coming from and how to read you. When you disclose, most others will open up. It broadens the bandwidth of the relationship leading to working better together. Almost all working relationships benefit from reasonable personal disclosure.

SECTION 2: LEARNING ON YOUR OWN

THESE SELF-DEVELOPMENT REMEDIES WILL HELP YOU BUILD YOUR SKILL(S)

SOME REMEDIES

☐ **1. What to disclose.** The kinds of disclosure that people enjoy are the reasons behind why you do what you do, your self appraisal, things you know behind what's happening in the business that they don't know – that you are at liberty to disclose, things both good and embarrassing that have happened to you in the past, commentary about what's going on around you – without being too negative about others, and things you are interested in and do outside of work. These are areas which you should learn to disclose more than you now do.

☐ **2. How to start.** Start with three things you can talk about with almost anyone without risking uncomfortable personal disclosure. Vacations, hobbies, business interests, your thinking on business issues, children, etc. Decide what they are and make a conscious effort to sprinkle them into some of your interactions with others you have generally had only a business relationship with before. Notice the reaction. Did they also share for the first time? Usually yes. And that's the point. Within limits, the more you know about each other, the better the working relationship will be.

☐ **3. Try to get to know three non-work things** about everybody – their interests or their children or something you can chat about with them other than the weather or the weekend sports results.

☐ **4. Observe someone who discloses a lot more than you do** and does it well. What do they disclose? What type of personal information do they share? How do they share? In what settings do they share? Then study someone who discloses less than you do. Which of the two do you work with the best?

☐ **5. Practice your disclosure skills with strangers** on airplanes or at social gatherings. Your goal is to disclose some things about yourself that you don't usually disclose in a work setting. Then see how many things you can get the other person to disclose. Test limits without irritating him/her. As he/she discloses more, you disclose more. After each event, ask yourself how that felt. What did the additional information about that person add to the temporary relationship? Would it be easier to work with that person now that you have some personal information?

☐ **6. Deeper disclosure.** More serious personal disclosure involves talking about your self appraisal. This involves talking about your personal strengths, weaknesses, limitations and beliefs. Most others are more comfortable with people who do reasonable disclosure. The funny thing about self-assessment disclosure is that most of the people around you already know what you're going to disclose! If you say, "I'm not the most organized person in the world," most around you will do a smiling nod because they suffer the consequences of your disorganization. But, that brief mention of a problem you have or a belief you hold will help the person feel more comfortable. This tells them they are not alone, that you have some of the same problems and worries they do.

☐ **7. Disclosing mistakes.** Learn to be more comfortable admitting your mistakes. This makes you more human, and it also establishes a routine of learning from our inevitable shortcomings. People who excel at dealing with their own mistakes usually do the following:

- Talk about mistakes matter of factly as quickly as possible.
- Volunteer the mistake and inform everyone affected what could occur.
- Publicly acknowledge the mistake if necessary.
- Demonstrate what they have learned so the mistake does not happen again.
- Move on; don't dwell on it.

☐ **8. Disclosing values.** When disclosing beliefs or values stances, always explain why you hold a belief – give reasons rather than just stating something. Statements cut off discussion and may make you look rigid or simplistic. Bold statements are those that are absolute and because of that limiting. There is no comeback to "never hire a friend" except to reject your disclosure. Saying "I had to fire someone once; this was the situation, my reasons, what I tried to do to help, and what I learned from it" sets up your belief statements. Making them first comes across as pronouncements ("Never hire a friend."). Try to start with moderate statements like, "This made me question how good an idea it is to hire a friend." That's a good disclosure. It invites discussion;

it may even lead to some insights: under what conditions a friend should or shouldn't be hired.

☐ **9. Audience sensitivity.** Try to balance your disclosure with what the other person is ready for. You start with a simple and short disclosure. What did the other person do? If he/she didn't respond with a disclosure, maybe the setting or situation isn't right for disclosure. If she/he acknowledged your disclosure and added one, then you disclose something else. Always check to see if your audience wants more.

☐ **10. Overdoing disclosure.** Avoid too much disclosure; it is probably worse than none. Set limits. Generally politics and religion are risky; ribald humor and anything ethnic or gender demeaning wouldn't be good and might end up in litigation. There are also people you can disclose to and some you shouldn't, since some people can't keep confidences. Be careful of putting someone in a counselor role or saying too much about an issue. Early in the process of disclosure, it's usually best for you to follow the lead of others and disclose about as much as they do.

SECTION 3: LEARNING FROM MORE FEEDBACK

THESE SOURCES WOULD GIVE YOU THE MOST ACCURATE AND DETAILED FEEDBACK ON YOUR SKILL(S)

☐ **Development Professionals**
Sometimes it might be valuable to get some analysis and feedback from a professional trained and certified in the area you're working on: possibly a career counselor, a therapist, clergy, a psychologist, etc.

☐ **Natural Mentors**
Natural mentors have a special relationship with you and are interested in your success and your future. Since they are usually not in your direct chain of command, you can have more open, relaxed, and fruitful discussions about yourself and your career prospects. They can be a very important source for candid or critical feedback others may not give you.

☐ **Spouse**
Spouses can be powerful sources of feedback on such things as interpersonal style, values, balance between work, career, and personal life, etc. Many participants attending development programs share their feedback with their spouses for value-adding confirmation or context and for specific examples.

SECTION 4: LEARNING FROM DEVELOP-IN-PLACE ASSIGNMENTS

THESE PART-TIME DEVELOP-IN-PLACE ASSIGNMENTS WILL HELP YOU BUILD YOUR SKILL(S)

- ☐ Attend a self-awareness/assessment course that includes feedback.
- ☐ Attend a course or event which will push you personally beyond your usual limits or outside your comfort zone (e.g., Outward Bound, language immersion training, sensitivity group, public speaking).
- ☐ Join a self-help or support group.
- ☐ Make peace with an enemy or someone you've disappointed with a product or service or someone you've had some trouble with or don't get along well with.
- ☐ Take on a task you dislike or hate to do.
- ☐ Manage a project team of people who are older and more experienced than you.
- ☐ Go to a campus as a recruiter.
- ☐ Teach a course, seminar, or workshop on something you don't know well.
- ☐ Become someone's assigned mentor, coach, sponsor, champion, or orienter.
- ☐ Manage an ad hoc, temporary group of people where the people in the group are towering experts but the temporary manager is not.

SECTION 5: LEARNING FROM FULL-TIME JOBS

Personal disclosure is not taught by any specific job.

SECTION 6: LEARNING MORE FROM YOUR PLAN

THESE ADDITIONAL REMEDIES WILL HELP MAKE THIS DEVELOPMENT PLAN MORE EFFECTIVE FOR YOU

Learning to Learn Better

- ☐ **Form a Learning Network With Others Working on the Same Problem**
  Look for people in similar situations, and create a process for sharing and learning together. Look for a variety of people inside and outside your organization. Give feedback to each other; try new and different things together; share successes and failures, lessons and learning.
- ☐ **Learn New and Frivolous Skills to Study How You Learn**
  Practice learning frivolous and fun skills (like juggling, square dancing, skeet shooting, video games, etc.) to see yourself under different and less personal or stressful learning conditions. Ask yourself why that was

easy while developing new personal/managerial skills is so hard. Try something harder with the same tactics.

- ☐ **Try Some New Things Out of Your Normal Comfort Zone**
Periodically, practice going against your grain (what's normal for you) and getting out of your comfort zone. Try something different and opposite to your nature; take a learning risk. Explore: if you're a thinker, act; if you're an action person, think. Test the unfamiliar; try the new; go beyond your self-determined limits and boundaries.

- ☐ **Work With a Development Partner**
Find a person you trust to be both candid and constructive and team up with him/her. Construct effective strategies together. Give each other feedback; role-play tactics with each other.

Learning from Experience, Feedback and Other People

- ☐ **Learning from Interviewing Others**
Interview others. Ask not only what they do, but how and why they do it. What do they think are the rules of thumb they are following? Where did they learn the behaviors? How do they keep them current? How do they monitor the effect they have on others?

- ☐ **Learning from Observing Others**
Observe others. Find opportunities to observe without interacting with your model. This enables you to objectively study the person, note what he/she is doing or not doing, and compare that with what you would typically do in similar situations. Many times you can learn more by watching than asking. Your model may not be able to explain what he/she does or may be an unwilling teacher.

- ☐ **Giving Feedback to Others**
Most managers complain they don't get enough useful feedback. Ironically, their direct reports and peers offer the same complaint! Getting serious about feedback for yourself involves giving more feedback to those around you. As you practice giving more feedback to others, you will receive more by the example you set and will become more sensitive and receptive to your own.

- ☐ **Learning from Mistakes**
Since we're human, we all make mistakes. The key is to focus on why you made the mistake. Spend more time locating causes and less worrying about the effects. Check how you react to mistakes. How much time do you spend being angry with yourself? Do you waste time stewing or do you move on? More importantly, do you learn? Ask why you made the mistake. Are you likely to repeat it under similar situations? Was it a lack of skill? Judgment? Style? Not enough data? Reading people? Misreading the challenge? Misreading the politics? Or was it just random? A good strategy that just didn't work? Others that let you down? The key is to avoid two common reactions to your

mistakes: 1) avoiding similar situations instead of learning and trying again, and 2) trying to repeat what you did, only more diligently and harder, hoping to break through the problem, making the same mistake again but with greater impact. Neither trap leaves us with better strategies for the future. Neither is a learning strategy. To learn and do something differently, focus on the patterns in your behavior that get you in trouble and go back to first causes, those that tell you something about your shortcomings. Facing ourselves squarely is always the best way to learn.

Learning from Courses

☐ **Insight Events**
These are courses designed around assessing skills and providing feedback to the participants. These events can be a powerful source of self-knowledge and can lead to significant development if done right. When selecting a self-insight course, consider the following: 1) Are the skills assessed the important ones? 2) Are the assessment techniques and instruments sound? 3) Are those who are providing the feedback trained and professional? 4) Is the feedback provided in a user-friendly and "actionable" format? 5) Does the feedback include development planning? 6) Is the setting comfortable and conducive to reflection and learning? 7) Are the other participants the kinds of people you could learn from? 8) Are you in the right frame of mind to learn from this kind of intense experience? Select events on the basis of positive answers to these eight questions.

☐ **Attitude Toward Learning**
In addition to selecting the right course, a learning attitude is required. Be open. Close down your "like/dislike" switch, your "agree/disagree" blinders, and your "like me/not like me" feelings toward the instructors. Learning requires new lessons, change, and new behaviors and perspectives – all scary stuff for most people. Don't resist. Take in all you can during the course. Ask clarifying questions. Discuss concerns with the other participants. Jot down what you learn as you go. After the course is over, take some reflective time to glean the meat. Make the practical decisions about what you can and cannot use.

SUGGESTED READINGS

Dilenschneider, Robert L. *A Briefing for Leaders: Communication as the ultimate exercise of power.* New York: HarperBusiness, 1992.

Dowse, Eileen. *The Naked Manager – How to build open relationships at work.* Greensboro, North Carolina: Oakhill Press, 1998.

Linver, Sandy. *The Leader's Edge – How to use communication to grow your business and yourself.* New York: Simon & Schuster, 1994.

PERSONAL LEARNING

SECTION 1: YOUR DEVELOPMENT NEED(S)

UNSKILLED

- ☐ Doesn't change or adapt to his/her surroundings or the situation
- ☐ May have a view that being true to oneself is all that matters
- ☐ May see adjusting to others as a sign of weakness
- ☐ May be a one thing at a time person or a person who only thinks about what he/she is doing, not how others are responding or what they need
- ☐ Doesn't pick up on the need for personal change
- ☐ Doesn't seek or listen to personal on-line feedback
- ☐ Not a people watcher or studier, doesn't see or understand their reactions to him/her
- ☐ May be arrogant or defensive

SKILLED

- ☐ Picks up on the need to change personal, interpersonal, and managerial behavior quickly
- ☐ Watches others for their reactions to his/her attempts to influence and perform, and adjusts
- ☐ Seeks feedback
- ☐ Is sensitive to changing personal demands and requirements and changes accordingly

OVERUSED SKILL

- ☐ May be seen as too changeable
- ☐ May shift situationally too easily and leave the impression of being wishy-washy
- ☐ May err toward doing things differently rather than remaining the same
- ☐ May confuse people by experimenting and being so adaptable

Select one to three of the competencies listed below to work on to compensate for an overuse of this skill.

COMPENSATORS: 5, 16, 17, 39, 46, 47, 50, 51, 52, 53, 58, 59, 62, 65

SOME CAUSES

- ☐ Arrogant/defensive
- ☐ Can't do more than one thing at a time
- ☐ No role models
- ☐ Poor observer of others
- ☐ Being true to yourself is an overriding concern
- ☐ Think consistency is a virtue
- ☐ Think others should adjust to you

THE MAP

We are all capable of a range of behaviors. Even a shy person can get up the courage and strength to be assertive once in a while. A loud person can be quiet. A smart person can act dumb. An action oriented person can reflect. How do you know where in your range of behaviors to be in any given situation? Observation and feedback. Ever watch people who always seem to know when to adjust their behavior and in what direction to adjust it? Just when a situation is about to turn bad, they change tactics. Such people are astute observers of the reactions of others to what they are doing. They select from their range of behaviors the tone and level that fits the situation. They are very customer and audience driven; they deliver what each customer wants. This competency is especially important in managing, developing and motivating others, and in tense situations like negotiating or political disputes.

SECTION 2: LEARNING ON YOUR OWN

THESE SELF-DEVELOPMENT REMEDIES WILL HELP YOU BUILD YOUR SKILL(S)

SOME REMEDIES

☐ **1. You must observe and listen to be good at this.** You must watch the reactions of people to what you are doing while you are doing it to gauge their response. Are they bored? Change the pace. Are they confused? State it in a different way. Are they angry? Stop and ask what the problem is. Are they too quiet? Stop and get them involved in what you are doing. Are they fidgeting, scribbling on their pads or staring out the window? They may not be interested in what you are doing. Move to the end of your presentation or task, end it, and exit. Check in with your audience frequently and select a different tactic if necessary. *More help? – See #33 Listening.*

☐ **2. Seek feedback.** Ask people for direct feedback on what you are doing while you are doing it and immediately after. People are reluctant to give you feedback, especially negative or corrective information. Generally, to get it you must ask for it. If people are reluctant to give criticism, help by making self appraisal statements rather than asking questions. Saying, "I think I talked too long on that topic in the meeting; what do you think?" is easier for most people to reply to than a question which asks them to volunteer this point. *More help? – See #55 Self-Knowledge.*

☐ **3. Select three people to observe** who are good in tense situations or good with interpersonal transactions and transitions. Write down what they say or do when problems arise. What kinds of words do they use? How do they monitor what's happening? Do they ask questions or make statements? Do they state things in hard, moderate or soft ways? How much time do they talk vs. others? Compare this with what you do in these same situations. What differences do you see? Interview these people to see if they can take you inside their minds and explain why they did what they did and especially why they changed tactics midstream.

- ☐ **4. Customer focus.** People who are good at this work from the outside (the customer, the audience, the person, the situation) in, not from the inside out ("What do I want to do in this situation; what would make me happy and feel good?"). Practice not thinking inside/out when you are around others. What are the demand characteristics of this situation? How does this person or audience best learn? Which of my approaches or styles would work best? How can I best accomplish my goals? How can I alter my approach and tactics to be the most effective? The one-trick pony can only perform once per show. If the audience doesn't like that particular trick, no oats for the pony.

- ☐ **5. Pay particular attention to non-verbal cues.** Common signals of trouble are changes in body posture (especially turning away), crossed arms, staring, or the telltale glancing at one's watch, scribbling on the pad, tapping fingers or the pencil, looking out the window, frowns and washboard foreheads. When this occurs, pause. Ask a question. Ask how we're doing. Do a live process check. Some people use the same body language to signal that they are done or not interested in what's going on. Get to know their signals. Construct an alternative plan for the five people you work with closely. When Bill begins to stare, I will... When Sally interrupts for the third time, I will....

- ☐ **6. Experiment with some new techniques.** Many excellent personal learners have a bag of techniques they use. They give reasons for everything they say, saving any solution statements for last. They ask lots of questions, speak briefly, summarize often, and when disagreeing they put it in conditional terms ("I don't think so, but what do you think?"). The point of these is to elicit as much information about the reactions of others as they can. They are loading their files so they can change behavior when needed.

- ☐ **7. Become a better student of people.** Observe more than you do now. See if you can predict what people are going to say and do before they do it. See if their behavior shows a pattern. What do they do over and over again? By scoping out people better, you can better adjust to their responses. *More help? – See #56 Sizing Up People.*

- ☐ **8. Expand your repertoire of behavior.** Try to stretch yourself. Do things that are not characteristic of you. Go to your limits and beyond. By expanding the number of behaviors you have access to, you can become more effective across a larger number of situations. *More help? – See #54 Self-Development.*

☐ **9. Arrogance is a major blockage to personal learning.** Many people who have a towering strength or lots of success get little feedback and roll along until their careers get in trouble. If you are arrogant (you devalue the contributions of others), you should work doubly hard at observing, reading about and Interview others. You will need to submerge your "what I want/think" demeanor and keep asking yourself, "What do they want; how are they reacting?" Writing down your observations is a must, since in your normal mode you pay scant attention to your impact on others. *More help? – See #104 Arrogant.*

☐ **10. Defensiveness is the other major blockage** to personal learning. If you are defensive, people will not offer course correction information. If you are defensive, the feedback won't get in. You will need to work on seeing yourself in a calm state prior to meetings, mentally rehearsing how you will react to tough situations before you go in, and developing automatic tactics to resist shutting down. Some useful tactics are to literally count to ten, tell yourself to think in slow motion (or see yourself doing it) or to temper the heat with stock questions like, "What do you think? Could you tell me more about that?" *More help? – See #108 Defensiveness.*

SECTION 3: LEARNING FROM MORE FEEDBACK

THESE SOURCES WOULD GIVE YOU THE MOST ACCURATE AND DETAILED FEEDBACK ON YOUR SKILL(S)

☐ **Development Professionals**
Sometimes it might be valuable to get some analysis and feedback from a professional trained and certified in the area you're working on: possibly a career counselor, a therapist, clergy, a psychologist, etc.

☐ **Direct Boss**
Your direct boss has important information about you, your performance, and your prospects. The challenge is to get this information. There are formal processes (e.g., performance appraisals). There are day-to-day opportunities. To help, signal your boss that you want and can handle direct and timely feedback. Many bosses have trouble giving feedback, so you will have to work at it over a period of time.

☐ **Direct Reports**
Across a variety of settings, your direct reports probably see you the most. They are the recipients of most of your managerial behaviors. They know your work. They can compare you with former bosses. Since they may hesitate to give you negative feedback, you have to set the atmosphere to make it easier for them. You have to ask.

☐ **Natural Mentors**
Natural mentors have a special relationship with you and are interested in your success and your future. Since they are usually not in your direct chain of command, you can have more open, relaxed, and fruit-

ful discussions about yourself and your career prospects. They can be a very important source for candid or critical feedback others may not give you.

- ☐ **Past Associates/Constituencies**
  When confronted with a present performance problem, some claim, "I wasn't like that before; it must be the current situation." When feedback is available from former associates, about 50% support that claim. In the other half of the cases, the people were like that before and probably didn't know it. It sometimes makes sense to access the past to clearly see the present.

SECTION 4: LEARNING FROM DEVELOP-IN-PLACE ASSIGNMENTS

THESE PART-TIME DEVELOP-IN-PLACE ASSIGNMENTS WILL HELP YOU BUILD YOUR SKILL(S)

- ☐ Attend a self-awareness/assessment course that includes feedback.
- ☐ Attend a course or event which will push you personally beyond your usual limits or outside your comfort zone (e.g., Outward Bound, language immersion training, sensitivity group, public speaking).
- ☐ Interview or work with a "tutor" or mentor on a skill you need to develop.
- ☐ Do a study of successful executives in your organization and report the findings to top management.
- ☐ Join a self-help or support group.
- ☐ Try to learn something frivolous and fun to see how good you can get (e.g., juggling, square dancing, magic).
- ☐ Go on a business trip to a foreign country you've not been to before.
- ☐ Teach/coach someone how to do something you are not an expert in.
- ☐ Take on a tough and undoable project, one where others who have tried it have failed.
- ☐ Make peace with an enemy or someone you've disappointed with a product or service or someone you've had some trouble with or don't get along well with.

SECTION 5: LEARNING FROM FULL-TIME JOBS

THESE FULL-TIME JOBS OFFER THE OPPORTUNITY TO BUILD YOUR SKILL(S)

- ☐ **Off-Shore Assignments**
  The core demands to qualify as an Off-Shore assignment are: 1) First time working in the country. 2) Significant challenges like new language, hardship location, unique business rules/practices, significant cultural/marketplace differences, different functional task, etc. 3) More

than a year assignment. 4) No automatic return deal. 5) Not necessarily a change in job challenge, technical content, or responsibilities.

☐ **Scope Assignments**
The core demands for a Scope (complexity) assignment are: 1) Significant increase in both internal and external scope or complexity. 2) Significant increase in visibility and/or bottom line responsibility. 3) Unfamiliar area, business, technology, or territory. Examples of Scope assignments involving shifts: 1) Switching into a new function/technology/business. 2) Moving to new organization. 3) Moving to overseas assignment. 4) Moving to new location. 5) Adding new products/services. 6) Moving between headquarters/field. 7) Switches in ownership/top management of the unit/organization. Examples of Scope assignments involving "firsts": 1) First-time manager. 2) First-time managing managers. 3) First-time executive. 4) First-time overseas. 5) First-time headquarters/field. 6) First-time team leader. 7) First-time new technology/business/function. Scope assignments involving increased complexity: 1) Managing a significant expansion of an existing product or service. 2) Managing adding new products/service into an existing unit. 3) Managing a reorganized and more diverse unit. 4) Managing explosive growth. 5) Adding new technologies.

SECTION 6: LEARNING MORE FROM YOUR PLAN

THESE ADDITIONAL REMEDIES WILL HELP MAKE THIS DEVELOPMENT PLAN MORE EFFECTIVE FOR YOU

Learning to Learn Better

☐ **Monitoring Yourself More Closely and Getting off Your Autopilot**
Past habits are a mixed blessing, sometimes helping, sometimes not. To avoid putting yourself on "autopilot," think afresh about each situation before acting. Consistently monitor yourself with questions. Is this task different? Ask why you would repeat a past action. Are you avoiding anything, like taking a chance? Is there something new you might try?

☐ **Examine Your Past for Parallels to the Current Situation**
Examine your past for similar or contrasting experiences that match with or counter the current situation. What has worked in the past that you've dropped? What hasn't worked that you're repeating? What "pearls" of wisdom did you take away from your successes and failures, which you could apply today?

☐ **Keep a Learning Journal**
Keep a learning log or diary about the issues and opportunities you've faced and how you've acted. Focus on how you've used your strengths and weaknesses. Deduce your effective and successful rules of thumb – what worked and what didn't, and how you would have done it differently.

- ☐ **Analyze How You Perform Under Several Roles**
Do an analysis of yourself as a contributor, boss, manager, professional, parent, spouse, and/or friend. Create a list of criteria for each role and evaluate yourself against it. Pick a few things to work on for each role to improve.

- ☐ **Do a Career Learning Timeline for Insights**
Do a timeline (a chronology from schooling to the present) for yourself in terms of the development of your thinking and problem-solving style and preferences. List the good and the bad times. What made the difference? What breakthroughs did you have? How have you developed as a learner? How did you get rid of previous blocks? Are you still growing?

- ☐ **Compare Notes and Views on a Single Problem From Multiple Sources**
List the facts, your opinions, your hunches, your intuitions, and your feelings about the same problem or issue, and check the overlap and the differences. How do the lists differ? How are your feelings and intuitions different from the facts and the views of others? What does that tell you about yourself?

- ☐ **Throw Yourself With More Vigor Than Usual Into Something New**
Throw yourself into a new area, something you've not done before so you will have to learn quickly, such as a new technical area, a new management practice, or a self-development project. Pick something that is out of your skill and strength set.

- ☐ **Debrief Someone Else After a Successful or Non-Successful Event**
Shortly after someone does something particularly well or badly, debrief them on the process they followed. Ask them about the decisions they made and why; find out what they would have done differently. See if you can glean some insights or rules of thumb from the experiences of others.

Learning from Experience, Feedback and Other People

- ☐ **Learning from Mistakes**
Since we're human, we all make mistakes. The key is to focus on why you made the mistake. Spend more time locating causes and less worrying about the effects. Check how you react to mistakes. How much time do you spend being angry with yourself? Do you waste time stewing or do you move on? More importantly, do you learn? Ask why you made the mistake. Are you likely to repeat it under similar situations? Was it a lack of skill? Judgment? Style? Not enough data? Reading people? Misreading the challenge? Misreading the politics? Or was it just random? A good strategy that just didn't work? Others that let you down? The key is to avoid two common reactions to your mistakes: 1) avoiding similar situations instead of learning and trying

again, and 2) trying to repeat what you did, only more diligently and harder, hoping to break through the problem, making the same mistake again but with greater impact. Neither trap leaves us with better strategies for the future. Neither is a learning strategy. To learn and do something differently, focus on the patterns in your behavior that get you in trouble and go back to first causes, those that tell you something about your shortcomings. Facing ourselves squarely is always the best way to learn.

Learning from Courses

☐ **Insight Events**

These are courses designed around assessing skills and providing feedback to the participants. These events can be a powerful source of self-knowledge and can lead to significant development if done right. When selecting a self-insight course, consider the following: 1) Are the skills assessed the important ones? 2) Are the assessment techniques and instruments sound? 3) Are those who are providing the feedback trained and professional? 4) Is the feedback provided in a user-friendly and "actionable" format? 5) Does the feedback include development planning? 6) Is the setting comfortable and conducive to reflection and learning? 7) Are the other participants the kinds of people you could learn from? 8) Are you in the right frame of mind to learn from this kind of intense experience? Select events on the basis of positive answers to these eight questions.

SUGGESTED READINGS

Archer, Dane. *How to expand your S.I.Q. (social intelligence quotient).* New York: M. Evans, 1980.

Bernstein, Albert J. and Sydney Craft Rozen. *Sacred Bull: the inner obstacles that hold you back at work and how to overcome them.* New York: Wiley, 1994.

Brooks, Michael. *Instant rapport.* New York: Warner Books, 1989.

Brothers, Joyce. *Positive Plus: the practical plan for liking yourself better.* New York: G.P. Putnam's Sons, 1994.

Burgoon, Judee K., David B. Buller, and W. Gill Woodall. *Nonverbal communication: the unspoken dialogue.* New York: Harper & Row, 1989.

Butler, Gillian Pd.D and Tony Hope, M.D. *Managing your Mind.* New York: Oxford University Press, 1995.

Carlson, Richard. *Don't sweat the small stuff – and it's all small stuff: simple ways to keep the little things from taking over your life.* New York: Hyperion, 1997.

Caro, Mike. *Books of tells – Mike Caro's book of tells: the body language of poker.* Hollywood, CA: Gambling Times; Secaucus, NJ: L. Stuart, 1984.

Conger, Jay A. *Learning to Lead.* San Francisco: Jossey-Bass, Inc., 1992.

Cooper, Robert K. and Ayman Sawaf. *Executive EQ: emotional intelligence in leadership and organizations.* New York: Grosset/Putnam, 1997.

Danzig, Robert J. *The Leader Within You.* Hollywood, FL: Lifetime Books, Inc. 1998.

Dimitrius, Jo-Ellan and Mark Mazzarella. *Reading people: how to understand people and predict their behavior – anytime, anyplace.* New York: Random House, 1998.

Fast, Julius. *Body language.* New York: MJF Books, 1992.

Gitlow, Abraham L. *Being the boss: the importance of leadership and power.* Homewood, IL: Business One Irwin, 1992.

Haas, Howard G. *The Leader Within – An empowering path to self discovery.* New York: HarperBusiness, 1992.

Ishiguro, Kazuo. *The Remains of the Day.* New York: Knopf: 1989.

Kouzes, James M. *Credibility: how leaders gain and lose it, why people demand it.* San Francisco: Jossey-Bass Publishers, 1993.

Morris, Desmond. *Bodytalk: the meaning of human gestures.* New York: Crown Trade Paperbacks, 1994.

Philippot, Pierre, Robert S. Feldman, and Erik J. Coats, editors. *The social context of nonverbal behavior.* Cambridge, U.K.; New York: Cambridge University Press; Paris: Editions de la Maison des Sciences de l'Homme, 1999.

Prochaska, James O., John C. Norcross and Carlo C. DiClemente. *Changing for Good.* New York: Avon Books, 1995.

Vargas, Marjorie Fink. *Louder than words: An introduction to nonverbal communication.* Ames, IA: Iowa State University.Press, 1986

46

PERSPECTIVE

SECTION 1: YOUR DEVELOPMENT NEED(S)

UNSKILLED

- ☐ Is narrow and parochial
- ☐ Has narrow views of issues and challenges
- ☐ Uses only one or a few lenses to view problems and opportunities
- ☐ Doesn't have far ranging interests, not well read
- ☐ Background may be narrow
- ☐ Isn't good at running "what if" scenarios
- ☐ Lacks interest in maybes and the future and how world events do and will affect his/her organization
- ☐ Won't be a good strategist or visionary
- ☐ A here and now person who is often surprised by unexpected change
- ☐ May be a single function/profession/technical area/skill person

SKILLED

- ☐ Looks toward the broadest possible view of an issue/challenge
- ☐ Has broad-ranging personal and business interests and pursuits
- ☐ Can easily pose future scenarios
- ☐ Can think globally
- ☐ Can discuss multiple aspects and impacts of issues and project them into the future

OVERUSED SKILL

- ☐ Might have some trouble concentrating on the here and now
- ☐ May leave others behind when he/she speculates on the broad view of an issue
- ☐ May not set practical priorities
- ☐ May always be reaching for too much and/or the ideal
- ☐ May see connections that aren't there

Select one to three of the competencies listed below to work on to compensate for an overuse of this skill.

COMPENSATORS: 5, 16, 17, 24, 35, 38, 47, 50, 51, 52, 53, 58, 59, 63, 65

SOME CAUSES

- ☐ Avoid risks
- ☐ Disadvantaged background
- ☐ Narrow interests
- ☐ Narrow upbringing
- ☐ Restricted experience base
- ☐ Tactically oriented

- ☐ Too comfortable
- ☐ Uncomfortable thinking/talking about future states

THE MAP

Ideas, perspectives and strategies don't come from raw intelligence or creativity. They come from a prepared mind, one broadened by lots of varied but disconnected experiences, exposures and interests. The broadest people usually win because they have a greater repertoire to draw from and more chances to make unusual connections to new ideas, cultures, events, etc. In the Sears studies of effectiveness across 35 years, one of the best predictors of success was range of interests.

SECTION 2: LEARNING ON YOUR OWN

THESE SELF-DEVELOPMENT REMEDIES WILL HELP YOU BUILD YOUR SKILL(S)

SOME REMEDIES

☐ **1. Read any of the *Megatrends* books** by John Naisbitt or *The Popcorn Report* by Faith Popcorn or the *Futurist*, the journal of the World Future Society. Pay less attention to the particulars and more to the organizing principles of the books. What are the trends at play and how do they affect your organization now and in the future? Can you back up what you conclude with facts from your own experience?

☐ **2. Study a few well known inventions of the past,** like the automobile (*The Machine That Changed the World* by James Womack and Associates at MIT is an excellent source). See how they use the past to predict the future. See how several unrelated inventions came together to form a bigger one. There is a series on cable called *Inventions*. Watch a few shows. Buy the series. How could you use the past of your organization – from 1960 to 1970; from 1970 to 1980, etc. – to predict the future?

☐ **3. Read the *Wall Street Journal*** and *Business Week* and write down three to five interesting things that have a parallel or an effect on your organization. Learn to connect what's out there to what's in here.

☐ **4. During World War II,** the military discovered the most creative groups were those where the members had little or nothing in common, and knew little about the issue. Their freewheeling approach yielded fresher solutions. They were not trapped by the past. Take a current challenge to the most disparate group you can find (an historian, a college student, a theologian, a salesperson, a plumber, etc.) and see what insights they have into it. Find some problems outside of your area and see what you can add.

☐ **5. Pick three unrelated things to study** and dabble in that you have not yet paid much attention to – opera, romance novels, technical journals out of your area, MTV, learn a new language, take a magic course, study archeology. Connections can come from anywhere – your brain doesn't care where it gets perspectives. Try to think about how the principles of one tie into the other.

- ☐ **6. Read international publications** like *The Economist*, the *International Herald Tribune*, *Commentary*, autobiographies of people like Kissinger; pick a country and study it; read a book on the fall of the Soviet Union or read "we present all sides" journals like *The Atlantic Monthly* to get the broadest possible view of issues. There are common underlying principles in everything. You need to expose yourself more broadly in order to find and apply those principles to what you're doing today.
- ☐ **7. Go on adventures.** Travel to places you have not been before. Never vacation at the same place again. Eat at different theme restaurants. Go to events and meetings of groups you have never really met. Go to ethnic festivals and sample the cultures. Go to athletic events you've never attended before. Each week, you and your family should go on a perspectives adventure.
- ☐ **8. Pick something you've never done,** but which would broaden your perspective off work: serve with a community group, volunteer to be a Big Sister/Brother, travel to an unvisited country, follow a group of ten-year-olds around for a few days.
- ☐ **9. At work, pick three tasks you've never done** and go do them. If you don't know much about customers, work in a store or handle customer complaints; if you don't know what engineering does, go find out; task trade with someone. Seek the broadest possible exposure inside the organization. Do lunch with counterparts of the organization and tell each other what you do.
- ☐ **10. Task Forces.** Task Forces/projects are a great opportunity. If the project is important, is multifunctional and has a real outcome which will be taken seriously (not a study group), it is one of the most common developmental events listed by successful executives. Such projects require learning other functions, businesses or nationalities well enough that in a tight timeframe you can appreciate how they think and why their area/position is important. In so doing, you get out of your own experience and start to see connections to a broader world – how international trade works, or more at home, how the pieces of your organization fit together. You can build perspective.

SECTION 3: LEARNING FROM MORE FEEDBACK

THESE SOURCES WOULD GIVE YOU THE MOST ACCURATE AND DETAILED FEEDBACK ON YOUR SKILL(S)

☐ **All Other Superiors**

Collectively important, your supervisors know about the organization and where you fit in. They have the power to decide on your progress. Productive relationships with senior managers help to foster the kind of feedback you need to grow and improve. Most people never get access to this kind of information.

☐ **Boss's Boss(es)**
From a process standpoint, your boss's boss probably has the most influence and control over your progress. He/she has a broader perspective, has more access to data, and stands at the center of decisions about you. To know what he/she thinks, without having to violate the canons of corporate due process to get that information, would be quite useful.

☐ **Natural Mentors**
Natural mentors have a special relationship with you and are interested in your success and your future. Since they are usually not in your direct chain of command, you can have more open, relaxed, and fruitful discussions about yourself and your career prospects. They can be a very important source for candid or critical feedback others may not give you.

SECTION 4: LEARNING FROM DEVELOP-IN-PLACE ASSIGNMENTS

THESE PART-TIME DEVELOP-IN-PLACE ASSIGNMENTS WILL HELP YOU BUILD YOUR SKILL(S)

☐ Serve for a year or more with a community agency.

☐ Become a volunteer for a year or more for an outside organization.

☐ Lobby for your organization on a contested issue in local, regional, state, or federal government.

☐ Act as a loaned executive to a charity, government, agency, etc.

☐ Work short rotations in other units, functions, or geographies you've not been exposed to before.

☐ Work on a project that involves travel and study of an issue, acquisition, or joint venture off-shore or overseas, with a report back to management.

☐ Manage a project team made up of nationals from a number of countries.

☐ Get involved with the negotiation of a contract or agreement with international consequences.

☐ Manage an ad hoc, temporary group of people where the people in the group are towering experts but the temporary manager is not.

☐ Assemble an ad hoc team of diverse people to accomplish a difficult task.

SECTION 5: LEARNING FROM FULL-TIME JOBS

THESE FULL-TIME JOBS OFFER THE OPPORTUNITY TO BUILD YOUR SKILL(S)

☐ **Cross-Moves**

The core demands necessary to qualify as a Cross-Move are: 1) Move to a very different set of challenges. 2) Abrupt jump-shift in tasks/activities. 3) Never been there before. 4) New setting/conditions. Examples of Cross-Moves are: 1) Changing divisions. 2) Changing functions. 3) Field/headquarters shifts. 4) Line/staff switches. 5) Country switches. 6) Working with all new people. 7) Changing lines of business.

☐ **Heavy Strategic Demands**

The core demands necessary to qualify as a Heavy Strategic Content assignment are: 1) Requires significant strategic thinking and planning most couldn't do. 2) Charts new ground strategically. 3) Plan must be presented, challenged, adopted, and implemented. 4) Exposure to significant decision makers and executives. 1) Strategic planning position. 2) Job involving repositioning of a product, service, or organization.

☐ **Off-Shore Assignments**

The core demands to qualify as an Off-Shore assignment are: 1) First time working in the country. 2) Significant challenges like new language, hardship location, unique business rules/practices, significant cultural/marketplace differences, different functional task, etc. 3) More than a year assignment. 4) No automatic return deal. 5) Not necessarily a change in job challenge, technical content, or responsibilities.

☐ **Scope Assignments**

The core demands for a Scope (complexity) assignment are: 1) Significant increase in both internal and external scope or complexity. 2) Significant increase in visibility and/or bottom line responsibility. 3) Unfamiliar area, business, technology, or territory. Examples of Scope assignments involving shifts: 1) Switching into a new function/technology/business. 2) Moving to new organization. 3) Moving to overseas assignment. 4) Moving to new location. 5) Adding new products/services. 6) Moving between headquarters/field. 7) Switches in ownership/top management of the unit/organization. Examples of Scope assignments involving "firsts": 1) First-time manager. 2) First-time managing managers. 3) First-time executive. 4) First-time overseas. 5) First-time headquarters/field. 6) First-time team leader. 7) First-time new technology/business/function. Scope assignments involving increased complexity: 1) Managing a significant expansion of an existing product or service. 2) Managing adding new products/service into an existing unit. 3) Managing a reorganized and more diverse unit. 4) Managing explosive growth. 5) Adding new technologies.

SECTION 6: LEARNING MORE FROM YOUR PLAN

THESE ADDITIONAL REMEDIES WILL HELP MAKE THIS DEVELOPMENT PLAN MORE EFFECTIVE FOR YOU

Learning to Learn Better

☐ **Consult With Expert in the Area of Concern for You**
Consult with an outside expert in the area you're dealing with, someone especially skilled and known; describe your situation the best you can and openly and receptively listen to the advice and counsel the expert provides. Try the advice before you reject it.

☐ **Model Someone Who Has What You Need**
Observe and emulate the behavior of one or more persons you respect who are models of the behavior you are trying to develop. Once you can do the behavior, try to make it permanent by finding the key learning and rules.

☐ **Try Some New Things Out of Your Normal Comfort Zone**
Periodically, practice going against your grain (what's normal for you) and getting out of your comfort zone. Try something different and opposite to your nature; take a learning risk. Explore: if you're a thinker, act; if you're an action person, think. Test the unfamiliar; try the new; go beyond your self-determined limits and boundaries.

☐ **Try New Things, Take Some Chances, Increase Personal Risk Taking**
Engage in some creative problem-solving activities such as brainstorming, free association, analogies to unrelated areas, nominal group techniques, etc. Let yourself go; let your thinking flow freely. Break down the restrictions on yourself; break through old barriers and blockages; try new ways of thinking.

☐ **Regularly Read Relevant Publications**
Read publications most relevant to you such as the *Wall Street Journal*, the *Harvard Business Review*, the *Economist*, *Fortune*, *Business Week*, etc. Track a single issue or trend to see as many sides of it as you can. What tactics and strategies are being followed? How is this similar to something you are doing? How could you use some of your insights?

☐ **Study Something Unusual or Unexpected**
Consider the odd and unusual facts or opinions that don't seem to fit in anywhere. If these anomalies comprised the majority opinion, where would that lead? What beliefs or facts would you have to have to state those unusual opinions?

☐ **Sort Through Information Multiple Ways**
Collect the data and arrange it in elements or pieces. Come up with definitions, and arrange the data in various ways: chronologically, from most to least, from biggest to smallest, from cold to hot, what you know most about and least about, from known to unknown, etc., until the meaning becomes obvious.

Learning from Experience, Feedback and Other People

☐ **Using Multiple Models**
Who do you know who exemplifies how to do whatever your need is? Who, for example, personifies decisiveness or compassion or strategic agility? Think more broadly than your current job and colleagues. For example, clergy, friends, spouses or community leaders are also good sources for potential models. Select your models not on the basis of overall excellence or likability, but on the basis of the one towering strength (or glaring weakness) you are interested in. Even people who are well thought of usually have only one or two towering strengths (or glaring weaknesses). Ordinarily, you won't learn as much from the whole person as you will from one characteristic.

Learning from Courses

☐ **Orientation Events**
Most organizations offer a variety of orientation events. They are designed to communicate strategies, charters, missions, goals, and general information and offer an opportunity for people to meet each other. They are short in duration and offer limited opportunities for learning anything beyond general context and background.

☐ **Strategic Courses**
There are a number of courses designed to stretch minds to prepare for future challenges. They include topics such as Workforce Diversity 2000, globalization, the European Union, competitive competencies and strategies, etc. Quality depends upon the following three factors: 1) The quality of the staff. Are they qualified? Are they respected in their fields? Are they strategic "gurus"? 2) The quality of the participants. Are they the kind of people you could learn from? 3) The quality of the setting. Is it comfortable and free from distractions? Can you learn there?

SUGGESTED READINGS

Soundview Executive Book Summaries. 10 LaCrue Avenue, Concordville, PA 19331 1-800-521-1227. 1-610-558-9495 (outside US and Canada) http://www.summary.com

Soundview Executive Book Summaries are 5,000-word, eight-page distillations of specially selected business books. Soundview Subscribers receive two or three eight-page Summaries of the best business books each month (30 per year); access to well over 200 Summaries on Soundview's backlist; and access to editors in Soundview's research department, for help in finding specific business book references.

The Atlantic Monthly. http://www.theatlantic.com

continued

Business Week. http://www.businessweek.com

Commentary Magazine. http://www.commentarymagazine.com

Futurist Magazine. http://www.wfs.org

The Economist. http://www.economist.com

International Herald Tribune. http://www.iht.com

Wall Street Journal. http://www.wsj.com

Badaracco, Joseph L. Jr. *Defining Moments – When managers must choose between right and right.* Boston: Harvard Business School Press, 1997.

Durant, Will. *The lessons of history.* New York: Simon and Schuster, 1968.

Gibbon, Edward, edited by Dero A. Saunders. *The portable Gibbon: The decline and fall of the Roman Empire.* New York: Viking Press, 1952.

...or...

Gibbon, Edward. *History of the decline and fall of the Roman Empire. A modern abridgment by Moses Hadas.* New York: Putnam, 1962.

Green, Peter. *Alexander of Macedon, 356–323 B.C. A historical biography.* Los Angeles: University of California Press, 1991.

Handy, Charles. *The Age of Unreason.* Boston: Harvard Business School Press, 1989.

Handy, Charles. *The Hungry Spirit.* New York: Doubleday, 1998.

Hendricks, Gay and Kate Ludeman. *The corporate mystic: a guidebook for visionaries with their feet on the ground.* New York: Bantam Books, 1996.

Kennedy, Paul M. *The rise and fall of the great powers: economic change and military conflict from 1500 to 2000.* New York, NY: Random House, 1987.

Kraus, Peter (Ed.). *The Book of Leadership Wisdom.* New York: John Wiley & Sons, Inc., 1998.

Montgomery, Cynthia A. and Michael E. Porter, Editors. *Strategy.* Boston: Harvard Business School Press, 1991.

Nixon, Richard M. *Leaders.* New York: Warner Books, 1982.

Popcorn, Faith. *The Popcorn report: Faith Popcorn on the future of your company, your world, your life.* New York: Doubleday, 1991.

continued

Popcorn, Faith. *The Popcorn report: Faith Popcorn on the future of your company, your world, your life [sound recording].* New York: Simon & Schuster Audio, 1991.

Price Waterhouse Change Integration Team. *Better Change.* Burr Ridge, IL: Irwin Professional Publishing, 1995.

Womack, James P. [et al.]. *The Machine that changed the world: Based on the Massachusetts Institute of Technology 5-million dollar 5-year study on the future of the automobile.* New York: Rawson Associates, 1990.

PLANNING

SECTION 1: YOUR DEVELOPMENT NEED(S)

UNSKILLED

- ☐ Doesn't plan for much
- ☐ May be a seat of the pants performer scratching it out at the last minute
- ☐ Doesn't follow an orderly method of setting goals and laying out work
- ☐ May be uncomfortable with structure and process flow
- ☐ May be disdainful of planning and come across to others as loose or too simple
- ☐ May not have the patience to establish goals and objectives, scope out difficulties, plan for task completion, develop schedules, and do roadblock management
- ☐ May be confusing to work for and with
- ☐ May be demotivating to others who work with him/her

SKILLED

- ☐ Accurately scopes out length and difficulty of tasks and projects
- ☐ Sets objectives and goals
- ☐ Breaks down work into the process steps
- ☐ Develops schedules and task/people assignments
- ☐ Anticipates and adjusts for problems and roadblocks
- ☐ Measures performance against goals
- ☐ Evaluates results

OVERUSED SKILL

- ☐ May be overly dependent on rules, regulations, procedures, and structure
- ☐ May leave out the human element of the work
- ☐ May be inflexible and have trouble with rapid change

Select one to three of the competencies listed below to work on to compensate for an overuse of this skill.

COMPENSATORS: 2, 3, 10, 14, 15, 26, 31, 32, 33, 40, 46, 57, 60, 64

SOME CAUSES

- ☐ Arrogant; don't need it
- ☐ Impatient
- ☐ Low sense of structure and process
- ☐ Need for simplicity
- ☐ Time management; just don't get around to it

THE MAP

Nothing helps move things along better than a good plan. It helps the people who have to work under the plan. It leads to better use of resources. It gets things done faster. It helps anticipate problems before they occur. It is one of the aspects of managing others that universally receives a positive response. A good plan leaves more time to do other things secure in the knowledge that things are on track and proceeding as planned.

SECTION 2: LEARNING ON YOUR OWN

THESE SELF-DEVELOPMENT REMEDIES WILL HELP YOU BUILD YOUR SKILL(S)

SOME REMEDIES

☐ **1. Lay out tasks and work.** Most successful projects begin with a good plan. What do I need to accomplish? What are the goals? What's the timeline? What resources will I need? How many of the resources do I control? Who controls the rest of the resources – people, funding, tools, materials, support – I need? Lay out the work from A to Z. Many people are seen as lacking a plan because they don't write down the sequence or parts of the work and leave something out. Ask others to comment on ordering and what's missing. *More help? – See #52 Process Management and #63 TQM/Re-Engineering.*

☐ **2. Set the plan.** Buy a flow charting software program like ABC FlowCharter® that does PERT and GANT charts. Become an expert in its use. Use the output of the software to communicate your plans to others. Use the flow charts in your presentations.

☐ **3. Set goals and measures.** Nothing keeps projects on time and on budget like a goal, a plan and a measure. Set goals for the whole project and the sub tasks. Plan for all. Set measures so you and others can track progress against the goals. *More help? – See #35 Managing and Measuring Work.*

☐ **4. Manage multiple plans or aspects of big plans.** Many attempts to accomplish complex plans involve managing parallel tracks or multiple tasks at the same time. It helps if you have a master plan. Good planning decreases the chances you will lose control by spreading yourself too thin.

☐ **5. Manage efficiently.** Plan the budget and manage against it. Spend carefully. Have a reserve if the unanticipated comes up. Set up a funding timeline so you can track ongoing expenditures against plan.

☐ **6. You need to match people and tasks.** People are different. They have different strengths and have differing levels of knowledge and experience. Instead of thinking of everyone as equal, think of them as different. Really equal treatment is giving people tasks to do that match their capacities. *More help? – See #56 Sizing Up People.*

☐ **7. Vision the plan in process.** What could go wrong? Run scenarios in your head. Think along several paths. Rank the potential problems from highest likelihood to lowest likelihood. Think about what you would do if the highest likelihood things were to occur. Create a contingency plan for each. Pay attention to the weakest links which are usually groups or elements you have the least interface with or control over (perhaps someone in a remote location, a consultant or supplier). Stay doubly in touch with the potential weak links. *More help? – See #51 Problem Solving.*

☐ **8. Set up a process to monitor progress against the plan.** How would you know if the plan is on time? Could you estimate time to completion or percent finished at any time? Give people involved in implementing the plan progress feedback as you go.

☐ **9. Find someone in your environment who is better at planning** than you are to see how it's done. How does that compare against what you typically do? Try to increase doing the things he/she does. Ask for feedback from some people who have had to follow your plans. What did they like? What did they find difficult?

☐ **10. Get others to help.** Share your ideas about the project with others, possibly the people you need to support you later. Get their input on the plan. Delegate creating the plan to people who are better at it than you are. You provide the goals and what needs to be done, and let others create the detailed plan. *More help? – See #18 Delegation and #33 Listening.*

SECTION 3: LEARNING FROM MORE FEEDBACK

THESE SOURCES WOULD GIVE YOU THE MOST ACCURATE AND DETAILED FEEDBACK ON YOUR SKILL(S)

☐ **Direct Boss**
Your direct boss has important information about you, your performance, and your prospects. The challenge is to get this information. There are formal processes (e.g., performance appraisals). There are day-to-day opportunities. To help, signal your boss that you want and can handle direct and timely feedback. Many bosses have trouble giving feedback, so you will have to work at it over a period of time.

☐ **Direct Reports**
Across a variety of settings, your direct reports probably see you the most. They are the recipients of most of your managerial behaviors. They know your work. They can compare you with former bosses. Since they may hesitate to give you negative feedback, you have to set the atmosphere to make it easier for them. You have to ask.

☐ **Past Associates/Constituencies**
When confronted with a present performance problem, some claim, "I wasn't like that before; it must be the current situation." When feed-

back is available from former associates, about 50% support that claim. In the other half of the cases, the people were like that before and probably didn't know it. It sometimes makes sense to access the past to clearly see the present.

☐ **Peers and Colleagues**
Peers and colleagues have a special social and working relationship. They attend staff meetings together, share private views, get feedback from the same boss, travel together, and are knowledgeable about each other's work. You perhaps let your guard down more around peers and act more like yourself. They can be a valuable source of feedback.

SECTION 4: LEARNING FROM DEVELOP-IN-PLACE ASSIGNMENTS

THESE PART-TIME DEVELOP-IN-PLACE ASSIGNMENTS WILL HELP YOU BUILD YOUR SKILL(S)

☐ Install a new process or system (computer system, new policies, new process, new procedures, etc.).

☐ Plan a new site for a building (plant, field office, headquarters, etc.).

☐ Plan an off-site meeting, conference, convention, trade show, event, etc.

☐ Manage the purchase of a major product, equipment, materials, program, or system.

☐ Run a company or unit picnic or annual outing.

☐ Manage the visit of a VIP (member of top management, government official, outside customer, foreign visitor, etc.).

☐ Seek out and use a seed budget to create and pursue a personal idea, product, or service.

☐ Work on a team writing a proposal to obtain significant government or foundation grants or funding of an activity.

☐ Design a training course in an area you're not an expert in.

☐ Work on a team that's deciding who to keep and who to let go in a layoff, shutdown, delayering, or divestiture.

SECTION 5: LEARNING FROM FULL-TIME JOBS

THESE FULL-TIME JOBS OFFER THE OPPORTUNITY TO BUILD YOUR SKILL(S)

☐ **Chair of Projects/Task Forces**
The core demands for qualifying as a Project/Task Force assignment are: 1) Full-time assignment. 2) Important and specific goal. 3) Tight deadline. 4) Success or failure will be evident. 5) High-visibility sponsor. 6) Learning something on the fly. 7) Must get others to cooperate. 8) Usually six months or more. Four types of Projects/Task Forces:

1) New ideas, products, services, or systems (e.g., product/service/program research and development, creation/installation/launch of a new system, new programs like Total Quality Management, positive discipline). 2) Formal negotiations and relationships (e.g., acquisitions, divestitures, agreements, joint ventures; licensing arrangements, franchising; dealing with unions, governments, communities, charities, customers, and relocations). 3) Big one-time events (e.g., working on a major presentation for the board, organizing significant meetings or conferences, disaster/damage control teams; reorganizations, mergers, acquisitions, or relocations, working on visions, charters, strategies, other time-urgent issues and problems). 4) Troubleshooting (e.g., problems, disasters, crises, product/service failures, accidents, illegal activities, damage control in public relations goofs, shut downs, downsizings, layoffs, abrupt changes in leadership).

☐ **Fix-its/Turnarounds**
The core demands to qualify as a Fix-it or Turnaround assignment are: 1) Cleaning up a mess. 2) Serious people issues/problems like credibility/performance/morale. 3) Tight deadline. 4) Serious business performance failure. 5) Last chance to fix. Four Types of Fix-its/Turnarounds: 1) Fixing a failed business/unit involving taking control, stopping losses, managing damage, planning the turnaround, dealing with people problems, installing new processes and systems, and rebuilding the spirit and performance of the unit. 2) Managing sizable disasters like mishandled labor negotiations and strikes, thefts, history of significant business losses, poor staff, failed leadership, hidden problems, fraud, public relations nightmares, etc. 3) Significant reorganization and restructuring (e.g., stabilizing the business, reforming unit, introducing new systems, making people changes, resetting strategy and tactics). 4) Significant system/process breakdown (e.g., MIS, financial coordination processes, audits, standards, etc.) across units requiring working to change something from a distant position, providing advice and counsel, and installing or implementing a major process improvement or system change outside your own unit and/or with customers outside the organization.

☐ **Scale Assignments**
Core requirements to qualify as a Scale (size) shift assignment are: 1) Sizable jump-shift in the size of the job in areas like: number of people, number of layers in organization, size of budget, number of locations, volume of activity, tightness of deadlines. 2) Medium to low complexity; mostly repetitive and routine processes and procedures. 3) Stable staff and business. 4) Stable operations. 5) Often slow, steady growth.

☐ **Start-ups**
The core demands to qualify as a start from scratch are: 1) Starting something new for you and/or for the organization. 2) Forging a new

team. 3) Creating new systems/facilities/staffs/programs/procedures. 4) Contextual adversity (e.g., uncertainty, government regulation, unions, difficult environment). Seven types of start from scratches: 1) Planning, building, hiring, and managing (e.g., building a new facility, opening up a new location, moving a unit or company). 2) Heading something new (e.g., new product, new service, new line of business, new department/function, major new program). 3) Take over a group/product/service/program that had existed for less than a year and was off to a fast start. 4) Establishing overseas operations. 5) Major new designs for existing systems. 6) Moving a successful program from one unit to another. 7) Installing a new organization-wide process as a full-time job (e.g., like Total Quality).

SECTION 6: LEARNING MORE FROM YOUR PLAN

THESE ADDITIONAL REMEDIES WILL HELP MAKE THIS DEVELOPMENT PLAN MORE EFFECTIVE FOR YOU

Learning to Learn Better

☐ **Plan Backwards from the Ideal**
Envision what an ideal outcome would look like and plan backwards. What is the series of events that would have to take place to get there? What would people do? What would have to be done? How would people react? How would things play out? Could you plan it forward and get to the same outcome?

☐ **Envision Yourself Succeeding**
Examine the image of success in detail: what you are doing, what you are feeling, how you are reacting to others, how others are reacting to you, how the parts fit together. Can you then play that out in the real situation and get to the same outcome?

☐ **Rehearse Successful Tactics/Strategies/Actions**
Mentally rehearse how you will act before going into the situation. Try to anticipate how others will react, what they will say, and how you'll respond. Check out the best and worst cases; play out both scenes. Check your feelings in conflict or worst-case situations; rehearse staying under control.

☐ **Study People Who Have Successfully Done What You Need to Do**
Interview people who have already done what you're planning to do and check your plan against what they did. Try to summarize their key tactics, strategies, and insights; adjust your plan accordingly.

☐ **Preview a Plan With a Test Audience**
Before committing to a plan, find someone agreeable to a wide-ranging discussion about the issue or problem you face. Explore all sides and options; go with the flow; let what you need to do emerge from the process; develop a plan as you go.

Learning from Experience, Feedback and Other People

- ☐ **Learning from Observing Others**
  Observe others. Find opportunities to observe without interacting with your model. This enables you to objectively study the person, note what he/she is doing or not doing, and compare that with what you would typically do in similar situations. Many times you can learn more by watching than asking. Your model may not be able to explain what he/she does or may be an unwilling teacher.

- ☐ **Getting Feedback from Bosses and Superiors**
  Many bosses are reluctant to give negative feedback. They lack the managerial courage to face people directly with criticism. You can help by soliciting feedback and setting the tone. Show them you can handle criticism and that you are willing to work on issues they see as important.

- ☐ **Getting Feedback from Direct Reports**
  Direct reports often fear reprisals for giving negative feedback about bosses, whether in a formal process, like a questionnaire, or informally and face-to-face. Even with a guarantee of confidentiality, some are still hesitant. If you want feedback from direct reports, you have to set a positive tone and never act out of revenge.

Learning from Courses

- ☐ **Job Skills**
  Most organizations and professional associations offer job skills training. The key is to find a course that has the right content and offers the opportunity for practicing the jobs skills. It's helpful if the instructors have actually performed the skills in situations similar to your own.

- ☐ **Sending Others to Courses**
  If you are responsible for managing someone else's development and, as part of that, sending them to courses, prepare them beforehand. Don't send them as tourists. Meet with them before and after the course. Tell them why they need this course. Tell them what you expect them to learn. Give them feedback on why you think they need the course. Agree ahead of time how you will measure and monitor learning after they return. If possible, offer a variety of courses for your employee to choose from. Have them give you a report shortly after they return. If appropriate, have them present what they learned to the rest of your staff. After they return, provide opportunities for using the new skills with safe cover and low risk. Give them practice time before expecting full exercise of the new skills. Be supportive during early unsteadiness. Give continuous feedback on progress.

SUGGESTED READINGS

Bandrowski, James F. *Corporate Imagination Plus.* New York: Macmillan, Inc., 1990.

Dutka, Alan F. *Competitive intelligence for the competitive edge.* Lincolnwood, Ill.: NTC Business Books, 1999.

Hamel, Gary and C.K. Prahalad. *Competing for the Future.* Boston: Harvard Business School Press, 1994.

Smith, Preston G. and Donald G. Reinertsen. *Developing Products in Half the Time.* New York: VanNostrand Reinhold, 1991.

Williams, Paul B. *Getting a Project Done on Time.* New York: AMACOM, 1996.

48

POLITICAL SAVVY

SECTION 1: YOUR DEVELOPMENT NEED(S)

UNSKILLED

- ☐ Doesn't know how to navigate smoothly and quietly through political waters
- ☐ Says and does things that cause political problems
- ☐ Doesn't understand how to deal with not invented here and territory protection
- ☐ Rejects politics and may view self as apolitical; others might see this as naive
- ☐ May not deal with upper management persuasively
- ☐ May be impatient with political process and make procedural errors
- ☐ May be too direct and not consider impact on others
- ☐ May not project out consequences of his/her actions well

SKILLED

- ☐ Can maneuver through complex political situations effectively and quietly
- ☐ Is sensitive to how people and organizations function
- ☐ Anticipates where the land mines are and plans his/her approach accordingly
- ☐ Views corporate politics as a necessary part of organizational life and works to adjust to that reality
- ☐ Is a maze-bright person

OVERUSED SKILL

- ☐ May be seen as excessively political
- ☐ May not be trusted
- ☐ May tell others what they are expecting to hear rather than what he/she knows to be true
- ☐ May overstate what he or she knows
- ☐ May be seen as manipulative and scheming

Select one to three of the competencies listed below to work on to compensate for an overuse of this skill.

COMPENSATORS: 4, 8, 12, 17, 22, 27, 29, 30, 34, 38, 44, 51, 53, 57, 63

SOME CAUSES

- ☐ Don't read others or their interests well
- ☐ Excessively direct and straightforward
- ☐ Misunderstanding of what political savvy is
- ☐ No patience with due process

- ☐ Poor interpersonal skills
- ☐ Poor negotiator
- ☐ Reject the necessity of "playing politics"
- ☐ Seen as an advocate
- ☐ Very action oriented
- ☐ Very ego/ethnocentric

THE MAP

Organizations are complex mazes of egos, constituencies, issues and rivalries. They are peopled with strong egos and empire driven individuals. Everyone builds his or her own sandbox and defends it from attack and influence from outsiders. There are many traps and dead ends in organizations. More ways to turn wrong than right. People who are politically savvy accept this as the human condition and deal with it. Not to be confused with being "political" which is a polite term for not being trusted or lacking in substance, political savvy involves getting things done in the maze with the least noise for the maximum benefit.

SECTION 2: LEARNING ON YOUR OWN

THESE SELF-DEVELOPMENT REMEDIES WILL HELP YOU BUILD YOUR SKILL(S)

SOME REMEDIES

☐ **1. How are you rated on** *#22 Ethics and Values* and *#29 Integrity and Trust*? If high, then don't read this tip. If either is average or lower, you may be seen as not helpful to others. Your attempts to influence will not be trusted. Are you viewed as a loner? You might be cutting corners to look good. You may slap things together to look good when what's underneath wouldn't pass the test. You may be trying to blame others for things you should take responsibility for. You may be seen as pushing narrow or personal interests. You may be making up excuses that are not real to cover your butt. You may be trying to make your rivals look bad so you look better. You may hedge when asked a tough question. You may indicate little or no concern for others. If you do any of these things or things like it, you will eventually be found out. Being more politically savvy may actually backfire on you. Others will trust you less. Before you work on political savvy, work on yourself. *More help? – See #22 Ethics and Values and #29 Integrity and Trust.*

☐ **2. People who are politically savvy work from the outside** (audience, person, group) in. They determine the demand characteristics or requirements of each situation and each person they face and select from among their various skills, tone, and styles to find the best approach to make things work. Practice not thinking inside/out when you are around others. *More help? – See #15 Customer Focus.*

☐ **3. With senior management.** In the special case of dealing with higher management, those who are best at it inform senior managers individually before the presentation/proposal. They often go to the toughest critic first to hone their ideas and get the worst case out first. Using sound political tactics with senior managers is complicated by people's comfort around top management. Sound political moves require a cool and clear head. *More help? – See #8 Comfort Around Higher Management.*

☐ **4. Organizations are politically complex.** They are peopled with strong egos and empire driven individuals. There are many political traps and dead ends. More ways to turn wrong than right. People who are politically savvy know the organization. They know how to get things done. They know who to rely on for expediting things. They know who the major gatekeepers are who control the flow of resources, information and decisions. *More help? – See #38 Organizational Agility.*

☐ **5. Being politically sensitive includes being people sensitive.** You have to be able to read people. You have to be able to predict how they are going to react to you and to what you are trying to get done. The magic and the complexity of life is that people are different. Each requires special consideration and treatment. If you are able to predict what individuals or groups will do, you will be able to select from among your various tactics, skills, and styles to get done what you need. *More help? – See #36 Motivating Others and #56 Sizing Up People.*

☐ **6. For close-in political savvy** (live in a meeting) you need to learn how to read non-verbals. Common signals of trouble are changes in body posture (especially turning away), crossed arms, staring, or the telltale glancing at one's watch, scribbling on the note pad, tapping one's fingers or a pencil, looking out the window, frowns and wash-board foreheads. When this occurs, pause. Ask a question. Ask how we're doing. Do a live process check.

☐ **7. Strong advocates for narrow views** don't usually fare well politically in organizations. Initially be tentative. Give others some room to maneuver. Make the business or organizational case first. Be prepared to counter arguments that your objective is less important than theirs. A lot of political noise is caused by making extreme statements right out of the box.

☐ **8. Selective savvy?** Is there a group or groups you have more trouble with politically than others? Is it because you don't like or are uncomfortable with them? To work better with problem groups, put yourself in their case. Turn off your "I like – I don't like; I agree – I don't agree" switch. Ask yourself why would you act that way? What do you think they're trying to achieve? Establish reciprocity. Relationships don't last unless you provide something and so do they. Find out what they want and tell them what you want. Strike a bargain.

☐ **9. Keep political conflicts small and concrete.** The more abstract it gets, the more unmanageable it becomes. Separate the people from the problem. Attack problems by looking at the nature of the problem, not the person presenting the problem. Avoid direct blaming remarks; describe the problem and its impact. If you can't agree on a solution, agree on procedure, or agree on a few things, and list all the issues remaining. This creates some motion and breaks political stalemates.

☐ **10. Be process flexible.** Always have a plan of attack but also have a contingency plan. Be ready for instant change. Expect the unexpected. People who are politically savvy are personally flexible. They care more about accomplishing the objective than staying true to the one true "me." *More help? – See #32 Learning on the Fly and #45 Personal Learning.*

SECTION 3: LEARNING FROM MORE FEEDBACK

THESE SOURCES WOULD GIVE YOU THE MOST ACCURATE AND DETAILED FEEDBACK ON YOUR SKILL(S)

☐ **Boss's Boss(es)**
From a process standpoint, your boss's boss probably has the most influence and control over your progress. He/she has a broader perspective, has more access to data, and stands at the center of decisions about you. To know what he/she thinks, without having to violate the canons of corporate due process to get that information, would be quite useful.

☐ **Direct Boss**
Your direct boss has important information about you, your performance, and your prospects. The challenge is to get this information. There are formal processes (e.g., performance appraisals). There are day-to-day opportunities. To help, signal your boss that you want and can handle direct and timely feedback. Many bosses have trouble giving feedback, so you will have to work at it over a period of time.

☐ **Human Resource Professionals**
Human Resource professionals have both a formal and informal feedback role. Since they have access to unique and confidential information, they can provide the right context for feedback you've received. Sometimes they may be "directed" to give you feedback. Other times, they may pass on feedback just to be helpful to you.

☐ **Natural Mentors**
Natural mentors have a special relationship with you and are interested in your success and your future. Since they are usually not in your direct chain of command, you can have more open, relaxed, and fruitful discussions about yourself and your career prospects. They can be a very important source for candid or critical feedback others may not give you.

- ☐ **Past Associates/Constituencies**
  When confronted with a present performance problem, some claim, "I wasn't like that before; it must be the current situation." When feedback is available from former associates, about 50% support that claim. In the other half of the cases, the people were like that before and probably didn't know it. It sometimes makes sense to access the past to clearly see the present.

SECTION 4: LEARNING FROM DEVELOP-IN-PLACE ASSIGNMENTS

THESE PART-TIME DEVELOP-IN-PLACE ASSIGNMENTS WILL HELP YOU BUILD YOUR SKILL(S)

- ☐ Serve for a year or more with a community agency.
- ☐ Lobby for your organization on a contested issue in local, regional, state, or federal government.
- ☐ Be a change agent; create a symbol for change; lead the rallying cry; champion a significant change and implementation.
- ☐ Relaunch an existing product or service that's not doing well.
- ☐ Serve on a junior or shadow board.
- ☐ Work on a team forming a joint venture or partnership.
- ☐ Prepare and present a proposal of some consequence to top management.
- ☐ Manage the assigning/allocating of office space in a contested situation.
- ☐ Take on a tough and undoable project, one where others who have tried it have failed.
- ☐ Do a postmortem on a failed project and present it to the people involved.

SECTION 5: LEARNING FROM FULL-TIME JOBS

THESE FULL-TIME JOBS OFFER THE OPPORTUNITY TO BUILD YOUR SKILL(S)

- ☐ **Chair of Projects/Task Forces**
  The core demands for qualifying as a Project/Task Force assignment are: 1) Full-time assignment. 2) Important and specific goal. 3) Tight deadline. 4) Success or failure will be evident. 5) High-visibility sponsor. 6) Learning something on the fly. 7) Must get others to cooperate. 8) Usually six months or more. Four types of Projects/Task Forces: 1) New ideas, products, services, or systems (e.g., product/service/program research and development, creation/installation/launch of a new system, new programs like Total Quality Management, positive discipline). 2) Formal negotiations and relationships (e.g., acquisitions, divestitures, agreements, joint ventures; licensing arrangements, fran-

chising; dealing with unions, governments, communities, charities, customers, and relocations). 3) Big one-time events (e.g., working on a major presentation for the board, organizing significant meetings or conferences, disaster/damage control teams; reorganizations, mergers, acquisitions, or relocations, working on visions, charters, strategies, other time-urgent issues and problems). 4) Troubleshooting (e.g., problems, disasters, crises, product/service failures, accidents, illegal activities, damage control in public relations goofs, shut downs, downsizings, layoffs, abrupt changes in leadership).

☐ **Fix-its / Turnarounds**
The core demands to qualify as a Fix-it or Turnaround assignment are: 1) Cleaning up a mess. 2) Serious people issues/problems like credibility/performance/morale. 3) Tight deadline. 4) Serious business performance failure. 5) Last chance to fix. Four Types of Fix-its/ Turnarounds: 1) Fixing a failed business/unit involving taking control, stopping losses, managing damage, planning the turnaround, dealing with people problems, installing new processes and systems, and rebuilding the spirit and performance of the unit. 2) Managing sizable disasters like mishandled labor negotiations and strikes, thefts, history of significant business losses, poor staff, failed leadership, hidden problems, fraud, public relations nightmares, etc. 3) Significant reorganization and restructuring (e.g., stabilizing the business, reforming unit, introducing new systems, making people changes, resetting strategy and tactics). 4) Significant system/process breakdown (e.g., MIS, financial coordination processes, audits, standards, etc.) across units requiring working to change something from a distant position, providing advice and counsel, and installing or implementing a major process improvement or system change outside your own unit and/or with customers outside the organization.

☐ **Influencing Without Authority**
The core demands to qualify as an Influence Without Authority are: 1) Significant challenge (e.g, start-up, fix-it, scope and/or scale assignment, strategic planning project, changes in management practices/ systems). 2) Insufficient direct authority to make it happen. 3) Tight deadlines. 4) Visible to significant others. 5) Sensitive politics.

☐ **Off-Shore Assignments**
The core demands to qualify as an Off-Shore assignment are: 1) First time working in the country. 2) Significant challenges like new language, hardship location, unique business rules/practices, significant cultural/marketplace differences, different functional task, etc. 3) More than a year assignment. 4) No automatic return deal. 5) Not necessarily a change in job challenge, technical content, or responsibilities.

SECTION 6: LEARNING MORE FROM YOUR PLAN

THESE ADDITIONAL REMEDIES WILL HELP MAKE THIS DEVELOPMENT PLAN MORE EFFECTIVE FOR YOU

Learning to Learn Better

☐ **Rehearse Successful Tactics/Strategies/Actions**
Mentally rehearse how you will act before going into the situation. Try to anticipate how others will react, what they will say, and how you'll respond. Check out the best and worst cases; play out both scenes. Check your feelings in conflict or worst-case situations; rehearse staying under control.

☐ **Examine Why You Judge People the Way You Do**
List the people you like and those you dislike and try to find out why. What do those you like have in common with each other and with you? What do those you dislike have in common with themselves and how do they differ from you? Are your "people buckets" logical and productive or do they interfere? Could you be more effective without putting people into buckets?

☐ **Sell Something to a Tough Group/Audience**
Think of the person or group who will be the toughest to sell, the most critical, skeptical, or resistant, and sell that person or group first. Take time to understand the opposing viewpoints. Find common ground and leverage points, line up your best data and arguments and go for it.

Learning from Experience, Feedback and Other People

☐ **Using Multiple Models**
Who do you know who exemplifies how to do whatever your need is? Who, for example, personifies decisiveness or compassion or strategic agility? Think more broadly than your current job and colleagues. For example, clergy, friends, spouses or community leaders are also good sources for potential models. Select your models not on the basis of overall excellence or likability, but on the basis of the one towering strength (or glaring weakness) you are interested in. Even people who are well thought of usually have only one or two towering strengths (or glaring weaknesses). Ordinarily, you won't learn as much from the whole person as you will from one characteristic.

☐ **Learning from Bosses**
Bosses can be an excellent and ready source for learning. All bosses do some things exceptionally well and other things poorly. Distance your feelings from the boss/direct report relationship and study things that work and things that don't work for your boss. What would you have done? What could you use, and what should you avoid?

☐ **Learning from Interviewing Others**
Interview others. Ask not only what they do, but how and why they do it. What do they think are the rules of thumb they are following? Where did they learn the behaviors? How do they keep them current? How do they monitor the effect they have on others?

☐ **Learning from Observing Others**
Observe others. Find opportunities to observe without interacting with your model. This enables you to objectively study the person, note what he/she is doing or not doing, and compare that with what you would typically do in similar situations. Many times you can learn more by watching than asking. Your model may not be able to explain what he/she does or may be an unwilling teacher.

☐ **Consolidating What You Learn from People**
After using any source and/or method of learning from others, write down or mentally note the new rules of thumb and the principles involved. How will you remind yourself of the new behaviors in similar situations? How will you prevent yourself from reacting on "autopilot"? How could you share what you have learned from others?

☐ **Learning from Bad Bosses**
First, what does he/she do so well to make him/her your boss? (Even bad bosses have strengths). Then, ask what makes this boss bad for you. Is it his/her behavior? Attitude? Values? Philosophy? Practices? Style? What is the source of the conflict? Why do you react as you do? Do others react the same? How are you part of the problem? What do you do that triggers your boss? If you wanted to, could you reduce the conflict or make it go away by changing something you do? Is there someone around you who doesn't react like you? How are they different? What can you learn from them? What is your emotional reaction to this boss? Why do you react like that? What can you do to cope with these feelings? Can you avoid reacting out of anger and frustration? Can you find something positive about the situation? Can you use someone else as a buffer? Can you learn from your emotions? What lasting lessons of managing others can you take away from this experience? What won't you do as a manager? What will you do differently? How could you teach these principles you've learned to others by the use of this example?

☐ **Learning from Bad Situations**
All of us will find ourselves in bad situations from time to time. Good intentions gone bad. Impossible tasks and goals. Hopeless projects. Even though you probably can't perform well, the key is to at least take away some lessons and insights. How did things get to be this way? What factors led to the impasse? How can you make the best of a bad situation? How can you neutralize the negative elements? How can you get the most out of yourself and your staff under the chilling situation? What can you salvage? How can you use coping strategies to minimize

the negatives? How can you avoid these situations going forward? In bad situations: 1) Be resourceful. Get the most you can out of the situation. 2) Try to deduce why things got to be that way. 3) Learn from both the situation you inherited and how you react to it. 4) Integrate what you learn into your future behavior.

SUGGESTED READINGS

Alessandra, Tony Ph.D. and Michael J. O'Connor, Ph.D. *The Platinum Rule.* New York: Warner Books, 1996

Aubuchon, Norbert. *The Anatomy of Persuasion.* New York: AMACOM, 1997.

Birnbaum, Jeffrey H. *The lobbyists: how influence peddlers get their way in Washington.* New York: Times Books, 1992.

Derber, Charles. *Corporation nation: how corporations are taking over our lives and what we can do about it.* New York: St. Martin's Press, 1998.

DuBrin, Andrew J. *Winning office politics: DuBrin's guide for the 90's.* Englewood Cliffs, NJ: Prentice Hall, 1990.

Edel, T. R. *Wake me when it's time to work: surviving meetings, office games, and the people who love them.* Houston, TX: Cashman Dudley, 1999.

Gunlicks, L. F. (Lynn F.). *The Machiavellian manager's handbook for success.* Washington, DC: Libey Pub.; Lanham, MD: Distributed to the trade by National Book Network, 1993.

Kissinger, Henry. *Diplomacy.* New York: Simon & Schuster, 1994.

Korten, David C. *When Corporations Rule The World.* San Francisco: Berrett-Koehler Publishers, 1995.

Lareau, William. *Dancing with the dinosaur: learning to live in the corporate jungle.* Clinton, NJ: New Win Publishing, 1994.

Machiavelli, Niccolò. *The prince.* Translated by W.K.Marriott. Introd. by Herbert Butterfield. [Abridged ed.]. Ann Arbor, MI: J. W. Edwards, [1946] [1968,1958]

Manchester, William. *On Mencken: Essays.* New York: Knopf, 1980.

Parekh, Bhikhu. *Gandhi's Political Philosophy*. Notre Dame, IN: University of Notre Dame Press, 1989.

Rogers, Will. [edited by] Bryan B. Sterling and Frances N. Sterling. *Will Rogers' World: America's foremost political humorist comments on the twenties and thirties–and eighties and nineties.* New York: M. Evans, 1989

continued

Roosevelt, Franklin D., Buhite, Russell D. and David W. Levy, Editors. *FDR's Fireside Chats.* Norman, Oklahoma: University of Oklahoma Press, 1992.

Rosner, Bob. *Working wounded: advice that adds insight to injury.* New York: Warner Books, 1998.

49

PRESENTATION SKILLS

SECTION 1: YOUR DEVELOPMENT NEED(S)

UNSKILLED

- ☐ Not a skilled presenter in varying situations
- ☐ May be shy
- ☐ May be disorganized, presentations lack focus
- ☐ May have a flat or grating style
- ☐ Doesn't listen to audience
- ☐ May have personal idiosyncrasies and habits that get in the way
- ☐ May be unprepared for or unable to handle tough questions
- ☐ May always present the same way, not adjusting to audiences
- ☐ May lose his/her cool during hot debate
- ☐ May be nervous, even scared when speaking

SKILLED

- ☐ Is effective in a variety of formal presentation settings: one-on-one, small and large groups, with peers, direct reports, and bosses
- ☐ Is effective both inside and outside the organization, on both cool data and hot and controversial topics
- ☐ Commands attention and can manage group process during the presentation
- ☐ Can change tactics midstream when something isn't working

OVERUSED SKILL

- ☐ May try to win with style and presentation skills over fact and substance
- ☐ May be able to wing it and dance without really being prepared
- ☐ May be able to sell things that shouldn't be sold

Select one to three of the competencies listed below to work on to compensate for an overuse of this skill.

COMPENSATORS: 5, 17, 22, 24, 30, 32, 33, 46, 51, 53, 57, 58, 61, 63, 65

SOME CAUSES

- ☐ Can't take the heat
- ☐ Disorganized
- ☐ Don't like open conflict
- ☐ Flat presenter
- ☐ Get nervous and emotional
- ☐ Scared to speak to larger groups
- ☐ Shy
- ☐ Spooked by AV
- ☐ Thrown by questions

THE MAP

There's presenting and being presentable presenting. Good presentations are those that achieve their objectives. Being presentable is being evaluated as being a good presenter with sufficient stage presence and audience sensitivity to give a good presentation.

SECTION 2: LEARNING ON YOUR OWN

THESE SELF-DEVELOPMENT REMEDIES WILL HELP YOU BUILD YOUR SKILL(S)

SOME REMEDIES

- ☐ **1. Preparing.** Make a checklist. What's your objective? What's your point? What are five things you want them to remember? What would the ideal audience member say if interviewed 15 minutes after you finish? Who's your audience? How much do they know? What are five techniques you will use to hold their attention? What AV would work best? What questions will the audience have? What's the setting? How much time do you have (always take a few minutes less, never more)? *More help? – See #47 Planning.*

- ☐ **2. Preparing the speech.** State your message or purpose in a single sentence. Then outline the three to five chunks of your argument to support your thesis. Any more and the audience won't follow it. What introduction will grab the audience and rivet them on your message? A story, a fact, a comparison, a quote, a photo, a cartoon? For example, one speaker selected a comparison to introduce a series of research findings on career success by saying, "How can you take identical twins, hired for the same entry job in the same organization, and 20 years later, one of them succeeds and one of them doesn't?" She then returned to the twins periodically as she went through her argument on the different developmental experiences they had with the corporation. In organizing your talk, you should resist telling them all you know. What are your priority points, and how will you explain them? Some points are made better by example, some by the logic of the argument, some by facts or stories. You should vary how you drive home your point because you will reach more people. One nasty shock many learning presenters experience is that writing is different than speaking. A well-written speech is one that sounds right spoken, not read. Do not fall in love with what you have written until you record it on tape and listen to it. The cadence and pace is different in writing than in speaking. Writing doesn't take breathing into account. If your computer has a speech synthesizer, let the computer say your speech. Or have someone else read it to you. Never deliver a written speech until you have heard it spoken. Subscribe to *The Executive Speechwriter Newsletter* (1-800-748-4472) for tips on writing better speeches.

- ☐ **3. Reading audiences.** Unfortunately, one speech generally does not play equally well across audiences. Many times you will have to adjust the tone, pace, style and even the message and how you couch it for different audiences. If you are giving the same speech (or delivering the same message) to multiple audiences, always ask yourself how are they different? Some differences among audiences include level of sophistication, friendly vs. unfriendly, the time sensitivity of the audience, how much the audience expects to participate, how much entertainment they expect, and whether a logical or emotional argument will play better. Adjust accordingly. *More help? – See #15 Customer Focus.*

- ☐ **4. Rehearsing.** If you are just building your presentation skills, rehearsals are very helpful. The best is to rehearse in the actual setting of the presentation. To get ready, practice in front of a video camera, in front of someone who can give you feedback, by using an audio tape, or worse case, in front of a mirror by yourself. Focus on time spent per major point – usually five to 10 minutes. For your longest point, did you go into too much detail? Vary your volume and tone – sameness lulls the audience. Use your hands and body. Vary facial expression – if the words and the music don't match, people don't buy the message. Use pauses – for effect, to drive in a point. Be careful of repeating the same words too often. If you're stumped for something to say, pause – uhs, ahs, and you knows distract and turn off some listeners. Avoid speaking too forcefully or using loaded terms that will annoy some audience members. The best speech is the one that looks totally natural. It is usually the one that has been rehearsed a lot. If you can deliver the presentation on autopilot, you can scan the audience and adjust as you go.

- ☐ **5. Questions.** Most fear being asked a question. There are infinite kinds of questions. Good questions and bad questions. Hot and cold questions. Good intention questions and dark intentioned questions. There are questions that come at a bad time and at good times. The ones we fear are the bad, hot, dark, at a bad time questions. Questions are all good because they tell you something about the audience and how successful you are being. In some settings, the arrangement is that questions are held until the end. In others, it's free speech. Think about the 10 most likely questions you could be asked. Rehearse what you would say. Some questions come out of nowhere. Some rules: if you are going to answer the question later, say, "Thanks for that great introduction to the next part of my talk; if you can hang on, I'll answer that in a minute or two." Don't disrupt your flow if you can help it. Practice 10 to 30 second answers. Then ask the questioner if that answered his/her question. Many new presenters spend too much time on the answers. Make sure you know what the question is. Many times presenters answer the wrong question. Ask one clarifying question before you answer – do you mean how would this product work in a foreign or domestic market? Only give two answers per question. The third time say, "I'm really sorry; I can't seem to give you the answer you're looking for; why don't you see me at the end and we can continue this exchange." If someone just won't let go, say, "We must really have different experiences. It's apparent we don't agree so let's just agree to disagree for now, but thanks for the debate." In rare situations, you can engage the audience. Say, "I'm stumped on that one; does anyone in the audience know?" If the question is hot, "Why are women so discriminated against in organizations?" extract the main issues and respond with, "Here are three things you can do about it." As a general rule, don't answer such questions as given because they are negative and stay away from classification – women, men, accountants – answers since they tend to split the audience into camps. Get it in your mind that questions are your friends. You just need five techniques to deal with them, including the dreaded "I don't know, but I'll find out and get back to you on that." Finally, Q & A sessions can be all over the place. Take a minute at the end to reinforce your key points only, or show an overhead which restates them.

☐ **6. Stage fright?** Nervous? Anxious? Didn't sleep well? Stomach's not working well? All normal. There is not a person in your audience who has not passed through that stage to become a competent presenter. Aside from death, speaking in front of large audiences is the most feared activity for adults. All of the things you think might happen don't. You won't pass out. You won't freeze and not be able to continue. You won't speak in tongues. You won't have to go to the bathroom midway through. You may run out of breath. Stop and breathe. Your mouth may get dry. Drink something. You may forget what you wanted to say. Refer to your notes. You may stumble on a word. Pause and repeat it. A sweat drop may run down your nose. Wipe it off. You may shake. Hold on to the podium. Look at three different people in the audience who are smiling and receptive. Avoid looking at frowners and head shakers.

☐ **7. Logistics.** Slides are nice but they lock you into a sequence you may want to change halfway through based upon audience reactions. Transparencies are good but they wed you to stand by the projector. Some rules of thumb. Ten lines only on slides and transparencies. Fewer lines if you can. Large type. Keep slides up for no more than 30 seconds. Don't read your slides. Don't put everything on the slide. Just put bullets and code or key words. There's nothing more boring than having someone present exactly what's on the slide. Have a handout for everyone if possible. Never give it out at the end, always before you start. Don't use slides that aren't in the handout unless they are cartoon or joke slides or proprietary slides (tell the audience before you put the slide up). Move around. Present left for awhile, then right. Keep eye contact with a specific person in the audience each small time period. Smile. Try to look relaxed even if you're not. Don't stand and hold on to the podium unless you're shaking and need support.

Pause here and there. There is nothing wrong with a little silence. If there are more than 25 people or there are poor acoustics in the room, always repeat questions before you answer them. Never say in conclusion or in summary or to wrap it up or I'm almost finished unless you are within 60 seconds of finishing. Don't turn off the projector between slides (besides being irritating, you may blow the bulb). Don't look at your watch. Find a wall clock or put your watch on the podium or have a friend signal you when there are five minutes left. Don't turn your back on the audience while you are speaking. If you have to look at the screen to remind you of something, stop talking for a moment and then continue after you have read the slide. Do thank the audience for their attention and questions if there were any.

- ☐ **8. Time management.** No one has ever run out of material. Everyone plans to get more in than they have time for. Always underplan. If that makes you nervous, bring along a slide or two for an encore. Don't go long. Everyone loves a person who is either right on time or even better, a few minutes short on the agenda. People don't appreciate you using more time than you have been allotted, especially if there are other speakers behind you or you are last on the agenda and are holding people who don't want to be there. You don't have to finish. There will always be another day. If you see that you're going to run over, go to your conclusion. Don't race through the rest of your slides. Or ask the audience for their preference. Say it's apparent I'm not going to get through all of this, what would you like in the time remaining?

- ☐ **9. Serious hecklers.** There are bad people who may want to embarrass you or anyone who presents to them. When heckled, bide time while asking the attacker to say more. If he or she gives you some data or opinion to work with, respond with something you both will agree on, paraphrase the person's argument and then respond, or simply acknowledge the disagreement. Generally, you won't win anyone over unless he or she truly misunderstood your argument. If that's the case, summarize it, then ask which part he/she disagrees with. If appropriate, you might ask others to respond to the attack if you can do it in a neutral problem oriented way. "That stumped me, does anyone have a response to that?" Don't take too much time responding to an attacker. The rule of 30 seconds, or two attempts, still applies. If you overdo your response, it may irritate others in the audience who have questions or who don't agree with the attacker. If the person persists, you should say that time is limited, you need to field other questions, and that the discussion can be continued later. If the person continues to be actively rude, you can ignore the insult and call for other questions.

☐ **10. Being presentable.** You are, after all, the one on stage. All eyes are on you. What is the impression they get by what you look like, how you carry yourself, how organized you appear to be, how prepared you are, how well you handle the AV. All these may not be germane to the message but they are reflections of you. Part of presenting is marketing yourself as someone others should listen to. Watch what you wear. Match the audience. Don't come casual to a business dress affair and don't wear a suit to a casual setting. What do you carry on to the stage? Presentation in a three ring binder or loose? Old frayed briefcase? If I didn't know you and haven't yet heard your speech, have you led me to any impression of you? Is it the one you want? If you're just starting to build your presentation skills, join your local Toastmasters Club where you can comfortably learn the basics in a low risk environment. Take a presentation skills course that uses video.

SECTION 3: LEARNING FROM MORE FEEDBACK

THESE SOURCES WOULD GIVE YOU THE MOST ACCURATE AND DETAILED FEEDBACK ON YOUR SKILL(S)

☐ **Direct Boss**
Your direct boss has important information about you, your performance, and your prospects. The challenge is to get this information. There are formal processes (e.g., performance appraisals). There are day-to-day opportunities. To help, signal your boss that you want and can handle direct and timely feedback. Many bosses have trouble giving feedback, so you will have to work at it over a period of time.

☐ **Internal and External Customers**
Customers interact with you as a person and as a supplier or vendor of products and services. You're important to them because you can either help address and solve their problems or stand in their way. As customer service and Total Quality programs gain importance, clients and customers become a more prominent source of feedback.

☐ **Natural Mentors**
Natural mentors have a special relationship with you and are interested in your success and your future. Since they are usually not in your direct chain of command, you can have more open, relaxed, and fruitful discussions about yourself and your career prospects. They can be a very important source for candid or critical feedback others may not give you.

☐ **Past Associates/Constituencies**
When confronted with a present performance problem, some claim, "I wasn't like that before; it must be the current situation." When feedback is available from former associates, about 50% support that claim. In the other half of the cases, the people were like that before and probably didn't know it. It sometimes makes sense to access the past to clearly see the present.

- ☐ **Peers and Colleagues**
  Peers and colleagues have a special social and working relationship. They attend staff meetings together, share private views, get feedback from the same boss, travel together, and are knowledgeable about each other's work. You perhaps let your guard down more around peers and act more like yourself. They can be a valuable source of feedback.

SECTION 4: LEARNING FROM DEVELOP-IN-PLACE ASSIGNMENTS

THESE PART-TIME DEVELOP-IN-PLACE ASSIGNMENTS WILL HELP YOU BUILD YOUR SKILL(S)

- ☐ Study humor in business settings; read books on the nature of humor; collect cartoons you could use in presentations; study funny people around you; keep a log of funny jokes and sayings you hear; read famous speeches and study how humor was used; attend comedy clubs; ask a funny person to act as your tutor; practice funny lines and jokes with others.
- ☐ Study and summarize a new trend, product, service, technique, or process and present and sell it to others.
- ☐ Make speeches/be a spokesperson for the organization on the outside.
- ☐ Represent the organization at a trade show, convention, exposition, etc.
- ☐ Represent the concerns of a group of nonexempt, clerical, or administrative employees to higher management to seek resolution of a difficult issue.
- ☐ Write a proposal for a new policy, process, mission, charter, product, service, or system, and present and sell it to top management.
- ☐ Seek out and use a seed budget to create and pursue a personal idea, product, or service.
- ☐ Teach a course, seminar, or workshop on something you know a lot about.
- ☐ Train customers in the use of the organization's products or services.
- ☐ Present the strategy of your unit to others not familiar with your business.

SECTION 5: LEARNING FROM FULL-TIME JOBS

THESE FULL-TIME JOBS OFFER THE OPPORTUNITY TO BUILD YOUR SKILL(S)

- ☐ **Chair of Projects/Task Forces**
  The core demands for qualifying as a Project/Task Force assignment are: 1) Full-time assignment. 2) Important and specific goal. 3) Tight deadline. 4) Success or failure will be evident. 5) High-visibility sponsor. 6) Learning something on the fly. 7) Must get others to cooperate.

8) Usually six months or more. Four types of Projects/Task Forces: 1) New ideas, products, services, or systems (e.g., product/service/ program research and development, creation/installation/launch of a new system, new programs like Total Quality Management, positive discipline). 2) Formal negotiations and relationships (e.g., acquisitions, divestitures, agreements, joint ventures; licensing arrangements, franchising; dealing with unions, governments, communities, charities, customers, and relocations). 3) Big one-time events (e.g., working on a major presentation for the board, organizing significant meetings or conferences, disaster/damage control teams; reorganizations, mergers, acquisitions, or relocations, working on visions, charters, strategies, other time-urgent issues and problems). 4) Troubleshooting (e.g., problems, disasters, crises, product/service failures, accidents, illegal activities, damage control in public relations goofs, shut downs, downsizings, layoffs, abrupt changes in leadership).

☐ **Influencing Without Authority**
The core demands to qualify as an Influence Without Authority are: 1) Significant challenge (e.g, start-up, fix-it, scope and/or scale assignment, strategic planning project, changes in management practices/ systems). 2) Insufficient direct authority to make it happen. 3) Tight deadlines. 4) Visible to significant others. 5) Sensitive politics.

☐ **Start-ups**
The core demands to qualify as a start from scratch are: 1) Starting something new for you and/or for the organization. 2) Forging a new team. 3) Creating new systems/facilities/staffs/programs/procedures. 4) Contextual adversity (e.g., uncertainty, government regulation, unions, difficult environment). Seven types of start from scratches: 1) Planning, building, hiring, and managing (e.g., building a new facility, opening up a new location, moving a unit or company). 2) Heading something new (e.g., new product, new service, new line of business, new department/function, major new program). 3) Take over a group/ product/service/program that had existed for less than a year and was off to a fast start. 4) Establishing overseas operations. 5) Major new designs for existing systems. 6) Moving a successful program from one unit to another. 7) Installing a new organization-wide process as a full-time job (e.g., like Total Quality).

SECTION 6: LEARNING MORE FROM YOUR PLAN

THESE ADDITIONAL REMEDIES WILL HELP MAKE THIS DEVELOPMENT PLAN MORE EFFECTIVE FOR YOU

Learning to Learn Better

☐ **Envision Yourself Succeeding**
Examine the image of success in detail: what you are doing, what you are feeling, how you are reacting to others, how others are reacting to

you, how the parts fit together. Can you then play that out in the real situation and get to the same outcome?

- ☐ **Rehearse Successful Tactics/Strategies/Actions**
  Mentally rehearse how you will act before going into the situation. Try to anticipate how others will react, what they will say, and how you'll respond. Check out the best and worst cases; play out both scenes. Check your feelings in conflict or worst-case situations; rehearse staying under control.

- ☐ **Study People Who Have Successfully Done What You Need to Do**
  Interview people who have already done what you're planning to do and check your plan against what they did. Try to summarize their key tactics, strategies, and insights; adjust your plan accordingly.

- ☐ **Pre-sell an Idea to a Key Stakeholder**
  Identify the key stakeholders – those who will be the most affected by your actions or the most resistant, or whose support you will most need. Collect the information each will find persuasive; marshal your arguments and try to pre-sell your conclusions, recommendations, and solutions.

Learning from Experience, Feedback and Other People

- ☐ **Using Multiple Models**
  Who do you know who exemplifies how to do whatever your need is? Who, for example, personifies decisiveness or compassion or strategic agility? Think more broadly than your current job and colleagues. For example, clergy, friends, spouses or community leaders are also good sources for potential models. Select your models not on the basis of overall excellence or likability, but on the basis of the one towering strength (or glaring weakness) you are interested in. Even people who are well thought of usually have only one or two towering strengths (or glaring weaknesses). Ordinarily, you won't learn as much from the whole person as you will from one characteristic.

- ☐ **Learning from Observing Others**
  Observe others. Find opportunities to observe without interacting with your model. This enables you to objectively study the person, note what he/she is doing or not doing, and compare that with what you would typically do in similar situations. Many times you can learn more by watching than asking. Your model may not be able to explain what he/she does or may be an unwilling teacher.

- ☐ **Getting Feedback from Bosses and Superiors**
  Many bosses are reluctant to give negative feedback. They lack the managerial courage to face people directly with criticism. You can help by soliciting feedback and setting the tone. Show them you can handle criticism and that you are willing to work on issues they see as important.

☐ **Getting Feedback from Peers/Colleagues**
Your peers and colleagues may not be candid if they are in competition with you. Some may not be willing to be open with you out of fear of giving you an advantage. Some may give you exaggerated feedback to deliberately cause you undue concern. You have to set the tone and gauge the trust level of the relationship and the quality of the feedback.

Learning from Courses

☐ **Courses with Feedback**
Many courses such as negotiating skills and personal influence offer feedback on the subject matter of the course in addition to the content. They either collect data ahead of time or collect it "live" during the course.

SUGGESTED READINGS

The Executive Speechwriter Newsletter. 1-802-748-4472

Antion, Tom. *Wake 'em up: how to use humor and other professional techniques to create alarmingly good business presentations.* Landover Hills, Md.: Anchor Pub.; Minneapolis, MN.: Creative Training Techniques Press, 1997.

Collins, Patrick J. *Say it with confidence.* New York: Prentice-Hall, 1998.

Decker, Bert with Jim Denney. *You've got to be believed to be heard.* New York: St. Martin's Press, 1992.

Griffin, Jack. *How to say it at work: Putting yourself across with power words, phrases, body language and communication secrets.* Paramus, NJ: Prentice-Hall, 1998.

Hendricks, Dr. William and Micki Holliday, Recie Mobley and Kristy Steinbrecher. *Secrets of Power Presentations.* Franklin Lakes, NJ: Career Press, 1996.

Pearce, Terry. *Leading out loud.* San Francisco: Jossey-Bass, 1995.

Rafe, Stephen C. *How to be prepared to think on your feet.* New York: HarperBusiness, 1990.

PRIORITY SETTING

SECTION 1: YOUR DEVELOPMENT NEED(S)

UNSKILLED

- ☐ Has little sense of what's mission-critical and what's just nice to do
- ☐ Doesn't identify the critical few well for self or others
- ☐ May believe that everything's equally important, may overwhelm others with unfocused activities
- ☐ May be addicted to action, do a little bit of everything quickly
- ☐ May be a poor time manager
- ☐ May not say no; wants to do everything
- ☐ Not good at figuring out how to eliminate a roadblock

SKILLED

- ☐ Spends his/her time and the time of others on what's important
- ☐ Quickly zeros in on the critical few and puts the trivial many aside
- ☐ Can quickly sense what will help or hinder accomplishing a goal
- ☐ Eliminates roadblocks
- ☐ Creates focus

OVERUSED SKILL

- ☐ May let the trivial many accumulate into a critical problem
- ☐ May too quickly reject the priorities of others
- ☐ May have a chilling effect on necessary complexity by requiring everything to be reduced to the simple
- ☐ May confuse simple with simplistic
- ☐ May be too dominant a force on priorities for the team

Select one to three of the competencies listed below to work on to compensate for an overuse of this skill.

COMPENSATORS: 2, 3, 12, 15, 17, 27, 30, 33, 38, 46, 52, 63, 65

SOME CAUSES

- ☐ Action junkie; always on the move
- ☐ Difficulty saying no
- ☐ Ego; overestimate capacity
- ☐ Perfectionist; need to do everything
- ☐ Short attention span; want to do a little bit of everything
- ☐ Time management; too busy to set priorities
- ☐ Trouble choosing

THE MAP

So much to do; so little time in which to do it. Finite resources; infinite needs. People to see, places to go, things to do. No time to say hello, good-bye, I'm late for a very important meeting. Sound familiar? That's life. Everyone has more to do than they can get to. Organizations have more opportunities than they have the resources to address. The higher up you go in the organization, the more you have to do and the less time you have to do it. Nobody can do it all. You have to set priorities to survive and prosper.

SECTION 2: LEARNING ON YOUR OWN

THESE SELF-DEVELOPMENT REMEDIES WILL HELP YOU BUILD YOUR SKILL(S)

SOME REMEDIES

☐ **1. Be clear about your goals and objectives.** What exactly is it you need to accomplish? Use the annual plan and the strategic plan to understand the mission-critical things that must happen. *More help? – See #47 Planning and #58 Strategic Agility.*

☐ **2. Using the goals, separate what you need to do** into mission-critical, important to get done, nice if there is time left over, and not central to what we are trying to achieve. When faced with choices or multiple things to do, apply the scale and always choose the highest level.

☐ **3. Watch out for the activity trap.** John Kotter, in *The General Managers*, found that effective managers spent about half their time working on one or two key priorities – priorities they described in their own terms, not in terms of what the business/organizational plan said. Further, they made no attempt to work as much on small but related issues that tend to add up to lots of activity. So rather than consuming themselves and others on 97 seemingly urgent and related smaller activities, they always returned to the few issues that would gain the most mileage long term.

☐ **4. Get help from others.** When faced with multiple good things to do, pass them by a few others around you for their opinion. You don't have to do what they say but having other perspectives is always better than having only your opinion. *More help? – See #33 Listening.*

☐ **5. Many times setting and operating on priorities** isn't a reflective task. You may not have much time for ruminating. Most of life's choices have to be made on the spot, without all of the data. Nobody is ever right all the time under that kind of pressure. Perfectionists have a problem with this. Wait as long as you can and then shoot your best shot. *More help? – See #16* Timely *Decision Making and #32 Learning on the Fly.*

☐ **6. Be careful not to be guided by just what you like** and what you don't like. That way of selecting priorities will probably not be successful over time. Use data, intuition and even feelings, but not feelings alone.

☐ **7. When you are stuck,** write down the pros and cons for each option. Check what effect each would have both on the short and long term. Are there cost differences? Is one resource more efficient than the other? Is one apt to be more successful than the other? Think about the interaction of both short and long-term goals. Sometimes what you decide to do today will hurt you or the organization downstream. When making either a short-term or long-term choice, stop for a second and ask what effect this might have on the other. Adjust as necessary. *More help? – See #65* Managing *Vision and Purpose.*

☐ **8. Be time sensitive.** Taking time to plan and set priorities actually frees up more time later than just diving into things hoping that you can get it done on time. Most people out of time claim they didn't have the time to plan their time. In the Stephen Covey *Seven Habits of Highly Successful People* sense, it's sharpening your saw. *More help? – See #62 Time Management.*

☐ **9. Avoiding making choices** actually leads to more choices downstream. Avoiding making choices actually makes life more difficult. You also miss opportunities. Basically, you can pay the price now or pay a bigger price tomorrow. *More help? – See #12 Conflict Management.*

☐ **10. Be sensitive to the time of others.** Generally, the higher up you go or the higher up the person you are interacting with is, the less time you and he/she have. Be time efficient with others. Use as little of their time as possible. Get to it and get done with it. Give them an opportunity to open new avenues for discussion or to continue but if they don't, say your good-byes and leave.

SECTION 3: LEARNING FROM MORE FEEDBACK

THESE SOURCES WOULD GIVE YOU THE MOST ACCURATE AND DETAILED FEEDBACK ON YOUR SKILL(S)

☐ **Direct Boss**
Your direct boss has important information about you, your performance, and your prospects. The challenge is to get this information. There are formal processes (e.g., performance appraisals). There are day-to-day opportunities. To help, signal your boss that you want and can handle direct and timely feedback. Many bosses have trouble giving feedback, so you will have to work at it over a period of time.

☐ **Direct Reports**
Across a variety of settings, your direct reports probably see you the most. They are the recipients of most of your managerial behaviors. They know your work. They can compare you with former bosses.

Since they may hesitate to give you negative feedback, you have to set the atmosphere to make it easier for them. You have to ask.

- ☐ **Past Associates/Constituencies**
When confronted with a present performance problem, some claim, "I wasn't like that before; it must be the current situation." When feedback is available from former associates, about 50% support that claim. In the other half of the cases, the people were like that before and probably didn't know it. It sometimes makes sense to access the past to clearly see the present.

SECTION 4: LEARNING FROM DEVELOP-IN-PLACE ASSIGNMENTS

THESE PART-TIME DEVELOP-IN-PLACE ASSIGNMENTS WILL HELP YOU BUILD YOUR SKILL(S)

- ☐ Plan a new site for a building (plant, field office, headquarters, etc.).
- ☐ Assign a project to a group with a tight deadline.
- ☐ Manage an ad hoc, temporary group of "green," inexperienced people as their coach, teacher, orienter, etc.
- ☐ Manage an ad hoc, temporary group of people where the people in the group are towering experts but the temporary manager is not.
- ☐ Manage the interface between consultants and the organization on a critical assignment.
- ☐ Help shut down a plant, regional office, product line, business, operation, etc.
- ☐ Prepare and present a proposal of some consequence to top management.
- ☐ Manage a cost-cutting project.
- ☐ Build a multifunctional project team to tackle a common business issue or problem.
- ☐ Work on a team looking at a reorganization plan where there will be more people than positions.

SECTION 5: LEARNING FROM FULL-TIME JOBS

THESE FULL-TIME JOBS OFFER THE OPPORTUNITY TO BUILD YOUR SKILL(S)

- ☐ **Chair of Projects/Task Forces**
The core demands for qualifying as a Project/Task Force assignment are: 1) Full-time assignment. 2) Important and specific goal. 3) Tight deadline. 4) Success or failure will be evident. 5) High-visibility sponsor. 6) Learning something on the fly. 7) Must get others to cooperate. 8) Usually six months or more. Four types of Projects/Task Forces: 1) New ideas, products, services, or systems (e.g., product/service/

program research and development, creation/installation/launch of a new system, new programs like Total Quality Management, positive discipline). 2) Formal negotiations and relationships (e.g., acquisitions, divestitures, agreements, joint ventures; licensing arrangements, franchising; dealing with unions, governments, communities, charities, customers, and relocations). 3) Big one-time events (e.g., working on a major presentation for the board, organizing significant meetings or conferences, disaster/damage control teams; reorganizations, mergers, acquisitions, or relocations, working on visions, charters, strategies, other time-urgent issues and problems). 4) Troubleshooting (e.g., problems, disasters, crises, product/service failures, accidents, illegal activities, damage control in public relations goofs, shut downs, downsizings, layoffs, abrupt changes in leadership).

- ☐ **Fix-its / Turnarounds**
  The core demands to qualify as a Fix-it or Turnaround assignment are: 1) Cleaning up a mess. 2) Serious people issues/problems like credibility/performance/morale. 3) Tight deadline. 4) Serious business performance failure. 5) Last chance to fix. Four Types of Fix-its/ Turnarounds: 1) Fixing a failed business/unit involving taking control, stopping losses, managing damage, planning the turnaround, dealing with people problems, installing new processes and systems, and rebuilding the spirit and performance of the unit. 2) Managing sizable disasters like mishandled labor negotiations and strikes, thefts, history of significant business losses, poor staff, failed leadership, hidden problems, fraud, public relations nightmares, etc. 3) Significant reorganization and restructuring (e.g., stabilizing the business, reforming unit, introducing new systems, making people changes, resetting strategy and tactics). 4) Significant system/process breakdown (e.g., MIS, financial coordination processes, audits, standards, etc.) across units requiring working to change something from a distant position, providing advice and counsel, and installing or implementing a major process improvement or system change outside your own unit and/or with customers outside the organization.

- ☐ **Heavy Strategic Demands**
  The core demands necessary to qualify as a Heavy Strategic Content assignment are: 1) Requires significant strategic thinking and planning most couldn't do. 2) Charts new ground strategically. 3) Plan must be presented, challenged, adopted, and implemented. 4) Exposure to significant decision makers and executives. 1) Strategic planning position. 2) Job involving repositioning of a product, service, or organization.

- ☐ **Scope Assignments**
  The core demands for a Scope (complexity) assignment are: 1) Significant increase in both internal and external scope or complexity. 2) Significant increase in visibility and/or bottom line responsibility.

3) Unfamiliar area, business, technology, or territory. Examples of Scope assignments involving shifts: 1) Switching into a new function/technology/business. 2) Moving to new organization. 3) Moving to overseas assignment. 4) Moving to new location. 5) Adding new products/services. 6) Moving between headquarters/field. 7) Switches in ownership/top management of the unit/organization. Examples of Scope assignments involving "firsts": 1) First-time manager. 2) First-time managing managers. 3) First-time executive. 4) First-time overseas. 5) First-time headquarters/field. 6) First-time team leader. 7) First-time new technology/business/function. Scope assignments involving increased complexity: 1) Managing a significant expansion of an existing product or service. 2) Managing adding new products/service into an existing unit. 3) Managing a reorganized and more diverse unit. 4) Managing explosive growth. 5) Adding new technologies.

☐ **Start-ups**
The core demands to qualify as a start from scratch are: 1) Starting something new for you and/or for the organization. 2) Forging a new team. 3) Creating new systems/facilities/staffs/programs/procedures. 4) Contextual adversity (e.g., uncertainty, government regulation, unions, difficult environment). Seven types of start from scratches: 1) Planning, building, hiring, and managing (e.g., building a new facility, opening up a new location, moving a unit or company). 2) Heading something new (e.g., new product, new service, new line of business, new department/function, major new program). 3) Take over a group/product/service/program that had existed for less than a year and was off to a fast start. 4) Establishing overseas operations. 5) Major new designs for existing systems. 6) Moving a successful program from one unit to another. 7) Installing a new organization-wide process as a full-time job (e.g., like Total Quality).

SECTION 6: LEARNING MORE FROM YOUR PLAN

THESE ADDITIONAL REMEDIES WILL HELP MAKE THIS DEVELOPMENT PLAN MORE EFFECTIVE FOR YOU

Learning to Learn Better

☐ **Teach Others Something You Don't Know Well**
Commit to a project like teaching something you don't know much about to force you to learn quickly to accomplish the task; pick something new, different, or unfamiliar.

☐ **Plan Backwards from the Ideal**
Envision what an ideal outcome would look like and plan backwards. What is the series of events that would have to take place to get there? What would people do? What would have to be done? How would people react? How would things play out? Could you plan it forward and get to the same outcome?

☐ **Study Yourself in Detail**
Study your likes and dislikes because they can drive a lot of your thinking, judging, and acting. Ask which like or dislike has gotten in the way or prevented you from moving to a higher level of learning. Are your likes and dislikes really important to you or have you just gone on "autopilot"? Try to address and understand a blocking dislike and change it.

☐ **Commit to a Tight Timeframe to Accomplish Something**
Set some specific goals and tighter than usual timeframes for yourself and go after them with all you've got. Push yourself to stick to the plan; get more done than usual by adhering to a tight plan.

☐ **Sort Through Information Multiple Ways**
Collect the data and arrange it in elements or pieces. Come up with definitions, and arrange the data in various ways: chronologically, from most to least, from biggest to smallest, from cold to hot, what you know most about and least about, from known to unknown, etc., until the meaning becomes obvious.

☐ **Look for the Simplest Explanation, Find the Essence**
Put all the complexity aside and ask yourself: what's the most obvious thing this problem could be. What is the most obvious thing to do? Who is the most obvious person to talk to? What is the simplest explanation possible? What's at the essence of the problem?

Learning from Experience, Feedback and Other People

☐ **Getting Feedback from Bosses and Superiors**
Many bosses are reluctant to give negative feedback. They lack the managerial courage to face people directly with criticism. You can help by soliciting feedback and setting the tone. Show them you can handle criticism and that you are willing to work on issues they see as important.

☐ **Getting Feedback from Direct Reports**
Direct reports often fear reprisals for giving negative feedback about bosses, whether in a formal process, like a questionnaire, or informally and face-to-face. Even with a guarantee of confidentiality, some are still hesitant. If you want feedback from direct reports, you have to set a positive tone and never act out of revenge.

Learning from Courses

☐ **Supervisory Courses**
Most new supervisors go through an "Introduction to Supervision" type course. They are designed to teach the common practices a first-line supervisor needs to know to be effective. The content of most of those courses is standard. There is general agreement on the principles of effective supervision. There are two common problems: 1) Do the

students have a strong motivation to learn? Do they know what they don't know? Is there any pain? Because motivated students with a need for the knowledge learn best, participants should have had some trying experiences and some supervisory pain and hardships before attending. 2) Are the instructors experienced supervisors? Have they practiced what they preach? Can they share powerful anecdotes to make key points? Can they answer questions credibly? If possible, select supervisory courses based on the instructors, since the content seems to be the much same for all such courses. Lastly, does the course offer the opportunity for practicing each skill? Does it contain simulations? Are there case studies you could easily identify with? Are there breakout groups? Is there opportunity for action learning? Search for the most interactive course.

☐ **Sending Others to Courses**
If you are responsible for managing someone else's development and, as part of that, sending them to courses, prepare them beforehand. Don't send them as tourists. Meet with them before and after the course. Tell them why they need this course. Tell them what you expect them to learn. Give them feedback on why you think they need the course. Agree ahead of time how you will measure and monitor learning after they return. If possible, offer a variety of courses for your employee to choose from. Have them give you a report shortly after they return. If appropriate, have them present what they learned to the rest of your staff. After they return, provide opportunities for using the new skills with safe cover and low risk. Give them practice time before expecting full exercise of the new skills. Be supportive during early unsteadiness. Give continuous feedback on progress.

SUGGESTED READINGS

Drucker, Peter F. *The Effective Executive.* New York: Harper & Row, 1996.

Drucker, Peter F. *The Effective Executive [sound recording].* New York: AMACOM, 1983.

Kofodimos, Joan. *Balancing Act – How managers can integrate successful careers and fulfilling personal lives.* San Francisco: Jossey-Bass Publishers, 1993.

Kotter, John P. *The General Managers.* New York: Free Press; London: Collier Macmillan, 1982.

Stalk, George Jr. and Thomas M. Hout. *Competing Against Time.* New York: Macmillan, Inc., 1990.

51

PROBLEM SOLVING

SECTION 1: YOUR DEVELOPMENT NEED(S)

UNSKILLED

- ☐ Not a disciplined problem solver; may be stuck in the past, wed to what worked before
- ☐ Many times has to come back and rework the problem a second time
- ☐ May be a fire-ready-aim type
- ☐ May get impatient and jump to conclusions too soon
- ☐ May not stop to define and analyze the problem; doesn't look under rocks
- ☐ May have a set bag of tricks and pull unfit solutions from it
- ☐ May miss the complexity of the issue and force fit it to what he/she is most comfortable with
- ☐ Unlikely to come up with the second and better solution, ask penetrating questions, or see hidden patterns

SKILLED

- ☐ Uses rigorous logic and methods to solve difficult problems with effective solutions
- ☐ Probes all fruitful sources for answers
- ☐ Can see hidden problems
- ☐ Is excellent at honest analysis
- ☐ Looks beyond the obvious and doesn't stop at the first answers

OVERUSED SKILL

- ☐ May tend toward analysis paralysis
- ☐ May wait too long to come to a conclusion
- ☐ May not set analysis priorities
- ☐ May get hung up in the process and miss the big picture
- ☐ May make things overly complex
- ☐ May do too much of the analysis personally

Select one to three of the competencies listed below to work on to compensate for an overuse of this skill.

COMPENSATORS: 1, 16, 18, 20, 35, 36, 50, 52, 55, 60

SOME CAUSES

- ☐ Disorganized
- ☐ Get emotional
- ☐ Impatient
- ☐ Jump to conclusions
- ☐ Perfectionist, need too much data
- ☐ Rely too much on historical solutions

THE MAP

Most people are smart enough to solve problems effectively. Most people know how. Most people don't do it right, however. They don't define the problem and jump to conclusions, or they go to the other extreme and analyze it to death without trying out anything. They also rely too much on themselves when multiple people usually have a better chance of solving the problem.

SECTION 2: LEARNING ON YOUR OWN

THESE SELF-DEVELOPMENT REMEDIES WILL HELP YOU BUILD YOUR SKILL(S)

SOME REMEDIES

☐ **1. Defining the problem.** Instant and early conclusions, solutions, statements, suggestions, how we solved it in the past, are the enemies of good problem solving. Studies show that defining the problem and taking action occur almost simultaneously for most people, so the more effort you put on the front end, the easier it is to come up with a good solution. Stop and first define what the problem is and isn't. Since providing solutions is so easy for everyone, it would be nice if they were offering solutions to the right problem. Figure out what causes it. Keep asking why, see how many causes you can come up with and how many organizing buckets you can put them in. This increases the chance of a better solution because you can see more connections. Be a chess master. Chess masters recognize thousands of patterns of chess pieces. Look for patterns in data; don't just collect information. Put it in categories that make sense to you. Ask lots of questions. Allot at least 50% of the time to defining the problem.

☐ **2. Results oriented impatience.** The style that chills sound problem solving the most is the results driven, time short and impatient person. He/she does not take the time to define problems and tends to take the first close enough solution that comes along. Studies have shown that on average, the solution somewhere between the second and third one generated is the best. Impatient people don't wait that long. Slow down. Discipline yourself to pause for enough time to define the problem better and always think of three solutions before you pick one.

☐ **3. Watch your biases.** Some people have solutions in search of problems. They have favorite solutions. They have biases. They have universal solutions to most situations. They pre-judge what the problem is without stopping to consider the nuances of this specific problem. Do honest and open analysis first. Did you state as facts things that are really assumptions or opinions? Are you sure these assertions are facts? Did you generalize from a single example? One of your solutions may in fact fit, but wait to see if you're right about the problem. *More help?* – Read *Six Thinking Hats* by Edward de Bono.

☐ **4. Get out of your comfort zone.** Many busy people rely too much on solutions from their own history. They rely on what has happened to them in the past. They see sameness in problems that isn't there. Beware of "I have always..." or "Usually I...." Always pause and look under rocks and ask yourself, is this really like the problems I have solved in the past?

☐ **5. Asking others for input.** Many try to do too much themselves. They don't delegate, listen or ask others for input. Even if you think you have the solution, ask some others for input just to make sure. Access your network. Find someone who makes a good sounding board and talk to her/him, not just for ideas, but to increase your understanding of the problem. Or do it more formally. Set up a competition between two teams, both acting as your advisors. Call a problem-solving meeting and give the group two hours to come up with something that will at least be tried. Find a buddy group in another function or organization that faces the same or a similar problem and both of you experiment.

☐ **6. Perfectionist?** Need or prefer or want to be 100% sure? Want to wait for all of the information to come in. Lots might prefer that. Beware of analysis paralysis. A good rule of thumb is to analyze patterns and causes to come up with alternatives. Many of us just collect data, which numerous studies show increases our confidence but doesn't increase decision accuracy. Perfectionism is tough to let go of because most people see it as a positive trait for them. Recognize your perfectionism for what it might be – collecting more information than others do to improve your confidence in making a fault-free decision and thereby avoiding risk and criticism. Try to decrease your need for data and your need to be right all the time slightly every week until you reach a more reasonable balance between thinking it through and taking action.

☐ **7. Incrementalism.** Sometimes the key to bigger problem-solving is to make them into a series of smaller problems. People who are good at this are incrementalists. They make a series of smaller decisions, get instant feedback, correct the course, get a little more data, move forward a little more, until the bigger problem is under control. They don't try to get it right the first time. Learn to break down problems into pieces and parts and solve them one at a time.

☐ **8. Learn some more problem-solving skills.** There are many different ways to think through and solve a problem.

- Ask more questions. In one study of problem solving, seven per cent of comments were questions and about half were answers. We jump to solutions based on what has worked in the past.
- To get fresh ideas, don't speedboat, look deeply instead. Tackle the most vexing problem of your job – carve out 20% of your time –

study it deeply, talk with others, look for parallels in other organizations and in remote areas totally outside your field.

- Complex problems are hard to visualize. They tend to be either oversimplified or too complex to solve unless they are put in a visual format. Cut the problem up into its component pieces. Examine the pieces to see if a different order would help, or how you could combine three pieces into one.
- Another technique is a pictorial chart called a storyboard where a problem is illustrated by its components being depicted as pictures.
- A variation of this is to tell stories that illustrate the +'s and -'s of a problem, then flow chart those according to what's working and not working. Another is a fishbone diagram used in Total Quality Management.
- Sometimes going to extremes helps. Adding every condition, every worse case you can think of sometimes will suggest a different solution. Taking the present state of affairs and projecting into the future may indicate how and where the system will break down.
- Are you or others avoiding making the tough points? In almost any group, there are topics so hot they can't be mentioned, let alone discussed. A technique, pioneered by Chris Argyris, can bubble them to the surface. Everyone takes three index cards and writes down three undiscussables. (Names are not used; the assumption is that the position has an effect on behavior, and even if people think the issue is personal, they are asked to see it in system or group terms.) The cards are then shuffled and each person receives a different three back. The cards are read, charted, and themes are arrayed for discussion. For more techniques, read *The Art of Problem Solving* by Russell Ackoff and *Lateral Thinking* by Edward de Bono.

☐ **9. Avoiding risks?** Develop a philosophical stance toward mistakes and failures in problem solving. After all, most innovations fail, most proposals fail, most change efforts fail, and the initial solutions to complex problems do not work. The best tack when a solution doesn't work is to say, "What can we learn from this?" and move on. The more tries, the more feedback and the more chances to find the best answer. *More help? – See #2* Dealing With *Ambiguity.*

☐ **10. Disorganized?** Problem solving involves using rigorous logic and disciplined methods. It involves going through checklists, looking under rocks, and probing all fruitful sources for answers. If you're disorganized, you need to set tight priorities. Focus on the mission-critical few. Don't get diverted by trivia. *More help? – See #47 Planning and #50 Priority Setting.*

SECTION 3: LEARNING FROM MORE FEEDBACK

THESE SOURCES WOULD GIVE YOU THE MOST ACCURATE AND DETAILED FEEDBACK ON YOUR SKILL(S)

☐ **Direct Boss**
Your direct boss has important information about you, your performance, and your prospects. The challenge is to get this information. There are formal processes (e.g., performance appraisals). There are day-to-day opportunities. To help, signal your boss that you want and can handle direct and timely feedback. Many bosses have trouble giving feedback, so you will have to work at it over a period of time.

☐ **Natural Mentors**
Natural mentors have a special relationship with you and are interested in your success and your future. Since they are usually not in your direct chain of command, you can have more open, relaxed, and fruitful discussions about yourself and your career prospects. They can be a very important source for candid or critical feedback others may not give you.

☐ **Past Associates/Constituencies**
When confronted with a present performance problem, some claim, "I wasn't like that before; it must be the current situation." When feedback is available from former associates, about 50% support that claim. In the other half of the cases, the people were like that before and probably didn't know it. It sometimes makes sense to access the past to clearly see the present.

SECTION 4: LEARNING FROM DEVELOP-IN-PLACE ASSIGNMENTS

THESE PART-TIME DEVELOP-IN-PLACE ASSIGNMENTS WILL HELP YOU BUILD YOUR SKILL(S)

☐ Integrate diverse systems, processes, or procedures across decentralized and/or dispersed units.

☐ Plan a new site for a building (plant, field office, headquarters, etc.).

☐ Study history and draw parallels for a current business issue or problem and present your findings to others for comment.

☐ Relaunch an existing product or service that's not doing well.

☐ Manage an ad hoc, temporary group of people where the people in the group are towering experts but the temporary manager is not.

☐ Assemble an ad hoc team of diverse people to accomplish a difficult task.

☐ Handle a tough negotiation with an internal or external client or customer.

☐ Take on a tough and undoable project, one where others who have tried it have failed.

- ☐ Resolve an issue in conflict between two people, units, geographies, functions, etc.
- ☐ Audit cost overruns to assess the problem and present your findings to the person or people involved.

SECTION 5: LEARNING FROM FULL-TIME JOBS

THESE FULL-TIME JOBS OFFER THE OPPORTUNITY TO BUILD YOUR SKILL(S)

☐ **Heavy Strategic Demands**
The core demands necessary to qualify as a Heavy Strategic Content assignment are: 1) Requires significant strategic thinking and planning most couldn't do. 2) Charts new ground strategically. 3) Plan must be presented, challenged, adopted, and implemented. 4) Exposure to significant decision makers and executives. 1) Strategic planning position. 2) Job involving repositioning of a product, service, or organization.

☐ **Scope Assignments**
The core demands for a Scope (complexity) assignment are: 1) Significant increase in both internal and external scope or complexity. 2) Significant increase in visibility and/or bottom line responsibility. 3) Unfamiliar area, business, technology, or territory. Examples of Scope assignments involving shifts: 1) Switching into a new function/technology/business. 2) Moving to new organization. 3) Moving to overseas assignment. 4) Moving to new location. 5) Adding new products/services. 6) Moving between headquarters/field. 7) Switches in ownership/top management of the unit/organization. Examples of Scope assignments involving "firsts": 1) First-time manager. 2) First-time managing managers. 3) First-time executive. 4) First-time overseas. 5) First-time headquarters/field. 6) First-time team leader. 7) First-time new technology/business/function. Scope assignments involving increased complexity: 1) Managing a significant expansion of an existing product or service. 2) Managing adding new products/service into an existing unit. 3) Managing a reorganized and more diverse unit. 4) Managing explosive growth. 5) Adding new technologies.

SECTION 6: LEARNING MORE FROM YOUR PLAN

THESE ADDITIONAL REMEDIES WILL HELP MAKE THIS DEVELOPMENT PLAN MORE EFFECTIVE FOR YOU

Learning to Learn Better

☐ **Find a Parallel to the Current Problem and Learn From It**
Find a parallel with similar situations, whether in your field or in other areas, past or present, and look for comparison or contrast points to see what else has or hasn't worked. Search especially for the reasons why certain things work and others don't across different situations; find the common and uncommon elements.

- ☐ **Keep a Rule of Thumb Journal**
In a journal, record your new knowledge and lessons, add to your rules of thumb, or revise old rules that no longer apply. Constantly assess the accuracy of your accumulated lessons; don't allow yourself to lapse into "autopilot."

- ☐ **Analyze Your Past Successes for Insights and Learnings**
Look at your accomplishments in detail. Ask why they came off well. What did you do that directly led to positive outcomes? Are they repeatable in other situations? How much was attributable to the context itself, how much to the work of others, and how much to you? Was it a windfall win? What lessons and rules of thumb can you take away from these successes?

- ☐ **Look Beyond Your First Solution to a Problem**
Don't always take the first action you think of. Look further for a second and third. What's different? Might the second or third be more effective? Research shows that the best solution lies somewhere between the second and third strategies or approaches. Your first solution is often an "autopilot" response and may not be the best.

- ☐ **Break Up Your Work Routine When You're Blocked**
When blocked on a problem, intersperse your work routine with dissimilar tasks, activities, or rest breaks. Turn to another task for awhile. In a sequence of tough work, string dissimilar tasks together so you can vary the types of skills used and the work done.

- ☐ **Become a Student of How People Learn**
Become a student of learning: Read some books and articles on child and adult learning; read about how the brain and mind work; study diverse learners of the past for insights; study the teaching techniques of expert teachers and coaches; attend a course on instructional design. Write and deliver a presentation on your findings.

- ☐ **Try New Things, Take Some Chances, Increase Personal Risk Taking**
Engage in some creative problem-solving activities such as brainstorming, free association, analogies to unrelated areas, nominal group techniques, etc. Let yourself go; let your thinking flow freely. Break down the restrictions on yourself; break through old barriers and blockages; try new ways of thinking.

- ☐ **Study Something Unusual or Unexpected**
Consider the odd and unusual facts or opinions that don't seem to fit in anywhere. If these anomalies comprised the majority opinion, where would that lead? What beliefs or facts would you have to have to state those unusual opinions?

Learning from Experience, Feedback and Other People

☐ **Learning from Interviewing Others**
Interview others. Ask not only what they do, but how and why they do it. What do they think are the rules of thumb they are following? Where did they learn the behaviors? How do they keep them current? How do they monitor the effect they have on others?

☐ **Learning from Mistakes**
Since we're human, we all make mistakes. The key is to focus on why you made the mistake. Spend more time locating causes and less worrying about the effects. Check how you react to mistakes. How much time do you spend being angry with yourself? Do you waste time stewing or do you move on? More importantly, do you learn? Ask why you made the mistake. Are you likely to repeat it under similar situations? Was it a lack of skill? Judgment? Style? Not enough data? Reading people? Misreading the challenge? Misreading the politics? Or was it just random? A good strategy that just didn't work? Others that let you down? The key is to avoid two common reactions to your mistakes: 1) avoiding similar situations instead of learning and trying again, and 2) trying to repeat what you did, only more diligently and harder, hoping to break through the problem, making the same mistake again but with greater impact. Neither trap leaves us with better strategies for the future. Neither is a learning strategy. To learn and do something differently, focus on the patterns in your behavior that get you in trouble and go back to first causes, those that tell you something about your shortcomings. Facing ourselves squarely is always the best way to learn.

SUGGESTED READINGS

Ackoff, Russell Lincoln. *The art of problem solving: Accompanied by Ackoff's fables.* New York: Wiley, 1978.

Allen, Roger E. and Stephen D. Allen. *Winnie-The-Pooh on Problem Solving – In which Pooh, Piglet and friends explore how to solve problems so you can too.* New York: Dutton, 1995.

De Bono, Edward. *Lateral thinking: creativity step by step.* New York: Harper & Row, 1970, 1973.

De Bono, Edward. *Six thinking hats.* Boston: Little, Brown, 1985.

Firestine, Roger L., Ph.D. *Leading on the Creative Edge – Gaining competitive advantage through the power of creative problem solving.* Colorado Springs, Colorado: Piñon Press, 1996.

Nadler, Gerald Ph.D. and Shozo Hibino Ph.D. *Breakthrough Thinking – The Seven Principles of Creative Problem Solving.* Rocklin, CA: Prima Publishing, 1998.

Nanus, Burt. *Visonary Leadership.* San Francisco: Jossey-Bass, Inc., 1992.

Quinlivan-Hall, Daniel and Peter Renner. *In Search of Solutions – 60 Ways to guide your problem solving group.* Vancouver: Training Associates, 1990.

52

PROCESS MANAGEMENT

SECTION 1: YOUR DEVELOPMENT NEED(S)

UNSKILLED

- ☐ Not good at figuring out effective and efficient ways to get things done
- ☐ Works in a disorganized fashion
- ☐ Doesn't take advantage of opportunities for synergy and efficiency with others
- ☐ Can't visualize effective processes in his/her head
- ☐ Lays out tasks for self and others in a helter skelter way
- ☐ Doesn't work to simplify things
- ☐ Uses more resources than others to get the same thing done
- ☐ Lacks attention to detail
- ☐ Doesn't anticipate the problems that will arise; not a systemic thinker

SKILLED

- ☐ Good at figuring out the processes necessary to get things done
- ☐ Knows how to organize people and activities
- ☐ Understands how to separate and combine tasks into efficient work flow
- ☐ Knows what to measure and how to measure it
- ☐ Can see opportunities for synergy and integration where others can't
- ☐ Can simplify complex processes
- ☐ Gets more out of fewer resources

OVERUSED SKILL

- ☐ May always be tinkering and refining – nothing is ever the same for long
- ☐ May have trouble explaining his/her vision of a process
- ☐ May never finish anything
- ☐ May always be dissatisfied because of unreasonably high standards and expectations of self and others
- ☐ May attempt to put too much together at once
- ☐ May misjudge the capacity of others to absorb change

Select one to three of the competencies listed below to work on to compensate for an overuse of this skill.

COMPENSATORS: 3, 14, 15, 19, 27, 33, 36, 41, 46, 47, 50, 56, 57, 58, 60, 63

SOME CAUSES

- ☐ Don't see through things easily
- ☐ Don't view things in terms of systems
- ☐ Impatient
- ☐ Inexperienced
- ☐ Not interested in details
- ☐ Reject the emerging science of people and organizations

THE MAP

Most things happen in orderly ways. Aside from maybe chaos, all things follow orderly rules about what happens first and what happens next. There are predictable "action gets reaction" rules. There are best ways to get something done – best in the sense of the highest probability of success, fewest resources, lowest costs, minimum noise. Each area in life and work have a set of these best ways or known process rules. In the physical world, the laws of physics and chemistry will almost always, if followed, produce a known result; H_2O will always be water. In the arena of people and organizations, the rules are a little more uncertain, but much is known. Those who know and follow the laws of due process almost always win and get what they need done.

SECTION 2: LEARNING ON YOUR OWN

THESE SELF-DEVELOPMENT REMEDIES WILL HELP YOU BUILD YOUR SKILL(S)

SOME REMEDIES

☐ **1. Subscribe to *The Systems Thinker*™,** Pegasus Communications, Inc., Cambridge, MA, 617-576-1231) This is a group dedicated to finding out how things work and why they work that way. They have a monthly publication as well as workshops, seminars and other materials available to help you see the world as a series of recurring systems or archetypes. They analyze everyday events and processes and try to see why they work the way they do.

☐ **2. Be a student of how organizations work.** Organizations can be complex mazes with many turns, dead ends, quick routes and choices. In most organizations, the best path to get somewhere is almost never a straight line. There is a formal organization – the one on the organization chart – where the path may look straight, and then there is the informal organization where all paths are zigzagged. Since organizations are staffed with people, they become all that more complex. There are gatekeepers, expediters, stoppers, resisters, guides, good Samaritans and influencers. All of these types live in the maze. The key to successful maneuvering through complex organizations is to find your way through the maze in the least amount of time making the least noise. The best way to do that is to accept the complexity of organizations rather than fighting it, and learn to be a maze-bright person. *More help? – See #38 Organizational Agility.*

☐ **3. Lay out the process.** Most well running processes start out with a plan. What do I need to accomplish? What's the timeline? What resources will I need? Who controls the resources – people, funding, tools, materials, support – I need? What's my currency? How can I pay for or repay the resources I need? Who wins if I win? Who might lose? Buy a flow charting software program like ABC FlowCharter® that does PERT and GANT charts. Become an expert in its use. Use the output of the software to communicate your plans to others. Use the flow charts in your presentations. Nothing helps move a process along better than a good plan. It helps the people who have to work under the plan. It leads to better use of resources. It gets things done faster. It helps anticipate problems before they occur. Lay out the work from A to Z. Many people are seen as lacking because they don't write the sequence or parts of the work and leave something out. Ask others to comment on ordering and what's missing. *More help? – See #47 Planning and #63 Total Quality Management/Re-Engineering.*

☐ **4. Some people know the steps** and the process necessary to get things done but they are too impatient to follow the process. Following a process to get things done includes stopping once in awhile to let things run their course. It may mean waiting until a major gatekeeper has the time to pay attention to your needs. Due process takes time. *More help? – See #41 Patience.*

☐ **5. Rally support.** Share the goals of your process with the people you need to support you. Try to get their input. People who are asked tend to cooperate more than people who are not asked. Figure out how the people who support your process can win along with you. It's easier to get things done when everybody is pulling in the same direction. It's easier to perform when you have all the tools and resources you need. It's easier to get things done when everyone you need in your corner is supportive and pulling for you. *More help? – See #36 Motivating Others and #60* Building Effective *Teams.*

☐ **6. Set goals and measures.** Nothing keeps processes on time and on budget like a goal and a measure. Set goals for the whole project and the sub tasks. Set measures so you and others can track progress against the goals. *More help? – See #35 Managing and Measuring Work.*

☐ **7. You need to match people and tasks** for processes to work well. People are different. They have different strengths and have differing levels of knowledge and experience. Instead of thinking of everyone as equal, think of them as different. Really equal treatment is giving each person tasks to do that match his/her capacities. *More help? – See #56 Sizing Up People.*

☐ **8. Envision the process unfolding.** What could go wrong? Run scenarios in your head. Think along several paths. Rank the potential problems from highest likelihood to lowest likelihood. Think about what you would do if the highest likelihood things were to occur. Create a contingency plan for each. Pay attention to the weakest links which are usually groups or elements you have the least interface with or control over – perhaps someone in a remote location, a consultant or supplier. Stay doubly in touch with the potential weak links. *More help? – See #51 Problem Solving.*

☐ **9. Set up a plan to monitor progress of the process.** How would you know if the process is unfolding on time? Could you estimate time to completion or percent finished at any time? Give people involved in implementing the process feedback as you go.

☐ **10. Find someone in your environment** who appears to do this skill well. Study what he/she does that you don't do. Ask how he/she goes about figuring out how things work.

SECTION 3: LEARNING FROM MORE FEEDBACK

THESE SOURCES WOULD GIVE YOU THE MOST ACCURATE AND DETAILED FEEDBACK ON YOUR SKILL(S)

☐ **Direct Reports**
Across a variety of settings, your direct reports probably see you the most. They are the recipients of most of your managerial behaviors. They know your work. They can compare you with former bosses. Since they may hesitate to give you negative feedback, you have to set the atmosphere to make it easier for them. You have to ask.

☐ **Internal and External Customers**
Customers interact with you as a person and as a supplier or vendor of products and services. You're important to them because you can either help address and solve their problems or stand in their way. As customer service and Total Quality programs gain importance, clients and customers become a more prominent source of feedback.

☐ **Past Associates/Constituencies**
When confronted with a present performance problem, some claim, "I wasn't like that before; it must be the current situation." When feedback is available from former associates, about 50% support that claim. In the other half of the cases, the people were like that before and probably didn't know it. It sometimes makes sense to access the past to clearly see the present.

SECTION 4: LEARNING FROM DEVELOP-IN-PLACE ASSIGNMENTS

THESE PART-TIME DEVELOP-IN-PLACE ASSIGNMENTS WILL HELP YOU BUILD YOUR SKILL(S)

☐ Install a new process or system (computer system, new policies, new process, new procedures, etc.).

- ☐ Integrate diverse systems, processes, or procedures across decentralized and/or dispersed units.
- ☐ Plan a new site for a building (plant, field office, headquarters, etc.).
- ☐ Monitor and follow a new product or service through the entire idea, design, test market, and launch cycle.
- ☐ Visit Malcolm Baldrige National Quality Award or Deming Prize winners and report back on your findings, showing how they would help your organization.
- ☐ Launch a new product, service, or process.
- ☐ Relaunch an existing product or service that's not doing well.
- ☐ Help shut down a plant, regional office, product line, business, operation, etc.
- ☐ Manage liquidation/sale of products, equipment, materials, a business, furniture, overstock, etc.
- ☐ Build a multifunctional project team to tackle a common business issue or problem.

SECTION 5: LEARNING FROM FULL-TIME JOBS

THESE FULL-TIME JOBS OFFER THE OPPORTUNITY TO BUILD YOUR SKILL(S)

- ☐ **Fix-its/Turnarounds**
  The core demands to qualify as a Fix-it or Turnaround assignment are: 1) Cleaning up a mess. 2) Serious people issues/problems like credibility/performance/morale. 3) Tight deadline. 4) Serious business performance failure. 5) Last chance to fix. Four Types of Fix-its/Turnarounds: 1) Fixing a failed business/unit involving taking control, stopping losses, managing damage, planning the turnaround, dealing with people problems, installing new processes and systems, and rebuilding the spirit and performance of the unit. 2) Managing sizable disasters like mishandled labor negotiations and strikes, thefts, history of significant business losses, poor staff, failed leadership, hidden problems, fraud, public relations nightmares, etc. 3) Significant reorganization and restructuring (e.g., stabilizing the business, reforming unit, introducing new systems, making people changes, resetting strategy and tactics). 4) Significant system/process breakdown (e.g., MIS, financial coordination processes, audits, standards, etc.) across units requiring working to change something from a distant position, providing advice and counsel, and installing or implementing a major process improvement or system change outside your own unit and/or with customers outside the organization.
- ☐ **Influencing Without Authority**
  The core demands to qualify as an Influence Without Authority are: 1) Significant challenge (e.g, start-up, fix-it, scope and/or scale assign-

ment, strategic planning project, changes in management practices/systems). 2) Insufficient direct authority to make it happen. 3) Tight deadlines. 4) Visible to significant others. 5) Sensitive politics.

☐ **Scale Assignments**
Core requirements to qualify as a Scale (size) shift assignment are: 1) Sizable jump-shift in the size of the job in areas like: number of people, number of layers in organization, size of budget, number of locations, volume of activity, tightness of deadlines. 2) Medium to low complexity; mostly repetitive and routine processes and procedures. 3) Stable staff and business. 4) Stable operations. 5) Often slow, steady growth.

☐ **Significant People Demands**
Core demands required to qualify as a Significant People Responsibilities assignment are: 1) A sizable increase in either the number of people managed and/or the complexity of the challenges involved 2) Longer-term assignment (two or more years). 3) Quality of people management critical to achieving results. 4) Involves groups not worked with before (e.g., union, new technical areas, nationalities).

SECTION 6: LEARNING MORE FROM YOUR PLAN

THESE ADDITIONAL REMEDIES WILL HELP MAKE THIS DEVELOPMENT PLAN MORE EFFECTIVE FOR YOU

Learning to Learn Better

☐ **Envision Doing Something Well in a Group**
Take the people you want or need to be involved through a envisioning/creativity exercise to come up with different ideas and solutions.

Learning from Experience, Feedback and Other People

☐ **Using Multiple Models**
Who do you know who exemplifies how to do whatever your need is? Who, for example, personifies decisiveness or compassion or strategic agility? Think more broadly than your current job and colleagues. For example, clergy, friends, spouses or community leaders are also good sources for potential models. Select your models not on the basis of overall excellence or likability, but on the basis of the one towering strength (or glaring weakness) you are interested in. Even people who are well thought of usually have only one or two towering strengths (or glaring weaknesses). Ordinarily, you won't learn as much from the whole person as you will from one characteristic.

☐ **Being a Teacher of Others**
Teaching others a skill you possess is a powerful way to learn from your students and about yourself. Decide what skill you have that you could teach direct reports, a child, or a friend. In what areas could you be a

mentor or tutor? Ask yourself why this is a strength for you. What are the first items you would teach as the keys to help others form umbrellas for understanding? Get feedback from others on why this is a strength for you and what you do behaviorally that makes it so. When teaching and coaching, watch the students carefully for their reactions. What works and doesn't work for you as a coach? Write down your rules of thumb on what works for you that helps others. Get feedback from your students on what you do well and not so well as a teacher/coach.

☐ **Learning from Observing Others**
Observe others. Find opportunities to observe without interacting with your model. This enables you to objectively study the person, note what he/she is doing or not doing, and compare that with what you would typically do in similar situations. Many times you can learn more by watching than asking. Your model may not be able to explain what he/she does or may be an unwilling teacher.

☐ **Consolidating What You Learn from People**
After using any source and/or method of learning from others, write down or mentally note the new rules of thumb and the principles involved. How will you remind yourself of the new behaviors in similar situations? How will you prevent yourself from reacting on "autopilot"? How could you share what you have learned from others?

☐ **Getting Feedback from Direct Reports**
Direct reports often fear reprisals for giving negative feedback about bosses, whether in a formal process, like a questionnaire, or informally and face-to-face. Even with a guarantee of confidentiality, some are still hesitant. If you want feedback from direct reports, you have to set a positive tone and never act out of revenge.

☐ **Getting Feedback from Peers/Colleagues**
Your peers and colleagues may not be candid if they are in competition with you. Some may not be willing to be open with you out of fear of giving you an advantage. Some may give you exaggerated feedback to deliberately cause you undue concern. You have to set the tone and gauge the trust level of the relationship and the quality of the feedback.

Learning from Courses

☐ **Survey Courses**
These are courses designed to give a general overview of an entire area (such as advertising), product or product line, division's activities, process (getting a product to market, Total Quality Management) or geography (doing business in "X"). These types of courses are good for general background and context.

☐ **The Role of Courses in Your Total Development Plan**
Seldom will a course alone be sufficient to fill a need or develop a strength. A course always has to be combined with practice back at work, feedback on your progress, other developmental assignments that feature the new skill, and integration with the rest of your portfolio. Always plan to do something in addition to the course.

SUGGESTED READINGS

The Systems Thinker™. Pegasus Communications, Inc., Waltham, MA. 781-398-9700

Carr, David K. and Henry J. Johansson. *Best Practices in Reengineering.* New York: McGraw-Hill, Inc., 1995.

Ghoshal, Sumantra and Christopher A. Bartlett. *The Individualized Corporation.* New York: HarperBusiness, 1997. Hammer, Michael and James Champy. Reengineering the Corporation. New York: HarperBusiness, 1993.

Hammer, Michael and James Champy. *Reengineering the Corporation [sound recording].* New York: Harper Audio, 1993.

Head, Christopher W. *Beyond corporate transformation: A whole systems approach to creating and sustaining high performance.* Portland, OR: Productivity Press, 1997.

Juran, J.M. *Juran on Leadership for Quality.* New York: Macmillan, 1989.

Keen, Peter G. W. *The Process Edge – Creating value where it counts.* Boston: Harvard Business School Press, 1998.

Rodgers, T.J. *No Excuses Management.* New York: Doubleday, 1992.

53

DRIVE FOR RESULTS

SECTION 1: YOUR DEVELOPMENT NEED(S)

UNSKILLED

- ☐ Doesn't deliver results consistently
- ☐ Doesn't get things done on time
- ☐ Wastes time and resources pursuing non-essentials
- ☐ Something always gets in the way – personal disorganization, failure to set priorities, underestimating timeframes, overcoming resistance
- ☐ Not bold or committed enough to push it through
- ☐ Procrastinates around whatever gets in his/her way
- ☐ Doesn't go all out to complete tasks
- ☐ Does the least to get by

SKILLED

- ☐ Can be counted on to exceed goals successfully
- ☐ Is constantly and consistently one of the top performers
- ☐ Very bottom-line oriented
- ☐ Steadfastly pushes self and others for results

OVERUSED SKILL

- ☐ May go for results at all costs without appropriate concern for people, teams, due process, or possibly norms and ethics
- ☐ May have high turnover under him/her due to the pressure for results
- ☐ May not build team spirit
- ☐ May not celebrate and share successes
- ☐ May be very self-centered

Select one to three of the competencies listed below to work on to compensate for an overuse of this skill.

COMPENSATORS: 3, 7, 19, 22, 23, 29, 31, 33, 36, 41, 46, 60, 64

SOME CAUSES

- ☐ Burned out
- ☐ Disorganized
- ☐ Inexperienced
- ☐ New to the job
- ☐ Not bold or innovative enough
- ☐ Not committed
- ☐ Not focused
- ☐ Perfectionist
- ☐ Procrastinate

THE MAP

Producing results means consistently hitting the goals and objectives set by you and others. It means pushing yourself and others to achieve stretch goals. It means keeping your eye on the ball and acting and talking as if you care about the bottom line.

SECTION 2: LEARNING ON YOUR OWN

THESE SELF-DEVELOPMENT REMEDIES WILL HELP YOU BUILD YOUR SKILL(S)

SOME REMEDIES

- ☐ **1. Setting priorities?** What's mission-critical? What are the three to five things that most need to get done to achieve your goals? Effective performers typically spend about half their time on a few mission-critical priorities. Don't get diverted by trivia and things you like doing but that aren't tied to the bottom line. *More help? – See #50 Priority Setting.*

- ☐ **2. Set goals for yourself and others.** Most people work better if they have a set of goals and objectives to achieve and a standard everyone agrees to measure accomplishments against. Most people like stretch goals. They like them even better if they have had a hand in setting them. Set checkpoints along the way to be able to measure progress. Give yourself and others as much feedback as you can. *More help? – See #35 Managing and Measuring Work.*

- ☐ **3. How to get things done.** Some don't know the best way to produce results. There is a well established set of best practices for producing results. Formally they are known as Total Quality Management and Process Re-Engineering. If you are not disciplined in how to design work flows and processes for yourself and others, buy one book on each of these topics. Go to one workshop on efficient and effective work design. Ask your Quality or Re-Engineering function for help. *More help? – See #52 Process Management and #63 Total Quality Management/Re-Engineering.*

- ☐ **4. Organizing?** Are you always short resources? Always pulling things together on a shoe string? Getting results means getting and using resources. People. Money. Materials. Support. Time. Many times it involves getting resources you don't control. You have to beg, borrow, but hopefully not steal. That means negotiating, bargaining, trading, cajoling, and influencing. What's the business case for the resources you need? What do you have to trade? How can you make it a win for everyone? *More help? – See #37 Negotiating and #39 Organizing.*

- ☐ **5. Getting work done through others?** Some people are not good managers of others. They can produce results by themselves but do less well when the results have to come from the team. Are you having trouble getting your team to work with you to get the results you need? You have the resources and the people but things just don't run well. Maybe you do too much work yourself. You don't delegate or empower. You don't communicate well. You don't motivate well. You don't plan well. You don't set priorities and goals well. If you are a struggling manager or a first time manager, there are well known and documented principles and practices of good managing. Do you share credit? Do you paint a clear picture of why this is important? Is their work challenging? Do you inspire or just hand out work? Read *Becoming a Manager* by Linda A. Hill. Go to one course on management. *More help? – See #18 Delegation, #20 Directing Others, #36 Motivating Others, and #60* Building Effective *Teams.*

☐ **6. Working across borders and boundaries?** Do you have trouble when you have to go outside your unit to reach your goals and objectives? This means that influence skills, understanding, and trading are the currency to use. Don't just ask for things; find some common ground where you can provide help. What do the peers you need need? Are your results important to them? How does what you're working on affect their results? If it affects them negatively, can you trade something, appeal to the common good, figure out some way to minimize the work – volunteering staff help, for example? Go into peer relationships with a trading mentality. To be seen as more cooperative, always explain your thinking and invite them to explain theirs. Generate a variety of possibilities first rather than stake out positions. Be tentative, allowing them room to customize the situation. Focus on common goals, priorities and problems. Invite criticism of your ideas. *More help? – See #42 Peer Relationships.*

☐ **7. Not bold enough?** Won't take a risk? Sometimes producing results involves pushing the envelope, taking chances and trying bold new initiatives. Doing those things leads to more misfires and mistakes but also better results. Treat any mistakes or failures as chances to learn. Nothing ventured, nothing gained. Up your risk comfort. Start small so you can recover more quickly. See how creative and innovative you can be. Satisfy yourself; people will always say it should have been done differently. Listen to them, but be skeptical. Conduct a postmortem immediately after finishing. This will indicate to all that you're open to continuous improvement whether the result was stellar or not. *More help? – See #2* Dealing With *Ambiguity, #14 Creativity, #28 Innovation Management, and #57 Standing Alone.*

☐ **8. Procrastinate?** Are you a lifelong procrastinator? Do you perform best in crises and impossible deadlines? Do you wait until the last possible moment? If you do, you will miss deadlines and performance targets. You might not produce consistent results. Some of your work will be marginal because you didn't have the time to do it right. You settled for a "B" when you could have gotten an "A" if you had one more day to work on it. Start earlier. Always do 10% of each task immediately after it is assigned so you can better gauge what it is going to take to finish the rest. Divide tasks and assignments into thirds and schedule time to do them spaced over the delivery period. Always leave more time than you think it's going to take. *More help? – See #47 Planning and #62 Time Management.*

☐ **9. Persistence?** Perseverance? Are you prone to give up on tough or repetitive tasks, have trouble going back the second and third time, lose motivation when you hit obstacles? Trouble making that last push to get it over the top? Attention span is shorter than it needs to be? Set mini-deadlines. Break down the task into smaller pieces so you can view your progress more clearly. Switch approaches. Do something totally different next time. Have five different ways to get the same outcome. Be prepared to do them all when obstacles arise. Task trade with someone who has your problem. Work on each other's tasks. *More help? – See #43 Perseverance.*

☐ **10. The stress and strain.** Producing results day after day, quarter after quarter, year after year is stressful. Some people are energized by moderate stress. They actually work better. Some people are debilitated by stress. They decrease in productivity as stress increases. Are you close to burnout? Dealing with stress and pressure is a known technology. Stress and pressure are actually in your head, not in the outside world. Some people are stressed by the same events others are energized by – losing a major account. Some people cry and some laugh at the same external event – someone slipping on a banana peel. Stress is how you look at events, not the events themselves. Dealing more effectively with stress involves reprogramming your interpretation of your work and about what you find stressful. There was a time in your life when spiders and snakes were life threatening and stressful to you. Are they now? Talk to your boss or mentor about getting some relief if you're about to crumble. Maybe this job isn't for you. Think about moving back to a less stressful job. *More help? – See #6 Career Ambition and #11 Composure.*

SECTION 3: LEARNING FROM MORE FEEDBACK

THESE SOURCES WOULD GIVE YOU THE MOST ACCURATE AND DETAILED FEEDBACK ON YOUR SKILL(S)

☐ **Boss's Boss(es)**

From a process standpoint, your boss's boss probably has the most influence and control over your progress. He/she has a broader perspective, has more access to data, and stands at the center of decisions about you. To know what he/she thinks, without having to violate the canons of corporate due process to get that information, would be quite useful.

☐ **Direct Boss**
Your direct boss has important information about you, your performance, and your prospects. The challenge is to get this information. There are formal processes (e.g., performance appraisals). There are day-to-day opportunities. To help, signal your boss that you want and can handle direct and timely feedback. Many bosses have trouble giving feedback, so you will have to work at it over a period of time.

☐ **Past Associates/Constituencies**
When confronted with a present performance problem, some claim, "I wasn't like that before; it must be the current situation." When feedback is available from former associates, about 50% support that claim. In the other half of the cases, the people were like that before and probably didn't know it. It sometimes makes sense to access the past to clearly see the present.

SECTION 4: LEARNING FROM DEVELOP-IN-PLACE ASSIGNMENTS

THESE PART-TIME DEVELOP-IN-PLACE ASSIGNMENTS WILL HELP YOU BUILD YOUR SKILL(S)

☐ Integrate diverse systems, processes, or procedures across decentralized and/or dispersed units.

☐ Manage the renovation of an office, floor, building, meeting room, warehouse, etc.

☐ Manage the purchase of a major product, equipment, materials, program, or system.

☐ Launch a new product, service, or process.

☐ Manage an ad hoc, temporary group of balky and resisting people through an unpopular change or project.

☐ Manage an ad hoc, temporary group of people where the people in the group are towering experts but the temporary manager is not.

☐ Manage an ad hoc, temporary group of people involved in tackling a fix-it or turnaround project.

☐ Manage liquidation/sale of products, equipment, materials, a business, furniture, overstock, etc.

☐ Manage a dissatisfied internal or external customer; troubleshoot a performance or quality problem with a product or service.

☐ Audit cost overruns to assess the problem and present your findings to the person or people involved.

SECTION 5: LEARNING FROM FULL-TIME JOBS

THESE FULL-TIME JOBS OFFER THE OPPORTUNITY TO BUILD YOUR SKILL(S)

☐ **Chair of Projects/Task Forces**

The core demands for qualifying as a Project/Task Force assignment are: 1) Full-time assignment. 2) Important and specific goal. 3) Tight deadline. 4) Success or failure will be evident. 5) High-visibility sponsor. 6) Learning something on the fly. 7) Must get others to cooperate. 8) Usually six months or more. Four types of Projects/Task Forces: 1) New ideas, products, services, or systems (e.g., product/service/program research and development, creation/installation/launch of a new system, new programs like Total Quality Management, positive discipline). 2) Formal negotiations and relationships (e.g., acquisitions, divestitures, agreements, joint ventures; licensing arrangements, franchising; dealing with unions, governments, communities, charities, customers, and relocations). 3) Big one-time events (e.g., working on a major presentation for the board, organizing significant meetings or conferences, disaster/damage control teams; reorganizations, mergers, acquisitions, or relocations, working on visions, charters, strategies, other time-urgent issues and problems). 4) Troubleshooting (e.g., problems, disasters, crises, product/service failures, accidents, illegal activities, damage control in public relations goofs, shut downs, downsizings, layoffs, abrupt changes in leadership).

☐ **Fix-its/Turnarounds**

The core demands to qualify as a Fix-it or Turnaround assignment are: 1) Cleaning up a mess. 2) Serious people issues/problems like credibility/performance/morale. 3) Tight deadline. 4) Serious business performance failure. 5) Last chance to fix. Four Types of Fix-its/Turnarounds: 1) Fixing a failed business/unit involving taking control, stopping losses, managing damage, planning the turnaround, dealing with people problems, installing new processes and systems, and rebuilding the spirit and performance of the unit. 2) Managing sizable disasters like mishandled labor negotiations and strikes, thefts, history of significant business losses, poor staff, failed leadership, hidden problems, fraud, public relations nightmares, etc. 3) Significant reorganization and restructuring (e.g., stabilizing the business, re-forming unit, introducing new systems, making people changes, resetting strategy and tactics). 4) Significant system/process breakdown (e.g., MIS, financial coordination processes, audits, standards, etc.) across units requiring working to change something from a distant position, providing advice and counsel, and installing or implementing a major process improvement or system change outside your own unit and/or with customers outside the organization.

☐ **Scope Assignments**
The core demands for a Scope (complexity) assignment are: 1) Significant increase in both internal and external scope or complexity. 2) Significant increase in visibility and/or bottom line responsibility. 3) Unfamiliar area, business, technology, or territory. Examples of Scope assignments involving shifts: 1) Switching into a new function/technology/business. 2) Moving to new organization. 3) Moving to overseas assignment. 4) Moving to new location. 5) Adding new products/services. 6) Moving between headquarters/field. 7) Switches in ownership/top management of the unit/organization. Examples of Scope assignments involving "firsts": 1) First-time manager. 2) First-time managing managers. 3) First-time executive. 4) First-time overseas. 5) First-time headquarters/field. 6) First-time team leader. 7) First-time new technology/business/function. Scope assignments involving increased complexity: 1) Managing a significant expansion of an existing product or service. 2) Managing adding new products/service into an existing unit. 3) Managing a reorganized and more diverse unit. 4) Managing explosive growth. 5) Adding new technologies.

SECTION 6: LEARNING MORE FROM YOUR PLAN

THESE ADDITIONAL REMEDIES WILL HELP MAKE THIS DEVELOPMENT PLAN MORE EFFECTIVE FOR YOU

Learning to Learn Better

☐ **Examine Your Past for Parallels to the Current Situation**
Examine your past for similar or contrasting experiences that match with or counter the current situation. What has worked in the past that you've dropped? What hasn't worked that you're repeating? What "pearls" of wisdom did you take away from your successes and failures, which you could apply today?

☐ **Learn to Compensate for a Weakness**
Some weaknesses just aren't correctable or at least are not worth the effort. Instead of ignoring what you can't change, try to create tactics to compensate for these weaknesses; be alert when these are needed. Use other people better than you to compensate for you in your weak areas; use a strength against your weakness.

☐ **Commit to a Tight Timeframe to Accomplish Something**
Set some specific goals and tighter than usual timeframes for yourself and go after them with all you've got. Push yourself to stick to the plan; get more done than usual by adhering to a tight plan.

Learning from Experience, Feedback and Other People

☐ **Getting Feedback from Bosses and Superiors**
Many bosses are reluctant to give negative feedback. They lack the managerial courage to face people directly with criticism. You can

help by soliciting feedback and setting the tone. Show them you can handle criticism and that you are willing to work on issues they see as important.

- ☐ **Feedback on What?**
  Although any feedback is useful, it's best to seek and receive feedback on skills the organization feels are the most important for your present and future success. Not all skills are equal in importance. Some common skills may not have much bearing on success at all. If the organization has an official success profile, that may be the best way to focus your growth efforts.

SUGGESTED READINGS

Drucker, Peter F. *Managing for the Future.* New York: Dutton, 1992.

Drucker, Peter F. *Managing for the Future [sound recording].* Beverly Hills, CA: Dove Audio, 1992.

Drucker, Peter F. *Managing for Results.* New York: HarperCollins, 1993.

Drucker, Peter F. *Managing for Results [sound recording].* New York: AMACOM, 1983.

Peters, Tom. *Thriving on Chaos.* New York: Knopf, Inc., 1987.

Peters, Tom. *Thriving on Chaos [sound recording].* New York: Random House, 1987.

Ulrich, David, Jack Zenger, Norman Smallwood. *Results-based leadership.* Boston, MA: Harvard Business School Press, 1999.

SELF-DEVELOPMENT

SECTION 1: YOUR DEVELOPMENT NEED(S)

UNSKILLED

- ☐ Doesn't put in the effort to grow and change
- ☐ Doesn't do anything to act on constructive feedback
- ☐ May not know what to work on or how
- ☐ May know what but doesn't act on it
- ☐ Doesn't adjust approach to different audiences and situations
- ☐ May be immune to negative feedback – arrogant or defensive
- ☐ May fear failure and the risk of admitting shortcomings
- ☐ May not believe people really change therefore it's not worth the effort
- ☐ May believe current skills will last
- ☐ May believe in development but is always too busy

SKILLED

- ☐ Is personally committed to and actively works to continuously improve him/herself
- ☐ Understands that different situations and levels may call for different skills and approaches
- ☐ Works to deploy strengths
- ☐ Works on compensating for weakness and limits

OVERUSED SKILL

- ☐ May be a self-help development junkie
- ☐ Can lead to navel-gazing
- ☐ May confuse others with constant efforts to improve and change
- ☐ May be too self-centered
- ☐ May be susceptible to self-help fads
- ☐ May spend too much time improving and too little time acting and performing

Select one to three of the competencies listed below to work on to compensate for an overuse of this skill.

COMPENSATORS: 1, 24, 43, 46, 50, 51, 53, 55, 57, 63

SOME CAUSES

- ☐ Arrogant; don't have any weaknesses
- ☐ Defensiveness
- ☐ Don't know what I should be developing
- ☐ Don't know what to do
- ☐ Don't need any development; I can make it on what I have
- ☐ Don't think people really change

☐ Fear of failure or of admitting shortcomings
☐ Too busy getting the work out

THE MAP

The bottom line is, those who learn, grow and change continuously across their careers are the most successful. Whatever skills you have now are unlikely to be enough in the future. Acquiring new skills is the best insurance you can get for an uncertain future. Some of us won't face our limitations; we make excuses, blame it on the boss or the job or the organization. Others are defensive and fight any corrective feedback. Some are just reluctant to do anything about our problems. Some of us want a quick fix; we don't have time for development. Some of us simply don't know what to do.

SECTION 2: LEARNING ON YOUR OWN

THESE SELF-DEVELOPMENT REMEDIES WILL HELP YOU BUILD YOUR SKILL(S)

SOME REMEDIES

☐ **1. Assessment.** First, get a good multi-source assessment, a 360° questionnaire, or poll 10 people who know you well to give you detailed feedback on what you do well and not well, what they'd like to see you keep doing, start doing and stop doing. You don't want to waste time on developing things that turn out not to be needs.

☐ **2. Next, divide your skills into these categories:**

- Clear strengths – Me at my best.
- Overdone strengths – I do too much of a good thing – "I'm so confident that I'm seen as arrogant."
- Hidden strengths – Others rate me higher than I rate myself.
- Blind spots – I rate myself higher than others rate me.
- Weaknesses – I don't do it well.
- Untested areas – I've never been involved in strategy formulation.
- Don't knows – I need more feedback.

☐ **3. What's important?** Find out what's important for your current job and the two or three next jobs you might have an opportunity to get. See if there are success profiles for those jobs. Compare the top requirements with your appraisal. If there are no success profiles, ask the Human Resources Department for help or ask one or two people who now have those jobs what skills they need and use to be successful.

☐ **4. Strengths.** Maintain the clear strengths you will need in the future by testing them in new task assignments. (You're good at conflict resolution – use this strength on a cross-functional problem-solving group while you learn about other functions.) Coach others in your strengths and ask for some help from them in their strengths.

- ☐ **5. Balance your overdone strengths in important areas.** If you're creative, telling yourself to do less of this won't work – it's the primary reason for your success to date. The key is to leave it alone and focus on the unintended consequences. (You're seen as lacking in detail orientation or disorganized.) Get the downside of your strength up to neutral; the goal is not to be good at it, but rather to see that it doesn't hurt you. Lominger's *FYI* lists the competencies that you can work on to balance your overused strengths.

- ☐ **6. Weaknesses.** *More help? – See #19 Developing Direct Reports* for how to work on your weaknesses. Weaknesses are best handled with a development plan which involves four keystones: stretching tasks in which you develop the skill or fail at the task (usually 70% of real development); continued feedback to help you understand how you're doing (usually 20% of learnings); building frameworks to understand through courses (about 10%); and ways to cement all your learning so you can repeat them next time.

- ☐ **7. You can also compensate for your weaknesses** rather than build the skill. We are all poor at something and beating on it is counterproductive. If you have failed repeatedly at sales, detail work or public speaking, find others who do this well, change jobs, or restructure your current job. Sometimes you can find indirect ways to compensate. Lincoln managed his temper by writing nasty letters, extracting the key points from the letters, tearing the letters up, then dealing with the key points contained in the letter when he regained composure.

- ☐ **8. Untested.** Get involved in small versions of your untested areas – write a strategic plan for your unit, then show it to people; negotiate the purchase of office furniture. Write down what you did well and what you didn't. Then try a second bigger task and again write down the +'s and -'s of your performance. At this point, you may want to read a book or attend a course in this area. Keep upping the size and stakes until you have the skill at the level you need it to be.

- ☐ **9. Blind spots.** Be very careful of blind spots, since you think you're much better at this than do others. Resist trying challenging tasks involving this skill until you clearly understand your behavior, have a target model of excellent behavior, and a plan so you don't get yourself into trouble. Collect more data. Ask someone you trust to monitor you and give you feedback each time. Study three people who are good at this and compare what you do with what they do. Don't rest until you have cleared up the blind spot.

- ☐ **10. Show others you take your development seriously.** State your developmental needs and ask for their help. Research shows that people are much more likely to help and give the benefit of the doubt to those who admit their shortcomings and try to do something about them. They know it takes courage. *More help? – See #44 Personal Disclosure.*

SECTION 3: LEARNING FROM MORE FEEDBACK

THESE SOURCES WOULD GIVE YOU THE MOST ACCURATE AND DETAILED FEEDBACK ON YOUR SKILL(S)

☐ **Human Resource Professionals**
Human Resource professionals have both a formal and informal feedback role. Since they have access to unique and confidential information, they can provide the right context for feedback you've received. Sometimes they may be "directed" to give you feedback. Other times, they may pass on feedback just to be helpful to you.

☐ **Natural Mentors**
Natural mentors have a special relationship with you and are interested in your success and your future. Since they are usually not in your direct chain of command, you can have more open, relaxed, and fruitful discussions about yourself and your career prospects. They can be a very important source for candid or critical feedback others may not give you.

☐ **Spouse**
Spouses can be powerful sources of feedback on such things as interpersonal style, values, balance between work, career, and personal life, etc. Many participants attending development programs share their feedback with their spouses for value-adding confirmation or context and for specific examples.

☐ **Yourself**
You are an important source of feedback on yourself. But some caution is appropriate. If you have not received much feedback, you may be less accurate than the other sources. We all have blind spots, defense shields, ideal self-views, and fantasies. Before acting on your own self-views, get outside confirmation from other appropriate sources.

SECTION 4: LEARNING FROM DEVELOP-IN-PLACE ASSIGNMENTS

THESE PART-TIME DEVELOP-IN-PLACE ASSIGNMENTS WILL HELP YOU BUILD YOUR SKILL(S)

☐ Attend a course or event which will push you personally beyond your usual limits or outside your comfort zone (e.g., Outward Bound, language immersion training, sensitivity group, public speaking).

☐ Teach a course, seminar, or workshop on something you don't know well.

- ☐ Manage an ad hoc, temporary group of people where the people in the group are towering experts but the temporary manager is not.
- ☐ Take on a task you dislike or hate to do.
- ☐ Make peace with an enemy or someone you've disappointed with a product or service or someone you've had some trouble with or don't get along well with.
- ☐ Do a study of failed executives in your organization, including interviewing people still with the organization who knew or worked with them, and report the findings to top management.
- ☐ Seek out and use a seed budget to create and pursue a personal idea, product, or service.
- ☐ Volunteer to fill an open management job temporarily until it's filled.
- ☐ Write a speech for someone higher up in the organization.
- ☐ Manage a project team of people who are older and more experienced than you.

SECTION 5: LEARNING FROM FULL-TIME JOBS

THESE FULL-TIME JOBS OFFER THE OPPORTUNITY TO BUILD YOUR SKILL(S)

☐ **Cross-Moves**

The core demands necessary to qualify as a Cross-Move are: 1) Move to a very different set of challenges. 2) Abrupt jump-shift in tasks/activities. 3) Never been there before. 4) New setting/conditions. Examples of Cross-Moves are: 1) Changing divisions. 2) Changing functions. 3) Field/headquarters shifts. 4) Line/staff switches. 5) Country switches. 6) Working with all new people. 7) Changing lines of business.

☐ **Off-Shore Assignments**

The core demands to qualify as an Off-Shore assignment are: 1) First time working in the country. 2) Significant challenges like new language, hardship location, unique business rules/practices, significant cultural/marketplace differences, different functional task, etc. 3) More than a year assignment. 4) No automatic return deal. 5) Not necessarily a change in job challenge, technical content, or responsibilities.

☐ **Scope Assignments**

The core demands for a Scope (complexity) assignment are: 1) Significant increase in both internal and external scope or complexity. 2) Significant increase in visibility and/or bottom line responsibility. 3) Unfamiliar area, business, technology, or territory. Examples of Scope assignments involving shifts: 1) Switching into a new function/technology/business. 2) Moving to new organization. 3) Moving to overseas assignment. 4) Moving to new location. 5) Adding new products/services. 6) Moving between headquarters/field. 7) Switches in ownership/top management of the unit/organization. Examples of Scope

assignments involving "firsts": 1) First-time manager. 2) First-time managing managers. 3) First-time executive. 4) First-time overseas. 5) First-time headquarters/field. 6) First-time team leader. 7) First-time new technology/business/function. Scope assignments involving increased complexity: 1) Managing a significant expansion of an existing product or service. 2) Managing adding new products/service into an existing unit. 3) Managing a reorganized and more diverse unit. 4) Managing explosive growth. 5) Adding new technologies.

☐ **Staff to Line Shifts**
Core demands necessary to qualify for a Staff to Line shift are: 1) Moving to a job with an easily determined bottom line or results. 2) Managing bigger scope and/or scale. 3) Requires new skills/perspectives. 4) Unfamiliar aspects of the assignment.

SECTION 6: LEARNING MORE FROM YOUR PLAN

THESE ADDITIONAL REMEDIES WILL HELP MAKE THIS DEVELOPMENT PLAN MORE EFFECTIVE FOR YOU

Learning to Learn Better

☐ **Form a Learning Network With Others Working on the Same Problem**
Look for people in similar situations, and create a process for sharing and learning together. Look for a variety of people inside and outside your organization. Give feedback to each other; try new and different things together; share successes and failures, lessons and learning.

☐ **Use a Tutor to Learn Something New**
Set up a tutor relationship in the areas you're working on; open up, listen, learn, and try new things. Learn from the tutoring/learning process. Do you learn more easily from a tutor or do you get blocked? Test out your thinking with the tutor; do debriefs after trying the tutor's advice.

☐ **Learn New and Frivolous Skills to Study How You Learn**
Practice learning frivolous and fun skills (like juggling, square dancing, skeet shooting, video games, etc.) to see yourself under different and less personal or stressful learning conditions. Ask yourself why that was easy while developing new personal/managerial skills is so hard. Try something harder with the same tactics.

☐ **Try Some New Things Out of Your Normal Comfort Zone**
Periodically, practice going against your grain (what's normal for you) and getting out of your comfort zone. Try something different and opposite to your nature; take a learning risk. Explore: if you're a thinker, act; if you're an action person, think. Test the unfamiliar; try the new; go beyond your self-determined limits and boundaries.

- ☐ **Do a Career Learning Timeline for Insights**
  Do a timeline (a chronology from schooling to the present) for yourself in terms of the development of your thinking and problem-solving style and preferences. List the good and the bad times. What made the difference? What breakthroughs did you have? How have you developed as a learner? How did you get rid of previous blocks? Are you still growing?
- ☐ **Throw Yourself With More Vigor Than Usual Into Something New**
  Throw yourself into a new area, something you've not done before so you will have to learn quickly, such as a new technical area, a new management practice, or a self-development project. Pick something that is out of your skill and strength set.

Learning from Experience, Feedback and Other People

- ☐ **Learning from Interviewing Others**
  Interview others. Ask not only what they do, but how and why they do it. What do they think are the rules of thumb they are following? Where did they learn the behaviors? How do they keep them current? How do they monitor the effect they have on others?
- ☐ **Learning from Observing Others**
  Observe others. Find opportunities to observe without interacting with your model. This enables you to objectively study the person, note what he/she is doing or not doing, and compare that with what you would typically do in similar situations. Many times you can learn more by watching than asking. Your model may not be able to explain what he/she does or may be an unwilling teacher.

Learning from Courses

- ☐ **Insight Events**
  These are courses designed around assessing skills and providing feedback to the participants. These events can be a powerful source of self-knowledge and can lead to significant development if done right. When selecting a self-insight course, consider the following: 1) Are the skills assessed the important ones? 2) Are the assessment techniques and instruments sound? 3) Are those who are providing the feedback trained and professional? 4) Is the feedback provided in a user-friendly and "actionable" format? 5) Does the feedback include development planning? 6) Is the setting comfortable and conducive to reflection and learning? 7) Are the other participants the kinds of people you could learn from? 8) Are you in the right frame of mind to learn from this kind of intense experience? Select events on the basis of positive answers to these eight questions.

☐ **Attitude Toward Learning**
In addition to selecting the right course, a learning attitude is required. Be open. Close down your "like/dislike" switch, your "agree/disagree" blinders, and your "like me/not like me" feelings toward the instructors. Learning requires new lessons, change, and new behaviors and perspectives – all scary stuff for most people. Don't resist. Take in all you can during the course. Ask clarifying questions. Discuss concerns with the other participants. Jot down what you learn as you go. After the course is over, take some reflective time to glean the meat. Make the practical decisions about what you can and cannot use.

SUGGESTED READINGS

Drucker, Peter F. *The Effective Executive.* New York: Harper & Row, 1996.

Drucker, Peter F. *The Effective Executive [sound recording].* New York: AMACOM, 1983.

Holton, Bill and Cher. *The Manager's Short Course. Thirty-three tactics to upgrade your career.* New York: John Wiley & Sons, 1992.

Maps, James J. *Quantum Leap Thinking.* Los Angeles: Dove Books, 1996.

Olesen, Erik. *12 Steps to Mastering the Winds of Change.* New York: Macmillan, 1993.

Pirsig, Robert M. *Zen and the Art of Motorcycle Maintenance.* New York: Bantam Books, 1984.

Stone, Florence M. and Randi T. Sachs. *The High-Value Manager – Developing the core competencies your organization needs.* New York: AMACOM, 1995.

55

SELF-KNOWLEDGE

SECTION 1: YOUR DEVELOPMENT NEED(S)

UNSKILLED

- ☐ Doesn't know him/herself well – strengths, weaknesses or limits
- ☐ Doesn't seek feedback – may be defensive or arrogant
- ☐ Doesn't listen to or learn from feedback
- ☐ May misestimate his/her performance – either too high or too low
- ☐ May rush in where he/she shouldn't, or not move when he/she should
- ☐ May be surprised by or not know own impact
- ☐ May know some shortcomings but will not share with others
- ☐ Avoids discussions about him/herself
- ☐ May assume he/she already knows when he/she doesn't
- ☐ May be an excuse maker and blamer; doesn't learn from mistakes
- ☐ Doesn't get much from personal insight exercises or performance discussions
- ☐ Is surprised by negative personal data

SKILLED

- ☐ Knows personal strengths, weaknesses, opportunities, and limits
- ☐ Seeks feedback
- ☐ Gains insights from mistakes
- ☐ Is open to criticism
- ☐ Isn't defensive
- ☐ Is receptive to talking about shortcomings
- ☐ Looks forward to balanced (+'s and -'s) performance reviews and career decisions

OVERUSED SKILL

- ☐ May be too self-critical, too open about self
- ☐ May not move past knowledge to improvement and action
- ☐ May spend too much time in self-insight activities
- ☐ May be too dependent upon waiting for feedback
- ☐ May overly solicit feedback

Select one to three of the competencies listed below to work on to compensate for an overuse of this skill.

COMPENSATORS: 1, 4, 11, 22, 27, 29, 33, 42, 44, 46, 48, 52, 54, 64

SOME CAUSES

- ☐ Arrogant
- ☐ Assume you know but others think you don't
- ☐ Defensive
- ☐ Don't get any feedback

☐ Don't know how to get feedback
☐ The only perfect person on the planet
☐ Too much success

THE MAP

Know thyself. (Socrates, 470–399 BC, didn't make much money teaching but wrote several 2000 year best-sellers.) Self-knowledge is strongly related to success in life and work. In one study, the best predictor of a high performance appraisal was seeing yourself as others see you; the best predictor of a low one was overrating your skills. Deploying yourself against life and work is greatly helped by really knowing what you're good, average and bad at, what you're untested in, and what you overdo or overuse. Known weaknesses don't get you in as much trouble as blind spots. You can loop around and compensate for a known weakness. A blind spot is the worst thing you can have. You can really get into performance or career trouble with a blind spot, because you don't know or are unwilling to admit you're not good at it. You will venture into areas that should make you cautious and humble, but you go in strutting and confident. Disaster soon follows. An important life and career goal is to have no blind spots.

SECTION 2: LEARNING ON YOUR OWN

THESE SELF-DEVELOPMENT REMEDIES WILL HELP YOU BUILD YOUR SKILL(S)

SOME REMEDIES

☐ **1. Get feedback.** People are reluctant to give you feedback, especially negative or corrective information. Generally, to get it, you must ask for it. Seeking negative feedback increases both the accuracy of our understanding and people's evaluation of our overall effectiveness. A person who wants to know the bad must be pretty good. People will increase their estimation of you as you seek out and accept more feedback. If people are reluctant to give criticism, help by making self appraisal statements rather than asking questions. Saying, "I think I focus too much on operations and miss some of the larger strategic connections; what do you think?" is easier for most people to reply to than a question which asks them to volunteer this point.

☐ **2. Confidential feedback** – a private discussion, a private 360° – tends to be more negative and more accurate than public – annual performance appraisal – feedback. Don't be lulled to sleep by your public feedback. For most of us, it's an excessively positive view. When the feedback giver knows results will be public, scores go up, accuracy goes down.

☐ **3. Seek feedback from more than one source.** Different types of raters are likely to know more about and be more accurate about different competencies. Fruitful areas for bosses usually include: strategic grasp, selling up skills, comfort around higher management, presentation of problems, solutions, clarity of thinking, team building, confronting and sizing up people skills. Customers generally know about responsiveness, listening, quality orientation, problem-solving skills, understanding of their business needs, persuasiveness. Peers know persuasion, selling, negotiation, listening to find common cause, keeping the interests of the organization in mind, follow-through on promises, and how well you maintain give and take in 50-50 relationships. Direct reports are best at the day to day behavior of leadership, management, team building, delegation, confronting, approachability, time use. When you get a piece of feedback, ask yourself if the person is in a position to know that about you. You may be the only one who doesn't know the truth about yourself. Other sources agree much more with one another about you than you will likely agree with any one of the sources. Even though your own view is important, don't accept it as fact until verified by more than one other person who should know.

- ☐ **4. In choosing people to give you feedback,** 360° or otherwise, focus on those who know you best to get the most accurate feedback. Try not to stack the deck, picking either those you do best with or worst with. Both friend and foe tend to pick similar competencies as strengths and weaknesses. Friends will use higher scores than foes but their highest and lowest competencies will usually be the same.

- ☐ **5. When getting feedback,** focus on the highest and lowest items or competency results from each group. Spend less time worrying about whether your scores are high or low in an absolute sense. In development, you should worry about you relative to you, not you relative to anyone else. Your goal is simply to know yourself better. To do this, answer the following questions: Why am I this way? How did my strengths get to be strengths? What experiences shaped my pattern? Do I have strengths tipping over into weaknesses – "I'm intelligent but make others feel less so;" "I'm creative but disorganized." If you are clearly poor at something, what's getting in your way? Many times you'll find you don't like it and have a poor understanding of why and how it's done well. Think of tough situations for you where your strengths and weaknesses play out. *More help? – See #54 Self-Development.*

- ☐ **6. Work to get continuous feedback;** don't wait for annual feedback events. There are three ways to get better continued, high quality feedback:

  - Prepare specific areas you are concerned about and ask people to respond anonymously in writing. List the areas where you need feedback and ask them what they would like for you to keep doing, start doing, and stop doing to improve.

  - Work with a development partner who knows what you're working on and gives up on-line feedback as you try new things.

- In areas you are working on, ask others who have watched you to debrief events with you shortly after they happen.

☐ **7. There will be three kinds of feedback:**

- Things others see that you also see that are true about you.
- Things others see that you don't see that are true about you – these will be strengths you have that you sell yourself short on and weaknesses you have that you deny or are unaware of (blind spots).
- Things others think they see, but you don't agree and are not really true about you. The perceptions of others are facts to them, even though they may not be true about you. On just those incorrect observations that really matter, try to demonstrate by actions, not words, that their perceptions are wrong.

☐ **8. Don't go it alone.** Regardless of how you get the feedback, get help in interpretation. Most 360° instruments can only be presented by a certified facilitator, but even if you get homegrown feedback, pick numerous people to talk with. Select people from each major constituency at work and people who know you best off work. Don't ask them for general reactions. Select a few things from your feedback, state what you think the issue is, see if they agree and ask them what they would like to see you do differently in this area.

☐ **9. Arrogance is a major blockage to self-knowledge.** Many people who have a towering strength or lots of success get little feedback and roll along until their careers get in trouble. If you are viewed as arrogant, you may have to repeatedly ask for feedback, and when you get it, there may be some anger with it. Almost by definition, arrogant people overrate themselves in the eyes of others. Others who think you are arrogant might rate you lower than neutral observers. If you devalue others, they will return the insult.

☐ **10. Defensiveness is the other major blockage** to self-knowledge. Here people suspect you really can't take it, that you are defending against something, probably by blaming it on others or the job context. Defensive people get less feedback, thereby fulfilling their dream of being perfect. To break this cycle, you will need to follow the rules of good listening (*More help? – See #33 Listening*), and give examples of the behavior being described to validate what people are saying. While this may sound unfair, you should initially accept all feedback as accurate, even when you know it isn't. On those matters that really count, you can go back and fix it later. *More help? – See #108 Defensiveness.*

SECTION 3: LEARNING FROM MORE FEEDBACK

THESE SOURCES WOULD GIVE YOU THE MOST ACCURATE AND DETAILED FEEDBACK ON YOUR SKILL(S)

- ☐ **Development Professionals**
  Sometimes it might be valuable to get some analysis and feedback from a professional trained and certified in the area you're working on: possibly a career counselor, a therapist, clergy, a psychologist, etc.
- ☐ **Human Resource Professionals**
  Human Resource professionals have both a formal and informal feedback role. Since they have access to unique and confidential information, they can provide the right context for feedback you've received. Sometimes they may be "directed" to give you feedback. Other times, they may pass on feedback just to be helpful to you.
- ☐ **Natural Mentors**
  Natural mentors have a special relationship with you and are interested in your success and your future. Since they are usually not in your direct chain of command, you can have more open, relaxed, and fruitful discussions about yourself and your career prospects. They can be a very important source for candid or critical feedback others may not give you.
- ☐ **Spouse**
  Spouses can be powerful sources of feedback on such things as interpersonal style, values, balance between work, career, and personal life, etc. Many participants attending development programs share their feedback with their spouses for value-adding confirmation or context and for specific examples.

SECTION 4: LEARNING FROM DEVELOP-IN-PLACE ASSIGNMENTS

THESE PART-TIME DEVELOP-IN-PLACE ASSIGNMENTS WILL HELP YOU BUILD YOUR SKILL(S)

- ☐ Attend a self-awareness/assessment course that includes feedback.
- ☐ Join a self-help or support group.
- ☐ Manage an ad hoc, temporary group of people where the people in the group are towering experts but the temporary manager is not.
- ☐ Take on a tough and undoable project, one where others who have tried it have failed.
- ☐ Make peace with an enemy or someone you've disappointed with a product or service or someone you've had some trouble with or don't get along well with.
- ☐ Do a study of failed executives in your organization, including interviewing people still with the organization who knew or worked with them, and report the findings to top management.

- ☐ Train and work as an assessor in an assessment center.
- ☐ Assemble an ad hoc team of diverse people to accomplish a difficult task.
- ☐ Take over for someone on vacation or a long trip.
- ☐ Volunteer to fill an open management job temporarily until it's filled.

SECTION 6: LEARNING MORE FROM YOUR PLAN

THESE ADDITIONAL REMEDIES WILL HELP MAKE THIS DEVELOPMENT PLAN MORE EFFECTIVE FOR YOU

Learning to Learn Better

☐ **Examine Your Past for Parallels to the Current Situation**
Examine your past for similar or contrasting experiences that match with or counter the current situation. What has worked in the past that you've dropped? What hasn't worked that you're repeating? What "pearls" of wisdom did you take away from your successes and failures, which you could apply today?

☐ **Learn to Compensate for a Weakness**
Some weaknesses just aren't correctable or at least are not worth the effort. Instead of ignoring what you can't change, try to create tactics to compensate for these weaknesses; be alert when these are needed. Use other people better than you to compensate for you in your weak areas; use a strength against your weakness.

☐ **Keep a Learning Journal**
Keep a learning log or diary about the issues and opportunities you've faced and how you've acted. Focus on how you've used your strengths and weaknesses. Deduce your effective and successful rules of thumb – what worked and what didn't, and how you would have done it differently.

☐ **Study Yourself in Detail**
Study your likes and dislikes because they can drive a lot of your thinking, judging, and acting. Ask which like or dislike has gotten in the way or prevented you from moving to a higher level of learning. Are your likes and dislikes really important to you or have you just gone on "autopilot"? Try to address and understand a blocking dislike and change it.

☐ **Examine Why You Judge People the Way You Do**
List the people you like and those you dislike and try to find out why. What do those you like have in common with each other and with you? What do those you dislike have in common with themselves and how do they differ from you? Are your "people buckets" logical and productive or do they interfere? Could you be more effective without putting people into buckets?

- ☐ **Study Your History of Conflicts for Insights**
  List the people and situations which cause you trouble. What are the common themes? Why do those kinds of people and/or those kinds of situations set you off? Do they have to? Was the conflict really important? Did it help or block your learning and getting things done? Try to anticipate those people/situations in the future.

- ☐ **Do a Career Learning Timeline for Insights**
  Do a timeline (a chronology from schooling to the present) for yourself in terms of the development of your thinking and problem-solving style and preferences. List the good and the bad times. What made the difference? What breakthroughs did you have? How have you developed as a learner? How did you get rid of previous blocks? Are you still growing?

- ☐ **Learning from Bad Situations**
  All of us will find ourselves in bad situations from time to time. Good intentions gone bad. Impossible tasks and goals. Hopeless projects. Even though you probably can't perform well, the key is to at least take away some lessons and insights. How did things get to be this way? What factors led to the impasse? How can you make the best of a bad situation? How can you neutralize the negative elements? How can you get the most out of yourself and your staff under the chilling situation? What can you salvage? How can you use coping strategies to minimize the negatives? How can you avoid these situations going forward? In bad situations: 1) Be resourceful. Get the most you can out of the situation. 2) Try to deduce why things got to be that way. 3) Learn from both the situation you inherited and how you react to it. 4) Integrate what you learn into your future behavior.

- ☐ **Learning from Mistakes**
  Since we're human, we all make mistakes. The key is to focus on why you made the mistake. Spend more time locating causes and less worrying about the effects. Check how you react to mistakes. How much time do you spend being angry with yourself? Do you waste time stewing or do you move on? More importantly, do you learn? Ask why you made the mistake. Are you likely to repeat it under similar situations? Was it a lack of skill? Judgment? Style? Not enough data? Reading people? Misreading the challenge? Misreading the politics? Or was it just random? A good strategy that just didn't work? Others that let you down? The key is to avoid two common reactions to your mistakes: 1) avoiding similar situations instead of learning and trying again, and 2) trying to repeat what you did, only more diligently and harder, hoping to break through the problem, making the same mistake again but with greater impact. Neither trap leaves us with better strategies for the future. Neither is a learning strategy. To learn and do something differently, focus on the patterns in your behavior that get you in trouble and go back to first causes, those that tell you

something about your shortcomings. Facing ourselves squarely is always the best way to learn.

Learning from Courses

☐ **Insight Events**
These are courses designed around assessing skills and providing feedback to the participants. These events can be a powerful source of self-knowledge and can lead to significant development if done right. When selecting a self-insight course, consider the following: 1) Are the skills assessed the important ones? 2) Are the assessment techniques and instruments sound? 3) Are those who are providing the feedback trained and professional? 4) Is the feedback provided in a user-friendly and "actionable" format? 5) Does the feedback include development planning? 6) Is the setting comfortable and conducive to reflection and learning? 7) Are the other participants the kinds of people you could learn from? 8) Are you in the right frame of mind to learn from this kind of intense experience? Select events on the basis of positive answers to these eight questions.

SUGGESTED READINGS

Barth, F. Diane. *Daydreaming: unlock the creative power of your mind.* New York: Viking, 1997.

Bennis, Warren. *On Becoming a Leader.* Reading, MA: Addison-Wesley, 1989.

Black, Jan and Greg Enns. *Better boundaries: owning and treasuring your life.* Oakland, CA: New Harbinger Publications, [Emeryville, CA]: Distributed in the U.S.A. by Publishers Group West, 1997.

Branden, Nathaniel. *The art of living consciously: the power of awareness to transform everyday life.* New York: Simon & Schuster, 1997.

Butler, Gillian Pd.D and Tony Hope, M.D. *Managing your Mind.* New York: Oxford University Press, 1995

Mason, Marilyn Ph.D. *Seven Mountains – The inner climb to commitment and caring.* New York: The Penguin Group, 1997.

Schechtman, Marya. *The constitution of selves.* Ithaca, NY: Cornell University Press, 1996.

Searing, Jill A. and Anne B. Lovett. *The career prescription: how to stop sabotaging your career and put it on a winning track.* Englewood Cliffs, NJ: Prentice-Hall, 1995.

Sternberg, Robert J. and John Kolligian, Jr., editors. *Competence considered.* New Haven, CT: Yale University Press, 1990.

56

SIZING UP PEOPLE

SECTION 1: YOUR DEVELOPMENT NEED(S)

UNSKILLED

- ☐ Isn't accurate in his/her appraisals of people
- ☐ Does not evaluate the strengths and weaknesses of others well
- ☐ Biases and stereotyping may play too much in his/her appraisals
- ☐ May have simplistic models of people
- ☐ May make instant judgments on almost no data
- ☐ Doesn't change after the initial appraisal
- ☐ His/her estimates and projections of what people will do in certain circumstances turn out to be wrong
- ☐ May be such a poor listener to and observer of others that he/she really doesn't know what they're like

SKILLED

- ☐ Is a good judge of talent
- ☐ After reasonable exposure, can articulate the strengths and limitations of people inside or outside the organization
- ☐ Can accurately project what people are likely to do across a variety of situations

OVERUSED SKILL

- ☐ May be hypercritical of others
- ☐ May be unwilling to alter an initial judgment about others
- ☐ May not look for or be open to further evidence
- ☐ May miss on slow starters and quiet and less expressive people

Select one to three of the competencies listed below to work on to compensate for an overuse of this skill.

COMPENSATORS: 19, 21, 31, 33, 38, 41, 46, 48, 60, 64

SOME CAUSES

- ☐ Anti-elitist; want all people to be equal
- ☐ Avoid making tough calls on people
- ☐ Impatient
- ☐ Inexperienced
- ☐ Only accept the moral equality argument; all people are the same
- ☐ Poor listener/observer
- ☐ Reject a science of people
- ☐ Time management; don't have the time to study people

THE MAP

Except from a moral viewpoint (everyone is equal in the eyes of their creator), all people are different. There is a rich variety and diversity of people. Physical is easy to see. Height. Weight. Speed. Strength. Some personal characteristics are easy as well. Smart; not so smart. Articulate; not so articulate. Warm; cold. Composed; emotional. Good presenter; poor presenter. Other human characteristics are harder. Motivated; not so motivated. Good values; not so good values. Integrity? Decisive? Fair? One key to getting anything of value done in the world of work is the ability to see differences in people and to manage against and use those differences for everyone's benefit.

SECTION 2: LEARNING ON YOUR OWN

THESE SELF-DEVELOPMENT REMEDIES WILL HELP YOU BUILD YOUR SKILL(S)

SOME REMEDIES

☐ **1. Read three texts on how people differ.** Go to a college bookstore and get an introductory textbook on the theory of personality. Find a copy of *Gifts Differing* by Isabel Myers, a book about the background of the Myers-Briggs Type Indicator. It outlines 16 different types of people, why they are different, and what those differences mean in the world of work. Find *Competencies at Work* by Spencer and Spencer which outlines 40 years of study on the differing characteristics people need to be successful in different jobs. Watch out for your personal biases – do you think you have a tendency to favor clones of yourself? Do you have a preference for people who think and act like you do? What characteristics do you value too much? What downsides do you ignore or excuse away? People good at this competency can see, describe and value the competencies of people not like them.

☐ **2. Understanding others starts with understanding self** (see Socrates!). Learn all you can about yourself. Volunteer for a 360° feedback process. Ask others to help you get the best picture of yourself that you can. As honestly as you can, outline your strengths and weaknesses as others see them and how you see them. Once you complete your assessment, you can use the level of your competencies as a benchmark in understanding others. Do they have more than, about the same, or less of this than you do? What difference do the differences make in behavior or effectiveness (How does poor listening play out, for example? How does it affect results? How about excellent listening?)? Watch out for personal insecurities as well. Sometimes we don't size up people different from us well because we'd rather not face how much better they are at something than we are. This is true – since no one has all possible strengths, chances are everyone you work with is better at something than you are. The key is to take this natural fear and use it as a positive. Observe people for different talents, study how they think, watch how they go about exercising their strengths, and use this knowledge to improve yourself.

- ☐ **3. Become a student of the people around you.** First try to outline their strengths and weakness, their preferences and beliefs. Watch out for traps – it is rarely general intelligence or pure personality that spells the difference in people. Most people are smart enough, and many personality characteristics don't matter that much for performance. Ask a second question. Look below surface descriptions of smart, approachable, technically skilled people, to describe specifics. Then try to predict ahead of time what they would do in specific circumstances. What percent of the time are your predictions correct? Try to increase the percent over time.
- ☐ **4. What differences make a difference?** For each job, role, task or assignment, try to create a success profile of what would be required for success. What skills, knowledge, and competencies would be mission-critical to getting the job done? This means that they differentiate superior from average performance. Don't include competencies that, while important, most people on a job would be expected to already have. (For example, integrity is a must, but if people already have it, it can't predict success. Similarly, time management and planning are important, but most people have demonstrated a reasonable proficiency in those in order to be employable. They wouldn't distinguish superior from average performers often.) Go for the critical few, not the important many. Which competencies don't make a difference?
- ☐ **5. You need to match people differences** and differences in task requirements. People are different; tasks are different. People have different strengths and have different levels of knowledge and experience. Instead of thinking of everyone as equal, think of them as different. Equal treatment is really giving each person tasks to do that match their capacities. Look at the success profile of each assignment and line it up with the capabilities of each person. Assign things based upon that match.
- ☐ **6. All people have positive and negative qualities.** People have the most trouble making public calls on the negative side. Most don't like giving people negative feedback. Negative reads on people have real life consequences. People could miss out on promotions or could even be released from the organization based on your negative read. If you are a supervisor or a manager, part of why you get paid more is to make those calls. It's just part of the requirements of management.
- ☐ **7. Volunteer to be part of an assessment center team.** You will be trained to observe and assess people as they are going through a number of tasks and assignments. As part of the process, you will compare your notes and assessments with others on the team. That way you will learn to calibrate your assessments.

☐ **8. Find two or three people** in your environment whom you can trust to share your people assessments with. In what areas are you different? What did you miss? What areas of behavior do you tend to misjudge?

☐ **9. Read a book and/or take a class** on how to interview others. That training will sharpen your observation skills and make you a more attentive listener for the signs of strengths and weaknesses in others.

☐ **10. Be cautious about early or rigid reads.** You may make a decent effort trying to read a person and form a reasonable judgment, but it may be wrong. Be willing to look at additional data. Be flexible; be willing to change as the information changes.

SECTION 3: LEARNING FROM MORE FEEDBACK

THESE SOURCES WOULD GIVE YOU THE MOST ACCURATE AND DETAILED FEEDBACK ON YOUR SKILL(S)

☐ **Direct Boss**
Your direct boss has important information about you, your performance, and your prospects. The challenge is to get this information. There are formal processes (e.g., performance appraisals). There are day-to-day opportunities. To help, signal your boss that you want and can handle direct and timely feedback. Many bosses have trouble giving feedback, so you will have to work at it over a period of time.

☐ **Human Resource Professionals**
Human Resource professionals have both a formal and informal feedback role. Since they have access to unique and confidential information, they can provide the right context for feedback you've received. Sometimes they may be "directed" to give you feedback. Other times, they may pass on feedback just to be helpful to you.

☐ **Natural Mentors**
Natural mentors have a special relationship with you and are interested in your success and your future. Since they are usually not in your direct chain of command, you can have more open, relaxed, and fruitful discussions about yourself and your career prospects. They can be a very important source for candid or critical feedback others may not give you.

SECTION 4: LEARNING FROM DEVELOP-IN-PLACE ASSIGNMENTS

THESE PART-TIME DEVELOP-IN-PLACE ASSIGNMENTS WILL HELP YOU BUILD YOUR SKILL(S)

☐ Go to a campus as a recruiter.

☐ Construct a success and derailment profile for a unit or the entire organization and present it to decision makers for adoption.

☐ Go on a business trip to a foreign country you've not been to before.

- ☐ Train and work as an assessor in an assessment center.
- ☐ Manage an ad hoc, temporary group of "green," inexperienced people as their coach, teacher, orienter, etc.
- ☐ Manage an ad hoc, temporary group of people involved in tackling a fix-it or turnaround project.
- ☐ Handle a tough negotiation with an internal or external client or customer.
- ☐ Work on a team that's deciding who to keep and who to let go in a layoff, shutdown, delayering, or divestiture.
- ☐ Resolve an issue in conflict between two people, units, geographies, functions, etc.
- ☐ Build a multifunctional project team to tackle a common business issue or problem.

SECTION 5: LEARNING FROM FULL-TIME JOBS

THESE FULL-TIME JOBS OFFER THE OPPORTUNITY TO BUILD YOUR SKILL(S)

☐ **Fix-its/Turnarounds**

The core demands to qualify as a Fix-it or Turnaround assignment are: 1) Cleaning up a mess. 2) Serious people issues/problems like credibility/performance/morale. 3) Tight deadline. 4) Serious business performance failure. 5) Last chance to fix. Four Types of Fix-its/ Turnarounds: 1) Fixing a failed business/unit involving taking control, stopping losses, managing damage, planning the turnaround, dealing with people problems, installing new processes and systems, and rebuilding the spirit and performance of the unit. 2) Managing sizable disasters like mishandled labor negotiations and strikes, thefts, history of significant business losses, poor staff, failed leadership, hidden problems, fraud, public relations nightmares, etc. 3) Significant reorganization and restructuring (e.g., stabilizing the business, reforming unit, introducing new systems, making people changes, resetting strategy and tactics). 4) Significant system/process breakdown (e.g., MIS, financial coordination processes, audits, standards, etc.) across units requiring working to change something from a distant position, providing advice and counsel, and installing or implementing a major process improvement or system change outside your own unit and/or with customers outside the organization.

☐ **Influencing Without Authority**

The core demands to qualify as an Influence Without Authority are: 1) Significant challenge (e.g, start-up, fix-it, scope and/or scale assignment, strategic planning project, changes in management practices/ systems). 2) Insufficient direct authority to make it happen. 3) Tight deadlines. 4) Visible to significant others. 5) Sensitive politics.

☐ **Significant People Demands**
Core demands required to qualify as a Significant People Responsibilities assignment are: 1) A sizable increase in either the number of people managed and/or the complexity of the challenges involved 2) Longer-term assignment (two or more years). 3) Quality of people management critical to achieving results. 4) Involves groups not worked with before (e.g., union, new technical areas, nationalities).

SECTION 6: LEARNING MORE FROM YOUR PLAN

THESE ADDITIONAL REMEDIES WILL HELP MAKE THIS DEVELOPMENT PLAN MORE EFFECTIVE FOR YOU

Learning to Learn Better

☐ **Use Objective Data When Judging Others**
Practice studying other people more than judging or evaluating them. Get the facts, the data, how they think, why they do things, without classifying them into your internal like/dislike or agree/disagree boxes, categories, or buckets. Try to project or predict how they would act/react in various situations and follow up to see how accurate you are.

☐ **Examine Why You Judge People the Way You Do**
List the people you like and those you dislike and try to find out why. What do those you like have in common with each other and with you? What do those you dislike have in common with themselves and how do they differ from you? Are your "people buckets" logical and productive or do they interfere? Could you be more effective without putting people into buckets?

☐ **Study One Person in Detail**
Pick one person you are around a lot. Study his/her actions and decisions. List what you think his/her rules of thumb are. Begin to try to predict how he/she will respond to future situations and events. See how accurate you can get; compare your analysis to your own methods of operating.

☐ **Pre-sell an Idea to a Key Stakeholder**
Identify the key stakeholders – those who will be the most affected by your actions or the most resistant, or whose support you will most need. Collect the information each will find persuasive; marshal your arguments and try to pre-sell your conclusions, recommendations, and solutions.

Learning from Experience, Feedback and Other People

☐ **Using Multiple Models**
Who do you know who exemplifies how to do whatever your need is? Who, for example, personifies decisiveness or compassion or strategic

agility? Think more broadly than your current job and colleagues. For example, clergy, friends, spouses or community leaders are also good sources for potential models. Select your models not on the basis of overall excellence or likability, but on the basis of the one towering strength (or glaring weakness) you are interested in. Even people who are well thought of usually have only one or two towering strengths (or glaring weaknesses). Ordinarily, you won't learn as much from the whole person as you will from one characteristic.

☐ **Learning from Observing Others**
Observe others. Find opportunities to observe without interacting with your model. This enables you to objectively study the person, note what he/she is doing or not doing, and compare that with what you would typically do in similar situations. Many times you can learn more by watching than asking. Your model may not be able to explain what he/she does or may be an unwilling teacher.

☐ **Consolidating What You Learn from People**
After using any source and/or method of learning from others, write down or mentally note the new rules of thumb and the principles involved. How will you remind yourself of the new behaviors in similar situations? How will you prevent yourself from reacting on "autopilot"? How could you share what you have learned from others?

☐ **Learning from Bad Bosses**
First, what does he/she do so well to make him/her your boss? (Even bad bosses have strengths). Then, ask what makes this boss bad for you. Is it his/her behavior? Attitude? Values? Philosophy? Practices? Style? What is the source of the conflict? Why do you react as you do? Do others react the same? How are you part of the problem? What do you do that triggers your boss? If you wanted to, could you reduce the conflict or make it go away by changing something you do? Is there someone around you who doesn't react like you? How are they different? What can you learn from them? What is your emotional reaction to this boss? Why do you react like that? What can you do to cope with these feelings? Can you avoid reacting out of anger and frustration? Can you find something positive about the situation? Can you use someone else as a buffer? Can you learn from your emotions? What lasting lessons of managing others can you take away from this experience? What won't you do as a manager? What will you do differently? How could you teach these principles you've learned to others by the use of this example?

☐ **Learning from Limited Staff**
Most managers either inherit or hire staff from time to time who are inexperienced, incompetent, not up to the task, resistant, or dispirited. Any of these may create a hardship for you. The lessons to be learned are how to get things done with limited resources and how to fix the people situation. In the short term, this hardship is best addressed by

assessing the combined strengths of the team and deploying the best you have against the problem. Almost everyone can do something well. Also, the team can contribute more than the combined individuals can. How can you empower and motivate the team? If you hired the troublesome staff, why did you err? What can you learn from your hiring mistakes? What wasn't there that you thought was present? What led you astray? How can you prevent that same hiring error in the future? What do you need to do to fix the situation? Quick development? Start over? If you inherited the problem, how can you fix it? Can you implement a program of accelerated development? Do you have to start over and get new people? What did the prior manager do or not do that led to this situation in the first place? What can you learn from that? What will you do differently? How does the staff feel? What can you learn from their frustrations over not being able to do the job? How can you be a positive force under negative circumstances? How can you rally them to perform? What lasting lessons can you learn from someone in distress and trouble? If you're going to try accelerated development, how can you get a quick assessment? How can you give the staff motivating feedback? How can you construct and implement development plans that will work? How can you get people on-line feedback for maximum growth? Do you know when to stop trying and start over? If you're going to turn over some staff, how can you do it both rapidly and with the least damage? How can you deliver the message in a constructive way? What can you learn from having to take negative actions against people? How can you prevent this from happening again?

Learning from Courses

☐ **Supervisory Courses**
Most new supervisors go through an "Introduction to Supervision" type course. They are designed to teach the common practices a first-line supervisor needs to know to be effective. The content of most of those courses is standard. There is general agreement on the principles of effective supervision. There are two common problems: 1) Do the students have a strong motivation to learn? Do they know what they don't know? Is there any pain? Because motivated students with a need for the knowledge learn best, participants should have had some trying experiences and some supervisory pain and hardships before attending. 2) Are the instructors experienced supervisors? Have they practiced what they preach? Can they share powerful anecdotes to make key points? Can they answer questions credibly? If possible, select supervisory courses based on the instructors, since the content seems to be the much same for all such courses. Lastly, does the course offer the opportunity for practicing each skill? Does it contain simulations? Are there case studies you could easily identify with? Are there breakout groups? Is there opportunity for action learning? Search for the most interactive course.

SUGGESTED READINGS

Bolton, Robert and Dorothy Grover Bolton. *People Styles at Work.* New York: AMACOM, 1996.

Brinkman, Rick, Ph.D. and Dr. Rick Kirschner. *Dealing with People You Can't Stand.* New York: McGraw-Hill, Inc., 1994.

Bromley, D. B. *Reputation, image, and impression management.* Chichester, England; New York: John Wiley & Sons, Inc., 1993.

Cornwell, Patricia Daniels. *Point of Origin.* New York: G.P. Putnam's Sons, 1998.

Douglas, John E. and Mark Olshaker. *Mindhunter: inside the FBI's elite serial crime unit.* New York: Scribner, 1995.

Kummerow, Jean M., Nancy J. Barger and Linda K. Kirby. *Work Types.* New York: Warner Books, 1997.

Myers, Isabel Briggs with Peter B. Myers. *Gifts differing: understanding personality type.* Palo Alto, CA: Davies-Black Pub., 1995.

Robinson, Ray. *American Original: A life of Will Rogers.* New York: Oxford University Press, 1996.

Smart, Bradford D. *The smart interviewer.* New York: John Wiley & Sons, Inc., 1989

Smart, Bradford D. Pd.D. *Topgrading – How Leading Companies Win Hiring, Coaching and Keeping the Best People.* New York: Prentice-Hall, Inc., 1999.

Yate, Martin. *Hiring the Best.* Holbrook, MA: Adams Media Corp, 1994.

Yate, Martin. *Keeping the Best.* Holbrook, MA: Adams Media Corp, 1991.

Wareham, John. *The New Secrets of a Corporate Headhunter.* New York: HarperBusiness, 1994.

57

STANDING ALONE

SECTION 1: YOUR DEVELOPMENT NEED(S)

UNSKILLED

- ☐ Isn't comfortable going it alone
- ☐ Prefers to be in the background
- ☐ May prefer to be one of many or be part of a team
- ☐ Doesn't take the lead on unpopular stands
- ☐ Doesn't take on controversial issues by him/herself
- ☐ May avoid and shrink from dispute and conflict
- ☐ May not have a passion, may be burned out

SKILLED

- ☐ Will stand up and be counted
- ☐ Doesn't shirk personal responsibility
- ☐ Can be counted on when times are tough
- ☐ Willing to be the only champion for an idea or position
- ☐ Is comfortable working alone on a tough assignment

OVERUSED SKILL

- ☐ May be a loner and not a good team player or team builder
- ☐ May not give appropriate credit to others
- ☐ May be seen as too self-centered
- ☐ May not wear well over time

Select one to three of the competencies listed below to work on to compensate for an overuse of this skill.

COMPENSATORS: 3, 4, 7, 15, 19, 27, 33, 36, 42, 60, 64

SOME CAUSES

- ☐ Can't take the heat
- ☐ Don't like to be out in front
- ☐ Don't relish working alone
- ☐ Laid back style
- ☐ Not identified strongly with any issue
- ☐ Not knowledgeable enough to take stands
- ☐ Not self confident
- ☐ Shy away from conflict

THE MAP

Standing alone involves being comfortable with the conflict inherent with being an individual champion. It means staking out tough and lonely positions, speaking out as a lone voice, and taking the buffeting that comes with that. It requires a strong sense of self and a lot of self confidence. Leading is many times standing alone.

SECTION 2: LEARNING ON YOUR OWN

THESE SELF-DEVELOPMENT REMEDIES WILL HELP YOU BUILD YOUR SKILL(S)

SOME REMEDIES

- ☐ **1. Not comfortable being out front?** Leading is riskier than following. While there are a lot of personal rewards for taking tough stands, it puts you into the limelight. Look at what happens to political leaders and the scrutiny they face. People who choose to stand alone have to be internally secure. Do you feel good about yourself? Can you defend to a critical and impartial audience the wisdom of what you're doing? They have to please themselves first that they are on the right track. They have to accept lightning bolts from detractors. Can you take the heat? People will always say it should have been done differently. Even great leaders are wrong sometimes. They accept personal responsibility for errors and move on to lead some more. Don't let criticism prevent you from taking a stand. Build up your heat shield. If you know you're right, standing alone is well worth the heat. If it turns out you're wrong, admit it and move on.

- ☐ **2. Against the grain tough stands.** Taking a tough stand demands confidence in what you're saying along with the humility that you might be wrong – one of life's paradoxes. To prepare to take the lead on a tough issue, work on your stand through mental interrogation until you can clearly state in a few sentences what your stand is and why you hold it. Build the business case. How do others win? Ask others for advice. Scope the problem, consider options, pick one, develop a rationale, then go with it until proven wrong. Consider the opposing view. Develop a strong case against your stand. Prepare responses to it. Expect pushback.

- ☐ **3. Selling your stand.** While some people may welcome what you say and what you do, others will go after you or even try to minimize you or the situation your stand relates to. Some will sabotage. To sell your views, keep your eyes on the prize but don't specify everything about how to get there. Give others room to maneuver. Present the outcomes, targets and goals without the how to's. Welcome ideas, good and bad. Any negative response is a positive if you learn from it. Invite criticism of what you're doing. Even though you're going it alone, you need the advice and support of others to get there. Stay away from personal clashes. *More help? – See #12 Conflict Management.*

☐ **4. Keep your cool.** Manage your emotional reactions. Sometimes your emotional reactions lead others to think you have problems with taking tough positions and stands. When this happens, what emotional reactions do you have? Do you show nervousness or non-verbals like increasing or wavering voice volume or fidgeting? Learn to recognize those as soon as they start. Ask a question to buy time. Pause. Or tell the person to tell you more about their point of view. *More help? – See #11 Composure and #107* Lack of *Composure.*

☐ **5. Develop a philosophical stance** toward being wrong or losing. After all, most innovations fail, most proposals fail, most efforts to lead change fail. Research says that successful general managers have made more mistakes in their careers than the people they were promoted over. They got promoted because they had the guts to stand alone, not because they were always right. Other studies suggest really good general managers are right about 65% of the time. Put errors, mistakes and failures on your menu. Everyone has to have some spinach for a balanced diet. Don't let the possibility of being wrong hold you back from standing alone when you believe it's right.

☐ **6. One-on-one combat.** Standing alone usually involves dealing with pure hand to hand confrontations. You believe one thing, they want something else. When that happens, keep it to any facts that are available. You won't always win. Stay objective. Make the business case. Listen as long as they will talk. Ask a lot of clarifying questions. Sometimes they talk themselves to your point of view if you let them talk long enough. Always listen to understand first, not judge. Restate their points until they say that's right. Find something to agree with, however small that may be. Then refute their points starting with the one you have the most objective information for first. Move down the line. You will always have points left that didn't get resolved. Acknowledge those. The objective is to get the list as small as possible. Then decide whether you are going to continue your stand, modify it or withdraw. *More help? – See #12 Conflict Management.*

☐ **7. Afraid of nasty questions or ones you can't answer?** Think about the 10 most likely questions you could be asked. Rehearse what you would say. Some rules. Practice 10 to 30 second answers. Ask the questioner if that answered his/her question. Many spend too much time on the answers. Make sure you know what the question is. Many answer the wrong question. Ask one clarifying question if you're unsure (do you mean how would this product work in a foreign or domestic market?). If someone just won't let go, say, "We must really have different experiences. It's apparent we don't agree so let's just agree to disagree for now, but thanks for the debate." If the question is hot, "Why are women so discriminated against in this organization?" extract the main issues and respond with, "Here are three things you can do about it." As a general rule, don't answer such questions as given because they are negative, and stay away from classification (women, men, accountants) answers. Get it in your mind that questions are your friends because they reveal opportunities to solve problems and headline the difficulties you face. You just need five techniques to deal with them including the dreaded "I don't know, but I'll find out and get back to you on that."

☐ **8. Don't like risk?** Standing alone involves pushing the envelope, taking chances and suggesting bold new initiatives. Doing those things leads to more misfires and mistakes. Treat any mistakes or failures as chances to learn. Nothing ventured, nothing gained. Up your risk comfort. Start small so you can recover more quickly. Go for small wins. Send up trial balloons. Don't blast into a major stand to prove your boldness. Break it down into smaller stands. Take the easiest one for you first. Then build up to the tougher ones. Review each one to see what you did well and not well, and set goals so you'll do something differently and better each time. Challenge yourself. See how inventive you can be in taking action a number of different ways. *More help? – See #2* Dealing With *Ambiguity, #14 Creativity, and #28 Innovation Management.*

☐ **9. Maybe there's nothing you care about deeply enough** to stand alone on. You stay in the background or within your group. This is OK, but most likely won't get you recognized or promoted. Leaders lead and take tough stands. Look around you – what's your passion? What do you have enthusiasm for or it deeply needs to be done? Identify it. Appoint yourself as champion. Throw out trial balloons to other units/groups to see if your notion strikes a chord or solves a common problem. Find an experimenter to go in with you. Bring in a heavy expert or someone with political clout to help you make your point. Plant seeds with others at every opportunity.

☐ **10. Taking personal responsibility.** Standing alone means taking the consequences alone. Both the credit and the heat. You won't always be right so you need to just be as quick to take the blame as the credit. Just say, "Yes you're right, my stand was wrong, sorry about that." Make it a practice to conduct postmortems immediately after milestone efforts – win or lose. This will indicate to all that you're interested in improvement and excellence whether the results are stellar or not. Don't let your missteps chill your courage to speak up, step into the breach, and stake out tough stands.

SECTION 3: LEARNING FROM MORE FEEDBACK

THESE SOURCES WOULD GIVE YOU THE MOST ACCURATE AND DETAILED FEEDBACK ON YOUR SKILL(S)

- ☐ **Direct Boss**
  Your direct boss has important information about you, your performance, and your prospects. The challenge is to get this information. There are formal processes (e.g., performance appraisals). There are day-to-day opportunities. To help, signal your boss that you want and can handle direct and timely feedback. Many bosses have trouble giving feedback, so you will have to work at it over a period of time.
- ☐ **Human Resource Professionals**
  Human Resource professionals have both a formal and informal feedback role. Since they have access to unique and confidential information, they can provide the right context for feedback you've received. Sometimes they may be "directed" to give you feedback. Other times, they may pass on feedback just to be helpful to you.
- ☐ **Past Associates/Constituencies**
  When confronted with a present performance problem, some claim, "I wasn't like that before; it must be the current situation." When feedback is available from former associates, about 50% support that claim. In the other half of the cases, the people were like that before and probably didn't know it. It sometimes makes sense to access the past to clearly see the present.

SECTION 4: LEARNING FROM DEVELOP-IN-PLACE ASSIGNMENTS

THESE PART-TIME DEVELOP-IN-PLACE ASSIGNMENTS WILL HELP YOU BUILD YOUR SKILL(S)

- ☐ Become a referee for an athletic league or program.
- ☐ Plan for and start up something small (secretarial pool, athletic program, suggestion system, program, etc.).
- ☐ Launch a new product, service, or process.
- ☐ Be a change agent; create a symbol for change; lead the rallying cry; champion a significant change and implementation.
- ☐ Manage an ad hoc, temporary group of people involved in tackling a fix-it or turnaround project.
- ☐ Prepare and present a proposal of some consequence to top management.
- ☐ Take on a tough and undoable project, one where others who have tried it have failed.
- ☐ Resolve an issue in conflict between two people, units, geographies, functions, etc.

- ☐ Do a postmortem on a failed project and present it to the people involved.
- ☐ Audit cost overruns to assess the problem and present your findings to the person or people involved.

SECTION 5: LEARNING FROM FULL-TIME JOBS

THESE FULL-TIME JOBS OFFER THE OPPORTUNITY TO BUILD YOUR SKILL(S)

☐ **Chair of Projects/Task Forces**

The core demands for qualifying as a Project/Task Force assignment are: 1) Full-time assignment. 2) Important and specific goal. 3) Tight deadline. 4) Success or failure will be evident. 5) High-visibility sponsor. 6) Learning something on the fly. 7) Must get others to cooperate. 8) Usually six months or more. Four types of Projects/Task Forces: 1) New ideas, products, services, or systems (e.g., product/service/program research and development, creation/installation/launch of a new system, new programs like Total Quality Management, positive discipline). 2) Formal negotiations and relationships (e.g., acquisitions, divestitures, agreements, joint ventures; licensing arrangements, franchising; dealing with unions, governments, communities, charities, customers, and relocations). 3) Big one-time events (e.g., working on a major presentation for the board, organizing significant meetings or conferences, disaster/damage control teams; reorganizations, mergers, acquisitions, or relocations, working on visions, charters, strategies, other time-urgent issues and problems). 4) Troubleshooting (e.g., problems, disasters, crises, product/service failures, accidents, illegal activities, damage control in public relations goofs, shut downs, downsizings, layoffs, abrupt changes in leadership).

☐ **Scope Assignments**

The core demands for a Scope (complexity) assignment are: 1) Significant increase in both internal and external scope or complexity. 2) Significant increase in visibility and/or bottom line responsibility. 3) Unfamiliar area, business, technology, or territory. Examples of Scope assignments involving shifts: 1) Switching into a new function/technology/business. 2) Moving to new organization. 3) Moving to overseas assignment. 4) Moving to new location. 5) Adding new products/services. 6) Moving between headquarters/field. 7) Switches in ownership/top management of the unit/organization. Examples of Scope assignments involving "firsts": 1) First-time manager. 2) First-time managing managers. 3) First-time executive. 4) First-time overseas. 5) First-time headquarters/field. 6) First-time team leader. 7) First-time new technology/business/function. Scope assignments involving increased complexity: 1) Managing a significant expansion of an existing product or service. 2) Managing adding new products/service into an existing unit. 3) Managing a reorganized and more diverse unit. 4) Managing explosive growth. 5) Adding new technologies.

- ☐ **Start-ups**
  The core demands to qualify as a start from scratch are: 1) Starting something new for you and/or for the organization. 2) Forging a new team. 3) Creating new systems/facilities/staffs/programs/procedures. 4) Contextual adversity (e.g., uncertainty, government regulation, unions, difficult environment). Seven types of start from scratches: 1) Planning, building, hiring, and managing (e.g., building a new facility, opening up a new location, moving a unit or company). 2) Heading something new (e.g., new product, new service, new line of business, new department/function, major new program). 3) Take over a group/product/service/program that had existed for less than a year and was off to a fast start. 4) Establishing overseas operations. 5) Major new designs for existing systems. 6) Moving a successful program from one unit to another. 7) Installing a new organization-wide process as a full-time job (e.g., like Total Quality).

SECTION 6: LEARNING MORE FROM YOUR PLAN

THESE ADDITIONAL REMEDIES WILL HELP MAKE THIS DEVELOPMENT PLAN MORE EFFECTIVE FOR YOU

Learning to Learn Better

- ☐ **Learn New and Frivolous Skills to Study How You Learn**
  Practice learning frivolous and fun skills (like juggling, square dancing, skeet shooting, video games, etc.) to see yourself under different and less personal or stressful learning conditions. Ask yourself why that was easy while developing new personal/managerial skills is so hard. Try something harder with the same tactics.
- ☐ **Do Something on Gut Feel More Than Analysis**
  Act on "gut feel;" go with your hunches instead of careful planning. Take a chance on a solution; take some risks; try a number of things by trial and error and learn to deal with making some mistakes.
- ☐ **Sell Something to a Tough Group/Audience**
  Think of the person or group who will be the toughest to sell, the most critical, skeptical, or resistant, and sell that person or group first. Take time to understand the opposing viewpoints. Find common ground and leverage points; line up your best data and arguments and go for it.

Learning from Experience, Feedback and Other People

- ☐ **Getting Feedback from Bosses and Superiors**
  Many bosses are reluctant to give negative feedback. They lack the managerial courage to face people directly with criticism. You can help by soliciting feedback and setting the tone. Show them you can handle criticism and that you are willing to work on issues they see as important.

☐ **Learning from Bad Things that Happen**
Bad things happen to everyone, sometimes because of what we do and sometimes with no help from us. We all have bad bosses, bad staffs, impossible and hopeless situations, impossible tasks, and unintended consequences. Aside from the trouble these bad things cause for you, the key is how can you learn from each of them.

☐ **Learning from Mistakes**
Since we're human, we all make mistakes. The key is to focus on why you made the mistake. Spend more time locating causes and less worrying about the effects. Check how you react to mistakes. How much time do you spend being angry with yourself? Do you waste time stewing or do you move on? More importantly, do you learn? Ask why you made the mistake. Are you likely to repeat it under similar situations? Was it a lack of skill? Judgment? Style? Not enough data? Reading people? Misreading the challenge? Misreading the politics? Or was it just random? A good strategy that just didn't work? Others that let you down? The key is to avoid two common reactions to your mistakes: 1) avoiding similar situations instead of learning and trying again, and 2) trying to repeat what you did, only more diligently and harder, hoping to break through the problem, making the same mistake again but with greater impact. Neither trap leaves us with better strategies for the future. Neither is a learning strategy. To learn and do something differently, focus on the patterns in your behavior that get you in trouble and go back to first causes, those that tell you something about your shortcomings. Facing ourselves squarely is always the best way to learn.

SUGGESTED READINGS

Badaracco, Joseph L. Jr. *Defining Moments – When managers must choose between right and right.* Boston: Harvard Business School Press, 1997.

Calvert, Gene. *Highwire Management.* San Francisco: Jossey-Bass, Inc., 1993.

Cox, Danny and John Hoover. *Leadership when the heat's on.* New York: McGraw-Hill, Inc., 1992.

Keneally, Thomas. *Schindler's List.* New York: Simon & Schuster, 1982.

Keneally, Thomas. *Schindler's List [sound recording].* Prince Frederick, MD: Recorded Books, 1990.

Truman, Harry S. edited by Margaret Truman. *Where the buck stops: the personal and private writings of Harry S. Truman.* New York: Warner Books, 1989.

58

STRATEGIC AGILITY

SECTION 1: YOUR DEVELOPMENT NEED(S)

UNSKILLED

- ☐ Doesn't think or talk strategy
- ☐ Can't put together a compelling strategic plan
- ☐ More comfortable in the tactical here and now
- ☐ Lacks the perspective to pull together varying elements into a coherent strategic view
- ☐ Can't weave a vision of the future
- ☐ May reject the usefulness of strategy, considering it pie in the sky
- ☐ May have narrow experience and not be knowledgeable of business and world events
- ☐ May try to simplify too much or be very tactical
- ☐ May lack the disciplined thought processes necessary to construct a strategic view

SKILLED

- ☐ Sees ahead clearly
- ☐ Can anticipate future consequences and trends accurately
- ☐ Has broad knowledge and perspective
- ☐ Is future oriented
- ☐ Can articulately paint credible pictures and visions of possibilities and likelihoods
- ☐ Can create competitive and breakthrough strategies and plans

OVERUSED SKILL

- ☐ May be seen as too theoretical
- ☐ May not be tolerant of or have patience with day-to-day details
- ☐ May over-complicate plans
- ☐ May not be able to communicate with tactical or less complex people

Select one to three of the competencies listed below to work on to compensate for an overuse of this skill.

COMPENSATORS: 5, 16, 17, 24, 27, 35, 38, 39, 46, 47, 50, 52, 53, 59, 61, 63

SOME CAUSES

- ☐ Don't like complexity
- ☐ Don't think the future is knowable
- ☐ Inexperienced
- ☐ Aren't comfortable speculating
- ☐ Lack of perspective
- ☐ Low risk taker; don't like uncertainty

- ☐ Low variety background
- ☐ New to the area
- ☐ Too busy with today's tasks
- ☐ Too laid back
- ☐ Too narrow
- ☐ Very tactical

THE MAP

There are a lot more people who can take a hill than there are people who can accurately predict which hill it would be best to take. There are more people good at producing results in the short term than there are visionary strategists. Both have value but we don't have enough strategists. It is more likely that your organization will be out maneuvered strategically than that it will be outproduced tactically. Most organizations do pretty well what they do today. It's what they need to be doing tomorrow that's the missing skill. Part of every manager's job is to be strategic. The higher you go, the more critical the requirement.

SECTION 2: LEARNING ON YOUR OWN

THESE SELF-DEVELOPMENT REMEDIES WILL HELP YOU BUILD YOUR SKILL(S)

SOME REMEDIES

☐ **1. Speaking strategically.** In some rare cases, we have found people who could think strategically who were not identified as such because they either didn't know, rejected or chose not to use what they considered the latest strategic buzzwords. Strategy is an emerging and ever changing field. At any time, there are gurus (at present probably Michael Porter, Ram Charan, C.K. Prahalad, Gary Hamel, Fred Weirsema and Vijay Govindarajan) in vogue, who create about 75 new words or concepts (values disciplines, strategic intent or destination, core capabilities, value migration, market oligarchy, co-evolution, strategic horizon) to describe strategic thinking. If you don't use these words, then I won't know you're being strategic. The words are to be found in books by these gurus, in the *Harvard Business Review* and *Strategy and Leadership*, a publication of the Strategic Leadership Forum. And yes, most of the words are bigger words for things we used to call something else before with smaller words. Nevertheless, if you want to be seen as more strategic, you have to talk more strategically. Every discipline has its lexicon. In order to be a member, you have to speak the code.

☐ **2. Reject strategy?** There are people who reject strategic formulation as so much folly. They have never seen a five year strategic plan actually happen as projected. They think the time they use to create and present strategic plans is wasted. They think it's where the rubber meets the sky. So much BS. While it's true that most strategic plans never work out as planned, that doesn't mean that it was a wasted effort. Strategic plans lead to choices about resources and deployment. They lead to different staffing actions and different financial plans. Without some strategic plans, it would be a total shot in the dark. Most failed companies got buried strategically not tactically. They were still making high quality buggy whips when they went under. They picked the wrong direction or too many. Not being able to produce a quality product or service today is generally not the problem.

☐ **3. Not curious?** Many managers are so wrapped up in today's problems that they aren't curious about tomorrow. They really don't care about the long-term future. They may not even be in the organization when the strategic plan is supposed to happen. They believe there won't be much of a future until we perform today. Being a visionary and a good strategist requires curiosity and imagination. It requires playing "what ifs." What if it turns out there is life on other planets, and we get the first message? What will that change? Will they need our products? What will happen when a larger percentage of the world's population is over the age of 65? What if cancer is cured? Heart disease? AIDS? Obesity? What if the government outlaws or severely regulates some aspect of your business? True, nobody knows the answers, but good strategists know the questions. Work at developing broader interests outside your business. Subscribe to different magazines. Pick new shows to watch. Meet different people. Join a new organization. Look under some rocks. Think about tomorrow. Talk to others about what they think the future will bring.

☐ **4. Narrow perspective?** Some are sharply focused on what they do and do it very well. They have prepared themselves for a narrow but satisfying career. Then someone tells them their job has changed, and they now have to be strategic. Being strategic requires a broad perspective. In addition to knowing one thing well, it requires that you know about a lot of things somewhat. You need to understand business. *More help? – See #5 Business Acumen*. You need to understand markets. *More help? – See #15 Customer Focus*. You need to understand how the world operates. *More help? – See #46 Perspective*. You need to put all that together and figure out what all that means to your organization. *More help? – See #32 Learning on the Fly and #51 Problem Solving*.

☐ **5. Too busy?** Strategy is always last on the list. Solving today's problems, of which there are many, is job one. You have to make time for strategy. A good strategy releases future time because it makes choices clear and leads to less wasted effort, but it takes time to do. Delegation is usually the main key. Give away as much tactical day-to-day stuff as you can. Ask your people what they think they could do to give you more time for strategic reflection. *More help? – See #18 Delegation*. Another key is better time management. Put an hour a week on your calendar for strategic reading and reflection throughout the year. Don't wait until one week before the strategic plan is due. *More help? – See #62 Time Management*. Keep a log of ideas you get from others, magazines, etc. Focus on how these impact your organization or function.

☐ **6. Avoid speculating?** Strategic planning is the most uncertain thing managers do next to managing people. It's speculating on the near unknown. It requires projections into foggy landscapes. It requires assumptions about the unknown. Many conflict avoiders and perfectionists don't like to make statements in public that they cannot back up with facts. Most strategies can be challenged and questioned. There are no clean ways to win a debate over strategy. It really comes down to one subjective estimate versus another. Sometimes it is the person who can talk the longest and loudest who wins. Join the World Future Society for a year and read their publication, *The Futurist*. *More help? – See #2* Dealing with *Ambiguity and #12 Conflict Management.*

☐ **7. Addicted to the simple?** Strategy ends up sounding simple. Five clean clear statements about where we want to go with a few tactics and decisions attached to each. Getting there is not simple. Good strategists are complexifiers. They extend everything to its extreme before they get down to the essence. Simplifiers close too early. They are impatient to get it done faster. They are very results oriented and want to get to the five simple statements before strategic due process has been followed. Be more tolerant of unlimited exploration and debate before you move to close.

☐ **8. Don't know how to be strategic?** The simplest problem is someone who wants to be strategic and wants to learn. Strategy is a reasonably well known field. Read the gurus (Michael Porter, Ram Charan, C.K. Prahalad, Gary Hamel, Fred Weirsema and Vijay Govindarajan). Scan the *Harvard Business Review* and *Sloan Review* regularly. Read the three to five strategic case studies in *Business Week* every issue. Go to a three day strategy course taught by one of the gurus. Get someone from the organization's strategic group to tutor you in strategy. Watch CEO's talk about their businesses on cable. Volunteer to serve on a task force on a strategic issue. Join the Strategic Leadership Forum for a year, read their publication, *Strategy and Leadership*, and attend one national convention. Attend The Conference Board's Annual Conference on strategy where CEO's talk about their companies. Read 10 annual reports a year outside your industry and study their strategies.

☐ **9. Can't think strategically?** Strategy is linking several variables together to come up with the most likely scenario. Think of it as the search for and application of relevant parallels. It involves making projections of several variables at once to see how they come together. These projections are in the context of shifting markets, international affairs, monetary movements and government interventions. It involves a lot of uncertainty, making risk assumptions, and understanding how things work together. How many reasons would account for sales going down? Up? How are advertising and sales linked? If the dollar is cheaper in Asia, what does that mean for our product in Japan? If the world population is aging and they have more money, how will that change buying patterns? Not everyone enjoys this kind of pie in the sky thinking and not everyone is skilled at doing it. *More help? – See #32 Learning on the Fly, #46 Perspective, and #51 Problem Solving.*

☐ **10. Don't want to be strategic?** Some just don't feel they want to ramp up and learn to be strategic. But they like their job and want to be considered strategically responsible. Hire a strategic consultant once a year to sit with you and your team and help you work out your strategic plan. Anderson Consulting. The Boston Consulting Group. McKinsey. Booz Allen. Strategos. GeoPartner Research. Corporate Decisions. Plus many more. Or delegate strategy to one or more in your unit who are more strategically capable. Or ask the strategic planning group to help. You don't have to be able to do everything to be a good manager. You like your nest? Some people are content in their narrow niche. They are not interested in being strategic. They just want to do their job and be left alone. They are interested in doing good work in their specialty and want to get as high as they can. That's OK. Just inform the organization of your wishes and don't take jobs that have a heavy strategic requirement.

SECTION 3: LEARNING FROM MORE FEEDBACK

THESE SOURCES WOULD GIVE YOU THE MOST ACCURATE AND DETAILED FEEDBACK ON YOUR SKILL(S)

☐ **Boss's Boss(es)**

From a process standpoint, your boss's boss probably has the most influence and control over your progress. He/she has a broader perspective, has more access to data, and stands at the center of decisions about you. To know what he/she thinks, without having to violate the canons of corporate due process to get that information, would be quite useful.

☐ **Direct Boss**

Your direct boss has important information about you, your performance, and your prospects. The challenge is to get this information. There are formal processes (e.g., performance appraisals). There are day-to-day opportunities. To help, signal your boss that you want and can handle direct and timely feedback. Many bosses have trouble giving feedback, so you will have to work at it over a period of time.

☐ **Natural Mentors**

Natural mentors have a special relationship with you and are interested in your success and your future. Since they are usually not in your direct chain of command, you can have more open, relaxed, and fruitful discussions about yourself and your career prospects. They can be a very important source for candid or critical feedback others may not give you.

- ☐ **Past Associates/Constituencies**
When confronted with a present performance problem, some claim, "I wasn't like that before; it must be the current situation." When feedback is available from former associates, about 50% support that claim. In the other half of the cases, the people were like that before and probably didn't know it. It sometimes makes sense to access the past to clearly see the present.

SECTION 4: LEARNING FROM DEVELOP-IN-PLACE ASSIGNMENTS

THESE PART-TIME DEVELOP-IN-PLACE ASSIGNMENTS WILL HELP YOU BUILD YOUR SKILL(S)

- ☐ Study history and draw parallels for a current business issue or problem and present your findings to others for comment.
- ☐ Do a competitive analysis of your organization's products or services or your position in the marketplace and present it to the people involved.
- ☐ Work short rotations in other units, functions, or geographies you've not been exposed to before.
- ☐ Monitor and follow a new product or service through the entire idea, design, test market, and launch cycle.
- ☐ Study and summarize a new trend, product, service, technique, or process and present and sell it to others.
- ☐ Visit Malcolm Baldrige National Quality Award or Deming Prize winners and report back on your findings, showing how they would help your organization.
- ☐ Work on a project that involves travel and study of an issue, acquisition, or joint venture off-shore or overseas, with a report back to management.
- ☐ Seek out and use a seed budget to create and pursue a personal idea, product, or service.
- ☐ Manage a study/project team on a significant issue and present the results to key people.
- ☐ Present the strategy of your unit to others not familiar with your business.

SECTION 5: LEARNING FROM FULL-TIME JOBS

THESE FULL-TIME JOBS OFFER THE OPPORTUNITY TO BUILD YOUR SKILL(S)

☐ **Heavy Strategic Demands**
The core demands necessary to qualify as a Heavy Strategic Content assignment are: 1) Requires significant strategic thinking and planning most couldn't do. 2) Charts new ground strategically. 3) Plan must be presented, challenged, adopted, and implemented. 4) Exposure to significant decision makers and executives. 1) Strategic planning position. 2) Job involving repositioning of a product, service, or organization.

☐ **Line To Staff Switches**
The core demands to qualify as a Line to Staff switch are: 1) Intellectually/strategically demanding. 2) Highly visible to others. 3) New area/perspective/method/culture/function. 4) Moving away from a bottom line. 5) Moving from field to headquarters. 6) Exposure to high-level executives. Examples: 1) Business/strategic planning. 2) Heading a staff department. 3) Assistant to/chief of staff to a senior executive. 4) Head of a task force. 5) Human resources role.

☐ **Scope Assignments**
The core demands for a Scope (complexity) assignment are: 1) Significant increase in both internal and external scope or complexity. 2) Significant increase in visibility and/or bottom line responsibility. 3) Unfamiliar area, business, technology, or territory. Examples of Scope assignments involving shifts: 1) Switching into a new function/technology/business. 2) Moving to new organization. 3) Moving to overseas assignment. 4) Moving to new location. 5) Adding new products/services. 6) Moving between headquarters/field. 7) Switches in ownership/top management of the unit/organization. Examples of Scope assignments involving "firsts": 1) First-time manager. 2) First-time managing managers. 3) First-time executive. 4) First-time overseas. 5) First-time headquarters/field. 6) First-time team leader. 7) First-time new technology/business/function. Scope assignments involving increased complexity: 1) Managing a significant expansion of an existing product or service. 2) Managing adding new products/service into an existing unit. 3) Managing a reorganized and more diverse unit. 4) Managing explosive growth. 5) Adding new technologies.

SECTION 6: LEARNING MORE FROM YOUR PLAN

THESE ADDITIONAL REMEDIES WILL HELP MAKE THIS DEVELOPMENT PLAN MORE EFFECTIVE FOR YOU

Learning to Learn Better

☐ **Regularly Read Relevant Publications**
Read publications most relevant to you such as the *Wall Street Journal*, the *Harvard Business Review*, the *Economist*, *Fortune*, *Business Week*,

etc. Track a single issue or trend to see as many sides of it as you can. What tactics and strategies are being followed? How is this similar to something you are doing? How could you use some of your insights?

Learning from Experience, Feedback and Other People

☐ **Using Multiple Models**
Who do you know who exemplifies how to do whatever your need is? Who, for example, personifies decisiveness or compassion or strategic agility? Think more broadly than your current job and colleagues. For example, clergy, friends, spouses or community leaders are also good sources for potential models. Select your models not on the basis of overall excellence or likability, but on the basis of the one towering strength (or glaring weakness) you are interested in. Even people who are well thought of usually have only one or two towering strengths (or glaring weaknesses). Ordinarily, you won't learn as much from the whole person as you will from one characteristic.

☐ **Learning from Interviewing Others**
Interview others. Ask not only what they do, but how and why they do it. What do they think are the rules of thumb they are following? Where did they learn the behaviors? How do they keep them current? How do they monitor the effect they have on others?

☐ **Learning from Observing Others**
Observe others. Find opportunities to observe without interacting with your model. This enables you to objectively study the person, note what he/she is doing or not doing, and compare that with what you would typically do in similar situations. Many times you can learn more by watching than asking. Your model may not be able to explain what he/she does or may be an unwilling teacher.

☐ **Getting Feedback from Bosses and Superiors**
Many bosses are reluctant to give negative feedback. They lack the managerial courage to face people directly with criticism. You can help by soliciting feedback and setting the tone. Show them you can handle criticism and that you are willing to work on issues they see as important.

Learning from Courses

☐ **Orientation Events**
Most organizations offer a variety of orientation events. They are designed to communicate strategies, charters, missions, goals, and general information and offer an opportunity for people to meet each other. They are short in duration and offer limited opportunities for learning anything beyond general context and background.

- ☐ **Strategic Courses**
  There are a number of courses designed to stretch minds to prepare for future challenges. They include topics such as Workforce Diversity 2000, globalization, the European Union, competitive competencies and strategies, etc. Quality depends upon the following three factors: 1) The quality of the staff. Are they qualified? Are they respected in their fields? Are they strategic "gurus"? 2) The quality of the participants. Are they the kind of people you could learn from? 3) The quality of the setting. Is it comfortable and free from distractions? Can you learn there?

SUGGESTED READINGS

Harvard Business Review. Phone: 800-988-0886 (U.S. and Canada). Fax: 617-496-1029. Mail: Harvard Business Review. Subscriber Services, P.O. Box 52623. Boulder, CO 80322-2623 USA. http://www.hbsp.harvard.edu/products/hbr

Futurist Magazine. http://www.wfs.org

Sloan management review. Cambridge, Mass.: Industrial Management Review Association at the Alfred P. Sloan School of Management, Massachusetts Institute of Technology. http://mitsloan.mit.edu/smr

Strategic Leadership Forum. 230 E. Ohio Street, Suite 400. Chicago, IL 60611 4067. (800) 873 5995 Fax: (312) 644 8557. http://www.slfnet.org

Annison, Michael H. *Managing the Whirlwind.* Englewood, CO: Medical Group Management Association, 1993.

Bandrowski, James F. *Corporate Imagination Plus.* New York: Macmillan, Inc., 1990.

Charan, Ram and Noel M. Tichy. *Every business is a growth business: how your company can prosper year after year.* New York: Times Business, 1998.

Fine, Charles H. *Clock Speed – Winning Industry Control in the Age of Temporary Advantage.* Reading, MA: Perseus Books, 1998.

Hamel, Gary and C.K. Prahalad. *Competing for the future.* Boston, Mass.: Harvard Business School Press, 1994.

Hayes, Robert H., Gary P. Pisaro and David Upton. *Strategic Operations – Competing through capabilities.* New York: Free Press, 1996.

Hickman, Craig and Michael A. Silva. *Creating Excellence.* New York: New American Library, 1984.

continued

Hope, Jeremy and Tony Hope. *Competing in the Third Wave – The ten key management issues of the information age.* Boston: Harvard Business School Press, 1997.

Kennedy, Paul M. *The rise and fall of the great powers: economic change and military conflict from 1500 to 2000.* New York: Random House, 1987.

Mohrman, Susan Albers, Jay R. Galbraith and Edward E. Lawler III and Associates. *Tomorrow's Organization – Crafting Winning Capabilities in a Dynamic World.* San Francisco: Jossey-Bass, Inc., 1998.

Montgomery, Cynthia A. and Michael E. Porter, Editors. *Strategy: seeking and securing competitive advantage.* Boston: Harvard Business School Press, 1991.

Ohmae, Kenichi. *The Mind of the Strategist.* New York: McGraw-Hill, Inc., 1982.

Porter, Michael E. *Competitive strategy: Techniques for analyzing industries and competitors.* New York: Free Press, 1980.

Porter, Michael E. *On competition.* Boston: Harvard Business, 1998.

Shank, John K. and Vijay Govindarajan. *Strategic Cost Management.* New York: Free Press, 1993.

Swinton, Ernest Dunlop. *The Defense of Duffer's Drift.* Washington, DC: U.S. Marine Corps, [1996]

Yoshiro, Michael and U. Srinivasa Ranga. *Strategic Alliances.* Boston: Harvard Business School Press, 1995.

59

MANAGING THROUGH SYSTEMS

SECTION 1: YOUR DEVELOPMENT NEED(S)

UNSKILLED

- ☐ Prefers hands on management
- ☐ Relies on personal intervention
- ☐ Has to physically be there for things to go well
- ☐ Doesn't think or manage in terms of policies, practices and systems
- ☐ Doesn't delegate much
- ☐ Doesn't really believe people can perform on their own
- ☐ Doesn't set up rules, procedures and tie breakers so people know what to do in his/her absence
- ☐ May be very controlling and a micromanager
- ☐ May not communicate clearly enough for people to know what to do without repeated inquiries of him/her

SKILLED

- ☐ Can design practices, processes, and procedures which allow managing from a distance
- ☐ Is comfortable letting things manage themselves without intervening
- ☐ Can make things work through others without being there
- ☐ Can impact people and results remotely

OVERUSED SKILL

- ☐ May be too hard to reach and talk to, out of touch with the details
- ☐ May get too comfortable having things run on autopilot
- ☐ May get surprised by negative events
- ☐ May be slow to change existing systems

Select one to three of the competencies listed below to work on to compensate for an overuse of this skill.

COMPENSATORS: 3, 10, 12, 14, 15, 21, 23, 31, 33, 36, 44, 60, 64

SOME CAUSES

- ☐ Don't delegate well
- ☐ Don't think in terms of systems
- ☐ Inexperienced
- ☐ Poor communicator
- ☐ Poor time management

THE MAP

For most managers, the quality of their impact on others and their work decreases as they become more remote. Most managers start as first line supervisors where all of their people sit around them on the floor. As you progress in management, your people and the operations you manage become more remote. Your people may be in different parts of the building, different parts of the country, or even different parts of the world. The key to being a good systems-based manager is to have the qualities you bring to managing people and work remain when you are not physically there. That's done by having a vision, goals, processes and practices to follow, two-way communication, and policies to guide remote decision making.

SECTION 2: LEARNING ON YOUR OWN

THESE SELF-DEVELOPMENT REMEDIES WILL HELP YOU BUILD YOUR SKILL(S)

SOME REMEDIES

☐ **1. Subscribe to *The Systems Thinker*™, Pegasus Communications, Inc., Cambridge, MA, 617-576-1231.** This is a group dedicated to finding out how things work and why they work that way. They have a monthly publication as well as workshops, seminars and other materials available to help you see the world as a series of recurring systems or archetypes. They analyze everyday events and processes and try to see why they work the way they do. The material will help you view things in terms of whole systems.

☐ **2. Try to picture things in the form of flows.** Buy a flow charting software program like ABC FlowCharter® that does PERT and GANT charts. Become an expert in its use. Use the output of the software to communicate the systems you manage to others. Use the flow charts in your presentations.

☐ **3. Be a student of how organizations work.** Organizations can be complex systems with many turns, dead ends, quick routes and choices. In most organizations, the best path to get somewhere is almost never a straight line. There is a formal organization – the one on the organization chart – where the path may look straight, and then there is the informal organization where all paths are zigzagged. Since organizations are staffed with people, they become all that more complex as systems. There are gatekeepers, expediters, stoppers, resisters, guides, good Samaritans and influencers. *More help? – See #38 Organizational Agility.*

☐ **4. Be a student of how to design rational and effective work flows and designs.** That technology can be found in *#35 Managing and Measuring Work, #47 Planning, #52 Process Management,* and *#63 Total Quality Management/Re-Engineering*.

☐ **5. Work on communicating.** Setting and communicating the vision creating a shared mindset is one key to remote management. *More help?* – See #65 Managing *Vision and Purpose*. Setting goals and establishing measures to guide decisions and work when you are not there is another key. *More help? – See #35 Managing and Measuring Work*. Being able to line up the resources you need to complete the work is the last key. *More help? – See #39 Organizing.*

☐ **6. Managing remotely is the true test of delegation and empowerment.** It's impossible for you to do it all. Successful managers report high involvement in setting parameters, exceptions they want to be notified of, and expected outcomes. They detail what requires their involvement and what doesn't. When people call them for a decision, they always ask, "What do you think? What impact will it have on you – customers, etc. – if we do this?" rather than just render a judgment. If you don't, people will begin to delegate upward, and you'll be a close-in manager from a remote location. Help people think things through, and trust them to follow the plan. Delegation requires this clear communication about expectations and releasing the authority to decide and act. *More help? – See #18 Delegation.*

☐ **7. Effective remote management requires plans, policies, practices and procedures to be in writing.** Verbal communication alone will seldom be sufficient. You need to write clearly and with as few words as you can. You may even have to write several versions of the same practice or policy to adapt to a remote location. Have someone else review your written work before you distribute it to check for clarity and purpose. *More help? – See #67 Written Communications.*

☐ **8. Another trick to effective remote management is involvement of those being managed** in the creation of the system. You need to rally support. Share your mission and goals with the people you need to support you. Get their input. People who are asked tend to cooperate more than people who are not asked. Let the people who will have to work under the system help design it. *More help? – See #18 Delegation and #38 Organizational Agility.*

☐ **9. Do an analysis of your remote management technology.** How do you sound over the phone? Are you coming across like you want to? What do your E-mail messages look and sound like? Ask trusted others for feedback. What do your speeches sound like when you visit remote locations? Do you change your message to adjust for local conditions? Who do you spend time with when you travel remotely? What kind of message does that leave? Do you meet just with top management or do you also find time for others? What do your memos look and sound like? Are they leaving the kind of message you intended?

☐ **10. Do you have a clean quick process set up for surfacing problems and getting to solutions remotely?** Is it a constructive process or is it punishing or blame oriented? How accessible are you to your remote locations? Do you think they would report that it is easy or hard to access you?

SECTION 3: LEARNING FROM MORE FEEDBACK

THESE SOURCES WOULD GIVE YOU THE MOST ACCURATE AND DETAILED FEEDBACK ON YOUR SKILL(S)

- ☐ **Boss's Boss(es)**
  From a process standpoint, your boss's boss probably has the most influence and control over your progress. He/she has a broader perspective, has more access to data, and stands at the center of decisions about you. To know what he/she thinks, without having to violate the canons of corporate due process to get that information, would be quite useful.
- ☐ **Direct Boss**
  Your direct boss has important information about you, your performance, and your prospects. The challenge is to get this information. There are formal processes (e.g., performance appraisals). There are day-to-day opportunities. To help, signal your boss that you want and can handle direct and timely feedback. Many bosses have trouble giving feedback, so you will have to work at it over a period of time.
- ☐ **Direct Reports**
  Across a variety of settings, your direct reports probably see you the most. They are the recipients of most of your managerial behaviors. They know your work. They can compare you with former bosses. Since they may hesitate to give you negative feedback, you have to set the atmosphere to make it easier for them. You have to ask.
- ☐ **Past Associates/Constituencies**
  When confronted with a present performance problem, some claim, "I wasn't like that before; it must be the current situation." When feedback is available from former associates, about 50% support that claim. In the other half of the cases, the people were like that before and probably didn't know it. It sometimes makes sense to access the past to clearly see the present.

SECTION 4: LEARNING FROM DEVELOP-IN-PLACE ASSIGNMENTS

THESE PART-TIME DEVELOP-IN-PLACE ASSIGNMENTS WILL HELP YOU BUILD YOUR SKILL(S)

- ☐ Integrate diverse systems, processes, or procedures across decentralized and/or dispersed units.
- ☐ Manage something "remote," away from your location.
- ☐ Assign a project to a group with a tight deadline.
- ☐ Help shut down a plant, regional office, product line, business, operation, etc.
- ☐ Install a new process or system (computer system, new policies, new process, new procedures, etc.).

- ☐ Manage the renovation of an office, floor, building, meeting room, warehouse, etc.
- ☐ Plan an off-site meeting, conference, convention, trade show, event, etc.
- ☐ Work on an affirmative action plan for the organization and present it to management for approval.
- ☐ Launch a new product, service, or process.
- ☐ Manage a cost-cutting project.

SECTION 5: LEARNING FROM FULL-TIME JOBS

THESE FULL-TIME JOBS OFFER THE OPPORTUNITY TO BUILD YOUR SKILL(S)

☐ **Line To Staff Switches**
The core demands to qualify as a Line to Staff switch are: 1) Intellectually/strategically demanding. 2) Highly visible to others. 3) New area/perspective/method/culture/function. 4) Moving away from a bottom line. 5) Moving from field to headquarters. 6) Exposure to high-level executives. Examples: 1) Business/strategic planning. 2) Heading a staff department. 3) Assistant to/chief of staff to a senior executive. 4) Head of a task force. 5) Human resources role.

☐ **Scale Assignments**
Core requirements to qualify as a Scale (size) shift assignment are: 1) Sizable jump-shift in the size of the job in areas like: number of people, number of layers in organization, size of budget, number of locations, volume of activity, tightness of deadlines. 2) Medium to low complexity; mostly repetitive and routine processes and procedures. 3) Stable staff and business. 4) Stable operations. 5) Often slow, steady growth.

☐ **Significant People Demands**
Core demands required to qualify as a Significant People Responsibilities assignment are: 1) A sizable increase in either the number of people managed and/or the complexity of the challenges involved 2) Longer-term assignment (two or more years). 3) Quality of people management critical to achieving results. 4) Involves groups not worked with before (e.g., union, new technical areas, nationalities).

SECTION 6: LEARNING MORE FROM YOUR PLAN

THESE ADDITIONAL REMEDIES WILL HELP MAKE THIS DEVELOPMENT PLAN MORE EFFECTIVE FOR YOU

Learning from Experience, Feedback and Other People

☐ **Getting Feedback from Direct Reports**
Direct reports often fear reprisals for giving negative feedback about bosses, whether in a formal process, like a questionnaire, or informally and face-to-face. Even with a guarantee of confidentiality, some are still

hesitant. If you want feedback from direct reports, you have to set a positive tone and never act out of revenge.

SUGGESTED READINGS

The Systems Thinker™. Pegasus Communications, Inc., Waltham, MA. 781-398-9700

Cooper, Robert K., Ph.D. *The Performance Edge: New strategies to maximize your work effectiveness and competitive advantage.* Boston: Houghton Mifflin Co., 1991.

Davidow, William H. and Michael S. Malone. *The Virtual Corporation.* New York: HarperBusiness, 1992.

Hammer, Michael. *Beyond reengineering: how the process-centered organization is changing our work and our lives.* New York: HarperBusiness, 1996.

Oshry, Barry. *Seeing Systems – Unlocking the mysteries of organizational life.* San Francisco: Berrett-Koehler Publishers, 1995.

Rodgers, T.J. *No Excuses Management.* New York: Doubleday, 1992.

60

BUILDING EFFECTIVE TEAMS

SECTION 1: YOUR DEVELOPMENT NEED(S)

UNSKILLED

- ☐ Doesn't assemble, build or manage in a team fashion
- ☐ Manages people on a one-to-one basis
- ☐ Doesn't create a common mindset or common challenge
- ☐ Rewards and compliments individuals, not the team
- ☐ May not hold many team meetings
- ☐ Doesn't create any synergies in the team; everyone works on his/her own projects
- ☐ Doesn't manage in a way that builds team morale or energy
- ☐ Doesn't have the skills or interest to build a team
- ☐ May be very action and control oriented and won't trust a team to perform

SKILLED

- ☐ Blends people into teams when needed
- ☐ Creates strong morale and spirit in his/her team
- ☐ Shares wins and successes
- ☐ Fosters open dialogue
- ☐ Lets people finish and be responsible for their work
- ☐ Defines success in terms of the whole team
- ☐ Creates a feeling of belonging in the team

OVERUSED SKILL

- ☐ May not treat others as unique individuals
- ☐ May slow down reasonable process by having everything open for debate
- ☐ May go too far in not hurting people's feelings and not making tough decisions
- ☐ May not develop individual leaders
- ☐ Might not provide take-charge leadership during tough times

Select one to three of the competencies listed below to work on to compensate for an overuse of this skill.

COMPENSATORS: 9, 12, 13, 18, 19, 20, 21, 34, 36, 56, 57, 64

SOME CAUSES

- ☐ A loner; an individual contributor
- ☐ Can't set common cause
- ☐ Control oriented manager
- ☐ Don't believe in or support teams
- ☐ Excessively action oriented
- ☐ Incentives are all based upon individual achievement
- ☐ Not a motivator
- ☐ Not a skilled process manager
- ☐ Poor time management
- ☐ The idea of a team is resisted by people
- ☐ Treat all people the same

THE MAP

Everyone would enjoy being on the dream team. That's a group of performers each skilled in his/her own specialties, pulling together accomplishing greater things than the added total of each performing separately. Most organizations talk teams, but primarily reward individual achievement. They also attract and promote people who sometimes resist the idea of tying their performance to that of others. But teams, although uncomfortable to some, are the best way to accomplish integrated tasks like creating systems, producing complex products or sustained coordinated efforts. They are also useful in cutting across boundaries to get things done. The key to successful team building lies in identifying roles, jobs, tasks, rewards and objectives with the team, not with individuals.

SECTION 2: LEARNING ON YOUR OWN

THESE SELF-DEVELOPMENT REMEDIES WILL HELP YOU BUILD YOUR SKILL(S)

SOME REMEDIES

☐ **1. Establish a common cause and a shared mindset.** A common thrust is what energizes dream teams. As in light lasers, alignment adds focus, power and efficiency. It's best to get each team member involved in setting the common vision. Establish goals and measures. Most people like to be measured. People like to have checkpoints along the way to chart their progress. Most people perform better with goals that are stretching. Again, letting the team participate in setting the goals is a plus. *More help? – See #35 Managing and Measuring Work.*

☐ **2. Once mission, outcomes and goals are established, create a plan.** In order to be resource efficient, a plan is necessary to avoid duplicate work and things falling through the cracks. *More help? – See #47 Planning.*

☐ **3. Follow the basic rules of inspiring team members** as outlined in classic books like *People Skills* by Robert Bolton or *Thriving on Chaos* by Tom Peters: tell people what they do is important, say thanks, offer help and ask for it, provide autonomy in how people do their work, provide a variety of tasks, "surprise" people with enriching, challenging assignments, show an interest in their work, adopt a learning attitude toward mistakes, celebrate successes, have visible accepted measures of achievement and so on. Each team member is different so good team managers deal with each person uniquely while being fair to all. *More help? – See #23 Fairness to Direct Reports and #36 Motivating Others.*

☐ **4. Create a climate of innovation and experimentation.** When how to do something is too rigidly specified, motivation and creativity decrease. How things are done should be as open as possible. Studies show that people work harder and are more effective when they have a sense of choice and ownership. Encourage quick short-cycle experiments. Many will fail so communicate a learning attitude toward mistakes and failures. *More help? – See #28 Innovation Management.*

☐ **5. To communicate with team members, work on understanding people without judging them.** You don't have to agree; you just have to understand. To build a team, invest in their learning, education, trips to customers, and time to think problems through. Give them the benefit of your thinking and particularly what the key objectives of an effort are. The goal is to have them say, "We did it." *More help? – See #27 Informing.*

☐ **6. Resistance to the idea of a team** is best overcome by focusing on common goals, priorities and problems, selling the logic of pulling together repeatedly, listening patiently to people's concerns, protecting people's feelings but also reinforcing the perspective of why the team is needed, inviting suggestions to reach the outcome, and showing patience toward the unconverted. Maintain a light touch. *More help? – See #13 Confronting Direct Reports.*

☐ **7. Build a sense of joy and fun for the team.** Even though some – including you – will resist it, parties, roasts, gag awards, picnics and outings build group cohesion. Working with the whole person tends to build better teams. Use humor and support it in others. Learn to celebrate wins.

☐ **8. Dream teams are usually made up of a variety of talent,** not sameness. While dream teams have all of the talent they need to accomplish the task, not any one member has all of the talent. High performing teams learn how to take advantage of each person's strengths and avoid unreasonable exposure to each person's weaknesses. High performing teams have more disclosure to one another about their self appraisal of strengths and weaknesses. A weakness is not considered bad. The team just adjusts to it and moves on. Successful teams specialize, cover for each other, and only sometimes demand that everyone participate in identical activities.

- ☐ **9. Allow roles within the team to evolve naturally.** Some research indicates that in well functioning teams people gravitate to eight roles. *More help? – See # 64 Understanding Others*. Generally each of the eight roles needs to be played by someone on the team for the whole team to be effective. One member can play more than one role.
- ☐ **10. Dream teams learn how to operate effectively and efficiently.** Read *Overcoming Organizational Defenses* by Chris Argyris. Half of the book is about some of the common problems teams run into that block peak performance, and the other half offers strategies and tactics for undoing those chilling team behaviors.

SECTION 3: LEARNING FROM MORE FEEDBACK

THESE SOURCES WOULD GIVE YOU THE MOST ACCURATE AND DETAILED FEEDBACK ON YOUR SKILL(S)

- ☐ **Direct Reports**
  Across a variety of settings, your direct reports probably see you the most. They are the recipients of most of your managerial behaviors. They know your work. They can compare you with former bosses. Since they may hesitate to give you negative feedback, you have to set the atmosphere to make it easier for them. You have to ask.
- ☐ **Human Resource Professionals**
  Human Resource professionals have both a formal and informal feedback role. Since they have access to unique and confidential information, they can provide the right context for feedback you've received. Sometimes they may be "directed" to give you feedback. Other times, they may pass on feedback just to be helpful to you.
- ☐ **Past Associates/Constituencies**
  When confronted with a present performance problem, some claim, "I wasn't like that before; it must be the current situation." When feedback is available from former associates, about 50% support that claim. In the other half of the cases, the people were like that before and probably didn't know it. It sometimes makes sense to access the past to clearly see the present.

SECTION 4: LEARNING FROM DEVELOP-IN-PLACE ASSIGNMENTS

THESE PART-TIME DEVELOP-IN-PLACE ASSIGNMENTS WILL HELP YOU BUILD YOUR SKILL(S)

- ☐ Create employee involvement teams.
- ☐ Manage an ad hoc, temporary group of "green," inexperienced people as their coach, teacher, orienter, etc.
- ☐ Manage an ad hoc, temporary group of balky and resisting people through an unpopular change or project.

- ☐ Manage an ad hoc, temporary group including former peers to accomplish a task.
- ☐ Manage an ad hoc, temporary group of people who are older and/or more experienced to accomplish a task.
- ☐ Manage an ad hoc, temporary group of people where the temporary manager is a towering expert and the people in the group are not.
- ☐ Manage an ad hoc, temporary group of people where the people in the group are towering experts but the temporary manager is not.
- ☐ Manage an ad hoc, temporary group of people involved in tackling a fix-it or turnaround project.
- ☐ Assemble an ad hoc team of diverse people to accomplish a difficult task.
- ☐ Manage a project team of people who are older and more experienced than you.

SECTION 5: LEARNING FROM FULL-TIME JOBS

THESE FULL-TIME JOBS OFFER THE OPPORTUNITY TO BUILD YOUR SKILL(S)

☐ **Fix-its/Turnarounds**

The core demands to qualify as a Fix-it or Turnaround assignment are: 1) Cleaning up a mess. 2) Serious people issues/problems like credibility/performance/morale. 3) Tight deadline. 4) Serious business performance failure. 5) Last chance to fix. Four Types of Fix-its/Turnarounds: 1) Fixing a failed business/unit involving taking control, stopping losses, managing damage, planning the turnaround, dealing with people problems, installing new processes and systems, and rebuilding the spirit and performance of the unit. 2) Managing sizable disasters like mishandled labor negotiations and strikes, thefts, history of significant business losses, poor staff, failed leadership, hidden problems, fraud, public relations nightmares, etc. 3) Significant reorganization and restructuring (e.g., stabilizing the business, reforming unit, introducing new systems, making people changes, resetting strategy and tactics). 4) Significant system/process breakdown (e.g., MIS, financial coordination processes, audits, standards, etc.) across units requiring working to change something from a distant position, providing advice and counsel, and installing or implementing a major process improvement or system change outside your own unit and/or with customers outside the organization.

☐ **Significant People Demands**

Core demands required to qualify as a Significant People Responsibilities assignment are: 1) A sizable increase in either the number of people managed and/or the complexity of the challenges involved 2) Longer-term assignment (two or more years). 3) Quality of people management critical to achieving results. 4) Involves groups not worked with before (e.g., union, new technical areas, nationalities).

☐ **Start-ups**
The core demands to qualify as a start from scratch are: 1) Starting something new for you and/or for the organization. 2) Forging a new team. 3) Creating new systems/facilities/staffs/programs/procedures. 4) Contextual adversity (e.g., uncertainty, government regulation, unions, difficult environment). Seven types of start from scratches: 1) Planning, building, hiring, and managing (e.g., building a new facility, opening up a new location, moving a unit or company). 2) Heading something new (e.g., new product, new service, new line of business, new department/function, major new program). 3) Take over a group/product/service/program that had existed for less than a year and was off to a fast start. 4) Establishing overseas operations. 5) Major new designs for existing systems. 6) Moving a successful program from one unit to another. 7) Installing a new organization-wide process as a full-time job (e.g., like Total Quality).

SECTION 6: LEARNING MORE FROM YOUR PLAN

THESE ADDITIONAL REMEDIES WILL HELP MAKE THIS DEVELOPMENT PLAN MORE EFFECTIVE FOR YOU

Learning to Learn Better

☐ **Form a Learning Network With Others Working on the Same Problem**
Look for people in similar situations, and create a process for sharing and learning together. Look for a variety of people inside and outside your organization. Give feedback to each other; try new and different things together; share successes and failures, lessons and learning.

☐ **Use a Tutor to Learn Something New**
Set up a tutor relationship in the areas you're working on; open up, listen, learn, and try new things. Learn from the tutoring/learning process. Do you learn more easily from a tutor or do you get blocked? Test out your thinking with the tutor; do debriefs after trying the tutor's advice.

☐ **Examine Why You Judge People the Way You Do**
List the people you like and those you dislike and try to find out why. What do those you like have in common with each other and with you? What do those you dislike have in common with themselves and how do they differ from you? Are your "people buckets" logical and productive or do they interfere? Could you be more effective without putting people into buckets?

☐ **Form an Advisory Group to Help You**
Assemble a one-time ad hoc group of people you respect and ask them for help solving or facing a significant issue. Outline what you know about it and ask the team to lay out a plan. Have them examine your thinking and suggest changes and improvements.

- [ ] **Envision Doing Something Well in a Group**
Take the people you want or need to be involved through a envisioning/creativity exercise to come up with different ideas and solutions.

- [ ] **Preview a Plan With a Test Audience**
Before committing to a plan, find someone agreeable to a wide-ranging discussion about the issue or problem you face. Explore all sides and options; go with the flow; let what you need to do emerge from the process; develop a plan as you go.

Learning from Experience, Feedback and Other People

- [ ] **Using Multiple Models**
Who do you know who exemplifies how to do whatever your need is? Who, for example, personifies decisiveness or compassion or strategic agility? Think more broadly than your current job and colleagues. For example, clergy, friends, spouses or community leaders are also good sources for potential models. Select your models not on the basis of overall excellence or likability, but on the basis of the one towering strength (or glaring weakness) you are interested in. Even people who are well thought of usually have only one or two towering strengths (or glaring weaknesses). Ordinarily, you won't learn as much from the whole person as you will from one characteristic.

- [ ] **Learning from Observing Others**
Observe others. Find opportunities to observe without interacting with your model. This enables you to objectively study the person, note what he/she is doing or not doing, and compare that with what you would typically do in similar situations. Many times you can learn more by watching than asking. Your model may not be able to explain what he/she does or may be an unwilling teacher.

- [ ] **Learning from Limited Staff**
Most managers either inherit or hire staff from time to time who are inexperienced, incompetent, not up to the task, resistant, or dispirited. Any of these may create a hardship for you. The lessons to be learned are how to get things done with limited resources and how to fix the people situation. In the short term, this hardship is best addressed by assessing the combined strengths of the team and deploying the best you have against the problem. Almost everyone can do something well. Also, the team can contribute more than the combined individuals can. How can you empower and motivate the team? If you hired the troublesome staff, why did you err? What can you learn from your hiring mistakes? What wasn't there that you thought was present? What led you astray? How can you prevent that same hiring error in the future? What do you need to do to fix the situation? Quick development? Start over? If you inherited the problem, how can you fix it? Can you implement a program of accelerated development? Do you have to start over and get new people? What did the prior manager do or not do

that led to this situation in the first place? What can you learn from that? What will you do differently? How does the staff feel? What can you learn from their frustrations over not being able to do the job? How can you be a positive force under negative circumstances? How can you rally them to perform? What lasting lessons can you learn from someone in distress and trouble? If you're going to try accelerated development, how can you get a quick assessment? How can you give the staff motivating feedback? How can you construct and implement development plans that will work? How can you get people on-line feedback for maximum growth? Do you know when to stop trying and start over? If you're going to turn over some staff, how can you do it both rapidly and with the least damage? How can you deliver the message in a constructive way? What can you learn from having to take negative actions against people? How can you prevent this from happening again?

Learning from Courses

☐ **Supervisory Courses**

Most new supervisors go through an "Introduction to Supervision" type course. They are designed to teach the common practices a first-line supervisor needs to know to be effective. The content of most of those courses is standard. There is general agreement on the principles of effective supervision. There are two common problems: 1) Do the students have a strong motivation to learn? Do they know what they don't know? Is there any pain? Because motivated students with a need for the knowledge learn best, participants should have had some trying experiences and some supervisory pain and hardships before attending. 2) Are the instructors experienced supervisors? Have they practiced what they preach? Can they share powerful anecdotes to make key points? Can they answer questions credibly? If possible, select supervisory courses based on the instructors, since the content seems to be the much same for all such courses. Lastly, does the course offer the opportunity for practicing each skill? Does it contain simulations? Are there case studies you could easily identify with? Are there breakout groups? Is there opportunity for action learning? Search for the most interactive course.

SUGGESTED READINGS

Team Management Briefings (monthly publication). P.O. Box 25755, Alexandria, VA 22313 1-800-722-9221 http://www.briefings.com/tm

Argyris,Chris. *Overcoming Organizational Defenses: Facilitating Organizational Learning.* Boston: Allyn and Bacon, 1990.

Deeprose, Donna. *The team coach: vital new skills for supervisors & managers in a team environment.* New York: American Management Association, 1995.

Frangos, Stephen J. and Steven J. Bennett. *Team Zebra.* Essex Junction, VT: Omneo Wight Publications, Inc., 1993.

Katzenbach, Jon R. and Douglas K. Smith. *The wisdom of teams: creating the high-performance organization*. Boston: Harvard Business School Press, 1993.

Katzenbach, Jon R., and Douglas K. Smith. *The wisdom of teams: creating the high-performance organization [sound recording].* New York: Harper Audio, 1994.

Lawler, E.E. *Strategies for High Performance Organizations.* San Francisco: Jossey-Bass, Inc., 1998.

Lipnack, Jessica and Jeffrey Stamps. *Virtual Teams – Reaching Across Space, Time, and Organizations with Technology.* New York: John Wiley & Sons, 1997.

Parker, Glenn M. *Cross-functional Teams.* San Francisco: Jossey-Bass, Inc., 1994.

Parker, Glenn M. T*eam Players and Teamwork.* San Francisco: Jossey-Bass, Inc., 1990.

Shank, James H. *Team-based Organizations.* Homewood, IL: Business One Irwin, 1992.

Sher, Barbara and Annie Gottlieb. *Teamworks: Building support groups that guarantee success.* New York: Warner Books, 1989.

Wellins, Richard, William C. Byham and George R. Dixon. *Inside Teams.* San Francisco: Jossey-Bass, Inc., 1994.

61

TECHNICAL LEARNING

SECTION 1: YOUR DEVELOPMENT NEED(S)

UNSKILLED

- ☐ Doesn't learn new technical skills readily
- ☐ Is among the last to learn or adopt new technology
- ☐ May be stuck and wed to past technologies and resist switching to new ones
- ☐ May be intimidated by technology
- ☐ May lack experience or exposure with new technologies
- ☐ May not be interested in things technical or areas involving lots of detail
- ☐ May not know how to or may reject using others to learn new technologies

SKILLED

- ☐ Picks up on technical things quickly
- ☐ Can learn new skills and knowledge
- ☐ Is good at learning new industry, company, product, or technical knowledge
- ☐ Does well in technical courses and seminars

OVERUSED SKILL

- ☐ May learn but not act
- ☐ May overdo learning at the expense of using it
- ☐ May be seen as too academic
- ☐ May not relate well to those who can't catch on as quickly

Select one to three of the competencies listed below to work on to compensate for an overuse of this skill.

COMPENSATORS: 1, 3, 5, 15, 26, 33, 36, 41, 45, 46, 53, 54, 57

SOME CAUSES

- ☐ Inexperienced; new to the area
- ☐ Fear of computers
- ☐ Lack of interest in technology
- ☐ Time management; haven't gotten around to it
- ☐ Stuck in a past technology

THE MAP

All areas of work have new and emerging technologies that underlie doing them well. The pace of new technologies seems to be increasing as more people sign on the Internet. Computers, printers, cell phones and video cameras all seem to last only a year or two before they are replaced with fresh features and technology. Keeping up with new technology is becoming more important as the world is moving faster and competition increasing.

SECTION 2: LEARNING ON YOUR OWN

THESE SELF-DEVELOPMENT REMEDIES WILL HELP YOU BUILD YOUR SKILL(S)

SOME REMEDIES

☐ **1. Find the master professional** in the technology you need and ask whether he/she would mind showing you the ropes and tutoring you lightly. Most people good at something don't mind having a few "apprentices" around. They like to be asked for help.

☐ **2. Almost all technologies have national, and sometimes regional, professional associations** made up of hundreds of people who do well every day the technology you need to learn. Sign up as a member. Buy some of the literature on emerging technologies. Go to some of their workshops featuring what's new. Go to the annual conference and attend those sessions featuring new technology.

☐ **3. Find the bible on technology in your area.** Almost every technology has a book people might call the "bible" in the area. It is the standard reference everyone looks to for knowledge about the new technology. There is probably a journal in any new technology. Subscribe for a year or more. See if they have back issues available.

☐ **4. Identify some national leaders in your technology** and buy their books, read their articles, and attend their lectures and workshops.

☐ **5. Your local college, university or trade school might have some nighttime or weekend courses** you could take in the new technology. Also, your organization may have training classes in the technology.

☐ **6. Find a consultant** in the technology and hire him/her to provide a private tutorial for you to accelerate your learning.

☐ **7. Be an early tester of new and emerging technology.** Don't wait until you have to hurry and catch up. Whenever a new technology surfaces, volunteer to learn and try it first. That gives you a head start and allows you to stumble a bit because you are the first.

☐ **8. Buy a computer for home.** Get a cell phone. Buy a digital camera. Get on the Internet. Buy a personal digital assistant. Go to technical trade shows. Find out what's coming and be the first one to suggest it back at work.

☐ **9. Practice by picking some technology somewhat related to your work** and quietly become an expert at it. Introduce it at work. Demonstrate it to your workmates. Market for others to learn it and adopt it for the business. Form a study group and take turns presenting on new, different or emerging technologies. Having to teach it will force you to conceptualize and understand it more deeply.

☐ **10. Learn to think as experts in technology do.** Take problems to them and ask what are the keys they look for; observe what they consider significant and not significant. Chunk data into categories so you can remember it better. Devise five key areas or questions you can consider each time a technical issue comes up. Don't waste your time learning facts; they won't be useful unless you have conceptual buckets to put them in.

SECTION 3: LEARNING FROM MORE FEEDBACK

THESE SOURCES WOULD GIVE YOU THE MOST ACCURATE AND DETAILED FEEDBACK ON YOUR SKILL(S)

☐ **Direct Boss**

Your direct boss has important information about you, your performance, and your prospects. The challenge is to get this information. There are formal processes (e.g., performance appraisals). There are day-to-day opportunities. To help, signal your boss that you want and can handle direct and timely feedback. Many bosses have trouble giving feedback, so you will have to work at it over a period of time.

☐ **Direct Reports**

Across a variety of settings, your direct reports probably see you the most. They are the recipients of most of your managerial behaviors. They know your work. They can compare you with former bosses. Since they may hesitate to give you negative feedback, you have to set the atmosphere to make it easier for them. You have to ask.

☐ **Internal and External Customers**

Customers interact with you as a person and as a supplier or vendor of products and services. You're important to them because you can either help address and solve their problems or stand in their way. As customer service and Total Quality programs gain importance, clients and customers become a more prominent source of feedback.

☐ **Peers and Colleagues**

Peers and colleagues have a special social and working relationship. They attend staff meetings together, share private views, get feedback from the same boss, travel together, and are knowledgeable about each other's work. You perhaps let your guard down more around peers and act more like yourself. They can be a valuable source of feedback.

SECTION 4: LEARNING FROM DEVELOP-IN-PLACE ASSIGNMENTS

THESE PART-TIME DEVELOP-IN-PLACE ASSIGNMENTS WILL HELP YOU BUILD YOUR SKILL(S)

- ☐ Do a problem-prevention analysis on a product or service and present it to the people involved.
- ☐ Plan a new site for a building (plant, field office, headquarters, etc.).
- ☐ Manage an ad hoc, temporary group of people where the people in the group are towering experts but the temporary manager is not.
- ☐ Build a multifunctional project team to tackle a common business issue or problem.
- ☐ Work on a process-simplification team to take steps and costs out of a process.
- ☐ Create a contingency plan for an anticipated event or crisis and present it to management for approval.
- ☐ Study and establish internal or external customer needs, requirements, specifications, and expectations and present it to the people involved.
- ☐ Help someone outside your unit or the organization solve a business problem.
- ☐ Benchmark innovative practices, processes, products, or services of competitors, vendors, suppliers, or customers and present a report to others to create recommendations for change.
- ☐ Represent the organization at a trade show, convention, exposition, etc.

SECTION 5: LEARNING FROM FULL-TIME JOBS

THESE FULL-TIME JOBS OFFER THE OPPORTUNITY TO BUILD YOUR SKILL(S)

☐ **Line To Staff Switches**

The core demands to qualify as a Line to Staff switch are: 1) Intellectually/strategically demanding. 2) Highly visible to others. 3) New area/perspective/method/culture/function. 4) Moving away from a bottom line. 5) Moving from field to headquarters. 6) Exposure to high-level executives. Examples: 1) Business/strategic planning. 2) Heading a staff department. 3) Assistant to/chief of staff to a senior executive. 4) Head of a task force. 5) Human resources role.

☐ **Member of Projects/Task Forces**

The core demands for qualifying as a Project/Task Force assignment are: 1) Full-time assignment. 2) Important and specific goal. 3) Tight deadline. 4) Success or failure will be evident. 5) High-visibility sponsor. 6) Learning something on the fly. 7) Must get others to cooperate. 8) Usually six months or more. Four types of Projects/Task Forces: 1) New ideas, products, services, or systems (e.g., product/service/program research and development, creation/installation/launch of a new system, new programs like Total Quality Management, positive discipline). 2) Formal negotiations and relationships (e.g., acquisitions, divestitures, agreements, joint ventures; licensing arrangements, franchising; dealing with unions, governments, communities, charities, customers, and relocations). 3) Big one-time events (e.g., working on a major presentation for the board, organizing significant meetings or conferences, disaster/damage control teams; reorganizations, mergers, acquisitions, or relocations, working on visions, charters, strategies, other time-urgent issues and problems). 4) Troubleshooting (e.g., problems, disasters, crises, product/service failures, accidents, illegal activities, damage control in public relations goofs, shut downs, downsizings, layoffs, abrupt changes in leadership).

- ☐ **Scope Assignments**
  The core demands for a Scope (complexity) assignment are: 1) Significant increase in both internal and external scope or complexity. 2) Significant increase in visibility and/or bottom line responsibility. 3) Unfamiliar area, business, technology, or territory. Examples of Scope assignments involving shifts: 1) Switching into a new function/technology/business. 2) Moving to new organization. 3) Moving to overseas assignment. 4) Moving to new location. 5) Adding new products/services. 6) Moving between headquarters/field. 7) Switches in ownership/top management of the unit/organization. Examples of Scope assignments involving "firsts": 1) First-time manager. 2) First-time managing managers. 3) First-time executive. 4) First-time overseas. 5) First-time headquarters/field. 6) First-time team leader. 7) First-time new technology/business/function. Scope assignments involving increased complexity: 1) Managing a significant expansion of an existing product or service. 2) Managing adding new products/service into an existing unit. 3) Managing a reorganized and more diverse unit. 4) Managing explosive growth. 5) Adding new technologies.

SECTION 6: LEARNING MORE FROM YOUR PLAN

THESE ADDITIONAL REMEDIES WILL HELP MAKE THIS DEVELOPMENT PLAN MORE EFFECTIVE FOR YOU

Learning to Learn Better

- ☐ **Study What and How You Learn**
  What are you good at and how did you get to be that way? What learning strategies and experiences led to you being an expert? Could those same strategies apply again in other areas? Can you gain expertise in other areas using the same techniques?

- ☐ **Teach Others Something You Don't Know Well**
  Commit to a project like teaching something you don't know much about to force you to learn quickly to accomplish the task; pick something new, different, or unfamiliar.

☐ **Become a Student of How People Learn**
Become a student of learning: read some books and articles on child and adult learning; read about how the brain and mind work; study diverse learners of the past for insights; study the teaching techniques of expert teachers and coaches; attend a course on instructional design. Write and deliver a presentation on your findings.

Learning from Experience, Feedback and Other People

☐ **Getting Feedback from Bosses and Superiors**
Many bosses are reluctant to give negative feedback. They lack the managerial courage to face people directly with criticism. You can help by soliciting feedback and setting the tone. Show them you can handle criticism and that you are willing to work on issues they see as important.

☐ **Getting Feedback from Direct Reports**
Direct reports often fear reprisals for giving negative feedback about bosses, whether in a formal process, like a questionnaire, or informally and face-to-face. Even with a guarantee of confidentiality, some are still hesitant. If you want feedback from direct reports, you have to set a positive tone and never act out of revenge.

☐ **Getting Feedback from Peers/Colleagues**
Your peers and colleagues may not be candid if they are in competition with you. Some may not be willing to be open with you out of fear of giving you an advantage. Some may give you exaggerated feedback to deliberately cause you undue concern. You have to set the tone and gauge the trust level of the relationship and the quality of the feedback.

☐ **Soliciting Feedback**
Almost everyone reports they receive less feedback than they need to achieve their career goals. While others may have some interest in your career, it is primarily up to you to take the initiative in soliciting feedback from multiple sources by any methods available. You're the stakeholder who needs feedback to improve and grow.

☐ **Openness to Feedback**
Nothing discourages feedback more than defensiveness, resistance, irritation, and excuses. People don't like giving feedback anyway, and much less to those who don't listen or are unreceptive. To help the feedback giver, be open, listen, ask for examples and details, take notes, keep a journal, and thank them for their interest.

Learning from Courses

- ☐ **Job Skills**
  Most organizations and professional associations offer job skills training. The key is to find a course that has the right content and offers the opportunity for practicing the jobs skills. It's helpful if the instructors have actually performed the skills in situations similar to your own.

- ☐ **Survey Courses**
  These are courses designed to give a general overview of an entire area (such as advertising), product or product line, division's activities, process (getting a product to market, Total Quality Management) or geography (doing business in "X"). These types of courses are good for general background and context.

SUGGESTED READINGS

Alesandrini, Kathryn. *Survive Information Overload – How to see the big picture.* Homewood, IL: Business One Irwin, 1992.

Annison, Michael H. *Managing the Whirlwind.* Englewood, CO: Medical Group Management Association, 1993.

Burris, Daniel. *Technotrends.* New York: HarperBusiness, 1995.

Currid, Cheryl. *Computing strategies for reengineering your organization.* Rocklin, CA: Prima Pub., 1994.

Epstein, Seymour, Ph.D. with Archie Brodsky. *You're Smarter Than You Think – How to develop your practical intelligence for success in living.* New York: Simon and Schuster, 1993.

Hruby, F. Michael. *Technoleverage.* New York: AMACOM, 1999.

Maps, James J. *Quantum Leap Thinking.* Los Angeles: Dove Books, 1996.

McConnell, Vicki C. and Karl Wm. Koch. *Computerizing the Corporation – The intimate link between people and machines.* New York: VanNostrand Reinhold, 1990.

Muirhead, Brian K. and William L. Simon. *High Velocity Leadership – The Mars Pathfinder Approach to Faster, Better, Cheaper.* New York: HarperBusiness, 1999.

Stewart, Thomas A. *Intellectual Capital – The new wealth of organizations.* New York: Doubleday, 1997.

Tobin, Daniel R. *Transformational Learning – Renewing your company through knowledge and skills.* New York: John Wiley & Sons, Inc., 1996.

62

TIME MANAGEMENT

SECTION 1: YOUR DEVELOPMENT NEED(S)

UNSKILLED

- ☐ Is disorganized and wastes time and resources
- ☐ Flits from activity to activity with little rhyme or reason
- ☐ Doesn't set priorities
- ☐ Can't say no
- ☐ Can only concentrate on one thing at a time
- ☐ Is very easily distracted
- ☐ Mostly reactive to what's hot at the moment
- ☐ Doesn't have or follow a plan or method for his/her time
- ☐ Can't cut off transactions politely
- ☐ Doesn't have a clock in his/her head
- ☐ May do all right on important priorities and issues, but not good with the little things

SKILLED

- ☐ Uses his/her time effectively and efficiently
- ☐ Values time
- ☐ Concentrates his/her efforts on the more important priorities
- ☐ Gets more done in less time than others
- ☐ Can attend to a broader range of activities

OVERUSED SKILL

- ☐ May be impatient with other people's agenda and pace
- ☐ May not take the time to stop and smell the roses
- ☐ May not give people rapport time with him/her to get comfortable

Select one to three of the competencies listed below to work on to compensate for an overuse of this skill.

COMPENSATORS: 2, 3, 7, 12, 14, 17, 26, 27, 31, 33, 36, 41, 46, 51, 60

SOME CAUSES

- ☐ Can't say no
- ☐ Disorganized
- ☐ Don't take time to plan time
- ☐ Impatient
- ☐ Not a planner
- ☐ Not time aware; not a good judge of time
- ☐ Poor closing skills; can't say good-bye
- ☐ Poor delegator
- ☐ Procrastinate

THE MAP

Who ever has enough time? So much to do; so little time in which to do it. Finite resources; infinite needs. People to see, places to go, things to do. No time to say hello, good-bye, I'm late for a very important meeting. Sound familiar? That's life and work. Everyone has more to do than they can get to. The higher up you go in the organization, the more you have to do and the less time you have to do it. Nobody can do it all. You have to set priorities and manage your time well to survive and prosper.

SECTION 2: LEARNING ON YOUR OWN

THESE SELF-DEVELOPMENT REMEDIES WILL HELP YOU BUILD YOUR SKILL(S)

SOME REMEDIES

- ☐ **1. Set goals.** Nothing manages time better then a goal, a plan and a measure. Set goals for yourself. These goals are essential for setting priorities. If you do not have goals, you can't set time priorities. Using the goals, separate what you need to do into mission-critical, important to get done, nice if there is time left over, and not central to what you are trying to achieve. When faced with choices or multiple things to do, apply the scale. *More help? – See #35 Managing and Measuring Work and #50 Priority Setting.*
- ☐ **2. Laying out tasks and work on a time line.** Most successful time managers begin with a good plan for time. What do I need to accomplish? What are the goals? What's mission-critical and what's trivial? What's the time line? How will I track it? Buy a flow charting software program like ABC FlowCharter® that does PERT and GANT charts. Become an expert in its use. Use the output of the software to plan your time. Alternatively, write down your work plan. Many people are seen as lacking time management skills because they don't write down the sequence or parts of the work and leave something out. Ask others to comment on ordering and what's missing.
- ☐ **3. Manage your time efficiently.** Plan your time and manage against it. Be time sensitive. Value time. Figure out what you are worth per hour and minute by taking your gross salary plus overhead and benefits. Attach a monetary value on your time. Then ask, is this worth $56 of my time? Figure out what your three largest time wasters are and reduce them 50% by batching activities and using efficient communications like E-mail and voice mail for routine matters.
- ☐ **4. Create more time for yourself.** Taking time to plan and set priorities actually frees up more time later than just diving into things, hoping that you can get it done on time. Most people out of time claim they didn't have the time to plan their time. In the Stephen Covey *Seven Habits of Highly Successful People* sense, it's sharpening your saw. *More help? – See #102* Poor *Administrator.*

- ☐ **5. Give away as much time-consuming work as you can.** This can be done by a little planning and by delegating things you don't have to do yourself. Try to give away as much as possible to others. The win-win is that people enjoy being delegated to and empowered. You win; they win. *More help? – See #18 Delegation.*
- ☐ **6. Find someone in your environment who is better at time management than you are.** Watch what he/she does and compare against what you typically do. Try to increase doing the things he or she does and doesn't do. Ask for feedback from some people who have commented on your poor time management. What did they find difficult?
- ☐ **7. Be careful not to be guided by just what you like** and what you don't like to do. That way of using your time will probably not be successful over time. Use data, intuition and even feelings to apportion your time, but not feelings alone.
- ☐ **8. Be sensitive to the time of others.** Generally, the higher up you go or the higher up the person you are interacting with is, the less time you and he/she has. Be time efficient with others. Use as little of their time as possible. Get to it and get done with it. Give them an opportunity to open new avenues for discussion or to continue, but if they don't, say your good-byes and leave.
- ☐ **9. Others will always ask you to do more than you can do.** An important time saver is the ability to constructively say no. One technique people use is to ask the requester which of the other things they have asked you to do would they like to cancel or delay in order to do the most recent request. That way you say both yes and no and let the requester choose.
- ☐ **10. Another common time waster is inadequate disengagement skills.** Some poor time managers can't shut down transactions. Either they continue to talk beyond what would be necessary, or more commonly, they can't get the other party to quit talking. When it's time to move on, just say, "I have to get on to the next thing I have to do; we can pick this up some other time."

SECTION 3: LEARNING FROM MORE FEEDBACK

THESE SOURCES WOULD GIVE YOU THE MOST ACCURATE AND DETAILED FEEDBACK ON YOUR SKILL(S)

- ☐ **Direct Boss**

  Your direct boss has important information about you, your performance, and your prospects. The challenge is to get this information. There are formal processes (e.g., performance appraisals). There are day-to-day opportunities. To help, signal your boss that you want and can handle direct and timely feedback. Many bosses have trouble giving feedback, so you will have to work at it over a period of time.

- ☐ **Direct Reports**
  Across a variety of settings, your direct reports probably see you the most. They are the recipients of most of your managerial behaviors. They know your work. They can compare you with former bosses. Since they may hesitate to give you negative feedback, you have to set the atmosphere to make it easier for them. You have to ask.
- ☐ **Past Associates/Constituencies**
  When confronted with a present performance problem, some claim, "I wasn't like that before; it must be the current situation." When feedback is available from former associates, about 50% support that claim. In the other half of the cases, the people were like that before and probably didn't know it. It sometimes makes sense to access the past to clearly see the present.
- ☐ **Spouse**
  Spouses can be powerful sources of feedback on such things as interpersonal style, values, balance between work, career, and personal life, etc. Many participants attending development programs share their feedback with their spouses for value-adding confirmation or context and for specific examples.

SECTION 4: LEARNING FROM DEVELOP-IN-PLACE ASSIGNMENTS

THESE PART-TIME DEVELOP-IN-PLACE ASSIGNMENTS WILL HELP YOU BUILD YOUR SKILL(S)

- ☐ Plan a new site for a building (plant, field office, headquarters, etc.).
- ☐ Plan an off-site meeting, conference, convention, trade show, event, etc.
- ☐ Manage an ad hoc, temporary group of people involved in tackling a fix-it or turnaround project.
- ☐ Work on a crisis management team.
- ☐ Launch a new product, service, or process.
- ☐ Teach a course, seminar, or workshop on something you don't know well.
- ☐ Volunteer to fill an open management job temporarily until it's filled.
- ☐ Manage a dissatisfied internal or external customer; troubleshoot a performance or quality problem with a product or service.
- ☐ Take on a task you dislike or hate to do.
- ☐ Build a multifunctional project team to tackle a common business issue or problem.

SECTION 5: LEARNING FROM FULL-TIME JOBS

THESE FULL-TIME JOBS OFFER THE OPPORTUNITY TO BUILD YOUR SKILL(S)

- ☐ **Chair of Projects/Task Forces**
  The core demands for qualifying as a Project/Task Force assignment are: 1) Full-time assignment. 2) Important and specific goal. 3) Tight deadline. 4) Success or failure will be evident. 5) High-visibility sponsor. 6) Learning something on the fly. 7) Must get others to cooperate. 8) Usually six months or more. Four types of Projects/Task Forces: 1) New ideas, products, services, or systems (e.g., product/service/program research and development, creation/installation/launch of a new system, new programs like Total Quality Management, positive discipline). 2) Formal negotiations and relationships (e.g., acquisitions, divestitures, agreements, joint ventures; licensing arrangements, franchising; dealing with unions, governments, communities, charities, customers, and relocations). 3) Big one-time events (e.g., working on a major presentation for the board, organizing significant meetings or conferences, disaster/damage control teams; reorganizations, mergers, acquisitions, or relocations, working on visions, charters, strategies, other time-urgent issues and problems). 4) Troubleshooting (e.g., problems, disasters, crises, product/service failures, accidents, illegal activities, damage control in public relations goofs, shut downs, downsizings, layoffs, abrupt changes in leadership).

- ☐ **Cross-Moves**
  The core demands necessary to qualify as a Cross-Move are: 1) Move to a very different set of challenges. 2) Abrupt jump-shift in tasks/activities. 3) Never been there before. 4) New setting/conditions. Examples of Cross-Moves are: 1) Changing divisions. 2) Changing functions. 3) Field/headquarters shifts. 4) Line/staff switches. 5) Country switches. 6) Working with all new people. 7) Changing lines of business.

- ☐ **Scope Assignments**
  The core demands for a Scope (complexity) assignment are: 1) Significant increase in both internal and external scope or complexity. 2) Significant increase in visibility and/or bottom line responsibility. 3) Unfamiliar area, business, technology, or territory. Examples of Scope assignments involving shifts: 1) Switching into a new function/technology/business. 2) Moving to new organization. 3) Moving to overseas assignment. 4) Moving to new location. 5) Adding new products/services. 6) Moving between headquarters/field. 7) Switches in ownership/top management of the unit/organization. Examples of Scope assignments involving "firsts": 1) First-time manager. 2) First-time managing managers. 3) First-time executive. 4) First-time overseas. 5) First-time headquarters/field. 6) First-time team leader. 7) First-time new technology/business/function. Scope assignments involving increased complexity: 1) Managing a significant expansion of an existing product or service. 2) Managing adding new products/service into

an existing unit. 3) Managing a reorganized and more diverse unit. 4) Managing explosive growth. 5) Adding new technologies.

- ☐ **Start-ups**
  The core demands to qualify as a start from scratch are: 1) Starting something new for you and/or for the organization. 2) Forging a new team. 3) Creating new systems/facilities/staffs/programs/procedures. 4) Contextual adversity (e.g., uncertainty, government regulation, unions, difficult environment). Seven types of start from scratches: 1) Planning, building, hiring, and managing (e.g., building a new facility, opening up a new location, moving a unit or company). 2) Heading something new (e.g., new product, new service, new line of business, new department/function, major new program). 3) Take over a group/product/service/program that had existed for less than a year and was off to a fast start. 4) Establishing overseas operations. 5) Major new designs for existing systems. 6) Moving a successful program from one unit to another. 7) Installing a new organization-wide process as a full-time job (e.g., like Total Quality).

SECTION 6: LEARNING MORE FROM YOUR PLAN

THESE ADDITIONAL REMEDIES WILL HELP MAKE THIS DEVELOPMENT PLAN MORE EFFECTIVE FOR YOU

Learning to Learn Better

- ☐ **Teach Others Something You Don't Know Well**
  Commit to a project like teaching something you don't know much about to force you to learn quickly to accomplish the task; pick something new, different, or unfamiliar.
- ☐ **Study People Who Have Successfully Done What You Need to Do**
  Interview people who have already done what you're planning to do and check your plan against what they did. Try to summarize their key tactics, strategies, and insights; adjust your plan accordingly.
- ☐ **Commit to a Tight Timeframe to Accomplish Something**
  Set some specific goals and tighter than usual timeframes for yourself and go after them with all you've got. Push yourself to stick to the plan; get more done than usual by adhering to a tight plan.

Learning from Experience, Feedback and Other People

- ☐ **Getting Feedback from Direct Reports**
  Direct reports often fear reprisals for giving negative feedback about bosses, whether in a formal process, like a questionnaire, or informally and face-to-face. Even with a guarantee of confidentiality, some are still hesitant. If you want feedback from direct reports, you have to set a positive tone and never act out of revenge.

Learning from Courses

- ☐ **Courses with Feedback**
  Many courses such as negotiating skills and personal influence offer feedback on the subject matter of the course in addition to the content. They either collect data ahead of time or collect it "live" during the course.

SUGGESTED READINGS

Blohowiak, Donald W. *How's all the work going to get done?.* Franklin Lakes, NJ: Career Press, 1995.

Fine, Charles H. *Clock Speed – Winning Industry Control in the Age of Temporary Advantage.* Reading, MA: Perseus Books, 1998.

Koch, Richard. *The 80/20 principle: the secret of achieving more with less.* New York: Currency/Doubleday, 1998.

McGee-Cooper, Ann with Duane Trammell. T*ime management for unmanageable people.* New York: Bantam Books, 1994.

Moskowitz, Robert. *How to organize your work and your life.* New York: Doubleday, 1993.

Mosvick, Roger K. and Robert B. Nelson. *We've got to start meeting like this.* Glenview, IL: Scott Foresman and Company, 1987.

Roesch, Roberta. *Time management for busy people.* New York: McGraw-Hill, 1998.

Sanitate, Frank. *Don't go to work unless it's fun! State-of-the- heart time management.* Santa Barbara, CA: Santa Barbara Press, 1994.

Sapadin, Linda with Jack Maguire. *It's about time!: the six styles of procrastination and how to overcome them.* New York: Viking, 1996.

Silber, Lee. *Time Management for the Creative Person.* New York: Three Rivers Press, 1998.

Smith, Hyrum W. *The 10 natural laws of successful time and life management: proven strategies for increased productivity and inner peace.* New York, NY: Warner Books, 1994.

Stalk, George Jr. and Thomas M. Hout. *Competing Against Time.* New York: Macmillan, Inc., 1990.

63

TQM / RE-ENGINEERING

SECTION 1: YOUR DEVELOPMENT NEED(S)

UNSKILLED

- ☐ Doesn't create effective and efficient work processes
- ☐ Isn't customer focused in how he/she designs and manages the work
- ☐ Isn't dedicated to continuous improvement of work processes
- ☐ Doesn't know the tools and techniques to improve work processes
- ☐ Sticks to the old and familiar rather than stepping back and seeing the larger pattern
- ☐ Isn't willing to scrap the past in favor of the new and improved
- ☐ Doesn't listen to employees about improving work design
- ☐ Doesn't empower others to design their own work processes
- ☐ Doesn't create an environment where the whole unit learns together how better to serve the customer

SKILLED

- ☐ Is dedicated to providing the highest quality products and services which meet the needs and requirements of internal and external customers
- ☐ Is committed to continuous improvement through empowerment and management by data
- ☐ Is willing to re-engineer processes from scratch
- ☐ Is open to suggestions and experimentation
- ☐ Creates a learning environment leading to the most efficient and effective work processes

OVERUSED SKILL

- ☐ May become a quality or re-engineering missionary to the exclusion of everything else
- ☐ May make marginal incremental changes which are more disruptive than helpful
- ☐ May reject others

Select one to three of the competencies listed below to work on to compensate for an overuse of this skill.

COMPENSATORS: 2, 32, 33, 40, 46, 57, 58

SOME CAUSES

- ☐ Don't delegate
- ☐ Don't listen
- ☐ Inexperienced
- ☐ Not a risk taker
- ☐ Not customer oriented

- ☐ Not planful and organized
- ☐ Not results oriented
- ☐ Stick to the old

THE MAP

There is a well understood and accepted technology for producing products and services that work the first time and that meet or exceed customer requirements. Countless organizations have implemented these best practices which have led to increased success in the marketplace. For every successful implementation of these techniques, three more have failed. The number one cause for failure has been that management didn't really understand and support the effort and, even more important, they didn't change their behavior to align with the new practices. They didn't walk the talk. There is no better way to be personally successful and lead your organization to success than to learn and use the principles of Total Quality Management and Process Re-Engineering.

SECTION 2: LEARNING ON YOUR OWN

THESE SELF-DEVELOPMENT REMEDIES WILL HELP YOU BUILD YOUR SKILL(S)

SOME REMEDIES

☐ **1. Learn the principles.** There are many sources available. Read about methods put forth by Deming, Juran, Crosby, Hammer and Champy and countless others. There are numerous conferences and workshops you can attend. It's best to get a sampling of what everybody thinks and then create your own version for your specific situation.

☐ **2. Be customer driven.** In a free enterprise system, the customer is king; those who please the customer best win. The same is true with internal customers; those who please them most will win. Winners are always customer oriented and responsive. Pleasing the reasonable needs of customers is fairly straightforward. First you need to know what they want and expect; the best way to do that is to ask them; then deliver that in a timely way at a price/value that's acceptable to them. Get in the habit of meeting with your internal or external customers on a regular basis to set up a dialogue; they need to feel free to contact you about problems and you need to be able to contact them for essential information. Also, get out in front of your customers; try to anticipate their needs for your products and services before they even know about them; provide your customers with positive surprises – features they weren't expecting; delivery in a shorter time; more than they ordered. *More help? – See #15 Customer Focus.*

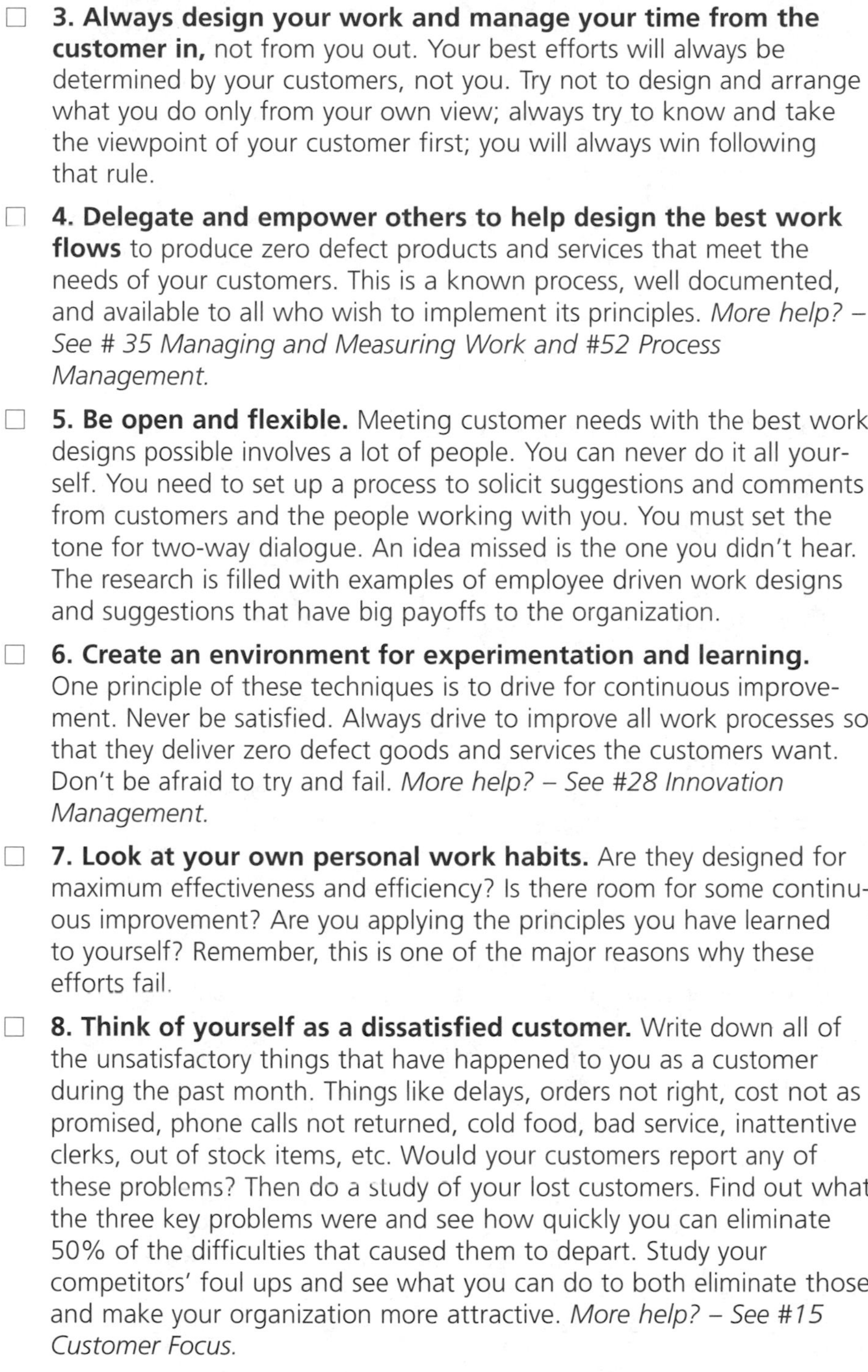

- ☐ **3. Always design your work and manage your time from the customer in,** not from you out. Your best efforts will always be determined by your customers, not you. Try not to design and arrange what you do only from your own view; always try to know and take the viewpoint of your customer first; you will always win following that rule.

- ☐ **4. Delegate and empower others to help design the best work flows** to produce zero defect products and services that meet the needs of your customers. This is a known process, well documented, and available to all who wish to implement its principles. *More help? – See # 35 Managing and Measuring Work and #52 Process Management.*

- ☐ **5. Be open and flexible.** Meeting customer needs with the best work designs possible involves a lot of people. You can never do it all yourself. You need to set up a process to solicit suggestions and comments from customers and the people working with you. You must set the tone for two-way dialogue. An idea missed is the one you didn't hear. The research is filled with examples of employee driven work designs and suggestions that have big payoffs to the organization.

- ☐ **6. Create an environment for experimentation and learning.** One principle of these techniques is to drive for continuous improvement. Never be satisfied. Always drive to improve all work processes so that they deliver zero defect goods and services the customers want. Don't be afraid to try and fail. *More help? – See #28 Innovation Management.*

- ☐ **7. Look at your own personal work habits.** Are they designed for maximum effectiveness and efficiency? Is there room for some continuous improvement? Are you applying the principles you have learned to yourself? Remember, this is one of the major reasons why these efforts fail.

- ☐ **8. Think of yourself as a dissatisfied customer.** Write down all of the unsatisfactory things that have happened to you as a customer during the past month. Things like delays, orders not right, cost not as promised, phone calls not returned, cold food, bad service, inattentive clerks, out of stock items, etc. Would your customers report any of these problems? Then do a study of your lost customers. Find out what the three key problems were and see how quickly you can eliminate 50% of the difficulties that caused them to depart. Study your competitors' foul ups and see what you can do to both eliminate those and make your organization more attractive. *More help? – See #15 Customer Focus.*

- ☐ **9. Think of yourself as a satisfied customer.** Write down all of the satisfactory things that have happened to you as a customer during the past month. What pleased you the most as a customer? Good value?

On time service? Courteousness? Returned phone calls? Are any of your customers experiencing any of these satisfactory transactions with you and your business? Study your successful customer transactions so they can be institutionalized. Then study what your competitors do well and see what you can also do to improve customer service. *More help? – See #15 Customer Focus.*

☐ **10. Be a student of the work flows and processes around you** at airports, restaurants, hotels, supermarkets, government services, etc. As a customer, how would you design those things differently to make them more effective and efficient? What principles would you follow? Apply those same principles to your own work.

SECTION 3: LEARNING FROM MORE FEEDBACK

THESE SOURCES WOULD GIVE YOU THE MOST ACCURATE AND DETAILED FEEDBACK ON YOUR SKILL(S)

☐ **Direct Boss**
Your direct boss has important information about you, your performance, and your prospects. The challenge is to get this information. There are formal processes (e.g., performance appraisals). There are day-to-day opportunities. To help, signal your boss that you want and can handle direct and timely feedback. Many bosses have trouble giving feedback, so you will have to work at it over a period of time.

☐ **Direct Reports**
Across a variety of settings, your direct reports probably see you the most. They are the recipients of most of your managerial behaviors. They know your work. They can compare you with former bosses. Since they may hesitate to give you negative feedback, you have to set the atmosphere to make it easier for them. You have to ask.

☐ **Internal and External Customers**
Customers interact with you as a person and as a supplier or vendor of products and services. You're important to them because you can either help address and solve their problems or stand in their way. As customer service and Total Quality programs gain importance, clients and customers become a more prominent source of feedback.

☐ **Peers and Colleagues**
Peers and colleagues have a special social and working relationship. They attend staff meetings together, share private views, get feedback from the same boss, travel together, and are knowledgeable about each other's work. You perhaps let your guard down more around peers and act more like yourself. They can be a valuable source of feedback.

SECTION 4: LEARNING FROM DEVELOP-IN-PLACE ASSIGNMENTS

THESE PART-TIME DEVELOP-IN-PLACE ASSIGNMENTS WILL HELP YOU BUILD YOUR SKILL(S)

- ☐ Work on a process-simplification team to take steps and costs out of a process.
- ☐ Do a problem-prevention analysis on a product or service and present it to the people involved.
- ☐ Study and establish internal or external customer needs, requirements, specifications, and expectations and present it to the people involved.
- ☐ Benchmark innovative practices, processes, products, or services of competitors, vendors, suppliers, or customers and present a report to others to create recommendations for change.
- ☐ Visit Malcolm Baldrige National Quality Award or Deming Prize winners and report back on your findings, showing how they would help your organization.
- ☐ Relaunch an existing product or service that's not doing well.
- ☐ Create employee involvement teams.
- ☐ Manage a cost-cutting project.
- ☐ Manage the purchase of a major product, equipment, materials, program, or system.
- ☐ Manage a dissatisfied internal or external customer; troubleshoot a performance or quality problem with a product or service.

SECTION 5: LEARNING FROM FULL-TIME JOBS

THESE FULL-TIME JOBS OFFER THE OPPORTUNITY TO BUILD YOUR SKILL(S)

- ☐ **Scale Assignments**
  Core requirements to qualify as a Scale (size) shift assignment are: 1) Sizable jump-shift in the size of the job in areas like: number of people, number of layers in organization, size of budget, number of locations, volume of activity, tightness of deadlines. 2) Medium to low complexity; mostly repetitive and routine processes and procedures. 3) Stable staff and business. 4) Stable operations. 5) Often slow, steady growth.

- ☐ **Significant People Demands**
  Core demands required to qualify as a Significant People Responsibilities assignment are: 1) A sizable increase in either the number of people managed and/or the complexity of the challenges involved 2) Longer-term assignment (two or more years). 3) Quality of people management critical to achieving results. 4) Involves groups not worked with before (e.g., union, new technical areas, nationalities).

SECTION 6: LEARNING MORE FROM YOUR PLAN

THESE ADDITIONAL REMEDIES WILL HELP MAKE THIS DEVELOPMENT PLAN MORE EFFECTIVE FOR YOU

Learning to Learn Better

- [ ] **Learn to Separate Opinions From Facts**
  Practice separating opinions, beliefs, feelings, attitudes and values from facts and data. Try to base more of your comments and actions on the data side. If there is a need to air subjective information, announce it as such, and label it for what it is. Don't present opinions with the look and sound of data.

- [ ] **Study People Who Have Successfully Done What You Need to Do**
  Interview people who have already done what you're planning to do and check your plan against what they did. Try to summarize their key tactics, strategies, and insights; adjust your plan accordingly.

Learning from Experience, Feedback and Other Pen

- [ ] **Using Multiple Models**
  Who do you know who exemplifies how to do whatever your need is? Who, for example, personifies decisiveness or compassion or strategic agility? Think more broadly than your current job and colleagues. For example, clergy, friends, spouses or community leaders are also good sources for potential models. Select your models not on the basis of overall excellence or likability, but on the basis of the one towering strength (or glaring weakness) you are interested in. Even people who are well thought of usually have only one or two towering strengths (or glaring weaknesses). Ordinarily, you won't learn as much from the whole person as you will from one characteristic.

- [ ] **Learning from Bosses**
  Bosses can be an excellent and ready source for learning. All bosses do some things exceptionally well and other things poorly. Distance your feelings from the boss/direct report relationship and study things that work and things that don't work for your boss. What would you have done? What could you use, and what should you avoid?

- [ ] **Learning from Interviewing Others**
  Interview others. Ask not only what they do, but how and why they do it. What do they think are the rules of thumb they are following? Where did they learn the behaviors? How do they keep them current? How do they monitor the effect they have on others?

- [ ] **Getting Feedback from Direct Reports**
  Direct reports often fear reprisals for giving negative feedback about bosses, whether in a formal process, like a questionnaire, or informally and face-to-face. Even with a guarantee of confidentiality, some are still hesitant. If you want feedback from direct reports, you have to set a positive tone and never act out of revenge.

Learning from Courses

- ☐ **Orientation Events**
  Most organizations offer a variety of orientation events. They are designed to communicate strategies, charters, missions, goals, and general information and offer an opportunity for people to meet each other. They are short in duration and offer limited opportunities for learning anything beyond general context and background.

- ☐ **Supervisory Courses**
  Most new supervisors go through an "Introduction to Supervision" type course. They are designed to teach the common practices a first-line supervisor needs to know to be effective. The content of most of those courses is standard. There is general agreement on the principles of effective supervision. There are two common problems: 1) Do the students have a strong motivation to learn? Do they know what they don't know? Is there any pain? Because motivated students with a need for the knowledge learn best, participants should have had some trying experiences and some supervisory pain and hardships before attending. 2) Are the instructors experienced supervisors? Have they practiced what they preach? Can they share powerful anecdotes to make key points? Can they answer questions credibly? If possible, select supervisory courses based on the instructors, since the content seems to be the much same for all such courses. Lastly, does the course offer the opportunity for practicing each skill? Does it contain simulations? Are there case studies you could easily identify with? Are there breakout groups? Is there opportunity for action learning? Search for the most interactive course.

- ☐ **Strategic Courses**
  There are a number of courses designed to stretch minds to prepare for future challenges. They include topics such as Workforce Diversity 2000, globalization, the European Union, competitive competencies and strategies, etc. Quality depends upon the following three factors: 1) The quality of the staff. Are they qualified? Are they respected in their fields? Are they strategic "gurus"? 2) The quality of the participants. Are they the kind of people you could learn from? 3) The quality of the setting. Is it comfortable and free from distractions? Can you learn there?

SUGGESTED READINGS

Brown, Mark Graham, Darcy Hitchcock and Marsha Willard. *Why TQM Fails.* Burr Ridge, IL: Irwin Professional Publishing, 1994.

Carr, David K. and Henry J. Johansson. *Best Practices in Reengineering.* New York: McGraw-Hill, Inc., 1995.

Ford, Henry. *Today and Tomorrow.* New York: Productivity Press, 1988.

Hammer, Michael. *Beyond Reengineering.* New York: HarperCollins, 1996.

Hammer, Michael and James Champy. *Reengineering the Corporation.* New York: HarperBusiness, 1993.

Hodgetts, Richard M. *Measures of quality and high performance.* New York: AMACOM, 1998.

Hronec, Steven M. and Arthur Anderson and Company. *Vital Signs – Using quality, time and cost performance measurements to chart your company's future.* New York: AMACOM, 1993.

Imai, Masaaki. *Gemba Kaizen.* New York: McGraw-Hill, Inc., 1997.

Lynch, Richard L. and Kevin F. Cross. *Measure Up! Yardsticks for continuous improvement.* Cambridge, MA: Basil Blackwell, 1991.

Merrill, Peter. *Do it right the second time: benchmarking best practices in the quality change process.* Portland, OR: Productivity press, 1997.

Risher, Howard and Charles Fay, Editors. *The Performance Imperative: Strategies for enhancing workforce effectiveness.* San Francisco: Jossey-Bass, 1995.

Schmidt, Warren H. and Jerome P. Finnigan. *The Race without a Finish Line.* San Francisco: Jossey-Bass, Inc., 1992.

Walton, Mary. *The Deming Management Method.* New York: Putnam Publishing, 1986.

Walton, Mary. *Deming Management at Work.* New York: Putnam Publishing, 1990.

Watson, Gregory H. *Strategic Benchmarking.* New York: John Wiley & Sons, Inc., 1993.

64

SECTION 1: YOUR DEVELOPMENT NEED(S)

UNSKILLED

- ☐ Doesn't read groups well
- ☐ Doesn't understand how groups operate or what purposes groups serve
- ☐ Can't predict what groups will do
- ☐ Stereotypes or pre-judges groups
- ☐ May only understand groups similar to him or her in purpose and characteristics
- ☐ Sees people as individuals only
- ☐ Doesn't understand how group membership affects people's views and behavior
- ☐ Prefers working one-on-one; can't reach or motivate groups
- ☐ May be a loner and not really a member of any voluntary groups

SKILLED

- ☐ Understands why groups do what they do
- ☐ Picks up the sense of the group in terms of positions, intentions, and needs; what they value and how to motivate them
- ☐ Can predict what groups will do across different situations

OVERUSED SKILL

- ☐ May spend too much time trying to analyze what a group might or might not do
- ☐ May generalize from his/her group appraisal to individuals, letting personal impressions of a group cover individuals as well
- ☐ May discount variety of opinion
- ☐ May have trouble dealing with individuals when he/she is in conflict with the group the individual belongs to
- ☐ May spend too much energy understanding and analyzing group actions

Select one to three of the competencies listed below to work on to compensate for an overuse of this skill.

COMPENSATORS: 1, 2, 12, 13, 16, 17, 21, 34, 37, 40, 50, 52, 53, 57, 59

SOME CAUSES

- ☐ A loner; not a joiner; hasn't experienced groups
- ☐ Dismiss the importance of groups
- ☐ Don't acknowledge groups
- ☐ Don't like people to form groups
- ☐ Don't understand how groups operate

- ☐ Judgmental about other groups
- ☐ Problems dealing with other functions/professions
- ☐ See groups as stereotypes

THE MAP

By knowing what group or groups a person belongs to, you can get a better handle on what the person believes, why, and what he or she might do in a given situation. Group members hold some but not all beliefs, assumptions about the world, habits and practices in common. Members of groups look alike because like minded people form and join groups and because groups educate and orient new members into the norms and standards of the group.

SECTION 2: LEARNING ON YOUR OWN

THESE SELF-DEVELOPMENT REMEDIES WILL HELP YOU BUILD YOUR SKILL(S)

SOME REMEDIES

☐ **1. Why do people belong to voluntary or advocacy groups?** If it is a voluntary/interest group, people usually belong for three reasons: the group fulfills social needs; provides a sense of belonging, gives emotional support and identification; and helps people achieve their goals by sharing information and helping each other. Groups are stronger than individuals and are natural to the human species. Being a loner is not. Belonging to voluntary groups is exceptionally important to most as they define our sense of what's worthwhile to a great degree. People go in and out of informal voluntary groups as their needs and interests change. Find out all you can about what groups people you need to deal with and manage belong to. It can help you deal with them and help them perform better.

☐ **2. Why do informal groups form?** Voluntary groups generally form because of a common interest, challenge, threat, or goal individual members can't deal with by themselves. Unions were a reaction to oppressive management. Civil Rights groups were a reaction to a lack of equal opportunities. The AMA was formed to set standards for the medical profession and protect it from charlatans and snake oil salespersons. A group of minorities might form inside your organization because they think they are being held to a double standard and not being given enough opportunities. Especially inside your organization, watch what groups and cliques form on their own. Try to work backward and determine why they formed. What groups do you belong to? Why did you join?

☐ **3. Categorical groups.** Some groups are forced by an involuntary category. There are gender and racial groups. There are country of origin groups. There is Mensa limited by a high tested IQ. There is a national Bald Person's Club. Any individual may or may not choose to join and partake in the activities of the group. Other people, however, have a tendency to stereotype people into their categorical groups, whether the person buys into that or not. While some aspects of categorical groups might help you read people better, it is important not to lump people into categories. First find out if they buy into the interests and practices of their category before you begin to use that in your assessment of them.

- ☐ **4. Other groups in organizations are not interest groups;** they are nominal functional/professional ones. They are formed to define and maintain the boundaries between one group – accountants, and the other – marketers. Formal groups maintain entry standards and have membership criteria. They support the development of specialized skills and help individual members succeed, guard the group against attack from the outside, and lobby for beneficial legislation. Membership in these groups is defined by your job, your organization's method of organizing itself and your profession. If your job changes, if you move from division A to division B, you will change nominal groups as soon as you cross the border.

- ☐ **5. Learn to be a cultural anthropologist.** In assessing groups, ask yourself what makes their blood boil? What do they believe? What are they trying to accomplish together? What do they smile at? What norms and customs do they have? What practices and behaviors do they share? Do they not like it if you stand too close? If you get right down to business? Do they like first names or are they more formal? If a Japanese manager presents his card, do you know what to do? Why do they have their cards printed in two languages and executives from the U.S. don't? Do you know what jokes are OK to tell? What do they believe about you and your group or groups? Positive? Neutral? Negative? What's been the history of their group and yours? Is this a first contact or a long history? Don't blunder in; nothing will kill you quicker with a group than showing utter disregard – read disrespect – for it and its norms or having no idea of how they view your group. Ask people who deal with this group often for insights. If it's an important group to you and your business, read about it. *More help? – See #21* Managing *Diversity.*

- ☐ **6. Be candid with yourself.** Is there a group or groups you don't like or are uncomfortable with? Do you judge individual members of that group without really knowing if your impressions and stereotype is true? Most of us do. Avoid putting groups in good and bad buckets. Many of us bucket groups as friendly or unfriendly. Once we do, we generally don't talk to the unfriendlies as much and may question their motives. Don't generalize about individuals. A person might belong to a group for many reasons, yet not typify stereotypes of the group. All accountants aren't detail driven introverts, for example. To deal with this put yourself in their shoes. Why would you act that way? What do you think they're trying to achieve? Assume that however they act is rational; it must have paid off or they wouldn't be doing it. Describe behavior and motives as neutrally as you can. Listen and observe to understand, not judge. If you are going to interact with a group you have trouble with, be on your guard and best behavior.

☐ **7. Roles inside groups.** All groups share a common set of things that happen inside the group. Groups aren't undifferentiated masses. Many errors in dealing with groups involve failures in seeing groups as sets of roles. A commonly accepted typology of eight group roles was developed by Belbin. You should know about it because spotting the role played tells you who to deal with as varying situations arise:

- Leader. Shapes the way in which group efforts are applied by focusing priorities and direction. Looked to when trouble comes.
- Process Manager. Focuses on process needed to reach team objectives.
- Innovator. Advances the new, challenges the old.
- Evaluator. The analyst; sifts through problems for the group.
- Finisher. Focuses on deadlines, commitments and urgency.
- Work organizer. Turns plans into procedures and sequences.
- Internal negotiator. Maintains relationships, builds team spirit.
- External negotiator. Scans outside for resources, ideas, contacts for deal making.

Additionally there are gatekeepers who protect and manage entry, clowns who manage tension relief, synergizers who bring disparate things together, enforcers who make sure members tow the line and so forth. So in addition to knowing what group or groups a person belongs to, you need to know what role or roles they play inside the group. Usually one person plays one role. Unless the group is very small or very hierarchical, you're better off going to the person who's most concerned with your issue or asking who that might be. Use the group's power. You will have little luck motivating a group by asking for something that asks them to go against a core reason for being in the group. Your best bet is to appeal to the person who plays the role you're interested in to exercise his/her power and influence. What role or roles do you usually play?

☐ **8. Working with groups.** To deal effectively with groups, establish reciprocity. Relationships don't last unless you provide something and so do they. Find out what they want and tell them what you want. Strike a bargain. If one group usually gets the benefit, the other group will eventually become uncooperative and balky. Learn their conceptual categories. People who went on to become successful executives often spoke of their first time dealing with another function. The most common tack for a marketing person dealing with finance for the first time was to show them something he/she was working on and ask them how they would analyze it. What questions would they ask? What are the key numbers and why? What were the four or five key factors they were looking at? Be able to speak their language. Speaking their language makes it easier for them to talk with you and shows respect. Tell them your conceptual categories. To deal with you they also need to know how you think and why. As in the tip above, tell them your perspective – the questions you ask, the factors you're interested in. If you can't explain your thinking, they won't know how to deal with you effectively.

☐ **9. Avoid early solution statements and extreme positions.** While the answer might be obvious to you, and might make perfect sense to someone in your field, it may either mean nothing or will be jarring to people in another function. Lay out your thinking, explain the alternatives, and keep them as maybes. Then invite them to apply their perspective to it. If you fire out solutions, you'll encourage them to reply in your terms. You'll never learn to understand them.

☐ **10. Getting groups to work together.** The keys are to find the common ground, downsize the differences that will get in the way and use the differences that add value to form an alliance. Even groups seemingly far apart will have some things in common. Announce that you would first like to see if there are any points on which the two sides could tentatively agree. List those on a board or flip chart. Then list the seemingly far aparts, the real differences. Take each difference and list it as adding value – we can do that and you can't, and you can do something we are not good at – or getting in the way. Use the differences that add value and throw a plan around minimizing the troublesome differences. Based on the common ground and the value adding differences, form a common mindset about how these groups can work together more effectively. *More help? – See #12 Conflict Management.*

SECTION 3: LEARNING FROM MORE FEEDBACK

THESE SOURCES WOULD GIVE YOU THE MOST ACCURATE AND DETAILED FEEDBACK ON YOUR SKILL(S)

☐ **Human Resource Professionals**
Human Resource professionals have both a formal and informal feedback role. Since they have access to unique and confidential information, they can provide the right context for feedback you've received. Sometimes they may be "directed" to give you feedback. Other times, they may pass on feedback just to be helpful to you.

☐ **Natural Mentors**
Natural mentors have a special relationship with you and are interested in your success and your future. Since they are usually not in your direct chain of command, you can have more open, relaxed, and fruit-

ful discussions about yourself and your career prospects. They can be a very important source for candid or critical feedback others may not give you.

- ☐ **Past Associates/Constituencies**
  When confronted with a present performance problem, some claim, "I wasn't like that before; it must be the current situation." When feedback is available from former associates, about 50% support that claim. In the other half of the cases, the people were like that before and probably didn't know it. It sometimes makes sense to access the past to clearly see the present.

- ☐ **Peers and Colleagues**
  Peers and colleagues have a special social and working relationship. They attend staff meetings together, share private views, get feedback from the same boss, travel together, and are knowledgeable about each other's work. You perhaps let your guard down more around peers and act more like yourself. They can be a valuable source of feedback.

SECTION 4: LEARNING FROM DEVELOP-IN-PLACE ASSIGNMENTS

THESE PART-TIME DEVELOP-IN-PLACE ASSIGNMENTS WILL HELP YOU BUILD YOUR SKILL(S)

- ☐ Integrate diverse systems, processes, or procedures across decentralized and/or dispersed units.
- ☐ Go to a campus as a recruiter.
- ☐ Go on a business trip to a foreign country you've not been to before.
- ☐ Create employee involvement teams.
- ☐ Work on a team forming a joint venture or partnership.
- ☐ Manage a dissatisfied internal or external customer; troubleshoot a performance or quality problem with a product or service.
- ☐ Resolve an issue in conflict between two people, units, geographies, functions, etc.
- ☐ Write a speech for someone higher up in the organization.
- ☐ Be a member of a union-negotiating or grievance-handling team.
- ☐ Manage a project team of people who are older and more experienced than you.

SECTION 5: LEARNING FROM FULL-TIME JOBS

THESE FULL-TIME JOBS OFFER THE OPPORTUNITY TO BUILD YOUR SKILL(S)

☐ **Cross-Moves**

The core demands necessary to qualify as a Cross-Move are: 1) Move to a very different set of challenges. 2) Abrupt jump-shift in tasks/activities. 3) Never been there before. 4) New setting/conditions. Examples of Cross-Moves are: 1) Changing divisions. 2) Changing functions. 3) Field/headquarters shifts. 4) Line/staff switches. 5) Country switches. 6) Working with all new people. 7) Changing lines of business.

☐ **Influencing Without Authority**

The core demands to qualify as an Influence Without Authority are: 1) Significant challenge (e.g, start-up, fix-it, scope and/or scale assignment, strategic planning project, changes in management practices/ systems). 2) Insufficient direct authority to make it happen. 3) Tight deadlines. 4) Visible to significant others. 5) Sensitive politics.

☐ **Line To Staff Switches**

The core demands to qualify as a Line to Staff switch are: 1) Intellectually/strategically demanding. 2) Highly visible to others. 3) New area/perspective/method/culture/function. 4) Moving away from a bottom line. 5) Moving from field to headquarters. 6) Exposure to high-level executives. Examples: 1) Business/strategic planning. 2) Heading a staff department. 3) Assistant to/chief of staff to a senior executive. 4) Head of a task force. 5) Human resources role.

☐ **Member of Projects/Task Forces**

The core demands for qualifying as a Project/Task Force assignment are: 1) Full-time assignment. 2) Important and specific goal. 3) Tight deadline. 4) Success or failure will be evident. 5) High-visibility sponsor. 6) Learning something on the fly. 7) Must get others to cooperate. 8) Usually six months or more. Four types of Projects/Task Forces: 1) New ideas, products, services, or systems (e.g., product/service/ program research and development, creation/installation/launch of a new system, new programs like Total Quality Management, positive discipline). 2) Formal negotiations and relationships (e.g., acquisitions, divestitures, agreements, joint ventures; licensing arrangements, franchising; dealing with unions, governments, communities, charities, customers, and relocations). 3) Big one-time events (e.g., working on a major presentation for the board, organizing significant meetings or conferences, disaster/damage control teams; reorganizations, mergers, acquisitions, or relocations, working on visions, charters, strategies, other time-urgent issues and problems). 4) Troubleshooting (e.g., problems, disasters, crises, product/service failures, accidents, illegal activities, damage control in public relations goofs, shut downs, downsizings, layoffs, abrupt changes in leadership).

SECTION 6: LEARNING MORE FROM YOUR PLAN

THESE ADDITIONAL REMEDIES WILL HELP MAKE THIS DEVELOPMENT PLAN MORE EFFECTIVE FOR YOU

Learning to Learn Better

☐ **Form a Learning Network With Others Working on the Same Problem**
Look for people in similar situations, and create a process for sharing and learning together. Look for a variety of people inside and outside your organization. Give feedback to each other; try new and different things together; share successes and failures, lessons and learning.

☐ **Use Objective Data When Judging Others**
Practice studying other people more than judging or evaluating them. Get the facts, the data, how they think, why they do things, without classifying them into your internal like/dislike or agree/disagree boxes, categories, or buckets. Try to project or predict how they would act/react in various situations and follow up to see how accurate you are.

☐ **Examine Why You Judge People the Way You Do**
List the people you like and those you dislike and try to find out why. What do those you like have in common with each other and with you? What do those you dislike have in common with themselves and how do they differ from you? Are your "people buckets" logical and productive or do they interfere? Could you be more effective without putting people into buckets?

☐ **Debrief Someone Else After a Successful or Non-Successful Event**
Shortly after someone does something particularly well or badly, debrief them on the process they followed. Ask them about the decisions they made and why; find out what they would have done differently. See if you can glean some insights or rules of thumb from the experiences of others.

☐ **Pre-sell an Idea to a Key Stakeholder**
Identify the key stakeholders – those who will be the most affected by your actions or the most resistant, or whose support you will most need. Collect the information each will find persuasive; marshal your arguments and try to pre-sell your conclusions, recommendations, and solutions.

☐ **Sell Something to a Tough Group/Audience**
Think of the person or group who will be the toughest to sell, the most critical, skeptical, or resistant, and sell that person or group first. Take time to understand the opposing viewpoints. Find common ground and leverage points; line up your best data and arguments and go for it.

Learning from Experience, Feedback and Other People

- ☐ **Using Multiple Models**
  Who do you know who exemplifies how to do whatever your need is? Who, for example, personifies decisiveness or compassion or strategic agility? Think more broadly than your current job and colleagues. For example, clergy, friends, spouses or community leaders are also good sources for potential models. Select your models not on the basis of overall excellence or likability, but on the basis of the one towering strength (or glaring weakness) you are interested in. Even people who are well thought of usually have only one or two towering strengths (or glaring weaknesses). Ordinarily, you won't learn as much from the whole person as you will from one characteristic.

- ☐ **Learning from a Coach or Tutor**
  Ask a person to coach or tutor you directly. This has the additional benefit of skill building coupled with correcting feedback. Also observe the teacher teaching you. How does he/she teach? How does he/she adjust to you as a learner? After the process, ask for feedback about you as a learner.

- ☐ **Consolidating What You Learn from People**
  After using any source and/or method of learning from others, write down or mentally note the new rules of thumb and the principles involved. How will you remind yourself of the new behaviors in similar situations? How will you prevent yourself from reacting on "autopilot"? How could you share what you have learned from others?

SUGGESTED READINGS

Hesselbein, Marshall Goldsmith, Richard Beckhard, Richard F. Schubert (The Drucker Foundation). *The Community of the Future.* San Francisco: Jossey-Bass, Inc., 1998.

Hunter, Dale, Anne Baile and Bill Taylor. *The Zen of groups: a handbook for people meeting with a purpose.* Tucson, AZ: Fisher Books, 1995.

Kiser, A. Glenn. *Masterful facilitation: becoming a catalyst for meaningful change.* New York: AMACOM, 1998.

Smith, Kenwyn K. and David N. Berg. *Paradoxes of Group Life.* San Francisco: Jossey-Bass, Inc., 1987.

Tagliere, Daniel A. *How to meet, think, and work to consensus.* Amsterdam; San Diego: Pfeiffer, 1993.

65

MANAGING VISION AND PURPOSE

SECTION 1: YOUR DEVELOPMENT NEED(S)

UNSKILLED

- ☐ Can't communicate or sell a vision
- ☐ Not a good presenter
- ☐ Can't turn a good phrase or create compelling one liners
- ☐ Uncomfortable speculating on the unknown future
- ☐ Isn't charismatic or passionate enough to excite and energize others
- ☐ Can't simplify enough to help people understand complex strategy
- ☐ May not understand how change happens
- ☐ Doesn't act like he/she really believes in the vision
- ☐ More comfortable in the here and now

SKILLED

- ☐ Communicates a compelling and inspired vision or sense of core purpose
- ☐ Talks beyond today
- ☐ Talks about possibilities
- ☐ Is optimistic
- ☐ Creates mileposts and symbols to rally support behind the vision
- ☐ Makes the vision sharable by everyone
- ☐ Can inspire and motivate entire units or organizations

OVERUSED SKILL

- ☐ May leave people behind
- ☐ May lack patience with those who don't understand or share his/her vision and sense of purpose
- ☐ May lack appropriate detail-orientation and concern for administrative routine
- ☐ May lack follow-through on the day-to-day tasks

Select one to three of the competencies listed below to work on to compensate for an overuse of this skill.

COMPENSATORS: 3, 5, 24, 27, 33, 35, 41, 52, 64, 67

NOTE:
This competency deals with communicating and implementing an existing vision; for creating a vision, see #58 *Strategic Agility*.

SOME CAUSES

- ☐ Can't create simple messages
- ☐ Can't deal with conflict
- ☐ Don't understand change

- ☐ Don't walk the talk
- ☐ Not committed
- ☐ Poor presenter
- ☐ Talk too long

THE MAP

Much research has shown that organizations with sound and inspiring missions and visions do better in the marketplace. Sound missions and visions motivate and guide people on how to allot their time and how to make choices. As important as the vision, mission and strategy might be, communicating and managing them is even more critical.

SECTION 2: LEARNING ON YOUR OWN

THESE SELF-DEVELOPMENT REMEDIES WILL HELP YOU BUILD YOUR SKILL(S)

SOME REMEDIES

☐ **1. Crafting the message.** C.K. Prahalad, one of the leading strategic consultants, believes that in order to qualify as a mission statement, it should take less than three minutes to explain it clearly to an audience. Really effective mission statements are simple, compelling and capable of capturing people's imagination. Mission statements should help everyone allot his/her time. They should signal what's mission- critical and explain what's rewarded in the organization and what's not. Create a simple obvious symbol, visual or slogan to make the cause come alive. Ford's "Quality is Job One" seems clear enough. Nordstrom's "The Customer is Always Right" tells employees how they should do their jobs. Although the actual mission and vision document would be longer, the message needs to be finely crafted to capture the essence of what's important around here. *More help? – See #27 Informing.*

☐ **2. Common mindset.** The power of a mission and vision communication is providing everyone in the organization with a roadmap on how they are going to be part of something grand and exciting. Establish common cause. Imagine what the change would look like if fully implemented, then describe the outcome often – how things will look in the future. Help people see how their efforts fit in by creating simple, obvious measures of achievement like bar or thermometer charts. Be succinct. People don't line up behind laundry lists or ambiguous objectives. Missions and visions should be more about where we are going and less about how we are going to get there. Keep your eyes on the prize.

☐ **3. Change management.** Most significant vision and mission statements represent a deviation from the past. They represent a rallying call for a departure from business as usual. They require that people are going to have to think, talk and act differently. For that reason, underneath the excitement will be apprehension, anxiety and fear of the unknown. All of the principles of change management apply to communicating a mission. Expect trouble and admit that 20–40% of time will be spent debugging, fixing mistakes and figuring out what went wrong. Treat each one as a chance to learn – document difficulties and learn from them. Without sounding like you're hedging, present it as a work in progress to be improved over time. How changes are made should be as open as possible. Studies show that people work harder and are more effective when they have a sense of choice over how they accomplish stretch goals and objectives. Invite multiple attacks, encourage experimentation, talk with people who have successfully pulled off changes. *More help? – See #28 Innovation Management.*

- ☐ **4. Walking your talk.** Many times employees listen more to what you do than to what you say. The largest reason change efforts fail is that the messenger does not act in line with the new vision and mission. Words are wonderful. Actions are stronger. If you want to be credible, make sure you incorporate the new thinking and behavior into your repertoire. Otherwise it will be gone as soon as the echoes of your words are gone. *More help? – See #22 Ethics and Values.*

- ☐ **5. Matching the audience.** Learn to adjust to your audience. Unfortunately, one vision and mission speech generally does not play equally well across audiences. Many times you will have to adjust the tone, pace, style and even the message and how you couch it for different audiences. If you are giving the mission speech – or delivering the same message – to multiple audiences, always ask yourself how are they different. The union? Managers? Individual producers? Already stressed out from the last mission that fizzled? Merged team? Adjust accordingly. *More help? – See #15 Customer Focus.*

- ☐ **6. Inspiring.** Missions and visions are meant to motivate. Don't threaten. Don't say this is our last chance. Don't blame the past. Visions are optimistic, inspirational, about possibilities, about getting to a grand place in the market. Paint a positive, "we can do it" picture. You have to blow a little smoke and use fairy dust. It's a performance. You have to get people to see what you see. This is all about how to present well (*More help? – See #49 Presentation Skills*) and motivate (*More help? – See #36 Motivating Others*). Always rehearse. Use a test group before you go public. See it yourself on video. Would you understand and be motivated?

- ☐ **7. Detractors and resisters.** There will always be those who don't buy it, have seen it all before, haven't yet seen a mission or vision come true. They may be private about it or come at you in public. Before you communicate the mission and vision, think about the 10 critical questions that might come up. "What happened to last year's brand-new mission that we've already abandoned? I don't think that will work. Our customers won't go for it." Be prepared for the most likely criticisms. Mentally rehearse how you might respond to questions. Listen patiently to people's concerns, protecting their feelings, but also reinforcing the perspective of why the change is needed. Attack positions, not the people. Show patience toward the unconverted; maintain a light touch. Remember, there was a time during the crafting of this vision that you were not convinced. Invite alternative suggestions to reach the same outcome. In the end, thank everyone for their time and input and just say the train is leaving. Rarely, you may have to pull a specific person aside and say, "I understand all your worries and have tried to respond to them, but the train is moving on. Are you on or off?" *More help? – See #12 Conflict Management.*

☐ **8. Managing vision and mission is a lot like selling.** You have a product you think others would buy if they knew about it. Each customer is a little different. What features and benefits would they be looking for? What would they be willing to pay in terms of time and commitment? What are their objections likely to be? How will you answer them? How are you going to ask for the order?

☐ **9. The very nature of missions and visions is that they are statements about the future.** A good manager of visions and purpose would have to be able to talk the future. The future in general. The future of the industry and the market. The future of this organization. Futuring is a series of educated "what ifs." What if there is life on other planets? Will they need our products? What if fusion is possible? Will cheaper energy impact us? When over 50% of the wealth in the U.S. is held by retired baby boomers, will that change anything we are doing? Will the green movement cause any opportunities for us? In order to get good at futuring, you need to read widely, especially outside of your industry. Read *The Futurist*, a magazine of the World Future Society. Watch *The Next Step*, *Connections*, *Inventions,* and *Innovation* on cable. Try to attend one meeting a year to hear futurists speculate on what they see. *More help? – See #46 Perspective.*

☐ **10. The loyal opposition.** Most of the time, you may be delivering someone else's view of the future. Top management and a consultant created the mission, vision and strategy off some where in the woods all by themselves. You may or may not have been asked for any input. You may even have some doubts about it yourself. Your role is to manage this vision and mission, not your personal one. Do not offer conditional statements to your audience, "I've got some concerns myself." Don't let it be known to others that you are not fully on board. Your job is to deliver and manage the message. While it's okay to admit your problems in dealing with change, it's not okay to admit them in dealing with this change. If you have better ideas, try to get them to the people who form missions in your organization. *More help? – See #22 Ethics and Values.*

SECTION 3: LEARNING FROM MORE FEEDBACK

THESE SOURCES WOULD GIVE YOU THE MOST ACCURATE AND DETAILED FEEDBACK ON YOUR SKILL(S)

- ☐ **Boss's Boss(es)**
  From a process standpoint, your boss's boss probably has the most influence and control over your progress. He/she has a broader perspective, has more access to data, and stands at the center of decisions about you. To know what he/she thinks, without having to violate the canons of corporate due process to get that information, would be quite useful.

- ☐ **Direct Boss**
  Your direct boss has important information about you, your performance, and your prospects. The challenge is to get this information. There are formal processes (e.g., performance appraisals). There are day-to-day opportunities. To help, signal your boss that you want and can handle direct and timely feedback. Many bosses have trouble giving feedback, so you will have to work at it over a period of time.

- ☐ **Natural Mentors**
  Natural mentors have a special relationship with you and are interested in your success and your future. Since they are usually not in your direct chain of command, you can have more open, relaxed, and fruitful discussions about yourself and your career prospects. They can be a very important source for candid or critical feedback others may not give you.

- ☐ **Past Associates/Constituencies**
  When confronted with a present performance problem, some claim, "I wasn't like that before; it must be the current situation." When feedback is available from former associates, about 50% support that claim. In the other half of the cases, the people were like that before and probably didn't know it. It sometimes makes sense to access the past to clearly see the present.

SECTION 4: LEARNING FROM DEVELOP-IN-PLACE ASSIGNMENTS

THESE PART-TIME DEVELOP-IN-PLACE ASSIGNMENTS WILL HELP YOU BUILD YOUR SKILL(S)

- ☐ Be a change agent; create a symbol for change; lead the rallying cry; champion a significant change and implementation.
- ☐ Relaunch an existing product or service that's not doing well.
- ☐ Manage an ad hoc, temporary group of "green," inexperienced people as their coach, teacher, orienter, etc.
- ☐ Build a multifunctional project team to tackle a common business issue or problem.

- ☐ Visit Malcolm Baldrige National Quality Award or Deming Prize winners and report back on your findings, showing how they would help your organization.
- ☐ Draft a mission statement, policy proposal, charter, or goal statement and get feedback from others.
- ☐ Manage a study/project team on a significant issue and present the results to key people.
- ☐ Serve on a junior or shadow board.
- ☐ Present the strategy of your unit to others not familiar with your business.
- ☐ Manage the interface between consultants and the organization on a critical assignment.

SECTION 5: LEARNING FROM FULL-TIME JOBS

THESE FULL-TIME JOBS OFFER THE OPPORTUNITY TO BUILD YOUR SKILL(S)

☐ **Heavy Strategic Demands**
The core demands necessary to qualify as a Heavy Strategic Content assignment are: 1) Requires significant strategic thinking and planning most couldn't do. 2) Charts new ground strategically. 3) Plan must be presented, challenged, adopted, and implemented. 4) Exposure to significant decision makers and executives. 1) Strategic planning position. 2) Job involving repositioning of a product, service, or organization.

☐ **Significant People Demands**
Core demands required to qualify as a Significant People Responsibilities assignment are: 1) A sizable increase in either the number of people managed and/or the complexity of the challenges involved 2) Longer-term assignment (two or more years). 3) Quality of people management critical to achieving results. 4) Involves groups not worked with before (e.g., union, new technical areas, nationalities).

☐ **Start-ups**
The core demands to qualify as a start from scratch are: 1) Starting something new for you and/or for the organization. 2) Forging a new team. 3) Creating new systems/facilities/staffs/programs/procedures. 4) Contextual adversity (e.g., uncertainty, government regulation, unions, difficult environment). Seven types of start from scratches: 1) Planning, building, hiring, and managing (e.g., building a new facility, opening up a new location, moving a unit or company). 2) Heading something new (e.g., new product, new service, new line of business, new department/function, major new program). 3) Take over a group/product/service/program that had existed for less than a year and was off to a fast start. 4) Establishing overseas operations. 5) Major new designs for existing systems. 6) Moving a successful program from one

unit to another. 7) Installing a new organization-wide process as a full-time job (e.g., like Total Quality).

SECTION 6: LEARNING MORE FROM YOUR PLAN

THESE ADDITIONAL REMEDIES WILL HELP MAKE THIS DEVELOPMENT PLAN MORE EFFECTIVE FOR YOU

Learning from Experience, Feedback and Other People

☐ **Using Multiple Models**
Who do you know who exemplifies how to do whatever your need is? Who, for example, personifies decisiveness or compassion or strategic agility? Think more broadly than your current job and colleagues. For example, clergy, friends, spouses or community leaders are also good sources for potential models. Select your models not on the basis of overall excellence or likability, but on the basis of the one towering strength (or glaring weakness) you are interested in. Even people who are well thought of usually have only one or two towering strengths (or glaring weaknesses). Ordinarily, you won't learn as much from the whole person as you will from one characteristic.

☐ **Being a Student of Others**
While many of us rely on others for information or advice, we do not really study the behavior of other people. Ask what a person does exceptionally well or poorly. What behaviors are particularly effective and ineffective for them? What works for them and what doesn't? As a student of others, you can deduce the rules of thumb for effective and ineffective behavior and include those in your own library. In comparing yourself with this person, in what areas could you most improve? What could you specifically do to improve in ways comfortable for you?

☐ **Learning from Bosses**
Bosses can be an excellent and ready source for learning. All bosses do some things exceptionally well and other things poorly. Distance your feelings from the boss/direct report relationship and study things that work and things that don't work for your boss. What would you have done? What could you use, and what should you avoid?

☐ **Learning from Interviewing Others**
Interview others. Ask not only what they do, but how and why they do it. What do they think are the rules of thumb they are following? Where did they learn the behaviors? How do they keep them current? How do they monitor the effect they have on others?

☐ **Learning from Observing Others**
Observe others. Find opportunities to observe without interacting with your model. This enables you to objectively study the person, note what he/she is doing or not doing, and compare that with what you

would typically do in similar situations. Many times you can learn more by watching than asking. Your model may not be able to explain what he/she does or may be an unwilling teacher.

- ☐ **Learning from Remote Models**
  Many times you can learn from people not directly available to you. You can read a book about them, watch tapes of public figures, read analyses of them, etc. The principles of learning are the same. Ask yourself what they do well or poorly and deduce their rules of thumb.

- ☐ **Getting Feedback from Bosses and Superiors**
  Many bosses are reluctant to give negative feedback. They lack the managerial courage to face people directly with criticism. You can help by soliciting feedback and setting the tone. Show them you can handle criticism and that you are willing to work on issues they see as important.

- ☐ **Getting Feedback from Direct Reports**
  Direct reports often fear reprisals for giving negative feedback about bosses, whether in a formal process, like a questionnaire, or informally and face-to-face. Even with a guarantee of confidentiality, some are still hesitant. If you want feedback from direct reports, you have to set a positive tone and never act out of revenge.

Learning from Courses

- ☐ **Orientation Events**
  Most organizations offer a variety of orientation events. They are designed to communicate strategies, charters, missions, goals, and general information and offer an opportunity for people to meet each other. They are short in duration and offer limited opportunities for learning anything beyond general context and background.

- ☐ **Strategic Courses**
  There are a number of courses designed to stretch minds to prepare for future challenges. They include topics such as Workforce Diversity 2000, globalization, the European Union, competitive competencies and strategies, etc. Quality depends upon the following three factors: 1) The quality of the staff. Are they qualified? Are they respected in their fields? Are they strategic "gurus"? 2) The quality of the participants. Are they the kind of people you could learn from? 3) The quality of the setting. Is it comfortable and free from distractions? Can you learn there?

SUGGESTED READINGS

Futurist Magazine. http://www.wfs.org

Belasco, James A. and Jerre Stead. *Soaring with the Phoenix – Renewing the vision, reviving the spirit, and re-creating the success of your company.* New York: Warner Books, 1999.

Belasco, James. *Teaching the Elephant to Dance – empowering change in your organization.* New York: Crown Publishers, 1990.

Belasco, James. *Teaching the Elephant to Dance – empowering change in your organization [sound recording].* Studio City, CA: Dove Books on Tape, 1990.

Chajet, Clive and Tom Shachtman. *Image by Design.* New York: Addison-Wesley, 1991.

Collins, James C. and Jerry I. Porras. *Built to Last.* New York: HarperBusiness, 1994.

Drucker, Peter F. *Managing the Non-Profit Organization.* New York: HarperCollins, 1990.

Kotter, John P. *Leading Change.* Boston: Harvard Business School Press, 1996.

Hickman, Craig and Michael A. Silva. *Creating Excellence.* New York: New American Library, 1984.

Price Waterhouse Change Integration Team. *Better Change.* Burr Ridge, IL: Irwin Professional Publishing, 1995.

Schwartz, Peter. *The Art of the Long View.* New York: Doubleday, 1991.

WORK / LIFE BALANCE

SECTION 1: YOUR DEVELOPMENT NEED(S)

UNSKILLED

- ☐ Lacks balance between work and personal life
- ☐ Overdoes one at the harmful expense of the other
- ☐ May be a workaholic
- ☐ May be bored off-work or can't relax
- ☐ May be a poor time manager and priority setter; may just react
- ☐ Can't turn off one area of life and fully concentrate on the other
- ☐ Can't keep multiple and mixed priorities going at one time
- ☐ Carries troubles from one area of life into the other
- ☐ Can only seem to manage one or the other

SKILLED

- ☐ Maintains a conscious balance between work and personal life so that one doesn't dominate the other
- ☐ Is not one-dimensional
- ☐ Knows how to attend to both
- ☐ Gets what he/she wants from both

OVERUSED SKILL

- ☐ May not be flexible enough when work or personal life demands change dramatically
- ☐ May not be willing to adjust one at the expense of the other
- ☐ May value balance over temporary discomfort
- ☐ May try to force his/her view of balance on others

Select one to three of the competencies listed below to work on to compensate for an overuse of this skill.

COMPENSATORS: 2, 6, 11, 12, 17, 22, 23, 32, 40, 45, 46, 50, 54, 55

SOME CAUSES

- ☐ A worrier
- ☐ Can't relax
- ☐ Off work is not exciting
- ☐ Overly ambitious
- ☐ Poor priority setting
- ☐ Time management
- ☐ Too intense
- ☐ Workaholic

THE MAP

Research on well-being shows that the best adjusted people are generally the busiest people, on and off work. Balance is not achieved only by people who are not busy and have the time. It's the off work part of balance that gives most people problems. With downsizing, wondering if you'll be in the next layoff, and 60 hour work weeks, many people are too exhausted to do much more than refuel off work. Nonetheless, frustration and feeling unidimensional are often the result of not forcing the issue of balance in one's life. There is special pressure on those with full dual responsibilities – they have full time jobs and they have full time care giver and home management duties.

SECTION 2: LEARNING ON YOUR OWN

THESE SELF-DEVELOPMENT REMEDIES WILL HELP YOU BUILD YOUR SKILL(S)

SOME REMEDIES

☐ **1. All your eggs in one basket?** Add things to your off-work life. This was a major finding of a stress study at AT&T of busy, high potential women and men. It may seem counterintuitive, but the best adjusted people forced themselves to structure off work activities just as much as on work activities. Otherwise work drives everything else out. Those with dual responsibilities (primary care giver and home manager and a full time job holder) need to use their management strengths and skills more at home. What makes your work life successful? Batch tasks, bundle similar activities together, delegate to children or set up pools with coworkers or neighbors to share tasks such as car pooling, soccer games, Scouts, etc. Pay to have some things done that are not mission-critical to your home needs. Organize and manage efficiently. Have a schedule. Set up goals and plans. Use some of your work skills more off work.

☐ **2. Balance has nothing to do with 50/50 or clock time.** It has to do with how we use the time we have. It doesn't mean for every hour of work, you must have an hour off work. It means finding what is a reasonable balance for you. Is it a few hours a week unencumbered by work worries? Is it four breaks a day? Is it some solitude before bedtime? Is it playing with your kids more? Is it having an actual (rather than "Did you remember the dry cleaning?") conversation with your spouse (partner) each day? Is it a community, religious or sports activity that you're passionate about. Schedule them; structure them into your life. Negotiate with your partner; don't just accept your life as a given. Define what balance is for you and include your spouse or friend or family in the definition.

☐ **3. There's time and there's focused time.** Busy people with not much time learn to get into the present tense without carrying the rest of their burdens, concerns and deadlines with them. When you have only one hour to read or play with the kids or play racquetball or sew – be there. Have fun. You won't solve any problems during the 60 minutes anyway. Train your mind to be where you are. Focus on the moment.

☐ **4. Create deadlines, urgencies and structures off work.** One tactic that helps is for people to use their strengths from work off work. If you are organized, organize something. If you are very personable, get together a regular group. If you are competitive, set up a regular match. As common sensical as this seems, AT&T found that people with poor off work lives did not use their strengths off work. They truly left them at the office.

☐ **5. What are your NOs?** If you don't have any, chances are you'll be frustrated on both sides of your life. Part of maturity is letting go of nice, even fun and probably valuable, activities. What are you hanging on to? What can't you say no to at the office that really isn't a priority? Where do you make yourself a patsy? If your saying no irritates people initially, this may be the price. You can usually soften it, however, by explaining what you are trying to do. Most people won't take it personally if you say you're going to pick up your child or maybe coach his/her soccer team or you can't help with this project because of a explicit priority which is critical to your unit. Give reasons that don't downgrade the activity you're giving up. It's not that it's insignificant; it just didn't quite make the cut.

☐ **6. Make your off work life more exciting.** Many of us want as little stress as we can get off work and seeking this comfort ends up as boredom. What are three really exciting things you and/or your family could do? Work will always be exciting or at least full of activity. Combating this stimulus overload means finding something you can be passionate about off the job.

☐ **7. If you can't relax once you leave work, schedule breakpoints or boundaries.** One of the great things about the human brain is that it responds to change; signal it that work is over – play music in your car, immediately play with your children, go for a walk, swim for 20 minutes – give your mind a clear and repetitious breakpoint. Try to focus all your energy where you are. At work, worry about work things and not life things. When you hit the driveway, worry about life things and leave work things at the office. Schedule a time every week for financial management and worries. Try to concentrate your worry time where it will do some good.

☐ **8. If your problem goes beyond that –** you're three days into vacation and still can't relax – write down what you're worried about, which is almost always unresolved problems. Write down everything you can think of. Don't worry about complete sentences – just get it down. You'll usually find it's hard to fill a page and there will be only three topics – work problems, problems with people, and a to-do list. Note any ideas that come up for dealing with them. This will usually shut off your worry response, which is nothing but a mental reminder of things unresolved. Since we're all creatures of habit, though, the same worries will pop up again. Then you have to say to yourself (as silly as this seems), "I've done everything I can do on that right now," or "That's right, I remember, I'll do it later." Obviously, this tactic works when we're not on vacation as well.

- ☐ **9. If you love work, and you're really a happy but unbalanced workaholic, try tip four.** If that doesn't work, you need to see yourself 20 years from now. Find three people who remind you of you but are 20 years older. Are they happy? How are their personal lives? Any problems with stress or depression? If this is OK with you, protect yourself with #7. If you don't do something to refresh yourself, your effectiveness will eventually suffer or you'll burn out.
- ☐ **10. Talk to people who have your best interests at heart,** who accept you for who you are and with whom you can be candid. What do they want for you? Ask them how they would change your balance.

SECTION 3: LEARNING FROM MORE FEEDBACK

THESE SOURCES WOULD GIVE YOU THE MOST ACCURATE AND DETAILED FEEDBACK ON YOUR SKILL(S)

- ☐ **Development Professionals**
  Sometimes it might be valuable to get some analysis and feedback from a professional trained and certified in the area you're working on: possibly a career counselor, a therapist, clergy, a psychologist, etc.
- ☐ **Direct Reports**
  Across a variety of settings, your direct reports probably see you the most. They are the recipients of most of your managerial behaviors. They know your work. They can compare you with former bosses. Since they may hesitate to give you negative feedback, you have to set the atmosphere to make it easier for them. You have to ask.
- ☐ **Family Members**
  On some issues, like interpersonal style or compassion, it might be helpful to ask various and multiple family members for feedback to add confirmation or context to feedback you've received in the workplace.
- ☐ **Natural Mentors**
  Natural mentors have a special relationship with you and are interested in your success and your future. Since they are usually not in your direct chain of command, you can have more open, relaxed, and fruitful discussions about yourself and your career prospects. They can be a very important source for candid or critical feedback others may not give you.

☐ **Yourself**
You are an important source of feedback on yourself. But some caution is appropriate. If you have not received much feedback, you may be less accurate than the other sources. We all have blind spots, defense shields, ideal self-views, and fantasies. Before acting on your own self-views, get outside confirmation from other appropriate sources.

SECTION 4: LEARNING FROM DEVELOP-IN-PLACE ASSIGNMENTS

THESE PART-TIME DEVELOP-IN-PLACE ASSIGNMENTS WILL HELP YOU BUILD YOUR SKILL(S)

☐ Attend a self-awareness/assessment course that includes feedback.

☐ Join a self-help or support group.

☐ Complete a self-study course or project in an important area for you.

☐ Attend a course or event which will push you personally beyond your usual limits or outside your comfort zone (e.g., Outward Bound, language immersion training, sensitivity group, public speaking).

☐ Act as a loaned executive to a charity, government, agency, etc.

☐ Become an active member of a professional organization.

☐ Work on a project that involves travel and study of an issue, acquisition, or joint venture off-shore or overseas, with a report back to management.

☐ Represent the organization at a trade show, convention, exposition, etc.

☐ Assign a project to a group with a tight deadline.

☐ Take over for someone on vacation or a long trip.

SECTION 5: LEARNING FROM FULL-TIME JOBS

THESE FULL-TIME JOBS OFFER THE OPPORTUNITY TO BUILD YOUR SKILL(S)

☐ **Cross-Moves**
The core demands necessary to qualify as a Cross-Move are: 1) Move to a very different set of challenges. 2) Abrupt jump-shift in tasks/activities. 3) Never been there before. 4) New setting/conditions. Examples of Cross-Moves are: 1) Changing divisions. 2) Changing functions. 3) Field/headquarters shifts. 4) Line/staff switches. 5) Country switches. 6) Working with all new people. 7) Changing lines of business.

☐ **Off-Shore Assignments**
The core demands to qualify as an Off-Shore assignment are: 1) First time working in the country. 2) Significant challenges like new language, hardship location, unique business rules/practices, significant cultural/marketplace differences, different functional task, etc. 3) More than a year assignment. 4) No automatic return deal. 5) Not necessarily a change in job challenge, technical content, or responsibilities.

- ☐ **Staff to Line Shifts**
  Core demands necessary to qualify for a Staff to Line shift are: 1) Moving to a job with an easily determined bottom line or results. 2) Managing bigger scope and/or scale. 3) Requires new skills/perspectives. 4) Unfamiliar aspects of the assignment.

SECTION 6: LEARNING MORE FROM YOUR PLAN

THESE ADDITIONAL REMEDIES WILL HELP MAKE THIS DEVELOPMENT PLAN MORE EFFECTIVE FOR YOU

Learning to Learn Better

- ☐ **Study Yourself in Detail**
  Study your likes and dislikes because they can drive a lot of your thinking, judging, and acting. Ask which like or dislike has gotten in the way or prevented you from moving to a higher level of learning. Are your likes and dislikes really important to you or have you just gone on "autopilot"? Try to address and understand a blocking dislike and change it.

Learning from Experience, Feedback and Other People

- ☐ **Learning from Ineffective Behavior**
  Seeing things done poorly can be a very potent source of learning for you, especially if the behavior or action affects others negatively. Many times the thing done poorly causes emotional reactions or pain in you and others. Distance yourself from the feelings and explore why the actions didn't work.
- ☐ **Learning from Interviewing Others**
  Interview others. Ask not only what they do, but how and why they do it. What do they think are the rules of thumb they are following? Where did they learn the behaviors? How do they keep them current? How do they monitor the effect they have on others?
- ☐ **Learning from Observing Others**
  Observe others. Find opportunities to observe without interacting with your model. This enables you to objectively study the person, note what he/she is doing or not doing, and compare that with what you would typically do in similar situations. Many times you can learn more by watching than asking. Your model may not be able to explain what he/she does or may be an unwilling teacher.
- ☐ **Feedback in Unusual Contexts/Situations**
  Temporary and extreme conditions and contexts may shade interpretations of your behavior and intentions. Demands of the job may drive you outside your normal mode of operating. Hence, feedback you receive may be inaccurate during those times. However, unusual contexts affect our behavior less than most assume. It's usually a weak excuse.

SUGGESTED READINGS

Carter, Steven and Julia Sokol. *Lives without balance.* New York: Villard Books, 1992.

Elliott, Miriam, Ph.D. and Susan Meltsner, MSW. *The Perfectionist Predicament.* New York: William Morrow and Company, Inc., 1991.

Kaplan, Robert E. with Wilfred H. Drath and Joan Kofodimos. *Beyond Ambition.* San Francisco: Jossey-Bass Publishers, 1991.

Kofodimos, Joan. *Balancing Act – How managers can integrate successful careers and fulfilling personal lives.* San Francisco: Jossey-Bass Publishers, 1993.

Lee, Deborah, Ph.D. *Having it all. Having Enough. How to create a career/family balance that works for you.* New York: AMACOM, 1997.

Sanitate, Frank. *Don't go to work unless it's fun! State-of-the-heart time management.* Santa Barbara, CA: Santa Barbara Press, 1994.

Schor, Juliet B. *The Overworked American – The unexpected decline of leisure.* New York: HarperCollins Publishers, 1991.

WRITTEN COMMUNICATIONS

SECTION 1: YOUR DEVELOPMENT NEED(S)

UNSKILLED

- ☐ Not a clear communicator in writing
- ☐ May be hard to tell what the point is
- ☐ May be too wordy or too terse or have grammar/usage problems
- ☐ May not construct a logical argument well
- ☐ May not adjust to different audiences; may have a single style of writing

SKILLED

- ☐ Is able to write clearly and succinctly in a variety of communication settings and styles
- ☐ Can get messages across that have the desired effect

OVERUSED SKILL

- ☐ May invest too much time crafting communications
- ☐ May too often try for perfection when something less would do the job
- ☐ May be overly critical of the written work of others

Select one to three of the competencies listed below to work on to compensate for an overuse of this skill.

COMPENSATORS: 1, 2, 3, 12, 15, 17, 27, 32, 38, 44, 46, 48, 50, 51, 53, 57, 62

SOME CAUSES

- ☐ Dull writing
- ☐ Too busy
- ☐ Too wordy; too long
- ☐ Hard to tell what your point is
- ☐ Disorganized
- ☐ Grammar/usage problems
- ☐ Don't write for the audience

THE MAP

You are what you write. Good writing is that which efficiently and effectively communicates to readers the points and messages you want them to know. No more. No less. It respects the time and the intelligence of the reader. Learn to write as if you had three minutes to present an argument to a group whose opinion is important to you. The border patrol has you stopped at a check point, has their guns trained on you, and has asked why you are there. What would you do? You would probably speak their language, make it clear what you want, use as few words as you could, sound plaintive, and reinforce key points that argue in your favor. Think of what you wouldn't do. You wouldn't ramble, expect them to guess your point or use vague words or jargon that would baffle them. Good writing is the same. Use the least amount of print possible to communicate your message.

SECTION 2: LEARNING ON YOUR OWN

THESE SELF-DEVELOPMENT REMEDIES WILL HELP YOU BUILD YOUR SKILL(S)

SOME REMEDIES

☐ **1. Preparing an outline before you write.** Too many people write without a plan. Go through a checklist. What's your objective? What are your main points? Outline your main points in logical support of the objective. What are five things you want them to know and remember about each point? When you write, any sentence that does not relate to the objective and the points shouldn't be there. What would the ideal reader say if interviewed 15 minutes after he/she finishes reading your piece? Who's your audience? How much do they know that you don't have to repeat? How much background should you include? What questions will the audience have when they read your piece? Are they covered? What's the setting for readers? How much time will they spend? How long can it be? Pick up something you've written lately and take a test. Does it have a thesis? Does each paragraph have a topic sentence – a subject? If you state one sentence per paragraph, do the statements follow logically? *More help? – See #47 Planning.*

☐ **2. Writing the piece.** Follow your outline. State your message or purpose in a lead single sentence or two early in the document. Any reader should immediately know why he/she is reading the piece. Then outline the three to five chunks of your argument to support your thesis. Any more and the readers won't follow it. What in the introduction will grab the reader and rivet him/her on your message? A story, a fact, a comparison, a quote, a photo, a cartoon? What are five techniques you will use to get and hold his/her attention? What style would work best? What are your priority points, and how will you explain them? Some points are made better by example, some by the logic of the argument, some by facts or stories. You should vary how you drive home your point because you will reach more people.

☐ **3. Writing for different audiences.** Unfortunately, one document generally does not play equally well across differing audiences. Many times you will have to adjust the length, tone, pace, style and even the message and how you couch it for different audiences. If you are writing a single message to multiple audiences, always ask yourself how are they different? Adjust accordingly. Writing for a higher level manager? Use an executive summary. One page. Just like your outline.

At the end, tell the person what decision you are asking him or her to make. If the executive indicates interest, follow with the longer document. A support group? What resources will you need to support this activity? They probably need detail to line up their schedules. Legal? They need why, the history, parallels in the marketplace, legal potholes. Direct reports? They need implementation detail to understand the goals and outcomes you are considering. In one sense, you need to write the entire document and then chunk it up for the various audiences. Don't try to make one document stretch. *More help? – See #15 Customer Focus.*

☐ **4. Don't drown the reader in detail he/she doesn't need or can't use.** Use detail only when it's essential to understanding your argument/thesis. What are five facts that show your point? Even if writing a lengthy report, those five facts should be highlighted in a paragraph or two, not revealed slowly. Readers will forget why they are reading about each problem since problems usually have more than one cause, and they will become distracted thinking about other matters. Few people read an almanac; if your argument is data driven, use the few; put the many in appendices.

☐ **5. Provide headlines and checkpoints for the reader, just as a newspaper does**. If the communication is more than two or three pages, break it into headings such as "The Purchasing Problem," "Why the Purchasing System is Breaking Down," "Purchasing Options," "Questions to Answer," etc.

☐ **6. Don't lose your readers with poor use of words.** Eliminate embellishing words such as very, great, exciting, etc. Most adjectives and adverbs add nothing, cause the reader to pause, or come across as overstatements. Arguments are carried by logic and facts, not filler. Avoid stringing abstract words together – usually nouns – such as "optimal personnel interface." Substitute common equivalents for these words. The numbing string of nouns above actually means "the best way for people to talk to each other." Since all word processing systems have a thesaurus embedded in them, use this if stumped. Use Spell Check to correct misspellings and to spot commonly used non-words such as "irregardless, prioritize, or orientate." Poor usage is more difficult to spot. Perhaps the easiest method is to have someone check your grammar. Another more difficult, but longer term, strategy is to get a copy of *The Elements of Style* by Strunk and White, a simple guide to the most common problems in grammar and what to do about them.

☐ **7. Action and visuals.** Pep up your writing. Use words that call up pictures whenever possible. Vivid, visual arguments are best remembered. (Can you make the reader see the purchasing problem? "The boxes were stacked to the ceiling, blocking two rows.") Vary sentence length and type. Too many writers fall into the trap of "The quick brown fox jumped over the lazy dog's back" – a string of simple sentences made long with lots of filler. Turning verbs into nouns makes writing dull – say X organized not, "the organization was accomplished by..." Use action – or active – words. Avoid "is" and "are," double negatives like "not bad" or veiled insults like "not very good." Say what you mean with active words: if a sentence has multiple commas, or multiple clauses, it may be too long. Say it out loud. Could you say it in half the words? Long, tortuous sentences usually come from turning the subject into the object of the sentence. In "Employees are inspired by X, Y, and Z," the employees are passive recipients of X, Y, and Z, which comprise the point of the sentence. Decide what inspires employees and put it first. Try a little drama. In contrast to the above point, if you want to emphasize something, put it last: "In conclusion, doing X increased profit 14%" is more likely to make the point than "Profit increased 14% by..."

☐ **8. If your writing is repetitious, usually your second or third statement or qualifier will be the best.** Often we write something, decides it needs clarification, and write another sentence or two to explain the first. In reading it over, we notice this and scratch out the later sentences, making the problem worse. First check the later statements to see if they are better statements; if not, combine the sentences into one.

☐ **9. Write like you speak.** Most people who don't write well, speak better than they write. Use this to your advantage. Talk out your argument with a friend, say it out loud, use a tape recorder, buy one of the new word recognition software programs. Then reduce your argument to the logical format required by writing.

☐ **10. Don't write like you speak.** Watch out for cute and humorous remarks. What is funny in person often seems cynical on paper. Watch out for strongly worded statements. While you may get away with them in person because you have a soft voice, they will come across as hard and uncompromising in writing. Watch out for jargon and other $1,000 words that bore readers or confuse them. This might be fine in person, because you can gauge reactions and clear up any furrowed brow responses; in writing, you can't see your audience. And don't ever, ever, write when you're angry. If you do, put it away overnight. Read it the next day, extract the points, rewrite it, then throw the original missile away. That's what Lincoln did and he was pretty successful.

SECTION 3: LEARNING FROM MORE FEEDBACK

THESE SOURCES WOULD GIVE YOU THE MOST ACCURATE AND DETAILED FEEDBACK ON YOUR SKILL(S)

☐ **Direct Boss**
Your direct boss has important information about you, your performance, and your prospects. The challenge is to get this information. There are formal processes (e.g., performance appraisals). There are day-to-day opportunities. To help, signal your boss that you want and can handle direct and timely feedback. Many bosses have trouble giving feedback, so you will have to work at it over a period of time.

☐ **Direct Reports**
Across a variety of settings, your direct reports probably see you the most. They are the recipients of most of your managerial behaviors. They know your work. They can compare you with former bosses. Since they may hesitate to give you negative feedback, you have to set the atmosphere to make it easier for them. You have to ask.

☐ **Internal and External Customers**
Customers interact with you as a person and as a supplier or vendor of products and services. You're important to them because you can either help address and solve their problems or stand in their way. As customer service and Total Quality programs gain importance, clients and customers become a more prominent source of feedback.

☐ **Peers and Colleagues**
Peers and colleagues have a special social and working relationship. They attend staff meetings together, share private views, get feedback from the same boss, travel together, and are knowledgeable about each other's work. You perhaps let your guard down more around peers and act more like yourself. They can be a valuable source of feedback.

SECTION 4: LEARNING FROM DEVELOP-IN-PLACE ASSIGNMENTS

THESE PART-TIME DEVELOP-IN-PLACE ASSIGNMENTS WILL HELP YOU BUILD YOUR SKILL(S)

☐ Plan a new site for a building (plant, field office, headquarters, etc.).

☐ Manage the purchase of a major product, equipment, materials, program, or system.

☐ Write public press (PR) releases for the organization.

☐ Write a proposal for a new policy, process, mission, charter, product, service, or system, and present and sell it to top management.

☐ Draft a mission statement, policy proposal, charter, or goal statement and get feedback from others.

☐ Seek out and use a seed budget to create and pursue a personal idea, product, or service.

- ☐ Work on a team writing a proposal to obtain significant government or foundation grants or funding of an activity.
- ☐ Design a training course in an area you're not an expert in.
- ☐ Design a training course in an area of expertise for you.
- ☐ Write a speech for someone higher up in the organization.

SECTION 5: LEARNING FROM FULL-TIME JOBS

THESE FULL-TIME JOBS OFFER THE OPPORTUNITY TO BUILD YOUR SKILL(S)

- ☐ **Heavy Strategic Demands**
  The core demands necessary to qualify as a Heavy Strategic Content assignment are: 1) Requires significant strategic thinking and planning most couldn't do. 2) Charts new ground strategically. 3) Plan must be presented, challenged, adopted, and implemented. 4) Exposure to significant decision makers and executives. 1) Strategic planning position. 2) Job involving repositioning of a product, service, or organization.

SECTION 6: LEARNING MORE FROM YOUR PLAN

THESE ADDITIONAL REMEDIES WILL HELP MAKE THIS DEVELOPMENT PLAN MORE EFFECTIVE FOR YOU

Learning from Experience, Feedback and Other People

- ☐ **Using Multiple Models**
  Who do you know who exemplifies how to do whatever your need is? Who, for example, personifies decisiveness or compassion or strategic agility? Think more broadly than your current job and colleagues. For example, clergy, friends, spouses or community leaders are also good sources for potential models. Select your models not on the basis of overall excellence or likability, but on the basis of the one towering strength (or glaring weakness) you are interested in. Even people who are well thought of usually have only one or two towering strengths (or glaring weaknesses). Ordinarily, you won't learn as much from the whole person as you will from one characteristic.
- ☐ **Getting Feedback from Bosses and Superiors**
  Many bosses are reluctant to give negative feedback. They lack the managerial courage to face people directly with criticism. You can help by soliciting feedback and setting the tone. Show them you can handle criticism and that you are willing to work on issues they see as important.

Learning from Courses

☐ **Courses with Feedback**
Many courses such as negotiating skills and personal influence offer feedback on the subject matter of the course in addition to the content. They either collect data ahead of time or collect it "live" during the course.

SUGGESTED READINGS

DeVries, Mary A. *Internationally yours – Writing and Communicating Successfully in Today's Global Marketplace.* Boston: Houghton Mifflin Co., 1994.

Ferrara, Cosmo F. Ed.D. *Writing on the Job – Quick practical solutions to all your business writing problems.* Englewood Cliffs, NJ: Prentice-Hall, 1995.

Gunning, Robert and Richard A. Kallan. *How to take the fog out of business writing.* Chicago: The Dartnell Corp., 1994.

Joseph, Albert. *Put it in Writing.* New York: McGraw-Hill, 1998.

Kaplan, Burton. *Strategic Communication – The art of making your ideas their ideas.* New York: HarperBusiness, 1991.

There are no competencies 68–80.
Those numbers are reserved for future additions.

THE NINE PERFORMANCE MANAGEMENT ARCHITECT® DIMENSIONS

QUANTITY OF OUTPUT OF WORK

SECTION 1: YOUR DEVELOPMENT NEED(S)

General Definition: Quantity or amount of work produced personally or from a group or team on assignments/tasks/ projects/products/or services without regard to any other factors like quality or timeliness of the work.

UNSKILLED

- ☐ Low amount of work produced
- ☐ Lags behind most other people or groups
- ☐ Significant goals are missed
- ☐ Productivity is lower than most others
- ☐ Makes a few goals but misses others

AVERAGE

- ☐ Amount of work produced is acceptable and about like most other people or similar groups
- ☐ Most production goals are met; a few may be missed
- ☐ Work output is at standard

SKILLED

- ☐ The amount of work produced by this person or group is simply amazing
- ☐ No matter how high the production or output goals are set, more is produced than expected in all areas
- ☐ Almost always number one in productivity
- ☐ Defines hard work for the rest

OVERUSED SKILL

- ☐ The amount of work coming from this person or group is so high that sometimes quality and morale suffer because things are so intense and the pace is so fast
- ☐ Can be so single mindedly focused on getting the most work out that all other matters including concern for others suffer

Select one to three of the competencies listed below to work on to compensate for an overuse of this skill.

COMPENSATORS: 7,17,20,23,33,36,41,42,50,52,60

SOME CAUSES

- ☐ Burned out
- ☐ Fights bosses
- ☐ Goals set too high
- ☐ Lack of ambition
- ☐ Lack of realistic resources
- ☐ New to the job or field
- ☐ Not aligned or committed
- ☐ Not focused or disciplined
- ☐ Not organized
- ☐ Organization politics
- ☐ Perfectionist
- ☐ Procrastinator

THE MAP

There is probably no substitute for getting things done. Most rewards in life go to those who produce. Being able to consistently produce covers a lot of other problems. Others are not very tolerant of excuses from those who consistently don't get things done. Once not getting things done surfaces as an issue, others begin to look for the reasons and begin finding other problems – real and imagined. It's a career death spiral. The best course of action is to concentrate fully on reaching the goals and objectives set for the task, project or job you are in or get out.

SECTION 2: LEARNING ON YOUR OWN

THESE SELF-DEVELOPMENT REMEDIES WILL HELP YOU BUILD YOUR SKILL(S)

SOME REMEDIES

☐ **1. Setting priorities?** What's mission-critical? What are the three to five things that most need to get done to achieve your goals? Effective performers typically spend about half their time on a few mission-critical priorities. Don't get diverted by trivia and things you like doing but that aren't tied to the bottom line. *More help? – See #50 Priority Setting.*

☐ **2. Set goals for yourself and others.** Most people work better if they have a set of goals and objectives to achieve and a standard everyone agrees to measure accomplishments against. Most people like stretch goals. They like them even better if they have had a hand in setting them. Set checkpoints along the way to be able to measure progress. Give yourself and others as much feedback as you can. *More help? – See #35 Managing and Measuring Work.*

☐ **3. How to get things done.** Some don't know the best way to produce results. There is a well established set of best practices for producing results. Formally they are known as Total Quality

Management and Process Re-Engineering. If you are not disciplined in how to design work flows and processes for yourself and others, buy one book on each of these topics. Go to one workshop on efficient and effective work design. Ask your Quality or Re-Engineering function for help. *More help? – See #52 Process Management and #63 Total Quality Management/Re-Engineering.*

☐ **4. Organizing?** Are you always short on resources? Always pulling things together on a shoe string? Getting results means getting and using resources. People. Money. Materials. Support. Time. Many times it involves getting resources you don't control. You have to beg, borrow, but hopefully not steal. That means negotiating, bargaining, trading, cajoling, and influencing. What's the business case for the resources you need? What do you have to trade? How can you make it a win for everyone? *More help? – See #37 Negotiating and #39 Organizing.*

☐ **5. Getting work done through others?** Some people are not good managers of others. They can produce results by themselves but do less well when the results have to come from the team. Are you having trouble getting your team to work with you to get the results you need? You have the resources and the people but things just don't run well. Maybe you do too much work yourself. You don't delegate or empower. You don't communicate well. You don't motivate well. You don't plan well. You don't set priorities and goals well. If you are a struggling manager or a first-time manager, there are well known and documented principles and practices of good managing. Do you share credit? Do you paint a clear picture of why this is important? Is their work challenging? Do you inspire or just hand out work? Read *Becoming a Manager* by Linda A. Hill. Go to one course on management. *More help? – See #20 Directing Others, #36 Motivating Others, #18 Delegation, and #60 Building Effective Teams.*

☐ **6. Working across borders and boundaries?** Do you have trouble when you have to go outside your unit to reach your goals and objectives? This means that influence skills, understanding, and trading are the currency to use. Don't just ask for things; find some common ground where you can provide help. What do the peers you need need? Are your results important to them? How does what you're working on affect their results? If it affects them negatively, can you trade something, appeal to the common good, figure out some way to minimize the work – volunteering staff help, for example? Go into peer relationships with a trading mentality. To be seen as more cooperative, always explain your thinking and invite them to explain theirs. Generate a variety of possibilities first rather than stake out positions. Be tentative, allowing them room to customize the situation. Focus on common goals, priorities and problems. Invite criticism of your ideas. *More help? – See #42 Peer Relationships.*

☐ **7. Not bold enough?** Won't take a risk? Sometimes producing results involves pushing the envelope, taking chances and trying bold new initiatives. Doing those things leads to more misfires and mistakes but also better results. Treat any mistakes or failures as chances to learn. Nothing ventured, nothing gained. Up your risk comfort. Start small so you can recover more quickly. See how creative and innovative you can be. Satisfy yourself; people will always say it should have been done differently. Listen to them, but be skeptical. Conduct a postmortem immediately after finishing. This will indicate to all that you're open to continuous improvement whether the result was stellar or not. *More help? – See #14 Creativity, #28 Innovation Management, #2 Dealing With Ambiguity, and #57 Standing Alone.*

☐ **8. Procrastinate?** Are you a lifelong procrastinator? Do you perform best in crises and impossible deadlines? Do you wait until the last possible moment? If you do, you will miss deadlines and performance targets. You might not produce consistent results. Some of your work will be marginal because you didn't have the time to do it right. You settled for a "B" when you could have gotten an "A" if you had one more day to work on it. Start earlier. Always do 10% of each task immediately after it is assigned so you can better gauge what it is going to take to finish the rest. Divide tasks and assignments into thirds and schedule time to do them spaced over the delivery period. Always leave more time than you think it's going to take. *More help? – See #47 Planning and #62 Time Management.*

☐ **9. Persistence?** Perseverance? Are you prone to give up on tough or repetitive tasks, have trouble going back the second and third time, lose motivation when you hit obstacles? Trouble making that last push to get it over the top? Attention span is shorter than it needs to be? Set mini-deadlines. Break down the task into smaller pieces so you can view your progress more clearly. Switch approaches. Do something totally different next time. Have five different ways to get the same outcome. Be prepared to do them all when obstacles arise. Task trade with someone who has your problem. Work on each other's tasks. *More help? – See #43 Perseverance.*

☐ **10. The stress and strain.** Producing results day after day, quarter after quarter, year after year is stressful. Some people are energized by moderate stress. They actually work better. Some people are debilitated by stress. They decrease in productivity as stress increases. Are you close to burnout? Dealing with stress and pressure is a known technology. Stress and pressure are actually in your head, not in the outside world. Some people are stressed by the same events others are energized by – losing a major account. Some people cry and some laugh at the same external event – someone slipping on a banana peel. Stress is how you look at events, not the events themselves. Dealing more effectively with stress involves reprogramming your interpretation of your work and about what you find stressful. There was a time in your life when spiders and snakes were life threatening and stressful to you. Are they now? Talk to your boss or mentor about getting some relief if you're about to crumble. Maybe this job isn't for you. Think about moving back to a less stressful job. *More help? – See #6 Career Ambition and #11 Composure.*

SECTION 3: LEARNING FROM MORE FEEDBACK

THESE SOURCES WOULD GIVE YOU THE MOST ACCURATE AND DETAILED FEEDBACK ON YOUR SKILL(S)

☐ **Direct Reports**
Across a variety of settings, your direct reports probably see you the most. They are the recipients of most of your managerial behaviors. They know your work. They can compare you with former bosses. Since they may hesitate to give you negative feedback, you have to set the atmosphere to make it easier for them. You have to ask.

☐ **Direct Boss**
Your direct boss has important information about you, your performance, and your prospects. The challenge is to get this information. There are formal processes (e.g., performance appraisals). There are day-to-day opportunities. To help, signal your boss that you want and can handle direct and timely feedback. Many bosses have trouble giving feedback, so you will have to work at it over a period of time.

☐ **Past Associates/Constituencies**
When confronted with a present performance problem, some claim, "I wasn't like that before; it must be the current situation." When feedback is available from former associates, about 50 percent support that claim. In the other half of the cases, the people were like that before and probably didn't know it. It sometimes makes sense to access the past to clearly see the present.

☐ **Peers and Colleagues**
Peers and colleagues have a special social and working relationship. They attend staff meetings together, share private views, get feedback from the same boss, travel together, and are knowledgeable about each other's work. You perhaps let your guard down more around peers and act more like yourself. They can be a valuable source of feedback.

☐ **Yourself**
You are an important source of feedback on yourself. But some caution is appropriate. If you have not received much feedback, you may be less accurate than the other sources. We all have blind spots, defense shields, ideal self-views, and fantasies. Before acting on your own self-views, get outside confirmation from other appropriate sources.

SECTION 4: LEARNING FROM DEVELOP-IN-PLACE ASSIGNMENTS

THESE PART-TIME DEVELOP-IN-PLACE ASSIGNMENTS WILL HELP YOU BUILD YOUR SKILL(S)

- ☐ Manage an ad hoc, temporary group of people involved in tackling a fix-it or turnaround project.
- ☐ Manage an ad hoc, temporary group of balky and resisting people through an unpopular change or project.
- ☐ Manage an ad hoc, temporary group of low-competence people through a task they couldn't do by themselves.
- ☐ Relaunch an existing product or service that's not doing well.
- ☐ Assign a project to a group with a tight deadline.
- ☐ Help shut down a plant, regional office, product line, business, operation, etc.
- ☐ Launch a new product, service, or process.
- ☐ Manage a group through a significant business crisis.
- ☐ Work short periods in customer service.
- ☐ Plan a new site for a building (plant, field office, headquarters, etc.).

SECTION 5: LEARNING FROM FULL-TIME JOBS

THESE FULL-TIME JOBS OFFER THE OPPORTUNITY TO BUILD YOUR SKILL(S)

- ☐ **Fix-its / Turnarounds**

  The core demands to qualify as a Fix-it or Turnaround assignment are: 1. Cleaning up a mess. 2. Serious people issues/problems like credibility/performance/morale. 3. Tight deadline. 4. Serious business performance failure. 5. Last chance to fix. Four Types of Fix-its / Turnarounds: 1. Fixing a failed business/unit involving taking control, stopping losses, managing damage, planning the turnaround, dealing with people problems, installing new processes and systems, and rebuilding the spirit and performance of the unit. 2. Managing sizable disasters like mishandled labor negotiations and strikes, thefts, history of significant business losses, poor staff, failed leadership, hidden problems, fraud, public relations nightmares, etc. 3. Significant reorganization and restructuring (e.g., stabilizing the business, reforming unit, introducing new systems, making people changes, resetting strategy and tactics). 4. Significant system/process breakdown (e.g,. MIS, financial coordination processes, audits, standards, etc.) across units requiring working to change something from a distant position, providing advice and counsel, and installing or implementing a major process improvement or system change outside your own unit and/or with customers outside the organization.

☐ **Start-ups**
The core demands to qualify as a start from scratch are: 1. Starting something new for you and/or for the organization. 2. Forging a new team. 3. Creating new systems/facilities/staffs/programs/procedures. 4. Contextual adversity (e.g., uncertainty, government regulation, unions, difficult environment). Seven types of start from scratches: 1. Planning, building, hiring, and managing (e.g., building a new facility, opening up a new location, moving a unit or company). Heading something new (e.g., new product, new service, new line of business, new department/function, major new program). 3. Take over a group/product/service/program that had existed for less than a year and was off to a fast start. 4. Establishing overseas operations. 5. Major new designs for existing systems. 6. Moving a successful program from one unit to another. 7. Installing a new organization-wide process as a full-time job (e.g., like Total Quality).

☐ **Scale Assignments**
Core requirements to qualify as a Scale (size) shift assignment are: 1. Sizable jump-shift in the size of the job in areas like:- Number of people. - Number of layers in organization. - Size of budget. - Number of locations. - Volume of activity. - Tightness of deadlines. 2. Medium to low complexity; mostly repetitive and routine processes and procedures. 3. Stable staff and business. 4. Stable operations. 5. Often slow, steady growth.

SECTION 6: LEARNING MORE FROM YOUR PLAN

THESE ADDITIONAL REMEDIES WILL HELP MAKE THIS DEVELOPMENT PLAN MORE EFFECTIVE FOR YOU

Learning to Learn Better

☐ **Teach Others Something You Don't Know Well**
Commit to a project like teaching something you don't know much about to force you to learn quickly to accomplish the task; pick something new, different, or unfamiliar.

☐ **Commit to a Tight Timeframe to Accomplish Something**
Set some specific goals and tighter than usual timeframes for yourself and go after them with all you've got. Push yourself to stick to the plan; get more done than usual by adhering to a tight plan.

☐ **Study People Who Have Successfully Done What You Need to Do**
Interview people who have already done what you're planning to do and check your plan against what they did. Try to summarize their key tactics, strategies, and insights; adjust your plan accordingly.

☐ **Plan Backwards from the Ideal**
Envision what an ideal outcome would look like and plan backwards. What is the series of events that would have to take place to get

there? What would people do? What would have to be done? How would people react? How would things play out? Could you plan it forward and get to the same outcome?

- ☐ **Rehearse Successful Tactics/Strategies/Actions**
  Mentally rehearse how you will act before going into the situation. Try to anticipate how others will react, what they will say, and how you'll respond. Check out the best and worst cases; play out both scenes. Check your feelings in conflict or worst-case situations; rehearse staying under control.

- ☐ **Study Yourself in Detail**
  Study your likes and dislikes because they can drive a lot of your thinking, judging, and acting. Ask which like or dislike has gotten in the way or prevented you from moving to a higher level of learning. Are your likes and dislikes really important to you or have you just gone on "autopilot"? Try to address and understand a blocking dislike and change it.

- ☐ **Do Something on Gut Feel More Than Analysis**
  Act on "gut feel"; go with your hunches instead of careful planning. Take a chance on a solution; take some risks; try a number of things by trial and error and learn to deal with making some mistakes.

- ☐ **Sort Through Information Multiple Ways**
  Collect the data and arrange it in elements or pieces. Come up with definitions, and arrange the data in various ways: chronologically, from most to least, from biggest to smallest, from cold to hot, what you know most about and least about, from known to unknown, etc., until the meaning becomes obvious.

Learning from Experience, Feedback and Other People

- ☐ **Learning from Bosses**
  Bosses can be an excellent and ready source for learning. All bosses do some things exceptionally well and other things poorly. Distance your feelings from the boss/direct report relationship and study things that work and things that don't work for your boss. What would you have done? What could you use, and what should you avoid?

- ☐ **Learning from Interviewing Others**
  Interviewing others. Not only ask what they do, but how and why they do it. What do they think are the rules of thumb they are following? Where did they learn the behaviors? How do they keep them current? How do they monitor the effect they have on others?

SUGGESTED READINGS

Blohowiak, Donald W. *How's all the work going to get done?.* Franklin Lakes, NJ: Career Press, 1995.

Henry, Lauchland A. *The Professional's Guide to Working Smarter.* Tenafly, NJ: Burrill-Ellsworth Associates, 1993.

Hickman, Craig, Craig Bott, Marlon Berrett and Brad Angus. *The Fourth Dimension.* New York: John Wiley & Sons, Inc., 1996.

Hill, Linda A. *Becoming a Manager: How new managers master the challenges of leadership.* New York: Penguin USA, 1993.

Lester, Richard K. *The Productive Edge: How U.S. Industries are pointing the way to a new era of economic growth.* New York: W.W. Norton, 1998.

TIMELINESS OF DELIVERY OF OUTPUT

SECTION 1: YOUR DEVELOPMENT NEED(S)

General Definition: Timely delivery of goods and services in terms of schedules, deadlines, goals and targets without regard to other factors like quality and resourcefulness.

UNSKILLED

- ☐ Always among the last to finish
- ☐ Misses important deadlines by a significant amount and barely meet standard for others
- ☐ Among the slowest people or groups around

AVERAGE

- ☐ Produces most work on time
- ☐ Timeliness is acceptable and at standard
- ☐ Meets deadlines on most work; may miss on a few
- ☐ About as timely as most other people or groups

SKILLED

- ☐ Always the first or among the first to finish
- ☐ Even unreasonable or difficult time targets and goals are met and some are actually exceeded
- ☐ Sets the speed standard for the rest

OVERUSED SKILL

- ☐ So committed to meeting deadlines and getting things done on time that things get too intense
- ☐ As the delivery target comes closer things like quality or costs or morale suffer at the last minute
- ☐ Getting it done on time becomes too important

Select one to three of the competencies listed below to work on to compensate for an overuse of this skill.

COMPENSATORS: 11,17,23,33,36,37,39,41,42,50,52

SOME CAUSES

- ☐ Can't say no
- ☐ Disorganized
- ☐ Doesn't delegate
- ☐ Doesn't set priorities
- ☐ Not focused
- ☐ Not resourceful
- ☐ Perfectionist
- ☐ Procrastinator
- ☐ Rejects help
- ☐ Slow to make decisions
- ☐ Won't contest deadlines

THE MAP

Second in importance only to producing results is producing them on time. No one is ever performing in a vacuum. Everyone's work is just a step in a bigger chain of tasks and work. The results picture is only as good as the weakest link in the productivity chain. If your project or report or service is a day late, everyone past you will feel the pain. All beyond you will have to change their expectations and schedule. Being late will always cause frustration and irritation of all of the people down the work chain. Being timely, even sometimes at the expense of completeness or even quality, is a key virtue in today's fast-paced world. As Woody Allen says, being there on time is half of life.

SECTION 2: LEARNING ON YOUR OWN

THESE SELF-DEVELOPMENT REMEDIES WILL HELP YOU BUILD YOUR SKILL(S)

SOME REMEDIES

☐ **1. Perfectionist?** Need or prefer or want to be 100% sure? Want to make sure that all or at least most of your decisions are right? A lot of people prefer that. Perfectionism is tough to let go of because most people see it as a positive trait for them. They pride themselves on never being wrong. Recognize perfectionism for what it might be – collecting more information than others do to improve confidence in making a fault-free decision and thereby avoiding the risk and criticism that would come from making decisions faster. Anyone with a brain, unlimited time and 100% of the data can make good decisions. The real test is who can act the soonest, being right the most, with less than all the data. Some studies suggest even successful general managers are about 65% correct. If you need to be more timely, you need to reduce your own internal need for data and the need to be perfect. Try to decrease your need for data and your need to be right all the time slightly every week until you reach a more reasonable balance between thinking it through and taking action. Try making some small decisions on little or no data. Trust your intuition more.

Your experience won't let you stray too far. Let your brain do the calculations.

☐ **2. Procrastinator?** Are you a procrastinator? Get caught short on deadlines? Do it all at the last minute? Not only will you not be timely, your decision quality and accuracy will be poor. Procrastinators miss deadlines and performance targets. If you procrastinate, you might not produce consistent decisions. Start earlier. Always do 10% of thinking about the decision immediately after it is assigned so you can better gauge what it is going to take to finish the rest. Divide decisions into thirds or fourths and schedule time to work on them spaced over the delivery period. Remember one of Murphy's Laws. It takes 90% of the time to do 90% of the project, and another 90% of the time to finish the remaining 10%. Always leave more time than you think it's going to take. Set up checkpoints for yourself along the way. Schedule early data collection and analysis. Don't wait until the last moment. Set an internal deadline one week before the real one. *More help? – See #47 Planning.*

☐ **3. Disorganized?** Don't always get to everything on time? Forget deadlines? Lose requests for decisions? Under time pressure and increased uncertainty, you have to put the keel in the water yourself. You can't operate helter skelter and make quality timely decisions. You need to set tighter priorities. Focus more on the mission-critical few decisions. Don't get diverted by trivial work and other decisions. Get better organized and disciplined. Keep a decision log. When a decision opportunity surfaces, immediately log it along with the ideal date it needs to be made. Plan backwards to the work necessary to make the decision on time. If you are not disciplined in how you work and are sometimes late making decisions and taking action because of it, buy a book on both Total Quality Management and Process Re-Engineering. Go to one workshop on efficient and effective work design. *More help? – See #50 Priority Setting, #52 Process Management, #62 Time Management and #63 Total Quality Management/ Re-Engineering.*

☐ **4. Too cautious and conservative?** Analysis paralysis? Break out of your examine-it-to-death and always-take-the-safest-path mode and just do it. Increasing timeliness will increase errors and mistakes but it also will get more done faster. Develop a more philosophical stance toward failure/criticism. After all, most innovations fail, most proposals fail, most change efforts fail; anything worth doing takes repeated effort. The best tack when confronted with a mistake is to say, "What can we learn from this?" Ask yourself if your need to be cautious matches the requirements for speed and timeliness of your job. *More help? – See #45 Personal Learning.*

☐ **5. Stress and conflict under time pressure.** Some are energized by time pressure. Some are stressed by time pressure. It actually slows us down. We lose our anchor. We are not at our best when we are pushed. We get more anxious, frustrated, upset. Does time pressure bring out your emotional response? Write down why you get anxious under time pressure. What fears does it surface? Don't want to make a mistake? Afraid of the unknown consequences? Don't have the confidence to decide? When you get stressed, drop the problem for a moment. Go do something else. Come back to it when you are under better control. Let your brain work on it while you do something safer. *More help? – See # 11 Composure and #107 Lack of Composure.*

☐ **6. Don't like risk?** Sometimes taking action involves pushing the envelope, taking chances and trying bold new initiatives. Doing those things leads to more misfires and mistakes. Research says that successful executives have made more mistakes in their careers than those who aren't successful. Treat any mistakes or failures as chances to learn. Nothing ventured, nothing gained. Up your risk comfort. Start small so you can recover more quickly. Go for small wins. Don't blast into a major task to prove your boldness. Break it down into smaller tasks. Take the easiest one for you first. Then build up to the tougher ones. Review each one to see what you did well and not well, and set goals so you'll do something differently and better each time. End up accomplishing the big goal and taking the bold action. Challenge yourself. See how creative you can be in taking action a number of different ways. *More help? – See #14 Creativity, #28 Innovation Management, and #2 Dealing with Ambiguity.*

☐ **7. Set better priorities.** You may not have the correct set of priorities. Some people take action but on the wrong things. Effective managers typically spend about half their time on two or three key priorities. What should you spend half your time on? Can you name five things that you have to do that are less critical? If you can't, you're not differentiating well. People without priorities see their jobs as 97 things that need to be done right now – that will actually slow you down. Pick a few mission critical things and get them done. Don't get diverted by trivia. *More help? – See #50 Priority Setting.*

☐ **8. Afraid to get others involved?** Taking action requires that you get others on board. Work on your influence and selling skills. Lay out the business reason for the action. Think about how you can help everybody win with the action. Get others involved before you have to take action. Involved people are easier to influence. Learn better negotiation skills. Learn to bargain and trade. *More help? – See #31 Interpersonal Savvy, #37 Negotiating, and #39 Organizing.*

☐ **9. Not committed?** Maybe you are giving as much to work as you care to give. Maybe you have made a life/work balance decision that leads you to a fair day's work for a fair day's pay mode of operating. No more. No less. That is an admirable decision, certainly one you can and should make. Problem is, you may be in a job where that's not enough. Otherwise people would not have given you this rating. You might want to talk to your boss to get transferred to a more comfortable job for you, one that doesn't take as much effort and require as much action initiation on your part. You may even think about moving down to the job level where your balance between quality of life and the effort and hours required of you at work are more balanced.

☐ **10. Lay out the process.** Most well running processes start out with a plan. What do I need to accomplish? What's the timeline? What resources will I need? Who controls the resources – people, funding, tools, materials, support – I need? What's my currency? How can I pay for or repay the resources I need? Who wins if I win? Who might lose? Buy a flow charting software program like ABC FlowCharter® that does PERT and GANT charts. Become an expert in its use. Use the output of the software to communicate your plans to others. Use the flow charts in your presentations. Nothing helps move a process along better than a good plan. It helps the people who have to work under the plan. It leads to better use of resources. It gets things done faster. It helps anticipate problems before they occur. Lay out the work from A to Z. Many people are seen as lacking because they don't write the sequence or parts of the work and leave something out. Ask others to comment on your ordering and note what's missing. *More help? – See #47 Planning and #63 Total Quality Management/Re-Engineering.*

SECTION 3: LEARNING FROM MORE FEEDBACK

THESE SOURCES WOULD GIVE YOU THE MOST ACCURATE AND DETAILED FEEDBACK ON YOUR SKILL(S)

☐ **Direct Reports**
Across a variety of settings, your direct reports probably see you the most. They are the recipients of most of your managerial behaviors. They know your work. They can compare you with former bosses. Since they may hesitate to give you negative feedback, you have to set the atmosphere to make it easier for them. You have to ask.

☐ **Direct Boss**
Your direct boss has important information about you, your performance, and your prospects. The challenge is to get this information. There are formal processes (e.g., performance appraisals). There are day-to-day opportunities. To help, signal your boss that you want and can handle direct and timely feedback. Many bosses have trouble giving feedback, so you will have to work at it over a period of time.

☐ **Past Associates/Constituencies**
When confronted with a present performance problem, some claim, "I wasn't like that before; it must be the current situation." When feedback is available from former associates, about 50 percent support that

claim. In the other half of the cases, the people were like that before and probably didn't know it. It sometimes makes sense to access the past to clearly see the present.

- ☐ **Natural Mentors**
Natural Mentors have a special relationship with you and are interested in your success and your future. Since they are usually not in your direct chain of command, you can have more open, relaxed, and fruitful discussions about yourself and your career prospects. They can be a very important source for candid or critical feedback others may not give you.

- ☐ **Peers and Colleagues**
Peers and colleagues have a special social and working relationship. They attend staff meetings together, share private views, get feedback from the same boss, travel together, and are knowledgeable about each other's work. You perhaps let your guard down more around peers and act more like yourself. They can be a valuable source of feedback.

SECTION 4: LEARNING FROM DEVELOP-IN-PLACE ASSIGNMENTS

THESE PART-TIME DEVELOP-IN-PLACE ASSIGNMENTS WILL HELP YOU BUILD YOUR SKILL(S)

- ☐ Manage a dissatisfied internal or external customer; troubleshoot a performance or quality problem with a product or service.
- ☐ Take on a tough and undoable project, one where others who have tried it have failed.
- ☐ Manage an ad hoc, temporary group of balky and resisting people through an unpopular change or project.
- ☐ Manage an ad hoc, temporary group of people involved in tackling a fix-it or turnaround project.
- ☐ Relaunch an existing product or service that's not doing well.
- ☐ Manage an ad hoc, temporary group of low-competence people through a task they couldn't do by themselves.
- ☐ Assign a project to a group with a tight deadline.
- ☐ Integrate diverse systems, processes, or procedures across decentralized and/or dispersed units.
- ☐ Manage a cost-cutting project.
- ☐ Manage the renovation of an office, floor, building, meeting room, warehouse, etc.

SECTION 5: LEARNING FROM FULL-TIME JOBS

THESE FULL-TIME JOBS OFFER THE OPPORTUNITY TO BUILD YOUR SKILL(S)

☐ **Fix-its/Turnarounds**

The core demands to qualify as a Fix-it or Turnaround assignment are: 1. Cleaning up a mess. 2. Serious people issues/problems like credibility/performance/morale. 3. Tight deadline. 4.Serious business performance failure. 5. Last chance to fix. Four Types of Fix-its / Turnarounds: 1. Fixing a failed business/unit involving taking control, stopping losses, managing damage, planning the turnaround, dealing with people problems, installing new processes and systems, and rebuilding the spirit and performance of the unit. 2. Managing sizable disasters like mishandled labor negotiations and strikes, thefts, history of significant business losses, poor staff, failed leadership, hidden problems, fraud, public relations nightmares, etc. 3. Significant reorganization and restructuring (e.g., stabilizing the business, reforming unit, introducing new systems, making people changes, resetting strategy and tactics). 4. Significant system/process breakdown (e.g,. MIS, financial coordination processes, audits, standards, etc.) across units requiring working to change something from a distant position, providing advice and counsel, and installing or implementing a major process improvement or system change outside your own unit and/or with customers outside the organization.

☐ **Start-ups**

The core demands to qualify as a start from scratch are: 1. Starting something new for you and/or for the organization. 2. Forging a new team. 3. Creating new systems/facilities/staffs/programs/procedures. 4. Contextual adversity (e.g., uncertainty, government regulation, unions, difficult environment). Seven types of start from scratches: 1. Planning, building, hiring, and managing (e.g., building a new facility, opening up a new location, moving a unit or company). 2. Heading something new (e.g., new product, new service, new line of business, new department/function, major new program). 3. Take over a group/product/service/program that had existed for less than a year and was off to a fast start. 4. Establishing overseas operations. 5. Major new designs for existing systems. 6. Moving a successful program from one unit to another. 7. Installing a new organization-wide process as a full-time job (e.g., like Total Quality).

☐ **Scale Assignments**

Core requirements to qualify as a Scale (size) shift assignment are: 1. Sizable jump-shift in the size of the job in areas like: - Number of people. - Number of layers in organization. - Size of budget. - Number of locations. - Volume of activity. - Tightness of deadlines. 2. Medium to low complexity; mostly repetitive and routine processes and procedures. 3. Stable staff and business. 4. Stable operations. 5. Often slow, steady growth.

SECTION 6: LEARNING MORE FROM YOUR PLAN

THESE ADDITIONAL REMEDIES WILL HELP MAKE THIS DEVELOPMENT PLAN MORE EFFECTIVE FOR YOU

Learning to Learn Better

☐ **Monitoring Yourself More Closely and Get Off Your Autopilot**
Past habits are a mixed blessing, sometimes helping, sometimes not. To avoid putting yourself on "autopilot," think afresh about each situation before acting. Consistently monitor yourself with questions. Is this task different? Ask why you would repeat a past action. Are you avoiding anything, like taking a chance? Is there something new you might try?

☐ **Be Alert to Learnings When Faced With Transitions**
To avoid applying rigid habits, be alert to situations that require a transition to a new set of conditions and reactions; check what's similar and what's different; think out which past lessons and rules apply and which need to be changed. Don't apply old solutions because you have missed subtle differences.

☐ **Plan Backwards from the Ideal**
Envision what an ideal outcome would look like and plan backwards. What is the series of events that would have to take place to get there? What would people do? What would have to be done? How would people react? How would things play out? Could you plan it forward and get to the same outcome?

☐ **Do Something on Gut Feel More Than Analysis**
Act on "gut feel"; go with your hunches instead of careful planning. Take a chance on a solution; take some risks; try a number of things by trial and error and learn to deal with making some mistakes.

☐ **Sort Through Information Multiple Ways**
Collect the data and arrange it in elements or pieces. Come up with definitions, and arrange the data in various ways: chronologically, from most to least, from biggest to smallest, from cold to hot, what you know most about and least about, from known to unknown, etc., until the meaning becomes obvious.

☐ **Look for the Simplest Explanation, Find the Essence**
Put all the complexity aside and ask yourself: what's the most obvious thing this problem could be. What is the most obvious thing to do? Who is the most obvious person to talk to? What is the simplest explanation possible? What's at the essence of the problem?

Learning from Experience, Feedback and Other People

☐ **Learning from Bosses**
Bosses can be an excellent and ready source for learning. All bosses do some things exceptionally well and other things poorly. Distance your feelings from the boss/direct report relationship and study things that

work and things that don't work for your boss. What would you have done? What could you use, and what should you avoid?

- ☐ **Methods of Learning from Others**
  Interviewing others. Not only ask what they do, but how and why they do it. What do they think are the rules of thumb they are following? Where did they learn the behaviors? How do they keep them current? How do they monitor the effect they have on others?

- ☐ **Learning from Observing Others**
  Observe others. Find opportunities to observe without interacting with your model. This enables you to objectively study the person, note what he/she is doing or not doing, and compare that with what you would typically do in similar situations. Many times you can learn more by watching than asking. Your model may not be able to explain what he/she does or may be an unwilling teacher.

Learning from Courses

- ☐ **Insight Events**
  These are courses designed around assessing skills and providing feedback to the participants. These events can be a powerful source of self-knowledge and can lead to significant development if done right. When selecting a self-insight course, consider the following: (1) Are the skills assessed the important ones? (2) Are the assessment techniques and instruments sound? (3) Are those who are providing the feedback trained and professional? (4) Is the feedback provided in a user-friendly and "actionable" format? (5) Does the feedback include development planning? (6) Is the setting comfortable and conducive to reflection and learning? (7) Are the other participants the kinds of people you could learn from? (8) Are you in the right frame of mind to learn from this kind of intense experience? Select events on the basis of positive answers to these 8 questions.

SUGGESTED READINGS

Fine, Charles H. *Clock Speed – Winning Industry Control in the Age of Temporary Advantage.* Reading, MA: Perseus Books, 1998.

Sapadin, Linda with Jack Maguire. *It's about time!: the six styles of procrastination and how to overcome them.* New York: Viking, 1996.

Smith, Hyrum W. *The 10 natural laws of successful time and life management: proven strategies for increased productivity and inner peace.* New York, NY: Warner Books, 1994.

Smith, Preston G. and Donald G. Reinertsen. *Developing Products in Half the Time.* New York: VanNostrand Reinhold, 1991.

Continued

Stalk, George Jr. and Thomas M. Hout. *Competing Against Time.* New York: Macmillan, Inc., 1990.

Williams, Paul B. *Getting a Project Done on Time.* New York: AMACOM, 1996.

Wright, Russell. *A little bit at a time.* Berkeley: Ten Speed Press, 1990.

83

QUALITY OF WORK OUTPUT

SECTION 1: YOUR DEVELOPMENT NEED(S)

General Definition: The quality of goods and services produced in terms of errors, waste and rework required to meet standards, not considering other things like timeliness or quantity.

UNSKILLED

- ☐ Produces work that's below the quality standard
- ☐ Contains notable and sloppy errors
- ☐ Usually requires rework before it can be used and then barely meets average minimum quality standards or specifications

AVERAGE

- ☐ Produces work that is of reasonable quality
- ☐ Most is acceptable, with a few errors and rework
- ☐ Occasionally not quite up to standard with some waste of time or resources

SKILLED

- ☐ The quality of the work from this person or group is always among the best
- ☐ Produces work that is mostly error free the first time with little waste or redone work

OVERUSED SKILL

- ☐ Produces very high quality work but perfectionism leads to lower productivity, some missed deadlines, using too many resources to finish or taking too long to get there
- ☐ Quality standards exceed what's reasonable

Select one to three of the competencies listed below to work on to compensate for an overuse of this skill.

COMPENSATORS: 1,2,16,39,40,51,52

SOME CAUSES

- ☐ Impatient
- ☐ Not aligned or committed
- ☐ Not customer oriented
- ☐ "Not invented here" behavior
- ☐ Not planful
- ☐ Not results oriented
- ☐ Not skilled enough
- ☐ Rejects help
- ☐ Rejects suggestions
- ☐ Stuck in the old ways
- ☐ Won't delegate

THE MAP

Things that work as expected please customers – internal or external. Doing things right, especially the first time, avoids waste, rework and the consequences of disappointment. Undershooting the expectations of the customers of your tasks, projects or services almost always will have bad downstream consequences for you and those you work with. Whatever price you save for yourself by producing or being part of producing below-standard work will just have to be redone at a higher cost than before. It will take you more time and resources in total to produce and fix your work than it would take to do it right the first time.

SECTION 2: LEARNING ON YOUR OWN

THESE SELF-DEVELOPMENT REMEDIES WILL HELP YOU BUILD YOUR SKILL(S)

SOME REMEDIES

☐ **1. Learn the principles.** There are many sources available. Read about methods put forth by Deming, Juran, Crosby, Hammer and Champy and countless others. There are numerous conferences and workshops you can attend. It's best to get a sampling of what everybody thinks and then create your own version for your specific situation.

☐ **2. Be customer driven.** In a free enterprise system, the customer is king; those who please the customer best win. The same is true with internal customers; those who please them most will win. Winners are always customer oriented and responsive. Pleasing the reasonable needs of customers is fairly straightforward. First you need to know what they want and expect; the best way to do that is to ask them, then deliver that in a timely way at a price/value that's acceptable to them. Get in the habit of meeting with your internal or external customers on a regular basis to set up a dialogue; they need to feel free to contact you about problems and you need to be able to contact them for essential information. Also, get out in front of your customers; try to anticipate their needs for your products and services before they even know about them; provide your customers with positive surprises – features they weren't expecting, delivery in a shorter time, more than they ordered. *More help? – See #15 Customer Focus.*

☐ **3. Always design your work and manage your time from the customer in, not from you out.** Your best efforts will always be determined by your customers, not you. Try not to design and arrange what you do only from your own view; always try to know and take the viewpoint of your customer first; you will always win following that rule.

☐ **4. Delegate and empower others to help design the best work flows** to produce zero defect products and services that meet the needs of your customers. This is a known process, well documented, and available to all who wish to implement its principles. *More help? – See # 35 Managing and Measuring Work and #52 Process Management.*

☐ **5. Look at your own personal work habits.** Are they designed for maximum effectiveness and efficiency? Is there room for some continuous improvement? Are you applying the principles you have learned to yourself? Remember, this is one of the major reasons why these efforts fail.

☐ **6. Think of yourself as a dissatisfied customer.** Write down all of the unsatisfactory things that have happened to you as a customer during the past month. Things like delays, orders not right, cost not as promised, phone calls not returned, cold food, bad service, inattentive clerks, out of stock items, etc. Would your customers report any of these problems? Then do a study of your lost customers. Find out what the three key problems were and see how quickly you can eliminate 50% of the difficulties that caused them to depart. Study your competitors' foul-ups and see what you can do to both avoid them in your own organization and make your organization more attractive. *More help? – See #15 Customer Focus.*

☐ **7. Lay out the process.** Most well running processes start out with a plan. What do I need to accomplish? What's the timeline? What resources will I need? Who controls the resources – people, funding, tools, materials, support – I need? What's my currency? How can I pay for or repay the resources I need? Who wins if I win? Who might lose? Buy a flow charting software program like ABC FlowCharter® that does PERT and GANT charts. Become an expert in its use. Use the output of the software to communicate your plans to others. Use the flow charts in your presentations. Nothing helps move a process along better than a good plan. It helps the people who have to work under the plan. It leads to better use of resources. It gets things done faster. It helps anticipate problems before they occur. Lay out the work from A to Z. Many people are seen as lacking because they don't write the sequence or parts of the work and leave something out. Ask others to comment on your ordering and note what's missing. *More help? – See #47 Planning and #63 Total Quality Management/Re-Engineering.*

☐ **8. Results oriented impatience.** The style that chills sound problem solving the most is the results driven, time short and impatient person. He/she does not take the time to define problems and tends to take the first close enough solution that comes along. Studies have shown that on average, the solution somewhere between the second and third one generated is the best. Impatient people don't wait that long. Slow down. Discipline yourself to pause for enough time to define the problem better and always think of three solutions before you pick one.

☐ **9. Asking others for input.** Many try to do too much themselves. They don't delegate, listen or ask others for input. Even if you think you have the solution, ask some others for input just to make sure. Access your network. Find someone who makes a good sounding board and talk to her/him, not just for ideas, but to increase your understanding of the problem. Or do it more formally. Set up a competition between two teams, both acting as your advisors. Call a problem-solving meeting and give the group two hours to come up with something that will at least be tried. Find a buddy group in another function or organization that faces the same or a similar problem and both of you experiment.

☐ **10. Are you organized and planful?** Can people follow what you want? Do you lay out work and tasks to be done clearly? Do you set clear goals and objectives that can guide their work? *More help? – See #35 Managing and Measuring Work and #47 Planning.*

SECTION 3: LEARNING FROM MORE FEEDBACK

THESE SOURCES WOULD GIVE YOU THE MOST ACCURATE AND DETAILED FEEDBACK ON YOUR SKILL(S)

☐ **Direct Boss**
Your direct boss has important information about you, your performance, and your prospects. The challenge is to get this information. There are formal processes (e.g., performance appraisals). There are day-to-day opportunities. To help, signal your boss that you want and can handle direct and timely feedback. Many bosses have trouble giving feedback, so you will have to work at it over a period of time.

☐ **Past Associates/Constituencies**
When confronted with a present performance problem, some claim, "I wasn't like that before; it must be the current situation." When feed-

back is available from former associates, about 50 percent support that claim. In the other half of the cases, the people were like that before and probably didn't know it. It sometimes makes sense to access the past to clearly see the present.

☐ **Direct Reports**
Across a variety of settings, your direct reports probably see you the most. They are the recipients of most of your managerial behaviors. They know your work. They can compare you with former bosses. Since they may hesitate to give you negative feedback, you have to set the atmosphere to make it easier for them. You have to ask.

☐ **Human Resource Professionals**
Human Resource professionals have both a formal and informal feedback role. Since they have access to unique and confidential information, they can provide the right context for feedback you've received. Sometimes they may be "directed" to give you feedback. Other times, they may pass on feedback just to be helpful to you.

☐ **Peers and Colleagues**
Peers and colleagues have a special social and working relationship. They attend staff meetings together, share private views, get feedback from the same boss, travel together, and are knowledgeable about each other's work. You perhaps let your guard down more around peers and act more like yourself. They can be a valuable source of feedback.

☐ **Internal and External Customers**
Customers interact with you as a person and as a supplier or vendor of products and services. You're important to them because you can either help address and solve their problems or stand in their way. As customer service and Total Quality programs gain importance, clients and customers become a more prominent source of feedback.

SECTION 4: LEARNING FROM DEVELOP-IN-PLACE ASSIGNMENTS

THESE PART-TIME DEVELOP-IN-PLACE ASSIGNMENTS WILL HELP YOU BUILD YOUR SKILL(S)

☐ Relaunch an existing product or service that's not doing well.

☐ Manage an ad hoc, temporary group of people involved in tackling a fix-it or turnaround project.

☐ Plan a new site for a building (plant, field office headquarters, etc.).

☐ Manage the purchase of a major product, equipment, materials, program, or system.

☐ Manage a dissatisfied internal or external customer; troubleshoot a performance or quality problem with a product or service.

- ☐ Visit Malcolm Baldrige National Quality Award or Deming prize winners and report back on your findings, showing how they would help your organization.
- ☐ Work on a team looking at a reorganization plan where there will be more people than positions.
- ☐ Do a competitive analysis of your organization's products or services or your position in the marketplace and present it to the people involved.
- ☐ Train customers in the use of the organization's products or services.
- ☐ Work on a process-simplification team to take steps and costs out of a process.

SECTION 5: LEARNING FROM FULL-TIME JOBS

THESE FULL-TIME JOBS OFFER THE OPPORTUNITY TO BUILD YOUR SKILL(S)

☐ **Start-ups**

The core demands to qualify as a start from scratch are: 1. Starting something new for you and/or for the organization. 2. Forging a new team. 3. Creating new systems/facilities/staffs/programs/procedures. 4. Contextual adversity (e.g., uncertainty, government regulation, unions, difficult environment). Seven types of start from scratches: 1. Planning, building, hiring, and managing (e.g., building a new facility, opening up a new location, moving a unit or company). 2. Heading something new (e.g., new product, new service, new line of business, new department/function, major new program). 3. Take over a group/product/service/program that had existed for less than a year and was off to a fast start. 4. Establishing overseas operations. 5. Major new designs for existing systems. 6. Moving a successful program from one unit to another. 7. Installing a new organization-wide process as a full-time job (e.g., like Total Quality).

☐ **Fix-its / Turnarounds**

The core demands to qualify as a Fix-it or Turnaround assignment are: 1. Cleaning up a mess. 2. Serious people issues/problems like credibility/performance/morale. 3. Tight deadline. 4. Serious business performance failure. 5. Last chance to fix. Four Types of Fix-its / Turnarounds: 1. Fixing a failed business/unit involving taking control, stopping losses, managing damage, planning the turnaround, dealing with people problems, installing new processes and systems, and rebuilding the spirit and performance of the unit. 2. Managing sizable disasters like mishandled labor negotiations and strikes, thefts, history of significant business losses, poor staff, failed leadership, hidden problems, fraud, public relations nightmares, etc. 3. Significant reorganization and restructuring (e.g., stabilizing the business, re-forming unit, introducing new systems, making people changes, resetting strategy and tactics). 4. Significant system/process breakdown (e.g,. MIS, financial coordination processes, audits, standards, etc.)

across units requiring working to change something from a distant position, providing advice and counsel, and installing or implementing a major process improvement or system change outside your own unit and/or with customers outside the organization.

- [ ] **Scale Assignments**
  Core requirements to qualify as a Scale (size) shift assignment are: 1. Sizable jump-shift in the size of the job in areas like: - Number of people. - Number of layers in organization. - Size of budget. - Number of locations. - Volume of activity. - Tightness of deadlines. 2. Medium to low complexity; mostly repetitive and routine processes and procedures. 3. Stable staff and business. 4. Stable operations. 5. Often slow, steady growth.

SECTION 6: LEARNING MORE FROM YOUR PLAN

THESE ADDITIONAL REMEDIES WILL HELP MAKE THIS DEVELOPMENT PLAN MORE EFFECTIVE FOR YOU

Learning to Learn Better

- [ ] **Find a Parallel to the Current Problem and Learn From It**
  Find a parallel with similar situations, whether in your field or in other areas, past or present, and look for comparison or contrast points to see what else has or hasn't worked. Search especially for the reasons why certain things work and others don't across different situations; find the common and uncommon elements.
- [ ] **Analyze Your Past Successes for Insights and Learnings**
  Look at your accomplishments in detail. Ask why they came off well. What did you do that directly led to positive outcomes? Are they repeatable in other situations? How much was attributable to the context itself, how much to the work of others, and how much to you? Was it a windfall win? What lessons and rules of thumb can you take away from these successes?
- [ ] **Analyze Your Past Failures for Insights and Learnings**
  Field-strip your mistakes and failures; ask what you did that contributed to the negative outcome; how could it have been avoided; how much was due to the context; what lessons and rules of thumb can you take away from the mistake or failure?
- [ ] **Analyze Mistakes Immediately and Learn from Them**
  Avoid mistakes, yes, but don't pass up the opportunity to learn from them. It's important to examine closely the reasons for the negative outcome. Do you need a small adjustment or a major change next time? Were there extenuating circumstances? How much an influence was the context, how much was you?

☐ **Plan Backwards from the Ideal**
Envision what an ideal outcome would look like and plan backwards. What is the series of events that would have to take place to get there? What would people do? What would have to be done? How would people react? How would things play out? Could you plan it forward and get to the same outcome?

☐ **Look Beyond Your First Solution to a Problem**
Don't always take the first action you think of. Look further for a second and third: What's different? Might the second or third be more effective? Research shows that the best solution lies somewhere between the second and third strategies or approaches. Your first solution is often an "autopilot" response and may not be the best.

☐ **Form an Advisory Group to Help You**
Assemble a one-time ad hoc group of people you respect and ask them for help solving or facing a significant issue. Outline what you know about it and ask the team to lay out a plan. Have them examine your thinking and suggest changes and improvements.

☐ **Sort Through Information Multiple Ways**
Collect the data and arrange it in elements or pieces. Come up with definitions, and arrange the data in various ways: chronologically, from most to least, from biggest to smallest, from cold to hot, what you know most about and least about, from known to unknown, etc., until the meaning becomes obvious.

Learning from Experience, Feedback and Other People

☐ **Using Multiple Models**
Who do you know who exemplifies how to do whatever your need is? Who, for example, personifies decisiveness or compassion or strategic agility? Think more broadly than your current job and colleagues. For example, ministers, friends, spouses or community leaders are also good sources for potential models. Select your models not on the basis of overall excellence or likeability, but on the basis of the one towering strength (or glaring weakness) you are interested in. Even people who are well thought of usually have only one or two towering strengths (or glaring weaknesses). Ordinarily, you won't learn as much from the whole person as you will from one characteristic.

☐ **Openness to Feedback**
Nothing discourages feedback more than defensiveness, resistance, irritation, and excuses. People don't like giving feedback anyway, and much less to those who don't listen or are unreceptive. To help the feedback giver, be open, listen, ask for examples and details, take notes, keep a journal, and thank them for their interest.

SUGGESTED READINGS

Byham, William C. and Jeff Cox. *HeroZ: empower yourself, your coworkers, your company.* New York: Harmony Books, 1994.

Hammer, Michael. *Beyond Reengineering.* New York: HarperCollins, 1996.

Hodgetts, Richard M. *Measures of quality and high performance.* New York: AMACOM, 1998.

Hronec, Steven M. and Arthur Anderson and Company. *Vital Signs – Using quality, time and cost performance measurements to chart your company's future.* New York: AMACOM, 1993.

Lynch, Richard L. and Kevin F. Cross. *Measure Up! Yardsticks for continuous improvement.* Cambridge, MA: Basil Blackwell, 1991.

Merrill, Peter. *Do it right the second time: benchmarking best practices in the quality change process.* Portland, OR: Productivity Press, 1997.

Risher, Howard and Charles Fay, Editors. *The Performance Imperative: Strategies for enhancing workforce effectiveness.* San Francisco: Jossey-Bass, 1995.

Walton, Mary. *The Deming Management Method.* New York: Putnam Publishing, 1986.

Walton, Mary. *Deming Management at Work.* New York: Putnam Publishing, 1990.

84

USE OF RESOURCES

SECTION 1: YOUR DEVELOPMENT NEED(S)

General Definition: The efficiency of use of time, money, materials and people to produce the required goods and services without considering other factors like timeliness or quality.

UNSKILLED

- ☐ Uses resources inefficiently and even with the additional resources, just meets minimum standards
- ☐ Usually over budget on everything or significantly over on some and on budget on others
- ☐ Wastes time, money, material and people's productivity

AVERAGE

- ☐ Most work comes in on budget, with efficient and as planned use of materials and people
- ☐ Some work may come in over budget
- ☐ About as resourceful as most other people or groups

SKILLED

- ☐ Uses fewer resources in terms of time, material, money and people than almost any other group
- ☐ Gets more things done with less
- ☐ A model of resourcefulness
- ☐ Always or almost always comes in significantly under budget in all areas

OVERUSED SKILL

- ☐ Although this person or group comes in on or even below budget, sometimes this is at the price of lower quantity or quality
- ☐ So concerned with making or beating the budget plan that other things suffer
- ☐ May cut corners on costs so tight that there are problems later in the work flow

Select one to three of the competencies listed below to work on to compensate for an overuse of this skill.

COMPENSATORS: 15,17,39,42,50,52,53,63

SOME CAUSES

- ☐ Difficulty saying no
- ☐ Disorganized
- ☐ Exceeds quality standards
- ☐ Impatient
- ☐ Inexperienced
- ☐ Not planful
- ☐ Poor delegation
- ☐ Rejects help
- ☐ Rejects suggestions
- ☐ Slow decision-making

THE MAP

Most anyone can produce results on time given infinite resources. The real trick is to get things done on time with the least resources you can. The rewards eventually go to those that get more done with less. There is an ever-increasing demand on limited resources. Downsizing. Trimming costs. Being the low cost producer. Many people and projects are competing for limited resources. Going global absorbs a lot of investment spending. Being resourceful includes realistic planning and estimating, clean goal setting and planning, smart and hard work, the efficient use of ready resources, the creative use of allied resources and the effective management of time.

SECTION 2: LEARNING ON YOUR OWN

THESE SELF-DEVELOPMENT REMEDIES WILL HELP YOU BUILD YOUR SKILL(S)

SOME REMEDIES

☐ **1. Set goals and measures.** Nothing keeps projects on time and on budget like a goal and a measure. Set goals for the whole project and the sub tasks. Set measures so you and others can track progress against the goals. *More help? – See #35 Managing and Measuring Work.*

☐ **2. Laying out the work.** Most resourcefulness starts out with a plan. What do I need to accomplish? What's the timeline? What resources will I need? Who controls the resources – people, funding, tools, materials, support – I need? What's my currency? How can I pay for or repay the resources I need? Who wins if I win? Who might lose? Lay out the work from A to Z. Many people are seen as disorganized because they don't write the sequence or parts of the work and leave something out. Ask others to comment on your ordering and note what's missing.

☐ **3. Bargaining for resources.** What do I have to trade? What can I buy? What can I borrow? What do I need to trade for? What do I need that I can't pay or trade for?

☐ **4. Delegating.** Getting long, complex or multi-tracked projects done involves accomplishing a series of tasks that lead up to the whole. One clear finding in the research is that empowered people work longer and harder. People like to have control over their work, determine how they are going to do it, and have the authority to make decisions. Give away as much as possible along with the authority that goes with it. Another clear finding is to pay attention to the weakest links – usually groups or elements you have the least interface with or control over – perhaps someone in a remote location, a consultant or supplier. Stay doubly in touch with the potential weak links.

☐ **5. Manage efficiently**. Watch the budget. Plan spending carefully. Have a reserve if the unanticipated comes up. Set up a funding timeline so you can track ongoing expenditures.

☐ **6. Be a student of the work flows** and processes around you at airports, restaurants, hotels, supermarkets, government services, etc. As a customer, how would you design those things differently to make them more effective and efficient? What principles would you follow? Apply those same principles to your own work.

☐ **7. More what and why, less how.** The best delegators are crystal clear on what and when, and more open on how. People are more motivated when they can determine the how for themselves. Inexperienced delegators include the hows, which turns the people into task automatons instead of an empowered and energized staff. Tell them what and when and for how long and let them figure out how on their own. Give them leeway. Encourage them to try things. Besides being more motivating, it's also more developmental for them. Add the larger context. Although knowing the context may not be necessary to get the task done, people are more motivated when they know where this task fits in the bigger picture. Take three extra minutes and tell them why this task needs to be done, where it fits in the grander scheme and its importance to the goals and objectives of the unit.

☐ **8. Manage your time efficiently.** Plan your time and manage against it. Be time sensitive. Value time. Figure out what you are worth per hour and minute by taking your gross salary plus overhead and benefits. Attach a monetary value on your time. Then ask, is this worth $56 of my time? Figure out what your three largest time wasters are and reduce them 50% by batching activities and using efficient communications like E-mail and voice mail for routine matters.

☐ **9. Others will always ask you to do more than you can do.** An important time saver is the ability to constructively say no. One technique you can use is to ask the requester which of the other things they have asked you to do would they like to cancel or delay in order to do the most recent request. That way you say both yes and no and let the requester choose.

☐ **10. Too dependent upon yourself.** Look at others' solutions more. Invite discussion and disagreement, welcome bad news, ask that people come up with the second and third solution. A useful trick is to assign issues and questions before you have given them any thought. Two weeks before you are due to decide, before you have a solution in mind, ask your people to examine the issue and report to you two days before you have to deal with it. This really motivates people and makes you look less impatient.

SECTION 3: LEARNING FROM MORE FEEDBACK

THESE SOURCES WOULD GIVE YOU THE MOST ACCURATE AND DETAILED FEEDBACK ON YOUR SKILL(S)

☐ **Past Associates/Constituencies**
When confronted with a present performance problem, some claim, "I wasn't like that before; it must be the current situation." When feedback is available from former associates, about 50 percent support that claim. In the other half of the cases, the people were like that before and probably didn't know it. It sometimes makes sense to access the past to clearly see the present.

☐ **Direct Reports**
Across a variety of settings, your direct reports probably see you the most. They are the recipients of most of your managerial behaviors. They know your work. They can compare you with former bosses. Since they may hesitate to give you negative feedback, you have to set the atmosphere to make it easier for them. You have to ask.

☐ **Direct Boss**
Your direct boss has important information about you, your performance, and your prospects. The challenge is to get this information. There are formal processes (e.g., performance appraisals). There are day-to-day opportunities. To help, signal your boss that you want and can handle direct and timely feedback. Many bosses have trouble giving feedback, so you will have to work at it over a period of time.

☐ **Natural Mentors**
Natural Mentors have a special relationship with you and are interested in your success and your future. Since they are usually not in your direct chain of command, you can have more open, relaxed, and fruitful discussions about yourself and your career prospects. They can be a very important source for candid or critical feedback others may not give you.

☐ **Peers and Colleagues**
Peers and colleagues have a special social and working relationship. They attend staff meetings together, share private views, get feedback from the same boss, travel together, and are knowledgeable about each other's work. You perhaps let your guard down more around

peers and act more like yourself. They can be a valuable source of feedback.

- ☐ **Human Resource Professionals**
  Human Resource professionals have both a formal and informal feedback role. Since they have access to unique and confidential information, they can provide the right context for feedback you've received. Sometimes they may be "directed" to give you feedback. Other times, they may pass on feedback just to be helpful to you.

SECTION 4: LEARNING FROM DEVELOP-IN-PLACE ASSIGNMENTS

THESE PART-TIME DEVELOP-IN-PLACE ASSIGNMENTS WILL HELP YOU BUILD YOUR SKILL(S)

- ☐ Plan a new site for a building (plant, field office, headquarters, etc.).
- ☐ Manage the purchase of a major product, equipment, materials, program, or system.
- ☐ Manage an ad hoc, temporary group of balky and resisting people through an unpopular change or project.
- ☐ Manage an ad hoc, temporary group of people involved in tackling a fix-it or turnaround project.
- ☐ Help shut down a plant, regional office, product line, business, operation, etc.
- ☐ Manage a dissatisfied internal or external customer; troubleshoot a performance or quality problem with a product or service.
- ☐ Manage a cost-cutting project.
- ☐ Plan for and start up something small (secretarial pool, athletic program, suggestion system, program, etc.).
- ☐ Install a new process or system (computer system, new policies, new process, new procedures, etc.).
- ☐ Work on a process-simplification team to take steps and costs out of a process.

SECTION 5: LEARNING FROM FULL-TIME JOBS

THESE FULL-TIME JOBS OFFER THE OPPORTUNITY TO BUILD YOUR SKILL(S)

- ☐ **Fix-its/Turnarounds**
  The core demands to qualify as a Fix-it or Turnaround assignment are: 1. Cleaning up a mess. 2. Serious people issues/problems like credibility/performance/morale. 3. Tight deadline. 4. Serious business performance failure. 5. Last chance to fix. Four Types of Fix-its / Turnarounds: 1. Fixing a failed business/unit involving taking control, stopping losses, managing damage, planning the turnaround, dealing with people problems, installing new processes and systems, and

rebuilding the spirit and performance of the unit. 2. Managing sizable disasters like mishandled labor negotiations and strikes, thefts, history of significant business losses, poor staff, failed leadership, hidden problems, fraud, public relations nightmares, etc. 3. Significant reorganization and restructuring (e.g., stabilizing the business, reforming unit, introducing new systems, making people changes, resetting strategy and tactics). 4. Significant system/process breakdown (e.g,. MIS, financial coordination processes, audits, standards, etc.) across units requiring working to change something from a distant position, providing advice and counsel, and installing or implementing a major process improvement or system change outside your own unit and/or with customers outside the organization.

☐ **Start-ups**
The core demands to qualify as a start from scratch are: 1. Starting something new for you and/or for the organization. 2. Forging a new team. 3. Creating new systems/facilities/staffs/ programs/procedures. 4. Contextual adversity (e.g., uncertainty, government regulation, unions, difficult environment). Seven types of start from scratches: 1. Planning, building, hiring, and managing (e.g., building a new facility, opening up a new location, moving a unit or company). 2. Heading something new (e.g., new product, new service, new line of business, new department/function, major new program). 3. Take over a group/product/service/program that had existed for less than a year and was off to a fast start. 4. Establishing overseas operations. 5. Major new designs for existing systems. 6. Moving a successful program from one unit to another. 7. Installing a new organization-wide process as a full-time job (e.g., like Total Quality).

☐ **Scope Assignments**
The core demands for a Scope (complexity) assignment are: 1. Significant increase in both internal and external scope or complexity. 2. Significant increase in visibility and/ or bottom line responsibility. 3. Unfamiliar area, business, technology, or territory. Examples of Scope assignments involving shifts: 1. Switching into a new function/technology/business. 2. Moving to new organization. 3. Moving to overseas assignment. 4. Moving to new location. 5. Adding new products/services. 6. Moving between headquarters/field. 7. Switches in ownership/top management of the unit/organization. Examples of Scope assignments involving "firsts": 1. First-time manager. 2. First-time managing managers. 3. First-time executive. 4. First-time overseas. 5. First-time headquarters/field. 6. First-time team leader. 7. First-time new technology/business/function. Scope assignments involving increased complexity: 1. Managing a significant expansion of an existing product or service. 2. Managing adding new products/service into an existing unit. 3. Managing a reorganized and more diverse unit. 4. Managing explosive growth. 5. Adding new technologies. 60 Influencing Without Authority The core demands to qualify as an

Influence Without Authority are: 1. Significant challenge (e.g, start-up, fix-it, scope and/or scale assignment, strategic planning project, changes in management practices/systems). 2. Insufficient direct authority to make it happen. 3. Tight deadlines. 4. Visible to significant others. 5. Sensitive politics.

SECTION 6: LEARNING MORE FROM YOUR PLAN

THESE ADDITIONAL REMEDIES WILL HELP MAKE THIS DEVELOPMENT PLAN MORE EFFECTIVE FOR YOU

Learning to Learn Better

- ☐ **Teach Others Something You Don't Know Well**
  Commit to a project like teaching something you don't know much about to force you to learn quickly to accomplish the task; pick something new, different, or unfamiliar.

- ☐ **Study Yourself in Detail**
  Study your likes and dislikes because they can drive a lot of your thinking, judging, and acting. Ask which like or dislike has gotten in the way or prevented you from moving to a higher level of learning. Are your likes and dislikes really important to you or have you just gone on "autopilot"? Try to address and understand a blocking dislike and change it.

- ☐ **Learn to Separate Opinions from Facts**
  Practice separating opinions, beliefs, feelings, attitudes and values from facts and data. Try to base more of your comments and actions on the data side. If there is a need to air subjective information, announce it as such, and label it for what it is. Don't present opinions with the look and sound of data.

- ☐ **Preview a Plan with a Test Audience**
  Before committing to a plan, find someone agreeable to a wide-ranging discussion about the issue or problem you face. Explore all sides and options; go with the flow; let what you need to do emerge from the process; develop a plan as you go.

Learning from Experience, Feedback and Other People

- ☐ **Using Multiple Models**
  Who do you know who exemplifies how to do whatever your need is? Who, for example, personifies decisiveness or compassion or strategic agility? Think more broadly than your current job and colleagues. For example, ministers, friends, spouses or community leaders are also good sources for potential models. Select your models not on the basis of overall excellence or likeability, but on the basis of the one towering strength (or glaring weakness) you are interested in. Even people who are well thought of usually have only one or two towering strengths (or

glaring weaknesses). Ordinarily, you won't learn as much from the whole person as you will from one characteristic.

☐ **Learning from Observing Others**
Observe others. Find opportunities to observe without interacting with your model. This enables you to objectively study the person, note what he/she is doing or not doing, and compare that with what you would typically do in similar situations. Many times you can learn more by watching than asking. Your model may not be able to explain what he/she does or may be an unwilling teacher.

☐ **Getting Feedback from Bosses and Superiors**
Many bosses are reluctant to give negative feedback. They lack the managerial courage to face people directly with criticism. You can help by soliciting feedback and setting the tone. Show them you can handle criticism and that you are willing to work on issues they see as important.

☐ **Getting Feedback from Direct Reports**
Direct Reports often fear reprisals for giving negative feedback about bosses, whether in a formal process, like a questionnaire, or informally and face-to-face. Even with a guarantee of confidentiality, some are still hesitant. If you want feedback from direct reports, you have to set a positive tone and never act out of revenge.

☐ **Getting Feedback from Peers/Colleagues**
Your peers and colleagues may not be candid if they are in competition with you. Some may not be willing to be open with you out of fear of giving you an advantage. Some may give you exaggerated feedback to deliberately cause you undue concern. You have to set the tone and gauge the trust level of the relationship and the quality of the feedback.

Learning from Courses

☐ **Supervisory Courses**
Most new supervisors go through an "Introduction to Supervision" type course. They are designed to teach the common practices a first-line supervisor needs to know to be effective. The content of most of those courses is standard. There is general agreement on the principles of effective supervision. There are two common problems: (1) Do the students have a strong motivation to learn? Do they know what they don't know? Is there any pain? Because motivated students with a need for the knowledge learn best, participants should have had some trying experiences and some supervisory pain and hardships before attending. (2) Are the instructors experienced supervisors? Have they practiced what they preach? Can they share powerful anecdotes to make key points? Can they answer questions credibly? If possible, select supervisory courses based on the instructors, since the content seems to be the much same for all such courses. Lastly, does the course

offer the opportunity for practicing each skill? Does it contain simulations? Are there case studies you could easily identify with? Are there breakout groups? Is there opportunity for action learning? Search for the most interactive course.

SUGGESTED READINGS

Brown, Mark Graham, Darcy E. Hitchcock and Marsha L. Willard. *RX for business: A troubleshooting guide for building a high performance organization.* Chicago: Irwin Professional Publishing, 1996.

Cooper, Robert K., Ph.D. *The Performance Edge: New strategies to maximize your work effectiveness and competitive advantage.* Boston: Houghton Mifflin Co., 1991.

Koch, Richard. *The 80/20 principle: the secret of achieving more with less.* New York: Currency/Doubleday, 1998.

Sibson, Robert. *Maximizing Employee Productivity.* New York: AMACOM, 1994.

85

CUSTOMER IMPACT / VALUE ADDED

SECTION 1: YOUR DEVELOPMENT NEED(S)

General Definition: The extent to which the goods and services produced meet the expectations of internal and external customers.

UNSKILLED

- ☐ Produces goods and services that don't meet the minimum standards and expectations of internal and external customers
- ☐ There are steady complaints and extensive rework is necessary to keep customers minimally happy

AVERAGE

- ☐ Produces goods and services that usually meet the normal standards of internal and external customers
- ☐ Most customers are happy, with a few customer complaints and some rework necessary to make all customers happy

SKILLED

- ☐ Produces goods and services that consistently meet and sometimes exceed the standards and expectations of internal and external customers
- ☐ Always up to date about customer needs and expectations
- ☐ The feedback from customers is almost always positive

OVERUSED SKILL

- ☐ Gives customers too much for what the organization receives in return
- ☐ Overly committed to produce goods and services that consistently meet and exceed the standards and expectations of internal and external customers
- ☐ Uses too many resources, loses sight of other important goals and objectives and becomes an unreasonable advocate for customers at the expense of other organizational values and policies

Select one to three of the competencies listed below to work on to compensate for an overuse of this skill.

COMPENSATORS: 5,9,12,34,35,38,39,42,50,51,52,53,57,58,59

SOME CAUSES

- ☐ Arrogant, always knows better
- ☐ Defensive in the face of complaints
- ☐ Difficulty saying no
- ☐ Nervous about negotiating with customers

- ☐ Not planful or organized
- ☐ Not results oriented
- ☐ Poor interpersonal skills
- ☐ Poor listening skills
- ☐ Poor time management
- ☐ Rejects input from customers
- ☐ Shy, afraid to ask

THE MAP

In a free enterprise system, the customer is king. Those win who consistently please internal and external customers best. Meeting customer expectations is the minimum standard. In order to do that, you would have to know or better yet negotiate customer expectations and standards, plan and align the resources needed to meet those expectations and then deliver. More advanced is anticipating customer needs and expectations even before customers know about them. That involves being creative and innovative with products and services, visioning the future and delivering now. You can seldom lose by being customer focused and delivery committed.

SECTION 2: LEARNING ON YOUR OWN

THESE SELF-DEVELOPMENT REMEDIES WILL HELP YOU BUILD YOUR SKILL(S)

REMEDIES

☐ **1. Keep in touch.** Pleasing the reasonable needs of customers is fairly straightforward. First you need to know what they want and expect. The best way to do that is to ask them. Then deliver that in a timely way at a price/value that's justified. Find ways to keep in touch with a broad spectrum of your customers to get a balanced view: face to face, phone surveys, questionnaires, response cards with the products and services you render, etc.

☐ **2. Customers complain; it's their job.** Be ready for the good news and the bad news; don't be defensive; just listen and respond to legitimate criticisms and note the rest. Vocal customers will usually complain more than compliment; you need to not get overwhelmed by the negative comments; people who have positive opinions speak up less.

☐ **3. Anticipate customer needs.** Get in the habit of meeting with your internal or external customers on a regular basis to set up a dialogue; they need to feel free to contact you about problems and you need to be able to contact them for essential information. Use this understanding to get out in front of your customers; try to anticipate their needs for your products and services before they even know about them; provide your customers with positive surprises, features they weren't expecting, delivery in a shorter time, more than they ordered.

☐ **4. Put yourself in your customer's shoes.** If you were a customer of yours, what would you expect; what kind of turnaround time would you tolerate; what price would you be willing to pay for the quality of product or service you provide; what would be the top three things you would complain about? Answer all calls from customers in a timely way; if you promise a response, do it; if the timeframe stretches, inform them immediately; after you have responded, ask them if the problem is fixed.

☐ **5. Think of yourself as a dissatisfied customer.** Write down all of the unsatisfactory things that have happened to you as a customer during the past month. Things like delays, orders not right, cost not as promised, phone calls not returned, cold food, bad service, inattentive clerks, out of stock items, etc. Are any of these things happening to your customers? Then do a study of your lost customers. Find out what the three key problems were and see how quickly you can eliminate 50% of the difficulties that caused them to depart. Study your competitor's foul-ups and see what you can do to both avoid them in your own organization and make your organization more attractive.

☐ **6. Think of yourself as a satisfied customer.** Write down all of the satisfactory things that have happened to you as a customer during the past month. What pleased you the most as a customer? Good value? On-time service? Courtesy? Returned phone calls? Are any of your customers experiencing any of these satisfactory transactions with you and your business? Study your successful customer transactions so they can be institutionalized. Then study what your competitors do well and see what you can also do to improve customer service.

☐ **7. Getting work done through others?** Some people are not good managers of others. They can produce results by themselves but do less well when the results have to come from the team. Are you having trouble getting your team to work with you to get the results you need? You have the resources and the people but things just don't run well. Maybe you do too much work yourself. You don't delegate or empower. You don't communicate well. You don't motivate well. You don't plan well. You don't set priorities and goals well. If you are a struggling manager or a first-time manager, there are well known and documented principles and practices of good managing. Do you share credit? Do you paint a clear picture of why this is important? Is their work challenging? Do you inspire or just hand out work? Read *Becoming a Manager* by Linda A. Hill. Go to one course on management. *More help? – See #20 Directing Others, #36 Motivating Others, #18 Delegation, and #60 Building Effective Teams.*

☐ **8. More what and why, less how.** The best delegators are crystal clear on what and when, and more open on how. People are more motivated when they can determine the how for themselves.

Inexperienced delegators include the hows, which turns the people into task automatons instead of an empowered and energized staff. Tell them what and when and for how long and let them figure out how on their own. Give them leeway. Encourage them to try things. Besides being more motivating, it's also more developmental for them. Add the larger context. Although knowing the context may not be necessary to get the task done, people are more motivated when they know where this task fits in the bigger picture. Take three extra minutes and tell them why this task needs to be done, where it fits in the grander scheme and its importance to the goals and objectives of the unit.

☐ **9. Listening under duress.** What if you're being criticized or attacked personally? What if people are wrong in what they are saying? The rules remain the same. You need to work on keeping yourself in a calm state when getting negative feedback. You need to shift your thinking. When getting the feedback, your only task is to accurately understand what the person is trying to tell you. It is not, at that point, to accept or refute. That comes later. Practice verbal Aikido, the ancient art of absorbing the energy of your opponent, and using it to manage him/her. Let the other side vent but don't react directly. Listen. Nod. Ask clarifying questions. But don't hit back. Don't judge. Keep him/her talking until he/she runs out of venom. Separate the person from the feedback. *See Tip #4 in #108 Defensiveness, for help on responding to negative attacks that aren't true. More help? – See #12 Conflict Management.*

☐ **10. You may be seen as rigid in your values stances and unwilling to accept, or even see, those of others.** *See Overdoing #22 Ethics and Values.* Rigid stances often come from childhood and early adult experiences. You may have reduced your beliefs to rigid commandments. You need to know why you hold these values and critically examine whether they are appropriate here. Statements of belief are pronouncements – a true value holds up to action scrutiny; you can say why you hold it, how it plays out in different situations, and what happens when it conflicts with other values.

SECTION 3: LEARNING FROM MORE FEEDBACK

THESE SOURCES WOULD GIVE YOU THE MOST ACCURATE AND DETAILED FEEDBACK ON YOUR SKILL(S)

☐ **Past Associates/Constituencies**

When confronted with a present performance problem, some claim, "I wasn't like that before; it must be the current situation." When feedback is available from former associates, about 50 percent support that claim. In the other half of the cases, the people were like that before and probably didn't know it. It sometimes makes sense to access the past to clearly see the present.

- ☐ **Direct Boss**
  Your direct boss has important information about you, your performance, and your prospects. The challenge is to get this information. There are formal processes (e.g., performance appraisals). There are day-to-day opportunities. To help, signal your boss that you want and can handle direct and timely feedback. Many bosses have trouble giving feedback, so you will have to work at it over a period of time.
- ☐ **Peers and Colleagues**
  Peers and colleagues have a special social and working relationship. They attend staff meetings together, share private views, get feedback from the same boss, travel together, and are knowledgeable about each other's work. You perhaps let your guard down more around peers and act more like yourself. They can be a valuable source of feedback.
- ☐ **Direct Reports**
  Across a variety of settings, your direct reports probably see you the most. They are the recipients of most of your managerial behaviors. They know your work. They can compare you with former bosses. Since they may hesitate to give you negative feedback, you have to set the atmosphere to make it easier for them. You have to ask.
- ☐ **Internal and External Customers**
  Customers interact with you as a person and as a supplier or vendor of products and services. You're important to them because you can either help address and solve their problems or stand in their way. As customer service and Total Quality programs gain importance, clients and customers become a more prominent source of feedback.

SECTION 4: LEARNING FROM DEVELOP-IN-PLACE ASSIGNMENTS

THESE PART-TIME DEVELOP-IN-PLACE ASSIGNMENTS WILL HELP YOU BUILD YOUR SKILL(S)

- ☐ Relaunch an existing product or service that's not doing well.
- ☐ Manage a dissatisfied internal or external customer; troubleshoot a performance or quality problem with a product or service.
- ☐ Launch a new product, service, or process.
- ☐ Plan a new site for a building (plant, field office, headquarters, etc.).
- ☐ Integrate diverse systems, processes, or procedures across decentralized and/or dispersed units.
- ☐ Study and establish internal or external customer needs, requirements, specifications, and expectations and present it to the people involved.
- ☐ Represent the organization at a trade show, convention, exposition, etc.

- ☐ Manage the interface between consultants and the organization on a critical assignment.
- ☐ Write a speech for someone higher up in the organization.
- ☐ Run (chair) a taskforce on a pressing problem.

SECTION 5: LEARNING FROM FULL-TIME JOBS

THESE FULL-TIME JOBS OFFER THE OPPORTUNITY TO BUILD YOUR SKILL(S)

☐ **Influencing Without Authority**

The core demands to qualify as an Influence Without Authority are: 1. Significant challenge (e.g, start-up, fix-it, scope and/or scale assignment, strategic planning project, changes in management practices/systems). 2. Insufficient direct authority to make it happen. 3. Tight deadlines. 4. Visible to significant others. 5. Sensitive politics.

☐ **Start-ups**

The core demands to qualify as a start from scratch are: 1. Starting something new for you and/or for the organization. 2. Forging a new team. 3. Creating new systems/facilities/staffs/ programs/procedures. 4. Contextual adversity (e.g., uncertainty, government regulation, unions, difficult environment). Seven types of start from scratches: 1. Planning, building, hiring, and managing (e.g., building a new facility, opening up a new location, moving a unit or company). 2. Heading something new (e.g., new product, new service, new line of business, new department/function, major new program). 3. Take over a group/product/service/program that had existed for less than a year and was off to a fast start. 4. Establishing overseas operations. 5. Major new designs for existing systems. 6. Moving a successful program from one unit to another. 7. Installing a new organization-wide process as a full-time job (e.g., like Total Quality).

☐ **Fix-its / Turnarounds**

The core demands to qualify as a Fix-it or Turnaround assignment are: 1. Cleaning up a mess. 2. Serious people issues/problems like credibility/performance/morale. 3. Tight deadline. 4. Serious business performance failure. 5. Last chance to fix. Four Types of Fix-its / Turnarounds: 1. Fixing a failed business/unit involving taking control, stopping losses, managing damage, planning the turnaround, dealing with people problems, installing new processes and systems, and rebuilding the spirit and performance of the unit. 2. Managing sizable disasters like mishandled labor negotiations and strikes, thefts, history of significant business losses, poor staff, failed leadership, hidden problems, fraud, public relations nightmares, etc. 3. Significant reorganization and restructuring (e.g., stabilizing the business, re-forming unit, introducing new systems, making people changes, resetting strategy and tactics). 4. Significant system/process breakdown (e.g,. MIS, financial coordination processes, audits, standards, etc.)

across units requiring working to change something from a distant position, providing advice and counsel, and installing or implementing a major process improvement or system change outside your own unit and/or with customers outside the organization.

☐ **Scope Assignments**
The core demands for a Scope (complexity) assignment are: 1. Significant increase in both internal and external scope or complexity. 2. Significant increase in visibility and/ or bottom line responsibility. 3. Unfamiliar area, business, technology, or territory. Examples of Scope assignments involving shifts: 1. Switching into a new function/technology/business. 2. Moving to new organization. 3. Moving to overseas assignment. 4. Moving to new location. 5. Adding new products/services. 6. Moving between headquarters/field. 7. Switches in ownership/top management of the unit/organization. Examples of Scope assignments involving "firsts": 1. First-time manager. 2. First-time managing managers. 3. First-time executive. 4. First-time overseas. 5. First-time headquarters/field. 6. First-time team leader. 7. First-time new technology/business/function. Scope assignments involving increased complexity: 1. Managing a significant expansion of an existing product or service. 2. Managing adding new products/service into an existing unit. 3. Managing a reorganized and more diverse unit. 4. Managing explosive growth. 5. Adding new technologies.

☐ **Member of Projects/Taskforces**
The core demands for qualifying as a Project/Taskforce assignment are: 1. Full-time assignment. 2. Important and specific goal. 3. Tight deadline. 4. Success or failure will be evident. 5. High-visibility sponsor. 6. Learning something on the fly. 7. Must get others to cooperate. 8. Usually 6 months or more. Four types of Projects/Taskforces: 1. New ideas, products, services, or systems (e.g., product/service/program research and development, creation/installation/launch of a new system, new programs like Total Quality Management, positive discipline). 2. Formal negotiations and relationships (e.g.,acquisitions; divestitures; agreements; joint ventures; licensing arrangements; franchising; dealing with unions, governments, communities, charities, customers, and relocations). 3. Big one-time events (e.g., working on a major presentation for the board; organizing significant meetings or conferences; disaster/damage control teams; reorganizations, mergers, acquisitions, or relocations; working on visions, charters, strategies, other time-urgent issues and problems). 4. Troubleshooting (e.g., problems, disasters, crises, product/service failures, accidents, illegal activities, damage control in public relations goofs, shut downs, downsizings, layoffs, abrupt changes in leadership).

SECTION 6: LEARNING MORE FROM YOUR PLAN

THESE ADDITIONAL REMEDIES WILL HELP MAKE THIS DEVELOPMENT PLAN MORE EFFECTIVE FOR YOU

Learning to Learn Better

☐ **Monitoring Yourself More Closely and Get Off Your Autopilot**
Past habits are a mixed blessing, sometimes helping, sometimes not. To avoid putting yourself on "autopilot," think afresh about each situation before acting. Consistently monitor yourself with questions. Is this task different? Ask why you would repeat a past action. Are you avoiding anything, like taking a chance? Is there something new you might try?

☐ **Plan Backwards from the Ideal**
Envision what an ideal outcome would look like and plan backwards. What is the series of events that would have to take place to get there? What would people do? What would have to be done? How would people react? How would things play out? Could you plan it forward and get to the same outcome?

☐ **Envision Yourself Succeeding**
Envision yourself succeeding. Examine the image in detail: what you are doing, what you are feeling, how you are reacting to others, how others are reacting to you, how the parts fit together. Can you then play that out in the real situation and get to the same outcome?

☐ **Look Beyond Your First Solution to a Problem**
Don't always take the first action you think of. Look further for a second and third: What's different? Might the second or third be more effective? Research shows that the best solution lies somewhere between the second and third strategies or approaches. Your first solution is often an "autopilot" response and may not be the best.

Sell Something to a Tough Group/Audience
Think of the person or group who will be the toughest to sell, the most critical, skeptical, or resistant, and sell that person or group first. Take time to understand the opposing viewpoints. Find common ground and leverage points; line up your best data and arguments and go for it.

Sort Through Information Multiple Ways
Collect the data and arrange it in elements or pieces. Come up with definitions, and arrange the data in various ways: chronologically, from most to least, from biggest to smallest, from cold to hot, what you know most about and least about, from known to unknown, etc., until the meaning becomes obvious.

Learning from Experience, Feedback and Other People

☐ **Using Multiple Models**
Who do you know who exemplifies how to do whatever your need is? Who, for example, personifies decisiveness or compassion or strategic agility? Think more broadly than your current job and colleagues. For example, ministers, friends, spouses or community leaders are also good sources for potential models. Select your models not on the basis of overall excellence or likeability, but on the basis of the one towering strength (or glaring weakness) you are interested in. Even people who are well thought of usually have only one or two towering strengths (or glaring weaknesses). Ordinarily, you won't learn as much from the whole person as you will from one characteristic.

☐ **Learning from Observing Others**
Observe others. Find opportunities to observe without interacting with your model. This enables you to objectively study the person, note what he/she is doing or not doing, and compare that with what you would typically do in similar situations. Many times you can learn more by watching than asking. Your model may not be able to explain what he/she does or may be an unwilling teacher.

☐ **Openness to Feedback**
Nothing discourages feedback more than defensiveness, resistance, irritation, and excuses. People don't like giving feedback anyway, and much less to those who don't listen or are unreceptive. To help the feedback giver, be open, listen, ask for examples and details, take notes, keep a journal, and thank them for their interest.

Learning from Courses

☐ **Courses with Feedback**
Many courses such as negotiating skills and personal influence offer feedback on the subject matter of the course in addition to the content. They either collect data ahead of time or collect it "live" during the course.

SUGGESTED READINGS

Albrecht, Karl. *The Only Thing that Matters.* New York: HarperCollins, 1992.

Albrecht, Karl and Ron Zemke. *Service America!.* Burr Ridge, IL: Irwin Professional Publishing, 1985.

Band, William A. *Creating value for customers: designing and implementing a total corporate strategy.* New York: John Wiley and Sons, 1991.

Connellan, Thomas K. and Ron Zemke. *Sustaining Knock Your Socks Off Service.* New York: AMACOM, 1993.

Heskett, James L., W. Earl Sasser, Jr., and Leonard A. Schlesinger. *The service profit chain: how leading companies link profit and growth to loyalty, satisfaction, and value.* New York: Free Press, 1997.

Keen, Peter G. W. *The Process Edge – Creating value where it counts.* Boston: Harvard Business School Press, 1998.

Reichheld, Frederick F. with Thomas Teal. *The Loyalty Effect: The hidden force behind growth, profits and lasting value.* Boston: Harvard Business School Press, 1996.

Schaaf, Dick. *Keeping the Edge.* New York: Dutton, 1995.

Whitely, Richard and Diane Hessan. *Customer-Centered Growth.* Reading, MA: Addison-Wesley Publishing Co. Inc., 1996.

SECTION 1: YOUR DEVELOPMENT NEED(S)

General Definition: The amount and intensity of supervision and support necessary to perform up to standard.

UNSKILLED

- ☐ Needs significantly more than average support and time from bosses and others to meet minimum standards
- ☐ Takes more maintenance and support than most people or groups to be able to contribute up to standard
- ☐ Not much time left for bosses to support other people or groups

AVERAGE

- ☐ Performs up to standard with the usual or reasonable amount of support, help and guidance from bosses and others
- ☐ As a proportion of support and time available, takes up a fair share

SKILLED

- ☐ Usually performs up to standard independently
- ☐ Takes minimal support from bosses and other sources and needs little unplanned guidance or help
- ☐ Independent, self starting
- ☐ Requires much less support than most other people or groups

OVERUSED SKILL

- ☐ So driven to work independently that is an unreasonable loner
- ☐ Doesn't want any help, goes own way and works on own objectives
- ☐ May waste time and resources working on the wrong things or in the wrong way

Select one to three of the competencies listed below to work on to compensate for an overuse of this skill.

COMPENSATORS: 3,15,33,42,50,53,60,65

SOME CAUSES

- ☐ Avoids criticism
- ☐ Avoids making decisions
- ☐ Avoids risk
- ☐ Doesn't experiment
- ☐ Fear of failure
- ☐ Inexperienced
- ☐ Not bold or innovative
- ☐ Not self confident
- ☐ Perfectionist
- ☐ Poor management
- ☐ Prefers structure

THE MAP

Performing as much on your own as you can while still meeting goals and targets is what most managers expect. With the exception of those managers who micro-manage, most like to set goals and assign tasks and authority and then move on to other managerial duties, leaving the rest to the skills and power of the people to perform. Asking for help and assistance because there is a real need is expected and acceptable. Depending upon direction and support due to weaknesses in your own make-up is not. Taking up the time and resources of others to get things done at high quality and on time is reasonable and laudable. Taking up the time of others to gain personal advantage or to cover a weakness is not. Doing things on your own in the gray zone is the winning career strategy.

SECTION 2: LEARNING ON YOUR OWN

THESE SELF-DEVELOPMENT REMEDIES WILL HELP YOU BUILD YOUR SKILL(S)

☐ **1. Selling your stand.** While some people may welcome what you say and what you do, others will go after you or even try to minimize you or the situation your stand relates to. Some will sabotage. To sell your views, keep your eyes on the prize but don't specify everything about how to get there. Give others room to maneuver. Present the outcomes, targets and goals without the how to's. Welcome ideas, good and bad. Any negative response is a positive if you learn from it. Invite criticism of what you're doing. Even though you're going it alone, you need the advice and support of others to get there. Stay away from personal clashes. *More help? – See #12 Conflict Management.*

☐ **2. Develop a philosophical stance toward being wrong or losing.** After all, most innovations fail, most proposals fail, most efforts to lead change fail. Research says that successful general managers have made more mistakes in their careers than the people they were promoted over. They got promoted because they had the guts to stand alone, not because they were always right. Other studies suggest really good general managers are right about 65% of the time. Put errors, mistakes and failures on your menu. Everyone has to have some spinach for a balanced diet. Don't let the possibility of being wrong hold you back from standing alone when you believe it's right.

☐ **3. Don't like risk?** Standing alone involves pushing the envelope, taking chances and suggesting bold new initiatives. Doing those things leads to more misfires and mistakes. Treat any mistakes or failures as chances to learn. Nothing ventured, nothing gained. Up your risk comfort. Start small so you can recover more quickly. Go for small wins. Send up trial balloons. Don't blast into a major stand to prove your boldness. Break it down into smaller stands. Take the easiest one for you first. Then build up to the tougher ones. Review each one to see what you did well and not well, and set goals so you'll do something differently and better each time. Challenge yourself. See how inventive you can be in taking action a number of different ways. *More help? – See #14 Creativity, #28 Innovation Management, and #2 Dealing With Ambiguity.*

☐ **4. Taking personal responsibility.** Standing alone means taking the consequences alone, both the credit and the heat. You won't always be right so you need to just be as quick to take the blame as the credit. Just say, "Yes, you're right, my stand was wrong, sorry about that." Make it a practice to conduct postmortems immediately after milestone efforts – win or lose. This will indicate to all that you're interested in improvement and excellence whether the results are stellar or not. Don't let your missteps chill your courage to speak up, step into the breach, and stake out tough stands.

☐ **5. Leading is riskier than following.** While there are a lot of personal rewards for leading, leading puts you in the limelight. Think about what happens to political leaders and the scrutiny they face. Leaders have to be internally secure. Do you feel good about yourself? They have to please themselves first and have confidence that they are on the right track. Can you defend to a critical and impartial audience the wisdom of what you're doing? They have to accept lightning bolts from detractors. Can you take the heat? People will always say it should have been done differently. Listen to them, but be skeptical. Even great leaders are wrong sometimes. They accept personal responsibility for errors and move on to lead some more. Don't let criticism prevent you from taking the lead. Build up your heat shield. Conduct a postmortem immediately after finishing milestone efforts. This will indicate to all that you're open to continuous improvement whether the result was stellar or not.

☐ **6. Haven't found your passion to lead?** Try small things. Try some leadership roles and tasks off work. Volunteer for a leadership role in your place of worship, school, or neighborhood. Volunteer to head a task force. Start up a credit union. Volunteer for the United Way drive. Start a softball league.

☐ **7. Too cautious and conservative?** Analysis paralysis? Break out of your examine-it-to-death and always-take-the-safest-path mode and just do it. Increasing timeliness will increase errors and mistakes but it also will get more done faster. Develop a more philosophical stance toward failure/criticism. After all, most innovations fail, most proposals fail, most change efforts fail; anything worth doing takes repeated effort. The best tack when confronted with a mistake is to say, "What can we learn from this?" Ask yourself if your need to be cautious matches the requirements for speed and timeliness of your job. *More help? – See #45 Personal Learning.*

☐ **8. Hesitate in the face of resistance and adverse reaction?** Conflict slows you down, shakes your confidence in your decision? Do you backpedal? Give in too soon? Try to make everyone happy? Do your homework first. Scope the problem, consider options, pick one, develop a rationale, then go to others. Be prepared to defend your selection; know what they will ask, what they will object to, how this decision will affect them. Listen carefully, invite criticism of your idea and revise accordingly in the face of real data. Otherwise, hold your ground.

☐ **9. Delegating.** Getting long, complex or multi-tracked projects done involves accomplishing a series of tasks that lead up to the whole. One clear finding in the research is that empowered people work longer and harder. People like to have control over their work, determine how they are going to do it, and have the authority to make decisions. Give away as much as possible along with the authority that goes with it. Another clear finding is to pay attention to the weakest links – usually groups or elements you have the least interface with or control over – perhaps someone in a remote location, a consultant or supplier. Stay doubly in touch with the potential weak links.

☐ **10. Be sensitive to the time of others.** Generally, the higher up you go or the higher up the person you are interacting with is, the less time you and he/she has. Be time efficient with others. Use as little of their time as possible. Get to it and get done with it. Give them an opportunity to open new avenues for discussion or to continue, but if they don't, say your good-byes and leave.

SECTION 3: LEARNING FROM MORE FEEDBACK

THESE SOURCES WOULD GIVE YOU THE MOST ACCURATE AND DETAILED FEEDBACK ON YOUR SKILL(S)

☐ **Direct Boss**
Your direct boss has important information about you, your performance, and your prospects. The challenge is to get this information. There are formal processes (e.g., performance appraisals). There are day-to-day opportunities. To help, signal your boss that you want and can handle direct and timely feedback. Many bosses have trouble giving feedback, so you will have to work at it over a period of time.

☐ **Past Associates/Constituencies**
When confronted with a present performance problem, some claim, "I wasn't like that before; it must be the current situation." When feedback is available from former associates, about 50 percent support that claim. In the other half of the cases, the people were like that before and probably didn't know it. It sometimes makes sense to access the past to clearly see the present.

☐ **Natural Mentors**
Natural Mentors have a special relationship with you and are interested in your success and your future. Since they are usually not in your direct chain of command, you can have more open, relaxed, and fruitful discussions about yourself and your career prospects. They can be a very important source for candid or critical feedback others may not give you.

☐ **Human Resource Professionals**
Human Resource professionals have both a formal and informal feedback role. Since they have access to unique and confidential information, they can provide the right context for feedback you've received. Sometimes they may be "directed" to give you feedback. Other times, they may pass on feedback just to be helpful to you.

☐ **Peers and Colleagues**
Peers and colleagues have a special social and working relationship. They attend staff meetings together, share private views, get feedback from the same boss, travel together, and are knowledgeable about each other's work. You perhaps let your guard down more around peers and act more like yourself. They can be a valuable source of feedback.

☐ **Yourself**
You are an important source of feedback on yourself. But some caution is appropriate. If you have not received much feedback, you may be less accurate than the other sources. We all have blind spots, defense shields, ideal self-views, and fantasies. Before acting on your own self-views, get outside confirmation from other appropriate sources.

☐ **Development Professionals**
Sometimes it might be valuable to get some analysis and feedback from a professional trained and certified in the area you're working on: possibly a career counselor, a therapist, a minister, a psychologist, etc.

SECTION 4: LEARNING FROM DEVELOP-IN-PLACE ASSIGNMENTS

THESE PART-TIME DEVELOP-IN-PLACE ASSIGNMENTS WILL HELP YOU BUILD YOUR SKILL(S)

☐ Launch a new product, service, or process.

☐ Take on a tough and undoable project, one where others who have tried it have failed.

☐ Prepare and present a proposal of some consequence to top management.

☐ Plan for and start up something small (secretarial pool, athletic program, suggestion system, program, etc.).

☐ Plan an off-site meeting, conference, convention, trade show, event, etc.

☐ Handle a tough negotiation with an internal or external client or customer.

☐ Be a change agent; create a symbol for change; lead the rallying cry; champion a significant change and implementation.

☐ Volunteer to fill an open management job temporarily until it's filled.

☐ Manage an ad hoc, temporary group of "green," inexperienced people as their coach, teacher, orienteer, etc.

☐ Make peace with an enemy or someone you've disappointed with a product or service or someone you've had some trouble with or don't get along well with.

SECTION 5: LEARNING FROM FULL-TIME JOBS

THESE FULL-TIME JOBS OFFER THE OPPORTUNITY TO BUILD YOUR SKILL(S)

☐ **Fix-its / Turnarounds**
The core demands to qualify as a Fix-it or Turnaround assignment are: 1. Cleaning up a mess. 2. Serious people issues/problems like credibility/performance/morale. 3. Tight deadline. 4. Serious business performance failure. 5. Last chance to fix. Four Types of Fix-its / Turnarounds: 1. Fixing a failed business/unit involving taking control, stopping losses, managing damage, planning the turnaround, dealing with people problems, installing new processes and systems, and rebuilding the spirit and performance of the unit. 2. Managing sizable disasters like mishandled labor negotiations and strikes, thefts, history of significant business losses, poor staff, failed leadership, hidden prob-

lems, fraud, public relations nightmares, etc. 3. Significant reorganization and restructuring (e.g., stabilizing the business, re-forming unit, introducing new systems, making people changes, resetting strategy and tactics). 4. Significant system/process breakdown (e.g,. MIS, financial coordination processes, audits, standards, etc.) across units requiring working to change something from a distant position, providing advice and counsel, and installing or implementing a major process improvement or system change outside your own unit and/or with customers outside the organization.

☐ **Scope Assignments**
The core demands for a Scope (complexity) assignment are: 1. Significant increase in both internal and external scope or complexity. 2. Significant increase in visibility and/ or bottom line responsibility. 3. Unfamiliar area, business, technology, or territory. Examples of Scope assignments involving shifts: 1. Switching into a new function/technology/business. 2. Moving to new organization. 3. Moving to overseas assignment. 4. Moving to new location. 5. Adding new products/services. 6. Moving between headquarters/field. 7. Switches in ownership/top management of the unit/organization. Examples of Scope assignments involving "firsts": 1. First-time manager. 2. First-time managing managers. 3. First-time executive. 4. First-time overseas. 5. First-time headquarters/field. 6. First-time team leader. 7. First-time new technology/business/function. Scope assignments involving increased complexity: 1. Managing a significant expansion of an existing product or service. 2. Managing adding new products/service into an existing unit. 3. Managing a reorganized and more diverse unit. 4. Managing explosive growth. 5. Adding new technologies.

☐ **Start-ups**
The core demands to qualify as a start from scratch are: 1. Starting something new for you and/or for the organization. 2. Forging a new team. 3. Creating new systems/facilities/staffs/programs/procedures. 4. Contextual adversity (e.g., uncertainty, government regulation, unions, difficult environment). Seven types of start from scratches: 1. Planning, building, hiring, and managing (e.g., building a new facility, opening up a new location, moving a unit or company). 2. Heading something new (e.g., new product, new service, new line of business, new department/function, major new program). 3. Take over a group/product/service/program that had existed for less than a year and was off to a fast start. 4. Establishing overseas operations. 5. Major new designs for existing systems. 6. Moving a successful program from one unit to another. 7. Installing a new organization-wide process as a full-time job (e.g., like Total Quality).

☐ **Chair of Projects/Taskforces**
The core demands for qualifying as a Project/Taskforce assignment are: 1. Full-time assignment. 2. Important and specific goal. 3. Tight dead-

line. 4. Success or failure will be evident. 5. High-visibility sponsor. 6. Learning something on the fly. 7. Must get others to cooperate. 8. Usually 6 months or more. Four types of Projects/Taskforces: 1. New ideas, products, services, or systems (e.g., product/service/program research and development, creation/installation/launch of a new system, new programs like Total Quality Management, positive discipline). 2. Formal negotiations and relationships (e.g., acquisitions; divestitures; agreements; joint ventures; licensing arrangements; franchising; dealing with unions, governments, communities, charities, customers, and relocations). 3. Big one-time events (e.g., working on a major presentation for the board; organizing significant meetings or conferences; disaster/damage control teams; reorganizations, mergers, acquisitions, or relocations; working on visions, charters, strategies, other time-urgent issues and problems). 4. Troubleshooting (e.g., problems, disasters, crises, product/service failures, accidents, illegal activities, damage control in public relations goofs, shut downs, downsizings, layoffs, abrupt changes in leadership).

☐ **Influencing Without Authority**
The core demands to qualify as an Influence Without Authority are: 1. Significant challenge (e.g, start-up, fix-it, scope and/or scale assignment, strategic planning project, changes in management practices/systems). 2. Insufficient direct authority to make it happen. 3. Tight deadlines. 4. Visible to significant others. 5. Sensitive politics.

SECTION 6: LEARNING MORE FROM YOUR PLAN

THESE ADDITIONAL REMEDIES WILL HELP MAKE THIS DEVELOPMENT PLAN MORE EFFECTIVE FOR YOU

Learning to Learn Better

☐ **Monitoring Yourself More Closely and Get Off Your Autopilot**
Past habits are a mixed blessing, sometimes helping, sometimes not. To avoid putting yourself on "autopilot," think afresh about each situation before acting. Consistently monitor yourself with questions. Is this task different? Ask why you would repeat a past action. Are you avoiding anything, like taking a chance? Is there something new you might try?

☐ **Teach Others Something You Don't Know Well**
Commit to a project like teaching something you don't know much about to force you to learn quickly to accomplish the task; pick something new, different, or unfamiliar.

☐ **Learn New and Frivolous Skills to Study How You Learn**
Practice learning frivolous and fun skills (like juggling, square dancing, skeet shooting, video games, etc.) to see yourself under different and less personal or stressful learning conditions. Ask yourself why that was easy while developing new personal/managerial skills is so hard. Try something harder with the same tactics.

- ☐ **Commit to a Tight Timeframe to Accomplish Something**
Set some specific goals and tighter than usual timeframes for yourself and go after them with all you've got. Push yourself to stick to the plan; get more done than usual by adhering to a tight plan.

- ☐ **Sell Something to a Tough Audience/Group**
Think of the person or group who will be the toughest to sell, the most critical, skeptical, or resistant, and sell that person or group first. Take time to understand the opposing viewpoints. Find common ground and leverage points; line up your best data and arguments and go for it.

- ☐ **Rehearse Successful Tactics/Strategies/Actions**
Mentally rehearse how you will act before going into the situation. Try to anticipate how others will react, what they will say, and how you'll respond. Check out the best and worst cases; play out both scenes. Check your feelings in conflict or worst-case situations; rehearse staying under control.

Learning from Experience, Feedback and Other People

- ☐ **Learning from Mistakes**
Since we're human, we all make mistakes. The key is to focus on why you made the mistake. Spend more time locating causes and less worrying about the effects. Check how you react to mistakes. How much time do you spend being angry with yourself? Do you waste time stewing or do you move on? More importantly, do you learn? Ask why you made the mistake. Are you likely to repeat it under similar situations? Was it a lack of skill? Judgement? Style? Not enough data? Reading people? Misreading the challenge? Misreading the politics? Or was it just random? A good strategy that just didn't work? Others that let you down? The key is to avoid two common reactions to your mistakes: (1) avoiding similar situations instead of learning and trying again, and (2) trying to repeat what you did, only more diligently and harder, hoping to break through the problem, making the same mistake again but with greater impact. Neither trap leaves us with better strategies for the future. Neither is a learning strategy. To learn and do something differently, focus on the patterns in your behavior that get you in trouble and go back to first causes, those that tell you something about your shortcomings. Facing ourselves squarely is always the best way to learn.

- ☐ **Using Multiple Sources**
The usefulness of feedback varies with the quality of the source and the content of the information. Some give better feedback than others. Feedback on skills directly tied to success is most useful. Different skills are best observed by different groups like peers, bosses, direct reports, or customers. Timing of feedback can be critical; some times to get feedback are better than others.

☐ **Learning from a Coach or Tutor**
Ask a person to coach or tutor you directly. This has the additional benefit of skill building coupled with correcting feedback. Also observe the teacher teaching you. How do they teach? How do they adjust to you as a learner? After the process, ask for feedback about you as a learner.

Learning from Courses

☐ **Insight Events**
These are courses designed around assessing skills and providing feedback to the participants. These events can be a powerful source of self-knowledge and can lead to significant development if done right. When selecting a self-insight course, consider the following: (1) Are the skills assessed the important ones? (2) Are the assessment techniques and instruments sound? (3) Are those who are providing the feedback trained and professional? (4) Is the feedback provided in a user-friendly and "actionable" format? (5) Does the feedback include development planning? (6) Is the setting comfortable and conducive to reflection and learning? (7) Are the other participants the kinds of people you could learn from? (8) Are you in the right frame of mind to learn from this kind of intense experience? Select events on the basis of positive answers to these 8 questions.

SUGGESTED READINGS

Boccialetti, Gene. *It takes two: managing yourself when working with bosses and authority figures.* San Francisco: Jossey-Bass, 1995.

DesRoches, Brian Ph.D. *Your Boss Is Not Your Mother – Creating autonomy, respect, and success at work.* New York: William Morrow and Company, 1995.

Kushel, Gerald and Peter Land. *Reaching the Peak: how to motivate yourself and others to excel.* New York: AMACOM 1994.

TEAM/UNIT CONTRIBUTION

SECTION 1: YOUR DEVELOPMENT NEED(S)

General Definition: Unrelated to personal or group performance, is helpful to others in the unit or organization in getting work done or setting a tone of cooperation.

UNSKILLED

- ☐ Rarely helpful to the rest of the team, unit or organization in getting work done or in cooperating with anyone
- ☐ May chill the efforts of the larger group by hesitating to get involved or even refusing to help
- ☐ Withholds resources and information from the others

AVERAGE

- ☐ Usually helpful to the rest of the team or other units in getting work done
- ☐ Will cooperate with others
- ☐ About as helpful as most people or groups are

SKILLED

- ☐ Always helpful to the rest of the team / other units
- ☐ Among the first to volunteer to help others succeed
- ☐ Will share anything if it's for the team or organization
- ☐ A model of sharing, caring and cooperation

OVERUSED SKILL

- ☐ Such a team player or players that own performance sometimes suffers
- ☐ Takes too much time and energy helping others succeed
- ☐ Sometimes runs out of time and resources for own work

Select one to three of the competencies listed below to work on to compensate for an overuse of this skill.

COMPENSATORS: 12,37,50,53,57

SOME CAUSES

- ☐ A Loner
- ☐ Arrogant
- ☐ Competitive
- ☐ Defensive
- ☐ Impatient with others
- ☐ Not personally productive
- ☐ Poor communications skills
- ☐ Poor interpersonal skills
- ☐ Poor negotiation skills
- ☐ Self-centered

THE MAP

While getting your own work done is always paramount, helping others get theirs done as well can also reap rewards downstream. There is reciprocity. You scratch my back and I'll scratch yours. Even though you may not need others today, you may need them tomorrow. There is the sharing of successes. If you succeed and others on your team stumble, this doesn't really help much over time. It's more fun and rewarding to part of a winner. There is learning. While helping others, you can always learn something useful that will help you in the future. There is personal satisfaction. Most people feel good about themselves when they have successfully helped others. If you don't help others because you don't know how, learn. If you don't help others because you don't think you have anything to contribute, ask. If you don't help others because you want to look superior, stop.

SECTION 2: LEARNING ON YOUR OWN

THESE SELF-DEVELOPMENT REMEDIES WILL HELP YOU BUILD YOUR SKILL(S)

SOME REMEDIES

☐ **1. Establish a common cause and a shared mindset.** A common thrust is what energizes dream teams. As in light lasers, alignment adds focus, power and efficiency. It's best to get each team member involved in setting the common vision. Establish goals and measures. Most people like to be measured. People like to have checkpoints along the way to chart their progress. Most people perform better with goals that are stretching. Again, letting the team participate in setting the goals is a plus. *More help? – See #35 Managing and Measuring Work.*

☐ **2. To communicate with team members, work on understanding people without judging them.** You don't have to agree; you just have to understand. To build a team, invest in their learning and education; take them on trips to customers, and give them time to think problems through. Give them the benefit of your thinking and particularly what the key objectives of an effort are. The goal is to have them say, "We did it." *More help? – See #27 Informing.*

☐ **3. Resistance to the idea of a team is best overcome by focusing on common goals, priorities and problems,** selling the logic of pulling together repeatedly, listening patiently to people's concerns, protecting people's feelings but also reinforcing the perspective of why the team is needed, inviting suggestions to reach the outcome, and showing patience toward the unconverted. Maintain a light touch. *More help? – See #13 Confronting Direct Reports.*

☐ **4. Dream teams learn how to operate effectively and efficiently.** Read *Overcoming Organizational Defenses* by Chris Argyris. Half of the book is about some of the common problems teams run into that block peak performance, and the other half offers strategies and tactics for undoing those chilling team behaviors.

☐ **5. Influencing.** Peers generally do not have power over each other. That means that influence skills, understanding, and trading is the currency to use. Don't just ask for things; find some common ground where you can provide help. What do the peers you're contacting need? Do you really know how they see the issue? Is it even important to them? How does what you're working on affect them? If it affects them negatively can you trade something, appeal to the common good, figure out some way to minimize the work (volunteering staff help, for example)? Go into peer relationships with a trading mentality.

☐ **6. Many times, negative personal styles get in the way of effective peer relationships.** People differ in the impression they leave. Those who leave positive impressions get more things done with peers than those who leave cold, insensitive or impersonal negative impressions. *More help? – See #33 Listening, #3 Approachability, and #31 Interpersonal Savvy.*

☐ **7. If peers see you as excessively competitive, they will cut you out of the loop** and may sabotage your cross border attempts. To be seen as more cooperative, always explain your thinking and invite them to explain theirs. Generate a variety of possibilities first, rather than staking out positions. Be tentative, allowing them room to customize the situation. Focus on common goals, priorities and problems. Invite criticism of your ideas.

☐ **8. If peers think you lack respect for them or what they do, try to keep conflicts as small and concrete as possible.** Separate the people from the problem. Don't get personal. Don't give peers the impression you're trying to dominate or push something on them. Without agreeing or disagreeing, try on their views for size. Can you understand their viewpoint? When peers blow off steam, don't react; return to facts and the problem, staying away from personal clashes. Allow others to save face; concede small points; don't try to hit a home run every time. When a peer takes a rigid position, don't reject it. Ask why – what are the principles behind the position, how do we know it's fair, what's the theory of the case? Play out what would happen if his/her position was accepted.

☐ **9. A loner.** Do you keep to yourself? Work alone or try to? Do you hold back information? Do you parcel out information on your schedule? Do you share information to get an advantage or to win favor? Do people around you know what you're doing and why? Are you aware of things others would benefit from but you don't take the time to communicate? In most organizations, these things and things like it will get you in trouble. Organizations function on the flow of information. Being on your own and preferring peace and privacy are OK as long as you communicate things to bosses, peers and teammates that they need to know and would feel better if they knew. Don't be the source of surprises.

☐ **10. Think equity.** Relationships that work are built on equity and considering the impact on others. Don't just ask for things; find some common ground where you can provide help, not just ask for it. What does the unit you're contacting need in the way of problem solving or information? Do you really know how they see the issue? Is it even important to them? How does what you're working on affect them? If it affects them negatively and they are balky, can you trade something, appeal to the common good, figure out some way to minimize the work or other impact (volunteering staff help, for example)? *More help? – See #42 Peer Relationships.*

SECTION 3: LEARNING FROM MORE FEEDBACK

THESE SOURCES WOULD GIVE YOU THE MOST ACCURATE AND DETAILED FEEDBACK ON YOUR SKILL(S)

☐ **Past Associates/Constituencies**

When confronted with a present performance problem, some claim, "I wasn't like that before; it must be the current situation." When feedback is available from former associates, about 50 percent support that claim. In the other half of the cases, the people were like that before and probably didn't know it. It sometimes makes sense to access the past to clearly see the present.

☐ **Peers and Colleagues**

Peers and colleagues have a special social and working relationship. They attend staff meetings together, share private views, get feedback from the same boss, travel together, and are knowledgeable about each other's work. You perhaps let your guard down more around peers and act more like yourself. They can be a valuable source of feedback.

- ☐ **Direct Boss**
  Your direct boss has important information about you, your performance, and your prospects. The challenge is to get this information. There are formal processes (e.g., performance appraisals). There are day-to-day opportunities. To help, signal your boss that you want and can handle direct and timely feedback. Many bosses have trouble giving feedback, so you will have to work at it over a period of time.
- ☐ **Direct Reports**
  Across a variety of settings, your direct reports probably see you the most. They are the recipients of most of your managerial behaviors. They know your work. They can compare you with former bosses. Since they may hesitate to give you negative feedback, you have to set the atmosphere to make it easier for them. You have to ask.
- ☐ **Internal and External Customers**
  Customers interact with you as a person and as a supplier or vendor of products and services. You're important to them because you can either help address and solve their problems or stand in their way. As customer service and Total Quality programs gain importance, clients and customers become a more prominent source of feedback.

SECTION 4: LEARNING FROM DEVELOP-IN-PLACE ASSIGNMENTS

THESE PART-TIME DEVELOP-IN-PLACE ASSIGNMENTS WILL HELP YOU BUILD YOUR SKILL(S)

- ☐ Be a change agent; create a symbol for change; lead the rallying cry; champion a significant change and implementation.
- ☐ Build a multifunctional project team to tackle a common business issue or problem.
- ☐ Work on a team that's deciding who to keep and who to let go in a layoff, shutdown, delayering, or divestiture.
- ☐ Assemble an ad hoc team of diverse people to accomplish a difficult task.
- ☐ Resolve an issue in conflict between two people, units, geographies, functions, etc.
- ☐ Manage an ad hoc, temporary group of "green," inexperienced people as their coach, teacher, orienteer, etc.
- ☐ Make peace with an enemy or someone you've disappointed with a product or service or someone you've had some trouble with or don't get along well with.
- ☐ Represent the concerns of a group of nonexempt, clerical, or administrative employees to higher management to seek resolution of a difficult issue.

- ☐ Coach a children's sports team.
- ☐ Serve for a year or more with a community agency.

SECTION 5: LEARNING FROM FULL-TIME JOBS

THESE FULL-TIME JOBS OFFER THE OPPORTUNITY TO BUILD YOUR SKILL(S)

☐ **Fix-its / Turnarounds**

The core demands to qualify as a Fix-it or Turnaround assignment are: 1. Cleaning up a mess. 2. Serious people issues/problems like credibility/performance/morale. 3. Tight deadline. 4. Serious business performance failure. 5. Last chance to fix. Four Types of Fix-its / Turnarounds: 1. Fixing a failed business/unit involving taking control, stopping losses, managing damage, planning the turnaround, dealing with people problems, installing new processes and systems, and rebuilding the spirit and performance of the unit. 2. Managing sizable disasters like mishandled labor negotiations and strikes, thefts, history of significant business losses, poor staff, failed leadership, hidden problems, fraud, public relations nightmares, etc. 3. Significant reorganization and restructuring (e.g., stabilizing the business, re-forming unit, introducing new systems, making people changes, resetting strategy and tactics). 4. Significant system/process breakdown (e.g,. MIS, financial coordination processes, audits, standards, etc.) across units requiring working to change something from a distant position, providing advice and counsel, and installing or implementing a major process improvement or system change outside your own unit and/or with customers outside the organization.

☐ **Influencing Without Authority**

The core demands to qualify as an Influence Without Authority are: 1. Significant challenge (e.g, start-up, fix-it, scope and/or scale assignment, strategic planning project, changes in management practices/systems). 2. Insufficient direct authority to make it happen. 3. Tight deadlines. 4. Visible to significant others. 5. Sensitive politics.

☐ **Scope Assignments**

The core demands for a Scope (complexity) assignment are: 1. Significant increase in both internal and external scope or complexity. 2. Significant increase in visibility and/ or bottom line responsibility. 3. Unfamiliar area, business, technology, or territory. Examples of Scope assignments involving shifts: 1. Switching into a new function/technology/business. 2. Moving to new organization. 3. Moving to overseas assignment. 4. Moving to new location. 5. Adding new products/services. 6. Moving between headquarters/field. 7. Switches in ownership/top management of the unit/organization. Examples of Scope assignments involving "firsts": 1. First-time manager. 2. First-time managing managers. 3. First-time executive. 4. First-time overseas. 5. First-time headquarters/field. 6. First-time team leader. 7.First-time new technology/business/function. Scope assignments involving increased complexity: 1. Managing a significant expansion of an existing product or service. 2. Managing adding new products/service into an existing unit. 3. Managing a reorganized and more diverse unit. 4. Managing explosive growth. 5. Adding new technologies.

☐ **Start-ups**
The core demands to qualify as a start from scratch are: 1. Starting something new for you and/or for the organization. 2. Forging a new team. 3. Creating new systems/facilities/staffs/ programs/procedures. 4. Contextual adversity (e.g., uncertainty, government regulation, unions, difficult environment). Seven types of start from scratches: 1. Planning, building, hiring, and managing (e.g., building a new facility, opening up a new location, moving a unit or company). 2. Heading something new (e.g., new product, new service, new line of business, new department/function, major new program). 3. Take over a group/product/service/program that had existed for less than a year and was off to a fast start. 4. Establishing overseas operations. 5. Major new designs for existing systems. 6. Moving a successful program from one unit to another. 7. Installing a new organization-wide process as a full-time job (e.g., like Total Quality).

☐ **Significant People Demands**
Core demands required to qualify as a Significant People Responsibilities assignment are: 1. A sizable increase in either the number of people managed and/or the complexity of the challenges involved 2. Longer-term assignment (2 or more years). 3. Quality of people management critical to achieving results. 4. Involves groups not worked with before (e.g., union, new technical areas, nationalities).

SECTION 6: LEARNING MORE FROM YOUR PLAN

THESE ADDITIONAL REMEDIES WILL HELP MAKE THIS DEVELOPMENT PLAN MORE EFFECTIVE FOR YOU

Learning to Learn Better

☐ **Form a Learning Network with Others Working on the Same Problem**
Look for people in similar situations, and create a process for sharing and learning together. Look for a variety of people inside and outside your organization. Give feedback to each other; try new and different things together; share successes and failures, lessons and learning.

☐ **Use a Tutor to Learn Something New**
Set up a tutor relationship in the areas you're working on; open up, listen, learn, and try new things. Learn from the tutoring/learning process. Do you learn more easily from a tutor or do you get blocked? Test out your thinking with the tutor; do debriefs after trying the tutor's advice.

- [ ] **Examine Why You Judge People the Way You Do**
List the people you like and those you dislike and try to find out why. What do those you like have in common with each other and with you? What do those you dislike have in common with themselves and how do they differ from you? Are your "people buckets" logical and productive or do they interfere? Could you be more effective without putting people into buckets?

- [ ] **Study People Who Have Successfully Done What You Need to Do**
Interview people who have already done what you're planning to do and check your plan against what they did. Try to summarize their key tactics, strategies, and insights; adjust your plan accordingly.

- [ ] **Work With a Development Partner**
Find a person you trust to be both candid and constructive and team up with him/her. Construct effective strategies together. Give each other feedback; role-play tactics with each other.

Learning from Experience, Feedback and Other People

- [ ] **Being a Teacher of Others**
Teaching others a skill you possess is a powerful way to learn from your students and about yourself. Decide what skill you have that you could teach direct reports, a child, or a friend. In what areas could you be a mentor or tutor? Ask yourself why this is a strength for you. What are the first items you would teach as the keys to help others form umbrellas for understanding? Get feedback from others on why this is a strength for you and what you do behaviorally that makes it so. When teaching and coaching, watch the students carefully for their reactions. What works and doesn't work for you as a coach? Write down your rules of thumb on what works for you that helps others. Get feedback from your students on what you do well and not so well as a teacher/coach.

- [ ] **Using Multiple Models**
Who do you know who exemplifies how to do whatever your need is? Who, for example, personifies decisiveness or compassion or strategic agility? Think more broadly than your current job and colleagues. For example, ministers, friends, spouses or community leaders are also good sources for potential models. Select your models not on the basis of overall excellence or likeability, but on the basis of the one towering strength (or glaring weakness) you are interested in. Even people who are well thought of usually have only one or two towering strengths (or glaring weaknesses). Ordinarily, you won't learn as much from the whole person as you will from one characteristic.

- [ ] **Learning from Ineffective Behavior**
Seeing things done poorly can be a very potent source of learning for you, especially if the behavior or action affects others negatively. Many

times the thing done poorly causes emotional reactions or pain in you and others. Distance yourself from the feelings and explore why the actions didn't work.

Learning from Courses

☐ **Insight Events**
These are courses designed around assessing skills and providing feedback to the participants. These events can be a powerful source of self-knowledge and can lead to significant development if done right. When selecting a self-insight course, consider the following: (1) Are the skills assessed the important ones? (2) Are the assessment techniques and instruments sound? (3) Are those who are providing the feedback trained and professional? (4) Is the feedback provided in a user-friendly and "actionable" format? (5) Does the feedback include development planning? (6) Is the setting comfortable and conducive to reflection and learning? (7) Are the other participants the kinds of people you could learn from? (8) Are you in the right frame of mind to learn from this kind of intense experience? Select events on the basis of positive answers to these 8 questions.

☐ **Soliciting Feedback**
Almost everyone reports they receive less feedback than they need to achieve their career goals. While others may have some interest in your career, it is primarily up to you to take the initiative in soliciting feedback from multiple sources by any methods available. You're the stakeholder who needs feedback to improve and grow.

SUGGESTED READINGS

Katzenbach, Jon R. and Douglas K. Smith. *The wisdom of teams: creating the high-performance organization.* Boston: Harvard Business School Press, 1993.

Parker, Glenn M. *Team Players and Teamwork.* San Francisco: Jossey-Bass, Inc., 1990.

Sher, Barbara and Annie Gottlieb. *Teamworks: Building support groups that guarantee success.* New York: Warner Books, 1989.

Wellins, Richard, William C. Byham and George R. Dixon. *Inside Teams.* San Francisco: Jossey-Bass, Inc., 1994.

PRODUCTIVE WORK HABITS

SECTION 1: YOUR DEVELOPMENT NEED(S)

General Definition: The extent to which overall work style is effective and productive in terms of time management, setting objectives and priorities, and following up on commitments across a variety of work challenges.

UNSKILLED

- ☐ Not orderly in approach to work
- ☐ Works on whatever comes up, gets easily diverted into less productive tasks
- ☐ Follow through is spotty
- ☐ Wastes a lot of energy and time due to being disorganized

AVERAGE

- ☐ Reasonably productive and organized in setting appropriate objectives and managing time
- ☐ Works on appropriate priorities to get the work out
- ☐ Follows through most of the time

SKILLED

- ☐ Very productive and efficient in planning and executing work
- ☐ Accurately scopes out the work, creates efficient workflows and processes, and assigns resources properly
- ☐ Consistently outperforms most other people or groups because of excellence at planning, priority setting and execution

OVERUSED SKILL

- ☐ So obsessed with doing things in a planned and orderly manner that work is sometimes late or exceeds even reasonable quality standards
- ☐ Easily thrown off balance by the unexpected and doesn't adjust well to change

Select one to three of the competencies listed below to work on to compensate for an overuse of this skill.

COMPENSATORS: 2,32,33,40,46,51,53

SOME CAUSES

- ☐ Disorganized
- ☐ Impatient
- ☐ Lack of commitment
- ☐ Lack of focus
- ☐ Lazy
- ☐ Not interested in details
- ☐ Not planful
- ☐ Poor follow-through
- ☐ Poor time management
- ☐ Procrastinator
- ☐ Slow

THE MAP

Sound personal work habits go a long way toward making many other positive things happen. Good planning skills, including the ability to estimate time and resource requirements, will always get things off to a good start and avoid having to plan later on the fly. Good goal setting skills set the standard against which decision making and resource allocation are made easier. Time management is golden. People never have enough time so the management of your and other people's time is a key skill. Follow-through saves the day. It gives you the data necessary to check the quality of your work and make the necessary adjustments before damage is done. These are lifelong habits that affect everything you do and can always use improvement.

SECTION 2: LEARNING ON YOUR OWN

THESE SELF-DEVELOPMENT REMEDIES WILL HELP YOU BUILD YOUR SKILL(S)

SOME REMEDIES

☐ **1. Lay out tasks and work.** Most successful projects begin with a good plan. What do I need to accomplish? What are the goals? What's the timeline? What resources will I need? How many of the resources do I control? Who controls the rest of the resources – people, funding, tools, materials, support – I need? Lay out the work from A to Z. Many people are seen as lacking a plan because they don't write down the sequence or parts of the work and leave something out. Ask others to comment on ordering and what's missing. *More help? – See #63 Total Quality Management/Re-Engineering and #52 Process Management.*

☐ **2. Watch out for the activity trap.** John Kotter, in *The General Managers*, found that effective managers spent about half their time working on one or two key priorities — priorities they described in their own terms, not in terms of what the business/organizational plan said. Further, they made no attempt to work as much on small but related issues that tend to add up to lots of activity. So rather than consuming themselves and others on 97 seemingly urgent and related smaller activities, they always returned to the few issues that would gain the most mileage long term.

- ☐ **3. Set goals and measures.** Nothing keeps projects on time and on budget like a goal, a plan and a measure. Set goals for the whole project and the sub tasks. Plan for all. Set measures so you and others can track progress against the goals. *More help? – See #35 Managing and Measuring Work.*

- ☐ **4. Manage efficiently.** Plan the budget and manage against it. Spend carefully. Have a reserve if the unanticipated comes up. Set up a funding timeline so you can track ongoing expenditures against plan.

- ☐ **5. Set up a process to monitor progress against the plan.** How would you know if the plan is on time? Could you estimate time to completion or percent finished at any time? Give progress feedback as you go to people involved in implementing the plan .

- ☐ **6. Lay out the process.** Most well running processes start out with a plan. What do I need to accomplish? What's the timeline? What resources will I need? Who controls the resources – people, funding, tools, materials, support – I need? What's my currency? How can I pay for or repay the resources I need? Who wins if I win? Who might lose? Buy a flow charting software program like ABC FlowCharter® that does PERT and GANT charts. Become an expert in its use. Use the output of the software to communicate your plans to others. Use the flow charts in your presentations. Nothing helps move a process along better than a good plan. It helps the people who have to work under the plan. It leads to better use of resources. It gets things done faster. It helps anticipate problems before they occur. Lay out the work from A to Z. Many people are seen as lacking because they don't write the sequence or parts of the work and leave something out. Ask others to comment on your ordering and note what's missing. *More help? – See #47 Planning and #63 Total Quality Management/Re-Engineering.*

- ☐ **7. Getting work done through others?** Some people are not good managers of others. They can produce results by themselves but do less well when the results have to come from the team. Are you having trouble getting your team to work with you to get the results you need? You have the resources and the people but things just don't run well. Maybe you do too much work yourself. You don't delegate or empower. You don't communicate well. You don't motivate well. You don't plan well. You don't set priorities and goals well. If you are a struggling manager or a first-time manager, there are well known and documented principles and practices of good managing. Do you share credit? Do you paint a clear picture of why this is important? Is their work challenging? Do you inspire or just hand out work? Read

Becoming a Manager by Linda A. Hill. Go to one course on management. *More help? – See #20 Directing Others, #36 Motivating Others, #18 Delegation, and #60 Building Effective Teams.*

☐ **8. Manage your time efficiently.** Plan your time and manage against it. Be time sensitive. Value time. Figure out what you are worth per hour and minute by taking your gross salary plus overhead and benefits. Attach a monetary value on your time. Then ask, is this worth $56 of my time? Figure out what your three largest time wasters are and reduce them 50% by batching activities and using efficient communications like E-mail and voice mail for routine matters.

☐ **9. Create more time for yourself.** Taking time to plan and set priorities actually frees up more time later, rather than just diving into things, hoping that you can get them done on time. Most people out of time claim they didn't have the time to plan their time. In the Stephen Covey *Seven Habits of Highly Successful People* sense, it's sharpening your saw.

☐ **10. Not committed?** Maybe you are giving as much to work as you care to give. Maybe you have made a life/work balance decision that leads you to a fair day's work for a fair day's pay mode of operating. No more. No less. That is an admirable decision, certainly one you can and should make. Problem is, you may be in a job where that's not enough. Otherwise people would not have given you this rating. You might want to talk to your boss to get transferred to a more comfortable job for you, one that doesn't take as much effort and require as much action initiation on your part. You may even think about moving down to the job level where your balance between quality of life and the effort and hours required of you at work are more balanced.

SECTION 3: LEARNING FROM MORE FEEDBACK

THESE SOURCES WOULD GIVE YOU THE MOST ACCURATE AND DETAILED FEEDBACK ON YOUR SKILL(S)

☐ **Direct Reports**

Across a variety of settings, your direct reports probably see you the most. They are the recipients of most of your managerial behaviors. They know your work. They can compare you with former bosses. Since they may hesitate to give you negative feedback, you have to set the atmosphere to make it easier for them. You have to ask.

☐ **Direct Boss**

Your direct boss has important information about you, your performance, and your prospects. The challenge is to get this information. There are formal processes (e.g., performance appraisals). There are day-to-day opportunities. To help, signal your boss that you want and can handle direct and timely feedback. Many bosses have trouble giving feedback, so you will have to work at it over a period of time.

☐ **Past Associates/Constituencies**
When confronted with a present performance problem, some claim, "I wasn't like that before; it must be the current situation."When feedback is available from former associates, about 50 percent support that claim. In the other half of the cases, the people were like that before and probably didn't know it. It sometimes makes sense to access the past to clearly see the present.

☐ **Peers and Colleagues**
Peers and colleagues have a special social and working relationship. They attend staff meetings together, share private views, get feedback from the same boss, travel together, and are knowledgeable about each other's work. You perhaps let your guard down more around peers and act more like yourself. They can be a valuable source of feedback.

☐ **Human Resource Professionals**
Human Resource professionals have both a formal and informal feedback role. Since they have access to unique and confidential information, they can provide the right context for feedback you've received. Sometimes they may be "directed" to give you feedback. Other times, they may pass on feedback just to be helpful to you.

☐ **Yourself**
You are an important source of feedback on yourself. But some caution is appropriate. If you have not received much feedback, you may be less accurate than the other sources. We all have blind spots, defense shields, ideal self-views, and fantasies. Before acting on your own self-views, get outside confirmation from other appropriate sources.

☐ **Internal and External Customers**
Customers interact with you as a person and as a supplier or vendor of products and services. You're important to them because you can either help address and solve their problems or stand in their way. As customer service and Total Quality programs gain importance, clients and customers become a more prominent source of feedback.

SECTION 4: LEARNING FROM DEVELOP-IN-PLACE ASSIGNMENTS

THESE PART-TIME DEVELOP-IN-PLACE ASSIGNMENTS WILL HELP YOU BUILD YOUR SKILL(S)

☐ Manage an ad hoc, temporary group of balky and resisting people through an unpopular change or project.

☐ Manage a cost-cutting project.

☐ Plan an off-site meeting, conference, convention, trade show, event, etc.

☐ Manage the purchase of a major product, equipment, materials, program, or system.

- ☐ Manage the renovation of an office, floor, building, meeting room, warehouse, etc.
- ☐ Manage the interface between consultants and the organization on a critical assignment.
- ☐ Install a new process or system (computer system, new policies, new process, new procedures, etc.).
- ☐ Work on a process-simplification team to take steps and costs out of a process.
- ☐ Manage a joint project with another unit, function, geography, etc.
- ☐ Become a member of a taskforce on a pressing problem.

SECTION 5: LEARNING FROM FULL-TIME JOBS

THESE FULL-TIME JOBS OFFER THE OPPORTUNITY TO BUILD YOUR SKILL(S)

☐ **Fix-its / Turnarounds**

The core demands to qualify as a Fix-it or Turnaround assignment are: 1. Cleaning up a mess. 2. Serious people issues/problems like credibility/performance/morale. 3. Tight deadline. 4. Serious business performance failure. 5. Last chance to fix. Four Types of Fix-its / Turnarounds: 1. Fixing a failed business/unit involving taking control, stopping losses, managing damage, planning the turnaround, dealing with people problems, installing new processes and systems, and rebuilding the spirit and performance of the unit. 2. managing sizable disasters like mishandled labor negotiations and strikes, thefts, history of significant business losses, poor staff, failed leadership, hidden problems, fraud, public relations nightmares, etc. 3. Significant reorganization and restructuring (e.g., stabilizing the business, reforming unit, introducing new systems, making people changes, resetting strategy and tactics). 4. Significant system/process breakdown (e.g,. MIS, financial coordination processes, audits, standards, etc.) across units requiring working to change something from a distant position, providing advice and counsel, and installing or implementing a major process improvement or system change outside your own unit and/or with customers outside the organization.

☐ **Start-ups**

The core demands to qualify as a start from scratch are: 1.Starting something new for you and/or for the organization. 2. Forging a new team. 3. Creating new systems/facilities/staffs/programs/procedures. 4. Contextual adversity (e.g., uncertainty, government regulation, unions, difficult environment). Seven types of start from scratches: 1. Planning, building, hiring, and managing (e.g., building a new facility, opening up a new location, moving a unit or company). 2. Heading something new (e.g., new product, new service, new line of business, new department/function, major new program). 3. Take over a group/product/service/program that had existed for less than a year and was off to a fast start. 4. Establishing overseas operations. 5. Major new designs for existing systems. 6. Moving a successful program from one unit to another. 7. Installing a new organization-wide process as a full-time job (e.g., like Total Quality).

☐ **Scale Assignments**
Core requirements to qualify as a Scale (size) shift assignment are: 1. Sizable jump-shift in the size of the job in areas like: - Number of people. - Number of layers in organization. - Size of budget. - Number of locations. - Volume of activity. - Tightness of deadlines. 2. Medium to low complexity; mostly repetitive and routine processes and procedures. 3. Stable staff and business. 4. Stable operations. 5. Often slow, steady growth.

☐ **Scope Assignments**
The core demands for a Scope (complexity) assignment are: 1. Significant increase in both internal and external scope or complexity. 2. Significant increase in visibility and/ or bottom line responsibility. 3. Unfamiliar area, business, technology, or territory. Examples of Scope assignments involving shifts: 1. Switching into a new function/technology/business. 2. Moving to new organization. 3. Moving to overseas assignment. 4. Moving to new location. 5. Adding new products/services. 6. Moving between headquarters/field. 7. Switches in ownership/top management of the unit/organization. Examples of Scope assignments involving "firsts": 1. First-time manager. 2. First-time managing managers. 3. First-time executive. 4. First-time overseas. 5. First-time headquarters/field. 6. First-time team leader. 7. First-time new technology/business/function. Scope assignments involving increased complexity: 1. Managing a significant expansion of an existing product or service. 2. Managing adding new products/service into an existing unit. 3. Managing a reorganized and more diverse unit. 4. Managing explosive growth. 5. Adding new technologies.

SECTION 6: LEARNING MORE FROM YOUR PLAN

THESE ADDITIONAL REMEDIES WILL HELP MAKE THIS DEVELOPMENT PLAN MORE EFFECTIVE FOR YOU

Learning to Learn Better

☐ **Monitoring Yourself More Closely and Get Off Your Autopilot**
Past habits are a mixed blessing, sometimes helping, sometimes not. To avoid putting yourself on "autopilot," think afresh about each situation before acting. Consistently monitor yourself with questions. Is this task different? Ask why you would repeat a past action. Are you avoiding anything, like taking a chance? Is there something new you might try?

☐ **Be Alert to Learnings When Faced With Transitions**
To avoid applying rigid habits, be alert to situations that require a transition to a new set of conditions and reactions; check what's similar and what's different; think out which past lessons and rules apply and which need to be changed. Don't apply old solutions because you have missed subtle differences.

☐ **Teach Others Something You Know Well**
Teach someone to do something you know how to do to check out your own thinking, knowledge, and rules. Watch in detail how others learn; the process will require breaking down your patterns into teachable steps.

☐ **Form a Learning Network with Others Working on the Same Thing**
Look for people in similar situations, and create a process for sharing and learning together. Look for a variety of people inside and outside your organization. Give feedback to each other; try new and different things together; share successes and failures, lessons and learning.

☐ **Sort Through Information Multiple Ways**
Collect the data and arrange it in elements or pieces. Come up with definitions, and arrange the data in various ways: chronologically, from most to least, from biggest to smallest, from cold to hot, what you know most about and least about, from known to unknown, etc., until the meaning becomes obvious.

☐ **Study Yourself in Detail**
Study your likes and dislikes because they can drive a lot of your thinking, judging, and acting. Ask which like or dislike has gotten in the way or prevented you from moving to a higher level of learning. Are your likes and dislikes really important to you or have you just gone on "autopilot"? Try to address and understand a blocking dislike and change it.

Learning from Experience, Feedback and Other People

☐ **Using Multiple Models**
Who do you know who exemplifies how to do whatever your need is? Who, for example, personifies decisiveness or compassion or strategic agility? Think more broadly than your current job and colleagues. For example, ministers, friends, spouses or community leaders are also good sources for potential models. Select your models not on the basis of overall excellence or likeability, but on the basis of the one towering strength (or glaring weakness) you are interested in. Even people who are well thought of usually have only one or two towering strengths (or glaring weaknesses). Ordinarily, you won't learn as much from the whole person as you will from one characteristic.

- ☐ **Learning from Observing Others**
  Observe others. Find opportunities to observe without interacting with your model. This enables you to objectively study the person, note what he/she is doing or not doing, and compare that with what you would typically do in similar situations. Many times you can learn more by watching than asking. Your model may not be able to explain what he/she does or may be an unwilling teacher.

- ☐ **Learning from Ineffective Behavior**
  Seeing things done poorly can be a very potent source of learning for you, especially if the behavior or action affects others negatively. Many times the thing done poorly causes emotional reactions or pain in you and others. Distance yourself from the feelings and explore why the actions didn't work.

Learning from Courses

- ☐ **Insight Events**
  These are courses designed around assessing skills and providing feedback to the participants. These events can be a powerful source of self-knowledge and can lead to significant development if done right. When selecting a self-insight course, consider the following: (1) Are the skills assessed the important ones? (2) Are the assessment techniques and instruments sound? (3) Are those who are providing the feedback trained and professional? (4) Is the feedback provided in a user-friendly and "actionable" format? (5) Does the feedback include development planning? (6) Is the setting comfortable and conducive to reflection and learning? (7) Are the other participants the kinds of people you could learn from? (8) Are you in the right frame of mind to learn from this kind of intense experience? Select events on the basis of positive answers to these 8 questions.

SUGGESTED READINGS

Dess, Gregory G. and Joseph C. Picken. *Beyond Productivity: How leading companies achieve superior performance by leveraging their human capital.* New York: AMACOM, 1999.

Dorland, Gil and John Dorland. *Duty, Honor, Company – West Point Fundamentals for Business Success.* New York: Henry Holt & Company, 1992.

Drucker, Peter F. *Managing for Results.* New York: HarperCollins, 1993.

Head, Christopher W. *Beyond corporate transformation: A whole systems approach to creating and sustaining high performance.* Portland, OR: Productivity Press, 1997.

continued

Hickman, Craig R. *The Productivity Game: An interactive business game where you make or break the company.* Englewood Cliffs, NJ: Prentice Hall, 1995.

Kaplan, Robert S. and David P. Norton. *The Balanced Scorecard: Translating strategy into action.* Boston: Harvard Business School Press, 1996.

Liker, Jeffrey K. *Becoming Lean: Inside stories of U.S.* Manufacturers. Portland, OR: Productivity Press, 1998.

Ott, Richard W. and Martin Snead. *Unleashing Productivity!.* Burr Ridge, IL: Irwin Professional Publishing, 1994.

Weimer, William A. *Masters & Patrons – Renaissance solutions for today's productivity problems.* Marietta, GA: Dogwood Publishing Co., 1992.

ADDING SKILLS AND CAPABILITIES

SECTION 1: YOUR DEVELOPMENT NEED(S)

General Definition: The extent to which any capabilities were added to the current portfolio of skills, attitudes and knowledge in order to get work done and build for the future.

UNSKILLED

- ☐ Shows little interest in learning and building new skills and knowledge
- ☐ Stuck in a comfort zone – getting out of date
- ☐ Appears content with skills as they are

AVERAGE

- ☐ Has about as much interest in learning new skills and knowledge as others do
- ☐ If it fits-in with the work, will learn when the opportunity is there
- ☐ Generally keeps up with near term new skill requirements

SKILLED

- ☐ Eagerly learns new skills and capabilities to improve for the future
- ☐ Makes learning new skills and capabilities a high priority
- ☐ More and better skilled at the end of the year than at the beginning

OVERUSED SKILL

- ☐ Spends so much time skill building that doesn't focus enough on day to day work
- ☐ Sometimes works on new skills that turn out to be only marginally helpful later

Select one to three of the competencies listed below to work on to compensate for an overuse of this skill.

COMPENSATORS: 1,16,17,32,50,51,53,58

SOME CAUSES

- ☐ Avoids criticism
- ☐ Comfortable with what is
- ☐ Doesn't admit to shortcomings
- ☐ Doesn't set forward priorities
- ☐ Low self-awareness
- ☐ Not a risk taker
- ☐ Not career oriented
- ☐ Not future oriented
- ☐ Procrastinator
- ☐ Too busy

THE MAP

It's hard enough to be totally prepared for today much less spend time and energy getting ready for tomorrow. But, there is no rest for the career minded individual. At the pace the world is moving, anticipating the knowledge and skill requirements on your path to where you want to go is essential. Jobs are getting more demanding and requiring higher level skills. Technology is exploding. Information is more available to all. Speed is increasing. There is no option. You have to block out time to keep up and more importantly get ahead of the career curve.

SECTION 2: LEARNING ON YOUR OWN

THESE SELF-DEVELOPMENT REMEDIES WILL HELP YOU BUILD YOUR SKILL(S)

SOME REMEDIES

☐ **1. Many people don't know how careers are built.** Most are put off by the popular myth of getting ahead. All of us have seen *How to Succeed in Business Without Really Trying* or something like it. It's easy to get cynical and believe that successful people are political or sell out, suck up, knife people in the back, it's who you know, and so on. The facts are dramatically different from this. Those behaviors get people in trouble eventually. What has staying power is performing and problem solving on the current job, having a few notable strengths, and seeking new tasks you don't know how to do. It's solving every problem with tenacity while looking for what you haven't yet done and getting yourself in a position to do it. Read *The Lessons of Experience* by McCall, Lombardo and Morrison for the careers of men and *Breaking the Glass Ceiling* by Morrison, White and Van Velsor for the careers of women to see how successful careers really happen.

☐ **2. Break out of your career comfort zone.** Maybe you haven't seen enough. Pick some activities you haven't done before but might find exciting. Take a course in a new area. Task trade – switch tasks with a peer. Volunteer for task forces and projects that are multi-functional or multi-business in nature. Read more broadly. *More help? – See #46 Perspective.*

☐ **3. Don't know what it takes?** Think of five successful people in your organization/field whom you know well and ask what drives them? What sorts of jobs have they held? What are their technical skills? Behavioral skills? Use the CAREER ARCHITECT® Portfolio Sort™ Cards to determine what the 10 key skills of each person are; compare this list with your own self assessment and feedback. Ask Human Resources if they have a success profile for some of the jobs you may be interested in. Make a list of what you need to work on next.

☐ **4. Not willing to make sacrifices?** Many people turn down career opportunities based upon current life comforts only to regret it later when they have been passed by. Studies indicate that the vast majority of moves successful general managers had to make during their careers were not seen as right for them at the time. They tried to turn them down. We all have the problems. Children in school. A house we like. A parent to take care of. A working spouse. A medical issue to manage. A good neighborhood. Most successful careers require moving around during the years that are the most inconvenient and painful – when we have kids in school, not much extra money, and aging parents to manage. Read *The Lessons of Experience* by McCall, Lombardo and Morrison for the careers of men and *Breaking the Glass Ceiling* by Morrison, White and Van Velsor for the careers of women to see how successful careers are really built. Set your mind to it. You must move to grow.

☐ **5. Assessment.** First, get a good multi-source assessment, a 360° questionnaire, or poll 10 people who know you well to give you detailed feedback on what you do well and not well, what they'd like to see you keep doing, start doing and stop doing. You don't want to waste time on developing things that turn out not to be needs.

☐ **6. Next, divide your skills into these categories**

- Clear strengths – Me at my best.
- Overdone strengths – I do too much of a good thing – "I'm so confident that I'm seen as arrogant."
- Hidden strengths – Others rate me higher than I rate myself.
- Blind spots – I rate myself higher than others rate me.
- Weaknesses – I don't do it well.
- Untested areas – I've never been involved in strategy formulation.
- Don't knows – I need more feedback.

☐ **7. What's important?** Find out what's important for your current job and the two or three next jobs you might have an opportunity to get. See if there are success profiles for those jobs. Compare the top requirements with your appraisal. If there are no success profiles, ask the Human Resources Department for help or ask one or two people who now have those jobs what skills they need and use to be successful.

☐ **8. Show others you take your development seriously.** State your developmental needs and ask for their help. Research shows that people are much more likely to help and give the benefit of the doubt to those who admit their shortcomings and try to do something about them. They know it takes courage. *More help? – See #44 Personal Disclosure.*

- ☐ **9. Arrogance is a major blockage to self knowledge.** Many people who have a towering strength or lots of success get little feedback and roll along until their careers get in trouble. If you are viewed as arrogant, you may have to repeatedly ask for feedback, and when you get it, there may be some anger with it. Almost by definition, arrogant people overrate themselves in the eyes of others. Others who think you are arrogant might rate you lower than neutral observers would. If you devalue others, they will return the insult.

- ☐ **10. Defensiveness is the other major blockage to self knowledge.** Here people suspect you really can't take it, that you are defending against something, probably by blaming it on others or the job context. Defensive people get less feedback, thereby fulfilling their dream of being perfect. To break this cycle, you will need to follow the rules of good listening (*see #33 Listening*) and give examples of the behavior being described to validate what people are saying. This may sound unfair, but you should initially accept all feedback as accurate, even when you know it isn't. On those matters that really count, you can go back and fix it later. *More help? – See #108 Defensiveness.*

SECTION 3: LEARNING FROM MORE FEEDBACK

THESE SOURCES WOULD GIVE YOU THE MOST ACCURATE AND DETAILED FEEDBACK ON YOUR SKILL(S)

☐ **Direct Boss**

Your direct boss has important information about you, your performance, and your prospects. The challenge is to get this information. There are formal processes (e.g., performance appraisals). There are day-to-day opportunities. To help, signal your boss that you want and can handle direct and timely feedback. Many bosses have trouble giving feedback, so you will have to work at it over a period of time.

☐ **Human Resource Professionals**

Human Resource professionals have both a formal and informal feedback role. Since they have access to unique and confidential information, they can provide the right context for feedback you've received. Sometimes they may be "directed" to give you feedback. Other times, they may pass on feedback just to be helpful to you.

☐ **Natural Mentors**

Natural Mentors have a special relationship with you and are interested in your success and your future. Since they are usually not in your direct chain of command, you can have more open, relaxed, and fruitful discussions about yourself and your career prospects. They can be a very important source for candid or critical feedback others may not give you.

- ☐ **Past Associates/Constituencies**
  When confronted with a present performance problem, some claim, "I wasn't like that before; it must be the current situation." When feedback is available from former associates, about 50 percent support that claim. In the other half of the cases, the people were like that before and probably didn't know it. It sometimes makes sense to access the past to clearly see the present.

- ☐ **Direct Reports**
  Across a variety of settings, your direct reports probably see you the most. They are the recipients of most of your managerial behaviors. They know your work. They can compare you with former bosses. Since they may hesitate to give you negative feedback, you have to set the atmosphere to make it easier for them. You have to ask.

SECTION 4: LEARNING FROM DEVELOP-IN-PLACE ASSIGNMENTS

THESE PART-TIME DEVELOP-IN-PLACE ASSIGNMENTS WILL HELP YOU BUILD YOUR SKILL(S)

- ☐ Do a study of failed executives in your organization, including interviewing people still with the organization who knew or worked with them, and report the findings to top management. Attend a self-awareness/assessment course that includes feedback. Work short rotations in other units, functions or geographies you've not been exposed to before. Train and work as an assessor in an assessment center.
- ☐ Launch a new product, service, or process.
- ☐ Seek out and use a seed budget to create and pursue a personal idea, product, or service.
- ☐ Manage an ad hoc, temporary group of people where the people in the group are towering experts but the temporary manager is not.
- ☐ Volunteer to fill an open management job temporarily until it's filled. Go on a business trip to a foreign country you've not been to before. Volunteer to do a special project for and with a person you admire and who has a skill you need to develop.

SECTION 5: LEARNING FROM FULL-TIME JOBS

THESE FULL-TIME JOBS OFFER THE OPPORTUNITY TO BUILD YOUR SKILL(S)

- ☐ **Cross Moves**
  The core demands necessary to qualify as a Cross-Move are: 1.Move to a very different set of challenges. 2. Abrupt jump-shift in tasks/activities. 3. Never been there before. 4. New setting/conditions. Examples of Cross-Moves are: 1. Changing divisions. 2. Changing functions. 3. Field/headquarters shifts. 4. Line/staff switches. 5. Country switches. 6. Working with all new people. 7. Changing lines of business.

☐ **Off-Shore Assignments**
The core demands to qualify as an Off-Shore assignment are: 1. First time working in the country. 2. Significant challenges like new language, hardship location, unique business rules/practices, significant cultural/marketplace differences, different functional task, etc. 3. More than a year assignment. 4. No automatic return deal. 5. Not necessarily a change in job challenge, technical content, or responsibilities.

☐ **Scope Assignments**
The core demands for a Scope (complexity) assignment are: 1.Significant increase in both internal and external scope or complexity. 2. Significant increase in visibility and/ or bottom line responsibility. 3. Unfamiliar area, business, technology, or territory. Examples of Scope assignments involving shifts: 1. Switching into a new function/technology/business. 2. Moving to new organization. 3. Moving to overseas assignment. 4. Moving to new location. 5. Adding new products/services. 6. Moving between headquarters/field. 7. Switches in ownership/top management of the unit/organization. Examples of Scope assignments involving "firsts": 1. First-time manager. 2. First-time managing managers. 3. First-time executive. 4. First-time overseas. 5. First-time headquarters/field. 6. First-time team leader. 7. First-time new technology/business/function. Scope assignments involving increased complexity: 1. Managing a significant expansion of an existing product or service. 2. Managing adding new products/service into an existing unit. 3. Managing a reorganized and more diverse unit. 4. Managing explosive growth.

☐ **Staff to Line Shifts**
Core demands necessary to qualify for a Staff to Line shift are: 1. Moving to a job with an easily determined bottom line or results. 2. Managing bigger scope and/or scale. 3. Requires new skills/perspectives. 4. Unfamiliar aspects of the assignment.

☐ **Start-ups**
The core demands to qualify as a start from scratch are: 1. Starting something new for you and/or for the organization. 2. Forging a new team. 3. Creating new systems/facilities/staffs/programs/procedures. 4. Contextual adversity (e.g., uncertainty, government regulation, unions, difficult environment). Seven types of start from scratches: 1. Planning, building, hiring, and managing (e.g., building a new facility, opening up a new location, moving a unit or company). 2. Heading something new (e.g., new product, new service, new line of business, new department/function, major new program). 3. Take over a group/ product/service/program that had existed for less than a year and was off to a fast start. 4. Establishing overseas operations. 5. Major new designs for existing systems. 6. Moving a successful program from one unit to another. 7. Installing a new organization-wide process as a full-time job (e.g., like Total Quality).

SECTION 6: LEARNING MORE FROM YOUR PLAN

THESE ADDITIONAL REMEDIES WILL HELP MAKE THIS DEVELOPMENT PLAN MORE EFFECTIVE FOR YOU

Learning to Learn Better

- ☐ **Teach Others Something You Don't Know Well**
  Commit to a project like teaching something you don't know much about to force you to learn quickly to accomplish the task; pick something new, different, or unfamiliar.

- ☐ **Keep a Learning Journal**
  Keep a learning log or diary about the issues and opportunities you've faced and how you've acted. Focus on how you've used your strengths and weaknesses. Deduce your effective and successful rules of thumb; what worked and what didn't, and how you would have done it differently.

- ☐ **Form a Learning Network with Others Working on the Same Thing**
  Look for people in similar situations, and create a process for sharing and learning together. Look for a variety of people inside and outside your organization. Give feedback to each other; try new and different things together; share successes and failures, lessons and learning.

- ☐ **Use a Tutor to Learn Something New**
  Set up a tutor relationship in the areas you're working on; open up, listen, learn, and try new things. Learn from the tutoring/ learning process. Do you learn more easily from a tutor or do you get blocked? Test out your thinking with the tutor; do debriefs after trying the tutor's advice.

- ☐ **Learn New and Frivolous Skills to Study How You Learn**
  Practice learning frivolous and fun skills (like juggling, square dancing, skeet shooting, video games, etc.) to see yourself under different and less personal or stressful learning conditions. Ask yourself why that was easy while developing new personal/managerial skills is so hard. Try something harder with the same tactics.

- ☐ **Regularly Read Relevant Publications**
  Read publications most relevant to you such as the Wall Street Journal, the Harvard Business Review, the Economist, Fortune, Business Week, etc. Track a single issue or trend to see as many sides of it as you can. What tactics and strategies are being followed? How is this similar to something you are doing? How could you use some of your insights?

- ☐ **Do a Career Learning Timeline for Insights**
  Do a timeline (a chronology from schooling to the present) for yourself in terms of the development of your thinking and problem-solving style and preferences. List the good and the bad times. What made the difference? What breakthroughs did you have? How have you developed as a learner? How did you get rid of previous blocks? Are you still growing?

Learning from Experience, Feedback and Other People

- [ ] **Being a Student of Others**
While many of us rely on others for information or advice, we do not really study the behavior of other people. Ask what a person does exceptionally well or poorly. What behaviors are particularly effective and ineffective for them? What works for them and what doesn't? As a student of others, you can deduce the rules of thumb for effective and ineffective behavior and include those in your own library. In comparing yourself with this person, in what areas could you most improve? What could you specifically do to improve in ways comfortable for you?

- [ ] **Learning from Remote Models**
Learning from remote models. Many times you can learn from people not directly available to you. You can read a book about them, watch tapes of public figures, read analyses of them, etc. The principles of learning are the same. Ask yourself what they do well or poorly and deduce their rules of thumb.

Learning from Courses

- [ ] **Insight Events**
These are courses designed around assessing skills and providing feedback to the participants. These events can be a powerful source of self-knowledge and can lead to significant development if done right. When selecting a self-insight course, consider the following: (1) Are the skills assessed the important ones? (2) Are the assessment techniques and instruments sound? (3) Are those who are providing the feedback trained and professional? (4) Is the feedback provided in a user-friendly and "actionable" format? (5) Does the feedback include development planning? (6) Is the setting comfortable and conducive to reflection and learning? (7) Are the other participants the kinds of people you could learn from? (8) Are you in the right frame of mind to learn from this kind of intense experience? Select events on the basis of positive answers to these 8 questions.

SUGGESTED READINGS

Hayes, Robert H., Gary P. Pisaro and David Upton. *Strategic Operations – Competing through capabilities.* New York: Free Press, 1996.

McCall, Morgan W., Michael M. Lombardo and Ann M. Morrison. *The Lessons of Experience.* Lexington, MA: Lexington Books, 1988.

Mohrman, Susan Albers, Jay R. Galbraith and Edward E. Lawler III and Associates. *Tomorrow's Organization – Crafting Winning Capabilities in a Dynamic World.* San Francisco: Jossey-Bass, Inc., 1998.

Morrison, Ann M., Randall P. White, Ellen Van Velsor, and the Center for Creative Leadership. *Breaking the glass ceiling: Can women reach the top of America's largest corporations?.* Reading, MA: Addison-Wesley Pub. Co., 1992.

Tobin, Daniel R. *Transformational Learning – Renewing your company through knowledge and skills.* New York: John Wiley & Sons, Inc., 1996.

There are no competencies 90–100.
Those numbers are reserved for future additions.

THE 19 CAREER STALLERS AND STOPPERS

101

UNABLE TO ADAPT TO DIFFERENCES

SECTION 1: YOUR DEVELOPMENT NEED(S)

A PROBLEM

- ☐ Has trouble working with and adapting to new or different bosses, strategies, plans and programs, cultures, and philosophies
- ☐ Might disagree inappropriately or too vocally with top management on mission, values, strategies, and tactics
- ☐ Would not do well with a person he/she disagreed with

NOT A PROBLEM

- ☐ Comfortable with change
- ☐ Challenges constructively but then goes along with change
- ☐ Can support things he/she doesn't totally agree with
- ☐ Easily makes transitions to the new and different
- ☐ Relates well to bosses
- ☐ Can deal with bad bosses reasonably well
- ☐ Can handle conflict evenhandedly
- ☐ Open to the views of others

SOME CAUSES

- ☐ Arrogant
- ☐ Can't handle conflicting views
- ☐ Defensive
- ☐ Hangs on hoping to make it without changing
- ☐ Like own ideas too much
- ☐ Low risk taker
- ☐ Narrow in scope and interests
- ☐ Not open to new approaches
- ☐ Not strategic
- ☐ Perfectionist
- ☐ Poor interpersonal skills
- ☐ Prefer the tried and true
- ☐ Problems with authority figures
- ☐ Problems with diversity
- ☐ Rigid values
- ☐ Too busy to change
- ☐ Too comfortable
- ☐ Very smart and successful

THE MAP

This has become one of, if not the, most common reasons promising people get in trouble. While you may be performing well now, people say you're inflexible or can't handle disagreement. You may have gotten in your comfort zone and be uncomfortable with change; there may be certain types of authority figures you have trouble dealing with. You are not updating and keeping yourself fresh.

SECTION 2: LEARNING ON YOUR OWN

THESE SELF-DEVELOPMENT REMEDIES WILL HELP YOU BUILD YOUR SKILL(S)

SOME REMEDIES

☐ **1. Defensiveness and arrogance are major blockages to adapting to change.** Defensive and arrogant people get less feedback from others. They don't listen. Interrupt. See change as a personal threat and an indictment of their current thinking and practices. People don't like working with or around defensive and arrogant people. Defensive and arrogant people are typically out of the information loop so they hear about the change late, which increases their defensive reaction. Even though it may not be true, defensiveness and arrogance are seen as resistance to input and therefore change. *More help? – See #104 Arrogant and #108 Defensiveness.*

☐ **2. Pure resistance to new ideas.** People say you're stuck in the past. For some reason, you resist anything or anybody new or different. You're the last to get on board a new initiative. You're from Missouri (the "Show Me" state); we have to prove it to you before you'll move. Surveys done with a major outplacement firm show that those most likely to be let go during a downsizing have good technical, individual skills, but are seen as not learning to do anything new or different, and resisting change. You can't survive today without keeping you and your skills fresh. There's not much room anymore for someone stuck in the past. In your day-to-day interactions with people, your style may make you appear closed or blocked to new or different points of view. Your first job is to turn off your evaluator/rejector program and learn to listen more. *More help? – See #33 Listening*. Ask more questions – "How did you conclude a change is necessary? Do you prefer the change to what we're now doing?" If you disagree, give your reasons first. Then invite criticism of your response. Turn the disagreement back to the nature of the problem or strategy the change is aimed at – "What are we trying to solve? What causes it? What questions should be asked and answered? What objective standards could we use to measure success?"

☐ **3. Answers. Solutions. Conclusions. Statements. Dictates.** That's the staple of resisters and dismissers. Instant output. Sharp reactions. This may be getting you in trouble. You jump to conclusions, categorically dismiss what others say about the need for change, use challenging words in an absolute tone. People then see you as closed or combative. More negatively, they may believe you think they're stupid or ill-informed because they suggested change. Use gentler words – "Another factor is...," "I see this a bit differently," "I think the problem is more one of...". People usually respond well to qualifiers; then you can state your point directly. Give people a chance to talk without interruption. If you're seen as intolerant or closed, people will often stumble over words in their haste to talk with you or shortcut their argument since they assume you're not listening anyway. Ask a question, invite them to disagree with you, present their argument back to them softly, let them save face no matter what. Add a 15-second pause into your transactions before you say anything and add two clarifying questions per transaction to signal you're listening and want to understand the need for change. *More help? – See #33 Listening and #41 Patience.*

☐ **4. You may be seen as rigid in your values stances** and unwilling to accept, or even see, those of others. *More help? – See Overdoing #22 Ethics and Values*. Rigid stances often come from childhood and early adult experiences. You need to know why you hold these values and critically examine if they are appropriate here. Statements of belief are pronouncements – a true value holds up to action scrutiny; you can say why you hold it, how it plays out in different situations, and what happens when it conflicts with other values. You may have reduced your beliefs to rigid commandments.

☐ **5. Selective resistance.** Do you adapt to some and not to others? You probably have good people buckets and bad people buckets and signal your disagreement with them to the bad bucket groups or individuals. You may have good group buckets and bad group buckets – gender, race, age, origin. Learn to understand without accepting or judging. Listen, take notes, ask questions, and be able to make their case as well as they can. Pick something in their argument you agree with. Present your argument in terms of the problem only – why you think this is the best manner to deal with a mutually agreed upon problem. A careful observer should not be able to tell your assessment of people or their arguments at the time. Find someone who is a fair observer and get a critique. Was I fair? Did I treat everyone the same? Were my objections based on reasoning against standards and not directed at people?

☐ **6. Too comfortable?** You may be caught in your comfort zone. You rely on historical, tried and true solutions. You use what you know and have seen or done before – so you naturally resist anything you yet don't know or understand. When faced with a new issue, challenge or problem, first figure out what causes it. Don't go to your past for the solution or conclusion first. Keep asking why, see how many causes you can come up with and how many organizing buckets you can put them in. This increases the chance of a better solution because you can see more connections. Look for patterns in data, don't just collect information. *More help? – See #51 Problem Solving.*

☐ **7. You may be highly intelligent and quite skilled in your area.** You may work around people who aren't as informed or educated as you are. You may be in a position of essentially dictating what should be done. When others less experienced than you suggest change, you may quickly dismiss it. But you don't have to make it demeaning or painful. Studies of creativity show that people less familiar with an area can contribute some unique and valuable suggestions because they are not trapped in the knowledge. You need to switch to an idea facilitator – tell him/her how you think about the need for change, don't just fire out solutions. Tell him/her what you think the problem is, what questions need to be asked and answered, how you would go about finding out, what you think some likely solutions might be. Listen to what he/she has to say.

☐ **8. It may be that you lack perspective.** First, see *#5 Business Acumen, #46 Perspective, and #58 Strategic Agility*. Then do an independent study of the issues in disagreement and come up with your own perspective. Do others the courtesy of analyzing their proposed solution as if it were valid as well.

☐ **9. Be an early adopter of a change.** Find some new thing, technique, software, tool, system, process or skill relevant to your activity. Privately become an expert in it. Read the books. Get certified. Visit somewhere where it's already being done. Then surprise everyone and be the first to introduce the change into your world. Sell it. Train others. Integrate it into your work.

☐ **10. The real fix.** Whatever applies in Some Causes, you will have to work on *#3 Approachability*, and *#31 Interpersonal Savvy*. Until you signal repeatedly that you are open to others, interested in what they have to say, share things you don't have to share, invite people to talk with you and then listen, little will come of this effort. You will have to persevere, endure some rejection, and perhaps some angry or dismissive remarks in order to balance the situation. Mentally rehearse so you're not blindsided by this. It would be a rare group of people who would respond to your overtures without making you squirm a bit because you have caused them pain in the past.

SECTION 3: LEARNING FROM MORE FEEDBACK

THESE SOURCES WOULD GIVE YOU THE MOST ACCURATE AND DETAILED FEEDBACK ON YOUR SKILL(S)

- ☐ **Boss's Boss(es)**
  From a process standpoint, your boss's boss probably has the most influence and control over your progress. He/she has a broader perspective, has more access to data, and stands at the center of decisions about you. To know what he/she thinks, without having to violate the canons of corporate due process to get that information, would be quite useful.

- ☐ **Development Professionals**
  Sometimes it might be valuable to get some analysis and feedback from a professional trained and certified in the area you're working on: possibly a career counselor, a therapist, clergy, a psychologist, etc.

- ☐ **Direct Boss**
  Your direct boss has important information about you, your performance, and your prospects. The challenge is to get this information. There are formal processes (e.g., performance appraisals). There are day-to-day opportunities. To help, signal your boss that you want and can handle direct and timely feedback. Many bosses have trouble giving feedback, so you will have to work at it over a period of time.

- ☐ **Human Resource Professionals**
  Human Resource professionals have both a formal and informal feedback role. Since they have access to unique and confidential information, they can provide the right context for feedback you've received. Sometimes they may be "directed" to give you feedback. Other times, they may pass on feedback just to be helpful to you.

- ☐ **Past Associates/Constituencies**
  When confronted with a present performance problem, some claim, "I wasn't like that before; it must be the current situation." When feedback is available from former associates, about 50% support that claim. In the other half of the cases, the people were like that before and probably didn't know it. It sometimes makes sense to access the past to clearly see the present.

SECTION 4: LEARNING FROM DEVELOP-IN-PLACE ASSIGNMENTS

THESE PART-TIME DEVELOP-IN-PLACE ASSIGNMENTS WILL HELP YOU BUILD YOUR SKILL(S)

- ☐ Go on a business trip to a foreign country you've not been to before.
- ☐ Work on a project that involves travel and study of an issue, acquisition, or joint venture off-shore or overseas, with a report back to management.

- ☐ Manage a project team made up of nationals from a number of countries.
- ☐ Represent the concerns of a group of nonexempt, clerical, or administrative employees to higher management to seek resolution of a difficult issue.
- ☐ Manage an ad hoc, temporary group of balky and resisting people through an unpopular change or project.
- ☐ Manage an ad hoc, temporary group of people where the people in the group are towering experts but the temporary manager is not.
- ☐ Handle a tough negotiation with an internal or external client or customer.
- ☐ Prepare and present a proposal of some consequence to top management.
- ☐ Manage a dissatisfied internal or external customer; troubleshoot a performance or quality problem with a product or service.
- ☐ Make peace with an enemy or someone you've disappointed with a product or service or someone you've had some trouble with or don't get along well with.

SECTION 5: LEARNING FROM FULL-TIME JOBS

THESE FULL-TIME JOBS OFFER THE OPPORTUNITY TO BUILD YOUR SKILL(S)

☐ **Chair of Projects/Task Forces**

The core demands for qualifying as a Project/Task Force assignment are: 1) Full-time assignment. 2) Important and specific goal. 3) Tight deadline. 4) Success or failure will be evident. 5) High-visibility sponsor. 6) Learning something on the fly. 7) Must get others to cooperate. 8) Usually six months or more. Four types of Projects/Task Forces: 1) New ideas, products, services, or systems (e.g., product/service/program research and development, creation/installation/launch of a new system, new programs like Total Quality Management, positive discipline). 2) Formal negotiations and relationships (e.g., acquisitions, divestitures, agreements, joint ventures; licensing arrangements, franchising; dealing with unions, governments, communities, charities, customers, and relocations). 3) Big one-time events (e.g., working on a major presentation for the board, organizing significant meetings or conferences, disaster/damage control teams; reorganizations, mergers, acquisitions, or relocations, working on visions, charters, strategies, other time-urgent issues and problems). 4) Troubleshooting (e.g., problems, disasters, crises, product/service failures, accidents, illegal activities, damage control in public relations goofs, shut downs, downsizings, layoffs, abrupt changes in leadership).

- [ ] **Influencing Without Authority**
  The core demands to qualify as an Influence Without Authority are: 1) Significant challenge (e.g, start-up, fix-it, scope and/or scale assignment, strategic planning project, changes in management practices/ systems). 2) Insufficient direct authority to make it happen. 3) Tight deadlines. 4) Visible to significant others. 5) Sensitive politics.

- [ ] **Off-Shore Assignments**
  The core demands to qualify as an Off-Shore assignment are: 1) First time working in the country. 2) Significant challenges like new language, hardship location, unique business rules/practices, significant cultural/marketplace differences, different functional task, etc. 3) More than a year assignment. 4) No automatic return deal. 5) Not necessarily a change in job challenge, technical content, or responsibilities.

- [ ] **Scope Assignments**
  The core demands for a Scope (complexity) assignment are: 1) Significant increase in both internal and external scope or complexity. 2) Significant increase in visibility and/or bottom line responsibility. 3) Unfamiliar area, business, technology, or territory. Examples of Scope assignments involving shifts: 1) Switching into a new function/technology/business. 2) Moving to new organization. 3) Moving to overseas assignment. 4) Moving to new location. 5) Adding new products/ services. 6) Moving between headquarters/field. 7) Switches in ownership/top management of the unit/organization. Examples of Scope assignments involving "firsts": 1) First-time manager. 2) First-time managing managers. 3) First-time executive. 4) First-time overseas. 5) First-time headquarters/field. 6) First-time team leader. 7) First-time new technology/business/function. Scope assignments involving increased complexity: 1) Managing a significant expansion of an existing product or service. 2) Managing adding new products/service into an existing unit. 3) Managing a reorganized and more diverse unit. 4) Managing explosive growth. 5) Adding new technologies.

- [ ] **Start-ups**
  The core demands to qualify as a start from scratch are: 1) Starting something new for you and/or for the organization. 2) Forging a new team. 3) Creating new systems/facilities/staffs/programs/procedures. 4) Contextual adversity (e.g., uncertainty, government regulation, unions, difficult environment). Seven types of start from scratches: 1) Planning, building, hiring, and managing (e.g., building a new facility, opening up a new location, moving a unit or company). 2) Heading something new (e.g., new product, new service, new line of business, new department/function, major new program). 3) Take over a group/product/service/program that had existed for less than a year and was off to a fast start. 4) Establishing overseas operations. 5) Major new designs for existing systems. 6) Moving a successful program from one unit to another. 7) Installing a new organization-wide process as a full-time job (e.g., like Total Quality).

SECTION 6: LEARNING MORE FROM YOUR PLAN

THESE ADDITIONAL REMEDIES WILL HELP MAKE THIS DEVELOPMENT PLAN MORE EFFECTIVE FOR YOU

Learning to Learn Better

☐ **Monitoring Yourself More Closely and Getting off Your Autopilot**
Past habits are a mixed blessing, sometimes helping, sometimes not. To avoid putting yourself on "autopilot," think afresh about each situation before acting. Consistently monitor yourself with questions. Is this task different? Ask why you would repeat a past action. Are you avoiding anything, like taking a chance? Is there something new you might try?

☐ **Be Alert to Learnings When Faced With Transitions**
To avoid applying rigid habits, be alert to situations that require a transition to a new set of conditions and reactions; check what's similar and what's different; think out which past lessons and rules apply and which need to be changed. Don't apply old solutions because you have missed subtle differences.

☐ **Use Objective Data When Judging Others**
Practice studying other people more than judging or evaluating them. Get the facts, the data, how they think, why they do things, without classifying them into your internal like/dislike or agree/disagree boxes, categories, or buckets. Try to project or predict how they would act/react in various situations and follow up to see how accurate you are.

☐ **Study Yourself in Detail**
Study your likes and dislikes because they can drive a lot of your thinking, judging, and acting. Ask which like or dislike has gotten in the way or prevented you from moving to a higher level of learning. Are your likes and dislikes really important to you or have you just gone on "autopilot"? Try to address and understand a blocking dislike and change it.

☐ **Examine Why You're Blocked on a Key Issue**
Examine what you are worrying/angry about and list all of your thoughts about it; ask why these feelings are holding you back. Why are the feelings overriding your thinking? How are they getting in the way? Why are they important to you? How can you move beyond them and learn to do something different?

☐ **Examine Why You Judge People the Way You Do**
List the people you like and those you dislike and try to find out why. What do those you like have in common with each other and with you? What do those you dislike have in common with themselves and how do they differ from you? Are your "people buckets" logical and productive or do they interfere? Could you be more effective without putting people into buckets?

Learning from Experience, Feedback and Other People

☐ **Using Multiple Models**
Who do you know who exemplifies how to do whatever your need is? Who, for example, personifies decisiveness or compassion or strategic agility? Think more broadly than your current job and colleagues. For example, clergy, friends, spouses or community leaders are also good sources for potential models. Select your models not on the basis of overall excellence or likability, but on the basis of the one towering strength (or glaring weakness) you are interested in. Even people who are well thought of usually have only one or two towering strengths (or glaring weaknesses). Ordinarily, you won't learn as much from the whole person as you will from one characteristic.

☐ **Learning from Bad Bosses**
First, what does he/she do so well to make him/her your boss? (Even bad bosses have strengths). Then, ask what makes this boss bad for you. Is it his/her behavior? Attitude? Values? Philosophy? Practices? Style? What is the source of the conflict? Why do you react as you do? Do others react the same? How are you part of the problem? What do you do that triggers your boss? If you wanted to, could you reduce the conflict or make it go away by changing something you do? Is there someone around you who doesn't react like you? How are they different? What can you learn from them? What is your emotional reaction to this boss? Why do you react like that? What can you do to cope with these feelings? Can you avoid reacting out of anger and frustration? Can you find something positive about the situation? Can you use someone else as a buffer? Can you learn from your emotions? What lasting lessons of managing others can you take away from this experience? What won't you do as a manager? What will you do differently? How could you teach these principles you've learned to others by the use of this example?

Learning from Courses

☐ **Insight Events**
These are courses designed around assessing skills and providing feedback to the participants. These events can be a powerful source of self-knowledge and can lead to significant development if done right. When selecting a self-insight course, consider the following: 1) Are the skills assessed the important ones? 2) Are the assessment techniques and instruments sound? 3) Are those who are providing the feedback trained and professional? 4) Is the feedback provided in a user-friendly and "actionable" format? 5) Does the feedback include development planning? 6) Is the setting comfortable and conducive to reflection and learning? 7) Are the other participants the kinds of people you could learn from? 8) Are you in the right frame of mind to learn from this kind of intense experience? Select events on the basis of positive answers to these eight questions.

☐ **Attitude Toward Learning**
In addition to selecting the right course, a learning attitude is required. Be open. Close down your "like/dislike" switch, your "agree/disagree" blinders, and your "like me/not like me" feelings toward the instructors. Learning requires new lessons, change, and new behaviors and perspectives – all scary stuff for most people. Don't resist. Take in all you can during the course. Ask clarifying questions. Discuss concerns with the other participants. Jot down what you learn as you go. After the course is over, take some reflective time to glean the meat. Make the practical decisions about what you can and cannot use.

SUGGESTED READINGS

Bern, Paula. *How to work for a woman boss even if you'd rather not.* New York: Dodd, Mead, 1987.

Blank, Renee and Sandra Slipp. *Voices of Diversity – Real people talk about problems and solutions in a workplace where everyone is not alike.* New York: AMACOM, 1994.

Brinkman, Rick, Ph.D. and Dr. Rick Kirschner. *Dealing with People You Can't Stand.* New York: McGraw-Hill, Inc., 1994.

Foster, D. Glenn and Mary Marshall. *How can I get through to you?: breakthrough communication beyond gender, beyond therapy, beyond deception.* New York: Hyperion, 1994.

Stone, Florence M. *The Manager's Balancing Act.* New York: AMACOM, 1997.

White, Randall P., Philip Hodgson, and Stuart Crainer. *The future of leadership: Riding the corporate rapids into the 21st century.* Washington, DC: Pitman Publishing, 1996.

102

POOR ADMINISTRATOR

SECTION 1: YOUR DEVELOPMENT NEED(S)

A PROBLEM

- ☐ Has low detail-orientation
- ☐ Lets things fall through the cracks
- ☐ Overcommits and underdelivers
- ☐ Misses key details
- ☐ Forgets undocumented commitments
- ☐ Has to scramble to pull things together at the last minute
- ☐ Moves on without completing the task

NOT A PROBLEM

- ☐ Well organized and detail skilled
- ☐ Reliable – keeps tabs on work in process; remembers commitments
- ☐ Good administrator
- ☐ Keeps things on track
- ☐ Sets tight priorities
- ☐ Uses time well
- ☐ Says no if he/she can't get to it
- ☐ Completes most things on time and in time

SOME CAUSES

- ☐ Can't say no to people; get overloaded
- ☐ Impatient
- ☐ Poor grasp of due process as seen by others
- ☐ Poor mental organization
- ☐ Poor sense of time
- ☐ Procrastinate
- ☐ Too busy to get organized

THE MAP

People differ widely on personal organization, ranging from the perfectionist with everything having to be just so, to the disorganized absent-minded professor never knowing where things are and never being on time with anything. There are really two issues. The first is personal disorganization. The fallout is having too much to do, being late on commitments, having to work longer hours to keep up, losing key documents, forgetting appointments, not doing things completely that have to be redone later, etc. It leads to personal inefficiency and ineffective use of personal time and resources. The second issue is many times worse than the first. It's the disruption your personal disorganization has on the processes managed by others. When your reports are late, others get delayed. When you're late, others have to wait. When the form isn't completed properly, someone else has to take the time to get it corrected. Many people go through life happily disorganized and disheveled. The key is its impact on the people around you.

SECTION 2: LEARNING ON YOUR OWN

THESE SELF-DEVELOPMENT REMEDIES WILL HELP YOU BUILD YOUR SKILL(S)

SOME REMEDIES

☐ **1. Do an upstream and downstream check on the people you work for,** work around and those who work for you, to create a list of the administrative slip-ups you do that give them the most trouble. Be sure to ask them for help creating the list. That way you have a focused list of the things you need to fix first. If you fix the top 10, maybe that will do and the rest of your habits can stay the same.

☐ **2. Personal time management is a known technology.** There are a number of books on the topic as well as a number of good personal time management courses you could attend. There are also personal organizer products on the market. Many of the courses include training in how to use the personal organizing books and software to be better organized. *More help? – See #62 Time Management.*

☐ **3. Put the things you have to do in two piles** – things I have to do that are for me, and things I have to do that are for others or that will affect others. Do the second pile first. Further divide the other pile into the mission-critical, important, and things that can wait. Do them in that order.

☐ **4. If you have the luxury of an assistant or a secretary,** select on the ability to organize him/herself and you. Pick someone who is candid, who will stand up to you and help you be successful.

☐ **5. Make your personal disorganization less obvious to others.** Get a roll top desk so you can close it when you have guests in your office or cubicle. If you are a pile manager, get shelving that has addressable cubbyholes so you can get your piles out of the way. Get an L-shaped desk, one for your piles and one that you keep clean for only the project you are working on at the moment. Put the pile table in back of you toward the wall. Have an area of your office, a couple of chairs and a table that you never put anything on, that you can use for visitors. Frame this saying and put it on your wall so others know you know you are not very organized: "If a cluttered desk is the sign of a cluttered mind, what is an empty desk the sign of?"

☐ **6. Don't work based upon your feelings.** Don't organize your work around what you like to do and put off what you don't like to do. That's one reason people get into organization problems. Use priorities of what needs to be done instead. *More help? – See #50 Priority Setting.*

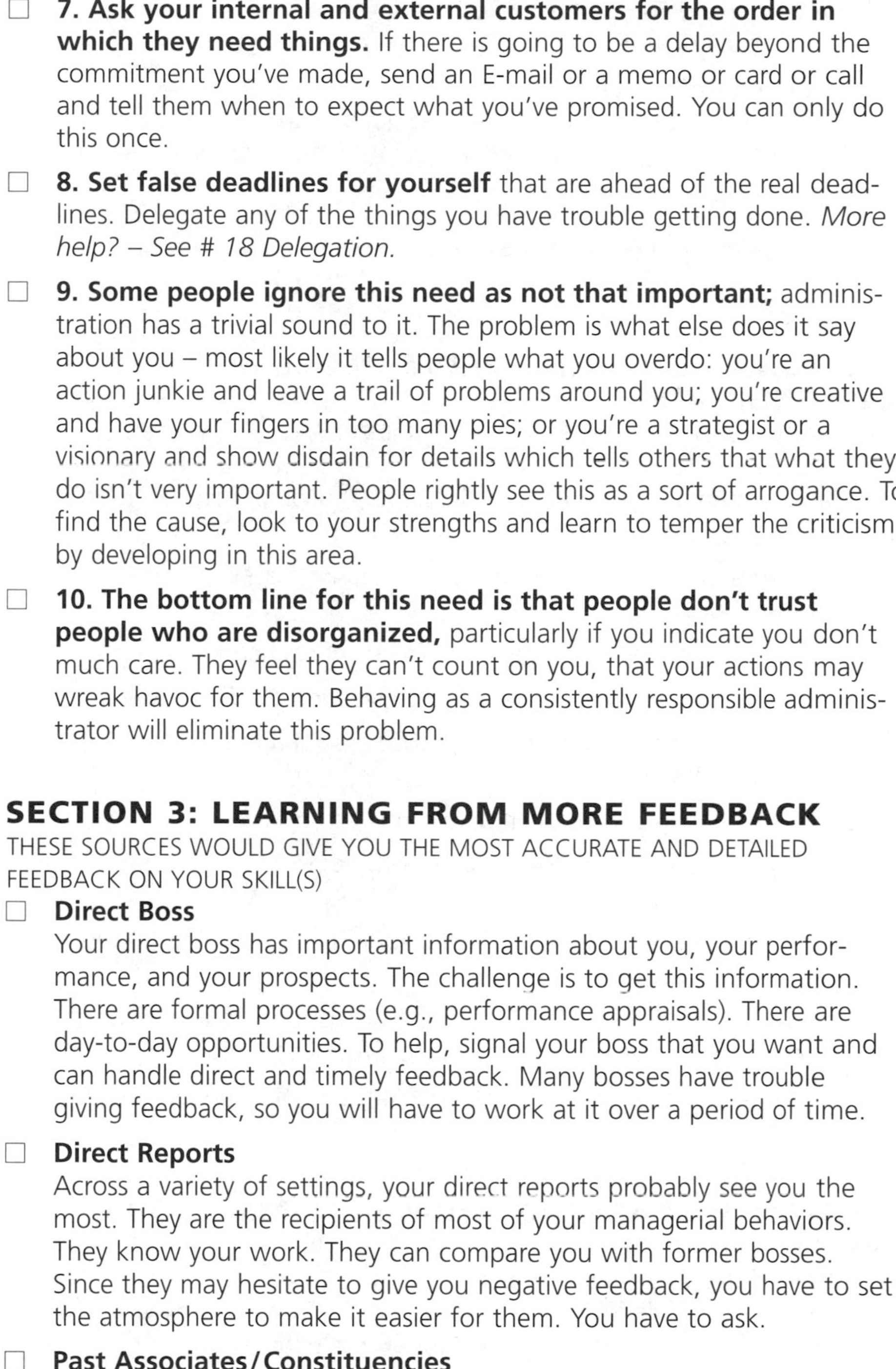

☐ **7. Ask your internal and external customers for the order in which they need things.** If there is going to be a delay beyond the commitment you've made, send an E-mail or a memo or card or call and tell them when to expect what you've promised. You can only do this once.

☐ **8. Set false deadlines for yourself** that are ahead of the real deadlines. Delegate any of the things you have trouble getting done. *More help? – See # 18 Delegation.*

☐ **9. Some people ignore this need as not that important;** administration has a trivial sound to it. The problem is what else does it say about you – most likely it tells people what you overdo: you're an action junkie and leave a trail of problems around you; you're creative and have your fingers in too many pies; or you're a strategist or a visionary and show disdain for details which tells others that what they do isn't very important. People rightly see this as a sort of arrogance. To find the cause, look to your strengths and learn to temper the criticism by developing in this area.

☐ **10. The bottom line for this need is that people don't trust people who are disorganized,** particularly if you indicate you don't much care. They feel they can't count on you, that your actions may wreak havoc for them. Behaving as a consistently responsible administrator will eliminate this problem.

SECTION 3: LEARNING FROM MORE FEEDBACK

THESE SOURCES WOULD GIVE YOU THE MOST ACCURATE AND DETAILED FEEDBACK ON YOUR SKILL(S)

☐ **Direct Boss**
Your direct boss has important information about you, your performance, and your prospects. The challenge is to get this information. There are formal processes (e.g., performance appraisals). There are day-to-day opportunities. To help, signal your boss that you want and can handle direct and timely feedback. Many bosses have trouble giving feedback, so you will have to work at it over a period of time.

☐ **Direct Reports**
Across a variety of settings, your direct reports probably see you the most. They are the recipients of most of your managerial behaviors. They know your work. They can compare you with former bosses. Since they may hesitate to give you negative feedback, you have to set the atmosphere to make it easier for them. You have to ask.

☐ **Past Associates/Constituencies**
When confronted with a present performance problem, some claim, "I wasn't like that before; it must be the current situation." When feedback is available from former associates, about 50% support that claim. In the other half of the cases, the people were like that before

and probably didn't know it. It sometimes makes sense to access the past to clearly see the present.

☐ **Peers and Colleagues**
Peers and colleagues have a special social and working relationship. They attend staff meetings together, share private views, get feedback from the same boss, travel together, and are knowledgeable about each other's work. You perhaps let your guard down more around peers and act more like yourself. They can be a valuable source of feedback.

SECTION 4: LEARNING FROM DEVELOP-IN-PLACE ASSIGNMENTS

THESE PART-TIME DEVELOP-IN-PLACE ASSIGNMENTS WILL HELP YOU BUILD YOUR SKILL(S)

☐ Manage the renovation of an office, floor, building, meeting room, warehouse, etc.

☐ Work on a process-simplification team to take steps and costs out of a process.

☐ Plan a new site for a building (plant, field office, headquarters, etc.).

☐ Plan an off-site meeting, conference, convention, trade show, event, etc.

☐ Manage the purchase of a major product, equipment, materials, program, or system.

☐ Design a training course in an area of expertise for you.

☐ Manage an ad hoc, temporary group of people involved in tackling a fix-it or turnaround project.

☐ Manage liquidation/sale of products, equipment, materials, a business, furniture, overstock, etc.

☐ Manage a dissatisfied internal or external customer; troubleshoot a performance or quality problem with a product or service.

☐ Audit cost overruns to assess the problem and present your findings to the person or people involved.

SECTION 5: LEARNING FROM FULL-TIME JOBS

THESE FULL-TIME JOBS OFFER THE OPPORTUNITY TO BUILD YOUR SKILL(S)

☐ **Chair of Projects/Task Forces**
The core demands for qualifying as a Project/Task Force assignment are: 1) Full-time assignment. 2) Important and specific goal. 3) Tight deadline. 4) Success or failure will be evident. 5) High-visibility sponsor. 6) Learning something on the fly. 7) Must get others to cooperate. 8) Usually six months or more. Four types of Projects/Task Forces: 1) New ideas, products, services, or systems (e.g., product/service/

program research and development, creation/installation/launch of a new system, new programs like Total Quality Management, positive discipline). 2) Formal negotiations and relationships (e.g., acquisitions, divestitures, agreements, joint ventures; licensing arrangements, franchising; dealing with unions, governments, communities, charities, customers, and relocations). 3) Big one-time events (e.g., working on a major presentation for the board, organizing significant meetings or conferences, disaster/damage control teams; reorganizations, mergers, acquisitions, or relocations, working on visions, charters, strategies, other time-urgent issues and problems). 4) Troubleshooting (e.g., problems, disasters, crises, product/service failures, accidents, illegal activities, damage control in public relations goofs, shut downs, downsizings, layoffs, abrupt changes in leadership).

☐ **Scale Assignments**
Core requirements to qualify as a Scale (size) shift assignment are: 1) Sizable jump-shift in the size of the job in areas like: number of people, number of layers in organization, size of budget, number of locations, volume of activity, tightness of deadlines. 2) Medium to low complexity; mostly repetitive and routine processes and procedures. 3) Stable staff and business. 4) Stable operations. 5) Often slow, steady growth.

☐ **Start-ups**
The core demands to qualify as a start from scratch are: 1) Starting something new for you and/or for the organization. 2) Forging a new team. 3) Creating new systems/facilities/staffs/programs/procedures. 4) Contextual adversity (e.g., uncertainty, government regulation, unions, difficult environment). Seven types of start from scratches: 1) Planning, building, hiring, and managing (e.g., building a new facility, opening up a new location, moving a unit or company). 2) Heading something new (e.g., new product, new service, new line of business, new department/function, major new program). 3) Take over a group/product/service/program that had existed for less than a year and was off to a fast start. 4) Establishing overseas operations. 5) Major new designs for existing systems. 6) Moving a successful program from one unit to another. 7) Installing a new organization-wide process as a full-time job (e.g., like Total Quality).

SECTION 6: LEARNING MORE FROM YOUR PLAN

THESE ADDITIONAL REMEDIES WILL HELP MAKE THIS DEVELOPMENT PLAN MORE EFFECTIVE FOR YOU

Learning to Learn Better

☐ **Plan Backwards from the Ideal**
Envision what an ideal outcome would look like and plan backwards. What is the series of events that would have to take place to get

there? What would people do? What would have to be done? How would people react? How would things play out? Could you plan it forward and get to the same outcome?

Learning from Experience, Feedback and Other People

☐ **Using Multiple Models**
Who do you know who exemplifies how to do whatever your need is? Who, for example, personifies decisiveness or compassion or strategic agility? Think more broadly than your current job and colleagues. For example, clergy, friends, spouses or community leaders are also good sources for potential models. Select your models not on the basis of overall excellence or likability, but on the basis of the one towering strength (or glaring weakness) you are interested in. Even people who are well thought of usually have only one or two towering strengths (or glaring weaknesses). Ordinarily, you won't learn as much from the whole person as you will from one characteristic.

☐ **Learning from Bosses**
Bosses can be an excellent and ready source for learning. All bosses do some things exceptionally well and other things poorly. Distance your feelings from the boss/direct report relationship and study things that work and things that don't work for your boss. What would you have done? What could you use, and what should you avoid?

☐ **Learning from Interviewing Others**
Interview others. Ask not only what they do, but how and why they do it. What do they think are the rules of thumb they are following? Where did they learn the behaviors? How do they keep them current? How do they monitor the effect they have on others?

☐ **Learning from Observing Others**
Observe others. Find opportunities to observe without interacting with your model. This enables you to objectively study the person, note what he/she is doing or not doing, and compare that with what you would typically do in similar situations. Many times you can learn more by watching than asking. Your model may not be able to explain what he/she does or may be an unwilling teacher.

Learning from Courses

☐ **Supervisory Courses**
Most new supervisors go through an "Introduction to Supervision" type course. They are designed to teach the common practices a first-line supervisor needs to know to be effective. The content of most of those courses is standard. There is general agreement on the principles of effective supervision. There are two common problems: 1) Do the students have a strong motivation to learn? Do they know what they don't know? Is there any pain? Because motivated students with a

need for the knowledge learn best, participants should have had some trying experiences and some supervisory pain and hardships before attending. 2) Are the instructors experienced supervisors? Have they practiced what they preach? Can they share powerful anecdotes to make key points? Can they answer questions credibly? If possible, select supervisory courses based on the instructors, since the content seems to be the much same for all such courses. Lastly, does the course offer the opportunity for practicing each skill? Does it contain simulations? Are there case studies you could easily identify with? Are there breakout groups? Is there opportunity for action learning? Search for the most interactive course.

☐ **Sending Others to Courses**
If you are responsible for managing someone else's development and, as part of that, sending them to courses, prepare them beforehand. Don't send them as tourists. Meet with them before and after the course. Tell them why they need this course. Tell them what you expect them to learn. Give them feedback on why you think they need the course. Agree ahead of time how you will measure and monitor learning after they return. If possible, offer a variety of courses for your employee to choose from. Have them give you a report shortly after they return. If appropriate, have them present what they learned to the rest of your staff. After they return, provide opportunities for using the new skills with safe cover and low risk. Give them practice time before expecting full exercise of the new skills. Be supportive during early unsteadiness. Give continuous feedback on progress.

SUGGESTED READINGS

Drucker, Peter F. *The Effective Executive.* New York: Harper & Row, 1996.

Henry, Lauchland A. *The Professional's Guide to Working Smarter.* Tenafly, NJ: Burrill-Ellsworth Associates, 1993.

Moskowitz, Robert. *How to organize your work and your life.* New York: Doubleday, 1993.

Sapadin, Linda with Jack Maguire. *It's about time!: the six styles of procrastination and how to overcome them.* New York: Viking, 1996.

103

OVERLY AMBITIOUS

SECTION 1: YOUR DEVELOPMENT NEED(S)

A PROBLEM

- ☐ Is focused excessively on self and on upward career movement, sometimes at the expense of others
- ☐ Is willing to politic for promotion and step on people on the way up
- ☐ Primarily manages up in order to market and position him/herself with management

NOT A PROBLEM

- ☐ Takes career advancement in stride
- ☐ Concentrates on performing well
- ☐ Lets results do the marketing
- ☐ Helps others advance
- ☐ Spreads credit for successes around
- ☐ Humble about his/her accomplishments

SOME CAUSES

- ☐ Loner
- ☐ Overly aggressive
- ☐ Poor political skills
- ☐ Problems with trust
- ☐ Unrealistic self assessment

THE MAP

Most people you and I know are ambitious. Ambition is good. It drives people to do well and want to improve themselves. Being overly ambitious means you make too big a deal out of it. You market yourself too actively. You make political mistakes in terms of whom you approach to inquire about being promoted. At the extremes, people wonder if you care about today's job at all because you are always talking about moving on. They wonder if you make yourself look good at the expense of others. They wonder if you position yourself on the class picture to cover your rival behind you. They wonder if you cut corners to get ahead. They wonder if you really care about others or are you just using people for your own purposes. Others may or may not agree on your overall worth, but they think you spend too much time and effort promoting yourself.

SECTION 2: LEARNING ON YOUR OWN

THESE SELF-DEVELOPMENT REMEDIES WILL HELP YOU BUILD YOUR SKILL(S)

SOME REMEDIES

- ☐ **1. The cream rises to the top.** Build a better mouse trap and the world will beat a path to your door. Maybe not, but good solid work will always attract attention. People who get ahead have two things going for themselves: they consistently perform well, and they market themselves enough to be noticed. The research is clear – over the long term, people who succeed are seen first and foremost as tenacious problem solvers in whatever job they're in. They pay far more attention to the present than the future. Their performance makes them visible, more than their words. Make sure your performance is stellar before you talk about or ask about your next job or complain about a promotion you think you missed. Also, make sure it won't be the view of others that almost anyone could have accomplished this. Make sure your achievements are unusual before you say anything – nothing will hurt you more than having managers think you don't know performance as usual from something exemplary.

- ☐ **2. Pick your battles carefully.** Self marketing needs to be done with great political care. Don't wear out your welcome. While people are usually positive about moderate self promotion, they turn off quickly to what they consider too much or self promotion that's too loud. Who really matters? Approach them once or twice carefully and with moderation. Don't share your ambitions with people who don't play a part in your future. And never, never bad mouth competitors for a promotion. This will say far more about you than it says about them. *More help? – See #38 Organizational Agility and #48 Political Savvy.*

- ☐ **3. How were, or what would be, your ratings on #22 *Ethics and Values* and #29 *Integrity and Trust*?** If they were or would be high, then don't read on. If they are average, you may be seen as not helpful enough to others. How much time do you spend helping others solve problems vs. pushing your own agenda? Are you viewed as a loner? Do you help peers, help direct reports develop, visibly work to build a team? If your ratings are low, you may be cutting corners to look good. You may be trying to blame others for things you should take responsibility for. You may be making up excuses that are not real to cover your butt. You may be trying to make your rivals look bad so that you look better. You may hedge when asked a tough question. You may slap things together to look good when what's underneath wouldn't pass the test. You may be disorganized and your actions cause problems for others. You may indicate little or no concern for others. If you do any of these things or things like it, you will eventually be found out and you will lose the future you have been marketing yourself for. Stop them all.

- ☐ **4. Make sure of what you're selling.** Get some real feedback. Volunteer for a 360° feedback process. Ask people you trust. Talk to a confidant in the Human Resources Department. Make sure you have the strengths you think you have. Make sure you do not deny your weaknesses. Generally, overly ambitious people overestimate their worth to the organization, and research indicates this is a primary cause of poor performance ratings. So don't rush into a negotiation believing yourself to be a superb negotiator unless you know that's true. *More help? – See #55 Self-Knowledge.*

- ☐ **5. If you don't have a mentor or confidant** higher up in the organization, work to get one. A mentor can offer unfiltered advice and counsel about you and your prospects in the organization.

- ☐ **6. The best two books on this subject** are *Career Mastery* by Harry Levinson and *What Color is Your Parachute?* by Richard Bolles. Get both and read them repeatedly until this problem goes away.

- ☐ **7. Overly ambitious people generally manage up more than down and sideways.** That leaves others to feel they are second-class citizens. You may well feel that way but you must never show that side of you. Make sure you make time for others. Make sure you don't position or peacock in front of others. Make sure you're not always the one who picks up the boss from the airport and gives the tour. Make sure you're not always seated at the boss's table.

- ☐ **8. Do you promote the careers of others as well as your own?** Do you help other people solve their problems or do they only help you solve yours? People will tolerate more ambition from you if you have a demonstrated track record of helping others get ahead as well. *More help? – See #19 Developing Direct Reports.*

- ☐ **9. Do you do all the presenting for your group to top management?** Sometimes that's a sign of being overly ambitious. Let others present sometimes. Try to gain stature with top management through the success of your people. Usually that's just as fast a track to a career as is doing everything yourself. Executives quickly notice people builders, those who surround themselves with high performers. *More help? – See #18 Delegation.*

- ☐ **10. How much time do you spend talking about yourself** and marketing yourself versus listening to others about what you need to improve to get ahead? The ratio should be at least 75% listening and 25% promoting. If it's not, work to get the ratio in line.

SECTION 3: LEARNING FROM MORE FEEDBACK

THESE SOURCES WOULD GIVE YOU THE MOST ACCURATE AND DETAILED FEEDBACK ON YOUR SKILL(S)

☐ **Direct Reports**
Across a variety of settings, your direct reports probably see you the most. They are the recipients of most of your managerial behaviors. They know your work. They can compare you with former bosses. Since they may hesitate to give you negative feedback, you have to set the atmosphere to make it easier for them. You have to ask.

☐ **Family Members**
On some issues, like interpersonal style or compassion, it might be helpful to ask various and multiple family members for feedback to add confirmation or context to feedback you've received in the workplace.

☐ **Natural Mentors**
Natural mentors have a special relationship with you and are interested in your success and your future. Since they are usually not in your direct chain of command, you can have more open, relaxed, and fruitful discussions about yourself and your career prospects. They can be a very important source for candid or critical feedback others may not give you.

☐ **Past Associates/Constituencies**
When confronted with a present performance problem, some claim, "I wasn't like that before; it must be the current situation." When feedback is available from former associates, about 50% support that claim. In the other half of the cases, the people were like that before and probably didn't know it. It sometimes makes sense to access the past to clearly see the present.

SECTION 4: LEARNING FROM DEVELOP-IN-PLACE ASSIGNMENTS

THESE PART-TIME DEVELOP-IN-PLACE ASSIGNMENTS WILL HELP YOU BUILD YOUR SKILL(S)

☐ Attend a self-awareness/assessment course that includes feedback.

☐ Do a study of failed executives in your organization, including interviewing people still with the organization who knew or worked with them, and report the findings to top management.

☐ Serve for a year or more with a community agency.

☐ Become a volunteer for a year or more for an outside organization.

☐ Teach/coach someone how to do something you are not an expert in.

☐ Manage an ad hoc, temporary group of people where the people in the group are towering experts but the temporary manager is not.

☐ Take on a tough and undoable project, one where others who have tried it have failed.

- ☐ Manage the visit of a VIP (member of top management, government official, outside customer, foreign visitor, etc.).
- ☐ Be a change agent; create a symbol for change; lead the rallying cry; champion a significant change and implementation.
- ☐ Make peace with an enemy or someone you've disappointed with a product or service or someone you've had some trouble with or don't get along well with.

SECTION 5: LEARNING FROM FULL-TIME JOBS

THESE FULL-TIME JOBS OFFER THE OPPORTUNITY TO BUILD YOUR SKILL(S)

☐ **Cross-Moves**

The core demands necessary to qualify as a Cross-Move are: 1) Move to a very different set of challenges. 2) Abrupt jump-shift in tasks/activities. 3) Never been there before. 4) New setting/conditions. Examples of Cross-Moves are: 1) Changing divisions. 2) Changing functions. 3) Field/headquarters shifts. 4) Line/staff switches. 5) Country switches. 6) Working with all new people. 7) Changing lines of business.

☐ **Influencing Without Authority**

The core demands to qualify as an Influence Without Authority are: 1) Significant challenge (e.g, start-up, fix-it, scope and/or scale assignment, strategic planning project, changes in management practices/systems). 2) Insufficient direct authority to make it happen. 3) Tight deadlines. 4) Visible to significant others. 5) Sensitive politics.

☐ **Start-ups**

The core demands to qualify as a start from scratch are: 1) Starting something new for you and/or for the organization. 2) Forging a new team. 3) Creating new systems/facilities/staffs/programs/procedures. 4) Contextual adversity (e.g., uncertainty, government regulation, unions, difficult environment). Seven types of start from scratches: 1) Planning, building, hiring, and managing (e.g., building a new facility, opening up a new location, moving a unit or company). 2) Heading something new (e.g., new product, new service, new line of business, new department/function, major new program). 3) Take over a group/product/service/program that had existed for less than a year and was off to a fast start. 4) Establishing overseas operations. 5) Major new designs for existing systems. 6) Moving a successful program from one unit to another. 7) Installing a new organization-wide process as a full-time job (e.g., like Total Quality).

SECTION 6: LEARNING MORE FROM YOUR PLAN

THESE ADDITIONAL REMEDIES WILL HELP MAKE THIS DEVELOPMENT PLAN MORE EFFECTIVE FOR YOU

Learning from Experience, Feedback and Other People

☐ **Using Multiple Models**
Who do you know who exemplifies how to do whatever your need is? Who, for example, personifies decisiveness or compassion or strategic agility? Think more broadly than your current job and colleagues. For example, clergy, friends, spouses or community leaders are also good sources for potential models. Select your models not on the basis of overall excellence or likability, but on the basis of the one towering strength (or glaring weakness) you are interested in. Even people who are well thought of usually have only one or two towering strengths (or glaring weaknesses). Ordinarily, you won't learn as much from the whole person as you will from one characteristic.

☐ **Learning from Mentors and Tutors**
Mentors and tutors offer a special case for learning since the relationship is specifically formed for learning. You need to be open and nondefensive. You need to solicit and accept feedback. This is a unique opportunity for you to get low-risk, honest, and direct feedback on what you do well and not so well.

☐ **Learning from Ineffective Behavior**
Seeing things done poorly can be a very potent source of learning for you, especially if the behavior or action affects others negatively. Many times the thing done poorly causes emotional reactions or pain in you and others. Distance yourself from the feelings and explore why the actions didn't work.

☐ **Learning from Observing Others**
Observe others. Find opportunities to observe without interacting with your model. This enables you to objectively study the person, note what he/she is doing or not doing, and compare that with what you would typically do in similar situations. Many times you can learn more by watching than asking. Your model may not be able to explain what he/she does or may be an unwilling teacher.

☐ **Learning from a Coach or Tutor**
Ask a person to coach or tutor you directly. This has the additional benefit of skill building coupled with correcting feedback. Also observe the teacher teaching you. How does he/she teach? How does he/she adjust to you as a learner? After the process, ask for feedback about you as a learner.

☐ **Getting Feedback from Direct Reports**
Direct reports often fear reprisals for giving negative feedback about bosses, whether in a formal process, like a questionnaire, or informally

and face-to-face. Even with a guarantee of confidentiality, some are still hesitant. If you want feedback from direct reports, you have to set a positive tone and never act out of revenge.

☐ **Getting Feedback from Peers/Colleagues**
Your peers and colleagues may not be candid if they are in competition with you. Some may not be willing to be open with you out of fear of giving you an advantage. Some may give you exaggerated feedback to deliberately cause you undue concern. You have to set the tone and gauge the trust level of the relationship and the quality of the feedback.

☐ **Soliciting Feedback**
Almost everyone reports they receive less feedback than they need to achieve their career goals. While others may have some interest in your career, it is primarily up to you to take the initiative in soliciting feedback from multiple sources by any methods available. You're the stakeholder who needs feedback to improve and grow.

☐ **Managing Your Own Future**
You can make a difference in the amount and quality of feedback you receive. The more you understand about feedback and the more initiative you take, the more feedback you will receive. From this, you can construct and execute better, on-target development and career plans.

☐ **Feedback on What?**
Although any feedback is useful, it's best to seek and receive feedback on skills the organization feels are the most important for your present and future success. Not all skills are equal in importance. Some common skills may not have much bearing on success at all. If the organization has an official success profile, that may be the best way to focus your growth efforts.

SUGGESTED READINGS

Bolles, Richard N. *What color is your parachute? 2000.* Berkeley, CA: Ten Speed Press, 1999.

Bridges, William. C*reating You & Co. – Finding work in the dejobbed workplace.* Reading, MA: Addison-Wesley Longman, 1995.

Brim, Gilbert. Ambition. *How we manage success and failure throughout our lives.* New York: Harper Collins, 1992.

Holton, Bill and Cher. *The Manager's Short Course. Thirty-three tactics to upgrade your career.* New York: John Wiley & Sons, 1992.

Hunt, Christopher W. and Scott A. Scanlon. *Navigating your Career.* New York: John Wiley & Sons, 1999.

continued

Johnson, Mike. *Getting a Grip on Tomorrow – Your Guide to Survival and Success in the Changed World of Work.* Newton, MA: Butterworth-Heinemann, 1997.

Kaplan, Robert E. with Wilfred H. Drath and Joan Kofodimos. *Beyond Ambition.* San Francisco: Jossey-Bass Publishers, 1991.

Kelley, Robert E. *How to be a Star at Work.* New York: Times Business, 1998.

Morrison, Ann M., Randall P. White, Ellen Van Velsor, and the Center for Creative Leadership. *Breaking the glass ceiling: Can women reach the top of America's largest corporations?.* Reading, MA: Addison-Wesley Pub. Co., 1992.

104

ARROGANT

SECTION 1: YOUR DEVELOPMENT NEED(S)

A PROBLEM

- ☐ Always thinks he/she has the right and only answer
- ☐ Discounts or dismisses the input of others
- ☐ Can be cold and aloof, makes others feel inferior
- ☐ May detach him/herself from others unless on his/her own terms
- ☐ Keeps distance between him/herself and others

NOT A PROBLEM

- ☐ Listens and responds to others
- ☐ Is approachable and warm
- ☐ Interested in others' views even if they counter his/hers
- ☐ Includes and builds others up
- ☐ Values the opinions of others
- ☐ Treats others as equal partners
- ☐ Shares credit with others
- ☐ Seldom pulls rank or tries to overpower others
- ☐ Gets close to some people and interacts with many more

SOME CAUSES

- ☐ Don't appear to like others much
- ☐ Lack of feedback
- ☐ Like own ideas too much
- ☐ Low personal disclosure
- ☐ Not very comfortable with people
- ☐ Poor interpersonal skills
- ☐ Poor reader of others
- ☐ Very smart and successful

THE MAP

Arrogant people are usually seen as distant loners who prefer their own ideas to anyone else's. Formally, being arrogant means to devalue others and the contributions of others. It usually results in people feeling diminished, rejected and angry. Arrogance is hard to fix for two reasons: it's hard to get feedback on what the problem specifically is since people hesitate giving arrogant people any feedback, and it's hard to change since you don't listen or read the reactions of others well. Nevertheless, people seen as arrogant usually get their expressed if not intended wish in the long term – they end up isolated and alone.

SECTION 2: LEARNING ON YOUR OWN

THESE SELF-DEVELOPMENT REMEDIES WILL HELP YOU BUILD YOUR SKILL(S)

SOME REMEDIES

☐ **1. Arrogance is a major blockage to building self-knowledge.** *More help? – see #55 Self-Knowledge*. Research says that successful people know themselves better. Many people who have a towering strength or lots of success get less feedback and roll along thinking they are perfect until their careers get in trouble. If you are viewed as arrogant, your best chance of understanding it is to get facilitated 360° feedback where the respondents can remain anonymous. It is unlikely you could get useful data from people directly since they don't think you listen and it has been painful in the past to try to influence you. Arrogant people typically overrate themselves. Their ratings from others may be lower than they should be because people believe they need to make it look worse than it is to get through your defiance shield. If you are seen as devaluing others, they will return the favor.

☐ **2. There are two possibilities:** you are really talented and near perfect and people just have had a hard time getting used to you mostly being right, or you're not perfect but you act as if you are. If you are in fact really, really bright and successful and knowledgeable and right most of the time, you have to stop making people feel bad and rejected because of your special gifts. If you're not almost perfect, there is no reason to act as if you are. In either case, you have to work on being more behaviorally open and approachable and help people deal with you comfortably.

☐ **3. Watch your non-verbals.** Arrogant people look, talk and act arrogantly. As you try to become less arrogant, you need to find out what your non-verbals are. All arrogant people do a series of things that can be viewed by a neutral party and judged to give off the signals of arrogance. Washboard brow. Facial expressions. Body shifting, especially turning away. Impatient finger or pencil tapping. False smile. Tight lips. Looking away. Find out from a trusted friend what you do and try to eliminate those behaviors.

☐ **4. Answers. Solutions. Conclusions. Statements. Dictates.** That's the staple of arrogant people. Instant output. Sharp reactions. This may be getting you in trouble. You jump to conclusions, categorically dismiss what others say, use challenging words in an absolute tone. People then see you as closed or combative. More negatively, they may believe you think they're stupid or ill-informed. Give people a chance to talk without interruption. If you're seen as intolerant or closed, people will often stumble over words in their haste to talk with you or short cut their argument since they assume you're not listening anyway. Ask a question, invite them to disagree with you, present their argument back to them softly, let them save face no matter what. Add a 15 second pause into your transactions before you say anything and add two clarifying questions per transaction to signal you're listening and want to understand. *More help? – See #33 Listening and #41 Patience.*

☐ **5. Read your audience.** Do you know what people look like when they are uncomfortable with your arrogance? Do they back up? Frown? Flush? Stumble over words? Shut down? Cringe? Stand at the door hoping not to get invited in? You should work doubly hard at observing others. Especially during the first three minutes of an important transaction, work to make one person or group comfortable with you before the agenda starts. Ask a question unrelated to the topic. Offer them something to drink. Tell them something you did last weekend that you found interesting.

☐ **6. Arrogant people keep their distance and don't share much personal data.** You may believe you shouldn't mix personal with business. You may believe it's wise to keep distance between you and others you work around and with. Since it's hard for others to relate to an arrogant person in the first place, your reputation may be based on only short unsatisfactory transactions. The kinds of disclosures people enjoy are: the reasons behind why you do and decide what you do; your self appraisal; things you know behind what's happening in the business that they don't know – that you are at liberty to disclose; things both good and embarrassing that have happened to you in the past; comments about what's going on around you – without being too negative about others; and things you are interested in and do outside of work. These are areas which you should learn to disclose more than you now do. *More help? – See #44 Personal Disclosure.*

☐ **7. You probably have good people buckets and bad people buckets** and signal to the bad bucket groups or individuals your disagreement with them. Learn to understand without either accepting or judging. Listen, take notes, ask questions, and be able to make their case as well as they can even though you don't agree. Pick something in their argument you agree with. Present your argument in terms of the problem only – why you think this is the best manner to deal with a mutually agreed upon problem.

☐ **8. You may be highly intelligent and quite skilled in your area.** You may work around people who aren't as informed or educated as you are. You may be in a position of essentially dictating what should be done. But you don't have to make it demeaning or painful. You need to switch to a teacher/guru role – tell them how you think about an issue, don't just fire out solutions. Tell them what you think the problem is, what questions need to be asked and answered, how you would go about finding out, what you think some likely solutions might be. Work to pass on your knowledge and skills.

☐ **9. Do you really want to leave the majority of people you deal with feeling stupid, inferior and unintelligent?** Most don't but that's what you do. Arrogant people may be looking for feedback that they are really superior, smart and knowledgeable. But they are looking for that affirmation in the wrong place. If you crave reinforcement of your excellence, perform better. Help others perform better. Produce tangible results. If your results don't measure up to your self view, your words and arrogant behavior certainly won't help you any. Don't try to feel good on the backs of others who are not your equal. Look at three people who you consider excellent performers, talented people, but who are not arrogant. What do they do and not do? Contrast this with your behavior.

☐ **10. The real fix.** Whatever applies in Some Causes, you will have to work on *#3 Approachability* and *#31 Interpersonal Savvy*. Until you signal repeatedly that you are open to others, interested in what they have to say, share things you don't have to share, invite people to talk with you and then listen, little will come of this effort. You will have to persevere, endure some rejection, and perhaps some angry or dismissive remarks in order to balance the situation. Mentally rehearse so you're not blindsided by this. It would be a rare group of people who would respond to your overtures without making you squirm a bit because you have caused them pain in the past.

SECTION 3: LEARNING FROM MORE FEEDBACK

THESE SOURCES WOULD GIVE YOU THE MOST ACCURATE AND DETAILED FEEDBACK ON YOUR SKILL(S)

☐ **Direct Reports**
Across a variety of settings, your direct reports probably see you the most. They are the recipients of most of your managerial behaviors. They know your work. They can compare you with former bosses. Since they may hesitate to give you negative feedback, you have to set the atmosphere to make it easier for them. You have to ask.

☐ **Human Resource Professionals**
Human Resource professionals have both a formal and informal feedback role. Since they have access to unique and confidential information, they can provide the right context for feedback you've received. Sometimes they may be "directed" to give you feedback. Other times, they may pass on feedback just to be helpful to you.

☐ **Natural Mentors**
Natural mentors have a special relationship with you and are interested in your success and your future. Since they are usually not in your direct chain of command, you can have more open, relaxed, and fruitful discussions about yourself and your career prospects. They can be a very important source for candid or critical feedback others may not give you.

- [ ] **Past Associates/Constituencies**
When confronted with a present performance problem, some claim, "I wasn't like that before; it must be the current situation." When feedback is available from former associates, about 50% support that claim. In the other half of the cases, the people were like that before and probably didn't know it. It sometimes makes sense to access the past to clearly see the present.

SECTION 4: LEARNING FROM DEVELOP-IN-PLACE ASSIGNMENTS

THESE PART-TIME DEVELOP-IN-PLACE ASSIGNMENTS WILL HELP YOU BUILD YOUR SKILL(S)

- [ ] Try to learn something frivolous and fun to see how good you can get (e.g., juggling, square dancing, magic).
- [ ] Manage an ad hoc, temporary group of balky and resisting people through an unpopular change or project.
- [ ] Manage an ad hoc, temporary group of people where the people in the group are towering experts but the temporary manager is not.
- [ ] Handle a tough negotiation with an internal or external client or customer.
- [ ] Manage a dissatisfied internal or external customer; troubleshoot a performance or quality problem with a product or service.
- [ ] Manage the outplacement of a group of people.
- [ ] Take on a task you dislike or hate to do.
- [ ] Make peace with an enemy or someone you've disappointed with a product or service or someone you've had some trouble with or don't get along well with.
- [ ] Write a speech for someone higher up in the organization.
- [ ] Manage a project team of people who are older and more experienced than you.

SECTION 5: LEARNING FROM FULL-TIME JOBS

THESE FULL-TIME JOBS OFFER THE OPPORTUNITY TO BUILD YOUR SKILL(S)

- [ ] **Cross-Moves**
The core demands necessary to qualify as a Cross-Move are: 1) Move to a very different set of challenges. 2) Abrupt jump-shift in tasks/activities. 3) Never been there before. 4) New setting/conditions. Examples of Cross-Moves are: 1) Changing divisions. 2) Changing functions. 3) Field/headquarters shifts. 4) Line/staff switches. 5) Country switches. 6) Working with all new people. 7) Changing lines of business.

- ☐ **Influencing Without Authority**
  The core demands to qualify as an Influence Without Authority are: 1) Significant challenge (e.g, start-up, fix-it, scope and/or scale assignment, strategic planning project, changes in management practices/ systems). 2) Insufficient direct authority to make it happen. 3) Tight deadlines. 4) Visible to significant others. 5) Sensitive politics.

- ☐ **Line To Staff Switches**
  The core demands to qualify as a Line to Staff switch are: 1) Intellectually/strategically demanding. 2) Highly visible to others. 3) New area/perspective/method/culture/function. 4) Moving away from a bottom line. 5) Moving from field to headquarters. 6) Exposure to high-level executives. Examples: 1) Business/strategic planning. 2) Heading a staff department. 3) Assistant to/chief of staff to a senior executive. 4) Head of a task force. 5) Human resources role.

- ☐ **Off-Shore Assignments**
  The core demands to qualify as an Off-Shore assignment are: 1) First time working in the country. 2) Significant challenges like new language, hardship location, unique business rules/practices, significant cultural/marketplace differences, different functional task, etc. 3) More than a year assignment. 4) No automatic return deal. 5) Not necessarily a change in job challenge, technical content, or responsibilities.

SECTION 6: LEARNING MORE FROM YOUR PLAN

THESE ADDITIONAL REMEDIES WILL HELP MAKE THIS DEVELOPMENT PLAN MORE EFFECTIVE FOR YOU

Learning to Learn Better

- ☐ **Analyze Your Past Failures for Insights and Learnings**
  Field-strip your mistakes and failures; ask what you did that contributed to the negative outcome; how could it have been avoided; how much was due to the context; what lessons and rules of thumb can you take away from the mistake or failure?

- ☐ **Put Yourself in Situations that Call for Your Weaknesses**
  Put yourself in situations where you must overcome or neutralize a weakness to be successful. Find opportunities to develop counter coping skills: if you're shy, attend functions where you don't know many people; if you're too aggressive, work with children, etc.

- ☐ **Form a Learning Network With Others Working on the Same Problem**
  Look for people in similar situations, and create a process for sharing and learning together. Look for a variety of people inside and outside your organization. Give feedback to each other; try new and different things together; share successes and failures, lessons and learning.

- ☐ **Use a Tutor to Learn Something New**
  Set up a tutor relationship in the areas you're working on; open up, listen, learn, and try new things. Learn from the tutoring/learning process. Do you learn more easily from a tutor or do you get blocked? Test out your thinking with the tutor; do debriefs after trying the tutor's advice.

Learning from Experience, Feedback and Other People

- ☐ **Using Multiple Models**
  Who do you know who exemplifies how to do whatever your need is? Who, for example, personifies decisiveness or compassion or strategic agility? Think more broadly than your current job and colleagues. For example, clergy, friends, spouses or community leaders are also good sources for potential models. Select your models not on the basis of overall excellence or likability, but on the basis of the one towering strength (or glaring weakness) you are interested in. Even people who are well thought of usually have only one or two towering strengths (or glaring weaknesses). Ordinarily, you won't learn as much from the whole person as you will from one characteristic.
- ☐ **Learning from Ineffective Behavior**
  Seeing things done poorly can be a very potent source of learning for you, especially if the behavior or action affects others negatively. Many times the thing done poorly causes emotional reactions or pain in you and others. Distance yourself from the feelings and explore why the actions didn't work.
- ☐ **Learning from Observing Others**
  Observe others. Find opportunities to observe without interacting with your model. This enables you to objectively study the person, note what he/she is doing or not doing, and compare that with what you would typically do in similar situations. Many times you can learn more by watching than asking. Your model may not be able to explain what he/she does or may be an unwilling teacher.
- ☐ **Learning from Mistakes**
  Since we're human, we all make mistakes. The key is to focus on why you made the mistake. Spend more time locating causes and less worrying about the effects. Check how you react to mistakes. How much time do you spend being angry with yourself? Do you waste time stewing or do you move on? More importantly, do you learn? Ask why you made the mistake. Are you likely to repeat it under similar situations? Was it a lack of skill? Judgment? Style? Not enough data? Reading people? Misreading the challenge? Misreading the politics? Or was it just random? A good strategy that just didn't work? Others that let you down? The key is to avoid two common reactions to your mistakes: 1) avoiding similar situations instead of learning and trying again, and 2) trying to repeat what you did, only more diligently and

harder, hoping to break through the problem, making the same mistake again but with greater impact. Neither trap leaves us with better strategies for the future. Neither is a learning strategy. To learn and do something differently, focus on the patterns in your behavior that get you in trouble and go back to first causes, those that tell you something about your shortcomings. Facing ourselves squarely is always the best way to learn.

Learning from Courses

☐ **Insight Events**

These are courses designed around assessing skills and providing feedback to the participants. These events can be a powerful source of self-knowledge and can lead to significant development if done right. When selecting a self-insight course, consider the following: 1) Are the skills assessed the important ones? 2) Are the assessment techniques and instruments sound? 3) Are those who are providing the feedback trained and professional? 4) Is the feedback provided in a user-friendly and "actionable" format? 5) Does the feedback include development planning? 6) Is the setting comfortable and conducive to reflection and learning? 7) Are the other participants the kinds of people you could learn from? 8) Are you in the right frame of mind to learn from this kind of intense experience? Select events on the basis of positive answers to these eight questions.

☐ **Attitude Toward Learning**

In addition to selecting the right course, a learning attitude is required. Be open. Close down your "like/dislike" switch, your "agree/disagree" blinders, and your "like me/not like me" feelings toward the instructors. Learning requires new lessons, change, and new behaviors and perspectives – all scary stuff for most people. Don't resist. Take in all you can during the course. Ask clarifying questions. Discuss concerns with the other participants. Jot down what you learn as you go. After the course is over, take some reflective time to glean the meat. Make the practical decisions about what you can and cannot use.

SUGGESTED READINGS

Autry, James A. *The Art of Caring Leadership.* New York: William Morrow and Company, Inc., 1991.

Bolton, Robert and Dorothy Grover Bolton. *People Styles at Work – Making bad relationships good and good relationships better.* New York: AMACOM, 1996.

DuBrin, Andrew J. *Personal Magnetism – Developing the charismatic qualities to influence others.* New York: AMACOM, 1997.

Dilenschneider, Robert L. A *Briefing for Leaders: Communication as the ultimate exercise of power.* New York: HarperBusiness, 1992.

Hornstein, Harvey Ph.D. *Brutal Bosses.* New York: Riverhead Books, 1996.

Peck, M. Scott, M.D. *A World Waiting to be Born: Civility Rediscovered.* New York: Bantam Books, 1993.

105

BETRAYAL OF TRUST

SECTION 1: YOUR DEVELOPMENT NEED(S)

A PROBLEM

- ☐ Says one thing and means or does another
- ☐ Is inconsistent and unpredictable at times
- ☐ Fails to follow through on commitments

NOT A PROBLEM

- ☐ Always follows through
- ☐ Keep confidences
- ☐ Walks his/her talk
- ☐ Does what he/she says he/she will do
- ☐ Finishes what he/she starts
- ☐ Is steady and predictable
- ☐ Checks back if there is going to be a problem

SOME CAUSES

- ☐ Avoid conflict
- ☐ Devious
- ☐ Disorganized/unpredictable
- ☐ Forgetful
- ☐ Not customer oriented
- ☐ Poor political skills
- ☐ Poor time management
- ☐ Spread too thin; can't say no
- ☐ Too anxious to make the sale
- ☐ Overly ambitious

THE MAP

Trust that you will do what you committed to and what is expected drives the world. Anything less than that leads to damaged or severed relationships, lost customers, unfinished projects, re-work and wasted time, and lots of noise. There is no up-side to betraying a trust.

SECTION 2: LEARNING ON YOUR OWN

THESE SELF-DEVELOPMENT REMEDIES WILL HELP YOU BUILD YOUR SKILL(S)

SOME REMEDIES

- ☐ **1. Simple commitments.** Do you return phones calls in a timely manner? Do you forward material you promised? Did you pass on information you promised to get? Did you carry through on a task you promised someone you would take care of? Failing to do things like this damages relationships. If you tend to forget things, write them down. If you run out of time, set up a specific time each day to follow through on commitments. If you are going to miss a deadline, let them know and give them a second date you will be sure to make.

☐ **2. Overcommiting.** A lot of trouble follows overcommiting. Overcommiting usually comes from wanting to please everyone or not wanting to face the conflict if you say no. You can only do so much. Only commit to that which you can actually do. Commit to a specific time for delivery. Write it down. Learn to say "no," pleasantly. Learn to pass it off to someone else who has the time – "Gee no, but I'm sure Susan could help you with that." Learn to say, "Yes, but it will take longer than you might want to wait," and give them the option of withdrawing the request. Learn to say ,"Yes, but what else that I have already committed to do for you would you like to delay to get this done?" *More help? – See #50 Priority Setting.*

☐ **3. Trying too hard to make the sale?** Does your enthusiasm to make the sale or get your point across cause you to commit to too many things in the heat of the transaction? The customers you get by unrealistic commitments are the customers you will lose forever when they find out you can't deliver.

☐ **4. Trying too hard to impress?** It's common for people to promise too much so others will be impressed. It's also common that people who do that repeatedly lose in the long term because others will learn to discount promises and only measure results.

☐ **5. Trying to avoid conflict?** Do you say what you need to say to get through the meeting or transaction but have little intention of doing what you said? Do you say things just to go along and not cause trouble? Do you say what you need to say to avoid disagreement or an argument? All these behaviors will eventually backfire when people find out you said something different in another setting or to another person, or they notice you didn't actually follow through and do what you said.

☐ **6. Intentionally say things to gain an advantage?** Do you actually know ahead of time that what you are saying is not really true or that you really don't think that? Do you say things you don't mean to gain an advantage or forward a relationship or get some resources? Do you forward your personal agenda ahead of that of the team or organization? Any of these will eventually catch up to you and cause you career disruption. *More help? – See #22 Ethics and Values and #29 Integrity and Trust.*

☐ **7. Have good days and bad days?** Many people are inconsistent in at least some of the things they do. Many follow through some days and weeks and not others. Some follow through up but not down in the organization. Some follow through with individuals they like and not with people they don't like. While all this is human nature, it's a losing strategy. Basically, if you can do it once, do it with one person, do it on one day, you should be able to do it much more often. *More help? – See #43 Perseverance.*

☐ **8. Leave things undone?** Very action oriented? Impatient? Fingers in many pies? Interest wanes if it takes too long? All of these result in unmet commitments. Try to discipline yourself to finish what you've started. Don't move on until it's done. Delegate finishing it to someone you trust. Check back to see that it was done. If you are not going to finish it, inform those concerned that you do not intend to complete the task with the reasons for your decision.

☐ **9. Always out of time?** Do you intend to get to things but never have the time? Do you always estimate shorter times to get things done that then take longer? There is a well established science and a set of best practices in time management. There are a number of books you can buy in any business book store, and there are a number of good courses you can attend. Delegating also helps you use your time more effectively. *More help? – See #62 Time Management.*

☐ **10. Perhaps you really aren't very trustworthy.** You hedge, sabotage others, play for advantage, set up others, don't intend to follow up. You justify it by saying that things are tough, that you're just doing your job, getting results. After all, the end justifies the means. You use others to get your agenda accomplished. First, you need to examine whether this view of the world is really right and whether it is the way you really want to be. Second, you need to find out if your career with this organization is salvageable. Have you burned too many bridges? The best way to do this is to admit you have regularly betrayed trusts and not followed through on your commitments. Talk with your boss or mentor to see if you can redeem yourself. If yes, meet with everyone you think you've alienated and see how they respond. Tell them what you're going to do differently. Ask them what you should stop doing. Ask them if the situation can be repaired.

SECTION 3: LEARNING FROM MORE FEEDBACK

THESE SOURCES WOULD GIVE YOU THE MOST ACCURATE AND DETAILED FEEDBACK ON YOUR SKILL(S)

☐ **Direct Boss**

Your direct boss has important information about you, your performance, and your prospects. The challenge is to get this information. There are formal processes (e.g., performance appraisals). There are day-to-day opportunities. To help, signal your boss that you want and can handle direct and timely feedback. Many bosses have trouble giving feedback, so you will have to work at it over a period of time.

- ☐ **Direct Reports**
  Across a variety of settings, your direct reports probably see you the most. They are the recipients of most of your managerial behaviors. They know your work. They can compare you with former bosses. Since they may hesitate to give you negative feedback, you have to set the atmosphere to make it easier for them. You have to ask.
- ☐ **Internal and External Customers**
  Customers interact with you as a person and as a supplier or vendor of products and services. You're important to them because you can either help address and solve their problems or stand in their way. As customer service and Total Quality programs gain importance, clients and customers become a more prominent source of feedback.
- ☐ **Natural Mentors**
  Natural mentors have a special relationship with you and are interested in your success and your future. Since they are usually not in your direct chain of command, you can have more open, relaxed, and fruitful discussions about yourself and your career prospects. They can be a very important source for candid or critical feedback others may not give you.
- ☐ **Past Associates/Constituencies**
  When confronted with a present performance problem, some claim, "I wasn't like that before; it must be the current situation." When feedback is available from former associates, about 50% support that claim. In the other half of the cases, the people were like that before and probably didn't know it. It sometimes makes sense to access the past to clearly see the present.
- ☐ **Peers and Colleagues**
  Peers and colleagues have a special social and working relationship. They attend staff meetings together, share private views, get feedback from the same boss, travel together, and are knowledgeable about each other's work. You perhaps let your guard down more around peers and act more like yourself. They can be a valuable source of feedback.

SECTION 4: LEARNING FROM DEVELOP-IN-PLACE ASSIGNMENTS

THESE PART-TIME DEVELOP-IN-PLACE ASSIGNMENTS WILL HELP YOU BUILD YOUR SKILL(S)

- ☐ Handle a tough negotiation with an internal or external client or customer.
- ☐ Manage a dissatisfied internal or external customer; troubleshoot a performance or quality problem with a product or service.
- ☐ Manage the assigning/allocating of office space in a contested situation.

- ☐ Make peace with an enemy or someone you've disappointed with a product or service or someone you've had some trouble with or don't get along well with.
- ☐ Represent the concerns of a group of nonexempt, clerical, or administrative employees to higher management to seek resolution of a difficult issue.
- ☐ Manage an ad hoc, temporary group of balky and resisting people through an unpopular change or project.
- ☐ Take on a tough and undoable project, one where others who have tried it have failed.
- ☐ Manage the outplacement of a group of people.
- ☐ Resolve an issue in conflict between two people, units, geographies, functions, etc.
- ☐ Be a member of a union-negotiating or grievance-handling team.

SECTION 5: LEARNING FROM FULL-TIME JOBS

THESE FULL-TIME JOBS OFFER THE OPPORTUNITY TO BUILD YOUR SKILL(S)

☐ **Chair of Projects/Task Forces**

The core demands for qualifying as a Project/Task Force assignment are: 1) Full-time assignment. 2) Important and specific goal. 3) Tight deadline. 4) Success or failure will be evident. 5) High-visibility sponsor. 6) Learning something on the fly. 7) Must get others to cooperate. 8) Usually six months or more. Four types of Projects/Task Forces: 1) New ideas, products, services, or systems (e.g., product/service/program research and development, creation/installation/launch of a new system, new programs like Total Quality Management, positive discipline). 2) Formal negotiations and relationships (e.g., acquisitions, divestitures, agreements, joint ventures; licensing arrangements, franchising; dealing with unions, governments, communities, charities, customers, and relocations). 3) Big one-time events (e.g., working on a major presentation for the board, organizing significant meetings or conferences, disaster/damage control teams; reorganizations, mergers, acquisitions, or relocations, working on visions, charters, strategies, other time-urgent issues and problems). 4) Troubleshooting (e.g., problems, disasters, crises, product/service failures, accidents, illegal activities, damage control in public relations goofs, shut downs, downsizings, layoffs, abrupt changes in leadership).

☐ **Influencing Without Authority**

The core demands to qualify as an Influence Without Authority are: 1) Significant challenge (e.g, start-up, fix-it, scope and/or scale assignment, strategic planning project, changes in management practices/systems). 2) Insufficient direct authority to make it happen. 3) Tight deadlines. 4) Visible to significant others. 5) Sensitive politics.

- ☐ **Start-ups**
  The core demands to qualify as a start from scratch are: 1) Starting something new for you and/or for the organization. 2) Forging a new team. 3) Creating new systems/facilities/staffs/programs/procedures. 4) Contextual adversity (e.g., uncertainty, government regulation, unions, difficult environment). Seven types of start from scratches: 1) Planning, building, hiring, and managing (e.g., building a new facility, opening up a new location, moving a unit or company). 2) Heading something new (e.g., new product, new service, new line of business, new department/function, major new program). 3) Take over a group/product/service/program that had existed for less than a year and was off to a fast start. 4) Establishing overseas operations. 5) Major new designs for existing systems. 6) Moving a successful program from one unit to another. 7) Installing a new organization-wide process as a full-time job (e.g., like Total Quality).

SECTION 6: LEARNING MORE FROM YOUR PLAN

THESE ADDITIONAL REMEDIES WILL HELP MAKE THIS DEVELOPMENT PLAN MORE EFFECTIVE FOR YOU

Learning from Experience, Feedback and Other People

- ☐ **Using Multiple Models**
  Who do you know who exemplifies how to do whatever your need is? Who, for example, personifies decisiveness or compassion or strategic agility? Think more broadly than your current job and colleagues. For example, clergy, friends, spouses or community leaders are also good sources for potential models. Select your models not on the basis of overall excellence or likability, but on the basis of the one towering strength (or glaring weakness) you are interested in. Even people who are well thought of usually have only one or two towering strengths (or glaring weaknesses). Ordinarily, you won't learn as much from the whole person as you will from one characteristic.

- ☐ **Being a Student of Others**
  While many of us rely on others for information or advice, we do not really study the behavior of other people. Ask what a person does exceptionally well or poorly. What behaviors are particularly effective and ineffective for them? What works for them and what doesn't? As a student of others, you can deduce the rules of thumb for effective and ineffective behavior and include those in your own library. In comparing yourself with this person, in what areas could you most improve? What could you specifically do to improve in ways comfortable for you?

- ☐ **Learning from Bosses**
  Bosses can be an excellent and ready source for learning. All bosses do some things exceptionally well and other things poorly. Distance your

feelings from the boss/direct report relationship and study things that work and things that don't work for your boss. What would you have done? What could you use, and what should you avoid?

- ☐ **Learning from Mentors and Tutors**
  Mentors and tutors offer a special case for learning since the relationship is specifically formed for learning. You need to be open and nondefensive. You need to solicit and accept feedback. This is a unique opportunity for you to get low-risk, honest, and direct feedback on what you do well and not so well.

- ☐ **Learning from Ineffective Behavior**
  Seeing things done poorly can be a very potent source of learning for you, especially if the behavior or action affects others negatively. Many times the thing done poorly causes emotional reactions or pain in you and others. Distance yourself from the feelings and explore why the actions didn't work.

- ☐ **Learning from Observing Others**
  Observe others. Find opportunities to observe without interacting with your model. This enables you to objectively study the person, note what he/she is doing or not doing, and compare that with what you would typically do in similar situations. Many times you can learn more by watching than asking. Your model may not be able to explain what he/she does or may be an unwilling teacher.

- ☐ **Learning from a Coach or Tutor**
  Ask a person to coach or tutor you directly. This has the additional benefit of skill building coupled with correcting feedback. Also observe the teacher teaching you. How does he/she teach? How does he/she adjust to you as a learner? After the process, ask for feedback about you as a learner.

- ☐ **Learning from Remote Models**
  Many times you can learn from people not directly available to you. You can read a book about them, watch tapes of public figures, read analyses of them, etc. The principles of learning are the same. Ask yourself what they do well or poorly and deduce their rules of thumb.

- ☐ **Consolidating What You Learn from People**
  After using any source and/or method of learning from others, write down or mentally note the new rules of thumb and the principles involved. How will you remind yourself of the new behaviors in similar situations? How will you prevent yourself from reacting on "autopilot"? How could you share what you have learned from others?

Learning from Courses

- ☐ **Insight Events**
  These are courses designed around assessing skills and providing feedback to the participants. These events can be a powerful source of

self-knowledge and can lead to significant development if done right. When selecting a self-insight course, consider the following: 1) Are the skills assessed the important ones? 2) Are the assessment techniques and instruments sound? 3) Are those who are providing the feedback trained and professional? 4) Is the feedback provided in a user-friendly and "actionable" format? 5) Does the feedback include development planning? 6) Is the setting comfortable and conducive to reflection and learning? 7) Are the other participants the kinds of people you could learn from? 8) Are you in the right frame of mind to learn from this kind of intense experience? Select events on the basis of positive answers to these eight questions.

SUGGESTED READINGS

Chambers, Harry E. *No fear management: rebuilding trust, performance, and commitment in the new American workplace.* Boca Raton, FL: St. Lucie Press, 1998.

Dosick, Rabbi Wayne. *The Business Bible – Ten new commandments for creating an ethical workplace.* New York: William Morrow and Company, Inc., 1993.

O'Toole, James. *Leading Change.* Boston: Harvard Business School Press, 1996.

Shaw, Robert Bruce. *Trust in the Balance – Building successful organizations on results, integrity and concern.* San Francisco: Jossey-Bass, Inc., 1997.

Sonnenberg, Frank K. *Managing with a Conscience – How to improve performance through integrity, trust and commitment.* New York: McGraw-Hill, Inc., 1994.

Zand, Dale E. *The Leadership Triad – Knowledge, Trust and Power.* New York: Oxford University Press, 1997.

BLOCKED PERSONAL LEARNER

SECTION 1: YOUR DEVELOPMENT NEED(S)

A PROBLEM

- ☐ Is closed to learning new personal, interpersonal, managerial, and leadership skills, approaches, and tactics
- ☐ Prefers staying the same, even when faced with new and different challenges
- ☐ Is narrow in interests and scope
- ☐ Uses few learning tactics
- ☐ Doesn't seek input
- ☐ Lacks curiosity
- ☐ Is not insightful about him/herself

NOT A PROBLEM

- ☐ Eager to learn; interested in what's new or better
- ☐ Has broad interests and perspective
- ☐ Seeks and listens to feedback
- ☐ Takes criticism to heart
- ☐ Always looking to improve him/herself
- ☐ Carefully observes others for their reactions and adjusts accordingly
- ☐ Reads people and groups well
- ☐ Picks up on subtle corrective cues from others
- ☐ Is sensitive to different challenges and changes accordingly

SOME CAUSES

- ☐ Hang on hoping to make it without changing
- ☐ Low risk taker
- ☐ May block change for others
- ☐ Narrow in scope and interests
- ☐ Not open to new approaches
- ☐ Perfectionist
- ☐ Prefer the tried and true
- ☐ Self learning/development interest is low
- ☐ Too busy to learn anything new
- ☐ Too comfortable

THE MAP

People say you're stuck in the past. For some reason, you resist learning new personal and managerial behaviors. You're the last to get on board a new initiative. You're from Missouri (the "Show Me" state); we have to prove it to you before you'll move. Surveys done with a major outplacement firm show that those most likely to be let go during a downsizing have good technical and individual skills, but poor learning to do anything new or different skills. You can't survive today without keeping you and your skills fresh. There's not much room anymore for someone stuck in the past.

SECTION 2: LEARNING ON YOUR OWN

THESE SELF-DEVELOPMENT REMEDIES WILL HELP YOU BUILD YOUR SKILL(S)

SOME REMEDIES

☐ **1. How do you select what you're going to do?** People who are good at this work from the outside – the customer, the audience, the person, the situation – in, not from the inside – What do I want to do in this situation? What would make me happy and feel good? – out. Practice not thinking inside/out when you are around others. What are the demand characteristics of this situation? How does this person or audience best learn? Which of my approaches or styles or skills or knowledge would work best? How can I best accomplish my goals? How can I alter my approach and tactics to be the most effective? The one-trick pony can only perform once per show. If the audience doesn't like that particular trick, no oats for the pony, no encore. *More help? – See #15 Customer Focus.*

☐ **2. You're probably caught in your comfort zone.** You rely on historical, tried and true solutions. You use what you know and have seen or done before. So when faced with a new issue, challenge or problem, first figure out what causes it. Don't go to the solution or conclusion first. Keep asking why, see how many causes you can come up with and how many organizing buckets you can put them in. This increases the chance of a better solution because you can see more connections. Look for patterns in data, don't just collect information or assume that you know what to do. People are telling you that you often don't. *More help? – See #51 Problem Solving.*

☐ **3. You must constantly observe others' reactions to you to be good at adjusting to others.** You must watch the reactions of people to what you are saying and doing while you are doing it in order to gauge their response. Are they bored? Change the pace. Are they confused? State it in a different way. Are they angry? Stop and ask what the problem is. Are they too quiet? Stop and get them involved in what you are doing. Are they fidgeting, scribbling on their pads or staring out the window? They may not be interested in what you are doing. Move to the end of your presentation or task, end it, and exit. Check in with your audience frequently and select a different tactic if necessary. *More help? – See #33 Listening and #45 Personal Learning.*

☐ **4. Whatever the causes are, people view you as not open to learning.** Until you signal repeatedly that you are open to others, interested in what they have to say, share things you don't have to share, invite people to talk with you and then listen, little will come of this effort. You will have to persevere, endure some rejection, and perhaps some angry or dismissive remarks in order to balance the situation. Mentally rehearse so you're not blindsided by this. It would be a rare group of people who would respond to your new overtures without making you squirm a bit because they have seen you as closed up to this point. *More help? – See #3 Approachability and #31 Interpersonal Savvy.*

- ☐ **5. Experiment with some new techniques with people.** Many excellent personal learners have a bag of engaging techniques they use: they give reasons for everything they say, saving any solution statements or conclusions for last. They ask more questions than make statements, speak briefly, summarize often, and when disagreeing they put it in conditional terms: "I don't think so, but what do you think?" The point of these is to elicit as much information about the reactions of others as they can. They are loading their files so they can change behavior when needed.

- ☐ **6. Expand your repertoire.** Stretch yourself. Do things that are not characteristic of you. Go to your limits and beyond. By expanding the number of behaviors you have access to, you can become more effective across a larger number of situations. *More help? – See #54 Self-Development.*

- ☐ **7. Be an early adopter of something.** Find some new thing, technique, software, tool, system, process or skill relevant to your activity. Privately become an expert in it. Read the books. Get certified. Visit somewhere where it's being done. Then surprise everyone and be the first to introduce it into your world. Sell it. Train others. Integrate it into your work.

- ☐ **8. Pick three tasks you've never done before and go do them.** If you don't know much about customers, work in a store or handle customer complaints; if you don't know what engineering does, go find out; task trade with someone. Meet with your colleagues from other areas and tell each other what, and more importantly, how you do what you do.

- ☐ **9. Volunteer for task forces.** Task Forces/projects are a great opportunity to learn new things in a low risk environment. Task Forces are one of the most common developmental events listed by successful executives. Such projects require learning other functions, businesses or nationalities well enough that in a tight timeframe you can appreciate how they think and why their area/position is important. In so doing, you get out of your own experience and start to see connections to a broader world – how international trade works, or more at home, how the pieces of your organization fit together.

☐ **10. Are you the same in your personal life?** Do you eat at the same restaurants? Vacation at the same places? Holidays are always done the same as in the past? Buy the same make or type car over and over again? Have the same insurance agent your father had? Expand yourself. Go on adventures with the family. Travel to places you have not been before. Never vacation at the same place again. Eat at different theme restaurants. Go to events and meeting of groups you have never really met. Go to ethnic festivals and sample the cultures. Go to athletic events you've never attended before. Each week, you and your family should go on a personal learning adventure. See how many different perspectives you can add to your knowledge.

SECTION 3: LEARNING FROM MORE FEEDBACK

THESE SOURCES WOULD GIVE YOU THE MOST ACCURATE AND DETAILED FEEDBACK ON YOUR SKILL(S)

☐ **Development Professionals**
Sometimes it might be valuable to get some analysis and feedback from a professional trained and certified in the area you're working on: possibly a career counselor, a therapist, clergy, a psychologist, etc.

☐ **Natural Mentors**
Natural mentors have a special relationship with you and are interested in your success and your future. Since they are usually not in your direct chain of command, you can have more open, relaxed, and fruitful discussions about yourself and your career prospects. They can be a very important source for candid or critical feedback others may not give you.

☐ **Human Resource Professionals**
Human Resource professionals have both a formal and informal feedback role. Since they have access to unique and confidential information, they can provide the right context for feedback you've received. Sometimes they may be "directed" to give you feedback. Other times, they may pass on feedback just to be helpful to you.

☐ **Past Associates/Constituencies**
When confronted with a present performance problem, some claim, "I wasn't like that before; it must be the current situation." When feedback is available from former associates, about 50% support that claim. In the other half of the cases, the people were like that before and probably didn't know it. It sometimes makes sense to access the past to clearly see the present.

SECTION 4: LEARNING FROM DEVELOP-IN-PLACE ASSIGNMENTS

THESE PART-TIME DEVELOP-IN-PLACE ASSIGNMENTS WILL HELP YOU BUILD YOUR SKILL(S)

- ☐ Attend a self-awareness/assessment course that includes feedback.
- ☐ Find and spend time with an expert to learn something new to you.
- ☐ Study some aspect of your job or a new technical area you haven't studied before that you need to be more effective.
- ☐ Work closely with a higher-level manager who is very good at something you need to learn.
- ☐ Attend a course or event which will push you personally beyond your usual limits or outside your comfort zone (e.g., Outward Bound, language immersion training, sensitivity group, public speaking).
- ☐ Study an admired person who has a skill you need.
- ☐ Volunteer to do a special project for and with a person you admire and who has a skill you need to develop.
- ☐ Teach a course, seminar, or workshop on something you don't know well.
- ☐ Teach/coach someone how to do something you are not an expert in.
- ☐ Take on a task you dislike or hate to do.

SECTION 5: LEARNING FROM FULL-TIME JOBS

THESE FULL-TIME JOBS OFFER THE OPPORTUNITY TO BUILD YOUR SKILL(S)

- ☐ **Cross-Moves**
  The core demands necessary to qualify as a Cross-Move are: 1) Move to a very different set of challenges. 2) Abrupt jump-shift in tasks/activities. 3) Never been there before. 4) New setting/conditions. Examples of Cross-Moves are: 1) Changing divisions. 2) Changing functions. 3) Field/headquarters shifts. 4) Line/staff switches. 5) Country switches. 6) Working with all new people. 7) Changing lines of business.
- ☐ **Heavy Strategic Demands**
  The core demands necessary to qualify as a Heavy Strategic Content assignment are: 1) Requires significant strategic thinking and planning most couldn't do. 2) Charts new ground strategically. 3) Plan must be presented, challenged, adopted, and implemented. 4) Exposure to significant decision makers and executives. 1) Strategic planning position. 2) Job involving repositioning of a product, service, or organization.
- ☐ **Scope Assignments**
  The core demands for a Scope (complexity) assignment are: 1) Significant increase in both internal and external scope or complexity. 2) Significant increase in visibility and/or bottom line responsibility.

3) Unfamiliar area, business, technology, or territory. Examples of Scope assignments involving shifts: 1) Switching into a new function/technology/business. 2) Moving to new organization. 3) Moving to overseas assignment. 4) Moving to new location. 5) Adding new products/services. 6) Moving between headquarters/field. 7) Switches in ownership/top management of the unit/organization. Examples of Scope assignments involving "firsts": 1) First-time manager. 2) First-time managing managers. 3) First-time executive. 4) First-time overseas. 5) First-time headquarters/field. 6) First-time team leader. 7) First-time new technology/business/function. Scope assignments involving increased complexity: 1) Managing a significant expansion of an existing product or service. 2) Managing adding new products/service into an existing unit. 3) Managing a reorganized and more diverse unit. 4) Managing explosive growth. 5) Adding new technologies.

SECTION 6: LEARNING MORE FROM YOUR PLAN

THESE ADDITIONAL REMEDIES WILL HELP MAKE THIS DEVELOPMENT PLAN MORE EFFECTIVE FOR YOU

Learning to Learn Better

☐ **Monitoring Yourself More Closely and Getting off Your Autopilot**
Past habits are a mixed blessing, sometimes helping, sometimes not. To avoid putting yourself on "autopilot," think afresh about each situation before acting. Consistently monitor yourself with questions. Is this task different? Ask why you would repeat a past action. Are you avoiding anything, like taking a chance? Is there something new you might try?

☐ **Examine Your Past for Parallels to the Current Situation**
Examine your past for similar or contrasting experiences that match with or counter the current situation. What has worked in the past that you've dropped? What hasn't worked that you're repeating? What "pearls" of wisdom did you take away from your successes and failures, which you could apply today?

☐ **Rehearse Successful Tactics/Strategies/Actions**
Mentally rehearse how you will act before going into the situation. Try to anticipate how others will react, what they will say, and how you'll respond. Check out the best and worst cases; play out both scenes. Check your feelings in conflict or worst-case situations; rehearse staying under control.

☐ **Keep a Learning Journal**
Keep a learning log or diary about the issues and opportunities you've faced and how you've acted. Focus on how you've used your strengths and weaknesses. Deduce your effective and successful rules of thumb – what worked and what didn't, and how you would have done it differently.

- ☐ **Examine Why You're Blocked on a Key Issue**
Examine what you are worrying/angry about and list all of your thoughts about it; ask why these feelings are holding you back. Why are the feelings overriding your thinking? How are they getting in the way? Why are they important to you? How can you move beyond them and learn to do something different?

- ☐ **Learn New and Frivolous Skills to Study How You Learn**
Practice learning frivolous and fun skills (like juggling, square dancing, skeet shooting, video games, etc.) to see yourself under different and less personal or stressful learning conditions. Ask yourself why that was easy while developing new personal/managerial skills is so hard. Try something harder with the same tactics.

- ☐ **Try New Things, Take Some Chances, Increase Personal Risk Taking**
Engage in some creative problem-solving activities such as brainstorming, free association, analogies to unrelated areas, nominal group techniques, etc. Let yourself go; let your thinking flow freely. Break down the restrictions on yourself; break through old barriers and blockages; try new ways of thinking.

- ☐ **Study One Person in Detail**
Pick one person you are around a lot. Study his/her actions and decisions. List what you think his/her rules of thumb are. Begin to try to predict how he/she will respond to future situations and events. See how accurate you can get; compare your analysis to your own methods of operating.

- ☐ **Learning from Bad Situations**
All of us will find ourselves in bad situations from time to time. Good intentions gone bad. Impossible tasks and goals. Hopeless projects. Even though you probably can't perform well, the key is to at least take away some lessons and insights. How did things get to be this way? What factors led to the impasse? How can you make the best of a bad situation? How can you neutralize the negative elements? How can you get the most out of yourself and your staff under the chilling situation? What can you salvage? How can you use coping strategies to minimize the negatives? How can you avoid these situations going forward? In bad situations: 1) Be resourceful. Get the most you can out of the situation. 2) Try to deduce why things got to be that way. 3) Learn from both the situation you inherited and how you react to it. 4) Integrate what you learn into your future behavior.

Learning from Courses

☐ **Insight Events**
These are courses designed around assessing skills and providing feedback to the participants. These events can be a powerful source of self-knowledge and can lead to significant development if done right. When selecting a self-insight course, consider the following: 1) Are the skills assessed the important ones? 2) Are the assessment techniques and instruments sound? 3) Are those who are providing the feedback trained and professional? 4) Is the feedback provided in a user-friendly and "actionable" format? 5) Does the feedback include development planning? 6) Is the setting comfortable and conducive to reflection and learning? 7) Are the other participants the kinds of people you could learn from? 8) Are you in the right frame of mind to learn from this kind of intense experience? Select events on the basis of positive answers to these eight questions.

SUGGESTED READINGS

Bernstein, Albert J. and Sydney Craft Rozen. *Sacred Bull: the inner obstacles that hold you back at work and how to overcome them.* New York: Wiley, 1994.

Brothers, Joyce. *Positive Plus: the practical plan for liking yourself better.* New York: G.P. Putnam's Sons, 1994.

Butler, Gillian Pd.D and Tony Hope, M.D. *Managing your Mind.* New York: Oxford University Press, 1995.

Carlson, Richard. *Don't sweat the small stuff – and it's all small stuff: simple ways to keep the little things from taking over your life.* New York: Hyperion, 1997.

Conger, Jay A. *Learning to Lead.* San Francisco: Jossey-Bass, Inc., 1992.

Cooper, Robert K. and Ayman Sawaf. *Executive EQ: emotional intelligence in leadership and organizations.* New York: Grosset/Putnam, 1997.

Danzig, Robert J. *The Leader Within You.* Hollywood, FL: Lifetime Books, Inc. 1998.

Gitlow, Abraham L. *Being the boss: the importance of leadership and power.* Homewood, IL: Business One Irwin, 1992.

Haas, Howard G. *The Leader Within – An empowering path to self discovery.* New York: HarperBusiness, 1992.

Ishiguro, Kazuo. *The Remains of the Day.* New York: Knopf: 1989.

Kouzes, James M. *Credibility: how leaders gain and lose it, why people demand it.* San Francisco: Jossey-Bass Publishers, 1993.

Prochaska, James O., John C. Norcross and Carlo C. DiClemente. *Changing for Good.* New York: Avon Books, 1995.

Searing, Jill A. and Anne B. Lovett. *The career prescription: how to stop sabotaging your career and put it on a winning track.* Englewood Cliffs, N.J.: Prentice-Hall, 1995.

Senge, Peter M. *The Fifth Discipline – The art and practice of the learning organization.* New York: Doubleday, 1998.

Wareham, John. *The anatomy of a great executive.* New York: HarperCollins, 1991.

LACK OF COMPOSURE

SECTION 1: YOUR DEVELOPMENT NEED(S)

A PROBLEM

- ☐ Does not handle pressure and stress well
- ☐ Gets emotional, subjective, and unpredictable when things don't go as planned
- ☐ May become hostile or sarcastic or withdraw from people as stress increases
- ☐ May make snap or poor decisions under pressure
- ☐ Performance degrades when things get tough

NOT A PROBLEM

- ☐ Cool under stress and pressure
- ☐ Can take conflict in stride
- ☐ Can absorb criticism and sarcasm without losing control
- ☐ Stays steady under pressure
- ☐ Keeps to the issues
- ☐ Doesn't fly off the handle when things don't go as expected
- ☐ Just tries harder when blocked
- ☐ Expects surprises
- ☐ Helps keep others calm in the storm

SOME CAUSES

- ☐ Defensive
- ☐ Easily overwhelmed
- ☐ In a bad set of circumstances you can't get out of
- ☐ Lack of self confidence
- ☐ Over your head
- ☐ Overly sensitive
- ☐ Perfectionist
- ☐ Too much going on
- ☐ Very control oriented
- ☐ Weak impulse control

THE MAP

Life is rough water. There are a lot of things that don't go right and are upsetting. There's lots to pay attention to. There are bad people. There are impossible situations. There are sad, catastrophic events. There is conflict and tension. There are contests and tests to win and pass. Sometimes you lose and it hurts. All unfortunately normal. On the other hand, losing one's cool and getting unduly upset isn't conducive to a successful career. Being able to function normally under stress and pressure is one of the mission-critical requirements for most managerial jobs. Impulse control and delay of gratification are skills that can be improved.

SECTION 2: LEARNING ON YOUR OWN

THESE SELF-DEVELOPMENT REMEDIES WILL HELP YOU BUILD YOUR SKILL(S)

SOME REMEDIES

☐ **1. First about emotions.** Emotions are electricity and chemistry. Emotions are designed to help you cope with emergencies and threats. Emotions trigger predictable body changes. Heart pumps faster and with greater pressure. Blood flows faster. Glucose is released into the bloodstream for increased energy and strength. Eyes dilate to take in more light. Breathing rate increases to get more oxygen. Why is that? To either fight or flee from Saber Toothed Tigers, of course. Emotions are designed to help us with the so-called fight or flight response. They makes the body faster and stronger temporarily. The price? In order to increase energy to the muscles, the emotional response decreases resources for the stomach – that's why we get upset stomachs under stress, and the thinking brain – that's why we say and do dumb things under stress. Even though we may be able to lift a heavy object off a trapped person, we can't think of the right thing to say in a tense meeting. Once the emotional response is triggered, it has to run its course. If no threat follows the initial trigger, it lasts from 45–60 seconds in most people. That's why your grandmother told you to count to 10. Trouble is, people have Saber Toothed Tigers in their heads. In modern times, thoughts can trigger this emotional response. Events which are certainly not physically threatening, like being criticized, can trigger the response. Even worse, people today have added a third "f" to the fight or flight response – freeze. Emotions can shut you down and leave you speechless, neither choosing to fight – argue, respond, nor flee – calmly shut down the transaction and exit.

☐ **2. Decreasing triggers.** Write down on 3" x 5" note cards or Post-it® Notes the last 25 times you lost your composure. Most people who have composure problems have three to five repeating triggers. Criticism. Loss of control. A certain kind of a person. An enemy. Being surprised. Spouse. Children. Money. Authority. Try to group 90% of the events into three to five categories. Once you have the groupings, ask yourself why these are problems. Is it ego? Losing face? Being caught short? Being found out? Causing you more work? In each grouping, what would be a more mature response? Mentally and physically rehearse a better response. Try to decrease by 10% a month the number of times you lose your composure.

☐ **3. Increasing impulse control.** People say and do dumb and inappropriate things when they lose their composure. The problem is that they say the first thing that occurs to them to say. They do the first thing that occurs to them to do. Research shows that generally somewhere between the second and third thing you think of to say or do is the best option. Practice holding back your first response long enough to think of a second. When you can do that, wait long enough to think of a third before you choose. By that time 50% of your composure problems should go away.

☐ **4. Count to 10.** Our thinking and judgment is not at its best during the emotional response. Create and practice delaying tactics. Go get a pencil out of your briefcase. Go get a cup of coffee. Ask a question and listen. Go up to the flip chart and write something. Take notes. Think of something you like. See yourself in a setting you find calming. Go to the bathroom. You need about a minute to regain your composure after the emotional response is triggered. Don't do or say anything until the minute has passed. *More help? – See #11 Composure.*

☐ **5. Delay of gratification.** Are you impatient? Do you get upset when the plane is delayed? The food is late? The car isn't ready? Your spouse is behind schedule? For most of us, life is one big delay. We always seem to be waiting for someone else to do something so we can do our something. People with composure problems often can't accept delay of what they want and think they deserve and have coming. When what they want is delayed, they get belligerent and demanding. They get emotional. Voice gets louder. Criticism of the blocking person or group goes up. Write down the last 25 delays that set you off. Group them into three to five categories. Create and rehearse a more mature response. Relax. Reward yourself with something enjoyable. Adopt a philosophical stance since there's little or nothing you can do about it. Think great thoughts while you're waiting. *More help? – See #41 Patience.*

☐ **6. Defensive?** A lot of loss of composure starts with an intended or even an unintended criticism. There are a lot of perfect people in this world who cannot deal with a piece of negative information about themselves or about something they have or have not done. You might be one of these perfect people. The rest of us have flaws that most around us know about and once in awhile tell us about. We even know that once in awhile unjust criticism is sent our way. Dealing constructively with criticism is a learnable skill. *More help? – See #108 Defensiveness.*

☐ **7. Control?** Are you somewhat of a perfectionist? Need to have everything just so? Create plans and expect them to be followed? Very jealous of your time? Another source of loss of composure is when things do not go exactly as planned. Put slack in your plans. Expect the unexpected. Lengthen the time line. Plan for delays. List worst case scenarios. Most of the time you will be pleasantly surprised and the rest of the time you won't get so upset.

☐ **8. Blame and vengeance?** Do you feel a need to punish the people and groups that set you off? Do you become hostile, angry, sarcastic or vengeful? While all that may be temporarily satisfying to you they will all backfire and you will lose in the long term. When someone attacks you, rephrase it as an attack on a problem. Reverse the argument – ask what they would do if they were in your shoes. When the other side takes a rigid position, don't reject it. Ask why – what are the principles behind the offer, how do we know it's fair, what's the theory of the case, play out what would happen if their position was accepted. Let the other side vent frustration, blow off steam, but don't react. When you do reply to an attack, keep it to the facts and their impact on you. It's fine for you to draw conclusions about the impact on yourself – "I felt blindsided;" it's not fine for you to tell others their motives – "You blindsided me" means you did it, probably meant to, and I know the meaning of your behavior. So state the meaning for yourself; ask others what their actions meant.

☐ **9. Get anxious and jump to conclusions?** Take quick action? Don't like ambiguity and uncertainty and act to wipe it out? Solutions first, understanding second? Take the time to really define the problem. Let people finish. Try not to interrupt. Don't finish others' sentences. Ask clarifying questions. Restate the problem in your own words to everyone's satisfaction. Ask them what they think. Throw out trial solutions for debate. Then decide.

☐ **10. Too much invested at work?** Find a release for your pent up emotions. Get a physical hobby. Start an exercise routine. Jog. Walk. Chop wood. Sometimes people who have flare tempers hold it in too much, the pressure builds, and the teakettle blows. The body stores energy. It has to go somewhere. Work on releasing your work frustration off-work.

SECTION 3: LEARNING FROM MORE FEEDBACK

THESE SOURCES WOULD GIVE YOU THE MOST ACCURATE AND DETAILED FEEDBACK ON YOUR SKILL(S)

☐ **Development Professionals**
Sometimes it might be valuable to get some analysis and feedback from a professional trained and certified in the area you're working on: possibly a career counselor, a therapist, clergy, a psychologist, etc.

☐ **Direct Reports**
Across a variety of settings, your direct reports probably see you the most. They are the recipients of most of your managerial behaviors. They know your work. They can compare you with former bosses. Since they may hesitate to give you negative feedback, you have to set the atmosphere to make it easier for them. You have to ask.

☐ **Human Resource Professionals**
Human Resource professionals have both a formal and informal feedback role. Since they have access to unique and confidential information, they can provide the right context for feedback you've received. Sometimes they may be "directed" to give you feedback. Other times, they may pass on feedback just to be helpful to you.

☐ **Past Associates/Constituencies**
When confronted with a present performance problem, some claim, "I wasn't like that before; it must be the current situation." When feedback is available from former associates, about 50% support that claim. In the other half of the cases, the people were like that before and probably didn't know it. It sometimes makes sense to access the past to clearly see the present.

☐ **Peers and Colleagues**
Peers and colleagues have a special social and working relationship. They attend staff meetings together, share private views, get feedback from the same boss, travel together, and are knowledgeable about each other's work. You perhaps let your guard down more around peers and act more like yourself. They can be a valuable source of feedback.

SECTION 4: LEARNING FROM DEVELOP-IN-PLACE ASSIGNMENTS

THESE PART-TIME DEVELOP-IN-PLACE ASSIGNMENTS WILL HELP YOU BUILD YOUR SKILL(S)

☐ Manage an ad hoc, temporary group of "green," inexperienced people as their coach, teacher, orienter, etc.

☐ Manage an ad hoc, temporary group of balky and resisting people through an unpopular change or project.

☐ Manage an ad hoc, temporary group of people where the people in the group are towering experts but the temporary manager is not.

☐ Handle a tough negotiation with an internal or external client or customer.

☐ Help shut down a plant, regional office, product line, business, operation, etc.

☐ Manage a dissatisfied internal or external customer; troubleshoot a performance or quality problem with a product or service.

- ☐ Manage the assigning/allocating of office space in a contested situation.
- ☐ Manage a group through a significant business crisis.
- ☐ Take on a tough and undoable project, one where others who have tried it have failed.
- ☐ Make peace with an enemy or someone you've disappointed with a product or service or someone you've had some trouble with or don't get along well with.

SECTION 5: LEARNING FROM FULL-TIME JOBS

THESE FULL-TIME JOBS OFFER THE OPPORTUNITY TO BUILD YOUR SKILL(S)

☐ **Chair of Projects/Task Forces**

The core demands for qualifying as a Project/Task Force assignment are: 1) Full-time assignment. 2) Important and specific goal. 3) Tight deadline. 4) Success or failure will be evident. 5) High-visibility sponsor. 6) Learning something on the fly. 7) Must get others to cooperate. 8) Usually six months or more. Four types of Projects/Task Forces: 1) New ideas, products, services, or systems (e.g., product/service/program research and development, creation/installation/launch of a new system, new programs like Total Quality Management, positive discipline). 2) Formal negotiations and relationships (e.g., acquisitions, divestitures, agreements, joint ventures; licensing arrangements, franchising; dealing with unions, governments, communities, charities, customers, and relocations). 3) Big one-time events (e.g., working on a major presentation for the board, organizing significant meetings or conferences, disaster/damage control teams; reorganizations, mergers, acquisitions, or relocations, working on visions, charters, strategies, other time-urgent issues and problems). 4) Troubleshooting (e.g., problems, disasters, crises, product/service failures, accidents, illegal activities, damage control in public relations goofs, shut downs, downsizings, layoffs, abrupt changes in leadership).

☐ **Influencing Without Authority**

The core demands to qualify as an Influence Without Authority are: 1) Significant challenge (e.g, start-up, fix-it, scope and/or scale assignment, strategic planning project, changes in management practices/systems). 2) Insufficient direct authority to make it happen. 3) Tight deadlines. 4) Visible to significant others. 5) Sensitive politics.

☐ **Start-ups**

The core demands to qualify as a start from scratch are: 1) Starting something new for you and/or for the organization. 2) Forging a new team. 3) Creating new systems/facilities/staffs/programs/procedures. 4) Contextual adversity (e.g., uncertainty, government regulation, unions, difficult environment). Seven types of start from scratches: 1) Planning, building, hiring, and managing (e.g., building a new facility, opening up a new location, moving a unit or company). 2) Heading something new (e.g., new product, new service, new line of business, new department/function, major new program). 3) Take over a group/product/service/program that had existed for less than a year and was off to a fast start. 4) Establishing overseas operations. 5) Major new designs for existing systems. 6) Moving a successful program from one unit to another. 7) Installing a new organization-wide process as a full-time job (e.g., like Total Quality).

SECTION 6: LEARNING MORE FROM YOUR PLAN

THESE ADDITIONAL REMEDIES WILL HELP MAKE THIS DEVELOPMENT PLAN MORE EFFECTIVE FOR YOU

Learning to Learn Better

- ☐ **Monitoring Yourself More Closely and Getting off Your Autopilot**
Past habits are a mixed blessing, sometimes helping, sometimes not. To avoid putting yourself on "autopilot," think afresh about each situation before acting. Consistently monitor yourself with questions. Is this task different? Ask why you would repeat a past action. Are you avoiding anything, like taking a chance? Is there something new you might try?

- ☐ **Rehearse Successful Tactics/Strategies/Actions**
Mentally rehearse how you will act before going into the situation. Try to anticipate how others will react, what they will say, and how you'll respond. Check out the best and worst cases; play out both scenes. Check your feelings in conflict or worst-case situations; rehearse staying under control.

- ☐ **Examine Why You're Blocked on a Key Issue**
Examine what you are worrying/angry about and list all of your thoughts about it; ask why these feelings are holding you back. Why are the feelings overriding your thinking? How are they getting in the way? Why are they important to you? How can you move beyond them and learn to do something different?

- ☐ **Study Your History of Conflicts for Insights**
List the people and situations which cause you trouble. What are the common themes? Why do those kinds of people and/or those kinds of situations set you off? Do they have to? Was the conflict really important? Did it help or block your learning and getting things done? Try to anticipate those people/situations in the future.

- ☐ **Learn to Separate Opinions From Facts**
Practice separating opinions, beliefs, feelings, attitudes and values from facts and data. Try to base more of your comments and actions on the data side. If there is a need to air subjective information, announce it as such, and label it for what it is. Don't present opinions with the look and sound of data.

Learning from Experience, Feedback and Other People

- ☐ **Using Multiple Models**
Who do you know who exemplifies how to do whatever your need is? Who, for example, personifies decisiveness or compassion or strategic agility? Think more broadly than your current job and colleagues. For example, clergy, friends, spouses or community leaders are also good sources for potential models. Select your models not on the basis of overall excellence or likability, but on the basis of the one towering strength (or glaring weakness) you are interested in. Even people who are well thought of usually have only one or two towering strengths (or glaring weaknesses). Ordinarily, you won't learn as much from the whole person as you will from one characteristic.

- ☐ **Learning from Ineffective Behavior**
Seeing things done poorly can be a very potent source of learning for you, especially if the behavior or action affects others negatively. Many times the thing done poorly causes emotional reactions or pain in you and others. Distance yourself from the feelings and explore why the actions didn't work.

- ☐ **Learning from Bad Situations**
All of us will find ourselves in bad situations from time to time. Good intentions gone bad. Impossible tasks and goals. Hopeless projects. Even though you probably can't perform well, the key is to at least take away some lessons and insights. How did things get to be this way? What factors led to the impasse? How can you make the best of a bad situation? How can you neutralize the negative elements? How can you get the most out of yourself and your staff under the chilling situation? What can you salvage? How can you use coping strategies to minimize the negatives? How can you avoid these situations going forward? In bad situations: 1) Be resourceful. Get the most you can out of the situation. 2) Try to deduce why things got to be that way. 3) Learn from both the situation you inherited and how you react to it. 4) Integrate what you learn into your future behavior.

- ☐ **Learning from Mistakes**
Since we're human, we all make mistakes. The key is to focus on why you made the mistake. Spend more time locating causes and less worrying about the effects. Check how you react to mistakes. How much time do you spend being angry with yourself? Do you waste time stewing or do you move on? More importantly, do you learn? Ask why you made the mistake. Are you likely to repeat it under similar situations? Was it a lack of skill? Judgment? Style? Not enough data? Reading people? Misreading the challenge? Misreading the politics? Or was it just random? A good strategy that just didn't work? Others that let you down? The key is to avoid two common reactions to your mistakes: 1) avoiding similar situations instead of learning and trying again, and 2) trying to repeat what you did, only more diligently and

harder, hoping to break through the problem, making the same mistake again but with greater impact. Neither trap leaves us with better strategies for the future. Neither is a learning strategy. To learn and do something differently, focus on the patterns in your behavior that get you in trouble and go back to first causes, those that tell you something about your shortcomings. Facing ourselves squarely is always the best way to learn.

Learning from Courses

☐ **Insight Events**

These are courses designed around assessing skills and providing feedback to the participants. These events can be a powerful source of self-knowledge and can lead to significant development if done right. When selecting a self-insight course, consider the following: 1) Are the skills assessed the important ones? 2) Are the assessment techniques and instruments sound? 3) Are those who are providing the feedback trained and professional? 4) Is the feedback provided in a user-friendly and "actionable" format? 5) Does the feedback include development planning? 6) Is the setting comfortable and conducive to reflection and learning? 7) Are the other participants the kinds of people you could learn from? 8) Are you in the right frame of mind to learn from this kind of intense experience? Select events on the basis of positive answers to these eight questions.

SUGGESTED READINGS

DuBrin, Andrew J. *Your Own Worst Enemy.* New York: AMACOM, 1992.

Elliot, Robert S., M.D. *From Stress to Strength.* New York: Doubleday, 1994.

Lee, John H. with Bill Stott. *Facing the fire: experiencing and expressing anger appropriately.* New York: Bantam Books, 1993.

Loehr, James E. *Stress for Success.* New York: Times Business, 1997.

Potter-Efron, Ronald T. *Working anger: preventing and resolving conflict on the job.* Oakland, CA: New Harbinger Publications, 1998.

Tavris, Carol. *Anger: the misunderstood emotion.* New York: Simon & Schuster, 1989.

108

DEFENSIVENESS

SECTION 1: YOUR DEVELOPMENT NEED(S)

A PROBLEM

- ☐ Is not open to criticism
- ☐ Denies mistakes and faults
- ☐ Rationalizes away failures
- ☐ Gets upset at the messenger who brings bad news
- ☐ Blames others for his/her own problems
- ☐ Doesn't listen to and doesn't hear negative feedback
- ☐ Doesn't share views of personal limitations with others
- ☐ Doesn't benefit much from formal feedback events or workshops

NOT A PROBLEM

- ☐ Takes criticism as a chance to learn
- ☐ Listens attentively to negative feedback
- ☐ Learns from feedback
- ☐ Admits flaws and mistakes
- ☐ Takes personal responsibility when things don't go well
- ☐ Learns from personal growth workshops and plans
- ☐ Thanks people for feedback

SOME CAUSES

- ☐ Blame others
- ☐ Can't read others
- ☐ Combative style
- ☐ Deny faults
- ☐ Doesn't seek feedback
- ☐ Don't share much
- ☐ Not approachable
- ☐ Perfectionist
- ☐ Rigid
- ☐ Shut down in the face of criticism

THE MAP

Self-knowledge is a mission-critical key to success and defensiveness takes away that key. People will give you less and less feedback and you'll rely increasingly on inaccurate self perception. Your blind spots – things they know about you that you deny or are unaware of – will multiply and eventually one of them will stall your career. The fix is to signal to others that you are open to listening to feedback, accurate or not, justified or not, and you'll take it all under advisement. Some of it you'll respond to with developmental efforts, some you will discard, and some you will refute. You can't do those three very constructive things until after you have taken it in.

SECTION 2: LEARNING ON YOUR OWN

THESE SELF-DEVELOPMENT REMEDIES WILL HELP YOU BUILD YOUR SKILL(S)

SOME REMEDIES

☐ **1. Defensiveness is a major blockage to accurate and comprehensive self-knowledge.** *More help? – See #55 Self-Knowledge.* Defensive people overrate themselves in the eyes of others. If you are seen as denying your faults, you may get jumped on when people finally get the chance to give you feedback. Their evaluations of you have to be lower than justified because they think the message has to be louder to get through your defense shields. Your best chance of getting real feedback as a defensive person is to get facilitated 360° feedback where the respondents remain anonymous or get a Human Resources professional to collect information for you and interpret it with you. If you ask for feedback directly, you are unlikely to find truth because of your history of being defensive in the face of negative criticism. Nobody enjoys giving even truthful and helpful criticism and feedback to a defensive person. It's just too painful.

☐ **2. Your defensive response.** You will need to work on keeping yourself in a calm state when getting negative feedback. You need to change your thinking. When getting the feedback, your only task is to accurately understand what people are trying to tell you. It is not your task at that point to accept or reject. That comes later. Mentally rehearse how you will calmly react to tough feedback situations before they happen. Develop automatic tactics to shut down or delay your usual emotional response. Some useful tactics are to slow down, take notes, ask clarifying questions, ask them for concrete examples, and thank them for telling you since you know it's not easy for them.

☐ **3. Getting feedback from others.** Remember, people suspect you really can't take feedback, that you believe yourself to be perfect, that you are defending against any suggestion to the contrary, and probably blaming the messenger of the feedback for the bad data. They expect the transaction to be painful for them and you. To break this cycle, you need to follow the rules of good listening. *More help? – See #33 Listening.* While this may sound unfair, you should initially accept all feedback as accurate, even when you know it isn't. You have to help others give you feedback in the beginning to overcome their fear of your defensiveness. On those matters that really count, you can go back and fix it later.

☐ **4. Once you have understood the feedback, and after the event, write down all of the criticisms** on 3" x 5" cards or Post-it® Notes. Create two piles. These criticisms are probably true of me and these are probably not. Ask someone you trust who knows you well to help you so you don't delude yourself. For those that are true, signal the people who gave you the feedback that you have understood, think it was accurate, and will try to do something about it. For those that are not true, resort the pile into criticisms that are important to you and those that are small and trivial or unimportant. Throw the unimportant pile away. With those that are probably not true but important, re-sort the pile into career threatening – if people above me really thought this was true about me, my career would be damaged, and not career stopping. Throw the not career stopping away. With the remaining pile, review them with your boss and/or mentor to see what the general opinion is about you. This leaves you with two piles: those that people do believe – even though they are not true – and those they don't. Throw the don't believe pile away. With the remaining pile, plot a strategy to convince people around you by deeds not words, that those criticisms are untrue of you.

☐ **5. Show others you take your development seriously.** Share your developmental needs and ask for their help. One of the best ways to avoid criticism is to bring it up yourself first and let others just fill in the details. Research shows that people are much more likely to help and give the benefit of the doubt to those who admit their shortcomings and try to do something about them. They know it takes courage. *More help? – See #44 Personal Disclosure.*

☐ **6. Resistance to new ideas.** A corollary to personal defensiveness is resistance to anything new or different. In your day-to-day interactions with people, your defensiveness may make you appear closed or blocked to new or different points of view. Your first job is to turn off your evaluator/rejector program and learn to listen more. *More help? – See #33 Listening*. Ask more questions – "How did you get there?" "Do you prefer this to that or to what we're now doing?" If you disagree, give your reasons first. Then invite criticism of your response. Turn the disagreement back to the nature of the problem or strategy – "What are we trying to solve? What causes it? What questions should be answered? What objective standards could we use to measure success?" Get the discussion off your view versus whomever and onto the criteria for making a decision. *More help? – See #12 Conflict Management*. Develop a more open style. You should work on *#3 Approachability* and *#31 Interpersonal Savvy*. Until you signal repeatedly that you are open to others, interested in what they have to say, share personal things you don't have to share, invite people to talk with you and then listen, little will come of this effort. You will have to persevere, endure some rejection, and perhaps some angry or dismissive remarks in order to balance the situation. Mentally rehearse so you're not blindsided by this. Since others think they will get a defensive reaction if they offer some criticism, you have to open the conversation.

- [ ] **7. Blind spots.** The thing that gets us in the most career trouble is a blind spot that matters. Blind spots are weaknesses we really have that we deny or reject. That means we go about performing as if we were very good at it when in fact we're not. Better to have a known and admitted weakness. We know we are not good at it so we try harder, ask for help, delegate it, get a consultant, get a tutor, read a book or loop around it. Your new life task is to have no blind spots. Turn all of your blind spots into known weaknesses and then the known weaknesses into skills. Make it a quest to find out what everybody really thinks about you. *More help? – See #55 Self-Knowledge.*

- [ ] **8. Disclosing more.** Defensive people tend to be shy or not very forthcoming with personal data, especially about possible weaknesses and mistakes. *More help? – See #44 Personal Disclosure*. The kinds of disclosures that people enjoy are the reasons behind why you do and decide what you do, your self appraisal, things you know behind what's happening in the business that they don't know – that you are at liberty to disclose, things both good and embarrassing that have happened to you in the past, comment about what's going on around you – without being too negative about others, and things you are interested in and do outside of work. These are areas which you should learn to disclose more than you now do. If you share your self appraisal of your possible weaknesses and shortcomings, that decreases the number of times you need to be defensive. These icebreakers open the door to the kind of relationships where you can get more feedback.

- [ ] **9. Avoid sharp and instant reactions.** This is very likely getting you into trouble. You may jump to conclusions, categorically dismiss what others say, use aggressive or inflammatory language or are quick to deny or blame. People then see you as closed or combative. More negatively, they may believe you think they're stupid or ill-informed. If you're seen as intolerant or closed or quick to jump, people will often stumble over words in their haste to talk with you or short cut their argument since they assume you're not listening anyway. The key is always to ask a clarifying question first to get you more information and to prepare a measured and calmer response.

- [ ] **10. Watch your non-verbals.** Most defensive people have one or more non-verbals that signal to others they don't accept what the person is saying. It could be the washboard brow, blank stare, flushing, body agitation, finger or pencil drumming, pointing, etc. Most around you know the signs. Do you? Ask someone you trust what it is that you do. Work on eliminating those chilling non-verbals.

SECTION 3: LEARNING FROM MORE FEEDBACK

THESE SOURCES WOULD GIVE YOU THE MOST ACCURATE AND DETAILED FEEDBACK ON YOUR SKILL(S)

- ☐ **Development Professionals**
  Sometimes it might be valuable to get some analysis and feedback from a professional trained and certified in the area you're working on: possibly a career counselor, a therapist, clergy, a psychologist, etc.
- ☐ **Direct Reports**
  Across a variety of settings, your direct reports probably see you the most. They are the recipients of most of your managerial behaviors. They know your work. They can compare you with former bosses. Since they may hesitate to give you negative feedback, you have to set the atmosphere to make it easier for them. You have to ask.
- ☐ **Human Resource Professionals**
  Human Resource professionals have both a formal and informal feedback role. Since they have access to unique and confidential information, they can provide the right context for feedback you've received. Sometimes they may be "directed" to give you feedback. Other times, they may pass on feedback just to be helpful to you.
- ☐ **Past Associates/Constituencies**
  When confronted with a present performance problem, some claim, "I wasn't like that before; it must be the current situation." When feedback is available from former associates, about 50% support that claim. In the other half of the cases, the people were like that before and probably didn't know it. It sometimes makes sense to access the past to clearly see the present.
- ☐ **Peers and Colleagues**
  Peers and colleagues have a special social and working relationship. They attend staff meetings together, share private views, get feedback from the same boss, travel together, and are knowledgeable about each other's work. You perhaps let your guard down more around peers and act more like yourself. They can be a valuable source of feedback.

SECTION 4: LEARNING FROM DEVELOP-IN-PLACE ASSIGNMENTS

THESE PART-TIME DEVELOP-IN-PLACE ASSIGNMENTS WILL HELP YOU BUILD YOUR SKILL(S)

- ☐ Attend a self-awareness/assessment course that includes feedback.
- ☐ Try to learn something frivolous and fun to see how good you can get (e.g., juggling, square dancing, magic).
- ☐ Be a change agent; create a symbol for change; lead the rallying cry; champion a significant change and implementation.

- ☐ Manage an ad hoc, temporary group of people where the people in the group are towering experts but the temporary manager is not.
- ☐ Manage a dissatisfied internal or external customer; troubleshoot a performance or quality problem with a product or service.
- ☐ Make peace with an enemy or someone you've disappointed with a product or service or someone you've had some trouble with or don't get along well with.
- ☐ Attend a course or event which will push you personally beyond your usual limits or outside your comfort zone (e.g., Outward Bound, language immersion training, sensitivity group, public speaking).
- ☐ Become a referee for an athletic league or program.
- ☐ Lobby for your organization on a contested issue in local, regional, state, or federal government.
- ☐ Create employee involvement teams.

SECTION 5: LEARNING FROM FULL-TIME JOBS

THESE FULL-TIME JOBS OFFER THE OPPORTUNITY TO BUILD YOUR SKILL(S)

☐ **Influencing Without Authority**

The core demands to qualify as an Influence Without Authority are: 1) Significant challenge (e.g, start-up, fix-it, scope and/or scale assignment, strategic planning project, changes in management practices/ systems). 2) Insufficient direct authority to make it happen. 3) Tight deadlines. 4) Visible to significant others. 5) Sensitive politics.

☐ **Line To Staff Switches**

The core demands to qualify as a Line to Staff switch are: 1) Intellectually/strategically demanding. 2) Highly visible to others. 3) New area/perspective/method/culture/function. 4) Moving away from a bottom line. 5) Moving from field to headquarters. 6) Exposure to high-level executives. Examples: 1) Business/strategic planning. 2) Heading a staff department. 3) Assistant to/chief of staff to a senior executive. 4) Head of a task force. 5) Human resources role.

☐ **Start-ups**

The core demands to qualify as a start from scratch are: 1) Starting something new for you and/or for the organization. 2) Forging a new team. 3) Creating new systems/facilities/staffs/programs/procedures. 4) Contextual adversity (e.g., uncertainty, government regulation, unions, difficult environment). Seven types of start from scratches: 1) Planning, building, hiring, and managing (e.g., building a new facility, opening up a new location, moving a unit or company). 2) Heading something new (e.g., new product, new service, new line of business, new department/function, major new program). 3) Take over a group/ product/service/program that had existed for less than a year and was off to a fast start. 4) Establishing overseas operations. 5) Major new designs for existing systems. 6) Moving a successful program from one unit to another. 7) Installing a new organization-wide process as a full-time job (e.g., like Total Quality).

SECTION 6: LEARNING MORE FROM YOUR PLAN

THESE ADDITIONAL REMEDIES WILL HELP MAKE THIS DEVELOPMENT PLAN MORE EFFECTIVE FOR YOU

Learning to Learn Better

- ☐ **Rehearse Successful Tactics/Strategies/Actions**
  Mentally rehearse how you will act before going into the situation. Try to anticipate how others will react, what they will say, and how you'll respond. Check out the best and worst cases; play out both scenes. Check your feelings in conflict or worst-case situations; rehearse staying under control.
- ☐ **Put Yourself in Situations that Call for Your Weaknesses**
  Put yourself in situations where you must overcome or neutralize a weakness to be successful. Find opportunities to develop counter coping skills: if you're shy, attend functions where you don't know many people; if you're too aggressive, work with children, etc.
- ☐ **Examine Why You're Blocked on a Key Issue**
  Examine what you are worrying/angry about and list all of your thoughts about it; ask why these feelings are holding you back. Why are the feelings overriding your thinking? How are they getting in the way? Why are they important to you? How can you move beyond them and learn to do something different?
- ☐ **Study Your History of Conflicts for Insights**
  List the people and situations which cause you trouble. What are the common themes? Why do those kinds of people and/or those kinds of situations set you off? Do they have to? Was the conflict really important? Did it help or block your learning and getting things done? Try to anticipate those people/situations in the future.
- ☐ **Learn to Separate Opinions From Facts**
  Practice separating opinions, beliefs, feelings, attitudes and values from facts and data. Try to base more of your comments and actions on the data side. If there is a need to air subjective information, announce it as such, and label it for what it is. Don't present opinions with the look and sound of data.
- ☐ **Learning from Bad Bosses**
  First, what does he/she do so well to make him/her your boss? (Even bad bosses have strengths). Then, ask what makes this boss bad for you. Is it his/her behavior? Attitude? Values? Philosophy? Practices? Style? What is the source of the conflict? Why do you react as you do? Do others react the same? How are you part of the problem? What do

you do that triggers your boss? If you wanted to, could you reduce the conflict or make it go away by changing something you do? Is there someone around you who doesn't react like you? How are they different? What can you learn from them? What is your emotional reaction to this boss? Why do you react like that? What can you do to cope with these feelings? Can you avoid reacting out of anger and frustration? Can you find something positive about the situation? Can you use someone else as a buffer? Can you learn from your emotions? What lasting lessons of managing others can you take away from this experience? What won't you do as a manager? What will you do differently? How could you teach these principles you've learned to others by the use of this example?

☐ **Learning from Bad Situations**
All of us will find ourselves in bad situations from time to time. Good intentions gone bad. Impossible tasks and goals. Hopeless projects. Even though you probably can't perform well, the key is to at least take away some lessons and insights. How did things get to be this way? What factors led to the impasse? How can you make the best of a bad situation? How can you neutralize the negative elements? How can you get the most out of yourself and your staff under the chilling situation? What can you salvage? How can you use coping strategies to minimize the negatives? How can you avoid these situations going forward? In bad situations: 1) Be resourceful. Get the most you can out of the situation. 2) Try to deduce why things got to be that way. 3) Learn from both the situation you inherited and how you react to it. 4) Integrate what you learn into your future behavior.

☐ **Learning from Mistakes**
Since we're human, we all make mistakes. The key is to focus on why you made the mistake. Spend more time locating causes and less worrying about the effects. Check how you react to mistakes. How much time do you spend being angry with yourself? Do you waste time stewing or do you move on? More importantly, do you learn? Ask why you made the mistake. Are you likely to repeat it under similar situations? Was it a lack of skill? Judgment? Style? Not enough data? Reading people? Misreading the challenge? Misreading the politics? Or was it just random? A good strategy that just didn't work? Others that let you down? The key is to avoid two common reactions to your mistakes: 1) avoiding similar situations instead of learning and trying again, and 2) trying to repeat what you did, only more diligently and harder, hoping to break through the problem, making the same mistake again but with greater impact. Neither trap leaves us with better strategies for the future. Neither is a learning strategy. To learn and do something differently, focus on the patterns in your behavior that get you in trouble and go back to first causes, those that tell you something about your shortcomings. Facing ourselves squarely is always the best way to learn.

Learning from Courses

☐ **Insight Events**
These are courses designed around assessing skills and providing feedback to the participants. These events can be a powerful source of self-knowledge and can lead to significant development if done right. When selecting a self-insight course, consider the following: 1) Are the skills assessed the important ones? 2) Are the assessment techniques and instruments sound? 3) Are those who are providing the feedback trained and professional? 4) Is the feedback provided in a user-friendly and "actionable" format? 5) Does the feedback include development planning? 6) Is the setting comfortable and conducive to reflection and learning? 7) Are the other participants the kinds of people you could learn from? 8) Are you in the right frame of mind to learn from this kind of intense experience? Select events on the basis of positive answers to these eight questions.

☐ **Attitude Toward Learning**
In addition to selecting the right course, a learning attitude is required. Be open. Close down your "like/dislike" switch, your "agree/disagree" blinders, and your "like me/not like me" feelings toward the instructors. Learning requires new lessons, change, and new behaviors and perspectives – all scary stuff for most people. Don't resist. Take in all you can during the course. Ask clarifying questions. Discuss concerns with the other participants. Jot down what you learn as you go. After the course is over, take some reflective time to glean the meat. Make the practical decisions about what you can and cannot use.

SUGGESTED READINGS

Bernstein, Albert J. and Sydney Craft Rozen. *Sacred Bull: the inner obstacles that hold you back at work and how to overcome them.* New York: Wiley, 1994.

Carson, Kerry, Ph.D. and Paula Phillips Carson, Ph.D. *Defective Bosses – Working for the Dysfunctional Dozen.* New York: The Haworth Press

DuBrin, Andrew J. *Your Own Worst Enemy.* New York: AMACOM, 1992.

Maslow, Abraham H. *Maslow on Management.* New York: John Wiley & Sons, Inc., 1998.

LACK OF ETHICS AND VALUES

SECTION 1: YOUR DEVELOPMENT NEED(S)

A PROBLEM

- ☐ Lacks the necessary sensitivity to the operating ethics and values of the organization
- ☐ Operates too close to the margins
- ☐ Pushes the limits of tolerance
- ☐ Doesn't operate within the norms

NOT A PROBLEM

- ☐ Values and ethics are generally aligned with the organization's
- ☐ Operates within boundaries most others would agree to
- ☐ Looked to for guidance on standards and norms
- ☐ Stays steady through crises involving close calls on ethics
- ☐ Can articulate own and other's values
- ☐ Helpful to others in making close calls on values/ethical matters
- ☐ Projects a consistent set of values

SOME CAUSES

- ☐ Inconsistent
- ☐ Operate close to the edge
- ☐ Overly ambitious
- ☐ Overly independent
- ☐ Pragmatic to a fault
- ☐ Set own rules of conduct
- ☐ Situational ethics

THE MAP

Being seen as having questionable ethics is a category killer. At the least it means the values and ethics you are operating under are not in line with the commonly held values and ethics of those around you. On the more negative side, it could mean you have unacceptable values and ethics in a more absolute sense; that is, most would reject them. You may hedge or operate too close to the edge for people to feel comfortable with you. Most of us haven't thought out our values/ethical stances well; we are on autopilot from childhood and our collective experience. People deduce your values and ethics by listening to what you say and more importantly watching what you do. Unless you address this issue now, your career with this organization might be in jeopardy.

SECTION 2: LEARNING ON YOUR OWN

THESE SELF-DEVELOPMENT REMEDIES WILL HELP YOU BUILD YOUR SKILL(S)

SOME REMEDIES

☐ **1. Fine tuning the problem.** Make sure you know exactly what your problem is. The range of possibilities is great. Get 360° feedback on this specific issue by having a Human Resource professional or outside consultant poll people to find out what your difficulty is. As a less severe problem, you may be just stubborn and rigid, tied to the values of the past, out of tune with the times, pragmatic to a fault, be seen as not helpful enough to others, pushing your own agenda, playing favorites, or being reluctant to speak up. As a more severe problem, you might be cutting corners to look good, setting your own rules, blaming others for things you should take responsibility for, sabotaging your rivals, hedging the truth, or showing little concern for others. *More help? – See #55 Self-Knowledge.*

☐ **2. The worst case.** Your ethics really are questionable. You hedge, sabotage others, play for advantage, set up others and make others look bad. You may be devious and scheming and overly political. You tell yourself it's OK because you are getting the results out on time. You really believe the end justifies the means. If any of this is true, this criticism should have also happened to you in the past. This is not something that develops overnight. You need to find out if your career with this organization is salvageable. The best way to do this is to admit that you know your ethics and values are not the same as the people you work with and ask a boss or a mentor whether it's fixable. If they say yes, contact everyone you think you've alienated and see how they respond. Tell them the things you're going to do differently. Ask them if the situation can be repaired. Longer term, you need to seek some professional counsel on your values and ethics.

☐ **3. Inconsistent or situational?** You might just be inconsistent in your value stances and actions. You change your mind based on mood or who you talked with last. That may confuse and bother people. You may express a pro people value in one instance – people you manage, and an anti people value in another – people from another unit. You may rigidly adhere to a high moral code in one transaction – with customers and play it close to the acceptable margin in another – with vendors. You may match your values with your audience when managing up and not when you're managing down. You may play favorites. People are more comfortable with consistency and predictability. Look for the three to five areas where you think these inconsistencies play out. Write down what you did with various people so you can compare. Did you do different things in parallel situations? Do you hold others to a different standard? Do you have so many values positions that they have to clash? Do you state so few that people have to fill in the blanks with guesses? Try to balance your behavior so that you are more consistent across situations.

- ☐ **4. Don't walk your good talk?** Another possibility is that there is a sizable gap between what you say about your ethics and values and what the ethics and values of others should be and what you actually do in those same situations. We have worked with many who get themselves in trouble by giving motivating values and ethics speeches, high toned, passionate, charismatic, gives you goose bumps until you watch that person do the opposite or something quite different in practice. Examine all the things you tend to say in speeches or in meetings or casual conversations that are values and ethics based. Write them down the left side of a legal pad. For each one, see if you can write three to five examples of when you acted exactly in line with that value or ethic. Can you write down any that are not exactly like that? If you can, it's the gap that's the problem. Either stop making values and ethics statements you can't model or bring your values into alignment with your own statements.

- ☐ **5. Don't walk your bad talk?** Another possibility is that there is a sizable gap between what you say and the language you use and what you actually think and do. We have worked with many who get themselves in trouble by using language and words that imply marginal values and ethics that are not real. Do you shoot for effect? Do you exaggerate? Do you push your statements to the extreme to make a point? Do you overstate negative views? Do you trash talk to fit in? Do you use demeaning words? What would others think your values were if they listened to you talk and didn't know what you actually do? Examine the words and the language you tend to use in speeches or in meetings or casual conversations that are values and ethics based. Write them down the left side of a legal pad. For each one, see if you can write three to five examples of when you acted exactly in line with those words. Do you really act like that? Do you really think that way? If you don't, it's the gap that's the problem. Stop using words and language that are not in line with your real thoughts and values.

- ☐ **6. Declaring your values.** You may not think in terms of values much, and your statements may not clearly state your values. To pass the test of a thoughtfully held value, you should be able to: state it in a sentence, give five examples of how it plays out, both the situation and consequences; state what is the opposite of the value – what is dishonesty, for example, and demonstrate how you follow the value. Since you are having trouble in this area, it may be a good exercise to try to capture your value system on paper so you can practice delivering a clear statement of it to others. If you ignore obvious values implications, people may assume you don't care.

☐ **7. Value clashes.** Sometimes people get in trouble because they don't understand the underlying mismatch between values. Few people have any trouble with clear cut value clashes; it's the close calls where ill-thought-through positions get us in trouble. You should be able to pro and con various values. You should be able to help people think through when to break a confidence or when loyalty to the organization supersedes loyalty to an individual. What are the common values clashes you deal with? In these situations, you need to be able to argue both sides of the question. Hedging on your tax return and padding of an expense account; is that the same or different? Working with or firing a marginal performer? Cutting quality or raising the price? Firing someone for drug abuse and serving alcohol at company functions? *More help? – See #12 Conflict Management.*

☐ **8. Too independent?** You set your own rules, smash through obstacles, see yourself as tough, action and results oriented. You get it done. The problem is, you wreak havoc for others; they don't know which of your actions will create headaches for them in their own unit or with customers. You don't often worry about whether others think like you do. You operate from the inside out. What's important to you is what you think and what you judge to be right and just. In a sense, admirable. In a sense, not smart. You live in an organization that has both formal and informal commonly held standards, belief, ethics and values. You can't survive long without knowing what they are and bending yours to fit. To find out, focus on the impact on others and how they see the issue. This will be hard at first since you spend your energy justifying your own actions.

☐ **9. Values or facts?** You may be a fact-based person. Since to you the facts dictate everything, you may be baffled as to why people would see it any differently than you do. The reason they see it differently is that there is a higher order of values at work. People compare across situations to check for common themes, equity and parity. They ask questions like who wins and loses here, who is being favored, is this a play for advantage? Since you are a here-and-now person, you will look inconsistent to them across slightly different situations. You need to drop back and ask what will others hear, not what you want to say. Go below the surface. Tell them why you're saying something. Ask them what they think.

☐ **10. Old values?** This is a tough one. Times change. Do values change? Some think not. That may be your stance. What about humor? Could you tell some ribald jokes 10 years ago that would get you in trouble today? Have dating practices and ages changed? Has television and 24 hour news changed our world view? Is there still lifelong employment? How long does a college education last today versus 20 years ago? Values run pretty deep. They don't change easily. When did you form your current values? Over 20 years ago? Maybe it's time to examine them in light of the new today to see whether you need to make any mid-course corrections.

SECTION 3: LEARNING FROM MORE FEEDBACK

THESE SOURCES WOULD GIVE YOU THE MOST ACCURATE AND DETAILED FEEDBACK ON YOUR SKILL(S)

☐ **Boss's Boss(es)**
From a process standpoint, your boss's boss probably has the most influence and control over your progress. He/she has a broader perspective, has more access to data, and stands at the center of decisions about you. To know what he/she thinks, without having to violate the canons of corporate due process to get that information, would be quite useful.

☐ **Direct Boss**
Your direct boss has important information about you, your performance, and your prospects. The challenge is to get this information. There are formal processes (e.g., performance appraisals). There are day-to-day opportunities. To help, signal your boss that you want and can handle direct and timely feedback. Many bosses have trouble giving feedback, so you will have to work at it over a period of time.

☐ **Direct Reports**
Across a variety of settings, your direct reports probably see you the most. They are the recipients of most of your managerial behaviors. They know your work. They can compare you with former bosses. Since they may hesitate to give you negative feedback, you have to set the atmosphere to make it easier for them. You have to ask.

☐ **Human Resource Professionals**
Human Resource professionals have both a formal and informal feedback role. Since they have access to unique and confidential information, they can provide the right context for feedback you've received. Sometimes they may be "directed" to give you feedback. Other times, they may pass on feedback just to be helpful to you.

☐ **Past Associates/Constituencies**
When confronted with a present performance problem, some claim, "I wasn't like that before; it must be the current situation." When feedback is available from former associates, about 50% support that claim. In the other half of the cases, the people were like that before and probably didn't know it. It sometimes makes sense to access the past to clearly see the present.

☐ **Peers and Colleagues**
Peers and colleagues have a special social and working relationship. They attend staff meetings together, share private views, get feedback from the same boss, travel together, and are knowledgeable about each other's work. You perhaps let your guard down more around

peers and act more like yourself. They can be a valuable source of feedback.

SECTION 4: LEARNING FROM DEVELOP-IN-PLACE ASSIGNMENTS

THESE PART-TIME DEVELOP-IN-PLACE ASSIGNMENTS WILL HELP YOU BUILD YOUR SKILL(S)

- ☐ Handle a tough negotiation with an internal or external client or customer.
- ☐ Help shut down a plant, regional office, product line, business, operation, etc.
- ☐ Manage a dissatisfied internal or external customer; troubleshoot a performance or quality problem with a product or service.
- ☐ Manage the assigning/allocating of office space in a contested situation.
- ☐ Manage a group through a significant business crisis.
- ☐ Make peace with an enemy or someone you've disappointed with a product or service or someone you've had some trouble with or don't get along well with.
- ☐ Manage an ad hoc, temporary group of balky and resisting people through an unpopular change or project.
- ☐ Resolve an issue in conflict between two people, units, geographies, functions, etc.
- ☐ Be a member of a union-negotiating or grievance-handling team.
- ☐ Work on a team looking at a reorganization plan where there will be more people than positions.

SECTION 5: LEARNING FROM FULL-TIME JOBS

THESE FULL-TIME JOBS OFFER THE OPPORTUNITY TO BUILD YOUR SKILL(S)

- ☐ **Fix-its/Turnarounds**

  The core demands to qualify as a Fix-it or Turnaround assignment are: 1) Cleaning up a mess. 2) Serious people issues/problems like credibility/performance/morale. 3) Tight deadline. 4) Serious business performance failure. 5) Last chance to fix. Four Types of Fix-its/Turnarounds: 1) Fixing a failed business/unit involving taking control, stopping losses, managing damage, planning the turnaround, dealing with people problems, installing new processes and systems, and rebuilding the spirit and performance of the unit. 2) Managing sizable disasters like mishandled labor negotiations and strikes, thefts, history of significant business losses, poor staff, failed leadership, hidden problems, fraud, public relations nightmares, etc. 3) Significant reorganization and restructuring (e.g., stabilizing the business, reforming unit, introducing new systems, making people changes, resetting strategy and tactics). 4) Significant system/process breakdown (e.g., MIS, financial coordination processes, audits, standards, etc.) across units requiring working to change something from a distant position, providing advice and counsel, and installing or implementing a major process improvement or system change outside your own unit and/or with customers outside the organization.

☐ **Scope Assignments**
The core demands for a Scope (complexity) assignment are: 1) Significant increase in both internal and external scope or complexity. 2) Significant increase in visibility and/or bottom line responsibility. 3) Unfamiliar area, business, technology, or territory. Examples of Scope assignments involving shifts: 1) Switching into a new function/technology/business. 2) Moving to new organization. 3) Moving to overseas assignment. 4) Moving to new location. 5) Adding new products/services. 6) Moving between headquarters/field. 7) Switches in ownership/top management of the unit/organization. Examples of Scope assignments involving "firsts": 1) First-time manager. 2) First-time managing managers. 3) First-time executive. 4) First-time overseas. 5) First-time headquarters/field. 6) First-time team leader. 7) First-time new technology/business/function. Scope assignments involving increased complexity: 1) Managing a significant expansion of an existing product or service. 2) Managing adding new products/service into an existing unit. 3) Managing a reorganized and more diverse unit. 4) Managing explosive growth. 5) Adding new technologies.

☐ **Start-ups**
The core demands to qualify as a start from scratch are: 1) Starting something new for you and/or for the organization. 2) Forging a new team. 3) Creating new systems/facilities/staffs/programs/procedures. 4) Contextual adversity (e.g., uncertainty, government regulation, unions, difficult environment). Seven types of start from scratches: 1) Planning, building, hiring, and managing (e.g., building a new facility, opening up a new location, moving a unit or company). 2) Heading something new (e.g., new product, new service, new line of business, new department/function, major new program). 3) Take over a group/product/service/program that had existed for less than a year and was off to a fast start. 4) Establishing overseas operations. 5) Major new designs for existing systems. 6) Moving a successful program from one unit to another. 7) Installing a new organization-wide process as a full-time job (e.g., like Total Quality).

SECTION 6: LEARNING MORE FROM YOUR PLAN

THESE ADDITIONAL REMEDIES WILL HELP MAKE THIS DEVELOPMENT PLAN MORE EFFECTIVE FOR YOU

Learning to Learn Better

☐ **Monitoring Yourself More Closely and Getting off Your Autopilot**
Past habits are a mixed blessing, sometimes helping, sometimes not. To avoid putting yourself on "autopilot," think afresh about each situation before acting. Consistently monitor yourself with questions. Is this task different? Ask why you would repeat a past action. Are you avoiding anything, like taking a chance? Is there something new you might try?

Learning from Experience, Feedback and Other People

☐ **Using Multiple Models**
Who do you know who exemplifies how to do whatever your need is? Who, for example, personifies decisiveness or compassion or strategic agility? Think more broadly than your current job and colleagues. For example, clergy, friends, spouses or community leaders are also good sources for potential models. Select your models not on the basis of overall excellence or likability, but on the basis of the one towering strength (or glaring weakness) you are interested in. Even people who are well thought of usually have only one or two towering strengths (or glaring weaknesses). Ordinarily, you won't learn as much from the whole person as you will from one characteristic.

☐ **Being a Student of Others**
While many of us rely on others for information or advice, we do not really study the behavior of other people. Ask what a person does exceptionally well or poorly. What behaviors are particularly effective and ineffective for them? What works for them and what doesn't? As a student of others, you can deduce the rules of thumb for effective and ineffective behavior and include those in your own library. In comparing yourself with this person, in what areas could you most improve? What could you specifically do to improve in ways comfortable for you?

☐ **Learning from Bosses**
Bosses can be an excellent and ready source for learning. All bosses do some things exceptionally well and other things poorly. Distance your feelings from the boss/direct report relationship and study things that work and things that don't work for your boss. What would you have done? What could you use, and what should you avoid?

☐ **Learning from Ineffective Behavior**
Seeing things done poorly can be a very potent source of learning for you, especially if the behavior or action affects others negatively. Many times the thing done poorly causes emotional reactions or pain in you and others. Distance yourself from the feelings and explore why the actions didn't work.

- ☐ **Learning from Observing Others**
  Observe others. Find opportunities to observe without interacting with your model. This enables you to objectively study the person, note what he/she is doing or not doing, and compare that with what you would typically do in similar situations. Many times you can learn more by watching than asking. Your model may not be able to explain what he/she does or may be an unwilling teacher.

- ☐ **Learning from Remote Models**
  Many times you can learn from people not directly available to you. You can read a book about them, watch tapes of public figures, read analyses of them, etc. The principles of learning are the same. Ask yourself what they do well or poorly and deduce their rules of thumb.

- ☐ **Consolidating What You Learn from People**
  After using any source and/or method of learning from others, write down or mentally note the new rules of thumb and the principles involved. How will you remind yourself of the new behaviors in similar situations? How will you prevent yourself from reacting on "autopilot"? How could you share what you have learned from others?

Learning from Courses

- ☐ **Insight Events**
  These are courses designed around assessing skills and providing feedback to the participants. These events can be a powerful source of self-knowledge and can lead to significant development if done right. When selecting a self-insight course, consider the following: 1) Are the skills assessed the important ones? 2) Are the assessment techniques and instruments sound? 3) Are those who are providing the feedback trained and professional? 4) Is the feedback provided in a user-friendly and "actionable" format? 5) Does the feedback include development planning? 6) Is the setting comfortable and conducive to reflection and learning? 7) Are the other participants the kinds of people you could learn from? 8) Are you in the right frame of mind to learn from this kind of intense experience? Select events on the basis of positive answers to these eight questions.

- ☐ **Attitude Toward Learning**
  In addition to selecting the right course, a learning attitude is required. Be open. Close down your "like/dislike" switch, your "agree/disagree" blinders, and your "like me/not like me" feelings toward the instructors. Learning requires new lessons, change, and new behaviors and perspectives – all scary stuff for most people. Don't resist. Take in all you can during the course. Ask clarifying questions. Discuss concerns with the other participants. Jot down what you learn as you go. After the course is over, take some reflective time to glean the meat. Make the practical decisions about what you can and cannot use.

SUGGESTED READINGS

Aguilar, Francis J. *Managing Corporate Ethics – Learning from America's ethical companies how to supercharge business performance.* New York: Oxford University Press, 1994.

Badaracco, Joseph L. Jr. *Defining Moments – When managers must choose between right and right.* Boston: Harvard Business School Press, 1997.

Clark, Ralph W. and Alice Darnell Lattal. *Workplace Ethics – Winning the integrity revolution.* Lanham, MD: Rowman and Littlefield Publishers, Inc., 1993.

Dosick, Rabbi Wayne. *The Business Bible – Ten new commandments for creating an ethical workplace.* New York: William Morrow and Company, Inc., 1993.

Sonnenberg, Frank K. *Managing with a Conscience – How to improve performance through integrity, trust and commitment.* New York: McGraw-Hill, Inc., 1994.

110

FAILURE TO BUILD A TEAM

SECTION 1: YOUR DEVELOPMENT NEED(S)

A PROBLEM

- ☐ Doesn't believe much in the value of teams
- ☐ Doesn't pull the group together to accomplish the task
- ☐ Delegates pieces and parts
- ☐ Doesn't resolve problems within the team
- ☐ Doesn't share credit for successes
- ☐ Doesn't celebrate
- ☐ Doesn't build team spirit
- ☐ Treats people more as a collection of individuals than as a team

NOT A PROBLEM

- ☐ Usually operates in a team format
- ☐ Talks we, us and the team versus I
- ☐ Gets the whole team motivated and enthused
- ☐ Runs participative meetings and processes
- ☐ Shares credit with the team for successes
- ☐ Adds people to strengthen the team
- ☐ Team performance doesn't suffer when a key person moves on
- ☐ Trusts the team to perform

SOME CAUSES

- ☐ Can't set common cause
- ☐ Can't resolve conflict among direct reports
- ☐ Don't believe in teams
- ☐ Don't have the time
- ☐ Don't want to deal with the conflict
- ☐ More comfortable one-on-one
- ☐ The idea of a team is resisted by people
- ☐ Time management; too busy
- ☐ Too serious and heavy

THE MAP

There is more talk of teams than there are well functioning teams. Most managers grow up as strong individual contributors. That's why they get promoted. They weren't like the rest of the members of the team. They were not raised in teams. They owe little of their success to teams. As a matter of fact, most of them could tell you stories about how some past team held them back from getting things done. But teams, although strange and uncomfortable to many, are the best way to accomplish some tasks such as creating systems that cross boundaries, producing complex products, or sustained coordinated efforts. It's really rewarding to be a member of a well functioning, high performance team. Well functioning teams can outproduce the collective of what each individual could do on his/her own. Most individuals would choose to work for a boss who was able to build a well functioning team.

SECTION 2: LEARNING ON YOUR OWN

THESE SELF-DEVELOPMENT REMEDIES WILL HELP YOU BUILD YOUR SKILL(S)

SOME REMEDIES

- ☐ **1. Don't believe in teams.** If you don't believe in teams, you are probably a strong individual achiever who doesn't like the mess and sometimes the slowness of due process relationships and team processes. You are very results oriented and truly believe the best way to do that is manage one person at a time. To balance this thinking, observe and talk with three excellent team builders and ask them why they manage that way. What do they consider rewarding about building teams? What advantages do they get from using the team format? Read *The Wisdom of Teams* by Katzenbach and Smith. If you can't see the value in teams, none of the following tips will help much.
- ☐ **2. Don't have the time; teaming takes longer.** That's true and not true. While building a team takes longer than managing one person at a time, having a well functioning team increases results, builds in a sustaining capability to perform, maximizes collective strengths and covers individual weaknesses, and actually releases more time for the manager because the team members help each other. Many managers get caught in the trap of thinking it takes up too much time to build a team and end up taking more time managing one-on-one. *More help? – See #62 Time Management.*
- ☐ **3. Not a people person?** Many managers are better with things, ideas, and projects than they are with people. They may be driven and very focused on producing results and have little time left to develop their people skills. It really doesn't take too much. There is communicating. People are more motivated and do better work when they know what's going on. They want to know more than just their little piece. *More help? – See #27 Informing*. There is listening. Nothing motivates more than a boss who will listen, not interrupt, not finish your sentences, and not complete your thoughts. Increase your listening time 30 seconds in each transaction. *More help? – See #33 Listening*. There is caring. Caring is questions. Caring is asking about me and what I think and what I feel. Ask one more question per transaction than you do now. *More help? – See #7 Caring About Direct Reports.*

☐ **4. Would like to build a team but don't know how.** High performance teams have four common characteristics: 1) They have a shared mindset. They have a common vision. Everyone knows the goals and measures. *More help? – See #35 Managing and Measuring Work*. 2) They trust one another. They know you will cover me if I get in trouble. They know you will pitch in and help even though it may be difficult for you. They know you will be honest with them. They know you will bring problems to them directly and won't go behind their backs. *More help? – See #29 Integrity and Trust*. 3) They have the talent collectively to do the job. While not any one member may have it all, collectively they have every task covered. *More help? – See #25 Hiring and Staffing*. 4) They know how to operate efficiently and effectively. They have good team skills. They run effective meetings. They have efficient ways to communicate. They have ways to deal with internal conflict. *More help? – See #52 Process Management and #63 TQM/Re-Engineering.*

☐ **5. Can't seem to get people motivated to be a team.** Follow the basic rules of inspiring others as outlined in classic books like *People Skills* by Robert Bolton or *Thriving on Chaos* by Tom Peters: communicate to people that what they do is important, say thanks, offer help and ask for it, provide autonomy in how people do their work, provide a variety of tasks, "surprise" people with enriching, challenging assignments, show an interest in their careers, adopt a learning attitude toward mistakes, celebrate successes, have visible accepted measures of achievement and so on. Try to get everyone to participate in the building of the team so they have a stake in the outcome. *More help? – See #36 Motivating Others.*

☐ **6. Cement relationships.** Even though some – maybe including you – will resist it, parties, roasts, gag awards, picnics and outings help build group cohesion. Allow roles to evolve naturally rather than being specified by job descriptions. Some research indicates that people gravitate naturally to eight roles – *See #64 Understanding Others*, and that successful teams are not those where everyone does the same thing. Successful teams specialize, cover for each other, and only sometimes demand that everyone participate in identical activities.

☐ **7. Not good at motivating people beyond being results oriented?** Play the motivation odds. According to research by Rewick and Lawler, the top motivators at work are: 1 – Job challenge; 2 – Accomplishing something worthwhile; 3 – Learning new things; 4 – Personal development; 5 – Autonomy. Pay (12th), Friendliness (14th), Praise (15th) or Chance of Promotion (17th) are not insignificant but are superficial compared with the five top motivators.Provide challenges, paint pictures of why this is worthwhile, set up chances to learn and grow, and provide autonomy and you'll hit the vast majority of people's hot buttons.

☐ **8. Have trouble delegating and empowering?** One true team builder is giving people tough tasks to do, the resources to do them and the authority to make decisions about it. Delegating increases motivation, releases your time to move on to other things, and gets more work done. Delegating is scary at first. They probably can't do it the first time as well as you can. But with coaching and support they will learn, and eventually either do it as well as you can or even better yet, do it better. *More help? – See #18 Delegation.*

☐ **9. Words and rewards.** Use we instead of I. Use the team, us, together, more. Say let us. Let's get together. We can do it. We're all in this together. Signal that you are thinking team. Do you talk teams and reward individuals? To the extent that you can, reward the team more. Take some incentive money and divide it equally among the team members. Set team goals and line up team rewards.

☐ **10. Create a climate of innovation and experimentation.** Don't prescribe how to do everything. How things are done should be as open as possible. Studies show that people work harder and are more effective when they have a sense of choice. Encourage quick experiments. Most innovations and experiments will fail so communicate a learning attitude toward mistakes and failures.

SECTION 3: LEARNING FROM MORE FEEDBACK

THESE SOURCES WOULD GIVE YOU THE MOST ACCURATE AND DETAILED FEEDBACK ON YOUR SKILL(S)

☐ **Direct Reports**
Across a variety of settings, your direct reports probably see you the most. They are the recipients of most of your managerial behaviors. They know your work. They can compare you with former bosses. Since they may hesitate to give you negative feedback, you have to set the atmosphere to make it easier for them. You have to ask.

☐ **Human Resource Professionals**
Human Resource professionals have both a formal and informal feedback role. Since they have access to unique and confidential information, they can provide the right context for feedback you've received. Sometimes they may be "directed" to give you feedback. Other times, they may pass on feedback just to be helpful to you.

☐ **Past Associates/Constituencies**
When confronted with a present performance problem, some claim, "I wasn't like that before; it must be the current situation." When feedback is available from former associates, about 50% support that claim. In the other half of the cases, the people were like that before and probably didn't know it. It sometimes makes sense to access the past to clearly see the present.

SECTION 4: LEARNING FROM DEVELOP-IN-PLACE ASSIGNMENTS

THESE PART-TIME DEVELOP-IN-PLACE ASSIGNMENTS WILL HELP YOU BUILD YOUR SKILL(S)

- ☐ Manage an ad hoc, temporary group of balky and resisting people through an unpopular change or project.
- ☐ Manage an ad hoc, temporary group of low-competence people through a task they couldn't do by themselves.
- ☐ Manage an ad hoc, temporary group of people who are older and/or more experienced to accomplish a task.
- ☐ Manage an ad hoc, temporary group of people where the temporary manager is a towering expert and the people in the group are not.
- ☐ Manage an ad hoc, temporary group of people where the people in the group are towering experts but the temporary manager is not.
- ☐ Assemble an ad hoc team of diverse people to accomplish a difficult task.
- ☐ Create employee involvement teams.
- ☐ Manage an ad hoc, temporary group of "green," inexperienced people as their coach, teacher, orienter, etc.
- ☐ Manage an ad hoc, temporary group of people involved in tackling a fix-it or turnaround project.
- ☐ Build a multifunctional project team to tackle a common business issue or problem.

SECTION 5: LEARNING FROM FULL-TIME JOBS

THESE FULL-TIME JOBS OFFER THE OPPORTUNITY TO BUILD YOUR SKILL(S)

- ☐ **Fix-its/Turnarounds**
  The core demands to qualify as a Fix-it or Turnaround assignment are: 1) Cleaning up a mess. 2) Serious people issues/problems like credibility/performance/morale. 3) Tight deadline. 4) Serious business performance failure. 5) Last chance to fix. Four Types of Fix-its/Turnarounds: 1) Fixing a failed business/unit involving taking control, stopping losses, managing damage, planning the turnaround, dealing with people problems, installing new processes and systems, and rebuilding the spirit and performance of the unit. 2) Managing sizable disasters like mishandled labor negotiations and strikes, thefts, history of significant business losses, poor staff, failed leadership, hidden problems, fraud, public relations nightmares, etc. 3) Significant reorganization and restructuring (e.g., stabilizing the business, reforming unit, introducing new systems, making people changes, resetting strategy and tactics). 4) Significant system/process breakdown (e.g., MIS, financial coordination processes, audits, standards, etc.)

across units requiring working to change something from a distant position, providing advice and counsel, and installing or implementing a major process improvement or system change outside your own unit and/or with customers outside the organization.

☐ **Scale Assignments**
Core requirements to qualify as a Scale (size) shift assignment are: 1) Sizable jump-shift in the size of the job in areas like: number of people, number of layers in organization, size of budget, number of locations, volume of activity, tightness of deadlines. 2) Medium to low complexity; mostly repetitive and routine processes and procedures. 3) Stable staff and business. 4) Stable operations. 5) Often slow, steady growth.

☐ **Significant People Demands**
Core demands required to qualify as a Significant People Responsibilities assignment are: 1) A sizable increase in either the number of people managed and/or the complexity of the challenges involved 2) Longer-term assignment (two or more years). 3) Quality of people management critical to achieving results. 4) Involves groups not worked with before (e.g., union, new technical areas, nationalities).

SECTION 6: LEARNING MORE FROM YOUR PLAN

THESE ADDITIONAL REMEDIES WILL HELP MAKE THIS DEVELOPMENT PLAN MORE EFFECTIVE FOR YOU

Learning to Learn Better

☐ **Form a Learning Network With Others Working on the Same Problem**
Look for people in similar situations, and create a process for sharing and learning together. Look for a variety of people inside and outside your organization. Give feedback to each other; try new and different things together; share successes and failures, lessons and learning.

☐ **Examine Why You Judge People the Way You Do**
List the people you like and those you dislike and try to find out why. What do those you like have in common with each other and with you? What do those you dislike have in common with themselves and how do they differ from you? Are your "people buckets" logical and productive or do they interfere? Could you be more effective without putting people into buckets?

☐ **Form An Advisory Group to Help You**
Assemble a one-time ad hoc group of people you respect and ask them for help solving or facing a significant issue. Outline what you know about it and ask the team to lay out a plan. Have them examine your thinking and suggest changes and improvements.

Learning from Experience, Feedback and Other People

- ☐ **Being a Student of Others**
While many of us rely on others for information or advice, we do not really study the behavior of other people. Ask what a person does exceptionally well or poorly. What behaviors are particularly effective and ineffective for them? What works for them and what doesn't? As a student of others, you can deduce the rules of thumb for effective and ineffective behavior and include those in your own library. In comparing yourself with this person, in what areas could you most improve? What could you specifically do to improve in ways comfortable for you?

- ☐ **Learning from Bosses**
Bosses can be an excellent and ready source for learning. All bosses do some things exceptionally well and other things poorly. Distance your feelings from the boss/direct report relationship and study things that work and things that don't work for your boss. What would you have done? What could you use, and what should you avoid?

- ☐ **Learning from Interviewing Others**
Interview others. Ask not only what they do, but how and why they do it. What do they think are the rules of thumb they are following? Where did they learn the behaviors? How do they keep them current? How do they monitor the effect they have on others?

- ☐ **Learning from Observing Others**
Observe others. Find opportunities to observe without interacting with your model. This enables you to objectively study the person, note what he/she is doing or not doing, and compare that with what you would typically do in similar situations. Many times you can learn more by watching than asking. Your model may not be able to explain what he/she does or may be an unwilling teacher.

- ☐ **Learning from Limited Staff**
Most managers either inherit or hire staff from time to time who are inexperienced, incompetent, not up to the task, resistant, or dispirited. Any of these may create a hardship for you. The lessons to be learned are how to get things done with limited resources and how to fix the people situation. In the short term, this hardship is best addressed by assessing the combined strengths of the team and deploying the best you have against the problem. Almost everyone can do something well. Also, the team can contribute more than the combined individuals can. How can you empower and motivate the team? If you hired the troublesome staff, why did you err? What can you learn from your hiring mistakes? What wasn't there that you thought was present? What led you astray? How can you prevent that same hiring error in the future? What do you need to do to fix the situation? Quick development? Start over? If you inherited the problem, how can you fix it? Can you implement a program of accelerated development? Do you have to start

over and get new people? What did the prior manager do or not do that led to this situation in the first place? What can you learn from that? What will you do differently? How does the staff feel? What can you learn from their frustrations over not being able to do the job? How can you be a positive force under negative circumstances? How can you rally them to perform? What lasting lessons can you learn from someone in distress and trouble? If you're going to try accelerated development, how can you get a quick assessment? How can you give the staff motivating feedback? How can you construct and implement development plans that will work? How can you get people on-line feedback for maximum growth? Do you know when to stop trying and start over? If you're going to turn over some staff, how can you do it both rapidly and with the least damage? How can you deliver the message in a constructive way? What can you learn from having to take negative actions against people? How can you prevent this from happening again?

Learning from Courses

☐ **Supervisory Courses**
Most new supervisors go through an "Introduction to Supervision" type course. They are designed to teach the common practices a first-line supervisor needs to know to be effective. The content of most of those courses is standard. There is general agreement on the principles of effective supervision. There are two common problems: 1) Do the students have a strong motivation to learn? Do they know what they don't know? Is there any pain? Because motivated students with a need for the knowledge learn best, participants should have had some trying experiences and some supervisory pain and hardships before attending. 2) Are the instructors experienced supervisors? Have they practiced what they preach? Can they share powerful anecdotes to make key points? Can they answer questions credibly? If possible, select supervisory courses based on the instructors, since the content seems to be the much same for all such courses. Lastly, does the course offer the opportunity for practicing each skill? Does it contain simulations? Are there case studies you could easily identify with? Are there breakout groups? Is there opportunity for action learning? Search for the most interactive course.

☐ **Sending Others to Courses**
If you are responsible for managing someone else's development and, as part of that, sending them to courses, prepare them beforehand. Don't send them as tourists. Meet with them before and after the course. Tell them why they need this course. Tell them what you expect them to learn. Give them feedback on why you think they need the course. Agree ahead of time how you will measure and monitor learning after they return. If possible, offer a variety of courses for your employee to choose from. Have them give you a report shortly after

they return. If appropriate, have them present what they learned to the rest of your staff. After they return, provide opportunities for using the new skills with safe cover and low risk. Give them practice time before expecting full exercise of the new skills. Be supportive during early unsteadiness. Give continuous feedback on progress.

SUGGESTED READINGS

Deeprose, Donna. *The team coach: vital new skills for supervisors & managers in a team environment.* New York: American Management Association, 1995.

Frangos, Stephen J. and Steven J. Bennett. *Team Zebra.* Essex Junction, VT: Omneo Wight Publications, Inc., 1993.

Katzenbach, Jon R. and Douglas K. Smith. *The wisdom of teams: creating the high-performance organization.* Boston: Harvard Business School Press, 1993.

Katzenbach, Jon R., and Douglas K. Smith. *The wisdom of teams: creating the high-performance organization [sound recording].* New York: Harper Audio, 1994.

Lawler, E.E. Strategies for High Performance Organizations. San Francisco: Jossey-Bass, Inc., 1998.

Lipnack, Jessica and Jeffrey Stamps. *Virtual Teams – Reaching Across Space, Time, and Organizations with Technology.* New York: John Wiley & Sons, 1997.

Parker, Glenn M. *Cross-functional Teams.* San Francisco: Jossey-Bass, Inc., 1994.

Parker, Glenn M. Team *Players and Teamwork.* San Francisco: Jossey-Bass, Inc., 1990.

Shank, James H. *Team-based Organizations.* Homewood, IL: Business One Irwin, 1992.

Sher, Barbara and Annie Gottlieb. *Teamworks: Building support groups that guarantee success.* New York: Warner Books, 1989.

Wellins, Richard, William C. Byham and George R. Dixon. *Inside Teams.* San Francisco: Jossey-Bass, Inc., 1994.

111

FAILURE TO STAFF EFFECTIVELY

SECTION 1: YOUR DEVELOPMENT NEED(S)

A PROBLEM

- ☐ Does not assemble skilled staff either from inside or outside the organization
- ☐ Uses inappropriate criteria and standards
- ☐ May select people too much like him/herself
- ☐ Is not a good judge of people
- ☐ Is consistently wrong on estimates of what others may do or become

NOT A PROBLEM

- ☐ Good judge of people
- ☐ Hires for diversity and balance of skills
- ☐ Describes people in a textured manner
- ☐ Uses a broad set of criteria in staffing
- ☐ Objective track record better than most on selections
- ☐ Takes his/her time to find the right person

SOME CAUSES

- ☐ Impatient
- ☐ Narrow perspective
- ☐ Non-strategic
- ☐ Poor people reading skills
- ☐ Unfocused
- ☐ Unwilling to take negative people actions

THE MAP

There is no substitute for a talented team all pulling in one direction accomplishing great things. Anything less than that is inefficient and ineffective. Getting there is a combination of hiring people against both a short-term and long-term staffing plan and having people with the necessary variety of skills and talents to do today's job with reserve to tackle tomorrow. You need the variety because no single profile or person is going to have it all.

SECTION 2: LEARNING ON YOUR OWN

THESE SELF-DEVELOPMENT REMEDIES WILL HELP YOU BUILD YOUR SKILL(S)

SOME REMEDIES

☐ **1. You try to hire good people but you keep getting negatively surprised** when they come on board. You need to develop one or more models of people to use in reading and sizing up others. There are a number of acceptable models available. *More help? – See #56 Sizing Up People and #64 Understanding Others*. Use The CAREER ARCHITECT® Portfolio Sort™ Cards to learn how to think in terms of competencies.

☐ **2. You just can't seem to make accurate appraisals** based upon interviews and reference checks. Sound interviewing is a known technology. Read a book on interviewing techniques and successful practices and go to a course that teaches interviewing skills, preferably one with videotaped practice and feedback. Also, have others interview the candidates using standard competency rating scales and seek their counsel.

☐ **3. You don't have a feel for what skills and talents are required.** Ask someone from Human Resources for help. Ask other bosses of units like yours what they look for. Benchmark with peers in other firms to see what they look for. *More help? – See #25 Hiring and Staffing.*

☐ **4. Your people choices work out in the short term but become less effective longer term.** This usually means you are using a success profile that is too narrow over time. *More help? – See #46 Perspective and #58 Strategic Agility*. It could also be that your organization only pays for current skills and you have trouble hiring the best people. In this case, try to hire people who have the current skills needed and are eager to learn new skills. *More help? – See #32 Learning on the Fly*. Add "What did you learn?" and "How have you applied that?" questions to your interviews to try to hire current doers and future learners.

☐ **5. You inherited the team** and some of the people are just not up to standard and you don't want to pull the trigger. If you don't, it just means more work for you and the rest of the team. The sooner you address people problems, the better off everyone will be, even the people involved. *More help? – See #13 Confronting Direct Reports* and *#16* Timely *Decision Making.*

☐ **6. You are impatient to fill empty spots on your team** and tend to take the first acceptable or near acceptable candidate that comes along. That means you will make compromises and probably never meet the best candidate. Always try to wait long enough for multiple candidates and a real choice. *More help? – See #41 Patience.*

☐ **7. You tend to hire too much in your own image.** You prefer working with people who think and act as you do so the team ends up skilled in only a few areas. You may load up on friends, people you have worked with in the past, or favorites. If you clone yourself in terms of skills, beliefs, background, or orientation, you and your team will not have the variety and diversity for truly great performance. *More help? – See #25 Hiring and Staffing.*

☐ **8. Look to teams around you that you feel are the best performing teams.** What does the talent look like? What does the hiring model look like? Are the team members more the same or are they different from one another? Do they have the same background or come from a variety of situations? How do those team managers hire? Ask them what they do when filling an opening.

☐ **9. You spend too little time worrying about improving the team.** You may as well just do the important things yourself and let the team fend for itself. This is a very short-term strategy – one that will usually get you in more trouble as the situation continues. A good rule of thumb to follow is that your team should spend 20% of its time working outside its, and perhaps your, comfort zone. Stretching assignments are the prime source or reason for improvement. *More help? – See #18 Delegation, #19 Developing Direct Reports, #50 Priority Setting, and #62 Time Management.*

☐ **10. You take the easy way out** and are hesitant to go against the grain and reject internal candidates. You can't say no to higher ups. You will be better able to do this if you have criteria for success for the job, ones that you can discuss easily. It's far easier to take a stand if you can say, "This candidate is strong in these competencies but not in these; we need someone who can do these as well." Discussions of criteria get discussions off individuals and on to what it takes to do the job. Beyond this, you have to take a stand. Prepare a brief list of what you are looking for and stick to it calmly. Invite input on criteria, not people. *More help? – See #34 Managerial Courage and #57 Standing Alone.*

SECTION 3: LEARNING FROM MORE FEEDBACK

THESE SOURCES WOULD GIVE YOU THE MOST ACCURATE AND DETAILED FEEDBACK ON YOUR SKILL(S)

☐ **Direct Boss**

Your direct boss has important information about you, your performance, and your prospects. The challenge is to get this information. There are formal processes (e.g., performance appraisals). There are day-to-day opportunities. To help, signal your boss that you want and can handle direct and timely feedback. Many bosses have trouble giving feedback, so you will have to work at it over a period of time.

☐ **Human Resource Professionals**

Human Resource professionals have both a formal and informal feedback role. Since they have access to unique and confidential information, they can provide the right context for feedback you've received. Sometimes they may be "directed" to give you feedback. Other times, they may pass on feedback just to be helpful to you.

- ☐ **Past Associates/Constituencies**
When confronted with a present performance problem, some claim, "I wasn't like that before; it must be the current situation." When feedback is available from former associates, about 50% support that claim. In the other half of the cases, the people were like that before and probably didn't know it. It sometimes makes sense to access the past to clearly see the present.

SECTION 4: LEARNING FROM DEVELOP-IN-PLACE ASSIGNMENTS

THESE PART-TIME DEVELOP-IN-PLACE ASSIGNMENTS WILL HELP YOU BUILD YOUR SKILL(S)

- ☐ Go to a campus as a recruiter.
- ☐ Do a study of successful executives in your organization and report the findings to top management.
- ☐ Do a study of failed executives in your organization, including interviewing people still with the organization who knew or worked with them, and report the findings to top management.
- ☐ Train and work as an assessor in an assessment center.
- ☐ Hire/staff a team from outside your unit or organization.
- ☐ Work on a team that's deciding who to keep and who to let go in a layoff, shutdown, delayering, or divestiture.
- ☐ Work on a team looking at a reorganization plan where there will be more people than positions.
- ☐ Plan for and start up something small (secretarial pool, athletic program, suggestion system, program, etc.).
- ☐ Manage the outplacement of a group of people.
- ☐ Build a multifunctional project team to tackle a common business issue or problem.

SECTION 5: LEARNING FROM FULL-TIME JOBS

THESE FULL-TIME JOBS OFFER THE OPPORTUNITY TO BUILD YOUR SKILL(S)

- ☐ **Fix-its/Turnarounds**
The core demands to qualify as a Fix-it or Turnaround assignment are: 1) Cleaning up a mess. 2) Serious people issues/problems like credibility/performance/morale. 3) Tight deadline. 4) Serious business performance failure. 5) Last chance to fix. Four Types of Fix-its/Turnarounds: 1) Fixing a failed business/unit involving taking control, stopping losses, managing damage, planning the turnaround, dealing with people problems, installing new processes and systems, and rebuilding the spirit and performance of the unit. 2) Managing sizable disasters like mishandled labor negotiations and strikes, thefts, history

of significant business losses, poor staff, failed leadership, hidden problems, fraud, public relations nightmares, etc. 3) Significant reorganization and restructuring (e.g., stabilizing the business, reforming unit, introducing new systems, making people changes, resetting strategy and tactics). 4) Significant system/process breakdown (e.g., MIS, financial coordination processes, audits, standards, etc.) across units requiring working to change something from a distant position, providing advice and counsel, and installing or implementing a major process improvement or system change outside your own unit and/or with customers outside the organization.

☐ **Significant People Demands**
Core demands required to qualify as a Significant People Responsibilities assignment are: 1) A sizable increase in either the number of people managed and/or the complexity of the challenges involved 2) Longer-term assignment (two or more years). 3) Quality of people management critical to achieving results. 4) Involves groups not worked with before (e.g., union, new technical areas, nationalities).

☐ **Start-ups**
The core demands to qualify as a start from scratch are: 1) Starting something new for you and/or for the organization. 2) Forging a new team. 3) Creating new systems/facilities/staffs/programs/procedures. 4) Contextual adversity (e.g., uncertainty, government regulation, unions, difficult environment). Seven types of start from scratches: 1) Planning, building, hiring, and managing (e.g., building a new facility, opening up a new location, moving a unit or company). 2) Heading something new (e.g., new product, new service, new line of business, new department/function, major new program). 3) Take over a group/product/service/program that had existed for less than a year and was off to a fast start. 4) Establishing overseas operations. 5) Major new designs for existing systems. 6) Moving a successful program from one unit to another. 7) Installing a new organization-wide process as a full-time job (e.g., like Total Quality).

SECTION 6: LEARNING MORE FROM YOUR PLAN

THESE ADDITIONAL REMEDIES WILL HELP MAKE THIS DEVELOPMENT PLAN MORE EFFECTIVE FOR YOU

Learning to Learn Better

☐ **Examine Why You Judge People the Way You Do**
List the people you like and those you dislike and try to find out why. What do those you like have in common with each other and with you? What do those you dislike have in common with themselves and how do they differ from you? Are your "people buckets" logical and productive or do they interfere? Could you be more effective without putting people into buckets?

Learning from Experience, Feedback and Other People

- ☐ **Using Multiple Models**
  Who do you know who exemplifies how to do whatever your need is? Who, for example, personifies decisiveness or compassion or strategic agility? Think more broadly than your current job and colleagues. For example, clergy, friends, spouses or community leaders are also good sources for potential models. Select your models not on the basis of overall excellence or likability, but on the basis of the one towering strength (or glaring weakness) you are interested in. Even people who are well thought of usually have only one or two towering strengths (or glaring weaknesses). Ordinarily, you won't learn as much from the whole person as you will from one characteristic.

- ☐ **Learning from Interviewing Others**
  Interview others. Ask not only what they do, but how and why they do it. What do they think are the rules of thumb they are following? Where did they learn the behaviors? How do they keep them current? How do they monitor the effect they have on others?

- ☐ **Learning from Observing Others**
  Observe others. Find opportunities to observe without interacting with your model. This enables you to objectively study the person, note what he/she is doing or not doing, and compare that with what you would typically do in similar situations. Many times you can learn more by watching than asking. Your model may not be able to explain what he/she does or may be an unwilling teacher.

- ☐ **Getting Feedback from Bosses and Superiors**
  Many bosses are reluctant to give negative feedback. They lack the managerial courage to face people directly with criticism. You can help by soliciting feedback and setting the tone. Show them you can handle criticism and that you are willing to work on issues they see as important.

- ☐ **Learning from Limited Staff**
  Most managers either inherit or hire staff from time to time who are inexperienced, incompetent, not up to the task, resistant, or dispirited. Any of these may create a hardship for you. The lessons to be learned are how to get things done with limited resources and how to fix the people situation. In the short term, this hardship is best addressed by assessing the combined strengths of the team and deploying the best you have against the problem. Almost everyone can do something well. Also, the team can contribute more than the combined individuals can. How can you empower and motivate the team? If you hired the troublesome staff, why did you err? What can you learn from your hiring mistakes? What wasn't there that you thought was present? What led you astray? How can you prevent that same hiring error in the future? What do you need to do to fix the situation? Quick development? Start over? If you inherited the problem, how can you fix it? Can you imple-

ment a program of accelerated development? Do you have to start over and get new people? What did the prior manager do or not do that led to this situation in the first place? What can you learn from that? What will you do differently? How does the staff feel? What can you learn from their frustrations over not being able to do the job? How can you be a positive force under negative circumstances? How can you rally them to perform? What lasting lessons can you learn from someone in distress and trouble? If you're going to try accelerated development, how can you get a quick assessment? How can you give the staff motivating feedback? How can you construct and implement development plans that will work? How can you get people on-line feedback for maximum growth? Do you know when to stop trying and start over? If you're going to turn over some staff, how can you do it both rapidly and with the least damage? How can you deliver the message in a constructive way? What can you learn from having to take negative actions against people? How can you prevent this from happening again?

Learning from Courses

☐ **Supervisory Courses**
Most new supervisors go through an "Introduction to Supervision" type course. They are designed to teach the common practices a first-line supervisor needs to know to be effective. The content of most of those courses is standard. There is general agreement on the principles of effective supervision. There are two common problems: 1) Do the students have a strong motivation to learn? Do they know what they don't know? Is there any pain? Because motivated students with a need for the knowledge learn best, participants should have had some trying experiences and some supervisory pain and hardships before attending. 2) Are the instructors experienced supervisors? Have they practiced what they preach? Can they share powerful anecdotes to make key points? Can they answer questions credibly? If possible, select supervisory courses based on the instructors, since the content seems to be the much same for all such courses. Lastly, does the course offer the opportunity for practicing each skill? Does it contain simulations? Are there case studies you could easily identify with? Are there breakout groups? Is there opportunity for action learning? Search for the most interactive course.

SUGGESTED READINGS

Bell, Arthur H. *Extraviewing – Innovative ways to hire the best.* Homewood, IL: Business One Irwin, 1992.

Canning, Miles B. *Ready, Aim, Hire!.* OakBrook, IL: PerSysCo. Publishing, Inc., 1992.

Half, Robert. *Finding, Hiring and Keeping the Best Employees.* New York: John Wiley & Sons, Inc., 1993.

Miller, Kathleen D. *Retraining the American Workforce.* Reading, MA: Addison-Wesley Publishing Co. Inc., 1989.

Smart, Bradford D. Pd.D. *Topgrading – How Leading Companies Win Hiring, Coaching and Keeping the Best People.* New York: Prentice-Hall, Inc., 1999.

Yate, Martin. *Hiring the Best.* Holbrook, MA: Adams Media Corp, 1994.

112

INSENSITIVE TO OTHERS

SECTION 1: YOUR DEVELOPMENT NEED(S)

A PROBLEM

- ☐ Has an intimidating style
- ☐ Makes others feel bad
- ☐ Doesn't care or doesn't think about how he/she affects others
- ☐ Doesn't follow interpersonal due process
- ☐ Doesn't care about the needs of others
- ☐ Doesn't ask and doesn't listen

NOT A PROBLEM

- ☐ Has a smooth and approachable style
- ☐ Shows empathy and caring
- ☐ Can tell when people are hurting
- ☐ Good at reading other people's hot buttons
- ☐ Listens
- ☐ Allows others to play out their agenda without interrupting
- ☐ Helpful toward others
- ☐ Asks others what they are feeling and thinking
- ☐ Sensitive to how he/she is coming across

SOME CAUSES

- ☐ Abuse others
- ☐ Action junkie
- ☐ Aggressive, results oriented
- ☐ Blow up under pressure
- ☐ Don't care
- ☐ No idea of impact
- ☐ Run over people
- ☐ Unrealistic standards
- ☐ Very successful

THE MAP

This evaluation may have been shocking for you, since few of us like to think of ourselves as insensitive. Chances are you see yourself as candid and forthright. Results oriented and matter of fact. Business oriented. Mostly right. Tough on slackers. Demanding manager. Focused and jealous of your time. Whatever your perception, others feel discounted and ignored. They don't find you pleasant to work with or for. You can get away with this only as long as your results are stellar. One stumble, and the sharks will be circling.

SECTION 2: LEARNING ON YOUR OWN

THESE SELF-DEVELOPMENT REMEDIES WILL HELP YOU BUILD YOUR SKILL(S)

SOME REMEDIES

- ☐ **1. Insensitivity is a catch-all term.** The authors have found 29 reasons why people might say this about you. Before you react to this evaluation and certainly before you try to do something about it, invest in 360° feedback or get a Human Resource specialist to talk with people and find out exactly why you are seen as insensitive, or talk to a mentor or someone you really trust will tell you the truth. It's unlikely that people will tell you directly, and even if they do, it's likely to be too general or too much based on one situation to do you much good. Of all needs, this one is probably the most complex to specify. Get a complete textured view of yourself. *More help? – See #55 Self-Knowledge*. The good news is that most people get this negative rating due only to a few aspects of insensitivity. It's also common to have some people view you as insensitive and others not. That makes it easier to address. Few are truly insensitive in 29 ways!

- ☐ **2. Loss of composure.** It may be that you blow up and are especially bullying or pressuring under stress. Avoid instant and sharp reactions. This is most likely what's getting you in trouble. You jump to conclusions, categorically dismiss what others say, use inflammatory words or something of the sort. People then see you as closed or combative when you probably want them to see you as reasonable. More negatively, they may believe you think they're stupid or ill-informed. Give people second chances. If you're seen as intolerant or closed, people will often stumble over words in their haste to talk with you or short cut their argument since they assume you're not listening anyway. Ask a question, invite them to disagree with you, present their argument back to them, let them save face no matter what. *More help? – See #11 Composure.*

- ☐ **3. Audience sensitivity.** In any situation, there are always multiple ways you can deliver messages and get things done. You could use a direct attack – candor and instant assessment. You could send a surrogate to deliver the message. You could wait until the next meeting to react. Some of these tactics are more effective and acceptable than others. Some people get into trouble because they act the same in all situations. They don't take the time to think about the most effective ways to get things done for each event and person. People who are seen as sensitive operate from the outside – audience, person, group, organization – in. They pick their pace, style, tone, timing and tactics based upon an evaluation of what would work best in each situation. It's the one-trick ponies that get into sensitivity trouble because they don't adjust what they say and do to each audience. *More help? – See #15 Customer Focus, #36 Motivating Others, and #45 Personal Learning.*

☐ **4. Being closed minded.** You may either be or may be signaling being stubborn, rigid and closed to new or different points of view. You must learn to turn off your instant evaluator/rejector filter and listen. Your first task is to understand, your second is to let the other person know you understand by repeating or rephrasing, and your third task can be to reject, with a fuller explanation of why than you now do. Ask more questions – "How did you get there?" "Do you prefer this to that or to what we're now doing?" If you disagree, give your reasons first. Then invite criticism. Turn the disagreement back to the nature of the problem or strategy – "What are we trying to solve? What causes it? What questions should be answered? What objective standards could we use to measure success?" *More help? – See #12 Conflict Management and #33 Listening.*

☐ **5. Impatience.** A lot of insensitivity is due to not taking the time to let others get more comfortable with you. Many insensitive people are very action oriented, results oriented and very agenda driven. There's not much rapport building. One third of the people who work around you prefer people like you. "Just the facts, ma'am. Let's get down to it." Two thirds need a little up front time to adjust to the situation before getting down to work. Usually three minutes is sufficient. You have to start by opening the discussion on a non-business topic. What did you do this weekend? How are the kids? Which college did your daughter pick? Did you see the Olympics? How do you like the new car? And then let them talk for awhile to give them time to get comfortable. *More help? – See #3 Approachability.*

☐ **6. Solutions first, understanding second?** You might be seen as someone who jumps to conclusions and solutions before others have had a chance to finish their statement of the problem. Take the time to really define the problem. Let people finish. Try not to interrupt. Don't finish other's sentences. Ask clarifying questions. Restate the problem in your own words to everyone's satisfaction. Then decide.

☐ **7. Interpersonally challenged?** You have to go first, no matter how shy you may be. Until you signal that you are open to others – listening with eye contact, interested in what they have to say – let them finish, share things you don't have to share – get personal, invite people to talk with you – ask questions – and then listen, little will come of this effort to be seen as more sensitive. You will have to persevere, endure some rejection and embarrassment to improve. *More help? – See #3 Approachability and #31 Interpersonal Savvy.*

☐ **8. Too smart?** You may be highly intelligent and quite skilled in your area. You may work around people who aren't as informed or skilled as you are. You may be in a position of essentially dictating what should be done because they don't know. In this case, you need to switch to a teacher role – tell them how you think about an issue, don't just fire out solutions. Tell them what you think the problem is, what questions need be asked, how you would go about finding out, what you think some likely solutions might be. Most important, invite their thinking. If you're the expert and they aren't, help them think better by showing them how you think. Be open to the fact that uninformed people in studies of creative problem solving usually come up with the most inventive solutions. Once immersed in the problem they bring a new perspective to it. Use that power. *More help? – See #18 Delegation.*

☐ **9. Don't think it matters?** Some hard charging managers just don't think it matters what people think of them. They think getting the results out on time and on budget is job one. They think good people can take it and those who are too sensitive aren't going to make it anyway and are not worth the time. Studies show that the vast majority of senior managers who fail do not fail because they can't get the work out. They fail because they damage people in the process. Think of the last ten people who were forced to leave your organization. Why were they fired or asked to leave? What were the real reasons? Most likely, the problem was in relationships with others. You really need to rethink your priorities.

☐ **10. Time management.** Some insensitivity is benign neglect. Usually it hits direct reports most. You manage your boss first. Your customers second. Issues and problems third. Your peers next. And your direct reports last. But it's now Friday at 4:50. Sensitivity takes time. Since insensitivity causes noise, unproductive transactions, a de-motivated team, and reworking communications and issues, increased sensitivity would actually buy you more time. Each week allot five additional minutes per direct report for just general conversation, their nickel. No agenda. No business. Just be there for them.

SECTION 3: LEARNING FROM MORE FEEDBACK

THESE SOURCES WOULD GIVE YOU THE MOST ACCURATE AND DETAILED FEEDBACK ON YOUR SKILL(S)

☐ **Development Professionals**
Sometimes it might be valuable to get some analysis and feedback from a professional trained and certified in the area you're working on: possibly a career counselor, a therapist, clergy, a psychologist, etc.

☐ **Direct Reports**
Across a variety of settings, your direct reports probably see you the most. They are the recipients of most of your managerial behaviors. They know your work. They can compare you with former bosses. Since they may hesitate to give you negative feedback, you have to set the atmosphere to make it easier for them. You have to ask.

☐ **Past Associates/Constituencies**
When confronted with a present performance problem, some claim, "I wasn't like that before; it must be the current situation." When feed-

back is available from former associates, about 50% support that claim. In the other half of the cases, the people were like that before and probably didn't know it. It sometimes makes sense to access the past to clearly see the present.

- ☐ **Peers and Colleagues**
Peers and colleagues have a special social and working relationship. They attend staff meetings together, share private views, get feedback from the same boss, travel together, and are knowledgeable about each other's work. You perhaps let your guard down more around peers and act more like yourself. They can be a valuable source of feedback.

- ☐ **Spouse**
Spouses can be powerful sources of feedback on such things as interpersonal style, values, balance between work, career, and personal life, etc. Many participants attending development programs share their feedback with their spouses for value-adding confirmation or context and for specific examples.

SECTION 4: LEARNING FROM DEVELOP-IN-PLACE ASSIGNMENTS

THESE PART-TIME DEVELOP-IN-PLACE ASSIGNMENTS WILL HELP YOU BUILD YOUR SKILL(S)

- ☐ Manage the renovation of an office, floor, building, meeting room, warehouse, etc.
- ☐ Plan an off-site meeting, conference, convention, trade show, event, etc.
- ☐ Represent the concerns of a group of nonexempt, clerical, or administrative employees to higher management to seek resolution of a difficult issue.
- ☐ Be a change agent; create a symbol for change; lead the rallying cry; champion a significant change and implementation.
- ☐ Create employee involvement teams.
- ☐ Help shut down a plant, regional office, product line, business, operation, etc.
- ☐ Manage a dissatisfied internal or external customer; troubleshoot a performance or quality problem with a product or service.
- ☐ Manage the outplacement of a group of people.
- ☐ Resolve an issue in conflict between two people, units, geographies, functions, etc.
- ☐ Make peace with an enemy or someone you've disappointed with a product or service or someone you've had some trouble with or don't get along well with.

SECTION 5: LEARNING FROM FULL-TIME JOBS

THESE FULL-TIME JOBS OFFER THE OPPORTUNITY TO BUILD YOUR SKILL(S)

☐ **Influencing Without Authority**
The core demands to qualify as an Influence Without Authority are: 1) Significant challenge (e.g, start-up, fix-it, scope and/or scale assignment, strategic planning project, changes in management practices/ systems). 2) Insufficient direct authority to make it happen. 3) Tight deadlines. 4) Visible to significant others. 5) Sensitive politics.

☐ **Off-Shore Assignments**
The core demands to qualify as an Off-Shore assignment are: 1) First time working in the country. 2) Significant challenges like new language, hardship location, unique business rules/practices, significant cultural/marketplace differences, different functional task, etc. 3) More than a year assignment. 4) No automatic return deal. 5) Not necessarily a change in job challenge, technical content, or responsibilities.

☐ **Significant People Demands**
Core demands required to qualify as a Significant People Responsibilities assignment are: 1) A sizable increase in either the number of people managed and/or the complexity of the challenges involved 2) Longer-term assignment (two or more years). 3) Quality of people management critical to achieving results. 4) Involves groups not worked with before (e.g., union, new technical areas, nationalities).

SECTION 6: LEARNING MORE FROM YOUR PLAN

THESE ADDITIONAL REMEDIES WILL HELP MAKE THIS DEVELOPMENT PLAN MORE EFFECTIVE FOR YOU

Learning to Learn Better

☐ **Monitoring Yourself More Closely and Getting off Your Autopilot**
Past habits are a mixed blessing, sometimes helping, sometimes not. To avoid putting yourself on "autopilot," think afresh about each situation before acting. Consistently monitor yourself with questions. Is this task different? Ask why you would repeat a past action. Are you avoiding anything, like taking a chance? Is there something new you might try?

☐ **Teach Others Something You Know Well**
Teach someone to do something you know how to do to check out your own thinking, knowledge, and rules. Watch in detail how others learn; the process will require breaking down your patterns into teachable steps.

☐ **Examine Why You Judge People the Way You Do**
List the people you like and those you dislike and try to find out why. What do those you like have in common with each other and with you? What do those you dislike have in common with themselves and how do they differ from you? Are your "people buckets" logical and

productive or do they interfere? Could you be more effective without putting people into buckets?

- ☐ **Pre-sell an Idea to a Key Stakeholder**
  Identify the key stakeholders – those who will be the most affected by your actions or the most resistant, or whose support you will most need. Collect the information each will find persuasive; marshal your arguments and try to pre-sell your conclusions, recommendations, and solutions.

- ☐ **Envision Doing Something Well in a Group**
  Take the people you want or need to be involved through a envisioning/creativity exercise to come up with different ideas and solutions.

- ☐ **Preview a Plan With a Test Audience**
  Before committing to a plan, find someone agreeable to a wide-ranging discussion about the issue or problem you face. Explore all sides and options; go with the flow; let what you need to do emerge from the process; develop a plan as you go.

Learning from Experience, Feedback and Other People

- ☐ **Learning from Ineffective Behavior**
  Seeing things done poorly can be a very potent source of learning for you, especially if the behavior or action affects others negatively. Many times the thing done poorly causes emotional reactions or pain in you and others. Distance yourself from the feelings and explore why the actions didn't work.

- ☐ **Learning from Observing Others**
  Observe others. Find opportunities to observe without interacting with your model. This enables you to objectively study the person, note what he/she is doing or not doing, and compare that with what you would typically do in similar situations. Many times you can learn more by watching than asking. Your model may not be able to explain what he/she does or may be an unwilling teacher.

Learning from Courses

- ☐ **Insight Events**
  These are courses designed around assessing skills and providing feedback to the participants. These events can be a powerful source of self-knowledge and can lead to significant development if done right. When selecting a self-insight course, consider the following: 1) Are the skills assessed the important ones? 2) Are the assessment techniques and instruments sound? 3) Are those who are providing the feedback trained and professional? 4) Is the feedback provided in a user-friendly and "actionable" format? 5) Does the feedback include development planning? 6) Is the setting comfortable and conducive to reflection and learning? 7) Are the other participants the kinds of people you could

learn from? 8) Are you in the right frame of mind to learn from this kind of intense experience? Select events on the basis of positive answers to these eight questions.

- ☐ **Attitude Toward Learning**
  In addition to selecting the right course, a learning attitude is required. Be open. Close down your "like/dislike" switch, your "agree/disagree" blinders, and your "like me/not like me" feelings toward the instructors. Learning requires new lessons, change, and new behaviors and perspectives – all scary stuff for most people. Don't resist. Take in all you can during the course. Ask clarifying questions. Discuss concerns with the other participants. Jot down what you learn as you go. After the course is over, take some reflective time to glean the meat. Make the practical decisions about what you can and cannot use.

SUGGESTED READINGS

Autry, James A. *The Art of Caring Leadership.* New York: William Morrow and Company, Inc., 1991.

Bolton, Robert and Dorothy Grover Bolton. *People Styles at Work – Making bad relationships good and good relationships better.* New York: AMACOM, 1996.

Daniels, Aubrey C. *Bringing out the Best in People.* New York: McGraw-Hill, Inc., 1994.

Garfield, Charles A. *Second to none: how our smartest companies put people first.* Homewood, IL: Business One Irwin, 1992.

Handy, Charles. *The Hungry Spirit.* New York: Doubleday, 1998.

Hornstein, Harvey Ph.D. *Brutal Bosses.* New York: Riverhead Books, 1996.

Hunsaker, Phillip L. and Anthony J. Alessandra. The art of managing people. New York: Simon & Schuster, 1986, 1980.

Peck, M. Scott, M.D. *A World Waiting to be Born: Civility Rediscovered.* New York: Bantam Books, 1993.

Peck, M. Scott, M.D. *A World Waiting to be Born: Civility Rediscovered [sound recording].* New York: Bantam Doubleday Dell Audio Pub., 1993.

Robertson, Arthur. *Language of Effective Listening.* Carmel, IN: ScottForesman Professional Books, 1991.

113

KEY SKILL DEFICIENCIES

SECTION 1: YOUR DEVELOPMENT NEED(S)

A PROBLEM

- ☐ Lacks one or more key job-required talents or skills needed to perform effectively

NOT A PROBLEM

- ☐ Skilled in most if not all of the mission-critical areas of the job
- ☐ Scopes out what skills are required to perform
- ☐ Works to improve and expand skill set
- ☐ Open to tutors, courses, any learning mode to improve proficiency

SOME CAUSES

- ☐ Counting backwards to retirement
- ☐ Inexperienced
- ☐ Lack of technical/functional skills
- ☐ Narrow perspective
- ☐ New to the job or function
- ☐ Not interested in self-development

THE MAP

New and different jobs, roles, geographies, business units, and organizations require new and different skills and abilities. Many times as we move up, in, out, down and sideways, we are caught without the requisite skills needed to perform well. Some go about the business of learning the new skills and others wait to see if they can get through without building new skills. Most of the time you can't wait. Those who wait too long get rated as having Key Skill Deficiencies.

SECTION 2: LEARNING ON YOUR OWN

THESE SELF-DEVELOPMENT REMEDIES WILL HELP YOU BUILD YOUR SKILL(S)

SOME REMEDIES

- ☐ **1. You need to find out what it is that people think you are missing.** The best way to do that is to volunteer for a 360° feedback process. Find out what skills others think are important to do the job and compare your feedback against that standard. You can also simply ask your boss for that gap information. *More help? – See #55 Self-Knowledge.*

- ☐ **2. Sometimes you miss essential feedback** about what you need to build because you didn't listen. Turn off your evaluator and listen to what you're being told. *More help? – See #33 Listening.*

- ☐ **3. Sometimes you hear the feedback but you choose not to do anything about it.** *More help? – See #45 Personal Learning and #54 Self-Development.*
- ☐ **4. Sometimes people try to deliver feedback to help you and you fight it.** *More help? – See #108 Defensiveness.*
- ☐ **5. Sometimes you know what you need to develop or build but you don't have the time.** *More help? – See #50 Priority Setting and #62 Time Management.*
- ☐ **6. Sometimes you know what you need and don't know how to go about building it.** *More help? – See #54 Self-Development.*
- ☐ **7. Look to what others in your role or job have that you don't have.** What skills do they apply to the job that you don't as yet have? Talk to your mentor and ask him/her for information about what you are missing.
- ☐ **8. Learn how to become a learner.** *More help? – See #32 Learning on the Fly and #45 Personal Learning.*
- ☐ **9. Sometimes the missing skills are functional.** *More help? – See #24 Functional/Technical Skills.*
- ☐ **10. Sometimes the missing skills are technical.** *More help? – See #24 Functional/Technical Skills and #61 Technical Learning.*

SECTION 3: LEARNING FROM MORE FEEDBACK

THESE SOURCES WOULD GIVE YOU THE MOST ACCURATE AND DETAILED FEEDBACK ON YOUR SKILL(S)

☐ **Direct Boss**

Your direct boss has important information about you, your performance, and your prospects. The challenge is to get this information. There are formal processes (e.g., performance appraisals). There are day-to-day opportunities. To help, signal your boss that you want and can handle direct and timely feedback. Many bosses have trouble giving feedback, so you will have to work at it over a period of time.

☐ **Human Resource Professionals**

Human Resource professionals have both a formal and informal feedback role. Since they have access to unique and confidential information, they can provide the right context for feedback you've received. Sometimes they may be "directed" to give you feedback. Other times, they may pass on feedback just to be helpful to you.

☐ **Past Associates/Constituencies**

When confronted with a present performance problem, some claim, "I wasn't like that before; it must be the current situation." When feedback is available from former associates, about 50% support that claim. In the other half of the cases, the people were like that before and probably didn't know it. It sometimes makes sense to access the past to clearly see the present.

SECTION 4: LEARNING FROM DEVELOP-IN-PLACE ASSIGNMENTS

THESE PART-TIME DEVELOP-IN-PLACE ASSIGNMENTS WILL HELP YOU BUILD YOUR SKILL(S)

- ☐ Find and spend time with an expert to learn something new to you.
- ☐ Study some aspect of your job or a new technical area you haven't studied before that you need to be more effective.
- ☐ Work closely with a higher-level manager who is very good at something you need to learn.
- ☐ Attend a course or event which will push you personally beyond your usual limits or outside your comfort zone (e.g., Outward Bound, language immersion training, sensitivity group, public speaking).
- ☐ Study an admired person who has a skill you need.
- ☐ Volunteer to do a special project for and with a person you admire and who has a skill you need to develop.
- ☐ Work short rotations in other units, functions, or geographies you've not been exposed to before.
- ☐ Study and summarize a new trend, product, service, technique, or process and present and sell it to others.
- ☐ Benchmark innovative practices, processes, products, or services of competitors, vendors, suppliers, or customers and present a report to others to create recommendations for change.
- ☐ Visit Malcolm Baldrige National Quality Award or Deming Prize winners and report back on your findings, showing how they would help your organization.

SECTION 5: LEARNING FROM FULL-TIME JOBS

THESE FULL-TIME JOBS OFFER THE OPPORTUNITY TO BUILD YOUR SKILL(S)

- ☐ **Chair of Projects/Task Forces**
  The core demands for qualifying as a Project/Task Force assignment are: 1) Full-time assignment. 2) Important and specific goal. 3) Tight deadline. 4) Success or failure will be evident. 5) High-visibility sponsor. 6) Learning something on the fly. 7) Must get others to cooperate. 8) Usually six months or more. Four types of Projects/Task Forces: 1) New ideas, products, services, or systems (e.g., product/service/program research and development, creation/installation/launch of a new system, new programs like Total Quality Management, positive discipline). 2) Formal negotiations and relationships (e.g., acquisitions, divestitures, agreements, joint ventures; licensing arrangements, fran-

chising; dealing with unions, governments, communities, charities, customers, and relocations). 3) Big one-time events (e.g., working on a major presentation for the board, organizing significant meetings or conferences, disaster/damage control teams; reorganizations, mergers, acquisitions, or relocations, working on visions, charters, strategies, other time-urgent issues and problems). 4) Troubleshooting (e.g., problems, disasters, crises, product/service failures, accidents, illegal activities, damage control in public relations goofs, shut downs, downsizings, layoffs, abrupt changes in leadership).

☐ **Cross-Moves**

The core demands necessary to qualify as a Cross-Move are: 1) Move to a very different set of challenges. 2) Abrupt jump-shift in tasks/activities. 3) Never been there before. 4) New setting/conditions. Examples of Cross-Moves are: 1) Changing divisions. 2) Changing functions. 3) Field/headquarters shifts. 4) Line/staff switches. 5) Country switches. 6) Working with all new people. 7) Changing lines of business.

☐ **Line To Staff Switches**

The core demands to qualify as a Line to Staff switch are: 1) Intellectually/strategically demanding. 2) Highly visible to others. 3) New area/perspective/method/culture/function. 4) Moving away from a bottom line. 5) Moving from field to headquarters. 6) Exposure to high-level executives. Examples: 1) Business/strategic planning. 2) Heading a staff department. 3) Assistant to/chief of staff to a senior executive. 4) Head of a task force. 5) Human resources role.

☐ **Staff to Line Shifts**

Core demands necessary to qualify for a Staff to Line shift are: 1) Moving to a job with an easily determined bottom line or results. 2) Managing bigger scope and/or scale. 3) Requires new skills/perspectives. 4) Unfamiliar aspects of the assignment.

SECTION 6: LEARNING MORE FROM YOUR PLAN

THESE ADDITIONAL REMEDIES WILL HELP MAKE THIS DEVELOPMENT PLAN MORE EFFECTIVE FOR YOU

Learning from Experience, Feedback and Other People

☐ **Using Multiple Models**

Who do you know who exemplifies how to do whatever your need is? Who, for example, personifies decisiveness or compassion or strategic agility? Think more broadly than your current job and colleagues. For example, clergy, friends, spouses or community leaders are also good sources for potential models. Select your models not on the basis of overall excellence or likability, but on the basis of the one towering strength (or glaring weakness) you are interested in. Even people who are well thought of usually have only one or two towering strengths (or glaring weaknesses). Ordinarily, you won't learn as much from the whole person as you will from one characteristic.

- ☐ **Getting Feedback from Bosses and Superiors**
  Many bosses are reluctant to give negative feedback. They lack the managerial courage to face people directly with criticism. You can help by soliciting feedback and setting the tone. Show them you can handle criticism and that you are willing to work on issues they see as important.

- ☐ **Feedback on What?**
  Although any feedback is useful, it's best to seek and receive feedback on skills the organization feels are the most important for your present and future success. Not all skills are equal in importance. Some common skills may not have much bearing on success at all. If the organization has an official success profile, that may be the best way to focus your growth efforts.

Learning from Courses

- ☐ **Job Skills**
  Most organizations and professional associations offer job skills training. The key is to find a course that has the right content and offers the opportunity for practicing the jobs skills. It's helpful if the instructors have actually performed the skills in situations similar to your own.

- ☐ **Survey Courses**
  These are courses designed to give a general overview of an entire area (such as advertising), product or product line, division's activities, process (getting a product to market, Total Quality Management) or geography (doing business in "X"). These types of courses are good for general background and context.

- ☐ **Personal Skills Courses**
  These are courses designed to teach one skill like negotiating or decision making. They are good for people with a need for that skill and a motivation to learn. The value of such courses depends upon the quality of instructors and the accuracy of the content. Check with others who have attended. Ask if they improved in the particular skill being taught.

SUGGESTED READINGS

Burris, Daniel. *Technotrends.* New York: HarperBusiness, 1995.

Epstein, Seymour, Ph.D. with Archie Brodsky. *You're Smarter Than You Think – How to develop your practical intelligence for success in living.* New York: Simon and Schuster, 1993.

Olesen, Erik. *12 Steps to Mastering the Winds of Change.* New York: Macmillan, 1993.

Stone, Florence M. and Randi T. Sachs. *The High-Value Manager – Developing the core competencies your organization needs.* New York: AMACOM, 1995.

114

NON-STRATEGIC

SECTION 1: YOUR DEVELOPMENT NEED(S)

A PROBLEM

- ☐ Can't create effective strategies
- ☐ Can't deal effectively with assignments that require strategic thinking
- ☐ Gets mired in tactics and details
- ☐ Prefers the tactical over the strategic, simple versus complex
- ☐ Isn't a visionary
- ☐ Lacks broad perspective

NOT A PROBLEM

- ☐ Can think and talk strategy with the best
- ☐ Intrigued and challenged by the complexity of the future
- ☐ Likes to run multiple "what if" scenarios
- ☐ Very broad perspective
- ☐ Counsels others on strategic issues
- ☐ Can juggle a lot of mental balls
- ☐ Isn't afraid to engage in wild speculation about the future
- ☐ Can bring several unrelated streams of information together to form a compelling vision
- ☐ Good at meaning making
- ☐ Produces distinctive and winning strategies

SOME CAUSES

- ☐ Don't like complexity
- ☐ Don't think the future is knowable
- ☐ Inexperienced
- ☐ Lack of perspective
- ☐ Low variety background
- ☐ Low risk taker; don't like uncertainty
- ☐ New to the area
- ☐ Too busy with today's tasks
- ☐ Too narrow
- ☐ Very tactical

THE MAP

There are a lot more people who can take a hill than there are people who can accurately predict which hill it would be best to take. There are more people good at producing results in the short term than there are visionary strategists. Both have value but we don't have enough strategists. It is more likely that your organization will be outmaneuvered strategically than that it will be outproduced tactically. Most organizations do pretty well what they do today. It's what they need to be doing tomorrow that's the missing skill. Part of every manager's job is to be strategic. The higher you go, the more critical the requirement.

SECTION 2: LEARNING ON YOUR OWN

THESE SELF-DEVELOPMENT REMEDIES WILL HELP YOU BUILD YOUR SKILL(S)

SOME REMEDIES

☐ **1. Using strategic language.** In some rare cases, we have found strategic thinkers who were not identified as such because they either didn't know, rejected or chose not to use what they considered the latest strategic buzzwords. Strategy is an emerging field. At any time, there are a small number of gurus (at present probably Michael Porter, Ram Charan, C.K. Prahalad, Gary Hamel, Fred Weirsema and Vijay Govindarajan) in vogue, who have created about 75 new words or concepts – values disciplines, strategic intent, value migration, co-evolution, market oligarchies, core capabilities, strategic horizon – to describe strategic thinking. If you don't use those words others won't know you're being strategic. The words are to be found in books by the gurus and in the *Harvard Business Review*. And yes, most of the words are bigger words for things we used to call something else before with smaller words. Nevertheless, if you want to be seen as strategic, you have to talk strategic. Every discipline has its lexicon. In order to be a member, you have to speak the code.

☐ **2. Reject strategy?** There are people who reject strategic formulation as so much folly. They have never seen a five-year strategic plan actually happen as projected. They think the time they use to create and present strategic plans is wasted. They think it's where the rubber meets the sky. So much BS. While it's true that most strategic plans never work out as planned, that doesn't mean that it was a wasted effort. Strategic plans lead to choices about resources and deployment. They lead to different staffing actions and different financial plans. Without some strategic plans, it would be a total shot in the dark. Most failed companies got buried strategically. They picked the wrong direction or too many. Not being able to produce a quality product or service today is generally not the problem.

☐ **3. Not curious?** Many managers are so wrapped up in today's problems they aren't curious about tomorrow. They really don't care about the future. They believe there won't be much of a future until we perform today. Being a visionary and a good strategist requires curiosity and imagination. It requires playing "what ifs." What if there is life on other planets and we get the first message? What will that change? What will happen when a larger percentage of the world's population is over the age of 65? What if cancer is cured? Heart disease? Obesity? What if the government outlaws or severely regulates some aspect of your business? True, nobody knows the answers, but good strategists know the questions. Work at developing eclectic interests outside your business. Subscribe to different magazines, pick new shows to watch, meet different people, join a new organization. Look under some rocks.

- ☐ **4. Narrow perspective?** Some are sharply focused on what they do and do it very well. They have prepared themselves for a narrow but satisfying career. Then someone tells them their job has changed and they now have to be strategic. Being strategic requires a broad perspective. In addition to knowing one thing well, it requires that you know about a lot of things somewhat. You need to understand business. *More help? – See #5 Business Acumen*. You need to understand markets. *More help? – See #15 Customer Focus*. You need to understand how the world operates. *More help? – See #46 Perspective*. You need to put all that together and figure out what it means to your organization. *More help? – See #32 Learning on the Fly and #51 Problem Solving*. And then you have to create a strategy. *More help? – See #58 Strategic Agility*.

- ☐ **5. Too busy?** Strategy is always last on the list. Solving today's problems, of which there are many, is job one. You have to make time for strategy. A good strategy releases future time because it makes choices clear and leads to less wasted effort, but it takes time to do. Delegation is usually the key. Give away as much tactical day-to-day stuff as you can. Ask your people what they think they could do to give you more time for strategic reflection. *More help? – See #18 Delegation*. Another key is better time management. Put an hour a week on your calendar for strategic reading and reflection throughout the year. Don't wait until one week before the plan is due. *More help? – See #62 Time Management*. Keep a log of ideas you get from others, magazines, etc. Focus on how these impact your organization or function.

- ☐ **6. Avoid risks?** Strategic planning is the most uncertain thing managers do. It's speculating on the near unknown. It requires projections into foggy landscapes. It requires assumptions about the unknown. Many conflict avoiders don't like to make statements in public that they cannot back up with facts. Most strategies can be questioned. There are no clean ways to win a debate over strategy. It really comes down to one subjective estimate versus another. *More help? – See #2* Dealing with *Ambiguity.*

- ☐ **7. Addicted to the simple?** Strategy ends up sounding simple – five clean clear statements about where we want to go with a few tactics and decisions attached to each. Getting there is not simple. Good strategists are complexifiers. They extend everything to its extreme before they get down to the essence. Simplifiers close too early. They are impatient to get it done faster. They are very results oriented and want to get to the five simple statements before strategic due process has been followed. Be more tolerant of unlimited exploration and debate before you move to close.

☐ **8. Don't know how to be strategic?** The simplest problem is someone who wants to be strategic and wants to learn. Strategy is a reasonably well known field. Read the gurus – Michael Porter, Ram Charan, C.K. Prahalad, Gary Hamel, Fred Weirsema and Vijay Govindarajan. Scan the *Harvard Business Review* regularly. Read the three to five strategic case studies in *Business Week*. Go to a three-day strategy course hopefully taught by one of the gurus. Get someone from the organization's strategic group to tutor you in strategy. Watch CEO's talk about their businesses on cable. Volunteer to serve on a task force on a strategic issue.

☐ **9. Can't think strategically?** Strategy is linking several variables together to come up with the most likely scenario. It involves making projections of several variables at once to see how they come together. These projections are in the context of shifting markets, international affairs, monetary movements and government interventions. It involves a lot of uncertainty, making risk assumptions, and understanding how things work together. How many reasons would account for sales going down? Up? How are advertising and sales linked? If the dollar is cheaper in Asia, what does that mean for our product in Japan? If the world population is aging and they have more money, how will that change buying patterns? Not everyone enjoys this kind of pie in the sky thinking and not everyone is skilled at doing it. *More help? – See #32 Learning on the Fly, #46 Perspective, and #51 Problem Solving.*

☐ **10. Don't want to be strategic?** Some just don't feel they want to ramp up and learn to be strategic. But they like their job and want to be considered strategically responsible. Hire a strategic consultant once a year to sit with you and your team and help you work out your strategic plan. Anderson Consulting. The Boston Consulting Group. McKinsey. Booz Allen. Plus many more. Or delegate strategy to one or more in your unit who are more strategically capable. Or ask the strategic planning group to help. You don't have to be able to do everything to be a good manager. You like your nest? Some people are content in their narrow niche. They are not interested in being strategic. They just want to do their job and be left alone. They are interested in doing good work in their specialty and want to get as high as they can. That's OK. Just inform the organization of your wishes and don't take jobs that have a heavy strategic requirement.

SECTION 3: LEARNING FROM MORE FEEDBACK

THESE SOURCES WOULD GIVE YOU THE MOST ACCURATE AND DETAILED FEEDBACK ON YOUR SKILL(S)

- ☐ **Boss's Boss(es)**
  From a process standpoint, your boss's boss probably has the most influence and control over your progress. He/she has a broader perspective, has more access to data, and stands at the center of decisions about you. To know what he/she thinks, without having to violate the canons of corporate due process to get that information, would be quite useful.

- ☐ **Direct Boss**
  Your direct boss has important information about you, your performance, and your prospects. The challenge is to get this information. There are formal processes (e.g., performance appraisals). There are day-to-day opportunities. To help, signal your boss that you want and can handle direct and timely feedback. Many bosses have trouble giving feedback, so you will have to work at it over a period of time.

- ☐ **Human Resource Professionals**
  Human Resource professionals have both a formal and informal feedback role. Since they have access to unique and confidential information, they can provide the right context for feedback you've received. Sometimes they may be "directed" to give you feedback. Other times, they may pass on feedback just to be helpful to you.

- ☐ **Natural Mentors**
  Natural mentors have a special relationship with you and are interested in your success and your future. Since they are usually not in your direct chain of command, you can have more open, relaxed, and fruitful discussions about yourself and your career prospects. They can be a very important source for candid or critical feedback others may not give you.

- ☐ **Past Associates/Constituencies**
  When confronted with a present performance problem, some claim, "I wasn't like that before; it must be the current situation." When feedback is available from former associates, about 50% support that claim. In the other half of the cases, the people were like that before and probably didn't know it. It sometimes makes sense to access the past to clearly see the present.

SECTION 4: LEARNING FROM DEVELOP-IN-PLACE ASSIGNMENTS

THESE PART-TIME DEVELOP-IN-PLACE ASSIGNMENTS WILL HELP YOU BUILD YOUR SKILL(S)

- ☐ Do a competitive analysis of your organization's products or services or your position in the marketplace and present it to the people involved.

- ☐ Do a postmortem on a successful project and present it to the people involved.
- ☐ Do a feasibility study on an important opportunity and make recommendations to those who will decide.
- ☐ Monitor and follow a new product or service through the entire idea, design, test market, and launch cycle.
- ☐ Study and summarize a new trend, product, service, technique, or process and present and sell it to others.
- ☐ Benchmark innovative practices, processes, products, or services of competitors, vendors, suppliers, or customers and present a report to others to create recommendations for change.
- ☐ Visit Malcolm Baldrige National Quality Award or Deming Prize winners and report back on your findings, showing how they would help your organization.
- ☐ Work on a project that involves travel and study of an issue, acquisition, or joint venture off-shore or overseas, with a report back to management.
- ☐ Serve on a product/service/project review committee.
- ☐ Work on a team forming a joint venture or partnership.

SECTION 5: LEARNING FROM FULL-TIME JOBS

THESE FULL-TIME JOBS OFFER THE OPPORTUNITY TO BUILD YOUR SKILL(S)

☐ **Heavy Strategic Demands**

The core demands necessary to qualify as a Heavy Strategic Content assignment are: 1) Requires significant strategic thinking and planning most couldn't do. 2) Charts new ground strategically. 3) Plan must be presented, challenged, adopted, and implemented. 4) Exposure to significant decision makers and executives. 1) Strategic planning position. 2) Job involving repositioning of a product, service, or organization.

☐ **Line To Staff Switches**

The core demands to qualify as a Line to Staff switch are: 1) Intellectually/strategically demanding. 2) Highly visible to others. 3) New area/perspective/method/culture/function. 4) Moving away from a bottom line. 5) Moving from field to headquarters. 6) Exposure to high-level executives. Examples: 1) Business/strategic planning. 2) Heading a staff department. 3) Assistant to/chief of staff to a senior executive. 4) Head of a task force. 5) Human resources role.

☐ **Scope Assignments**

The core demands for a Scope (complexity) assignment are: 1) Significant increase in both internal and external scope or complexity. 2) Significant increase in visibility and/or bottom line responsibility.

3) Unfamiliar area, business, technology, or territory. Examples of Scope assignments involving shifts: 1) Switching into a new function/technology/business. 2) Moving to new organization. 3) Moving to overseas assignment. 4) Moving to new location. 5) Adding new products/services. 6) Moving between headquarters/field. 7) Switches in ownership/top management of the unit/organization. Examples of Scope assignments involving "firsts": 1) First-time manager. 2) First-time managing managers. 3) First-time executive. 4) First-time overseas. 5) First-time headquarters/field. 6) First-time team leader. 7) First-time new technology/business/function. Scope assignments involving increased complexity: 1) Managing a significant expansion of an existing product or service. 2) Managing adding new products/service into an existing unit. 3) Managing a reorganized and more diverse unit. 4) Managing explosive growth. 5) Adding new technologies.

SECTION 6: LEARNING MORE FROM YOUR PLAN

THESE ADDITIONAL REMEDIES WILL HELP MAKE THIS DEVELOPMENT PLAN MORE EFFECTIVE FOR YOU

Learning to Learn Better

☐ **Monitoring Yourself More Closely and Getting off Your Autopilot**
Past habits are a mixed blessing, sometimes helping, sometimes not. To avoid putting yourself on "autopilot," think afresh about each situation before acting. Consistently monitor yourself with questions. Is this task different? Ask why you would repeat a past action. Are you avoiding anything, like taking a chance? Is there something new you might try?

☐ **Find a Parallel to the Current Problem and Learn From It**
Find a parallel with similar situations, whether in your field or in other areas, past or present, and look for comparison or contrast points to see what else has or hasn't worked. Search especially for the reasons why certain things work and others don't across different situations; find the common and uncommon elements.

☐ **Regularly Read Relevant Publications**
Read publications most relevant to you such as the *Wall Street Journal*, the *Harvard Business Review*, the *Economist*, *Fortune*, *Business Week*, etc. Track a single issue or trend to see as many sides of it as you can. What tactics and strategies are being followed? How is this similar to something you are doing? How could you use some of your insights?

Learning from Experience, Feedback and Other People

☐ **Using Multiple Models**
Who do you know who exemplifies how to do whatever your need is? Who, for example, personifies decisiveness or compassion or strategic agility? Think more broadly than your current job and colleagues. For example, clergy, friends, spouses or community leaders are also good

sources for potential models. Select your models not on the basis of overall excellence or likability, but on the basis of the one towering strength (or glaring weakness) you are interested in. Even people who are well thought of usually have only one or two towering strengths (or glaring weaknesses). Ordinarily, you won't learn as much from the whole person as you will from one characteristic.

- ☐ **Learning from Interviewing Others**
Interview others. Ask not only what they do, but how and why they do it. What do they think are the rules of thumb they are following? Where did they learn the behaviors? How do they keep them current? How do they monitor the effect they have on others?

- ☐ **Learning from Observing Others**
Observe others. Find opportunities to observe without interacting with your model. This enables you to objectively study the person, note what he/she is doing or not doing, and compare that with what you would typically do in similar situations. Many times you can learn more by watching than asking. Your model may not be able to explain what he/she does or may be an unwilling teacher.

- ☐ **Getting Feedback from Bosses and Superiors**
Many bosses are reluctant to give negative feedback. They lack the managerial courage to face people directly with criticism. You can help by soliciting feedback and setting the tone. Show them you can handle criticism and that you are willing to work on issues they see as important.

Learning from Courses

- ☐ **Orientation Events**
Most organizations offer a variety of orientation events. They are designed to communicate strategies, charters, missions, goals, and general information and offer an opportunity for people to meet each other. They are short in duration and offer limited opportunities for learning anything beyond general context and background.

- ☐ **Sending Others to Courses**
If you are responsible for managing someone else's development and, as part of that, sending them to courses, prepare them beforehand. Don't send them as tourists. Meet with them before and after the course. Tell them why they need this course. Tell them what you expect them to learn. Give them feedback on why you think they need the course. Agree ahead of time how you will measure and monitor learning after they return. If possible, offer a variety of courses for your employee to choose from. Have them give you a report shortly after they return. If appropriate, have them present what they learned to the rest of your staff. After they return, provide opportunities for using the new skills with safe cover and low risk. Give them practice time before

expecting full exercise of the new skills. Be supportive during early unsteadiness. Give continuous feedback on progress.

- ☐ **Strategic Courses**
  There are a number of courses designed to stretch minds to prepare for future challenges. They include topics such as Workforce Diversity 2000, globalization, the European Union, competitive competencies and strategies, etc. Quality depends upon the following three factors: 1) The quality of the staff. Are they qualified? Are they respected in their fields? Are they strategic "gurus"? 2) The quality of the participants. Are they the kind of people you could learn from? 3) The quality of the setting. Is it comfortable and free from distractions? Can you learn there?

SUGGESTED READINGS

Annison, Michael H. *Managing the Whirlwind.* Englewood, CO: Medical Group Management Association, 1993.

Bandrowski, James F. Corporate *Imagination Plus.* New York: Macmillan, Inc., 1990.

Charan, Ram and Noel M. Tichy. *Every business is a growth business: how your company can prosper year after year.* New York: Times Business, 1998.

Fine, Charles H. *Clock Speed – Winning Industry Control in the Age of Temporary Advantage.* Reading, MA: Perseus Books, 1998.

Hamel, Gary and C.K. Prahalad. *Competing for the future.* Boston, Mass.: Harvard Business School Press, 1994.

Hickman, Craig and Michael A. Silva. *Creating Excellence.* New York: New American Library, 1984.

Kennedy, Paul M. *The rise and fall of the great powers: economic change and military conflict from 1500 to 2000.* New York: Random House, 1987.

Montgomery, Cynthia A. and Michael E. Porter, Editors. *Strategy: seeking and securing competitive advantage.* Boston: Harvard Business School Press, 1991.

Ohmae, Kenichi. *The Mind of the Strategist.* New York: McGraw-Hill, Inc., 1982.

Swinton, Ernest Dunlop. *The Defense of Duffer's Drift.* Washington, DC: U.S. Marine Corps, [1996]

Yoshiro, Michael and U. Srinivasa Ranga. *Strategic Alliances.* Boston: Harvard Business School Press, 1995.

115

OVERDEPENDENCE ON AN ADVOCATE

SECTION 1: YOUR DEVELOPMENT NEED(S)

A PROBLEM

- ☐ Has been with the same boss, champion, mentor, advocate too long
- ☐ Isn't seen as independent
- ☐ Others question whether he/she could stand up to a tough assignment or situation without help
- ☐ Might not do well in the organization if the advocate lost interest, lost out him/herself, or left the organization

NOT A PROBLEM

- ☐ Has largely done it on his/her own
- ☐ Has multiple advocates and champions
- ☐ No one questions whether he/she could go it alone
- ☐ Independent, resourceful person
- ☐ Doesn't use a champion's influence to get things done
- ☐ Has moved around a lot
- ☐ Has not been with one boss very long
- ☐ Has survived an advocate or two leaving the organization

SOME CAUSES

- ☐ Dependent
- ☐ Don't get results alone
- ☐ Has gotten lazy
- ☐ Narrow experience base
- ☐ Not tough
- ☐ Overly loyal

THE MAP

The most successful men in studies of managerial success usually didn't have a single long-term mentor or advocate. They were more likely to have multiple advocates at various stages of their careers. Women have reported a higher incidence of having single mentors because of being pioneers into a new arena. They needed one to get into the "Club." There's good news and bad news. Having an advocate/mentor is a great way to get into the mainstream of an organization, be privy to fresh information and get advantages – promotions, choice assignments, invitations to events, etc. Having a strong advocate is also one of the best ways to stall your career long term. People wonder if you can do it on your own; can you stand alone without the advocate and be successful? How much of your success was windfall? What would happen to you if your advocate/mentor left or fell from grace?

SECTION 2: LEARNING ON YOUR OWN

THESE SELF-DEVELOPMENT REMEDIES WILL HELP YOU BUILD YOUR SKILL(S)

SOME REMEDIES

☐ **1. Being trapped with an advocate/mentor starts innocently enough.** Two people take a liking to each other. They respect each other. A bond is formed. One helps the other break in. The other works hard to reward the advocate/mentor. The advocate/mentor gets promoted. He/she takes you along. You pass up other opportunities to stay with this positive and supportive person. The advocate/mentor doesn't put you up for other jobs because he or she really appreciates what you can do. And it's so easy working for each other. Each of you is in the groove and in your comfort zone. How long is too long? When others begin to question whether you could perform alone. When your advocate/mentor turns down opportunities for you. When your advocate/mentor keeps you for his or her own comfort. When you aren't learning anything new. When you don't have to push yourself to please him or her. Then it's time to break free. Volunteer for a job change. Ask your advocate/mentor for help in getting another assignment. Ask Human Resources how to market yourself for another opportunity.

☐ **2. Can't change jobs?** Volunteer for task forces/projects your advocate/mentor is not involved in. If the project is important, is multifunctional and has a real outcome which will be taken seriously, it is one of the most common developmental events listed by successful executives. Such projects require learning other functions, businesses or nationalities. You can get out of your own experience and start to see connections to a broader world – how international trade works or how the pieces of your organization fit together. Your performance will also be seen as yours and part of the project's and not connected with your advocate/mentor. *More help? – See #46 Perspective.*

☐ **3. Do things in your job that you have not done before.** Broaden your experience base. In your unit there are things to start up or fix, problems to confront, etc. Pick three tasks you've never done and volunteer to do them. If you don't know much about customers, work in a store or handle customer complaints; if you don't know what engineering does, go find out; task trade with someone; write a strategic plan for your unit. *More help? – See #54 Self-Development.*

☐ **4. Locate some additional role models.** You have learned great stuff from your advocate/mentor but it's time to add some new stuff. Pick a person in the organization who is different in some aspects from your advocate/mentor. Observe what he/she does and how he/she does it. He/she is as successful as your advocate/mentor but does it in other ways. If possible, ask for a meeting/lunch to discuss his/her success and the things he/she has learned. See if he/she has any interest in teaching you something and being a temporary coach. Get to know other potential advocates on and off work. Go for maximum variety in the towering strengths they possess.

☐ **5. Perform more independently.** What do you take for granted that your advocate/mentor does for you? How is he/she helpful? Helps you make final decisions? Start making the decisions yourself. Gets you invitations to special events? Get them on your own. Shares interesting information? Get it from other sources. Helps you prepare important presentations? Do a few by yourself. Covers your mistakes? Fix them yourself. Passes on feedback from others to you? Go talk to the originators on your own. Try to think about all the things you rely on your advocate/mentor for and try to begin to perform more independently from him or her.

☐ **6. Avoiding overusing your advocate/mentor.** One common problem of being with a boss or advocate too long is that you might get in the habit of acting in his/her absence or on his/her behalf. You may take on his/her authority. You might even get in the lazy habit of saying "Larry" would like it this way or "Larry" would approve or not approve of this when that isn't literally true. People may get in the habit of passing information to you because they know it will get to Larry. People may pass things by you and ask you how you think Larry would react to it. People may ask you what Larry is really like because they are having some difficulty with him. All of these types of things are natural consequences of your special relationship with Larry, but they can just as well backfire longer term in your career. Don't use Larry's name, use your own.

☐ **7. If you have trouble standing alone** because you have been overly dependent upon an advocate/mentor, increase the risks you take on your own. Stake out a position on an issue that will require some courage and where you know there will be some detractors. Prepare by rehearsing for tough questions, attacks, and countering views. Don't use your advocate/mentor. Talk to yourself. Pump yourself up by focusing on your strengths. *More help? – See #34 Managerial Courage and #57 Standing Alone.*

☐ **8. Breaking out of a habit or a rut.** Stuck in the ways the advocate/mentor passed on to you? Do you approach situations much the same every time? Then switch approaches. Do something totally different next time. If you visited the office of someone you have difficulties with, invite him/her to your office next time. Compare the situations and see which was more valuable. Develop three different ways to get the same outcome. For example, to push a decision through, you could meet with stakeholders first, go to a key stakeholder, study and present the problem to a group, call a problem-solving session, or call in an outside expert. Be prepared to do them all when obstacles arise.

☐ **9. Women and minorities only.** Here's the catch-22. If you are different or new or a first timer or a member of any minority, you need a mentor, guide, orienter or advocate to get invited in. That's the only way you are going to get the information you need to be effective. That's the only way you can get invited to attend important meetings. It's the only way, aside from stellar performance, you will be considered for career progression. The trick is to take advantage of this special relationship long enough to get plugged in and comfortable and not long enough to question whether you could have done it on your own. That usually means unplugging before you want to. Before you become too comfortable. Before the mentor has taught you everything you need to know. Before you get evaluated as being overdependent on an advocate. Start early to find multiple models, multiple advocates. Make sure at least five key figures know who you are and what you can do.

☐ **10. Saying farewell.** One situation involves what to do when your advocate/mentor stumbles, falls, fails or leaves. Many times the person may ask you to join him or her in the next company. Think very carefully about that. There are many cases of entourages of people following a general manager from company to company. You will be an outsider. Your career will be closely tied to the person you are following. The same thing will happen to you in the next company, only faster. If he/she falls out of favor but stays, be supportive but keep out of it. It's not your problem. Don't go around defending your advocate/mentor. You will get tainted, too. The other situation occurs when you decide to change jobs within your organization. Advocate/mentors may not buy the fact that you have to establish a performance track on your own to be truly successful. They may think or say that they can counsel you to the top. You don't need to take another job. You don't need to work for someone else. Remember that these kinds of wonderful relationships have advantages for both sides. They get things they need from you also. You are in no way rejecting or devaluing your advocate/mentor by breaking free. In a sense it's a celebration of the success the advocate/mentor has had with you. You are now fully prepared to go it on your own. Be appreciative. Keep a light in the window. And move on to new vistas.

SECTION 3: LEARNING FROM MORE FEEDBACK

THESE SOURCES WOULD GIVE YOU THE MOST ACCURATE AND DETAILED FEEDBACK ON YOUR SKILL(S)

☐ **All Other Superiors**

Collectively important, your supervisors know about the organization and where you fit in. They have the power to decide on your progress. Productive relationships with senior managers help to foster the kind of feedback you need to grow and improve. Most people never get access to this kind of information.

- ☐ **Boss's Boss(es)**
  From a process standpoint, your boss's boss probably has the most influence and control over your progress. He/she has a broader perspective, has more access to data, and stands at the center of decisions about you. To know what he/she thinks, without having to violate the canons of corporate due process to get that information, would be quite useful.
- ☐ **Direct Boss**
  Your direct boss has important information about you, your performance, and your prospects. The challenge is to get this information. There are formal processes (e.g., performance appraisals). There are day-to-day opportunities. To help, signal your boss that you want and can handle direct and timely feedback. Many bosses have trouble giving feedback, so you will have to work at it over a period of time.
- ☐ **Human Resource Professionals**
  Human Resource professionals have both a formal and informal feedback role. Since they have access to unique and confidential information, they can provide the right context for feedback you've received. Sometimes they may be "directed" to give you feedback. Other times, they may pass on feedback just to be helpful to you.
- ☐ **Natural Mentors**
  Natural mentors have a special relationship with you and are interested in your success and your future. Since they are usually not in your direct chain of command, you can have more open, relaxed, and fruitful discussions about yourself and your career prospects. They can be a very important source for candid or critical feedback others may not give you.

SECTION 4: LEARNING FROM DEVELOP-IN-PLACE ASSIGNMENTS

THESE PART-TIME DEVELOP-IN-PLACE ASSIGNMENTS WILL HELP YOU BUILD YOUR SKILL(S)

- ☐ Plan an off-site meeting, conference, convention, trade show, event, etc.
- ☐ Become a referee for an athletic league or program.
- ☐ Plan for and start up something small (secretarial pool, athletic program, suggestion system, program, etc.).
- ☐ Launch a new product, service, or process.
- ☐ Be a change agent; create a symbol for change; lead the rallying cry; champion a significant change and implementation.
- ☐ Run (chair) a task force on a pressing problem.
- ☐ Manage an ad hoc, temporary group of balky and resisting people through an unpopular change or project.
- ☐ Handle a tough negotiation with an internal or external client or customer.

- ☐ Manage a dissatisfied internal or external customer; troubleshoot a performance or quality problem with a product or service.
- ☐ Take on a tough and undoable project, one where others who have tried it have failed.

SECTION 5: LEARNING FROM FULL-TIME JOBS

THESE FULL-TIME JOBS OFFER THE OPPORTUNITY TO BUILD YOUR SKILL(S)

☐ **Cross-Moves**
The core demands necessary to qualify as a Cross-Move are: 1) Move to a very different set of challenges. 2) Abrupt jump-shift in tasks/activities. 3) Never been there before. 4) New setting/conditions. Examples of Cross-Moves are: 1) Changing divisions. 2) Changing functions. 3) Field/headquarters shifts. 4) Line/staff switches. 5) Country switches. 6) Working with all new people. 7) Changing lines of business.

☐ **Off-Shore Assignments**
The core demands to qualify as an Off-Shore assignment are: 1) First time working in the country. 2) Significant challenges like new language, hardship location, unique business rules/practices, significant cultural/marketplace differences, different functional task, etc. 3) More than a year assignment. 4) No automatic return deal. 5) Not necessarily a change in job challenge, technical content, or responsibilities.

SECTION 6: LEARNING MORE FROM YOUR PLAN

THESE ADDITIONAL REMEDIES WILL HELP MAKE THIS DEVELOPMENT PLAN MORE EFFECTIVE FOR YOU

Learning to Learn Better

☐ **Read About a Model Who has What You Need**
Read about someone who was in a similar or contrasting situation and find the keys to their successes and failures. What rules of thumb can you take away and apply to your own situation?

☐ **Interview a Model of What You Need to Learn**
Find someone you consider a model in the area you're trying to work on and observe him/her performing successfully. Interview him/her for keys, rules of thumb, and insights. Ask how he/she became good at it. Test their thinking: How does he/she assess situations to determine when and how to use the skills in this area?

☐ **Envision the Ideal Person/Behavior for Insights**
Try to imagine what the best or ideal person would be able to do; check how close you could get to that by using what you have. How much could you learn in a short period of time to reach the ideal? How real is the ideal? Is it worth the effort?

Learning from Experience, Feedback and Other People

- ☐ **Using Multiple Models**
Who do you know who exemplifies how to do whatever your need is? Who, for example, personifies decisiveness or compassion or strategic agility? Think more broadly than your current job and colleagues. For example, clergy, friends, spouses or community leaders are also good sources for potential models. Select your models not on the basis of overall excellence or likability, but on the basis of the one towering strength (or glaring weakness) you are interested in. Even people who are well thought of usually have only one or two towering strengths (or glaring weaknesses). Ordinarily, you won't learn as much from the whole person as you will from one characteristic.

- ☐ **Learning from Mentors and Tutors**
Mentors and tutors offer a special case for learning since the relationship is specifically formed for learning. You need to be open and nondefensive. You need to solicit and accept feedback. This is a unique opportunity for you to get low-risk, honest, and direct feedback on what you do well and not so well.

- ☐ **Learning from Ineffective Behavior**
Seeing things done poorly can be a very potent source of learning for you, especially if the behavior or action affects others negatively. Many times the thing done poorly causes emotional reactions or pain in you and others. Distance yourself from the feelings and explore why the actions didn't work.

- ☐ **Learning from a Coach or Tutor**
Ask a person to coach or tutor you directly. This has the additional benefit of skill building coupled with correcting feedback. Also observe the teacher teaching you. How does he/she teach? How does he/she adjust to you as a learner? After the process, ask for feedback about you as a learner.

- ☐ **Getting Feedback from Bosses and Superiors**
Many bosses are reluctant to give negative feedback. They lack the managerial courage to face people directly with criticism. You can help by soliciting feedback and setting the tone. Show them you can handle criticism and that you are willing to work on issues they see as important.

- ☐ **Getting Feedback from Peers/Colleagues**
Your peers and colleagues may not be candid if they are in competition with you. Some may not be willing to be open with you out of fear of giving you an advantage. Some may give you exaggerated feedback to deliberately cause you undue concern. You have to set the tone and gauge the trust level of the relationship and the quality of the feedback.

Learning from Courses

☐ **Strategic Courses**
There are a number of courses designed to stretch minds to prepare for future challenges. They include topics such as Workforce Diversity 2000, globalization, the European Union, competitive competencies and strategies, etc. Quality depends upon the following three factors: 1) The quality of the staff. Are they qualified? Are they respected in their fields? Are they strategic "gurus"? 2) The quality of the participants. Are they the kind of people you could learn from? 3) The quality of the setting. Is it comfortable and free from distractions? Can you learn there?

SUGGESTED READINGS

Barner, Robert. *Lifeboat strategies: how to keep your career above water during tough times—or any time.* New York: American Management Association, 1994.

Bell, Chip R. *Managers as mentors: building partnerships for learning.* San Francisco, CA:Berrett-Koehler Publishers, 1996.

Boccialetti, Gene. *It takes two: managing yourself when working with bosses and authority figures.* San Francisco: Jossey-Bass, 1995.

Fuller, George T. *The workplace survival guide: tools, tips and techniques for succeeding on the job.* Englewood Cliffs, NJ: Prentice Hall, 1996.

Hendricks, William [et al.]. *Coaching, mentoring, and managing.* Franklin Lakes, NJ: Career Press, 1996.

Hughes, Marylou. *Keeping your job while your bosses are losing theirs.* Binghamton, New York: William Neil Publishing, 1998.

Johnson, Harold E. *Mentoring for exceptional performance.* Glendale, CA.: Griffin Pub., 1997.

Searing, Jill A. and Anne B. Lovett. *The career prescription: how to stop sabotaging your career and put it on a winning track.* Englewood Cliffs, N.J.: Prentice-Hall, 1995.

Stern, Paul G. and Tom Schactman. *Straight to the top: beyond loyalty, gamesmanship, mentors, and other corporate myths.* New York: Warner Books, 1990.

116

OVERDEPENDENCE ON A SINGLE SKILL

SECTION 1: YOUR DEVELOPMENT NEED(S)

A PROBLEM

- ☐ Relies too much on a single strength for performance and career progression
- ☐ Uses the same core talent, function, or technology to leverage him/herself
- ☐ Acts as if he/she can make it all the way on one strength

NOT A PROBLEM

- ☐ Has a broad and varied background
- ☐ Has moved around a lot
- ☐ Relies on several different skills to get the job done
- ☐ Has multiple functional exposures
- ☐ Has worked in different business units
- ☐ Always looking to learn more
- ☐ Works on adding more skills

SOME CAUSES

- ☐ Counting backwards to retirement
- ☐ Inexperienced
- ☐ Lazy
- ☐ Lives in the glory of the past
- ☐ Narrow perspective
- ☐ Not interested in broadening or self-development
- ☐ Too comfortable

THE MAP

We are comfort zone creatures. We build nests. We go where it feels safe and good. Most of us don't like taking chances. Most of us don't venture on to alien ground comfortably. For those reasons, many of us take the safe career track, we think, of learning one thing and doing that well. In our early careers, that gets us good pay and promotions up the career ladder. We pass up people who are not as deeply skilled as we. We play the one skill, one technology, one business, one function or one talent (e.g. selling) all the way. Trouble is, it doesn't go all the way. All things change. One of the requirements for higher level management and career fulfillment is broadness and diversity. If you succeed long enough, you'll manage or work closely with new functions and businesses. A single skill is never enough.

SECTION 2: LEARNING ON YOUR OWN

THESE SELF-DEVELOPMENT REMEDIES WILL HELP YOU BUILD YOUR SKILL(S)

SOME REMEDIES

- ☐ **1. Think carefully about your next natural point for an assignment change.** This time, press your boss, business unit or organization for something different. Could be different geography, same job but different business unit, same job but different assignments, or a completely different job. Sometimes if you have been in something too long, you may have to take a lateral or even a short-term downgrading to get on a different track.
- ☐ **2. Volunteer for task forces and study teams outside your area.**
- ☐ **3. Attend off-sites and meetings of functions and units other than yours.**
- ☐ **4. In addition to the literature you now read in your specialty, expand to a broader selection of journals and magazines.**
- ☐ **5. Take a seminar or workshop outside your area just for the fun of it.**
- ☐ **6. Vacation more broadly than you now do.** Get out of your comfort zone and explore new places. If you can arrange it, vacation outside of your home country.
- ☐ **7. Find someone who is as specialized as you are** who also is seeking expansion and teach your specialties to each other. Get together a small group; have each person agree to present a new technology or business topic each month to the group. Teaching something new for you is one of the best ways to learn it yourself.
- ☐ **8. Look to some people in your area who are in higher level jobs than you are.** Are they as specialized as you are? Are they struggling in their new roles because they are as specialized as you are? Read *Career Mastery* by Harry Levinson. *More help? – See #6 Career Ambition and #54 Self-Development.*
- ☐ **9. Find some experts in what you need to learn.** Interview them; find out how they think about their area. Take something to them in their area and ask them how they figure it out. What are the five key things they look for?
- ☐ **10. Pick three people who are broadly skilled.** Ask them how they got to be that way. What job experiences have they had? What do they read? Watch on TV? Who do they like to learn from?

SECTION 3: LEARNING FROM MORE FEEDBACK

THESE SOURCES WOULD GIVE YOU THE MOST ACCURATE AND DETAILED FEEDBACK ON YOUR SKILL(S)

☐ **Direct Boss**
Your direct boss has important information about you, your performance, and your prospects. The challenge is to get this information. There are formal processes (e.g., performance appraisals). There are day-to-day opportunities. To help, signal your boss that you want and can handle direct and timely feedback. Many bosses have trouble giving feedback, so you will have to work at it over a period of time.

☐ **Human Resource Professionals**
Human Resource professionals have both a formal and informal feedback role. Since they have access to unique and confidential information, they can provide the right context for feedback you've received. Sometimes they may be "directed" to give you feedback. Other times, they may pass on feedback just to be helpful to you.

☐ **Natural Mentors**
Natural mentors have a special relationship with you and are interested in your success and your future. Since they are usually not in your direct chain of command, you can have more open, relaxed, and fruitful discussions about yourself and your career prospects. They can be a very important source for candid or critical feedback others may not give you.

SECTION 4: LEARNING FROM DEVELOP-IN-PLACE ASSIGNMENTS

THESE PART-TIME DEVELOP-IN-PLACE ASSIGNMENTS WILL HELP YOU BUILD YOUR SKILL(S)

☐ Find and spend time with an expert to learn something new to you.

☐ Study some aspect of your job or a new technical area you haven't studied before that you need to be more effective.

☐ Work closely with a higher-level manager who is very good at something you need to learn.

☐ Attend a course or event which will push you personally beyond your usual limits or outside your comfort zone (e.g., Outward Bound, language immersion training, sensitivity group, public speaking).

☐ Study an admired person who has a skill you need.

☐ Volunteer to do a special project for and with a person you admire and who has a skill you need to develop.

☐ Work short rotations in other units, functions, or geographies you've not been exposed to before.

☐ Study and summarize a new trend, product, service, technique, or process and present and sell it to others.

- ☐ Benchmark innovative practices, processes, products, or services of competitors, vendors, suppliers, or customers and present a report to others to create recommendations for change.
- ☐ Visit Malcolm Baldrige National Quality Award or Deming Prize winners and report back on your findings, showing how they would help your organization.

SECTION 5: LEARNING FROM FULL-TIME JOBS

THESE FULL-TIME JOBS OFFER THE OPPORTUNITY TO BUILD YOUR SKILL(S)

☐ **Chair of Projects/Task Forces**

The core demands for qualifying as a Project/Task Force assignment are: 1) Full-time assignment. 2) Important and specific goal. 3) Tight deadline. 4) Success or failure will be evident. 5) High-visibility sponsor. 6) Learning something on the fly. 7) Must get others to cooperate. 8) Usually six months or more. Four types of Projects/Task Forces: 1) New ideas, products, services, or systems (e.g., product/service/program research and development, creation/installation/launch of a new system, new programs like Total Quality Management, positive discipline). 2) Formal negotiations and relationships (e.g., acquisitions, divestitures, agreements, joint ventures; licensing arrangements, franchising; dealing with unions, governments, communities, charities, customers, and relocations). 3) Big one-time events (e.g., working on a major presentation for the board, organizing significant meetings or conferences, disaster/damage control teams; reorganizations, mergers, acquisitions, or relocations, working on visions, charters, strategies, other time-urgent issues and problems). 4) Troubleshooting (e.g., problems, disasters, crises, product/service failures, accidents, illegal activities, damage control in public relations goofs, shut downs, downsizings, layoffs, abrupt changes in leadership).

☐ **Cross-Moves**

The core demands necessary to qualify as a Cross-Move are: 1) Move to a very different set of challenges. 2) Abrupt jump-shift in tasks/activities. 3) Never been there before. 4) New setting/conditions. Examples of Cross-Moves are: 1) Changing divisions. 2) Changing functions. 3) Field/headquarters shifts. 4) Line/staff switches. 5) Country switches. 6) Working with all new people. 7) Changing lines of business.

☐ **Line To Staff Switches**

The core demands to qualify as a Line to Staff switch are: 1) Intellectually/strategically demanding. 2) Highly visible to others. 3) New area/perspective/method/culture/function. 4) Moving away from a bottom line. 5) Moving from field to headquarters. 6) Exposure to high-level executives. Examples: 1) Business/strategic planning. 2) Heading a staff department. 3) Assistant to/chief of staff to a senior executive. 4) Head of a task force. 5) Human resources role.

- [ ] **Staff to Line Shifts**
Core demands necessary to qualify for a Staff to Line shift are: 1) Moving to a job with an easily determined bottom line or results. 2) Managing bigger scope and/or scale. 3) Requires new skills/perspectives. 4) Unfamiliar aspects of the assignment.

SECTION 6: LEARNING MORE FROM YOUR PLAN

THESE ADDITIONAL REMEDIES WILL HELP MAKE THIS DEVELOPMENT PLAN MORE EFFECTIVE FOR YOU

Learning to Learn Better

- [ ] **Study What and How You Learn**
What are you good at and how did you get to be that way? What learning strategies and experiences led to you being an expert? Could those same strategies apply again in other areas? Can you gain expertise in other areas using the same techniques?

- [ ] **Put Yourself in Situations that Call for Your Weaknesses**
Put yourself in situations where you must overcome or neutralize a weakness to be successful. Find opportunities to develop counter coping skills: if you're shy, attend functions where you don't know many people; if you're too aggressive, work with children, etc.

- [ ] **Throw Yourself With More Vigor Than Usual Into Something New**
Throw yourself into a new area, something you've not done before so you will have to learn quickly, such as a new technical area, a new management practice, or a self-development project. Pick something that is out of your skill and strength set.

Learning from Experience, Feedback and Other People

- [ ] **Using Multiple Models**
Who do you know who exemplifies how to do whatever your need is? Who, for example, personifies decisiveness or compassion or strategic agility? Think more broadly than your current job and colleagues. For example, clergy, friends, spouses or community leaders are also good sources for potential models. Select your models not on the basis of overall excellence or likability, but on the basis of the one towering strength (or glaring weakness) you are interested in. Even people who are well thought of usually have only one or two towering strengths (or glaring weaknesses). Ordinarily, you won't learn as much from the whole person as you will from one characteristic.

- [ ] **Learning from Ineffective Behavior**
Seeing things done poorly can be a very potent source of learning for you, especially if the behavior or action affects others negatively. Many times the thing done poorly causes emotional reactions or pain in you and others. Distance yourself from the feelings and explore why the actions didn't work.

- ☐ **Learning from Interviewing Others**
  Interview others. Ask not only what they do, but how and why they do it. What do they think are the rules of thumb they are following? Where did they learn the behaviors? How do they keep them current? How do they monitor the effect they have on others?

- ☐ **Learning from Observing Others**
  Observe others. Find opportunities to observe without interacting with your model. This enables you to objectively study the person, note what he/she is doing or not doing, and compare that with what you would typically do in similar situations. Many times you can learn more by watching than asking. Your model may not be able to explain what he/she does or may be an unwilling teacher.

- ☐ **Learning from Remote Models**
  Many times you can learn from people not directly available to you. You can read a book about them, watch tapes of public figures, read analyses of them, etc. The principles of learning are the same. Ask yourself what they do well or poorly and deduce their rules of thumb.

Learning from Courses

- ☐ **Supervisory Courses**
  Most new supervisors go through an "Introduction to Supervision" type course. They are designed to teach the common practices a first-line supervisor needs to know to be effective. The content of most of those courses is standard. There is general agreement on the principles of effective supervision. There are two common problems: 1) Do the students have a strong motivation to learn? Do they know what they don't know? Is there any pain? Because motivated students with a need for the knowledge learn best, participants should have had some trying experiences and some supervisory pain and hardships before attending. 2) Are the instructors experienced supervisors? Have they practiced what they preach? Can they share powerful anecdotes to make key points? Can they answer questions credibly? If possible, select supervisory courses based on the instructors, since the content seems to be the much same for all such courses. Lastly, does the course offer the opportunity for practicing each skill? Does it contain simulations? Are there case studies you could easily identify with? Are there breakout groups? Is there opportunity for action learning? Search for the most interactive course.

- ☐ **Survey Courses**
  These are courses designed to give a general overview of an entire area (such as advertising), product or product line, division's activities, process (getting a product to market, Total Quality Management) or geography (doing business in "X"). These types of courses are good for general background and context.

SUGGESTED READINGS

Drucker, Peter F. *The Effective Executive.* New York: Harper & Row, 1996.

Drucker, Peter F. The Effective Executive [sound recording]. New York: AMACOM, 1983.

Levinson, Harry. *Career Mastery.* San Francisco: Berrett-Koehler Publishers, 1992.

Olesen, Erik. *12 Steps to Mastering the Winds of Change.* New York: Macmillan, 1993.

Stone, Florence M. and Randi T. Sachs. *The High-Value Manager – Developing the core competencies your organization needs.* New York: AMACOM, 1995.

117

OVERMANAGING

SECTION 1: YOUR DEVELOPMENT NEED(S)

A PROBLEM

- ☐ Overcontrols and meddles
- ☐ Doesn't empower others
- ☐ Doesn't get the most out of people
- ☐ Doesn't develop subordinates well
- ☐ Does too much of the work him/herself
- ☐ Is a poor delegator

NOT A PROBLEM

- ☐ Delegates and empowers
- ☐ Lets others finish their work once assigned
- ☐ Checks in infrequently unless there is a problem
- ☐ Assigns enough authority for people to make their own decisions
- ☐ Lets others contribute to how the work is to be done
- ☐ Works to do less personally and trust others more
- ☐ Usually helps only when needed or asked

SOME CAUSES

- ☐ Don't have any good people
- ☐ Excessively action oriented
- ☐ Impatient
- ☐ Isn't willing to trust others
- ☐ Know too much about the work
- ☐ Perfectionist
- ☐ Very control driven

THE MAP

Most of us really prefer depending upon ourselves to get important things done. It's probably more uncommon to comfortably delegate and empower. Overmanaging means you don't trust your people to perform against standards and on time. You may feel they are not qualified or that they are not motivated. Both of those, of course, are your responsibilities. The catch-22 is that the more time you spend managing and re-managing, the less time you will have left to do what you need to do and the less they will develop.

SECTION 2: LEARNING ON YOUR OWN

THESE SELF-DEVELOPMENT REMEDIES WILL HELP YOU BUILD YOUR SKILL(S)

SOME REMEDIES

☐ **1. If you are overmanaging because you don't think your people are good enough** to do what you need doing, look to the plan for *#25 Hiring and Staffing* and *#56 Sizing Up People* for tips on upgrading the selections you make. Look to *#13 Confronting Direct Reports* for help on making tough calls and taking actions, and look to *#19 Developing Direct Reports* for help in upgrading the skills level of your team. Any manager of a marginal team would have to overmanage to survive but that's a very poor long-term strategy.

☐ **2. If you are overmanaging because you are too busy to communicate** with your people about what you need and would rather do it yourself or delegate it and then monitor it to death, read *#18 Delegation*, *#27 Informing* and *#62 Time Management*. Poor communicators always have to take up more time managing.

☐ **3. Let your team help you.** Periodically, send out a memo asking each person whether there is anything he or she thinks he/she could do that you are now doing or monitoring too closely. Pick one or two things per person and empower them to do it on their own. Make sure the up front communication is adequate for them to perform well. Explain your standards – what the outcome should be, the key things that need to be taken care of, then ask them to figure out how to do it themselves.

☐ **4. If you are impatient and find yourself checking in too frequently,** set up a timetable with your people with agreed upon checkpoints and in-progress checks. Let them initiate this on a schedule you are comfortable with. Ask yourself who your most motivating bosses were. Chances are they gave you a lot of leeway, encouraged you to try things, were good sounding boards, and cheered your successes. Do what they did with you. *More help? – See #41 Patience.*

☐ **5. Are you hanging on to too much?** Are you a perfectionist, wanting everything to be just so? Do you have unrealistic expectations of others? Someone made you leader because you are probably better at doing what the team does than some or most of the members. Be careful to set the goals and objectives in a realistic and motivating manner. *More help? – See #35 Managing and Measuring Work.*

☐ **6. Do you delegate but withhold the power and authority to get the job done?** Delegating the work without the authority to make process or how-to decisions is de-motivating. People grow if they have a chance to decide and succeed or fail on their own. *More help? – See #18 Delegation.*

- ☐ **7. What skill do you have that you could pass on to others?** Ask yourself why this is a strength for you. What are the first items you would teach as the keys to help others form umbrellas for understanding? Watch others carefully for their reactions when teaching and coaching. What works and doesn't for you as a coach? Reveal things that people don't need to know to do their jobs, but which will be interesting to them – and help them feel valued.
- ☐ **8. Do you feel guilty handing out tough work to do?** Do you keep it yourself because you feel bad about giving them too much work? They would have to stay late or work on weekends to get it done. Most people enjoy being busy and on the move. If you think the workload is too much, ask. *More help? – See #36 Motivating Others.*
- ☐ **9. Do things go better when you are there** than when you are on a trip, at a meeting or on vacation? It should be the same. You should have informed and delegated in such a way that the work can be completed without any further guidance from you. *More help? – See #59* Managing Through *Systems*. It could also be that you are a one-on-one, face-to-face manager. You focus your attention on single tasks and on individuals one at a time. That means there is not a feeling of team or a greater purpose or shared mindset. In your absence, there are no left behind principles to follow and the team members can't help each other. *More help? – See #60* Building Effective *Teams.*
- ☐ **10. Read this only if your ratings would be – or are – OK to high on most of the preceding remedies and reference competencies.** Sometimes good managers overmanage, too. Are you so good and know so much that you overwhelm others and make them dependent on you? Have you become arrogant? Have you given up on passing on your knowledge and skills to your people? In this, switch to a teacher role and pay particular attention to *#18 Delegation* and *#19 Developing Direct Reports*.

SECTION 3: LEARNING FROM MORE FEEDBACK

THESE SOURCES WOULD GIVE YOU THE MOST ACCURATE AND DETAILED FEEDBACK ON YOUR SKILL(S)

- ☐ **Direct Reports**
  Across a variety of settings, your direct reports probably see you the most. They are the recipients of most of your managerial behaviors. They know your work. They can compare you with former bosses. Since they may hesitate to give you negative feedback, you have to set the atmosphere to make it easier for them. You have to ask.
- ☐ **Human Resource Professionals**
  Human Resource professionals have both a formal and informal feedback role. Since they have access to unique and confidential information, they can provide the right context for feedback you've

received. Sometimes they may be "directed" to give you feedback. Other times, they may pass on feedback just to be helpful to you.

- ☐ **Past Associates/Constituencies**
  When confronted with a present performance problem, some claim, "I wasn't like that before; it must be the current situation." When feedback is available from former associates, about 50% support that claim. In the other half of the cases, the people were like that before and probably didn't know it. It sometimes makes sense to access the past to clearly see the present.

SECTION 4: LEARNING FROM DEVELOP-IN-PLACE ASSIGNMENTS

THESE PART-TIME DEVELOP-IN-PLACE ASSIGNMENTS WILL HELP YOU BUILD YOUR SKILL(S)

- ☐ Create employee involvement teams.
- ☐ Manage an ad hoc, temporary group of people where the people in the group are towering experts but the temporary manager is not.
- ☐ Manage a project team of people who are older and more experienced than you.
- ☐ Manage something "remote," away from your location.
- ☐ Assign a project to a group with a tight deadline.
- ☐ Manage an ad hoc, temporary group of balky and resisting people through an unpopular change or project.
- ☐ Manage an ad hoc, temporary group including former peers to accomplish a task.
- ☐ Assemble an ad hoc team of diverse people to accomplish a difficult task.
- ☐ Take over for someone on vacation or a long trip.
- ☐ Build a multifunctional project team to tackle a common business issue or problem.

SECTION 5: LEARNING FROM FULL-TIME JOBS

THESE FULL-TIME JOBS OFFER THE OPPORTUNITY TO BUILD YOUR SKILL(S)

- ☐ **Chair of Projects/Task Forces**
  The core demands for qualifying as a Project/Task Force assignment are: 1) Full-time assignment. 2) Important and specific goal. 3) Tight deadline. 4) Success or failure will be evident. 5) High-visibility sponsor. 6) Learning something on the fly. 7) Must get others to cooperate. 8) Usually six months or more. Four types of Projects/Task Forces: 1) New ideas, products, services, or systems (e.g., product/service/program research and development, creation/installation/launch of a

new system, new programs like Total Quality Management, positive discipline). 2) Formal negotiations and relationships (e.g., acquisitions, divestitures, agreements, joint ventures; licensing arrangements, franchising; dealing with unions, governments, communities, charities, customers, and relocations). 3) Big one-time events (e.g., working on a major presentation for the board, organizing significant meetings or conferences, disaster/damage control teams; reorganizations, mergers, acquisitions, or relocations, working on visions, charters, strategies, other time-urgent issues and problems). 4) Troubleshooting (e.g., problems, disasters, crises, product/service failures, accidents, illegal activities, damage control in public relations goofs, shut downs, downsizings, layoffs, abrupt changes in leadership).

☐ **Influencing Without Authority**
The core demands to qualify as an Influence Without Authority are: 1) Significant challenge (e.g, start-up, fix-it, scope and/or scale assignment, strategic planning project, changes in management practices/ systems). 2) Insufficient direct authority to make it happen. 3) Tight deadlines. 4) Visible to significant others. 5) Sensitive politics.

☐ **Scale Assignments**
Core requirements to qualify as a Scale (size) shift assignment are: 1) Sizable jump-shift in the size of the job in areas like: number of layers in organization, size of budget, number of locations, volume of activity, tightness of deadlines. 2) Medium to low complexity; mostly repetitive and routine processes and procedures. 3) Stable staff and business. 4) Stable operations. 5) Often slow, steady growth.

☐ **Scope Assignments**
The core demands for a Scope (complexity) assignment are: 1) Significant increase in both internal and external scope or complexity. 2) Significant increase in visibility and/or bottom line responsibility. 3) Unfamiliar area, business, technology, or territory. Examples of Scope assignments involving shifts: 1) Switching into a new function/technology/business. 2) Moving to new organization. 3) Moving to overseas assignment. 4) Moving to new location. 5) Adding new products/ services. 6) Moving between headquarters/field. 7) Switches in ownership/top management of the unit/organization. Examples of Scope assignments involving "firsts": 1) First-time manager. 2) First-time managing managers. 3) First-time executive. 4) First-time overseas. 5) First-time headquarters/field. 6) First-time team leader. 7) First-time new technology/business/function. Scope assignments involving increased complexity: 1) Managing a significant expansion of an existing product or service. 2) Managing adding new products/service into an existing unit. 3) Managing a reorganized and more diverse unit. 4) Managing explosive growth. 5) Adding new technologies.

SECTION 6: LEARNING MORE FROM YOUR PLAN

THESE ADDITIONAL REMEDIES WILL HELP MAKE THIS DEVELOPMENT PLAN MORE EFFECTIVE FOR YOU

Learning to Learn Better

☐ **Monitoring Yourself More Closely and Getting off Your Autopilot**
Past habits are a mixed blessing, sometimes helping, sometimes not. To avoid putting yourself on "autopilot," think afresh about each situation before acting. Consistently monitor yourself with questions. Is this task different? Ask why you would repeat a past action. Are you avoiding anything, like taking a chance? Is there something new you might try?

☐ **Form An Advisory Group to Help You**
Assemble a one-time ad hoc group of people you respect and ask them for help solving or facing a significant issue. Outline what you know about it and ask the team to lay out a plan. Have them examine your thinking and suggest changes and improvements.

☐ **Envision Doing Something Well in a Group**
Take the people you want or need to be involved through a envisioning/creativity exercise to come up with different ideas and solutions.

Learning from Experience, Feedback and Other People

☐ **Using Multiple Models**
Who do you know who exemplifies how to do whatever your need is? Who, for example, personifies decisiveness or compassion or strategic agility? Think more broadly than your current job and colleagues. For example, clergy, friends, spouses or community leaders are also good sources for potential models. Select your models not on the basis of overall excellence or likability, but on the basis of the one towering strength (or glaring weakness) you are interested in. Even people who are well thought of usually have only one or two towering strengths (or glaring weaknesses). Ordinarily, you won't learn as much from the whole person as you will from one characteristic.

☐ **Being a Student of Others**
While many of us rely on others for information or advice, we do not really study the behavior of other people. Ask what a person does exceptionally well or poorly. What behaviors are particularly effective and ineffective for them? What works for them and what doesn't? As a student of others, you can deduce the rules of thumb for effective and ineffective behavior and include those in your own library. In comparing yourself with this person, in what areas could you most improve? What could you specifically do to improve in ways comfortable for you?

☐ **Learning from Interviewing Others**
Interview others. Ask not only what they do, but how and why they do it. What do they think are the rules of thumb they are following? Where did they learn the behaviors? How do they keep them current? How do they monitor the effect they have on others?

☐ **Learning from Observing Others**
Observe others. Find opportunities to observe without interacting with your model. This enables you to objectively study the person, note what he/she is doing or not doing, and compare that with what you would typically do in similar situations. Many times you can learn more by watching than asking. Your model may not be able to explain what he/she does or may be an unwilling teacher.

☐ **Consolidating What You Learn from People**
After using any source and/or method of learning from others, write down or mentally note the new rules of thumb and the principles involved. How will you remind yourself of the new behaviors in similar situations? How will you prevent yourself from reacting on "autopilot"? How could you share what you have learned from others?

Learning from Courses

☐ **Supervisory Courses**
Most new supervisors go through an "Introduction to Supervision" type course. They are designed to teach the common practices a first-line supervisor needs to know to be effective. The content of most of those courses is standard. There is general agreement on the principles of effective supervision. There are two common problems: 1) Do the students have a strong motivation to learn? Do they know what they don't know? Is there any pain? Because motivated students with a need for the knowledge learn best, participants should have had some trying experiences and some supervisory pain and hardships before attending. 2) Are the instructors experienced supervisors? Have they practiced what they preach? Can they share powerful anecdotes to make key points? Can they answer questions credibly? If possible, select supervisory courses based on the instructors, since the content seems to be the much same for all such courses. Lastly, does the course offer the opportunity for practicing each skill? Does it contain simulations? Are there case studies you could easily identify with? Are there breakout groups? Is there opportunity for action learning? Search for the most interactive course.

☐ **Sending Others to Courses**
If you are responsible for managing someone else's development and, as part of that, sending them to courses, prepare them beforehand. Don't send them as tourists. Meet with them before and after the course. Tell them why they need this course. Tell them what you expect them to learn. Give them feedback on why you think they need the

course. Agree ahead of time how you will measure and monitor learning after they return. If possible, offer a variety of courses for your employee to choose from. Have them give you a report shortly after they return. If appropriate, have them present what they learned to the rest of your staff. After they return, provide opportunities for using the new skills with safe cover and low risk. Give them practice time before expecting full exercise of the new skills. Be supportive during early unsteadiness. Give continuous feedback on progress.

SUGGESTED READINGS

Albright, Mary and Clay Carr. *101 biggest mistakes managers make and how to avoid them.* Paramus, N.J.: Prentice Hall, 1997.

Belker, Loren B. *The first-time manager.* New York: AMACOM, 1997.

Carr, Clay. *The new manager's survival manual.* New York: John Wiley & Sons, Inc., 1995.

Fuller, George. *The first-time supervisor's survival guide.* Englewood Cliffs, NJ: Prentice Hall, 1995.

Harvard Business Review. *On Managing People.* Boston: Harvard Business School Press, 1999.

Hunsaker, Phillip L. and Anthony J. Alessandra. *The art of managing people.* New York: Simon & Schuster, 1986, 1980.

Montgomery, Vickie. *The woman manager's troubleshooter: pinpointing the causes & cures of today's tough supervisory problems.* Englewood Cliffs, NJ: Prentice Hall, 1996.

Mullen, James X. *The simple art of greatness: building, managing and motivating a kick-ass workforce.* New York: Viking, 1995.

Robinson, Margot. *Egos & eggshells: managing for success in today's workplace.* Greensboro, NC: Stanton & Harper Books, 1993.

Simmons, Annette. *Territorial games: understanding and ending turf wars at work.* New York: American Management Association, 1998.

PERFORMANCE PROBLEMS

SECTION 1: YOUR DEVELOPMENT NEED(S)

A PROBLEM

- ☐ Does not consistently hit targets and objectives
- ☐ Doesn't produce results across a variety of situations

NOT A PROBLEM

- ☐ Consistently produces results
- ☐ Meets all goals and targets
- ☐ Plans and sets priorities well
- ☐ Is organized and gets things done on time and in time
- ☐ Has produced results under a variety of conditions

SOME CAUSES

- ☐ Don't deliver consistently
- ☐ Inexperienced
- ☐ New to the job
- ☐ Not bold or innovative
- ☐ Procrastinate
- ☐ Scramble at the last minute

THE MAP

Performance problems can come from a number of causes. Exactly what is getting in your way must be determined before you can do much about this. Something in the situation, the people dealt with or yourself, causes you not to deliver as expected and on time. People think you're not doing enough to get results.

SECTION 2: LEARNING ON YOUR OWN

THESE SELF-DEVELOPMENT REMEDIES WILL HELP YOU BUILD YOUR SKILL(S)

SOME REMEDIES

- ☐ **1. Priorities?** You don't have a correct set of priorities. Some people get results, but on the wrong things. Effective managers typically spend about half their time on two or three key priorities. What should you spend half your time on? Can you name five things that are less critical? If you can't, you're not differentiating well. Or even if you know the priorities, your team doesn't. You communicate that everything's important and has a deadline of yesterday. They see their jobs as 97 things that need to be done right now. To deal with this: ask yourself what would happen if they only did four or five things today? What would they be? Ask what the three things they spend the most time on are, and what they would be if we were doing things better? Find out what the 10–20% most time consuming activities are and either eliminate them or structure them through processes and policies to take less time. *More help? – See #50 Priority Setting.*

- ☐ **2. Procrastinate?** Are you a lifelong procrastinator? Do you perform best in crises and impossible deadlines? Do you wait until the last possible moment? If you do, you will miss some deadlines and performance targets. You might not produce consistent results. Some of your work will be marginal because you didn't have the time to do it right. You settled for a "B" when you could have gotten an "A" if you had one more day to work on it. Start earlier. Always do 10% of each task immediately after it is assigned so you can better gauge what it is going to take to finish the rest. Divide tasks and assignments into thirds or fourths and schedule time to do them spaced over the delivery period. Remember Murphy's Law. It takes 90% of the time to do 90% of the project, and another 90% of the time to finish the remaining 10%. Always leave more time than you think it's going to take. *More help? – See #47 Planning.*

- ☐ **3. Process?** Some don't know the best way to get things done. There is a well established set of best practices for getting work done efficiently and effectively. Formally they are known as Total Quality Management and Process Re-Engineering. If you are not disciplined in how you design work for yourself and others, buy one book on each of these topics. Go to one workshop on efficient and effective work design. *More help? – See #52 Process Management and #63 Total Quality Management/Re-Engineering.*

- ☐ **4. Organizing?** Are you always short resources? Always pulling things together on a shoe string? Getting results means getting and using resources. People. Money. Materials. Support. Time. Many times it involves getting resources you don't control. You have to beg, borrow but hopefully not steal. That means negotiating, bargaining, trading, cajoling, and influencing. What's the business case for the resources? What do I have to trade? How can I make it a win for everyone? *More help? – See #37 Negotiating and #38 Organizational Agility.*

- ☐ **5. Getting work done through others?** Some people are not good managers. Are you having trouble getting your team to work with you to get the results you need? You have the resources and the people but things just don't run well. You do too much work yourself. You don't delegate or empower. You don't communicate well. You don't motivate well. You don't plan well. You don't set priorities and goals well. If you are a struggling manager, there are well known and documented principles and practices of good managing. Do you share credit? Do you paint a clear picture of why this is important? Is their work challenging? Do you inspire or just hand out work? Read two books on managing. Go to one course on management. Get 360° feedback on your current management skills. Pick a few to work on. *More help? – See #18 Delegation, #20 Directing Others, #36 Motivating Others, and #60* Building Effective *Teams.*

☐ **6. Too new to the job?** Sometimes you can't produce results because you keep moving around from job to job and never have the time to get smart in the business of the unit. How about general business principles that would go across all jobs? Do you understand how businesses operate? Do you know what causes what in organizations? Do you know what's going on in the market? Do you know what future trends might be? If you are shaky on any of these, read *Business Week* regularly. Scan the *Harvard Business Review*. Subscribe to the *Wall Street Journal*. Watch a show or two on a cable business channel each week. *More help? – See #5 Business Acumen*. Never quite up to speed in the functional skills? Work on your ability to learn more quickly. Use seasoned pros in the technology to tutor you from the start. Hire a consultant. Delegate more. *More help? – See #32 Learning on the Fly, #61 Technical Learning, and #24 Functional/Technical Skills.*

☐ **7. Not bold enough?** Won't take a risk? Sometimes producing results involves pushing the envelope, taking chances and trying bold new initiatives. Doing those things leads to more misfires and mistakes. Treat any mistakes or failures as chances to learn. Nothing ventured, nothing gained. Up your risk comfort. Start small so you can recover quickly. Make it fun. Challenge yourself. See how creative and innovative you can be. *More help? – See #2* Dealing With *Ambiguity, #14 Creativity, and #28 Innovation Management.*

☐ **8. Stuck in old habits and comfortable ways?** You're a creature of habit. You do things too much the same way. You're not very flexible. Just as you use the same style, you gravitate toward the same tasks again and again. You've gotten stale. Shake things up. Off-work, force yourself to shift gears. Go from a civic meeting to a water fight with your kids, for example. Go for maximum variety at work. Take a risk, play it safe. Set yourself tasks that force you to shift gears such as being a spokesperson for your organization when tough questions are expected, making peace with an enemy or managing people who are novices at a task. If you already have these tasks as part of your job, use them to observe yourself and try new behavior. Switch approaches. Do something totally different next time. Have five different ways to get the same outcome. For example, to push a decision through, you could meet with stakeholders first, go to a key stakeholder, study and present the problem to a group, call a problem-solving session, or call in an outside expert. Be prepared to do them all when obstacles arise. Whatever you are doing, it doesn't seem to be working. It may have worked in the past but it's now time to change. *More help? – See #45 Personal Learning.*

☐ **9. Working across borders and boundaries?** You have trouble when you have to go outside your unit. This means that influence skills, understanding, and trading is the currency to use. Don't just ask for things; find some common ground where you can provide help, not just ask for it. What do the peers you're contacting need? Do you really know how they see the issue? Is it even important to them? How does what you're working on affect them? If it affects them negatively can you trade something, appeal to the common good, figure out some way to minimize the work – volunteering staff help, for example? Go into peer relationships with a trading mentality. To be seen as more cooperative, always explain your thinking and invite them to explain theirs. Generate a variety of possibilities first rather than stake out positions. Be tentative, allowing them room to customize the situation. Focus on common goals, priorities and problems. Invite criticism of your ideas. *More help? – See #42 Peer Relationships.*

☐ **10. The stress and strain.** Producing results day after day, quarter after quarter, year after year is pressureful. Nothing is ever good enough. Bar is always rising. Goals are set higher. Have to learn new ways and new methods. Lots of stress. Some people are energized by moderate stress. They actually work better. Some people are debilitated by stress. They decrease in productivity as stress increases. Dealing with stress and pressure is a known technology. Stress and pressure are actually in your head, not in the outside world. Some people are stressed by the same events others are energized about – losing a major account. Some people cry and some laugh at the same external event – someone slipping on a banana peel. Stress is how you look at events, not the events themselves. Dealing more effectively with stress involves reprogramming your interpretation of your work and about what you find stressful. There was a time in your life where spiders and snakes were life threatening and stressful to you. Are they now? *More help? – See #11 Composure and #107* Lack of *Composure.*

SECTION 3: LEARNING FROM MORE FEEDBACK

THESE SOURCES WOULD GIVE YOU THE MOST ACCURATE AND DETAILED FEEDBACK ON YOUR SKILL(S)

☐ **Boss's Boss(es)**

From a process standpoint, your boss's boss probably has the most influence and control over your progress. He/she has a broader perspective, has more access to data, and stands at the center of decisions about you. To know what he/she thinks, without having to violate the canons of corporate due process to get that information, would be quite useful.

☐ **Direct Boss**

Your direct boss has important information about you, your performance, and your prospects. The challenge is to get this information.

There are formal processes (e.g., performance appraisals). There are day-to-day opportunities. To help, signal your boss that you want and can handle direct and timely feedback. Many bosses have trouble giving feedback, so you will have to work at it over a period of time.

☐ **Human Resource Professionals**
Human Resource professionals have both a formal and informal feedback role. Since they have access to unique and confidential information, they can provide the right context for feedback you've received. Sometimes they may be "directed" to give you feedback. Other times, they may pass on feedback just to be helpful to you.

☐ **Internal and External Customers**
Customers interact with you as a person and as a supplier or vendor of products and services. You're important to them because you can either help address and solve their problems or stand in their way. As customer service and Total Quality programs gain importance, clients and customers become a more prominent source of feedback.

☐ **Natural Mentors**
Natural mentors have a special relationship with you and are interested in your success and your future. Since they are usually not in your direct chain of command, you can have more open, relaxed, and fruitful discussions about yourself and your career prospects. They can be a very important source for candid or critical feedback others may not give you.

☐ **Past Associates/Constituencies**
When confronted with a present performance problem, some claim, "I wasn't like that before; it must be the current situation." When feedback is available from former associates, about 50% support that claim. In the other half of the cases, the people were like that before and probably didn't know it. It sometimes makes sense to access the past to clearly see the present.

SECTION 4: LEARNING FROM DEVELOP-IN-PLACE ASSIGNMENTS

THESE PART-TIME DEVELOP-IN-PLACE ASSIGNMENTS WILL HELP YOU BUILD YOUR SKILL(S)

☐ Install a new process or system (computer system, new policies, new process, new procedures, etc.).

☐ Plan an off-site meeting, conference, convention, trade show, event, etc.

☐ Plan for and start up something small (secretarial pool, athletic program, suggestion system, program, etc.).

☐ Help shut down a plant, regional office, product line, business, operation, etc.

- ☐ Take on a tough and undoable project, one where others who have tried it have failed.
- ☐ Work on a process-simplification team to take steps and costs out of a process.
- ☐ Manage the purchase of a major product, equipment, materials, program, or system.
- ☐ Visit Malcolm Baldrige National Quality Award or Deming Prize winners and report back on your findings, showing how they would help your organization.
- ☐ Assign a project to a group with a tight deadline.
- ☐ Manage a dissatisfied internal or external customer; troubleshoot a performance or quality problem with a product or service.

SECTION 5: LEARNING FROM FULL-TIME JOBS

THESE FULL-TIME JOBS OFFER THE OPPORTUNITY TO BUILD YOUR SKILL(S)

☐ **Chair of Projects/Task Forces**

The core demands for qualifying as a Project/Task Force assignment are: 1) Full-time assignment. 2) Important and specific goal. 3) Tight deadline. 4) Success or failure will be evident. 5) High-visibility sponsor. 6) Learning something on the fly. 7) Must get others to cooperate. 8) Usually six months or more. Four types of Projects/Task Forces: 1) New ideas, products, services, or systems (e.g., product/service/program research and development, creation/installation/launch of a new system, new programs like Total Quality Management, positive discipline). 2) Formal negotiations and relationships (e.g., acquisitions, divestitures, agreements, joint ventures; licensing arrangements, franchising; dealing with unions, governments, communities, charities, customers, and relocations). 3) Big one-time events (e.g., working on a major presentation for the board, organizing significant meetings or conferences, disaster/damage control teams; reorganizations, mergers, acquisitions, or relocations, working on visions, charters, strategies, other time-urgent issues and problems). 4) Troubleshooting (e.g., problems, disasters, crises, product/service failures, accidents, illegal activities, damage control in public relations goofs, shut downs, downsizings, layoffs, abrupt changes in leadership).

☐ **Fix-its/Turnarounds**

The core demands to qualify as a Fix-it or Turnaround assignment are: 1) Cleaning up a mess. 2) Serious people issues/problems like credibility/performance/morale. 3) Tight deadline. 4) Serious business performance failure. 5) Last chance to fix. Four Types of Fix-its/Turnarounds: 1) Fixing a failed business/unit involving taking control, stopping losses, managing damage, planning the turnaround, dealing with people problems, installing new processes and systems, and rebuilding the spirit and performance of the unit. 2) Managing sizable disasters like mishandled labor negotiations and strikes, thefts, history of significant business losses, poor staff, failed leadership, hidden problems, fraud, public relations nightmares, etc. 3) Significant reorganization and restructuring (e.g., stabilizing the business, reforming unit, introducing new systems, making people changes, resetting strategy and tactics). 4) Significant system/process breakdown (e.g., MIS, financial coordination processes, audits, standards, etc.) across units requiring working to change something from a distant position, providing advice and counsel, and installing or implementing a major process improvement or system change outside your own unit and/or with customers outside the organization.

☐ **Scope Assignments**
The core demands for a Scope (complexity) assignment are: 1) Significant increase in both internal and external scope or complexity. 2) Significant increase in visibility and/or bottom line responsibility. 3) Unfamiliar area, business, technology, or territory. Examples of Scope assignments involving shifts: 1) Switching into a new function/technology/business. 2) Moving to new organization. 3) Moving to overseas assignment. 4) Moving to new location. 5) Adding new products/ services. 6) Moving between headquarters/field. 7) Switches in ownership/top management of the unit/organization. Examples of Scope assignments involving "firsts": 1) First-time manager. 2) First-time managing managers. 3) First-time executive. 4) First-time overseas. 5) First-time headquarters/field. 6) First-time team leader. 7) First-time new technology/business/function. Scope assignments involving increased complexity: 1) Managing a significant expansion of an existing product or service. 2) Managing adding new products/service into an existing unit. 3) Managing a reorganized and more diverse unit. 4) Managing explosive growth. 5) Adding new technologies.

☐ **Start-ups**
The core demands to qualify as a start from scratch are: 1) Starting something new for you and/or for the organization. 2) Forging a new team. 3) Creating new systems/facilities/staffs/programs/procedures. 4) Contextual adversity (e.g., uncertainty, government regulation, unions, difficult environment). Seven types of start from scratches: 1) Planning, building, hiring, and managing (e.g., building a new facility, opening up a new location, moving a unit or company). 2) Heading something new (e.g., new product, new service, new line of business, new department/function, major new program). 3) Take over a group/ product/service/program that had existed for less than a year and was off to a fast start. 4) Establishing overseas operations. 5) Major new designs for existing systems. 6) Moving a successful program from one unit to another. 7) Installing a new organization-wide process as a full-time job (e.g., like Total Quality).

SECTION 6: LEARNING MORE FROM YOUR PLAN

THESE ADDITIONAL REMEDIES WILL HELP MAKE THIS DEVELOPMENT PLAN MORE EFFECTIVE FOR YOU

Learning to Learn Better

- ☐ **Analyze Your Past Failures for Insights and Learnings**
  Field-strip your mistakes and failures; ask what you did that contributed to the negative outcome; how could it have been avoided; how much was due to the context; what lessons and rules of thumb can you take away from the mistake or failure?
- ☐ **Learn to Compensate for a Weakness**
  Some weaknesses just aren't correctable or at least are not worth the effort. Instead of ignoring what you can't change, try to create tactics to compensate for these weaknesses; be alert when these are needed. Use other people better than you to compensate for you in your weak areas; use a strength against your weakness.
- ☐ **Envision Yourself Succeeding**
  Examine the image of success in detail: what you are doing, what you are feeling, how you are reacting to others, how others are reacting to you, how the parts fit together. Can you then play that out in the real situation and get to the same outcome?
- ☐ **Commit to a Tight Timeframe to Accomplish Something**
  Set some specific goals and tighter than usual timeframes for yourself and go after them with all you've got. Push yourself to stick to the plan; get more done than usual by adhering to a tight plan.

Learning from Experience, Feedback and Other People

- ☐ **Using Multiple Models**
  Who do you know who exemplifies how to do whatever your need is? Who, for example, personifies decisiveness or compassion or strategic agility? Think more broadly than your current job and colleagues. For example, clergy, friends, spouses or community leaders are also good sources for potential models. Select your models not on the basis of overall excellence or likability, but on the basis of the one towering strength (or glaring weakness) you are interested in. Even people who are well thought of usually have only one or two towering strengths (or glaring weaknesses). Ordinarily, you won't learn as much from the whole person as you will from one characteristic.
- ☐ **Learning from Ineffective Behavior**
  Seeing things done poorly can be a very potent source of learning for you, especially if the behavior or action affects others negatively. Many times the thing done poorly causes emotional reactions or pain in you and others. Distance yourself from the feelings and explore why the actions didn't work.

- ☐ **Learning from Observing Others**
  Observe others. Find opportunities to observe without interacting with your model. This enables you to objectively study the person, note what he/she is doing or not doing, and compare that with what you would typically do in similar situations. Many times you can learn more by watching than asking. Your model may not be able to explain what he/she does or may be an unwilling teacher.
- ☐ **Openness to Feedback**
  Nothing discourages feedback more than defensiveness, resistance, irritation, and excuses. People don't like giving feedback anyway, and much less to those who don't listen or are unreceptive. To help the feedback giver, be open, listen, ask for examples and details, take notes, keep a journal, and thank them for their interest.
- ☐ **Learning from Bad Things that Happen**
  Bad things happen to everyone, sometimes because of what we do and sometimes with no help from us. We all have bad bosses, bad staffs, impossible and hopeless situations, impossible tasks, and unintended consequences. Aside from the trouble these bad things cause for you, the key is how can you learn from each of them.

Learning from Courses

- ☐ **Strategic Courses**
  There are a number of courses designed to stretch minds to prepare for future challenges. They include topics such as Workforce Diversity 2000, globalization, the European Union, competitive competencies and strategies, etc. Quality depends upon the following three factors: 1) The quality of the staff. Are they qualified? Are they respected in their fields? Are they strategic "gurus"? 2) The quality of the participants. Are they the kind of people you could learn from? 3) The quality of the setting. Is it comfortable and free from distractions? Can you learn there?

SUGGESTED READINGS

Drucker, Peter F. *Managing for the Future.* New York: Dutton, 1992.

Drucker, Peter F. *Managing for the Future [sound recording].* Beverly Hills, CA: Dove Audio, 1992.

Drucker, Peter F. *Managing for Results.* New York: HarperCollins, 1993.

Drucker, Peter F. *Managing for Results [sound recording].* New York: AMACOM, 1983.

Peters, Tom. *Thriving on Chaos.* New York: Knopf, Inc., 1987.

continued

Peters, Tom. *Thriving on Chaos [sound recording].* New York: Random House, 1987.

Ulrich, David, Jack Zenger, Norman Smallwood. *Results-based leadership.* Boston, MA: Harvard Business School Press, 1999.

119

POLITICAL MISSTEPS

SECTION 1: YOUR DEVELOPMENT NEED(S)

A PROBLEM

- ☐ Can't get things done in complex political settings and environments
- ☐ Lacks sensitivity to people and organizational politics
- ☐ Doesn't recognize political due process requirements
- ☐ Says and does the wrong things
- ☐ Shares sensitive information and opinions with the wrong people

NOT A PROBLEM

- ☐ Is politically smooth and noiseless;
- ☐ Reads individuals and groups well; knows how they are effected
- ☐ Modifies approach when resistance is met
- ☐ Keeps confidences
- ☐ Can maneuver through rough water without getting wet
- ☐ Uses multiple ways to get things done
- ☐ Adjusts to the realities of the political situation
- ☐ Counsels others on political approaches
- ☐ Usually knows the right thing to do and say

SOME CAUSES

- ☐ Competitive with peers
- ☐ Don't read others or their interests well
- ☐ May be too candid to curry favor
- ☐ May share wrong/sensitive information
- ☐ Misunderstanding of what political savvy is
- ☐ No patience with due process
- ☐ Poor impulse control
- ☐ Poor interpersonal skills
- ☐ Poor negotiator
- ☐ Seen as a strident advocate

THE MAP

Organizations are a complex maze of constituencies, issues and rivalries peopled by strong egos, sensitivities and empire protectors. People who are politically savvy accept this as the human condition and deal with it by considering the impact of what they say and do on others. This is not to be confused with "political," which is a polite term for not being trusted or lacking in substance; political savvy involves getting things done in the maze with the minimum of noise. Political mistakes come in a variety of shapes and sizes. The most common is saying things that you shouldn't. This comes in two shapes – you knew it was wrong but you couldn't hold it back, or you didn't know it was wrong to say and were surprised at the reaction. Next are actions that are politically out of line and not right for the context. Worst are politically unacceptable moves, initiatives, tactics and strategies. You tried to get something done in the organization and went about it in the wrong way. Last are unnecessary conflicts, tensions, misunderstandings and rivalries created because you took after a specific person or group.

SECTION 2: LEARNING ON YOUR OWN

THESE SELF-DEVELOPMENT REMEDIES WILL HELP YOU BUILD YOUR SKILL(S)

SOME REMEDIES

- ☐ **1. Impulse control.** Many people get into political trouble because they have a lot of trouble holding things back. It's not that they didn't know what they were about to say was going to cause noise, they just have weak impulse control. They say almost everything that occurs to them to say. It's even possible that others in the room or in the meeting were thinking the same thing; the difference is that they kept it to themselves. When you dump everything before you put it through a political filter, much of what you say will cause noise and will be seen as poor political judgment by others. One rule is to let others speak first and follow their lead before you dump. *More help? – See #11 Composure and #41 Patience.*

- ☐ **2. Humor.** Many people get into political trouble with their humor. Times have changed drastically in the past decade. Humor that was seen as positive 10 years ago in organizations is now politically unacceptable. The rules now are real simple. Any humor that hurts others, demeans others, or makes fun of the difficulties others are having is out. No humor that is critical or sarcastic is acceptable. No ribald or off-color humor. No ethnic humor. No gender humor. No religious humor. No humor about people's disabilities. No humor about people in other countries. What's left? You can tell clean jokes, make fun of yourself, tell funny stories, and laugh with others. *More help? – See #26 Humor.*

- ☐ **3. Attitudes and beliefs.** Many people confuse the terms political savvy and being political. When someone criticizes you for not being political, you might interpret it as the bad political. Being bad political means that your motives should not be trusted. Being bad political means saying one thing and meaning another. It means being devious and scheming. Being politically savvy means saying and doing things that fit into the commonly held beliefs people have around you about what's appropriate and wise and what is not. It's about a set of standards most around you would agree to. Being politically savvy means you can transact with others and get things done in the maze with minimum noise and without triggering an unnecessary negative reaction from others.

☐ **4. Political due process.** In any culture or organization, there are multiple ways you can get things done. You could use a direct attack. You could get an ally first. You could send in a more acceptable substitute for yourself. Some of these tactics are more effective and acceptable than others. Some people get into trouble because they treat all situations the same. They don't do any research about the most effective ways to get things done for each event. People who are politically savvy operate from the outside – audience, person, group, organization – in. They pick their pace, style, tone and tactics based upon an evaluation of what would work best in each situation. We all have a number of ways in which we can behave if we want to. It's the one-trick ponies that get into political trouble because they don't adjust what they say and do to each audience. *More help? – See #15 Customer Focus and #45 Personal Learning.*

☐ **5. The special case of candor.** Candor can be a mission-critical requirement in a 9 a.m. meeting and politically unwise and unacceptable in a 10 a.m. meeting. Many people get themselves in political trouble with either too much candor that ends up hurting others and causing noise, or too little candor seen as holding back something important. Many often say, "I just say what I think. I've always believed in saying exactly what I mean. Consequences be damned. If they don't like it, they shouldn't have asked me about it." While that might get good marks for integrity, it would fail the political savvy test. Each situation must be examined on the candor scale. Are the right people here? Is this the best time for candor? Should I let someone else start before I do? Did the speaker who asked for candor really mean it? *More help? – See #56 Sizing Up People and #64 Understanding Others.*

☐ **6. Understanding the politics of the organization.** Who are the movers and shakers in the organization? Who are the major gatekeepers who control the flow of resources, information and decisions? Who are the guides and the helpers? Get to know them better. Do lunch. Who are the major resisters and stoppers? Try to avoid or go around them or make peace with them. Every maze has its solution. Being politically savvy means finding that least distant path through the organizational maze. *More help? – See #38 Organizational Agility.*

☐ **7. Impropriety.** Are you sharing things inappropriately to cement a relationship, to get something you need, to feel like an important insider, or because you just don't think it through? Monitor yourself closely and ask these questions: "Why am I sharing this? Does it move a problem along? Do people really need to know this? Will this make someone else look bad or will it be obvious where I got it? Am I name dropping? Have I labeled facts as facts and opinions as opinions? Will this be considered grousing, gossiping or cutting down another person or group? In the worst case how could this person use this information that would reflect badly on me?" A general rule of thumb is you can be as candid as you like as long as comments refer to specific problems/issues and you're not violating confidences and the person you are giving the information to can be trusted.

☐ **8. Gossiping.** A lot of political noise comes from sharing private views of others in the wrong settings and with the wrong people. All things come around that go around. In closed organizations, people quickly find out what you have said about them. If you are having trouble with this, the simplest rule is never to share any negative information about another person unless it is a formal evaluation process in the organization.

☐ **9. In the special case of dealing with top management,** sensitivities are high, egos are big, sensitivity traps are set and tensions can be severe. There is a lot of room for making statements or acting in ways that would be seen as exhibiting poor political judgment. There usually isn't a second chance to make a good first impression. *More help? – See #8 Comfort Around Higher Management.*

☐ **10. Strident advocates don't usually fare well in organizations** because their perspectives are seen as rigid and narrow. To avoid being seen this way, make the business or organizational case first. Be more tentative than you actually are so others have room to get comfortable and negotiate and bargain. People who have trouble with this state things in such an extreme that others are turned off and can't save face even if they agree with more than 50% of what you are pushing for. *More help? – See #37 Negotiating.*

SECTION 3: LEARNING FROM MORE FEEDBACK

THESE SOURCES WOULD GIVE YOU THE MOST ACCURATE AND DETAILED FEEDBACK ON YOUR SKILL(S)

☐ **Boss's Boss(es)**
From a process standpoint, your boss's boss probably has the most influence and control over your progress. He/she has a broader perspective, has more access to data, and stands at the center of decisions about you. To know what he/she thinks, without having to violate the canons of corporate due process to get that information, would be quite useful.

☐ **Direct Boss**
Your direct boss has important information about you, your performance, and your prospects. The challenge is to get this information. There are formal processes (e.g., performance appraisals). There are day-to-day opportunities. To help, signal your boss that you want and can handle direct and timely feedback. Many bosses have trouble giving feedback, so you will have to work at it over a period of time.

- ☐ **Human Resource Professionals**
  Human Resource professionals have both a formal and informal feedback role. Since they have access to unique and confidential information, they can provide the right context for feedback you've received. Sometimes they may be "directed" to give you feedback. Other times, they may pass on feedback just to be helpful to you.

- ☐ **Natural Mentors**
  Natural mentors have a special relationship with you and are interested in your success and your future. Since they are usually not in your direct chain of command, you can have more open, relaxed, and fruitful discussions about yourself and your career prospects. They can be a very important source for candid or critical feedback others may not give you.

- ☐ **Past Associates/Constituencies**
  When confronted with a present performance problem, some claim, "I wasn't like that before; it must be the current situation." When feedback is available from former associates, about 50% support that claim. In the other half of the cases, the people were like that before and probably didn't know it. It sometimes makes sense to access the past to clearly see the present.

SECTION 4: LEARNING FROM DEVELOP-IN-PLACE ASSIGNMENTS

THESE PART-TIME DEVELOP-IN-PLACE ASSIGNMENTS WILL HELP YOU BUILD YOUR SKILL(S)

- ☐ Integrate diverse systems, processes, or procedures across decentralized and/or dispersed units.
- ☐ Manage the renovation of an office, floor, building, meeting room, warehouse, etc.
- ☐ Plan a new site for a building (plant, field office, headquarters, etc.).
- ☐ Manage an ad hoc, temporary group of people where the people in the group are towering experts but the temporary manager is not.
- ☐ Manage an ad hoc, temporary group of people involved in tackling a fix-it or turnaround project.
- ☐ Manage the interface between consultants and the organization on a critical assignment.
- ☐ Prepare and present a proposal of some consequence to top management.
- ☐ Manage the assigning/allocating of office space in a contested situation.
- ☐ Work on a team that's deciding who to keep and who to let go in a layoff, shutdown, delayering, or divestiture.

SECTION 5: LEARNING FROM FULL-TIME JOBS

THESE FULL-TIME JOBS OFFER THE OPPORTUNITY TO BUILD YOUR SKILL(S)

☐ **Chair of Projects/Task Forces**
The core demands for qualifying as a Project/Task Force assignment are: 1) Full-time assignment. 2) Important and specific goal. 3) Tight deadline. 4) Success or failure will be evident. 5) High-visibility sponsor. 6) Learning something on the fly. 7) Must get others to cooperate. 8) Usually six months or more. Four types of Projects/Task Forces: 1) New ideas, products, services, or systems (e.g., product/service/program research and development, creation/installation/launch of a new system, new programs like Total Quality Management, positive discipline). 2) Formal negotiations and relationships (e.g., acquisitions, divestitures, agreements, joint ventures; licensing arrangements, franchising; dealing with unions, governments, communities, charities, customers, and relocations). 3) Big one-time events (e.g., working on a major presentation for the board, organizing significant meetings or conferences, disaster/damage control teams; reorganizations, mergers, acquisitions, or relocations, working on visions, charters, strategies, other time-urgent issues and problems). 4) Troubleshooting (e.g., problems, disasters, crises, product/service failures, accidents, illegal activities, damage control in public relations goofs, shut downs, downsizings, layoffs, abrupt changes in leadership).

☐ **Influencing Without Authority**
The core demands to qualify as an Influence Without Authority are: 1) Significant challenge (e.g, start-up, fix-it, scope and/or scale assignment, strategic planning project, changes in management practices/systems). 2) Insufficient direct authority to make it happen. 3) Tight deadlines. 4) Visible to significant others. 5) Sensitive politics.

☐ **Line To Staff Switches**
The core demands to qualify as a Line to Staff switch are: 1) Intellectually/strategically demanding. 2) Highly visible to others. 3) New area/perspective/method/culture/function. 4) Moving away from a bottom line. 5) Moving from field to headquarters. 6) Exposure to high-level executives. Examples: 1) Business/strategic planning. 2) Heading a staff department. 3) Assistant to/chief of staff to a senior executive. 4) Head of a task force. 5) Human resources role.

SECTION 6: LEARNING MORE FROM YOUR PLAN

THESE ADDITIONAL REMEDIES WILL HELP MAKE THIS DEVELOPMENT PLAN MORE EFFECTIVE FOR YOU

Learning to Learn Better

☐ **Monitoring Yourself More Closely and Getting off Your Autopilot**
Past habits are a mixed blessing, sometimes helping, sometimes not. To avoid putting yourself on "autopilot," think afresh about each situation

before acting. Consistently monitor yourself with questions. Is this task different? Ask why you would repeat a past action. Are you avoiding anything, like taking a chance? Is there something new you might try?

- ☐ **Edit Your Thinking On-Line Before You Talk**
  Edit your thinking as you go; ask why you think the way you do; ask common questions: "Am I avoiding anything? Am I objectively reading the facts? Am I considering others? Are my feelings helping or blocking? How would others I respect think? Would others around me think the same? Is my past helping or hurting?"

- ☐ **Rehearse Successful Tactics/Strategies/Actions**
  Mentally rehearse how you will act before going into the situation. Try to anticipate how others will react, what they will say, and how you'll respond. Check out the best and worst cases; play out both scenes. Check your feelings in conflict or worst-case situations; rehearse staying under control.

- ☐ **Pre-sell an Idea to a Key Stakeholder**
  Identify the key stakeholders – those who will be the most affected by your actions or the most resistant, or whose support you will most need. Collect the information each will find persuasive; marshal your arguments and try to pre-sell your conclusions, recommendations, and solutions.

Learning from Experience, Feedback and Other People

- ☐ **Using Multiple Models**
  Who do you know who exemplifies how to do whatever your need is? Who, for example, personifies decisiveness or compassion or strategic agility? Think more broadly than your current job and colleagues. For example, clergy, friends, spouses or community leaders are also good sources for potential models. Select your models not on the basis of overall excellence or likability, but on the basis of the one towering strength (or glaring weakness) you are interested in. Even people who are well thought of usually have only one or two towering strengths (or glaring weaknesses). Ordinarily, you won't learn as much from the whole person as you will from one characteristic.

- ☐ **Learning from Bosses**
  Bosses can be an excellent and ready source for learning. All bosses do some things exceptionally well and other things poorly. Distance your feelings from the boss/direct report relationship and study things that work and things that don't work for your boss. What would you have done? What could you use, and what should you avoid?

- ☐ **Learning from Observing Others**
  Observe others. Find opportunities to observe without interacting with your model. This enables you to objectively study the person, note what he/she is doing or not doing, and compare that with what you

would typically do in similar situations. Many times you can learn more by watching than asking. Your model may not be able to explain what he/she does or may be an unwilling teacher.

☐ **Learning from Bad Bosses**
First, what does he/she do so well to make him/her your boss? (Even bad bosses have strengths). Then, ask what makes this boss bad for you. Is it his/her behavior? Attitude? Values? Philosophy? Practices? Style? What is the source of the conflict? Why do you react as you do? Do others react the same? How are you part of the problem? What do you do that triggers your boss? If you wanted to, could you reduce the conflict or make it go away by changing something you do? Is there someone around you who doesn't react like you? How are they different? What can you learn from them? What is your emotional reaction to this boss? Why do you react like that? What can you do to cope with these feelings? Can you avoid reacting out of anger and frustration? Can you find something positive about the situation? Can you use someone else as a buffer? Can you learn from your emotions? What lasting lessons of managing others can you take away from this experience? What won't you do as a manager? What will you do differently? How could you teach these principles you've learned to others by the use of this example?

☐ **Learning from Bad Situations**
All of us will find ourselves in bad situations from time to time. Good intentions gone bad. Impossible tasks and goals. Hopeless projects. Even though you probably can't perform well, the key is to at least take away some lessons and insights. How did things get to be this way? What factors led to the impasse? How can you make the best of a bad situation? How can you neutralize the negative elements? How can you get the most out of yourself and your staff under the chilling situation? What can you salvage? How can you use coping strategies to minimize the negatives? How can you avoid these situations going forward? In bad situations: 1) Be resourceful. Get the most you can out of the situation. 2) Try to deduce why things got to be that way. 3) Learn from both the situation you inherited and how you react to it. 4) Integrate what you learn into your future behavior.

Learning from Courses

☐ **Strategic Courses**
There are a number of courses designed to stretch minds to prepare for future challenges. They include topics such as Workforce Diversity 2000, globalization, the European Union, competitive competencies and strategies, etc. Quality depends upon the following three factors: 1) The quality of the staff. Are they qualified? Are they respected in their fields? Are they strategic "gurus"? 2) The quality of the participants. Are they the kind of people you could learn from? 3) The quality

of the setting. Is it comfortable and free from distractions? Can you learn there?

SUGGESTED READING

Alessandra, Tony Ph.D. and Michael J. O'Connor, Ph.D. *The Platinum Rule.* New York: Warner Books, 1996

Aubuchon, Norbert. *The Anatomy of Persuasion.* New York: AMACOM, 1997.

Birnbaum, Jeffrey H. The lobbyists: how influence peddlers get their way in Washington. New York: Times Books, 1992.

Derber, Charles. *Corporation nation: how corporations are taking over our lives and what we can do about it.* New York: St. Martin's Press, 1998.

DuBrin, Andrew J. *Winning office politics: DuBrin's guide for the 90's.* Englewood Cliffs, NJ: Prentice Hall, 1990.

Edel, T. R. *Wake me when it's time to work: surviving meetings, office games, and the people who love them.* Houston, TX: Cashman Dudley, 1999.

Gunlicks, L. F. (Lynn F.). *The Machiavellian manager's handbook for success.* Washington, D.C.: Libey Pub.; Lanham, MD: Distributed to the trade by National Book Network, 1993.

Kissinger, Henry. *Diplomacy.* New York: Simon & Schuster, 1994.

Korten, David C. *When Corporations Rule The World.* San Francisco: Berrett-Koehler Publishers, 1995.

Lareau, William. *Dancing with the dinosaur: learning to live in the corporate jungle.* Clinton, NJ: New Win Publishing, 1994.

Machiavelli, Niccolò. The prince. Translated by W.K.Marriott. Introd. by Herbert Butterfield. [Abridged ed.]. Ann Arbor, MI: J. W. Edwards, [1946] [1968,1958]

Manchester, William. *On Mencken: Essays.* New York: Knopf, 1980.

Parekh, Bhikhu. *Gandhi's Political Philosophy.* Notre Dame, IN: University of Notre Dame Press, 1989.

Rogers, Will. [edited by] Bryan B. Sterling and Frances N. Sterling. *Will Rogers' World: America's foremost political humorist comments on the twenties and thirties–and eighties and nineties.* New York: M. Evans, 1989

continued

Roosevelt, Franklin D., Buhite, Russell D. and David W. Levy, Editors. *FDR's Fireside Chats.* Norman, Oklahoma: University of Oklahoma Press, 1992.

Rosner, Bob. *Working wounded: advice that adds insight to injury.* New York: Warner Books, 1998.

APPENDIX A

MY PERSONAL DEVELOPMENT PLAN

SECTION 1 – MY BEFORE AND AFTER PICTURE

SECTION 1A – SOME CAUSES FOR ME

SECTION 1B – NEW LEARNINGS FROM "THE MAP" FOR ME

SECTION 2 – LEARNING ON MY OWN

SECTION 2A – TAILORING THE REMEDIES

SECTION 3 – LEARNING FROM FEEDBACK
SOURCES FOR ME TO ASK ABOUT MY NEEDS

SECTION 3A – NOTES ON BEST SOURCES FOR FEEDBACK

SECTION 4 – LEARNING FROM DEVELOP-IN-PLACE ASSIGNMENTS

SECTION 5 – LEARNING FROM FULL TIME JOBS
JOBS THAT WILL HELP ME DEVELOP MY SKILLS

SECTION 5A – MY PLAN FOR JOBS

SECTION 6 – LEARNING MORE FROM MY PLAN

SECTION 1 – MY BEFORE AND AFTER PICTURE

Look to the Unskilled Definitions (from – I am more like this now) and the Skilled Definitions (to – I would like to be more like this in the future).

1. I want to go from: ____________________

   ____

   ____

   To looking and acting more like: ____________________

   ____

   ____

2. From: ____________________

   ____

   ____

   To: ____________________

   ____

   ____

3. From: ____________________

   ____

   ____

   To: ____________________

   ____

   ____

4. From: ____________________

   ____

   ____

   To: ____________________

   ____

   ____

5. From: ____________________

   ____

   ____

   To: ____________________

   ____

   ____

SECTION 1 – MY BEFORE AND AFTER PICTURE
Look to the Unskilled Definitions (from – I am more like this now) and the Skilled Definitions (to – I would like to be more like this in the future).

1. I want to go from: ______________________________

____

____

To looking and acting more like: ______________________________

____

____

2. From: ______________________________

____

____

To: ______________________________

____

____

3. From: ______________________________

____

____

To: ______________________________

____

____

4. From: ______________________________

____

____

To: ______________________________

____

____

5. From: ______________________________

____

____

To: ______________________________

____

____

SECTION 1 – MY BEFORE AND AFTER PICTURE
Look to the Unskilled Definitions (from – I am more like this now) and the Skilled Definitions (to – I would like to be more like this in the future).

6. From: ______________________________

____

____

To: ______________________________

____

____

7. From: ______________________________

____

____

To: ______________________________

____

____

8. From: ______________________________

____

____

To: ______________________________

____

____

9. From: ______________________________

____

____

To: ______________________________

____

____

10. From: ______________________________

____

____

To: ______________________________

____

____

SECTION 1 – MY BEFORE AND AFTER PICTURE

Look to the Unskilled Definitions (from – I am more like this now) and the Skilled Definitions (to – I would like to be more like this in the future).

6. From: ________________________________

   To: ________________________________

7. From: ________________________________

   To: ________________________________

8. From: ________________________________

   To: ________________________________

9. From: ________________________________

   To: ________________________________

10. From: ________________________________

   To: ________________________________

SECTION 1A – SOME CAUSES FOR ME
Why am I like this? Why do I do things this way?
Look to "Some Causes" for clues.

1.Cause?: ______________________________

Comments: ______________________________

____

____

____

2.Cause?: ______________________________

Comments: ______________________________

____

____

____

3.Cause?: ______________________________

Comments: ______________________________

____

____

____

4.Cause?: ______________________________

Comments: ______________________________

____

____

____

5.Cause?: ______________________________

Comments: ______________________________

____

____

____

SECTION 1A – SOME CAUSES FOR ME
Why am I like this? Why do I do things this way?
Look to "Some Causes" for clues.

1.Cause?: ______

Comments: ______

2.Cause?: ______

Comments: ______

3.Cause?: ______

Comments: ______

4.Cause?: ______

Comments: ______

5.Cause?: ______

Comments: ______

SECTION 1B – NEW LEARNINGS FROM "THE MAP" FOR ME

1. __________

2. __________

3. __________

4. __________

5. __________

SECTION 1B – NEW LEARNINGS FROM "THE MAP" FOR ME

1. ______________________________

2. ______________________________

3. ______________________________

4. ______________________________

5. ______________________________

SECTION 2 – LEARNING ON MY OWN
Which remedies make the most sense for me?

Write in the Competency or Stallers and Stoppers Numbers Below *Write the Remedy Numbers in the boxes*

▼

Competency / Stallers and Stoppers Number							
______	☐	☐	☐	☐	☐	☐	☐
______	☐	☐	☐	☐	☐	☐	☐
______	☐	☐	☐	☐	☐	☐	☐
______	☐	☐	☐	☐	☐	☐	☐
______	☐	☐	☐	☐	☐	☐	☐
______	☐	☐	☐	☐	☐	☐	☐
______	☐	☐	☐	☐	☐	☐	☐

SECTION 2 – LEARNING ON MY OWN

Which remedies make the most sense for me?

Write in the Competency or Stallers and Stoppers Numbers Below *Write the Remedy Numbers in the boxes*

▼

SECTION 2A – TAILORING THE REMEDIES

From: ____________
(Competency #)

To: [ ]
(Remedy #)

From: ____________
(Competency #)

To: [ ]
(Remedy #)

From: ____________
(Competency #)

To: [ ]
(Remedy #)

From: ____________
(Competency #)

To: [ ]
(Remedy #)

SECTION 2A – TAILORING THE REMEDIES

From: ____________
(Competency #)

To: [ ]
(Remedy #)

From: ____________
(Competency #)

To: [ ]
(Remedy #)

From: ____________
(Competency #)

To: [ ]
(Remedy #)

From: ____________
(Competency #)

To: [ ]
(Remedy #)

SECTION 3 – LEARNING FROM FEEDBACK
SOURCES FOR ME TO ASK ABOUT MY NEEDS

	Write in Competencies / Stallers and Stoppers Numbers Below							*Total Times ✔'d*	*My Rank Order of Best Sources for Me*
	____	____	____	____	____	____	____		
Bosses	☐	☐	☐	☐	☐	☐	☐	____	☐
Boss's Boss(es)	☐	☐	☐	☐	☐	☐	☐	____	☐
Internal and External Customers	☐	☐	☐	☐	☐	☐	☐	____	☐
Development Professionals	☐	☐	☐	☐	☐	☐	☐	____	☐
Family Members	☐	☐	☐	☐	☐	☐	☐	____	☐
Human Resource Professionals	☐	☐	☐	☐	☐	☐	☐	____	☐
Assigned Mentors/Sponsors	☐	☐	☐	☐	☐	☐	☐	____	☐
Natural Mentors	☐	☐	☐	☐	☐	☐	☐	____	☐
Off-work Friends/Associates	☐	☐	☐	☐	☐	☐	☐	____	☐
Past Associates	☐	☐	☐	☐	☐	☐	☐	____	☐
Peers and Colleagues	☐	☐	☐	☐	☐	☐	☐	____	☐
All Other Superiors	☐	☐	☐	☐	☐	☐	☐	____	☐
Spouse	☐	☐	☐	☐	☐	☐	☐	____	☐
Direct Reports	☐	☐	☐	☐	☐	☐	☐	____	☐
Yourself	☐	☐	☐	☐	☐	☐	☐	____	☐

SECTION 3 – LEARNING FROM FEEDBACK
SOURCES FOR ME TO ASK ABOUT MY NEEDS

	Write in Competencies/Stallers and Stoppers Numbers Below							*Total Times ✔'d*	*My Rank Order of Best Sources for Me*
	____	____	____	____	____	____	____		
Bosses	☐	☐	☐	☐	☐	☐	☐	____	☐
Boss's Boss(es)	☐	☐	☐	☐	☐	☐	☐	____	☐
Internal and External Customers	☐	☐	☐	☐	☐	☐	☐	____	☐
Development Professionals	☐	☐	☐	☐	☐	☐	☐	____	☐
Family Members	☐	☐	☐	☐	☐	☐	☐	____	☐
Human Resource Professionals	☐	☐	☐	☐	☐	☐	☐	____	☐
Assigned Mentors/Sponsors	☐	☐	☐	☐	☐	☐	☐	____	☐
Natural Mentors	☐	☐	☐	☐	☐	☐	☐	____	☐
Off-work Friends/Associates	☐	☐	☐	☐	☐	☐	☐	____	☐
Past Associates	☐	☐	☐	☐	☐	☐	☐	____	☐
Peers and Colleagues	☐	☐	☐	☐	☐	☐	☐	____	☐
All Other Superiors	☐	☐	☐	☐	☐	☐	☐	____	☐
Spouse	☐	☐	☐	☐	☐	☐	☐	____	☐
Direct Reports	☐	☐	☐	☐	☐	☐	☐	____	☐
Yourself	☐	☐	☐	☐	☐	☐	☐	____	☐

SECTION 3A – NOTES ON BEST SOURCES FOR FEEDBACK

Source (from Section #3)

Order

Source (from Section #3)

Order

Source (from Section #3)

Order

Source (from Section #3)

Order

Source (from Section #3)

Order

Source (from Section #3)

Order

SECTION 3A – NOTES ON BEST SOURCES FOR FEEDBACK

Source (from Section #3)

Order

Source (from Section #3)

Order

Source (from Section #3)

Order

Source (from Section #3)

Order

Source (from Section #3)

Order

Source (from Section #3)

Order

SECTION 4 – LEARNING FROM DEVELOP-IN-PLACE ASSIGNMENTS

Which Assignment would be useful and practical for me?

Write in the Competency or Stallers and Stoppers Numbers Below

▼

________ Assignment ____

____

____

____

________ Assignment ____

____

____

____

________ Assignment ____

____

____

____

________ Assignment ____

____

____

____

________ Assignment ____

____

____

____

________ Assignment ____

____

____

____

SECTION 4 – LEARNING FROM DEVELOP-IN-PLACE ASSIGNMENTS

Which Assignment would be useful and practical for me?

Write in the Competency or Stallers and Stoppers Numbers Below
▼

_______ Assignment ____________________________________

_______ Assignment ____________________________________

_______ Assignment ____________________________________

_______ Assignment ____________________________________

_______ Assignment ____________________________________

_______ Assignment ____________________________________

SECTION 5 – LEARNING FROM FULL TIME JOBS THAT WILL HELP ME DEVELOP MY SKILLS

	Write in Competencies / Stallers and Stoppers Numbers Below							*Total Times ✔'d*	*My Rank Order of Best Jobs for Me*
	____	____	____	____	____	____	____		
Chair of Projects/Taskforces	☐	☐	☐	☐	☐	☐	☐	____	☐
Cross-Moves	☐	☐	☐	☐	☐	☐	☐	____	☐
Fix-Its/Turnarounds	☐	☐	☐	☐	☐	☐	☐	____	☐
Heavy Strategic Demands	☐	☐	☐	☐	☐	☐	☐	____	☐
Influencing Without Authority	☐	☐	☐	☐	☐	☐	☐	____	☐
Line to Staff Switches	☐	☐	☐	☐	☐	☐	☐	____	☐
Member of Projects/Taskforces	☐	☐	☐	☐	☐	☐	☐	____	☐
Off-Shore Assignments	☐	☐	☐	☐	☐	☐	☐	____	☐
Scale Assignments	☐	☐	☐	☐	☐	☐	☐	____	☐
Scope Assignments	☐	☐	☐	☐	☐	☐	☐	____	☐
Significant People Demands	☐	☐	☐	☐	☐	☐	☐	____	☐
Staff to Line Shifts	☐	☐	☐	☐	☐	☐	☐	____	☐
Start-Ups	☐	☐	☐	☐	☐	☐	☐	____	☐

SECTION 5 – LEARNING FROM FULL TIME JOBS THAT WILL HELP ME DEVELOP MY SKILLS

	Write in Competencies/Stallers and Stoppers Numbers Below							*Total Times ✔'d*	*My Rank Order of Best Jobs for Me*
	____	____	____	____	____	____	____		
Chair of Projects/Taskforces	☐	☐	☐	☐	☐	☐	☐	____	☐
Cross-Moves	☐	☐	☐	☐	☐	☐	☐	____	☐
Fix-Its/Turnarounds	☐	☐	☐	☐	☐	☐	☐	____	☐
Heavy Strategic Demands	☐	☐	☐	☐	☐	☐	☐	____	☐
Influencing Without Authority	☐	☐	☐	☐	☐	☐	☐	____	☐
Line to Staff Switches	☐	☐	☐	☐	☐	☐	☐	____	☐
Member of Projects/Taskforces	☐	☐	☐	☐	☐	☐	☐	____	☐
Off-Shore Assignments	☐	☐	☐	☐	☐	☐	☐	____	☐
Scale Assignments	☐	☐	☐	☐	☐	☐	☐	____	☐
Scope Assignments	☐	☐	☐	☐	☐	☐	☐	____	☐
Significant People Demands	☐	☐	☐	☐	☐	☐	☐	____	☐
Staff to Line Shifts	☐	☐	☐	☐	☐	☐	☐	____	☐
Start-Ups	☐	☐	☐	☐	☐	☐	☐	____	☐

SECTION 5A – MY PLAN FOR JOBS

____
Job (from Section #5)

Order

____
Job (from Section #5)

Order

____
Job (from Section #5)

Order

____
Job (from Section #5)

Order

____
Job (from Section #5)

Order

____
Job (from Section #5)

Order

SECTION 5A – MY PLAN FOR JOBS

Job (from Section #5)

Order

Job (from Section #5)

Order

Job (from Section #5)

Order

Job (from Section #5)

Order

Job (from Section #5)

Order

Job (from Section #5)

Order

SECTION 6 – LEARNING MORE FROM MY PLAN

Write in the Competency or Stallers and Stoppers Numbers Below
▼

_______ Action ______________________________

____

____

____

_______ Action ______________________________

____

____

____

_______ Action ______________________________

____

____

____

_______ Action ______________________________

____

____

____

_______ Action ______________________________

____

____

____

_______ Action ______________________________

____

____

____

SECTION 6 – LEARNING MORE FROM MY PLAN

Write in the Competency or Stallers and Stoppers Numbers Below

▼

________ Action ____

________ Action ____

________ Action ____

________ Action ____

________ Action ____

________ Action ____

SECTION 7 – MY SUGGESTED READINGS

Competency # ______________________________

Readings: ______________________________

____

____

____

Competency # ______________________________

Readings: ______________________________

____

____

____

Competency # ______________________________

Readings: ______________________________

____

____

____

Competency # ______________________________

Readings: ______________________________

____

____

____

Competency # ______________________________

Readings: ______________________________

____

____

____

Competency # ______________________________

Readings: ______________________________

____

____

____

SECTION 7 – MY SUGGESTED READINGS

Competency # ____

Readings: ____

Competency # ____

Readings: ____

Competency # ____

Readings: ____

Competency # ____

Readings: ____

Competency # ____

Readings: ____

Competency # ____

Readings: ____

To get more information about the LEADERSHIP ARCHITECT® Suite of Integrated Tools, visit the Lominger Limited, Inc. World Wide Web site at http://www.lominger.com, contact the person in your company in charge of these products, or contact the Lominger Business Office at 5320 Cedar Lake Road South, Minneapolis, MN 55416.